THE WPA DALLAS GUIDE AND HISTORY

FOUNDERS OF DALLAS

John Neely Bryan
1810–1877

Margaret Beeman Bryan
1825–1919

George Mifflin Dallas
1792–1864

Commander Alexander James Dallas
1791–1844

THE WPA DALLAS GUIDE AND HISTORY

Written and compiled from 1936 to 1942 by the workers
of the Writers' Program of the Work Projects Administration
in the City of Dallas

Introduction by Gerald D. Saxon

Edited for publication by
Maxine Holmes
Dallas Public Library
and
Gerald D. Saxon
The University of Texas at Arlington

Dallas Public Library
Texas Center for the Book
University of North Texas Press

1992

Printed in the United States of America

10 9 8 7 6 5 4 3 2

The paper in this book meets the minimum requirements of the
American National Standard for Permanence of Paper for Printed
Library Materials, z39.48-1984.

Library of Congress Cataloging-in-Publication Data

WPA Dallas guide and history / introduction by Gerald Saxon
    p. cm.
    Includes bibliographical references and index.
    ISBN 0-929398-31-9
    1. Dallas (Tex.)—Guidebooks.   2. Dallas (Tex.)—History.
    I. United States. Work Projects Administration.
    F314.D213W8   1992
    976.4'2811—dc20   92-4505
                                                   CIP

TABLE ㊏ CONTENTS

I. GENERAL BACKGROUND

II. ECONOMIC DEVELOPMENT

III. CULTURAL DEVELOPMENT

IV. SOCIAL DEVELOPMENT

V. CITY ADDENDA

VI. POINTS OF INTEREST

MAPS

INTRODUCTION

The WPA Dallas Guide and History was a product of the Great Depression. When "Black Tuesday" (October 29, 1929) triggered the start of a save-who-may scramble on Wall Street, the United States began an economic decline of unprecedented proportions. In short order, the "Roaring Twenties" gave way to the "Depressing Thirties." The stock market crash precipitated a business depression that closed factories, put millions of people out of work, ruined many banks, and tested the collective will of the country. A contemporary jingle ran:

> Mellon pulled the whistle,
> Hoover rang the bell
> Wall Street gave the signal
> And the country went to hell.

With several million men and women looking for work and hearing, "We're firing, not hiring," the federal government intervened. Under the imaginative leadership of President Franklin Delano Roosevelt, Congress laid the legislative groundwork for the New Deal, a program aimed at the Three Rs—relief, recovery, and reform. The *Dallas Guide* was researched and written by the staff of one of Roosevelt's alphabetical relief agencies, the Works Progress Administration (WPA).

Begun in 1935 to put people back to work at government expense, the WPA during its eight-year existence provided jobs for nearly nine million people at a cost of $11 billion. The agency subsidized both blue and white collar workers—plumbers and playwrights, window washers and writers, unskilled and skilled. While critics sneered that WPA meant "We Provide Alms," the agency bolstered the shaken confidence of millions of the unemployed by providing them with meaningful jobs. The *Dallas Guide* was written under the auspices of the Federal Writers' Project, a WPA program designed to employ writers, journalists, historians, map makers, researchers, archaeologists, and office workers.

The Federal Writers' Project was created in 1935 and directed by journalist Henry G. Alsberg. One of the project's original goals was to publish a multi-volume American Guide. The guide was to emphasize history, folklore, the speech and mores of the common people, and the contributions of ethnic groups to the nation. When research for the American Guide seemed to bog down, the Writers' Project abandoned the national guide in order to publish state and local guides. By the close of the project in 1942, federal relief employees had completed 276 volumes (including a guide for every state), 701 pamphlets, and 340 miscellaneous publications, such as leaflets, articles, and radio scripts. Overall, the quality of the writing was quite good, prompting literary critic Van Wyck Brooks to comment that "the American Guide Series will still be going strong when most of our current books are dead and forgotten." In addition to the hundreds of published items, countless other manuscripts were in various stages of completion when the program ended. The *Dallas Guide* was one of these.

The Dallas office of the Writers' Project opened in the Allen Building in 1936 under the supervision of Milton H. Saul, a former publicity director for Dallas Power and Light. In 1939, Dallas journalist and social reformer Louis P. Head assumed management of the local office, an office that employed on the average of ten to fifteen people at any one time. The Dallas staff was to research, write, and forward to the state office in San Antonio selections on North Texas to be included in the Texas guide (published as *Texas: A Guide to the Lone Star State*, New York: Hastings House, 1940). The local office also was charged with preparing for publication guides to Denison, Sherman, Paris, Gainesville, Greenville, Denton, and, of course, Dallas. Of these, only *The Denison Guide* (Denison: Chamber of Commerce, 1939) made it through the Writers' Project bureaucratic and editing maze to reach publication. Ironically, the *Dallas Guide* was essentially complete in 1940, some two years before the project ended, but fell victim to a host of problems that prevented its publication. Among these problems were the project's total reorganization in 1939, the constantly changing editorial and format rules adopted in Washington, D. C., the inability to locate a Dallas sponsor to underwrite the book, and the untimely death of supervisor Head in February, 1942.

Confusion and hesitation on both the local and national level followed the reorganization of the Federal Writers' Project in 1939. As early as 1936, Republicans and conservative Democrats, disenchanted with Roosevelt's social experiments and upset with some of the writers' radical philosophies, bitterly attacked the Writers' Project as a "festering sore of communism." Influential Texas Congressman Martin Dies charged in October, 1938, that the writers were "doing more to spread Communist propaganda than the Communist Party itself." Because of attacks like these and the anxieties produced by a rampaging Hitler, the Roosevelt administration began to de-emphasize its Depression-oriented programs. At the president's suggestion, Congress relieved the Works Progress Administration of its independent status, changed its name to the Work Projects Administration, and withdrew federal sponsorship of the Writers' Project. In order for state projects to continue, a sponsor had to be found that would contribute at least twenty-five percent of the total cost of the program. The Bureau of Research in the Social Sciences at The University of Texas at Austin sponsored the Texas project after this reorganization.

With this reorganization and change in sponsorship came new rules, new personnel in the national office at Washington, and new confusion. Once again the Dallas manuscript began the long editorial road toward final approval. The extant office memoranda reflect a deep-seated frustration in Dallas with these policy changes, a frustration shared by project employees nationwide. Indeed, California writer Miriam Allen deFord perhaps best summarized this feeling:

> I think that I have never tried
> A job as painful as the guide.
> A guide which changes every day
> Because our betters feel that way.
> A guide whose deadlines come so fast
> Yet no one lives to see the last.
> A guide to which we give our best
> To hear: "This stinks like all the rest!"
> There's no way out but suicide
> For only God can end the guide.

While the San Antonio office edited the manuscript, Head looked for a local sponsor to underwrite the printing and marketing costs of the volume. Despite protracted discussions with a number of groups and organizations, including the Dallas Centennial Committee, the Dallas Historical Society, the Dallas Citizens Council, the Junior Chamber of Commerce, and the City of Dallas, he was unable to locate a sponsor with the means and the willingness to support the book. In 1942 Head died in the midst of his search, and shortly after his death, the local office closed its doors as the nation mobilized for World War II. Work relief programs were no longer needed. In the summer of 1942 a manuscript draft of the *Dallas Guide* was deposited with the Dallas Public Library, and the local and state files of the Writers' Project in Texas were transferred to the library of The University of Texas at Austin.

Researchers have used the unpublished guide for the past fifty-plus years, and have lauded it as an excellent and exhaustive study of Dallas to 1940. The manuscript provides a comprehensive look at Dallas' economic, cultural, and social development as well as a discussion of points of interest in the city and county in 1940. The *Dallas Guide* was the first serious history of the city to be based on a variety of documentary and oral sources. Surprisingly, while Dallas has undergone dramatic growth in the five decades since the manuscript was written, the city's character has changed little. The federal writers' view that Dallas is a "young, vigorous, rich city" that has "almost obliterated every vestige of the past" still holds true. Moreover, the comparison of Dallas to Zenith, the hometown of Sinclair Lewis' Babbitt and a city American enterprise created, seems particularly apt. And who does not think of many young residents of today in reading that the "average Dallasite wants the latest fashions" and "the newest model of cars." Fortunately, not everything in Dallas has remained the same. The rigid racial barriers of pre-World War II Dallas depicted in the manuscript have been lowered somewhat, paving the way for new social and economic opportunities for African Americans, Hispanics, and other ethnic groups.

Aware that the Dallas Public Library owned a local historical treasure, and wanting to make it available to a wider audience, the staff of the Texas/Dallas History and Archives Division, as Louis Head had done some fifty years before, began looking for a way to publish the manuscript. Fran Vick of the University of North Texas Press read the manuscript and enthusiastically agreed to publish the *Dallas Guide*. Prior to UNT Press' involvement, library staff had decided to edit the manuscript only for grammatical mistakes, typographical errors, and consistency. The integrity of the writers' work, in short, has been preserved.

Readers should keep in mind that the tone and point of view of the book reflect the Dallas of 1940, not of today. Readers also may find inaccuracies in the manuscript, but it was our intention to publish the book as it was written, based on the sources available in the late 1930s and early 1940s. Photographs collected for the book by the federal writers were included when possible, but many could not be found in the WPA archives at the Barker Texas History Center of The University of Texas at Austin. Additional photographs have come primarily from the collections of the Dallas Public Library, Dallas Historical Society, and DeGolyer Library of Southern Methodist University.

The WPA Dallas Guide and History is as much a historical document as it is a history. Its format closely follows the guidelines established in Washington for local guides, while its interpretive framework mirrors the concerns and opinions prevalent in Dallas during the Depression. Its pages, moreover, reflect the ambitious goals of a work relief program which affirmed for the first time in American history that those who follow learning are as important to the nation as those who follow other callings. Ralph Thompson summarized the legacy of the Federal Writers' Project when he wrote in the September 14, 1938, issue of *The New York Times*:

> For when we of this generation are all dust and ashes and forgotten . . . the American Guide Series will be still very much in evidence. And not only in evidence but in use: our children will be thankful for it, and their children, and their children's children.

With the publication of *The WPA Dallas Guide and History*, the children of the local relief writers will finally be able to enjoy—indeed, be able to learn from—the prodigious labor of their parents. This book now joins the others in the American Guide Series as a lasting legacy of the Great Depression.

Gerald D. Saxon
February, 1992

ACKNOWLEDGEMENTS

Everyone who has worked on or been associated with the *WPA Dallas Guide and History* will agree that at times—too many times it seemed—the manuscript was cursed and destined never to be published. The WPA staff who researched and wrote the main body of text was unable to find a publisher in the late-1930s and early-1940s. When a number of us at the Central Dallas Public Library confidently decided to take the manuscript on as a Texas sesquicentennial project (remember the sesquicentennial in 1986?), we had no idea that it would be 1992 before the manuscript would be published. In the mid-1980s, we came close a couple of times to having the *Dallas Guide* published, but each time negotiations with a potential publisher collapsed. It wasn't until 1990 that Fran Vick of the University of North Texas Press and Patrick O'Brien, director of Dallas Public Library, reached an agreement which finally laid the legal and financial groundwork for this book. Both of them deserve special thanks for having the insight to recognize the historical importance of the *Dallas Guide* and the fortitude to support its publication.

The debts that we accrued in editing and shepherding the manuscript through the publication process are tremendous, and a simple thank you seems terribly inadequate. Nevertheless, a sincere expression of our appreciation will have to do. To our library colleagues, past and present, who have played a role in this publication, we offer our thanks. We want to especially recognize the fine work done by Paula Barber, Lucile Boykin, Travis Dudley, Allison Esposito, Wayne Gray, Jean Hudon, Gary Jennings, Pam Lange, Cheryl Siebert, Michael Sours, and the entire staff of the Word Processing Section. We are also deeply appreciative of the financial support the *Dallas Guide* received from the Texas Center for the Book, which is partially funded by the Ida M. Green Fund. Without this support, quite simply, this book would not have found a publisher.

A number of librarians, archivists, and curators in the state deserve special thanks for helping us locate photographs and giving us permission to include them here. These people are Kate Adams, Don Carleton, and Ralph Elder at the Barker Texas History Center at The University of Texas at Austin; Kay Bost, David Farmer, and Dawn Letson, DeGolyer Library, Southern Methodist University; and Michael Hazel and Mary Ellen Holt at the Dallas Historical Society.

Finally, we would be remiss if we did not mention the many staff members, whose names unfortunately we do not know, who worked on the *Dallas Guide* in the 1930s and 1940s. This is their book plain and simple, and it is both a pleasure and a relief to finally have it published.

Maxine Holmes   xiii   Gerald Saxon

DALLAS
GUIDE AND HISTORY

Written and Compiled by the Dallas Unit
of the Texas Writers' Project
of the
Work Projects Administration

AMERICAN GUIDE SERIES
ILLUSTRATED

1940

FEDERAL WORKS AGENCY
WORK PROJECTS ADMINISTRATION
F. C. Harrington, Commissioner
Florence Kerr, Assistant Commissioner
J. Frank Davis, State Supervisor

PREFACE

The compilation of the *Dallas Guide and History* has in a very real sense been a community undertaking, enlisting not only the cooperation of its official local sponsors, but of various institutions, public and private, and of numerous interested individuals who have given generously of their time and special knowledge to make this volume an authoritative source of information on everything pertaining to Dallas.

City and county officials, the Dallas Public Library, Southern Methodist University, the Dallas Historical Society, *The Dallas Morning News,* the *Daily Times Herald,* the Chamber of Commerce, and Dr. William E. Howard and G. J. Signaigo, owners of valuable private collections, have thrown their records, files, and archives open to the staff of the Texas Writers' Project and provided a body of primary source material without which this book would have been impossible. Libraries of the State and of the University of Texas at Austin also were prolific sources of historical data.

This material has been supplemented with countless personal recollections of the Dallas of other days, and arranged and edited with the aid of expert opinion in various specialized fields. Without this assistance numerous omissions, discrepancies, and errors of interpretation would have been unavoidable.

Professor Herbert Gambrell of the Dallas Historical Society and Sam Acheson of *The Dallas Morning News* aided in correlating the historical portions of the manuscript, while Epps G. Knight and August Guillot, lineal descendants of Dallas pioneers, checked the parts of which they had first-hand knowledge.

Hilton R. Greer of the Texas Poetry Society helped piece together the story of literary expression in Dallas. John Rosenfield, dramatic critic on *The Dallas Morning News,* Louis O. Bullman of the Majestic Theater, Mrs. Besa Short of the Interstate Theater Circuit, and Charles Meredith and Irma Mangold of the Dallas Little Theater enormously enriched the theater section with names, dates, and anecdotes of the local stage. John William Rogers, in his double capacity of critic and playwright, served as an ever-ready and authoritative consultant in both fields.

Ralph Bryan and George L. Dahl supplied much of the technical descriptive material on Dallas architecture and the former also read the completed chapter. Reveau Bassett, Olin Travis, Frank Reaugh, Jerry Bywaters, and Alexandre Hogue—all well-known Dallas artists—rendered valuable services in the field of painting; and Mike Owen and Allie V. Tennant, local sculptors, contributed to the preparation of the material on their particular medium.

Dr. Robert T. Hill and Ellis W. Schuler of Southern Methodist University furnished the scientific data on the geology and paleontology of Dallas County, and the latter read the finished chapter. Dr. J. W. Bass and Dr. E. H. Cary supplied facts and figures on Dallas as a medical center.

George White and Jerry Hayes, leading sports writers, checked the record of professional and amateur sports in Dallas. Dr. J. F. Kimball's long experience as a Dallas schoolman was utilized in rounding out the chapter on education. Wallace Reilly and Roy James of the Dallas Central Labor Council helped to reconstruct the history of organized labor in the city. Adolfo G. Dominguez, formerly Mexican Consul, assisted in evaluating the local economic and social status of his people; and A. Maceo Smith opened up many interesting aspects of Negro life in Dallas.

Besides these, there have been many others whose names and services are too numerous and diversified to mention but to all of whom the Texas Writers' Project is indebted in preparing this *Guide History*.

PHOTOGRAPHS

FOUNDERS OF DALLAS

John Neely Bryan (1810–1877)
Margaret Beeman Bryan (1825–1919)
Dallas Public Library

George Mifflin Dallas (1792–1864)
Dallas Public Library

Commander Alexander James Dallas (1791–1844)
Dallas Public Library

I. DALLAS, TODAY AND YESTERDAY

Skyline from Houston Street Viaduct
Dallas Public Library

Downtown Dallas by Night, ca. 1930
Dallas Public Library

Theater Row on Elm Street
Dallas Public Library

Triple Underpass—Where Dallas Was Born
Barker Texas History Center

Peak Hour Shopping Crowds
Dallas Public Library

Suburban Residential Street, ca. 1930
Dallas Public Library

John Neely Bryan's Third Cabin
Barker Texas History Center

Delord House, Last of La Reunion
Barker Texas History Center

Main Street East from Scollard Alley, ca. 1887
Dallas Public Library

Main Street East from Akard, ca. 1935
Dallas Public Library

IV. INDIGENOUS CULTURE

V. SOUTHWESTERN SOCIAL PATTERNS

VI. STREAMLINED AMERICAN CITY

Dallas County Courthouse
Dallas Public Library

Parkland City-County Hospital
Dallas Public Library

Dallas County Criminal Courts Building
Dallas Public Library

Dallas City Hall
Dallas Public Library

Federal Building and Post Office
Dallas Public Library

Medical Arts Building
Dallas Public Library

Dallas Cotton Exchange
Dallas Public Library

Magnolia Petroleum Building
Dallas Public Library

Tower Petroleum Building
Dallas Public Library

Santa Fe Building (first three units)
Dallas Public Library

VII. SETTINGS FOR SIGHTSEEING

Esplanade of State during State Fair
Dallas Public Library

Hall of State, Fair Park
Dallas Public Library

Museum of Fine Arts, Fair Park
Barker Texas History Center

Museum of Natural History, Fair Park
Barker Texas History Center

Aquarium, Fair Park
Barker Texas History Center

Horticultural Museum, Fair Park
Dallas Public Library

Education Building, Fair Park
Barker Texas History Center

Bandshell and Amphitheater, Fair Park
Barker Texas History Center

Globe Theater (reproduction), Fair Park
Barker Texas History Center

Arlington Recreated, Robert E. Lee Park
Dallas Public Library

White Rock Lake, Man-made Inland Resort
Barker Texas History Center

Along Scenic Turtle Creek Drive
Barker Texas History Center

MAPS

DOWNTOWN POINTS OF INTEREST

CITY OF DALLAS

FAIR PARK

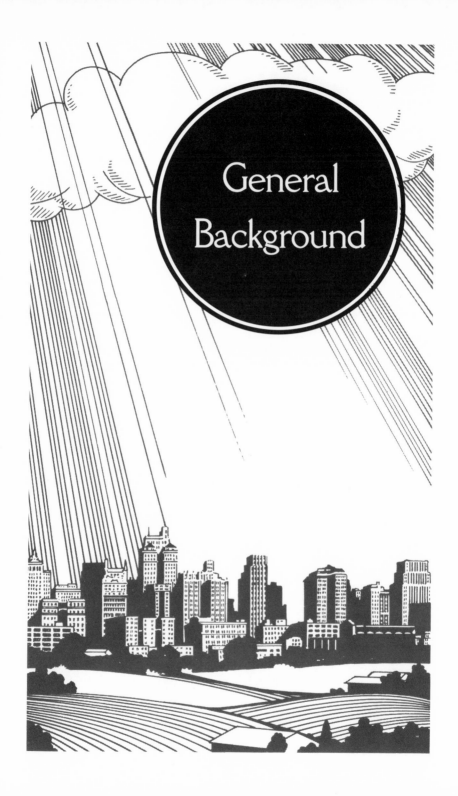

General

Background

PORTRAIT OF A CITY: DALLAS TODAY

By usual urban standards, Dallas, an inland metropolis with over 300,000 inhabitants, is an overgrown youth of a city not yet a hundred years old and looking even younger, so completely contemporary is it in appearance—a young, vigorous, rich city.

Situated in the blackland prairie region of North Texas, Dallas embraces 43.64 square miles within its corporate limits, and extends irregularly from northeast to southwest on both sides of the Trinity River. Its many skyscrapers have earned it the name of City of Towers, and recurrent waves of building have almost obliterated every vestige of the past. The use of natural gas as a fuel has made it a well-nigh smokeless city, and its pyramided downtown skyline, dominated by the twenty-nine-story bulk of the Magnolia Building with its distinctive observation tower rises on the east bank of the Trinity like a segment of lower Manhattan, sharp and clean-cut against the blue Texas sky.

In downtown Dallas an early-day clinging to river and railroads, reinforced by a local impulse to adopt the imperious urban pattern of New York, is more apparent than the million acres that lie in the city's dooryard. Practically the entire business district, retail and wholesale, is piled up in the crowded mile between the Trinity River and the Houston & Texas Central Railroad tracks, marking the route of the first railroad. The three principal streets—Commerce, Main, and Elm—are narrow thoroughfares of the streetcar and horse and buggy era, stemming from the city's birthplace on the banks of the river.

The city's most congested area lies along these streets, in the skyscraper district extending from Field to Ervay Streets, and centered at Akard

3

Street. Here the tallest buildings are jammed together in the space of a few blocks. The streets are literally choked at peak hours with motor traffic and shopping crowds, the almost complete lack of alleys further increasing congestion by necessitating delivery of merchandise and removal of refuse from the front entrances of stores.

Few old buildings are to be seen in the downtown area above Lamar Street, and ultramodern store fronts display an unusually wide and up-to-the-minute range of merchandise. There are a few buildings dating back to the 1870s and 1880s in the neighborhood of the courthouse and the surrounding wholesale district—none, however, antedating 1860, when almost the entire town was destroyed by fire.

Around the edges of the business district the retreating residential section has left a fringe of boarding- and rooming-houses that were once the homes of socially prominent families. Streets in this area bore names to conjure with in the old days—Akard, Ervay, and Harwood to the south, and Bryan, Live Oak, Swiss, Ross, and Maple to the north. A number of the old residences that then faced them still stand, "sound in body" and replete with many-angled gables, decorative cornices, cupolas, wide verandas, ornamental iron fences, and old-fashioned flower gardens—a tribute to the sturdy, honest workmanship that went into their construction, and an expression of the architectural exuberance of the period that produced them. They are almost the only reminders left of the old city of the 1880s, 1890s, and early 1900s.

Also lying close to the business section are many of Dallas' slum areas, Little Mexico, parts of South Dallas, and a belt of Negro neighborhoods that extends across the north central part of the city—where the poor are lodged in squalid, dilapidated shanties and frame houses of the "shotgun" type, some without the most elementary conveniences and almost unfit for human habitation. A low-income group, the majority of the Negroes are compelled to live in dwellings of this sort, although many are home-owners, particularly in the exclusively Negro neighborhoods. An extensive Federal housing program designed to relieve these slum conditions among both whites and Negroes was projected in the late 1930s.

Beyond this ring of squalor and decayed opulence, the city climbs rapidly out of the lowlands and spills out fanwise north, east, and south, across the rolling prairies in an irregularly distributed jigsaw patchwork of new residential additions, most of them laid out independently with little organic interrelationship. These newer residential sections, especially toward the north and east, are well protected with zoning ordinances and building restrictions and are smart, neat, and attractive in appearance, displaying a variety of architectural trends with no one prevailing type.

To the east the city is split by the wedge of Fair Park—since 1936 almost a city within a city. To the northeast Dallas reaches out and encircles the broad, shining surface of White Rock Lake, a man-made inland resort for fishing and aquatic sports. On the north the city merges into the landscaped

4

town estates, winding drives, and smart, severely restricted shopping centers that compose the fashionable suburbs of Highland Park, University Park, and Preston Hollow, all independent municipalities—University Park being the site of Southern Methodist University. To the northwest another long fingerlike suburban development, largely industrial in character and marked by manufacturing plants, surrounded by rows of barrack-like workmen's houses, stretches out along the Denton Road to take in the municipal airport of Love Field.

On the west side of the river lies Oak Cliff, settled in the 1840s, developed as a residential suburb in the 1880s, and organized as a separate township in 1891, but a part of greater Dallas since 1903. Today this suburb calls itself with peculiar fitness the Brooklyn of the Southwest. It has a population in its own right of 100,000 or more, a number of restricted and landscaped residential additions with many fine homes, a series of thriving shopping centers along Jefferson Avenue (its main thoroughfare), a medical-dental office building, a large hospital, and several big apartment hotels rising conspicuously from the wooded bluffs that border the western edge of the Trinity bottoms. These forested "cliffs," covered with a growth of post oaks, are generally credited with having given this section of the city its name.

On the same side of the Trinity as Oak Cliff are Trinity Heights to the south, and West Dallas to the north. Trinity Heights is a scattered middle-class residential district extending south along US 77 to the small trading center of Lisbon, now also embraced within the city limits. The area loosely designated as West Dallas is a straggling suburban section that extends along the Eagle Ford Road west of the river between the city and the large cement plant and cluster of company houses that constitute Cement City. This district has during the last decade been unfavorably publicized as the breeding ground and hideout of Clyde Barrow, Bonnie Parker, and other notorious criminals of the Southwest.

Through the mile-wide strip of bottom lands that separate Dallas proper from its western suburbs flows the Trinity River from north to south, cutting the city almost squarely in half. For many years the murky river, winding its lazy, tortuous way through dense growths of trees and underbrush, constituted a serious flood hazard to Dallas. An insignificant trickle during most of the year, in flood times it became a raging, swirling torrent that swept over the lowlands, causing untold property loss. Since the completion of the $18,000,000 city-county improvement program in 1933, however, the treacherous stream has been straitjacketed between levees and flows docilely in a straight and narrow channel through the middle of the valley. The trees and underbrush along its banks have been cut away, and more than 10,000 acres of land in the shadow of the city's skyscrapers reclaimed for industrial uses. Through the length of the valley runs the broad cement ribbon of the new Industrial Boulevard, paralleling the tangle of railroad yards that fringe the valley's eastern edge. Four gleaming

5

white steel and concrete viaducts, with underpasses leading directly into the heart of downtown Dallas, have been built from east to west through the bottoms, supplementing the original Houston Street viaduct built in 1912, and accommodating the continuous streams of traffic that flow between the city proper and Oak Cliff.

In this reclamation and improvement project are to be seen evidences of Dallas' maturing Kessler City Plan. This program and its principles are also seen in the opening of crooked and dead-end streets, in the creation of the broad new boulevards that encircle the outer edges of the city, and in the numerous parks that provide newer residential sections with space for breath and beauty. Slowly for three decades it has been imposing a coherent, metropolitan, motor-age pattern on the face of a city congested by too-rapid growth and marred by streets that followed the routes of preexistent Indian and buffalo trails.

The most phenomenal aspect of Dallas has been its swift and continuous growth, marked by neither slumps nor booms. In 1842 Dallas was a frontier trading post and ferry crossing with ten or twelve people living in two log cabins on the banks of the Trinity River. In 1872–73 it was a sprawling railhead village and market for buffalo hides from the western plains, with a population of less than 3,000. A score of Texas communities within a hundred-mile radius showed equal promise of becoming large cities. Following the arrival of the first railroads Dallas had a brief boom period, the population increasing from 3,000 in 1870 to over 10,000 in 1880; since that time its growth has been a steady climb, spanning a period of rapid urban development in Texas. In the 1880s and 1890s the city achieved an outstanding position as a distributing center for a rapidly expanding trade territory demanding great quantities of farm implements, machinery for mills and factories, household equipment, clothing, and other merchandise. Northern and eastern manufacturers established branch houses, and Dallas became literally a vast warehouse from which an army of drummers went forth by rail and buggy to supply the needs of Texas and the Southwest.

During this period Dallas grew steadily and absorbed various neighboring communities such as East Dallas, South Dallas, and North Dallas, giving the city its present composite neighborhood character. By 1900 Dallas had rococo hotels, theaters that attracted the best talent, ornate public buildings, big-city ambitions expressing themselves in habitual superlatives, and a population of 42,683. The census of 1910 showed a population of 92,104 and civic leaders prepared for further growth by the adoption of the Kessler Plan. By 1920 the city had grown during the intervening World War decade to 158,176, and since that time has progressed in seven-league strides—becoming a commercial, industrial, educational, medical, convention, and travel center with tentacles of trade stretching out to South America, England, Continental Europe, India, China, and Japan, as well as to Mexico and all parts of the United States. In 1940 the population of greater Dallas was estimated on the basis of the city directory at 380,927.

Dallas has never known the financial panics that have halted the growth of some cities and the long lean years of industrial stagnation that have decimated others. It has never ceased to grow, and even during the recent depression decade its unimpaired wealth has enabled it to avail itself generously of Federal aid for civic improvements. Federal grants for streets, sewers, buildings, and parks by August 1939 amounted to $4,833,270, which the city had matched with $5,387,344.

Almost in the geographical center of the Southwest, Dallas reaches out to a vast trade area embracing the five states of Texas, Louisiana, Arkansas, Oklahoma, and New Mexico, with a combined population of nearly fourteen million, and abounding in cotton, cattle, wheat, oil, timber, orchards, truck gardens, citrus fruits, sheep, goats, swine, quarries, and mines. Economically Dallas depends on no one industry or source of wealth, offering instead a spectacle of well-balanced development that closely links it with other business, financial, and industrial centers of the nation.

Cotton and oil are particularly important. The fertile, waxy black lands that surround the city bloom annually into a fluffy white sea of cotton. Virtually half of America's annual cotton crop is grown within a radius of 300 miles. Dallas is the largest inland spot cotton market in the world, the cotton exchange handling 2,000,000 bales every year. An abundance of capital combined with its strategic geographical position in relation to the major oil fields of the Southwest also make the city the center of the mid-continent oil industry. Oil fields containing 25,000 producing wells are exploited from home or regional offices in Dallas, for the housing of which some of the city's principal skyscrapers have been built. One large Dallas bank estimates that 20 percent of its deposits can be attributed directly to the oil industry, 1,382 units of which, including major and independent producers, oil and gas pipelines, lease brokers, geophysical survey services, royalty owners, equipment and supply companies, operate in the city.

Financially, Dallas is recognized as the undisputed money capital of the Southwest. The Federal Reserve Bank for the Eleventh District is located here; two Dallas banks rank among the 100 largest in the nation; the city stands fourth among the insurance centers of the country; and various governmental loan agencies, such as the Home Owners' Loan Corporation, the Federal Housing Administration, and the Farm Security Administration, have their regional headquarters in the city. Large amounts of capital available in Dallas have served materially to develop the natural resources of the trade area of which it is the center, and this in turn has served to develop the city as a distributing point.

In the manufacturing field the city is important for the production of consumer goods. Dallas has become one of the apparel and fashion centers of the nation and also manufactures food products, storage batteries, automobiles, automobile accessories, furniture and home furnishings, leather goods and harness, chemicals, paints, cosmetics, gasoline and oils, building materials, paper and paper products, printing, and cottonseed products. In the manufacture of cotton gins and gin machinery Dallas leads the world.

In effective buying income per family Dallas stood second in 1939 among 101 metropolitan areas in the country. As a wholesale market it ranks fourteenth in the nation, and as a retail market twenty-third. In both fields it is easily first in the Southwest. Likewise, it surpasses any other Southwestern city in transportation facilities, being on nine United States highways, eight trunk line railroads, and three airlines. By air it is within twelve to eighteen hours of any major city in North America. All of these elements have combined to make Dallas a favorite location for conventions and expositions and to give the city a cosmopolitan character with modern hotels, smart shops, theaters, clubs, dining and dancing places, golf courses, and major annual sports events. Sophisticated world travelers choose Dallas to stop, while they are en route from New York and the East to Los Angeles and the West Coast, or between other distant points.

An assertion made in the city directory of 1875 is still largely true, perhaps more today than in the frontier boom times when it was written. "Probably no city in the state," declared this directory, "enjoys a more enviable reputation for morality than this. Her people are honorable, law-abiding, and progressive, and contribute as liberally as any in the South for the support of schools and churches."

Dallas is definitely a church-going community, ranking high among the nation's cities in church attendance. Here several nationally famous denominational leaders have developed; and evangelists find the city a fruitful field for their labors. The influence of the churches is also apparent in the lack of the more spectacular forms of legalized vice, a strong liquor prohibition sentiment that upholds the state law against the sale of intoxicating beverages by the drink, and frequent crusades against betting, bookmaking, bucket shops, slot machines, pool halls, and other forms of gambling. The general tone of the community life is decidedly on the moral and respectable side.

Dallas' cultural assets are also numerous. Among these are two large universities, a modern and well-supported public school system with high scholastic standards, fine buildings and handsome athletic stadia; numerous private and parochial schools; seventeen hospitals recognized by the leading hospital and medical associations of the country, the largest county medical society in the state; a public library containing 148,635 volumes, with five branch libraries; the Civic Federation, described by the *Encyclopedia Britannica* as "perhaps the best example in the country of a private educational venture for adults"; the Dallas Little Theater, thrice winner of the Belasco Cup; the Dallas Symphony Orchestra; and the $3,000,000 Civic Center at Fair Park, consisting of the Museum of Fine Arts, the Museum of Natural History, the Aquarium, Amphitheater and Bandshell, Texas Museum of Natural Resources, and Hall of State with its extensive collection of Texas historical material. Dallas every year has a full season of plays, operas, concerts, lectures by nationally and internationally famous figures, and other attractions of a cultural nature. All of these enterprises are formally patronized through sponsorship and participation by Dallas society and liberally supported by business and financial interests.

However, in a recent survey published under the title of *Your City*, Dr. E. L. Thorndike of Columbia University ranked Dallas eighteenth among the cities of America in "general goodness of life for good people," finding the city below standard in good reading, home ownership, and continuance in school, and with a relatively high proportion of illiterates and child labor. It also ranks relatively high in its number of homicides and for the prevalence of venereal disease. Its slum areas tend to breed criminals, and its position as a crossroads of the Southwest attracts undesirable elements from other parts of the country. The cheap unskilled white, Negro, and Mexican labor which has gravitated to the city has attracted many industrialists from other states, but has of recent years ceased to be a wholly unmixed asset, the condition has created a serious relief problem marked by recurrent crises.

Wages for unskilled labor are low, as in most Southern cities, and this, combined with a comparatively high cost of living—according to the figures of the United States Department of Labor the fourth highest in the country—often creates distress and places an added strain on relief and welfare agencies.

Culture in Dallas tends to be imitative rather than dynamic and creative. Several of the leading spokesmen for so-called indigenous culture make their homes in Dallas. But the movement is more often found in discussions and isolated artistic experiments than as a genuine expression of Texas folkways. Of real folk culture there is comparatively little except for the preservation of a few native customs and traditions by Mexicans and other racial groups.

Dallas has no Greenwich Village, Left Bank, or French Quarter, and most of its so-called bohemians have independent incomes, or prosaically earn their bread and butter by commercial art, journalism, or teaching.

The city as a whole is inclined to be indifferent to new political, economic, and religious ideas, particularly those of a radical nature; it has a better record than some Southern cities as regards freedom of speech and assembly.

The average Dallasite wants the latest fashions from Fifth Avenue, Bond Street, and the Rue de la Paix; the newest models in cars; and the best in functionally constructed, electrified, air-conditioned homes—but prefers old-time religion with comfortable modern trimmings, and old-fashioned Jeffersonian democracy. The city usually votes with the Solid South, but has twice in its history voted Republican in national elections. Locally, politics is usually tepidly nonpartisan. The schools and universities, churches, and newspapers all lean strongly in the direction of conservatism. Labor organizers complain that they find the open-shop psychology almost as firmly rooted among the workers as among the employers, and clashing contemporary "isms" find in Dallas only a faint response.

Dallas has been repeatedly called cosmopolitan, and some have accused it of lacking soul and individual character. Neither is quite accurate. Though externally cosmopolitan, it retains many of the characteristics of Main Street. Nor is it altogether lacking in individuality. Its very lack of indigenous features gives it a certain character peculiar to itself. It has been called a "Northern city under a Southern sun and in a Southern setting." Its setting and climate are Southern; its purposeful, high-pressure activity and solid enterprise are Northern; its sophistication and modishness Eastern; and its civic pride and youthful, confident spirit, delighting in newness and bigness for their own sake, Western. It is a sort of archetypal American city, like Zenith, the home town of Babbitt in Sinclair Lewis's novels—a city created by American business enterprise for its own special and individual purposes of pride and profit, according to the stereotyped pattern of the American city, relatively unmodified by geographical, racial, or other factors.

Regionalists seek in vain for the explanation of such a city as Dallas in terms of the open range or of the Spanish-American traditions of the Southwestern frontier. Neither is its explanation to be found in the strategy of its location at the three forks of the Trinity River, no river trade having swelled the volume of its commerce. Even its setting in the rich and prolific blacklands of North Central Texas does not adequately explain its growth and character, hundreds of other towns in the region having had equal access to the natural assets on which it has drawn.

Some students of the city's life believe that the key lies in the character of its citizenship and the high degree of civic consciousness and local patriotism which was manifest even among the first settlers. From its earliest days, Dallas has had few transients or drifters; its people have come to build homes and businesses. The city began as a trading post and has been essentially the creation of shrewd, energetic, and far-seeing merchants, industrialists, bankers, and salesmen from the older sections of the United States. They had both imagination and practical business sense; they were attracted to Dallas by the wealth of natural resources within easy reach and made the most of these resources. From the very outset Dallas has been built by men of this stamp and caliber, and the city built to meet their expanding needs bears in its every feature the mark of their special gifts and limitations.

The first settlers were solid, sober, middle-class citizens who believed in schools and churches, and had a decent respect for the processes of orderly government. They came to stay and to prosper, and their descendants have stayed and prospered, establishing new enterprises as new opportunities arose, rather than retiring to form a leisure class. Their numbers have been increased by newcomers with essentially the same outlook. In nearly all cases, except possibly that of a French colony of the 1850s, these newcomers have been drawn to Dallas by the opportunities it offered to make money and get ahead in the world rather than by a spirit of adventure or by an idealistic search for the good life. The bonds that created the city in the first place and which have kept it together since have been almost purely economic ones, but each successive generation has shown vision, civic pride, and public-mindedness, apparently justifying the dictum of Adam Smith and the classical economists that the greatest good for the greatest number results from the spontaneous interaction of independent and unrestrained individual agents actuated only by intelligent self-interest.

Thus has been built the modern, prosperous, and partially planned metropolis that is the Dallas of today. Externally at least it retains to an unusual degree the optimistic and expansive trend that marked the American boom years after the World War; the depression has sobered it somewhat but it is as yet comparatively untouched by the socially critical and experimental spirit of the past decade. The city is young yet, however—very young as cities go—and has the virtues and vices of youth. The forces of change are constantly at work in it, and what it will become in another ten or twenty years no one can, with confidence, say.

GENERAL INFORMATION

Area: 45.64 sq. mi.

Altitude: 512 feet in the city, ranging to 750 feet in parts of the county.

Population: U.S. 1930 Census:

Dallas proper	260,475
Highland Park	8,422
University Park	4,200
	273,097

As of January 1, 1940, estimated metropolitan population 380,927.

Railroad Stations: Union Railway Passenger Terminal, Houston St. bet. Jackson and Young Sts., for Chicago, Rock Island & Gulf Ry. (Rock Island Lines); Fort Worth & Denver City Ry. (Burlington Lines); St. Louis & San Francisco Ry. (Frisco); Gulf, Colorado & Santa Fe Ry. (Santa Fe); Missouri-Kansas-Texas R.R. (Katy); St. Louis-Southwestern Ry. (Cotton Belt); Texas & New Orleans R.R. (Southern Pacific Lines); Texas & Pacific Ry. (Missouri Pacific System). Highland Park Station, Abbott Ave. at Knox St., Missouri-Kansas-Texas (Katy).

Airports: Love Field Airport, 3630 Love Field Dr., Lemmon Ave. to Denton Dr., 278 acres, owned and operated by the City of Dallas. By auto, 6 mi. NW. from downtown on Lemmon Ave., or Denton Dr. (US 77-SH 40). Love Field Coach, 7¢; taxi from downtown, 90¢. Operating airlines transport passengers to and from field for 50¢, for American Airlines, Inc.; Delta Air Lines; Braniff Airways, Inc. Complete facilities for servicing aircraft day and night; charter and ambulance service. Hensley Field (US Army Airport), 13-1/2 mi. SW. of Dallas, about 1/4 mi. to left of US 80. Owned by City of Dallas, but used exclusively by army under lease to war department.

Bus Stations: Union Bus Depot and Interurban Terminal, Jackson and Browder Sts. (Interurban Bldg.) for Dixie Motor Coaches Corp., Bowen Motor Coaches, Dallas-Celina-Sherman Bus Lines, Sunshine Bus Lines, Inc., Texas Motor Coaches, Inc.; Greyhound Union Bus Terminal, 812 Commerce St. at Lamar, for Southwestern Greyhound Lines, Inc., Texas Motor Coaches, Inc. (westbound only); Bowen Motor Coaches; Dallas-Celina-Sherman Bus Lines; Sunshine Bus Lines, Inc.; Dixie Motor Coaches Corp.; Texas Motor Coaches, Inc.; All-American Bus Lines Depot, 1001 Commerce St., for All-American Bus Lines, Inc. Bus sightseeing trips arranged at Dallas Railway & Terminal Co. (Interurban Bldg.)

Interurban Electric Service: Interurban Terminal and Union Bus Depot, Jackson and Browder Sts. (Interurban Bldg.) Cars operated between Dallas and Denison N. through McKinney and Sherman, and S. to Corsicana and Waco. Fares, Dallas to terminals: Denison $1.50, Waco $1.70, Corsicana $1.10; round-trip regular fare less 10 percent.

City Streetcar and Bus Service: Streetcar service supplemented by buses. Fare 7¢, five tokens 30¢. Children under 12, 3¢; school students with tickets 3¢ during term.

Taxicabs: 35¢ (1 or 4 persons) for first 2 1/2 mi., 10¢ each additional mi. Taxi stands in downtown district.

Traffic Regulations: Downtown traffic controlled by officers and signal lights. At intersections where signals are located, left turn on green, and right turn on red permitted only when so indicated by sign at bottom of signal light. Out-of-state vehicle licenses good in city 30 days. A booklet of traffic rules may be secured free of charge at police traffic bureau, City Hall; 1,500 parking meters downtown: 5¢ fee for varying periods from 15 minutes to one hour between 7 a.m. and 6 p.m. except legal holidays and Sundays, no fee. No parking under any conditions between 2 a.m. and 5 a.m. in metropolitan district bounded by Central Railroad, Houston St., Young St., and Pacific Ave. Outside metered districts, parking limit indicated on curb. Ample parking space on streets, and in centrally located parking stations downtown. Speed limit 20 miles an hour; 45 miles outside city limits in environs. Left turn where permitted must be made from inside white dividing line indicated on pavement; right turn where permitted must be made from as near right curb as possible.

Street Order and Numbering: Trinity River divides city into east and west sections; principal business district and app. two-thirds of Dallas population E. of river. Oak Cliff (W. of river) has several large business and shopping areas. Main St., running E. from river, is dividing line for N. and S. street numbers for 44 blocks east, thence Columbia Ave. becomes dividing line. In Oak Cliff, Beckley Ave. is dividing line for E. and W. street numbers, Tenth St. for N. and S. (only W. of Beckley Ave.)

Shopping Facilities: Central shopping district largely confined to three downtown streets, Elm, Main, and Commerce, bet. Houston and Harwood Sts., E. and W. Numerous neighborhood business and shopping centers over city. In Oak Cliff, four districts along Jefferson Ave. In Highland Park, Knox Street shopping area and the

Spanish Village shopping center, the architectural motif of which was derived from the Barcelona Exposition.

Theaters and Motion Picture Houses: Downtown, three first-run motion picture theaters, five modern second- and extended-run houses, three of which offer occasional road shows, opera, etc.; all between Akard and Harwood Sts. (E. and W.) on Elm St.; one legitimate theater, one Little Theater, and more than twenty neighborhood theaters.

Auditoriums: Fair Park Auditorium, Parry and Second Aves. (Seats 4,309); McFarlin Auditorium, Southern Methodist University, Mockingbird Lane and Hillcrest St. (Seats 3,000); City Hall Auditorium, City Hall, Harwood and Commerce Sts. (Seats 1,100)

Radio Stations: WFAA, 800 kc., (open 7 a.m.-10 p.m.), third floor Baker Hotel, Commerce St. at Akard St.; KRLD, 1040 kc., (open 6 a.m.-12 midnight), mezzanine floor Adolphus Hotel, Commerce St. at Akard St.; KGKO, 570 kc., (open 9 a.m.-5 p.m.), studios, Thomas Bldg., 1314 Wood St., station, Arlington, Texas; WRR, 1280 kc., (open 7 a.m.-12 midnight), owned by city of Dallas, studios and plant, Municipal Radio Building, Fair Park; KVP, 1712 kc., Dallas Police Radio Station, basement City Hall.

Information Bureaus: American Automobile Association, main office, Adolphus Hotel, phone 2−3411; branch office, Baker Hotel, phone 2−5131; Auto Club of Dallas, Adolphus Hotel, phone 2−3411; Better Business Bureau, 1000 Main St., phone 7−5109; Chamber of Commerce, Chamber of Commerce Bldg., 1101 Commerce St., phone 7−8451; Mexican Consulate, 1002 Main St. (Fidelity Bldg.), phone 7−6264. Travel and other information on Mexico.

National Service Clubs: Civitan Club, Thursday noon, Adolphus Hotel; Cooperative Club, Wednesday noon, Adolphus Hotel; Exchange Club, Wednesday noon, Adolphus Hotel; Kiwanis Club, Tuesday noon, Adolphus Hotel; Knights of the Round Table, Friday noon, Adolphus Hotel; Lions Club, Friday noon, Adolphus Hotel; Optimist Club, Thursday noon, Dallas Athletic Club; Real Estate Board, Thursday noon, Baker Hotel; Rotary Club, Wednesday noon, Baker Hotel; Traffic Club, 2nd and 4th Mondays noon, Dallas Athletic Club; Zonta Club of Dallas, every other Friday noon, Baker Hotel.

Local Luncheon Clubs: Advertising League, Tuesday noon, Adolphus Hotel; Agricultural Club, Monday noon, Jefferson Hotel; Bonehead Club, Friday noon, Baker Hotel; Electric Club, Monday noon, Baker Hotel; High Noon Club (Masonic), Thursday noon, Adolphus Hotel; Junior Chamber of Commerce, Wednesday noon, Adolphus Hotel; Motor Freight Traffic Club, Thursday noon, Cliff Towers; Retail Credit Men's Association, Thursday noon, Adolphus Hotel; Salesmanship Club, Thursday noon, Dallas Athletic Club; Technical Club, Tuesday noon, Adolphus Hotel; Texas A&M Club, Friday noon, Adolphus Hotel; Variety Club, Monday noon, Adolphus Hotel.

HOTEL AND OTHER ACCOMMODATIONS

Hotels

The Adolphus, 1321 Commerce St. at Akard St.; 825 rooms (275 air-conditioned); $2 up. European plan; air-conditioned dining room and coffee shop, four banquet halls, roof garden, bar, and writing room. (Home of Radio Station KRLD)

Baker Hotel, 1400 Commerce St. at Akard St.; 700 rooms (300 air-conditioned); $2 up. European plan; air-conditioned dining room, six banquet and meeting rooms, coffee shop, and cafeteria. (Home of Radio Station WFAA)

White-Plaza Hotel, 1933 Main St. at Harwood St.; 325 rooms (175 air-conditioned); $1.50 up. European plan; coffee shop.

Jefferson Hotel, 312 S. Houston St. at Wood St.; 450 rooms; $1.50 up. European plan; coffee shop and roof garden.

Scott Hotel, 302 S. Houston St. at Jackson St.; 175 rooms; $2 up. European plan; coffee shop. Garage service.

Southland Hotel, 1200 Main St. at Murphy St. through to Commerce St.; 200 rooms (70 air-conditioned); $1.50 up. European plan; dining room, coffee shop, and meeting room. Garage service.

Hotel Whitmore, 1019 Commerce St. at Martin St.; 120 rooms (75 air-conditioned); $2 up. European plan; dining room and coffee shop. Garage service.

Apartment Hotels

The Ambassador, 1312 S. Ervay St. bet. Pocahontas St. and Sullivan Park (Ervay car on Elm or Main St.); 50 apartments, 110 rooms; hotel rates $2 up, apartments $60 per month up. Modern coffee shop. Garage.

Cliff Towers, Zang Blvd. and Colorado St. (Seventh St. car on Main St.); 125 units. Rooms $2 up, apartments $3 per day, $65 per month up. Coffee shop. Garage.

The Highlander, 4217 Loma Alto Dr. at Roland (University or Greenway Parks

15

Coach on Elm St.); 46 four-room apartments; $135 per month up. Coffee shop, sun deck on 8th floor for solar baths; air-conditioned throughout. Garage.

Maple Terrace, 3001 Maple Ave. at Carlisle St. (Love Field or Greenway Parks Coach on Elm St.); 28 bachelor apartments $60 up; 56 four- and five-room apartments; furnished $125 up, unfurnished $115 up per month. Garage. Dining room accommodations at Stoneleigh Court across street; 18-acre flower and rock garden and tennis courts in rear of building.

Melrose Court, 3015 Oak Lawn Ave. at Cedar Springs Rd. (Oak Lawn car on Commerce or Elm St.); 149 units from one to five rooms. Single room $60 up, apartments $75 per month up. Air-conditioned. Garage.

Sanger Hotel and Apartments, 1611 Canton St. at Ervay St. (Ervay car on Elm or Main St.); 188 single rooms and 48 apartments. Rooms $2 up, apartments $65 per month up. Air-conditioned lobby, coffee shop.

Stoneleigh Court, 2927 Maple Ave. at Carlisle St. (Love Field or Greenway Parks Coach on Elm St.); 136 units, apartments $85 per month up; bachelor apartments $55 up. Air-conditioned. Maid service, dining room, grill. Garage.

YMCA and YWCA

YMCA, 605 N. Ervay St. bet. Patterson Ave. and San Jacinto St. (Oak Lawn car on Commerce or Elm St.); 238 rooms for local and visiting members only. Grill room, dining room, recreational facilities. $1 per day for single room; weekly $4 up. Double rooms $5 up.

YWCA Residence, 1206 N. Haskell Ave. bet. Live Oak St. and Swiss Ave. (Belmont car on Main or Elm St.); 69 rooms, private, double and dormitories (4 beds); dining room. Rooms $5 up (weekly). American plan.

Tourist Camps

Numerous modern tourist camps are located in the city and environs on all Federal and state highways.

Accommodations for Negroes

Lone Star Hotel, 2602 State St. at Routh St. (State car on Elm St.); 12 rooms, 2 baths, hot and cold water, rates $3.50 weekly.

Powell Hotel and Court, 3115 State St., bet. Hugo and Ellis Sts. (State car on Elm St.); 73 rooms, 2 baths on each floor, hot and cold water. European plan; $1 up; dining room and bar. Garage.

YMCA Moorland Branch, 2700 Flora St. at Boll St. (Vickery Coach on Elm St.); 37 rooms, 28 single, 9 double, with hot and cold water. European plan; cafe. Rates 75¢, $1 daily, $2 weekly.

RECREATIONAL FACILITIES

Parks

Lake Cliff Park, Crawford, Colorado, Fifth Sts., and Blaylock Dr. (Seventh St. car on Main St. or Beckley Coach on Elm St.) Municipal swimming pool and bathhouse, concession stand; baseball and softball diamonds, football and soccer fields, cinder track, tennis courts, play apparatus, boating and picnic facilities. Site of annual municipal tennis, track, and swimming meets. City open tennis tournaments are held here.

Bachman's Lake and Park, Maple Ave. and Shorecrest Dr. (Love Field Coach, Ervay at Elm or Elm at Akard St.) By auto 7.1 mi. downtown E. on Main St. to Lamar St., N. on Lamar to McKinney Ave., E. on McKinney to Orange St., NE. on Orange to Cedar Springs Ave., N. on Cedar Springs to Maple Ave. (US 77-SH 40), NW. on Maple to M-K-T R. R., where Denton Dr. begins, NW. on Denton to Shorecrest Dr. on right. Boating, fishing, picnic facilities, bridle path, and tennis courts. On N. shore are Salesmanship Club Recreation Camp for Underprivileged Children, City Federation of Women's Clubs Camp, Dallas Tuberculosis Association Camp for Undernourished Children, and Dallas Camp Fire Lodge. Swimming pool and complete playground equipment at Salesmanship Camp.

Kiest Park, bounded by Wheatland (Hampton) Rd., Inner Kessler Blvd., and Five-Mile Creek. (Hampton Place car on Commerce St.) By auto 7 mi. from downtown, S. on Houston St., cross viaduct to Zang Blvd., SW. on Zang to Davis St., W. on Davis to Edgefield St., S. on Edgefield to Clarendon Dr., W. on Clarendon to Hampton Rd., S. on Hampton to park on left. Contains 247 acres, given to city by Edwin J. Kiest, as a memorial to his wife, Elizabeth Patterson Kiest. Landscaped around water rills and sunken garden with shrubbery and flower beds. Equipped playgrounds, tennis courts, baseball diamonds, archery triangle, football and soccer fields, bridle path, picnic facilities, shelter house, barbecue pits and ovens. Field house available for private parties and dances for $5 per night. The remainder of the acreage is maintained in its naturally wooded state.

17

Tenison Park, Samuell Blvd. (East Pike) and East Grand Ave. (Mt. Auburn car on Main St.) By auto 4.6 mi. from downtown, E. on Commerce St. to Second Ave., SE. on Second to Parry Ave., N. on Parry to Haskell Ave., E. on Haskell to East Grand Ave., NE. on East Grand to Samuell Blvd., E. on Samuell Blvd. to entrance on left. The 122 acres in this park were given to the city in 1923 by E. O. Tenison and wife as a memorial to their son, Edward Hugh Tenison, and since that time about 100 acres more have been added. Tennis courts, baseball diamonds, football and soccer fields. Natural wooded picnic grounds with brick ovens and other facilities; comfort stations and play apparatus. Municipal golf course.

Stevens Park, N. Mont Clair and Kessler Parkway. (Stevens Park Coach, Commerce St. at Lamar) Tennis courts, picnic facilities, and shelter and play apparatus. Municipal golf course.

White Rock Lake Park, Old Garland Rd. (Parkview or Junius Heights cars on Main St.) By auto 6.4 mi. NE. of courthouse, E. on Pacific Ave. to Hawkins St., where Gaston Ave. (US 67) begins, continue NE. to Lawther Dr. *(see POINTS OF INTEREST, White Rock Lake Park)*

Marsalis Park, bounded by Opera St., Clarendon Dr., Ewing and Storey Aves. (Sunset or Hampton cars on Commerce St.) *(see POINTS OF INTEREST, Dallas Zoological Gardens)*

Reverchon Park, Maple Ave., at W. end of Turtle Creek Blvd. (Greenway Parks or Love Field Coach, Ervay at Elm or Elm at Akard St.) *(see POINTS OF INTEREST, Reverchon Park)*

Sullivan Park (Browder Springs 1876, City Park 1881–1936), Ervay and Pocahontas Sts., Park Ave., and Gano St. (Ervay car on Elm, Main, or Ervay Sts.) *(see POINTS OF INTEREST, Sullivan Park)*

Robert E. Lee Park, Hall St. and Turtle Creek Blvd. (Oak Lawn car on Commerce St. westbound or on Elm St. eastbound) *(see POINTS OF INTEREST, Robert E. Lee Park)*

Exline Park (Community Center), Pine, Eugene, and Latimer Sts. (Ervay car on Elm, Main, or Ervay Sts.) Wading pool, softball diamonds, play apparatus with supervised play, community house with free baths.

Fretz Park (Community Center known as Cotton Mills Playground, later as Trinity Play Park), S. Lamar St. bet. Corinth and Montgomery Sts. (Myrtle car on Elm St.) This park was the first community center in the city, provided for the many children in this industrial district. Kindergarten, day nursery, milk station, wading pool, baseball diamond, tennis courts, apparatus with supervised play, auditorium and field house with free baths.

Lagow Park (Community Center), Second Ave. and Carpenter St. (Second Ave. car on Commerce St.) Wading pool, tennis courts, baseball diamonds, library, roque court, apparatus with supervised play, picnic facilities, community house with free baths.

Pike Park (Community Center), Randall, Turney, and Payne Sts. in Little Mexico. (Lake Ave. Coach on Elm at Field St.) Community house and auditorium in center of park. Tennis courts, softball diamonds, football and soccer fields, wading pool, apparatus with supervised play, free baths. *(see LITTLE MEXICO: OUTPOST FOR MANANA)*

Walford Park (Community Center for small children), Haskell Ave., Roseland and Ripley Sts. (Vickery Coach on Elm St.) Park enclosed, under supervision of a playground director. Softball, volleyball, baseball diamonds, sand beds, swings, and library.

In addition to these listed there are in Dallas 27 smaller neighborhood parks and playgrounds for white persons, many of which have modern equipment. (For information, call Park Board, 7–9731.)

Clubs

Dallas Athletic Club, Liberty Bank Bldg., St. Paul and Elm Sts. *(see POINTS OF INTEREST, Dallas Athletic Club)*

Young Men's Christian Association, 605 N. Ervay St. bet. Patterson and San Jacinto Sts. (Oak Lawn car on Commerce or Elm St.) *(see POINTS OF INTEREST, Young Men's Christian Association)*

Young Women's Christian Association, 1709 Jackson St. bet. Prather and Ervay St. From Commerce St. walk one block S. on Ervay or Prather St. *(see POINTS OF INTEREST, Young Women's Christian Association)*

Jewish Community Center, 1817½ Pocahontas St. and Park Ave. (Ervay car on Main or Elm St.) Gymnasium, auditorium, basketball court, volleyball court, and ping-pong tables. Facilities for members and guests.

Baseball and Softball

Twenty-eight baseball and 87 softball diamonds are provided in various city parks and playgrounds.

Boating

Boats may be rented from concessionaires at White Rock Lake, Bachman's Lake, and Lake Cliff Park, all municipally owned. *(see PARKS)*

Bowling

Hap Morse Bowling Alleys, 1515 Young St., bet. Browder and Ervay Sts. Twenty-seven alleys. Largest in the South without a post; air-conditioned summer and winter. Modern equipment; floodlighted; 22 regular leagues patronize these alleys. Play for both men and women.

Brantley-Burton Bowling Alleys, 1807 N. Harwood St. Sixteen alleys; 14 regular leagues patronize this alley. Drop light system; instructors for both men and women.

Golf Courses—Country Clubs

Tenison Park and Golf Course (Municipal), bounded by Samuell Blvd. (East Pike) and East Grand Ave. (Mt. Auburn car on Main St.) Eighteen holes, grass greens; 50¢ weekdays, 75¢ Saturdays, Sundays, and holidays. Annual membership $15.

Stevens Park Golf Course (Municipal), N. Mont Clair and Kessler Parkway. (Stevens Park Coach, Commerce at Lamar) Eighteen holes, grass greens; 50¢ weekdays, 75¢ Saturdays, Sundays, and holidays. Annual membership $15.

El Tivoli Golf Course, W. Davis (Fort Worth Pike) bet. Kessler Blvd. and Cliffdale Ave. By auto 4 ½ mi. from courthouse S. on Houston St. over viaduct to Zang Blvd., SW. on Zang to Davis St., W. on Davis to club on right. Eighteen-hole golf course, grass greens; 50¢ weekdays, 75¢ Saturdays, Sundays, and holidays.

Bob-O-Link Golf Course, 3120 Abrams Rd. By auto app. 5 mi. from downtown,

E. on Pacific Ave. to Hawkins St., where Gaston Ave. (US 67) begins, to Abrams Rd., turn left (N.) on Abrams Rd. and continue to golf course on right. Eighteen-hole golf course, grass greens; 35¢ weekdays, 50¢ Saturdays, Sundays, and holidays.

Crescent Golf Course, Lemmon Ave. at Maple Lawn. (Lemmon Ave. Coach on Elm St., bet. Olive and Hawkins Sts.) Eighteen-hole golf course, grass greens; 50¢ weekdays, 75¢ Saturdays, Sundays, and holidays.

Cedar Lake Golf Course, SE. of Dallas, left of Scyene Rd. (SH 183) and left (W.) of Buckner Blvd. By auto 7½ mi. SE. from downtown, E. on Commerce St. to Second Ave., SE. on Second to Scyene Rd., E. on Scyene to Buckner Blvd., course on left. Nine holes, sand greens; 35¢ for 18 holes.

Brook Hollow Country Club (Private), Grauwyler and Brook Hollow Rd. By auto 6 mi. from downtown, N. on Akard St. to McKinney Ave., NE. on McKinney to Maple Ave., left (W.) on Maple (Denton Dr. after leaving Hudnall) to Lovers Lane, left (W.) on Lovers Lane to clubhouse. Golf course, tennis courts, outdoor swimming pool, putting greens, card room, grill, and dining room.

Cedar Crest Golf and Country Club (Private), Cedar Crest Blvd. and Sutherland Ave. By auto 5 mi. from downtown, S. on Forest Ave. across bridge and continue to Cedar Crest Blvd. to club entrance. Eighteen holes, grass greens, putting greens, lunch and card rooms; 75¢ weekdays, $1 Saturdays, Sundays, and holidays.

Columbian Club (Jewish—Private), NE. of Dallas on Garland Rd. (US 67) about 1 mi. past White Rock Lake on left side of highway. By auto 7 1/2 mi. from downtown, E. on Pacific Ave. to Hawkins St., where Gaston Ave. (US 67) begins, passing lake, and to club on left of highway. Outdoor swimming pool, sand beach, tennis court, putting greens, dining room and cafe, ballroom and cocktail lounge, playground equipment for children.

Dallas Country Club (Private), Preston Rd. and Beverly Dr. (Highland Park car on Elm St.) Golf course, outdoor swimming pool, tennis courts, driving range, putting greens, restaurant, and card room. Swimming meets of the Dallas Country Clubs are held here each year.

Glen Lakes Golf and Country Club (Private), NE. of Dallas, about 1/2 mi. NW. of town of Vickery. By auto 7 mi. from downtown, NE. on Ross Ave. to Greenville Ave., N. on Greenville (Richardson Rd., US 75-SH 6) to Southwestern Blvd, turn left (W.) on Southwestern Blvd. to Coit Rd., turn right (N.) on Coit Rd. and continue to club entrance on right. Golf course, putting greens, swimming pool, dining room, grill room and bar, card room, and ballroom.

Lakewood Country Club (Private), Gaston Ave. near Abrams Rd. (Junius Heights car on Main St.) Golf course, outdoor swimming pool, tennis courts, putting greens, grill, ballroom, and card room. Site of annual Lakewood invitation golf tournament.

Parkdale Country Club, SE. of Dallas, left of Scyene Rd. 1/4 mi. beyond White Rock Creek. By auto 5 1/2 mi. from downtown, E. on Commerce St. to Second Ave., SE. on Second to Scyene Rd., left (E.) on Scyene past White Rock Creek to club on left. Eighteen holes, grass greens; 50¢ weekdays, Saturdays, Sundays, and holidays; 25¢ Monday through Friday after 5 p.m.

Walnut Hill Country Club, NW. of Dallas, Lemmon Ave. and Northwest Highway. By auto 8 mi. from downtown, E. on Main St. to Lamar St., N. on Lamar to McKinney Ave., E. on McKinney to Lemmon Ave., N. on Lemmon past Northwest

Highway short distance to club on right. Eighteen holes, grass greens; 50¢ weekdays, 75¢ Saturdays, Sundays, and holidays.

Gymnasiums

Dallas Athletic Club. *(see POINTS OF INTEREST, Dallas Athletic Club)*

YMCA. *(see POINTS OF INTEREST, YMCA)*

YWCA. *(see POINTS OF INTEREST, YWCA)*

Jewish Community Center. Classes Monday through Thursday evening 8 to 10. Wednesday night classes are for young people over 12 years.

SMU Gymnasiums and Basketball Pavilion, on campus at Hillcrest St. and Mockingbird Lane. (Highland Park car on Elm St.) Men's gymnasium, complete with basketball court for Southwestern conference games; seating capacity 3,500. Classes in fencing and other indoor sports. Women's swimming pool and gymnasium, complete college gymnasium equipment, with basketball court; seating capacity 1,000.

Dallas Labor Temple Gymnasium, 1727 Young St., available to public for training. Amateurs free, professional $1 per week.

High School Gymnasiums. All Dallas high schools have completely equipped gymnasiums.

Riding

Rendezvous Stables, Northwest Highway, near Lemmon Ave. By auto app. 8 mi. from downtown, E. on Main St. to Lamar St., N. on Lamar to McKinney Ave., E. on McKinney to Lemmon Ave., N. on Lemmon to Northwest Highway; turn right on Northwest Highway about 1/4 mi., stables on right. Regulation size riding ring with floodlights for night riding; club rooms with showers, picnic grounds, and picnic pits. Country roads and access to Bachman's municipal path. Six hours riding for $5, or $1 per hour.

Palace Riding Academy, 7900 Denton Dr. at Mabel Ave. By auto 5½ mi. from downtown, E. on Main St. to Lamar St., N. on Lamar to McKinney Ave., E. on McKinney to Maple Ave., N. on Maple to Denton Dr. (US 77-SH 40) to stable entrance, visible from Denton Dr. Country roads and access to Bachman's municipal path. Instructor; 75¢ hr.

Horseshoe Stables, Abrams Rd. N. of McCommas Ave. By auto 5 mi. from downtown, E. on Main St. to Lamar St., N. on Lamar to Pacific Ave., E. on Pacific to Hawkins St., where Gaston Ave. (US 67) begins, to Abrams Rd., N. on Abrams to McCommas, stables on left. One-eighth-mile floodlighted riding path for rides at night. Bridle path within easy reach of municipal path at White Rock Lake. Instructor and trainer on grounds; 75¢ hr. weekdays, $1 Sundays.

Blue Bonnet Riding Stables, Abrams Rd. south of M-K-T R. R. By auto 6 mi. from downtown, E. on Main St. to Lamar St., N. on Lamar to Pacific Ave., E. on Pacific to Hawkins St., where Gaston Ave. (US 67) begins, to Abrams Rd., N. on Abrams past Mockingbird Lane and continue to stable, entrance on left. Private bridle path and access to municipal path at White Rock Lake. Private instructor; 50¢ hr. weekdays, 75¢ hr. Sundays.

White Rock Bridle Path (Municipal), runs N. and S. bet. White Rock Lake and Lawther Dr. *(see POINTS OF INTEREST, White Rock Lake Park)*

Bachman's Bridle Path (Municipal), along S. shore of lake, and among trees and hills on eastern side of lake, 11 miles in length. *(see PARKS)*

Kiest Park Bridle Path (Municipal), through park and small hills and along Five-Mile Creek. *(see PARKS)*

Stadiums

Cotton Bowl Stadium, in Fair Park, Parry and Second Aves. (Second or Forest Ave. cars on Commerce St., or Parkview or Mt. Auburn cars on Main St.) Seating capacity 46,400. Football, rodeo, concerts, community and mass singings. Press box, broadcasting room, electrically operated score board, public address system, and floodlighting for night playing.

Dal-Hi Field, bet. Reagan St. and Oak Lawn Blvd., left (W.) of Maple Ave. (Greenway Parks or Love Field Coach on Ervay at Elm St.) Field house; seating capacity 3,500, contains basketball, volleyball, handball, and indoor tennis courts. Boxing and wrestling rooms; press box; broadcasting room, equipped with public speaker system. Stadium seating capacity 27,000; cinder track with 220-yd. straightaway track, quarter mi. circle track; three tennis courts and baseball diamond, illuminated for night games. Three broadcasting rooms, press box seating 45. All-weather parking area for 7,000 cars.

Highland Park High School Stadium, 4200 Emerson Ave., bet. Westchester and Douglas St. (Highland Park car or University Park Coach on Elm St.) Seating capacity 6,000; press box used as broadcasting room for public address system; floodlights for night playing; rifle range for ROTC practice. Home of Highlanders football team.

Ownby Stadium, SMU Campus near Airline Rd. and Mockingbird Lane. (Highland Park car or University Park Coach on Elm St.) Seating capacity 20,000. Conference and nonconference football games of SMU played here. Cinder track inside entire oval. During track season stadium is used for field and track meets.

Dallas Baseball Stadium (Rebel Field), 1500 E. Jefferson Ave. at Colorado St., in Oak Cliff. (Hampton Place, Sunset, or Trinity Heights cars on Commerce St.) Home of Dallas Rebels, Texas League baseball team. Seating capacity 16,500. Parking accommodations for 1,500 cars.

Swimming

White Rock Lake Bathing Beach (Municipal), Old Garland Rd. (US 67-SH 1). By auto 9.8 mi. NE. from courthouse, E. on Main St. to Lamar St., N. on Lamar to Pacific Ave., E. on Pacific to Hawkins St., where Gaston Ave. (US 67) begins; continue NE. on Gaston to White Rock Dr., circling lake on east. Bathing beach, diving boards, and other facilities. Open 6 a.m. to 10 p.m. daily June 1 to September 1; 25¢, children 15¢.

Lake Cliff Swimming Pool (Municipal), Colorado St. and Zang Blvd., Crawford St. and Blaylock Dr. in Oak Cliff. (Seventh St. car on Main St.) Diving boards, water top, and other facilities; children's wading pool. Open 6 a.m. to 10 p.m. June 1 to September 1; 25¢, children 15¢.

Fair Park Swimming Pool (Municipal), in Fair Park, Parry and Second Aves. (Second or Forest Ave. cars on Commerce St.) Diving boards and other facilities. Open 6 a.m. to 10 p.m. June 1 to September 1; 25¢, children 15¢.

Highland Park Swimming Pool (Municipal), Lexington Ave. at Drexel Dr. in

Highland Park. (Highland Park car on Elm St.) Wading pool for children, diving boards, and other facilities. Open 6 a.m. to 10 p.m. daily from last week in May until cool weather. Membership fee for residents of Highland Park. Guests may be taken on invitation of members for fee of 25¢.

University Park Swimming Pool (Municipal), Westminster Ave. at Dickens St. (University Park Coach on Elm St.) Wading pool for children, diving boards, and other facilities. Open 6 a.m. to 10 p.m. daily from first week in June until cool weather. Membership fee for residents of University Park. Guests may be taken by members for fee of 50¢.

Kidd Springs, Canty and Tyler Sts., in Oak Cliff. (Seventh St. car on Main St.) Wading pool for children, diving boards, chute, bathing beach, 20-foot diving tower, water tops, and spring boards. Open 6 a.m. to 12 p.m. daily, from May 14 through Labor Day.

YMCA Swimming Pool. Members and guests only.

YWCA Swimming Pool. Members and guests only.

(For other swimming facilities, see Golf Courses—Country Clubs.)

Tennis

Cedar Springs Tennis Club, 4500 Cedar Springs Rd., bet. Herschel St. and Cotton Belt R. R. (Greenway Parks Coach on Ervay at Elm St.) Seven tennis courts, concrete practice court, and clubhouse with showers for members. Club tournaments are held regularly.

Dallas Lawn Tennis Club, 201 E. Colorado St., bet. Zang Blvd. and Englewood St. (Seventh St. car on Main St.) Use of the eight courts and clubhouse restricted to members and guests. Club tournaments held annually.

There are 90 public tennis courts located in the different parks in the city and ten other courts on grounds of the various schools. Reservations made at Fretz Community Center, Corinth and Cochran Sts. Phone 4–7151. All Country Clubs also have tennis courts.

Trap Shooting

Trinity Rifle Club and Shooting Range, west end of Oak Cliff viaduct, to the right (N.). Open Saturdays and Sundays; 25¢ fee for nonmembers.

Dallas Skeet Club, west end of Oak Cliff viaduct, to the right. Open at all times; $1.35 for round including 25 birds with box of ammunition.

Horseshoe Pitching, Dominoes, and Checkers

Horseshoe pitching in practically all Dallas parks. Equipment for dominoes and checkers supplied by the Park Department in the following parks: Buckner, Exall, Fretz, Garrett, Kiest, Lagow, Lake Cliff, Robert E. Lee, Marsalis, Pike, Reverchon, and Sullivan.

NEGRO RECREATIONAL FACILITIES

YMCA (Moorland Branch), 2700 Flora St. at Boll St. (Vickery Coach on Elm St.) Swimming pool, gymnasium, basketball court, pool and billiard tables for men, pool, billiard and cue roque tables for boys, two game rooms for boys.

YWCA (Maria Morgan), 2503 N. Washington Ave. at State St. (State car on Elm St.) Game room, ping-pong tables, tap dancing and calisthenics for children. Employment department, classes in household management, and Bible study. Uses facilities of Negro YMCA for swimming, during summer months from June through August, Mondays, Wednesdays, Fridays, 8 a.m. and Tuesdays and Thursdays, 9 a.m. Facilities available to nonmembers.

Baseball

Baseball and softball diamonds are provided in various parks and playgrounds.

Softball

League Softball is played on the grounds of the Booker T. Washington High School, located at Flora and Burford Sts. (State car on Elm St.) Under the supervision of the YMCA.

Basketball

Basketball is played by amateur leagues, by boys and girls of the YMCA and YWCA in the gymnasium of the YMCA, and by the Booker T. Washington and Lincoln High School teams in their school gymnasiums.

Football

Football games are played by the Booker T. Washington High School (Bulldogs) and Lincoln High School (Tigers) at Dal-Hi Field. Two games are played on Negro Day at the State Fair in the Cotton Bowl. In the afternoon an annual game is played between Wiley College of Marshall, and Prairie View State Normal, Prairie View. The Booker T. Washington Bulldogs play Lincoln Tigers or some other outstanding colored high school team at night.

Gymnasiums

YMCA Gymnasium (Moorland Branch), gymnasium classes Monday, Wednesday, Friday mornings. Boxing, Monday, Wednesday, Friday 8:30 a.m. Swimming classes, Monday, Wednesday, Friday 10:30 a.m. Gymnasium classes in the Booker T. Washington High School and the Lincoln High School.

Parks

Hall Street Park (Community Center), Hall at Cochran St. and H&TC R.R. (State car on Elm St.) Swimming pool and bathhouse, free baths, tennis courts, baseball diamonds, play apparatus, and supervised play.

Wahoo Lake and Park (Community Center), Spring Ave. and Foreman St. By auto 4.9 mi. from downtown, E. on Commerce St. to Second Ave., SE. on Second to Spring Ave., NE. on Spring to Foreman St. to park entrance on left. Park is operated the year round as a center for recreation for both adults and children. The annual field day for Negro children is held in the park under the supervision of the Park Department. Community house, picnic facilities, baseball diamonds, tennis courts, play apparatus, children's wading pool. Fishing allowed, 25¢ fee; open to public but used exclusively by Negroes.

Eighth Street Park, Eighth St. (Bosley) and Rockefeller Blvd., Oak Cliff. (Trinity Heights car on Commerce St.) Field house, baseball diamonds, picnic grounds, and play apparatus.

Two other parks afford park and playground facilities.

Swimming

Hall Street Swimming Pool (Municipal). Swimming pool and bathhouse. Open 6 a.m. to 10 p.m. daily from June 1 to September 1.

YMCA (Moorland Branch). Swimming classes, Mondays, Wednesdays, and Fridays. Members and their guests.

YWCA (Maria Morgan). Uses facilities of the YMCA swimming pool on Mondays, Wednesdays, and Fridays 8 a.m., Tuesdays and Thursdays 9 a.m. Facilities are available to nonmembers.

Tennis

Tennis is played in the various Negro parks, with elimination held at Hall Street Negro Park annually under the supervision of the Park Department.

Track and Field Meets

Track and Field Meets are held annually at the Booker T. Washington High School and Lincoln High School.

Athletic Meets

Winning teams in park and community center athletic competitions engage in annual finals.

Amateur Sports Events

Baseball is played in season Saturdays and Sundays by a number of amateur teams in the following places: Kiest Park, Lake Cliff Park, Randall Park, Reverchon Park, and Tenison Park. High school and other amateur teams of the city play on these diamonds. There are two junior baseball leagues in the city divided into 24 teams and composed of boys from 15 to 17, playing regulation baseball.

League Softball is played every night in season, 8 and 9 o'clock, at the Railton Softball Park, in Fair Park, bet. Fair Park Auditorium and the swimming pool. There are 60 teams that use this field and in a season attract as high as three-quarters of a million people. Softball is played on 87 other diamonds located in the various city parks. Forty-eight softball teams in the Church League play softball at Lion Field, on the west side of Industrial Blvd., two miles north of the triple underpass. This plant was acquired early in 1939 by the Lions Club of Dallas for use of the church players.

Basketball games, by Southern Methodist University (Mustangs) in Southwest Conference schedule, high schools and private preparatory schools. Numerous amateur men's and women's leagues play in the Automobile Building at Fair Park. YMCA has four leagues, three playing in the Central YMCA, one on a municipal court.

Bowling Tournaments are held semiannually at Hap Morse Bowling Alley, 1515 Young St., with outstanding amateurs competing.

Boxing contests are staged under the auspices of the Southwestern Amateur Athletic Union, at the Dallas Athletic Club, Liberty Bank Bldg., St. Paul and Elm

Sts. Boxing and wrestling tournaments also are held in Dallas and in Oak Cliff YMCA.

Football games of sectional and interstate importance are played by Southern Methodist University (Mustangs) in Southwest Conference schedule at Ownby Stadium on the university campus. Intersectional games are played at the Cotton Bowl at Fair Park. These include an annual Thanksgiving Day game between the University of Texas and the University of Oklahoma, and the Cotton Bowl game on New Year's Day between the winner of the Southwest Conference title and an invited team representing another conference. High schools, beginning with the 1939 season, played at the new Dal-Hi Field. Preparatory schools and professional teams play usually at the Cotton Bowl. There are two leagues of boys under 15 and not on any high school team playing softball, in addition to 12 teams playing soccer, which is popular as a playground sport in Dallas.

Golf Tournaments—Men's City Tournament and the Women's City Tournament are held annually at various country clubs in the city. (*see Golf Courses—Country Clubs* for locations of links.) Admission free. Lakewood Country Club invitation golf tournament is held annually. Municipal championship tournament held annually at one of the municipal courses.

Polo at Hawes Park, Denton Dr. and Mabel Ave., Tuesdays and Fridays at 3 p.m., Sunday, 3:30 p.m. Tournaments in spring and fall with teams from Texas, comprising the Southwest Circuit. Admission free, except for final elimination games. Ample parking space along both sides of the playing field.

Tennis—Municipal senior and junior tennis tournaments are staged annually in various parks, with eliminations held at Lake Cliff Park. A number of privately sponsored tournaments are held each year, under general supervision of Dallas Park Board, while tournament matches are held at the country clubs and private tennis clubs.

Track and Field Meets—Municipal senior and junior track and field meets are held annually in various parks, with track eliminations at Lake Cliff Park. High school track and field meets at Dal-Hi Field. SMU track and field meets at Ownby Stadium.

Swimming Meet eliminations held in each park with winners taking part in the city meet at Lake Cliff Park.

Elimination contests in **croquet, horseshoe pitching,** and **roque** also are held at Lake Cliff Park.

Professional Sports Events
Baseball

Dallas Baseball Stadium (Rebel Field), 1500 E. Jefferson Ave. at Colorado St. in Oak Cliff. (Hampton Place, Sunset, or Trinity Heights car on Commerce St.) Home of the Dallas team in the Texas Baseball League. Night games during week, day game Sundays. Seating capacity 16,500. Admission: boxes $1.10; grandstand 80¢; pavilion 55¢; bleachers 40¢. Parking accommodations for 1,500 cars.

26

Boxing and Wrestling

Sportatorium, Cadiz St. and Industrial Blvd. (Myrtle car on Elm St.) Program usually four preliminaries (three events of four rounds, one event of six rounds) and main event of ten rounds. Section for Negroes. Bouts are held Thursday evenings 8:30. Heavyweight wrestling matches Tuesday evenings 8:30. Five bouts usually held. The first three events are 20-minutes, one-fall matches, and the other two events are two-hour limit, two out of three falls. Seating capacity 9,600.

Hunting and Fishing: Time and Place

Hunting

General Information—Dallas County is in the North Zone in the division of the state for seasonal hunting of migratory birds. Licenses (1940)—It is unlawful to hunt outside the county of your residence in Texas without a state license. ($2, dated Sept. 1, good for 1 year, required of resident hunters over 17 years old. Nonresident license, $25). Duck hunters required to have Federal license ($1). Unlawful (1940) to hunt from automobile or motorboat, to possess more than 50 game birds of all kinds at one time, to hunt under license of another, to hire another to hunt for you, to hunt with shotgun larger than 10 gauge, to hunt with automatic or repeating gun that is not plugged for 3 shells only, to bait for waterfowl or doves, to use live duck or geese decoys regardless of distance bait may be from shooter, to hunt before 7 a.m. or after sundown.

Game Animals listed under the Federal and state laws are deer, elk, antelope, bear, wild sheep, squirrels, and peccaries.

Game Birds listed are turkeys, geese, ducks, brant, grouse, prairie chickens, pheasants, quail or partridges, wild pigeons, doves, snipe, chachalaca, plover, and shore birds of all kinds.

No Open Season on antelope, wood duck, plover, or prairie chicken (1940).

Open Season and Bag Limit (North Zone, 1940)—**Doves**, Sept. 1 to Oct. 31 inc.; 15 in 1 day, 15 in possession at one time. **Quail**, Dec. 1 to Jan. 16 inc.; 12 in 1 day, 36 in calendar week. **Turkeys**, Nov. 16 to Dec. 31 inc.; 3 gobblers in one season, some exceptions. **Deer**, Nov. 16 to Dec. 31 inc.; 2 bucks in 1 season. **Squirrels**, May, June, and July; Oct., Nov., and Dec.; 10 in 1 day, 20 in possession at one time, some exceptions. **Ducks and Geese**, Nov. 15 to Dec. 29 inc.; 10 ducks in 1 day, 4 geese in 1 day; possession 20 ducks at one time, 8 geese at one time. In 1939 season you may have 3 canvasbacks, redheads, buffleheads, or ruddy ducks in the 10-bag limit, or an aggregate of 3 ducks of these different species. Not more than 2 days' bag limit of lawfully taken and possessed ducks and geese can be transported in one calendar week.

Where to Hunt—Rabbits (cottontails) are not listed as game animals and are not covered by the wildlife conservation laws. They may be hunted in the fields and marshes of Dallas and adjoining counties. It is necessary to obtain permission from land owners and farmers before entering these fields, as most of them are posted against trespassing. Doves are found in almost any field (see above warning against trespassing). Squirrels usually may be found (in season) in the oak, elm, cotton-wood, and pecan groves along the Trinity River and its tributary streams in Dallas and adjoining counties.

Ducks and geese appear on the lakes and streams in the Dallas district as they fly southward in September and October, northward in late January and February, with "flybacks" of ducks from coastal regions between these main flights. Mallard, pintail, bluebill, widgeon, redhead, canvasback, and teal are the most plentiful among the migratory birds. Geese appear only in the early southward and late northward flights. Club lakes in Dallas County *(see Fishing section in HUNTING AND FISHING: TIME AND PLACE)* have blinds, boats, accommodations for members and invited guests. Hunting and fishing camps at Lake Dallas, Eagle Mountain Lake, Lake Bridgeport *(see Fishing section)* have boats, blinds, guides, and cabin accommodations. There are a number of small lakes in Dallas and adjoining counties where "bank hunting" may be had, notably Murphy's Lake at Crandall, Kaufman County (US 175, 27 mi. E. of Dallas); lakes at Waxahachie (US 77, 30 mi. S. of Dallas); Ennis (US 75, 35 mi. S. of Dallas); and Corsicana (US 75, 55 mi. S. of Dallas). Duck hunting is not allowed at White Rock Lake and Bachman's Lake in Dallas County, these lakes being in the city limits of Dallas.

While bear and deer are not to be found in the Dallas area of the state, numbers of Dallas hunters annually go out for this game and visitors may wish to be informed as to the nearest section in which they may be hunted.

Since these game animals range only in the sparsely inhabited regions of East and West Texas, it is advisable for the hunter to consult information bureaus of the sporting goods houses, where hunting lodges and camps are listed each season and detailed information as to routes, guides, accommodations, and rates are kept. Dallas hunters have found the regions about Kerrville, 64 mi. NW. of San Antonio, and Mason, 124 mi. NW. of Austin, good deer hunting grounds. Deer and bear are found in Big Thicket, a wild swampy region near Kountze, Hardin County, 26 mi. N. of Beaumont.

Fishing

Freshwater fishing in season (May to Feb.) is available in two lakes in the immediate vicinity of Dallas, **White Rock Lake** and **Bachman's Lake** (see below), and in a number of large lakes within a radius of 70 miles of Dallas. The Dallas lakes are restocked annually by the Dallas Park Board and those in the outlying area by the Texas Game, Fish & Oyster Commission. Bass, crappie (white perch), bream (green perch), and channel catfish are the species used for restocking by both agencies. In each of the lakes in the region it is not unusual for the angler to catch the legal limit daily in the protected species, under these laws and regulations by the Commission:

Bass (not less than 11 in.) 15 per day; white perch (not less than 7 in.) 15; bream, 35; goggle-eye, 35; total of 15 bass and white perch, or total of 50 of all protected species. Residents of Texas when fishing with artificial bait or lures must have a license for same, $1.10; nonresidents must have a nonresident fishing license, $5.00 per year, $1.10 for five days. Licenses may be obtained at sporting goods stores or at the larger fishing camps on the lakes.

White Rock Lake, 6.4 mi. NE. of Dallas County Courthouse, on Gaston Ave. (continuation of Pacific Ave.), a clearwater lake covering 1,347 acres with boat concessions along the shoreline where permits to fish (25¢), minnows and other bait may be obtained. Boat hire, 50¢ per day. Bass, crappie, bream, and channel catfish are the species mainly sought by anglers, but carp, blue catfish, yellow catfish, and drum are taken. A fish hatchery operated by the Dallas Park Board is located on the SW. shore, containing 26 breeding pools with an annual production of more than 1,000,000 fish to be distributed in White Rock and Bachman's Lakes.

Bachman's Lake, 6¼ mi. NW. of Dallas County Courthouse, on Denton Dr. (continuation of Maple Ave.) and Lemmon Ave. A clearwater lake covering 142 acres with a boat concession on the S. shore where permit to fish ($1 per year), tackle, minnows and other bait may be obtained. Boat hire 50¢ per day. Bass, crappie, and bream are most frequently taken but channel catfish are often added to the catch.

Mountain Creek Lake, 9 mi. SW. of Dallas County Courthouse, on Blue Cut Rd.; take Fort Worth Pike (US 80) to 7.5 mi. at Blue Cut Rd., left to lake on right, 1½ mi. A clearwater lake covering 3,500 acres. (In 1938 privately owned and operated by Dallas Power & Light Co., public not admitted, but proposed operation in 1940 under Dallas Park Board, same as White Rock Lake.)

Lake Dallas, 30 mi. N. of Dallas, on US 77. Town of Lake Dallas is entering point to numerous fishing and boat camps along the shorelines. A clearwater lake covering 11,000 acres. Bass, crappie, bream, all species of catfish common to Texas waters, carp, buffalo, and drum. Boat hire, 50¢ per day. A state fish hatchery is located near the dam, operated by the Texas Game, Fish & Oyster Commission, with an annual production of fish adequate to supply North Texas lakes with restocking.

Eagle Mountain Lake, 49 mi. NW. of Dallas, on SH 34. (Take US 80 to Fort Worth, 33 mi.; SH 34 to town of Azle, at 16 mi. At Azle, right to lake, 1 mi.) A clearwater lake covering 9,600 acres. Bass, crappie, all species of catfish common to Texas waters. Boat and fishing camps along the shoreline where tackle, minnows and other bait may be obtained. Boat hire, 50¢ per day.

Lake Bridgeport, 67 mi. NW. of Dallas. US 77 to 7 mi., left on SH 114 (Northwest Highway) through Rhome to Bridgeport, 60 mi. A clearwater lake covering 13,000 acres. This is one of the largest lakes in North Texas and anglers consider it one of the best for freshwater fishing. Bass, crappie, all species of catfish common to Texas waters. Several boat and fishing camps along the shoreline. (Obtain information as to routes from Bridgeport to lake camps at any store in Bridgeport.) Boat hire, 50¢ per day.

Fin and Feather Club Lake (Private to membership; guests of member admitted on guest fee). 12½ mi. SE. of Dallas County Courthouse. US 75 to Hutchins, 11 mi.; left on Cleveland Rd. to lake, 1½ mi. Bass and crappie. Clubhouse open the year round.

Dallas Hunting and Fishing Club (Private to membership; guests admitted only when accompanied by member). 13½ mi. SE. of Dallas County Courthouse. US 75 to Hutchins, 11 mi.; left on Dowdy Ferry Rd. to lake, 2½ mi. Bass and crappie.

While saltwater fishing is not available in the Dallas district, large numbers of Dallas fishermen enjoy the sport in the waters of the Gulf of Mexico. Visitors who would like to indulge in this exciting pastime may do so at a number of points along the Texas gulf coast, from Galveston to Corpus Christi. Any of these places are reached by practically overnight trains, or by auto over excellent highways. From May to December saltwater fishermen, with favorable weather and water conditions, usually make good hauls of mackerel, redfish, red snapper, sea trout, and at times huge groupers, known as Jewfish. Tarpon fishing is enjoyed all along the coast, with annual tarpon rodeos at each port in the summer months, usually June, July, or August. Boats with guides, tackle, and bait are obtainable at the docks in each port.

From Dallas to Galveston, by auto, 294 mi.; to Freeport, 308 mi.; to Aransas Pass (internationally known for its excellent gulf fishing), 420 mi.; to Corpus Christi, 420 mi. Chamber of Commerce at any of these gulf ports will on request wire information (collect) on weather and general fishing conditions.

CALENDAR OF EVENTS

NOTE: *nfd means no fixed date.*

Jan. 1	*Cotton Bowl*	Intersectional football game.
Feb., nfd		Spring Southwestern Style Show.
Apr. 1	*Southern Methodist University*	Piker's Day.
nfd		Garden Pilgrimage.
Sat. before Easter	*City Parks*	Easter Egg Hunt.
May 5	*Pike Park*	Cinco de Mayo Celebration (Mexican fiesta).
2nd week	*Cotton Bowl*	Reserve Officers Training Corps competitive drill.
nfd		Southwestern Shoe Style Show.
nfd	*Civic Center, Fair Park*	Dallas Art Carnival.
June 19	*Fair Park*	Emancipation Day Celebration.
July 4	*White Rock Lake*	Fireworks display.
19–20	*Sokol Hall, 3700 Carl Street*	Czechoslovakian Celebration.
nfd	*White Rock Lake*	Sailing and Motor Boat Regatta.
nfd	*Kidd Springs*	Oak Cliff Goodwill Picnic.
Aug., nfd	*Lakewood Country Club*	Invitation Golf Tournament.
nfd		Municipal Golf Championship Tournament.
nfd		Fall Southwestern Style Show.
Sept., 1st Mon.	*Cotton Bowl*	"Dream" football game be-

31

		tween Southwestern College All-Stars and a professional team.
nfd	*Robert E. Lee Park*	Dallas Pioneer Society Meeting.
Sept. 15, 16, 17	*Pike Park*	Mexican Independence Day.
Oct., nfd	*Fair Park*	State Fair of Texas.
1st Tues.	*State Fair*	Dallas Day.
2nd Fri.	*State Fair*	High School Day.
2nd Mon.	*State Fair*	Negro Day.
nfd	*State Fair*	Fall Flower Show.
2nd Sat.	*State Fair, Cotton Bowl*	Football game—University of Texas vs. University of Oklahoma.
Nov. 11		Armistice Day Parade.
nfd	*Dal-Hi Field*	Thanksgiving football game, Washington Bulldogs and Lincoln Tigers (Negroes).
nfd	*Fair Park*	Charity Horse Show.
Dec., nfd		Christmas Lighting and Decoration Contest.

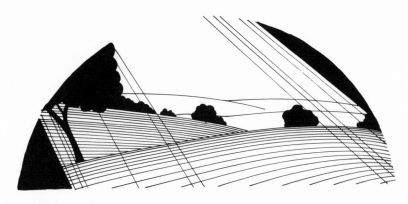

NATURAL SETTING: BLACK LAND, WHITE ROCK

Geography—The city of Dallas is located in almost the exact center of the county of the same name, in the north central part of the state, approximately between the parallels 32° 40' and 32° 50' north latitude, and the meridians 96° 43' and 96° 53' west longitude. The total area of the city proper is 45.351 miles, its greatest length north to south 12.5 miles and east and west 9 miles. Area of the county is 859 square miles. Average altitude within the city is 512 feet, and in the county ranges from 450 to 750 feet.

Topography—Topographically, Dallas County lies largely within the area known as the Black Prairie, the city in its center on high, rolling terrain bisected by the Trinity River. The Black Prairie is a southwestward extension of the nation's great central plain, and with the Grand Prairie, beginning some thirty-five miles west of the city, forms the outermost landward margin of the Gulf Coastal plain. The "black waxy" soil characteristic of the county is a rich dark earth derived from the upper Cretaceous limestone.

Topography of the county, according to Ellis W. Shuler's *The Geology of Dallas County*, is dominated by the underlying rock structure. The outstanding feature is a well-defined "cuesta," or tilted mesa, developed on an indurated chalk and limestone marl formation called "white rock." Shuler describes this formation at more length: "In a region where the underlying beds of rock dip at a low angle in one general direction, if there is a difference in the resistant beds to erosion—that is, if they are harder than others, such resistant beds will stand up as hills while valleys will be etched out on the softer beds. The hills will be on the side toward which the beds dip at a long, gentle slope, often spoken of as the dip plain, and on the other side a short, steep slope. Such an unsymmetrical hill is called a 'cuesta'. The white rock cuesta in Dallas County occupies a belt some ten miles wide running east of north and south of west across the middle of the county, and almost centrally through the city. The west face is steep and rough. The east slope is gentle."

Other topographic features include the valleys of the Trinity River. The valleys of the West Fork and the Elm Fork of the Trinity are from three to five miles wide, except where the river cuts across the white rock of Dallas. Here the flood plain is less than a mile wide, but beyond this constriction it widens again.

33

The Eagle Ford Prairie covers the western and northern parts of the county, and for the most part is typical open prairie. The Black Prairie in the eastern part of the county is a clay soil noted for its "waxy" character. "The Black Prairie," says Shuler, "is an open, rolling plain which dips slightly but gradually to the southeast. It is cut by narrow, shallow, sluggish streams with steep banks, which are rather widely spaced over the area. These streams, with the exception of White Rock Creek, follow the general slope of the dip plain."

All parts of the county are reached by these creeks or small branches, and the drainage is adequate over the greater part of the uplands, though on some level areas water stands after rains. On many of the side-valley slopes the runoff is rapid enough to cause serious erosion. The bottom lands are subject to overflow, except where protected by levees.

The supply of drinking water is adequate over all parts of the county. Artesian wells supply water from two sands at depths of from 250 feet on the west side of the county to 1,700 feet on the east for the shallow sand, and from 2,000 to 3,000 feet for the deeper sands. Water from the shallow sands is less desirable than that from the deeper strata.

Dallas, while using artesian water to some extent, depends for its chief supply upon Lake Dallas, in Denton County, twenty-six miles north, where it has impounded 63,000,000,000 gallons of surface water from the Elm Fork watershed of the Trinity.

Climate—With a mean annual temperature of 65.5° and average wind velocity of 10.2 miles, the climate of Dallas is equable, despite occasional sudden drops in winter temperature called "northers" and periods of sustained high temperatures in summer, tempered by gulf breezes. Annual average rainfall is 35.9 inches, the average snowfall .113 inches. Average dates of killing frosts are: first, November 14, last, March 18 (see DALLAS WEATHER: WINDS OVER THE PRAIRIE).

Geology—The rocks underlying Dallas County are a part of a belt across the whole Central Texas region, from Red River to the Rio Grande, called the Black and Grand Prairie country. The surfaces of these belts are the soil-covered rock formations of one of the greater divisions of geologic time, the Cretaceous (chalky) period.

This land in ancient geologic time was alternately submerged and raised above sea level, and the soils and rocks are largely the muds of what were once old sea bottoms. Geologists assert the present site of Dallas was once at least 5,000 feet below sea level, and it was also once covered by many other layers of sea muds of the same epoch which have been washed away as the site again rose to its present level.

These ocean muds, as they were elevated and infiltered by chemical solutions, were hardened and became the rocks and soils of the land called in Texas pack sands, joint clays, and white rock when freshly exposed. When weathered they form the soils known as red sands, black lands, and black waxy soil.

Geologists, among them Dr. Robert T. Hill of Dallas, also assert there were two great chalky periods involved in the Dallas County formations, the Comanchean and the Gulf series. Their aspects as revealed in the region are called the hard and soft lime rock area. By driving west from Elmo, Kaufman County, across Dallas County to Millsap, Parker County, the two series of rock sheets of the Cretaceous period may be seen in descending order, the layers dipping to the southeast at a low angle. Only the upper series of rocks come to the surface within the county.

34

Among the geological formations described and named by Dr. Hill are the Woodbine, found in the western part of the county and consisting, when weathered, of red and brown sandy soils. On the eastern side of the county are the Upper and Lower Taylor groups which weather into the rich prairie soils. The central belt is underlain by Austin chalk (white rock), which forms the foundations of the city of Dallas. Firmer than the sticky mud, it attracted the pioneer settlers, and together with the Eagle Ford shales to the west, affords the principal ingredient of the cement industry in Dallas County. This chalk weathers into a rich soil.

Paleontology (Fossils)—One-sixth of Dallas County is covered with alluvial deposits transported to their present location by the Trinity River. These give it rich soils and gravel and sand deposits of importance. The Trinity River flood plain, one mile wide at Dallas but broader to the east and west, has a depth of about thirty-four feet.

Within the alluvial deposits many interesting fossils of large size have been found. The chief depository of these fossils is Southern Methodist University in Dallas, though numbers of disjointed and unidentified specimens are held by private individuals. Skulls and other bones of twenty-one elephants *(Elephas columbi and Elephas imperator)* have been dug up at various times since 1887. In most cases these have been tossed aside to be destroyed by weathering. One complete skeleton (restored) is preserved in the Peabody Museum of Yale University, and two skulls (unmounted) are in the possession of Southern Methodist University.

Exceptionally complete remains of a sea lizard *(Elasmosaurus Serpentinus Cope)* having an estimated length of thirty-seven feet are on display at Southern Methodist University. This specimen, secured near Cedar Hill from the Eagle Ford shales, flourished in the Upper Cretaceous period, approximately sixty million years ago. It has fifty-nine cervical vertebrae, a head twenty-two inches long, a neck eighteen feet long. Fossil parts of the lizard actually secured cover twenty-five feet of its total estimated length.

At Southern Methodist University are also the partial remains of the Texas horse *(Equus scotti)*, the saber-toothed tiger, camels, and various reptiles, as well as numerous invertebrates.

The occurrence of human remains along with Pleistocene fossils in a Dallas sandpit is considered probable by geologists who examined bones unearthed on October 26, 1920. They were human bones and an analysis showed the degree of fossilization of the human skull and that of a camel found there were approximately the same.

35

PROLOGUE: BEFORE THE SETTLERS CAME

Indians of the Caddo tribes roamed the plains of North Texas long before the advent of the white man. The Anadarkos, one of the Caddo clans, were found in the area immediately about what is now Dallas, living in villages of thatched huts along the Trinity River, which they called the Arkikosa. Here the squaws tended crops of maize, beans, calabashes, and tobacco, and the braves hunted the buffalo.

The first Caucasian to visit the neighborhood is believed to have been Luis Moscoso, second in command to the ill-fated Hernando DeSoto, discoverer of the Mississippi, who after DeSoto's death in Arkansas in 1541 sought to guide the expedition to Mexico City. The Moscoso expedition passed across the northeastern corner of the present Dallas County in the early summer of 1542.

From the west, in the same year, Captain Francisco Vasquez de Coronado came into the section, leading the earliest of several Spanish expeditions in search of the Seven Cities of Cibolo and Gran Quivira, the fabled land of gold mentioned in the writings of the amazing Cabeza de Vaca.

These white men were in Texas before the Pilgrim Fathers were born, but disappointed in what they found or failed to find, they left the country to the aborigines for another 170 years.

Then the Caddo nomads were again disturbed by the white man, ever seeking gold and the wealth to be more tediously acquired by trade with the Indians. This time the visitors were French traders, Antoine Crozat and Bernard de La Harpe, who came from the colonies of their nation in Louisiana. They visited the Anadarkos on the Trinity in 1712 and again in 1719. Another trader, François Herve, in 1752 established a trading post, Fort St. Louis de Carloretto, on the Red River near the later Arthur City, but this was abandoned in 1770.

In 1760 Friar Calahorra y Saenz, a Roman Catholic missionary from Nacogdoches, passed through the territory, making treaties with the Indians. The Trinity was then given its modern name because of the three forks that combined to form the stream. After Louisiana had been transferred to Spain by France, Athanase de Mezieres, a French trader acting as agent for the Spaniards, in 1771 concluded a treaty with all of the Indians in the region in which Dallas, Waco, and Wichita Falls now are situated. De Mezieres spent ten years in establishing Spanish sovereignty in the Dallas area. Appointed as governor of the Texas territory in 1779, he died in San Antonio before assuming office.

Though Claiborne Wright of Tennessee had crossed the Red River and founded the Pecan Point settlement at the mouth of the Kiamichi in 1816, it was more than two decades later before Americans set foot upon the soil of the present Dallas and its environs.

In 1818 the vicinity of the three forks of the Trinity was the scene of a battle between the Caddo Indians and the Cherokees, who had migrated from Arkansas into the territory of the Caddos, and the Cherokees were defeated and driven eastward toward Nacogdoches, but the neighborhood of the Red River long remained the hinterland for North Texas pioneers.

From 1836 to 1840, in the first years of the Republic of Texas, Indian warfare was one of the many problems confronting the settlers. To make the region safe for white immigrants, the Republic in 1837 sent a company of eighteen mounted Rangers into North Texas, under command of Lieutenant A. B. Benthuysons, on a scouting expedition against the Indians. On November 10 of that year the Rangers had an engagement with 150 Indians near the headwaters of the Trinity, fifty miles north of Dallas in what is now Wise County. Ten Rangers were killed, among them Lieutenant Alfred H. Miles, second-in-command.

The surviving scouts moved southward along the river and camped, first at the mouth of Turtle Creek and later at a spring on the site of the present Santa Fe Building, in the heart of today's downtown Dallas. These Rangers are believed to have been the first Anglo-Americans in Dallas.

HISTORY
River Camp to Village: 1840–1860

In the year 1840 the stage of history was set for the appearance of the first permanent settlers in the region around the three forks of the Trinity River—a spot in the wilderness soon to become the city and county of Dallas. The frontier Republic of Texas had won its independence at the decisive Battle of San Jacinto four years before, and, harassed by constant Indian uprisings on its borders, was vainly seeking admission to the Union. Its second President, Mirabeau B. Lamar, in the face of bitter opposition, had just removed his capital from Houston to the village of Austin in Central Texas, and South Texas was rapidly being populated.

Goods and settlers were beginning to flow in steadily increasing streams through the flourishing port of Galveston, and the town of Houston was firmly established. To the north and west, however, beyond the termini of the navigable rivers and the old Spanish roads, all was still virgin wilderness, penetrated as yet only by a few scouting parties and a slow infiltration of settlers up the valley of the Red River from Shreveport. The logic of history pointed unmistakably to the fertile prairie lands south of the Red River as the area in which the next phase of the Anglo-American colonization of the Southwest was to take place.

It was in the autumn of 1840 that a young Tennessee-bred lawyer and frontier adventurer from Arkansas, John Neely Bryan, accompanied by a Cherokee Indian guide and a bear dog, pitched camp on the east bank of the Trinity River, where the city of Dallas stands today. Born of Scotch-Irish stock at Fayetteville, Tennessee, December 24, 1810, John Neely Bryan was one of the restless, enterprising, and frequently well-educated sons of the Old South who in the pioneer annals of the Southwest are the equivalents of the *voyageurs* and *coureurs de bois* of early frontier history in the North, and of the hunters and scouts who played such a prominent role in the later winning of the West. He had apparently read law in Tennessee in the approved fashion of the day, but when still very young crossed over into Arkansas to recover from the debilitating effects of an attack of the cholera; he lived with the Indians and adopted their mode of life. Little is known of his movements in the years immediately following except that he acquired an extensive acquaintance with native languages and customs.

A Pioneer Pitches Camp

Entering Texas in 1839 from Van Buren, Arkansas, where he had substantial interests—including a share in a coal mine—Bryan had been attracted to the Dallas region by visions of profitable trading with the Indians and white settlers who would traverse a projected military highway from Austin to the Red River. This road, according to an act of the Congress of the Republic of Texas (May 26, 1838), would cross the Trinity River "at or near its three forks." After his preliminary survey in 1840 of the possibilities of a trading post on the Trinity, Bryan returned to Van Buren, disposed of his holdings there and came again, this time alone, to the Texas site he had chosen, arriving later in November, 1841. He built a rude shelter against the bluff that formed the eastern bank of the river. Around the site of this habitation grew first the village, then the town, and finally the city of Dallas.

Survey of the military road northward had been begun September 14, 1840, by Colonel W. G. Cooke of the Texas army. His party, after great hardships, in mid-October completed the route to the mouth of the Kiamichi on Red River, crossing the Trinity River near the western end of the present Gulf, Colorado & Santa Fe railway bridge in Dallas. This road was staked through the prairies and blazed through the timber. The southern section was opened in 1843, and in this year the "citizens at and near the three forks of the Trinity," including Bryan, petitioned the Congress of the Republic for the completion of the road. As a result the northern leg—designated as the Texas Central National Highway, authorized February 5, 1844—was opened in 1845, following the Cooke survey from the Trinity to the Red River.

The territory east of the Trinity River was then a part of Nacogdoches County, that on the west Robertson County. As a settler Bryan received a grant of 640 acres in the former county, comprising a strip along the Trinity River, and adjoining on the east a 4,605-acre tract previously granted to John Grigsby of Houston County. Owing to complications arising out of the proximity of the two grants, Bryan's title was not finally confirmed by the State of Texas until February 16, 1854, while litigation over the Grigsby grant occupied the courts of the state for many years.

While Bryan was absent on his return trip to Arkansas, Rangers sent into North Texas by President Lamar to drive out the Indians had largely completed their task. When Bryan again arrived on the banks of the Trinity, the redskins on whom he had counted as customers had departed.

Consequently, he abandoned his original idea of a trading post in favor of establishing a permanent settlement. He learned from friendly Indians remaining in the vicinity that there were a number of white people twenty-two miles to the northwest at Bird's Fort (near the present Birdville in Tarrant County), survivors of a military camp established in 1840. Bryan invited these pioneers to join him on the lower river.

Beginnings of Settlement

On April 8, 1842, John Beeman, an earlier immigrant from Illinois, came with his family from Bird's Fort, settling eight miles to the southeast on White Rock Creek. Here a half-brother, James Beeman, joined him in that year. The Beemans planted the first corn in present-day Dallas County. Captain Mabel Gilbert, a former Mississippi River steamboat operator whom Bryan had known before coming to Texas, brought his family down river in canoes and located south of Bryan's cabin on the west side of the Trinity. Tom Keenan, a former Texas Ranger from Bird's Fort, and Isaac B. Webb, an immigrant from Green County, Missouri, established themselves on Mustang Branch, north of Bryan's place in the same year. These men and their families were, with Bryan, the founders of the city and county of Dallas.

The next additions to the community were settlers brought by the Texan Emigration Land Company of Louisville, Kentucky. This company was headed by William S. Peters, Henry J. Peters, Joseph Carroll, and others, with whom the Republic of Texas had contracted on August 30, 1841 (under an act approved February 4, 1841), for settlement of at least 600 families in that section of its domains now embraced in the counties of Dallas, Denton, Collin, Cooke, Grayson, and parts of Ellis and Wise. The earliest of these immigrants established homesteads in the region around Bryan's settlement, which for a time was known by the general designation of Peters' Colony. Earlier it had been referred to as "the colony in the Cross Timbers."

Glowing and farfetched tales spread abroad by one of the Peters' Colony agents of a thriving prairie paradise of rich black land, tall grass, and great navigable rivers plied by steamboats flowing to the Gulf—with the thriving city of Dallas in its center—impelled five brothers named Billingsley to emigrate from Missouri to the promised land of Texas by way of Arkansas. They arrived at Dallas in November, 1842, to learn that the Peters' Colony promoter had said nothing of the hardships, Indian raids, and devastating prairie fires that "cleaned the country of the only substance there was for the cattle, buffalo, deer, antelope, and everything that existed on the native grass."

City of Two Cabins

"The great City of Dallas," as the brothers found it, is described thus by John B. Billingsley, author of the family journal:

> We had heard a great deal about the three forks of the Trinity River and the town of Dallas. This was the center of attraction. It sounded big in the far-off states. We had heard of it often, yes, the place, but the town, where was it? Two small log cabins, the logs just as nature formed them, the walls just high enough for the doorhead, the covering of clapboards held to their place with poles, chimneys made of sticks and mud and old mother earth serving as floors; a shelter made on four sticks for a smith shop, a garden fenced in with brush and mortar in which they beat their corn into meal. This was the town of Dallas, and two families, ten or twelve souls, was its population. . . . After taking in the town the next thing to see was the river. A few yards away and we were on its banks. One deep, narrow and crooked channel was all we could see of the far-famed Trinity River.

A number of incoming Peters' Colony settlers in 1843 joined Keenan and Webb on Mustang Branch, which was soon renamed Farmers Branch, since it was here that the first wheat, peaches, hogs, and chickens in the colony were produced. The richness of the soil and the abundant crops moved one homesteader to declare, as quoted later by William Cochran, "I can drive a stake down within one hundred feet of where the Garden of Eden was located." Although twelve miles removed from the central settlement, the residents of Farmers Branch were closely identified with Bryan's townsite on the Trinity, already known as Dallas.

When John Beeman joined Bryan at Dallas he brought his wife and ten children, including two daughters, Elizabeth and Margaret, in a covered wagon, the first wheeled vehicle the village knew. Beeman's impedimenta proved a double attraction for the bachelor pioneer, Bryan, who first borrowed his wagon and oxen to go to Preston on the Red River for merchandise, and later paid court to his younger daughter, Margaret. On his trip to Preston, Bryan followed the route, later the old Preston Road (now State Highway 14), which he had blazed along the western edge of the Cross Timbers on his first trip to and from the site of Dallas. On February 26, 1843, he married Margaret Beeman. The couple tilled the land about a second and better habitation the young husband had erected for his bride, using his Indian pony and a crude bois d'arc plow. Harness for the horse was made from buffalo hide, and, when necessary, the couple crossed the river in a canoe hewn from a cottonwood tree. This second cabin was washed away in a great Trinity River flood in the spring of 1844, which threatened to destroy the village, and Bryan and his wife lived in a tent made of wagon sheets until a new and larger log house could be erected.

Civilization Invades Wilderness

The first settlers in and around Dallas were typical of the westward-moving pioneers of the time. They lived in log houses and dressed in garments made of buckskin sewed with deer tendons and handwoven cloth. "Buckskin pants, hunting shirts, and moccasins were the common garb of frontier men, and the women had to spin and weave their everyday wear," a local chronicler writes. Their weapons for hunting and defense against the Indians were mostly old muzzleloading rifles, with flintlocks. Hard labor and ingenuity, aided only by the most elementary of tools, were combined to produce the necessities of existence as civilization invaded the wilderness.

That the supply of wild game was more than sufficient for the needs of the scattered homesteaders is indicated by this entry in the Billingsley diary:

> About the first of June the buffalo came in from the western plains and the prairies were alive with them. Thousands of them were to be seen. Deer, antelope, wild horses, and wolves were numerous. Bear, wild turkeys and all kinds of wild varmints ranged the bottoms and the thickets along the water courses.

Supplementing the flesh and fowl thus generously afforded, wild honey was used in lieu of sugar, flour and meal were made from the wheat and corn planted, harvested, and ground with primitive implements. Not until 1846 was there even a gristmill in the district. There was no glass for the windows of the first cabins; tallow dips and homemade beeswax candles afforded light at night. The rich but heavy black land was broken with prairie plows requiring five yokes of oxen to pull them, while old-fashioned bulltongue and halfshovel plows sufficed for cultivation. The first corn was planted "Missouri style"—by sticking axes in the sod, dropping in the corn, and closing the hole with the foot.

"Life in Dallas," noted a writer of this period, "moved on primitive lines. An old-fashioned hand mill, brought by one of the settlers to grind the corn with, was in such demand that it was allotted to the applicants one day at a time. One sewing machine served the village for years."

There were some consolations for the hardships of the wilderness, however, for John H. Cochran in his *History of Dallas County* records that whiskey was soon to be bought at the pioneer distillery of Gold & Donaldson at Cedar Springs for fifteen cents a quart or fifty cents a gallon, and another memoir stated that jerked venison could be had for three cents a pound. An entire saddle of a deer cost forty cents, and while no buffaloes were seen east of the Trinity after 1846, an ample supply of meat from these animals continued to come in from the west for some years. A buffalo hunt was held not far from Dallas as late as Christmas, 1860. Dried buffalo tongues were part of every freighter's cargo.

Treaty Pacifies Indians

Fortunately the newcomers were little annoyed by Indians. Hampton Rattan, one of the settlers at Bird's Fort, was slain by Indians near the present town of Carrollton in Dallas County on Christmas Day, 1841. Following near-starvation during an early and bitter winter, the Bird's Fort colony had sent wagons to Paris in Lamar County for supplies, and it was to meet this supply train on its return journey that Rattan had left the protection of the settlement with two companions, Alex Webb and Solomon Silkwood. While cutting down a bee-tree to secure honey and fuel, they were ambushed, and Rattan and one Indian were killed in the resulting battle. A Dr. Calder, newly come to the Cedar Springs settlement, was killed early in 1843, and in the autumn of that year David Chubb, a Texas military scout, was killed a few miles south of Dallas. These three were the only deaths charged to Indians in the history of Dallas County. The signing of a treaty of peace between the Republic of Texas and the North Texas tribes, concluded at Bird's Fort while President Sam Houston maintained temporary field headquarters at Grapevine Springs (or Grapevine Prairie) in the northwestern part of Dallas County, on September 29, 1843, tended to remove the menace of Indian depredations, though occasional forays involving the theft of horses and cattle continued until 1846 *(see DALLAS COUNTY TOUR, Grapevine Springs Park)*.

While there is no recorded date when the name Dallas was first applied to Bryan's settlement, there is reason to believe that it was so named early in 1842. William Beeman, who arrived in the spring of that year, asserted afterward that Bryan named his settlement at the suggestion of Beeman's father, John Beeman. Corroboration of this claim, even though meager, is found in a quotation from the diary of one "W.A.F.," published later in the *Dallas Herald*:

> In the spring of 1842, streams again flooded; worked below Dallas, on the Trinity, visited Dallas in May, 1842; found Col. John M. Bryan and three or four others encamped on the present site of Dallas; there was at that time one solitary log cabin constructed. Captain Gilbert made a small crop of corn in the river bottom opposite Dallas, which was good.

The Billingsley brothers, coming to the community in November of that year (1842), recorded not only that it then was called Dallas, but that it had been so known to them as the place they had left Missouri to find.

Townsite Called Dallas

Confirmation of the naming of the settlement as Dallas by 1843 is also found in the diary of Edward W. Parkinson, who in the summer of that year was a member of the party accompanying President Sam Houston from Washington-on-the-Brazos to Bird's Fort, where Houston expected to make a treaty with the Indians. Parkinson wrote:

> I then went on (after leaving the Houston party) to another settler's cabin on the banks of the Trinity River, the projected site for a town called Dallas, inhabited by a man named Bryan, who had settled in the wilderness previous to its being chartered for a colony, and

who seemed to anticipate some trouble from the heads of the colony wishing to assume his lands, a choice spot on the Elm Fork, which he had located previous to the colonial grant by virtue of his headright. He was a hardy backwoodsman and a sensible, industrious, ingenious, and hospitable man. He as well as others complained bitterly of the colonial management, there being no agents or surveyors there to attend to the immigrants when they arrived or point out the lands available for them. He informed me there were only about thirty families spread over a space of as many miles in length and breadth.

That the village was called Dallas prior to November 16, 1843, is shown by an item in the *Morning Star* of Houston, published on this date:

We have recently learned that the number of families now settled within the limits of Peters & Company (Colony) is only twenty-five. These are settled near the mouth of Elm Creek (Elm Fork of the Trinity) and the houses are scattered from Bird's Fort, a distance of seventeen miles, along the east bank of the river. Bird's Fort is situated about twelve miles above the mouth of Elm Creek and Dallas five miles below it.

Bryan himself used the name of Dallas when he first laid out a townsite. Under date of July 29, 1903, Coho Smith, then 77 years old and residing at Argyle in Denton County, wrote the *Dallas News* that in 1844 he had assisted Bryan in a preliminary survey of the town, using a homemade instrument built around a pocket compass. The place was then known as Dallas, Smith declared. Later, in 1846, Bryan, assisted by J. P. Dumas, a surveyor, formally platted the town. This plat, later filed in the county records, embodied a tract one-half-mile square, extending eastward from the river. An entire block for a courthouse, donated by Bryan, was set apart in the center of the townsite.

Origin of Name Obscure

The origin of the town's name is not definitely known. Lacking any commitment by John Neely Bryan himself except the assertion attributed to him by Frank M. Cockrell in his memoirs, that "the town was named for my friend Dallas," the particular Dallas thus honored still lacks positive identification and remains a subject of speculation and wide differences of opinion among local historians.

There is general unanimity of opinion that the county of Dallas was named in honor of George Mifflin Dallas, Vice-President of the United States during the administration of James K. Polk (1845–49), a conclusion unsupported by actual records but made fairly obvious by the circumstance that Polk County was created by legislative enactment and named specifically in honor of the President on the same day that Dallas County came into existence. The natural assumption is that the Vice-President was equally honored in the naming of Dallas County. Well-grounded objections, however, have been raised against the widely accepted and plausible corollary that the town of Dallas, which bore that name at least three, and probably four, years before the county was created, also was named for the distinguished Philadelphian.

Available records do not indicate that Bryan had ever heard of George Mifflin Dallas when the little settlement was named for "my friend Dallas." At that time Dallas was a practicing lawyer in Philadelphia, having served from 1835 to 1839 as minister to Russia, and had neither personal nor political interest in Texas. He received the Democratic nomination for Vice-President at the Baltimore convention in May, 1844, only after it had been refused by Silas Wright of New York. His first interest in the campaign inspired by Andrew Jackson to bring Texas into the Union was revealed only casually in a letter to Senator Robert J. Walker of Mississippi, dated February 1, 1844, wherein he mentioned favoring annexation.

In the voluminous genealogy of the Dallas family there is no reference which would give credence to the theory that George Mifflin Dallas knew John Neely Bryan or, at the time of its naming, had any knowledge of the little village of some forty souls on the Trinity.

Many students of local history, while in agreement upon the origin of the county's name, point to the fact that there were a number of persons named Dallas who figured in affairs much nearer Bryan's settlement, and thus were more likely candidates for the designation of "my friend Dallas" than was Lawyer Dallas in remote Philadelphia.

Colonel J. M. Morphis in his *History of Texas from its Discovery and Settlement* (1874) says that, "The town of Dallas was named for Commodore Dallas of the United States Navy, and the county for George Mifflin Dallas." The commodore mentioned was Commander Alexander James Dallas, a brother of George Mifflin, for a time stationed in the Gulf of Mexico combating piracy in these waters. The colonel did not go into particulars as to the naming of either county or city, but later revealed that he was "around there [Dallas] in 1846," so that he should have had benefit of firsthand knowledge.

Another theory is that the town was named either for Walter R. Dallas, who fought at San Jacinto, or his brother James L. Dallas, one-time Texas Ranger. These two men were sons of James L. Dallas of Maryland and Elizabeth (Reed) Dallas, whom he married in Kentucky in 1813. This family settled at Washington-on-the-Brazos before the Texas Revolution and after the father's death both the boys and their mother received land grants in McLennan, Hill, and Burleson Counties for services to the Texas Republic. Their holdings were near enough to those of Bryan for them to have been known to him.

Still another Dallas who flashed across early history for a brief period could very logically have been the friend of Bryan for whom the town was named. This man was Joseph Dallas, who came to Cedar Springs—near Bryan's little village—in April, 1843, from Washington County, Arkansas, which adjoined Bryan's former home county of Crawford. A likely supposition is that the two men knew each other and that Joseph Dallas, upon Bryan's invitation, followed his friend to Texas and thus became, "unhonored and unsung" and very probably unconcerned at the time, the man to whom Dallas is indebted for its name.

One-Man Community

During the first few years of Dallas' existence Bryan embodied practically all official community functions in his own person. He was first postmaster and a notary public, and his cabin home, which was also a store selling powder and lead, tobacco and whiskey, was utilized both as post office and courthouse prior to the formation of Dallas County and for some time thereafter.

The learned professions began early to be represented. Dr. John Cole and Dr. W. W. Conover were the first physicians in the district, arriving in 1843, the former from Arkansas and the latter from Kentucky, both settling at Cedar Springs. Dr. A. D. Rice appears to have been the first physician in the village itself. John C. McCoy, an Indianan who became the founder of the Dallas bar, came from Louisville, Kentucky, as field representative for the Peters colonization company, arriving at the village early in 1845. He had reached New Orleans by going down the

Ohio and Mississippi Rivers and thence by ship to Houston, where he expected to find a steamboat to bring him up the Trinity. This mode of transportation being lacking, he came overland, as he later said, "navigating the Trinity on foot," and was met by John Neely Bryan, "clad in buckskin leggings and mocassins [sic] and a red and black blanket cut in 'highwater style,'" who, aided by "the inevitable gourd, the contents of which could readily be guessed," welcomed McCoy and a traveling companion.

John M. Crockett, second lawyer in the community, recorded that on his arrival with his law library in his saddlebags, "the place sustained only thirty-nine souls, half a dozen cabins or dwellings, a dramshop, an open-air tenpin alley, a double log tavern and scarce a lot under fence." Nat M. Burford, another attorney who followed shortly after Crockett, wrote in 1848 that "twelve adult males then composed the sovereignty of Dallas." Each of these three lawyers served the community as judge at one time or another.

By 1845, when the question of the annexation of Texas to the United States and adoption of a State Constitution was submitted to the people on October 13, the town of Dallas had thirty-two residents qualified to vote, twenty-nine of whom favored annexation. The three opposing votes were cast by Roderick A. Rawlins, Alexander Harwood, and John C. McCoy. The transition to statehood was finally approved by the Congress of the United States on December 29.

County Is Organized

On March 30, 1846, the county was organized and on April 18 the town of Dallas designated as the temporary seat of government. William H. Beeman later recorded that he rode 140 miles to Franklin, then county seat of Robertson County, to secure the official court order for the creation of Dallas County. In the election of officers that followed, John Thomas was made chief justice, Dr. John Cole probate judge, John C. McCoy district clerk, William M. Cochran county clerk, John R. Huitt sheriff, Anson McCrackin coroner, and Benjamin Merrill assessor. A log cabin, 10x10 feet, became the temporary courthouse.

Among the first acts of the new county court, August 31, 1846, was the fixing of the tax rate and the granting of a ferry license to John Neely Bryan and William Baker, with legal fees for ferriage. The ad valorem tax rate was set at five cents on every $100 of property value. Ferry charges were dependent on the stage of water in the river. When the stream was within its banks, $1.25 was fixed as the charge for two-horse wagons and carriages; when in flood, an additional 25 cents was permitted to be charged. The fee for horse and rider was 20 cents, for loose horses 10 cents each, and for footmen 10 cents. The ferry was made of large cottonwood logs hollowed out canoe-fashion, and covered with puncheon flooring. The rope for pulling it across the stream was woven of buffalo hair, and stretched from bank to bank.

The administration of justice was first provided by the Sixth District Court in 1846, with William B. Ochiltree as circuit judge, and later by the Ninth Court, with Bennett H. Martin as judge. Despite the profuse use of legal terminology in the records of the day, the actual operations of the courts appear to have been rather informal. The first Dallas grand jury returned sixty-one indictments, fifty-one of which were for gaming. The others included one for murder, one for challenging to a duel, and four for assault and battery. The first divorce case—Charlotte M. Dalton vs. Joseph Dalton—was heard by a jury in the Sixth District Court in 1846.

45

The wife paid costs of the suit, and winning a decree, married Henderson Couch, foreman of the jury, a few hours afterward. On a later occasion when most of the leading citizens of the village were arraigned in the Ninth District Court, charged with gaming in William Walton's saloon, those first convicted served in turn as jurors in trying the others. Each of the defendants was fined the sum of $10.

Other events during the crowded year of 1846 included the appointment of Charles H. Durgin as the first United States postmaster, the establishment of improved mail service, and the opening of the town's first hotel, the Dallas Inn, a small log structure operated by James B. Bryan, brother of John Neely Bryan. The first private schools were also established in both county and village in this year, and the first church congregations organized. Webb's Chapel was founded at Farmers Branch, a Methodist mission in Dallas proper, and a Christian church at Hord's Ridge, across the Trinity. A definite social life was developing.

"Doll Village" in 1847

Though growing, Dallas at this period held its prestige chiefly because it was the temporary county seat and because of the leadership of its founder. Its physical aspect was not impressive, even by contemporary frontier standards. What the place was actually like is indicated by the description of Mrs. Addie (Dye) McDermott, who arrived in 1847:

> We found Dallas a sort of doll village. The houses were small log cabins, the largest not exceeding 21x14 feet. The courthouse was a cabin 10x10 feet. It had one door and one window, puncheon floor, and hewn logs for benches. The showy building (there is always one, you know, in every town) was Uncle Jack Smith's (Smith & Patterson) store, the only store in town. It was a small one-story structure built of boards, and differing from the rest in higher finish of material rather than in size. There were no streets. A network of only winding paths, more or less weed- and grass-grown, connected the houses. The central figure, and general overseer of things was John Neely Bryan, the proud founder of the settlement. He wore moccasins and buckskin breeches, which for ornament had a strip of untanned deerskin running up and down the legs.

Though small, the settlement had responded with enthusiasm to war's alarm in the spring of 1846, and the new county and its capital village joined with Fannin and Collin Counties in raising a company of 110 men for Colonel John C. (Jack) Hays' Second Texas Regiment of Rangers for service in the war between the United States and Mexico. Next in command to Hays was Peter H. Bell as lieutenant-colonel and Alfred Truitt as major, with John S. Ford as adjutant. Among those enlisting from Dallas County were Peter Haught, Samuel A. Haught, John Herald, Andrew Sloan Jackson, William C. Jackson, John McCommas, Burke McCommas, George Mounts, George Markham, John Newton, John L. Pulliam, Benjamin Prigmore, Alexander A. Thomas, and Calaway A. Patrick. The return of survivors among these fighters after their command was disbanded in May of 1848 was an event of note in the community.

The discovery of gold in California in 1849 notably affected Dallas. So many gold seekers came through the county en route to the West Coast that the name California Crossing was given to a ford of the Trinity seven miles north of Dallas, and has persisted to this day. This ford was used in preference to the Dallas crossing because it enabled the travelers to avoid several other streams farther to the west. John Neely Bryan was one of the group from Dallas who joined the gold rush, remaining in the Far West for several months. Believing that they could find gold closer to home, some eighty other residents of Dallas and vicinity organized an expedition in August, 1849, to explore the Wichita Mountains in the land occupied by the Creek Nation, Indian Territory (just north of the present site of Ardmore, Oklahoma), but their efforts were unrewarded.

First Newspaper Established

These comings and goings to and through Dallas kept the growing population busy and maintained contacts with the outside world. Stories of the new town on the Trinity were being carried to various parts of Texas, and its prospects so appealed to J. Wellington (Weck) Latimer, who had been publishing the *Western Star* at Paris, that in 1849 this journalist loaded his printing equipment into an oxcart, together with his wife's piano, and came to Dallas where he established the first newspaper, the *Cedar Snag*, shortly renamed the *Herald*.

During 1849 the farmers in the Dallas area encountered a new hazard in the myriads of wheatbirds (*otocoris alpestris* or horned lark)—small birds between a hummingbird and a snowbird in size, related to the ricebirds of South Texas—that invaded the region in the spring of this year. Just at the time that the wheat was in the milk these birds appeared like a swarm of devouring locusts and, by sucking the juice from the grain, destroyed almost the entire crop. Such were their numbers that it was impossible to drive them from a wheat field, once they had settled on it, or to save any part of it from their ravages. The farmers rallied against these feathered foes as against an invading army and pitched battles were fought between man and bird, but with the invariable defeat of the former. A newspaper account a decade later gives a stirring picture of one of these battles:

> It is related by a farmer in this county, as a fact, that when the birds attacked his wheat in 1849, he sought by gun and shot, ringing bells, beating tin pans, and every other available noise-maker, to frighten them from his grounds. For this purpose, bringing his whole force, big and little, into requisition, with these motley weapons, he stationed the little army over the field. Finding that his efforts were unavailing, he thought to compromise with the enemy by giving up part of the field, and concentrating his force on the remaining, and defend it more effectively. The rapacious gluttons soon made a clean sweep of the relinquished spoils, and swooped down on the other. After a dispirited struggle, our farmer concluded to relinquish the half of that, and give the other to the birds. No sooner had they finished the second section of the crop, than they solidly demanded the balance. A gallant stand was made by the farmer to save this, but his little force could do nothing against the legion of the invaders. He finally thought he would save enough for seed, and retreated and took the position on an acre; they resolved to "do or die." It became a hand to hand fight, but while shotguns were firing, pans sounding, and bludgeons waving around the heads of the little urchins, the birds would swarm over them, light in their midst, and actually destroyed the last of his acre of wheat before his eyes, and in defiance of all his efforts.

Periodic forays of these wheatbirds continued around Dallas up through the last of the fifties.

Settlers Cross the Trinity

The first settlement on the west side of the Trinity opposite Bryan's settlement in what was then Robertson County had been made by Judge William H. Hord of Tennessee, a Peters' Colony immigrant, January 12, 1845. This area was thereafter

47

known as Hord's Ridge and became a part of the new county of Dallas, now constituting the populous Oak Cliff section of the city. So large had the community of Hord's Ridge become by 1850 that, with Cedar Springs, another newer settlement north of Dallas, it contended with Dallas in an election to determine the permanent seat of the county government.

After Cedar Springs had been eliminated in the first voting, Dallas won over Hord's Ridge by a majority of only 28 votes in a total of 460. This was on August 31, 1850. The county government had to borrow the $100 needed to pay for the transcription of records at the former county seat at Nacogdoches pertaining to the area now transferred to the new county of Dallas.

Later in the year the first courthouse was built, a one-story frame structure 16x32 feet. This served chiefly as a repository for records and for offices, sessions of the district court at times being held at various more commodious places. Among these temporary seats of justice was the barroom of one Adolphus F. Goughnant, to whom on August 17, 1850, the county commissioners allowed $7.50 as "rental for the use of his saloon for the holding of the last term of the district court."

The Federal census of 1850, the first taken after the settlement of Dallas County, gave the county a population of 2,743, and the town a population of 430. There were, according to this census, nine lawyers and five physicians in Dallas. These, with one dentist, formed the professional group in the community. The lawyers were Samuel G. Newton, John J. Elkins, Felix Eakens, John C. McCoy, Nat M. Burford, J. W. Latimer (editor of the *Herald*), John M. Crockett, Smith Elkins, and John Neely Bryan. The doctors were S. B. Pryor, six years later elected the town's first mayor, Samuel T. Bledsoe, Perry Dakans, S. B. McCommas, and A. D. Rice. The dentist was James B. Bryan.

Only three men were listed as merchants in the 1850 census—James M. Patterson and John W. Smith, partners, and Madison M. Miller. There were three wagonmakers, Edward Mills, B. F. Barrow, and Gide Pemberton, while Charles Newton chose the somewhat higher sounding appellation of carriage-maker. John Shurlock was the community's one chair-maker, and Thomas Crutchfield the one hotel proprietor. Adam Haught, who had started the first saloon, preferred to list himself as ferryman, since he also operated a craft on the Trinity. B. O. C. Pound was a saddletree-maker. William M. Wallis was a printer, presumably employed on Latimer's *Herald*. Aaron McDaniel was a gunsmith, while J. W. Lyttle, A. J. Marvin, Robert Ray, and E. T. Myers were the village blacksmiths. William Briton and John A. Jackson were put down as traders, with A. M. Keen as the lone surveyor. Wormley Carter gave hunting as his means of livelihood. The oddest occupation enumerated, lacking any notation identifying the man's actual work, was that of coffeesmith, given William McDermitt.

First Cotton Planted

Earlier citizens of Dallas and the wilderness roundabout of necessity blazed new trails in their economic development. The principal crops in the region were first those necessary to provide a food supply, and thus it was that cotton, already the mainstay of the Old South, was not widely planted until nearly a decade after settlement began. Slave labor, required by large-scale plantation cultivation of money crops, was never to become an important factor in the development of the region around Dallas, for while the first slave was sold in the town in 1845, the total number in the county at the outbreak of the Civil War was only 1,080, of whom 97 were in the town. William M. Cochran planted the first cotton at Farmers Branch in 1846. The first gin in the county was built at Farmers Branch in 1849. Soon thereafter cotton became the chief money resource of the farmers around Dallas as elsewhere in the South, and the town began to draw trade which hitherto had gone to Jefferson, Shreveport, Preston, and to Houston.

The forebodings of John Neely Bryan, expressed to Parkinson in 1843, of trouble between the settlers and the Texan Emigration Land Company were realized in 1852, when there was an organized revolt against the colonization company's policies and practices. Under the contract between the company and the Republic of Texas the former was to receive an alternate section of land for every section upon which a settler was placed. Many of the newcomers had taken up land other than that specified in their grants, a fact said to account for the meanderings of some of the county's older roads, which were laid out to bring some of these scattered tracts together.

Differences over these apportionments between the settlers and the land company precipitated a controversy when the company asked the legislature to fulfill the terms of the contract by sectionizing the alternate tracts and deeding them to the company. Many of the immigrants, fearing themselves about to be ousted, objected and elected John M. Crockett of Dallas to the legislature to lead their fight against dispossession. Crockett was alleged to have threatened agents of the company with lynching when he spoke in Austin in defense of the settlers' claims.

Some of the more aggressive landholders of the Dallas area armed themselves and under the leadership of Captain John J. Good marched to the land company's office at Stewartville in Denton County. Of this episode John H. Reagan in his memoirs asserts that "but for the efforts of Col. M. T. Johnson of Tarrant County, the Hon. John M. Crockett of Dallas, and myself, violent measures against the agent of the company would certainly have been adopted." Many of the company's records were seized and brought to Dallas, where they disappeared. After this demonstration the legislators reversed their first decision to validate the old contract and instead gave the settlers title to the lands they occupied.

Growth Brings Manufacture

The growth of the town during this period and the increasing influx of travelers led to the building of what was for many years to be a widely known hotel, the Crutchfield House. Thomas F. Crutchfield had for a time rented the old Dallas Tavern from William Beeman, but in 1852 erected a new and larger building at the northwest corner of Main and Houston Streets, on the courthouse square. At this hostelry were entertained many of the notables of the day, among them Sam Houston, Thomas J. Rusk, General Jubal A. Early, Bishop Robert Paine of the Methodist Church, Senator Robert Toombs of Georgia, and Prince Paul of Williamsburg, Germany. Guests of the Crutchfield House might wander afar in the town, assured they would be notified of mealtime by the ringing of a large bell swung from a post in the hotel yard. This bell was finally shot down while being used as a target by a tipsy visiting gunman. The Crutchfield House was celebrated as a purveyor of the substantial provender of the Old South, supplemented by a plenitude of wild game, often brought in by the proprietor himself, a Nimrod of some note. "Square meals" could be had at the Crutchfield House for twenty-five cents, with board and room at from $12.50 to $15 a month. The Crutchfield House burned in the fire of 1860, was rebuilt, and finally perished in another blaze in 1888.

The year 1852 brought to Dallas its first manufacturing plant, a wagon factory opened by Maxime Guillot, a Frenchman who had come to Texas in 1847 from Angiers, France, by way of New Orleans, in search of the brother of his sweetheart. Guillot's wagon factory was followed in 1853 by a brickyard, wherein were produced the first permanent materials for a construction boom that lasted until the eve of the Civil War.

Dallas was now definitely emerging from its status, noted a short time before by a local historian, as a "shaggy little village, whose streets are but winding paths and wagon roads through woods, stumps, and small cedars and oaks." It was already approaching proportions to justify the claim of the town newspaper a few years later that "our little settlement bids fair to become a considerable inland town."

It was in 1853 that the first legal execution took place in the county. This was the hanging of Jane Elkins, a slave who had murdered a man named Wisdom at Farmers Branch. After a trial before Judge John H. Reagan, most notable jurist of his time, the woman was hanged May 27, 1853.

The next year was marked by the arrival on April 26 of the advance guard of La Reunion colonists, a dozen men who had come, inspired by the roseate Utopian theories of Charles Francois Fourier, to arrange for locating their fellow Frenchmen and Belgians on 1,200 acres of land purchased earlier on the western side of the Trinity in present Oak Cliff. The whole population of Dallas turned out to celebrate the arrival June 16, 1855, of the main body of these idealistic European immigrants, and they were welcomed by a committee headed by their fellow countryman Maxime Guillot, who acted as interpreter *(see LA REUNION: ADVENTURE IN UTOPIA)*. In October of this year contract was let for a new courthouse, to be of brick, 50x50 feet and two stories in height.

Capitalist Finds Opportunity

By the mid-fifties the stage had been set for a capitalist with resources to promote a more rapid and comprehensive expansion of the community. Alexander Cockrell, a Kentuckian, filled the need. He had taken up 640 acres of land west of Dallas in the Peters' Colony and had married Sarah Horton, whose parents had come from Tennessee to settle at Hord's Ridge. In 1852 Cockrell contracted for the purchase of the remainder of John Neely Bryan's holdings, including about one-third of the townsite of Dallas and ferry rights, for $7,000, the property being finally deeded to him in 1854.

Always something of a visionary, Bryan had wasted the better part of the townsite in wedding presents to young married couples and the like, and the lots he sold had brought little return. He became morbid and depressed, took to drink, and was several times hauled into court for minor offenses. Following his return empty-handed from California in 1850 he became involved in a shooting affray, and believing erroneously that he had killed a man, fled to the reservation of the Creek Nation in 1855, where he took up his residence with Jesse Chisholm, Indian trader. Leaving his affairs in the hands of Cockrell and others, he began a series of wanderings through the West that led him to Stockton, California, in 1858, then to Colorado, and then back to California in 1859.

He finally returned to Dallas, his fortunes and outlook considerably improved. At the outbreak of the Civil War in 1861 he enlisted in a cavalry regiment, but was discharged in 1862 as physically unfit for active service. After the war he tried farming, but was committed to the State Lunatic Asylum at Austin February 20,

1877, and died on September 8 of that year. Bryan's widow survived him 42 years, dying at Thorndale, Clay County, September 6, 1919, at the age of 93.

Trinity River Is Bridged

Assuming Bryan's position of leadership in the community after the latter's departure in 1855, Alexander Cockrell immediately initiated a program of building and industrial development. He formed the Dallas Bridge & Causeway Company and within the year built a bridge over the Trinity at the foot of Commerce Street, making it usable by the construction of a plank road through the river bottoms. The Cockrell sawmill, south of the Cockrell bridge, supplied much of the lumber for the building of the town. The two-story brick commercial building erected by Cockrell on the southeast corner of the town square attracted the Hopkins County firm of Hirsh & Shireck, who opened a large general store there in 1857. The first steam-powered flour mill, with a capacity of fifty barrels daily, and the St. Nicholas Hotel, at the northeast corner of Commerce and Broadway, were built by his widow, Sarah, after Cockrell's death in a gun duel with the city marshal, Andrew M. Moore, April 3, 1858, in which Moore also was killed. The St. Nicholas Hotel was destroyed in the 1860 fire. The new bridge opened a large trade territory to Dallas, drawing both business and population from the north and west. Labor was attracted by the increase in industries, and saloons and gambling halls sprung up to cater to the influx of newcomers.

While Dallas never developed the "Wild West" atmosphere of frequent brawls and gunfights to the extent that characterized some other early Texas towns, there was enough lawlessness in the community to bring about a demand in 1856 for incorporation to provide better government and police protection. On February 2 of that year Dr. Samuel Pryor was elected mayor, with a total of fewer than a hundred votes cast in the election. Dallas had become a political entity less than fifteen years after the arrival of the first settler.

By the following year the newborn town was beginning to develop the incipient growing pains of urban life—a consciousness of crime and culture. A log jail was erected, and on February 20 the Commissioners Court decreed that persons convicted of vagrancy in the county should be put to work on the roads for periods not to exceed three weeks for each offense. By September a lyceum, characteristic cultural institution of nineteenth-century America, was in existence, and the citizens were invited through the news columns of the *Dallas Herald* to contribute books or money to the village library. Dallas County was also availing itself of the state monies apportioned for the support of public education, collecting $3,710.42 for the children taught in the county during the scholastic year ending October 31, 1857.

The year 1858 stands out as a period of calamity in the history of Dallas and Dallas County, a succession of natural disasters occurring one after another. In the spring the village suffered a serious flood; the swollen river causing collapse of the new bridge—a forerunner of numerous other overflows marking Dallas' long struggle to tame the Trinity. The summer brought a drought of unprecedented length and severity, during which the grass on the prairies was parched and burned, livestock perished from thirst, and the gristmills on White Rock Creek were idle for lack of water to turn their wheels. This summer was followed by one of the hardest winters in the history of the region, with heavy falls of rain, snow, and sleet. The winter wheat crop was retarded and cattle running the open range suffered severely from the restricted pasturage. There were renewed depredations of wheatbirds during the year, inspiring an article in the *Herald* on the habits of this voracious pest and its history in the region.

Stage Lines Bring Trade

However, despite such setbacks as these, town and county continued to grow in population and prosperity. A state census taken in 1858 showed a county population of 6,981, which by 1860 had increased to 8,655. By the same date the town of Dallas had an estimated population of 2,000. In 1850 there had been only 7,305 acres under cultivation in the county; by 1858 the acreage under cultivation had increased to 35,107. Manufactories in Dallas by the end of the decade included a wool carding and rolling plant, flour and lumber mills, and the brick plant. Dallas-milled flour was being sold over a wide area. The increasing population in the county added to the growing volume of trade in the town. Several stage lines had by 1858 made Dallas a breaking point or terminus, extending the town's communication facilities in every direction. The Houston & Texas Central Railroad was approaching from the south, and railroad connections for Dallas were definitely within the category of reasonable expectation.

By 1859 Dallas was enjoying many of the amenities and facilities of civilized mid-nineteenth-century American life. In September the town acquired its first barber shop, "an institution the want of which had long been seriously felt," according to the *Herald*. Mr. Wester from New Orleans was the first barber and erected "a very neat building . . . on the vacant lot east of the Crutchfield House," apparently with an eye to the transient trade. S. A. Galleher, a photographer, had also taken temporary quarters earlier in the year "in Mrs. Cockrell's Building on the South East Corner Public Square," where he advertised the making of "ambrotypes, put up in all the different styles of the day . . . satisfaction guaranteed. Price of the pictures, from $1.50 up, owing to quality of case." By November the newspaper boasted that the town had "two hotels, an exchange office by Nicholson & Ferris, two livery stables, two drug stores, seven large mercantile houses, two brick yards, two blacksmith shops, one carriage factory, one jeweler (with another about to locate), one insurance agency by John M. Crockett, one boot and shoe store, two saddler's shops, two mechanic's shops, one barber shop, one tinner, one cabinetmaker, one milliner, two schools, two drinking saloons, and the prospect of a lager beer establishment, one steam sawmill, and last but not least, one printing office." The lack of a baker and tailor was still felt, however. There was a universal cry of hard times, and the individual who could get "enough 'hard' to buy sugar and coffee for his family" was declared "thrice fortunate and supremely happy." The town square nevertheless presented "a gay and animated scene . . . carriages drawn up before the doors of our merchants, fashionable and elegant ladies shopping."

Merchants Organize Fair

Among the events that highlighted the year 1859 were the exhibition in May by Eldred's Great Circus and Menageries of a collection of lions, tigers, hyenas, and other wild animals; an old-fashioned Fourth of July celebration featuring the "firing of monster guns and the anvil chorus played in a rather different style from the role in *Trovatore*"; the arrival in September of a caravan of Mexicans from San Antonio in high-wheeled, ox-drawn carts thatched with straw, come to trade for Dallas-milled flour; and as a climax of the year the first annual fair of the Dallas

County Agricultural and Mechanical Association, organized by businessmen to display the community's products and resources. The fair opened October 25, at Commerce and Preston Streets on what was then the extreme eastern edge of the city, and ran three days. This was the first of a long series of Dallas fairs culminating in the State Fair of Texas. The fair ended with a tournament and ball. By 1860 such sophisticated diversions as musical soirees were being enjoyed in the city.

As the frontier epoch during which Dallas had progressed from a solitary cabin on the banks of the Trinity to a thriving agricultural and trading community neared its close, signs of the heightened tension and sectional feeling that presaged the approach of the war between the states began to manifest themselves in the region. Dallas was strongly Southern in its sympathies, and as early as May 18, 1859, a strong drift of sentiment was indicated by ironical editorializing in the news columns of the *Herald*. Under this date the passage of a herd of cattle through the town en route to distant markets was reported as follows:

> Yesterday a drove of 2,000 beef cattle passed through Dallas, to feed our abolition neighbors. We hope that Southern diet may agree with them.

C. R. Pryor, John C. McCoy, and N. H. Darnell of Dallas County were appointed during the spring of 1859 to attend the Southern Convention at Vicksburg, Mississippi, and by the end of the year secession was being generally discussed. The Dallas Lyceum announced for December 28 a public debate on the question: "Under the political aspect of affairs in the United States would the election of a black Republican President in 1860 be just cause for the South to secede from the Union?" The affirmative side in this debate was taken by C. M. Loving and T. M. Waller and the negative by R. W. Lindsay and John W. Lane.

As the year 1860 opened, signs of the times multiplied. On February 11 "a public meet irrespective of party" was held "for a free interchange of opinion on the great questions that now agitate the country," at which Nat M. Burford was the chief speaker. By April there were concrete preparations for war. A company of volunteers had been raised in Dallas County by order of General Nicholas H. Darnell, and others were urged to join.

Fire Devastates Town

As a spectacular climax to this period of increasing alarms and mounting passions, there occurred on July 8 a fire which destroyed most of the buildings in Dallas' business district, entailing a loss of $300,000. The fire originated about two o'clock on a hot Sunday afternoon, in a pile of boxes in front of the W. W. Peak & Brother Drug Store, and in less than five minutes the building was enveloped in flames. Whipped by a strong southwest wind, the fire spread rapidly to other buildings, including the *Herald* office, the St. Nicholas Hotel, and the Crutchfield House, and soon the whole square was a blazing mass of ruins. Judge Nat Burford records that when he returned the next morning from Waxahachie, where he had held court, there was only one building, a brick structure, standing on the Dallas town square—and residences had been consumed in every direction. A death-like stillness hung over the town. Citizens were grim and determined.

The crucial three-cornered campaign, with Abraham Lincoln arrayed against Stephen A. Douglas and John C. Breckinridge, was in full swing, and the people of Dallas were in no mood to accept the conflagration—heralded in headlines throughout the state—as an act of God. The fire was almost immediately laid to a slave plot, fomented by two white abolitionist preachers from Iowa. After having been called upon by a committee composed of Judge W. H. Hord, W. B. Miller, and Obadiah Knight, these two men were confined in the county jail, and after being publicly whipped, were told to quit the country.

A committee of fifty-two members was formed to mete out vigilante justice to the Negro slaves of the county—all except three of whom were said to be involved in the plot. The extremists on this committee favored hanging every Negro in the county, but at a mass meeting in the courthouse the moderates prevailed, and only three were executed—Pat Jennings, who had allegedly ignited the pile of trash outside the drug store; Sam Smith, a preacher; and "Old Cato, who had always borne a bad name in the county." Old Cato was convicted on the testimony of a Negro boy who declared he had had prior knowledge of the fire, and he in turn implicated the other two Negroes. The trio were hanged two days later on the banks of the Trinity at the foot of Main Street, near the present site of the Triple Underpass. According to a newspaper account published in Houston, the doomed men "betrayed no discomposure in view of the awful fate before them," and "Pat positively refused to say anything and died with as much indifference as if he had been about his ordinary occupation. With apparent nonchalance he retained his chew of tobacco in his mouth and died with it there." A fourth Negro was driven out of the county and the remaining slaves, more out of consideration for their property value than for reasons of humanity, were let off with a sound flogging.

Opinion in the county as to the origin of the fire and the guilt of the Negroes was by no means unanimous. The temperature on the day it had broken out had reached an unofficial maximum of 112 degrees, and observers believed it could easily have been caused by spontaneous combustion of the trash pile in which it originated. At least one member of the vigilance committee who sentenced the three slaves to hang (Judge James Bentley) later declared that in his opinion they were innocent, but added that because of the inflamed state of the public mind, "someone had to be hanged."

Portents of War

In the election of November 6, 1860, when the divided Democratic party went down in defeat before Lincoln, squarely precipitating the issue of Southern secession, the Dallas County vote was as follows:

For Breckinridge and Lane 403
For fusion 75
Democratic majority 328

"A glorious day for State Rights Democracy . . . The people of Dallas sensible to the last," the *Herald* proclaimed proudly.

News of Lincoln's election was apparently some time in reaching North Texas, however, as on November 14 a mass meeting was called in the courthouse to consider the course that Texas should pursue in the event of Lincoln's election to the presidency. The *Herald* on the same date predicted that his election would result in the dissolution of the Union and the formation of two nations, the South having "all the advantages of commerce and the respect of the world."

By November 22 the issue no longer remained in doubt, and the temper of the community on receipt of the news that the candidate of the Northern abolitionists had triumphed, is accurately reflected in a *Herald* editorial published on this date:

> From every exchange on our table we see notices of the simultaneous and unanimous movement of the people of Texas upon the announcement of the late presidential election. At various points in the state the banner of the Lone Star State floats proudly in the breezes of Heaven, indicative of the will and desire of our people to assert their independence rather than remain in vassalage and a state of dependent inequality under black Republican rule. We hear from all sides news of preparations. Military companies are forming and the drum and fife are calling the clans together to the pibroch of "Liberty and equality in the Union, or Independence out of it." We hear the mustering of squadrons in all parts of the South and whole districts and states are on a war basis. Not because we are menaced by a foreign foe, but because those whom we looked upon as brothers refuse to render us our just dues under the constitution. It is a defensive movement on our part against domestic enemies, and the resistance we make is unlike that of any other people, for we maintain our liberties and our rights against the wishes of those who dwell with us under the same roof.

Under this editorial appeared a dispatch stating that the Lone Star flag had been run up amidst intense enthusiasm at Galveston, Houston, Richmond, Huntsville, Gonzales, Navasota, and Waco.

Citizens of Dallas were organizing a cavalry company under the direction of George W. Baird, and by December 12 the Dallas Minute Men were drilling under arms at the Masonic Hall.

At the close of 1860 Dallas had recovered almost completely from the ravages of the fire. New and more substantial hotels and business houses, some of them fireproof, were being erected, the rapidly growing population had created a serious housing shortage, and an optimistic newspaper notice on December 26 declared:

> Within six months Dallas has risen almost like a dream from its ruins. Our merchants have all a full and excellent stock of goods and from the numbers we see daily in their houses, we augur a profitable season to them. Many of them are crowded into small rooms, while their large houses are being completed. We need not fear to suffer for anything to eat, drink, or wear this winter unless we become "depressed in financial matters."

These visions of prosperity were not to be realized until after more than a decade of war and Reconstruction.

War and Reconstruction: 1860–1880

On January 28, 1861, the convention that voted for Texas' secession from the Union met in Galveston, attended by Thomas J. Nash, Pleasant Taylor, E. P. Nicholson, and W. S. J. Adams as delegates from Dallas. When these men had been elected earlier in the month, the die of civil war had already been cast. The question which they went to Galveston to help decide was not the preservation of peace—that was already regarded as a thing of history—but whether Texas should stand with the North or South in the coming struggle. In the subsequent state referendum on February 23, the citizens of Dallas County voted, 741 to 237, in favor of secession and a state of war was proclaimed on June 8.

Enthusiasm for the Confederate cause ran high during the spring of 1861. The town was full of excitement and military display—parades, the booming of artillery salutes, and festive illuminations of the town square in honor of secession. Even before the state convention had acted, several military companies had been formed and were busily drilling. Among these were Captain John Good's Dallas Light Artillery and a cavalry company, General Ashley Carter's Lone Star Company of picked men from the eastern part of the county—who, the *Herald* recorded, voted "in solid phalanx for the secession ticket"—and the Dallas Minute Company, numbering eighty or ninety men and commanded by the mayor of Dallas, Colonel John M. Crockett. Later the Davis Light Infantry Company was formed under the command of Captain Thomas Flynn. President Lincoln's proclamation calling up the militia in several Northern states was answered in Dallas County by the enrollment of hundreds in the Confederate army, many joining General John B. Hood's hardfighting brigade, which was then forming. In April the Dallas Artillery and Dallas Cavalry companies had marched to Austin to tender their services to the now sovereign state government.

Of all the Southern states Texas was the most remote from the theater of war, its strategic isolation and freedom from devastation earning it later the title of the "granary of the Confederacy." Men were needed, however, to repel wild bands of Indians, and forces of Mexicans who were taking advantage of the division among their traditional Anglo-American foes to make destructive border forays. Dallas County, despite its small population and the hope of many conservative people that armed conflict between the North and the South might still be avoided, responded generously to the call for volunteers. Boys still in their early teens ran away from home to join the army. One volunteer of twelve was restrained from enlisting only by a promise from his parents to allow him to enlist as a drummer boy in the next company that was formed, with the added privilege of wearing a revolver along with his drumsticks. At least one Dallas youth, James Kinnard, printer's devil in the office of the *Dallas Herald*, served at Manassas.

Later in the war the Fair Grounds at Dallas was made an army cantonment, and served as a concentration point for Confederate volunteers and supplies. Several regiments of cavalry and artillery were organized and sent to the fighting front from Dallas and the vicinity. These included most of the recruits for the Sixth, Thirteenth, Eighteenth, Nineteenth, and Thirty-first Texas Cavalry regiments and the First Texas Artillery, first under the command of John J. Good and later of J. P. Douglas. Dallas men who attained the rank of colonel in the Confederate forces were Nicholas H. Darnell, B. Warren Stone, T. C. Hawpe, Nat M. Burford, John J. Good, John T. Coit, and W. S. Hughes. Dallas furnished the first lieutenant-governor to the Confederate State of Texas in the person of John M. Crockett; and Dr. Charles R. Pryor served four years as secretary of state, from May 2, 1865.

Gold Given to Confederacy

Dallas County not only gave its sons freely to the cause, but its material wealth as well. On May 4, 1861, the county voted, 516 to 3, to contribute to the Confederacy $5,000 in gold held in the county treasury. The three opposing voters asked to be so recorded. They were Adam Haught, H. H. Hall, and William Burton. The sequel to this action came after the war, when in 1865 a suit was filed against Edward W. Hunt, county treasurer when the money was donated, compelling him to restore the funds, entailing a severe hardship upon Hunt and his bondsmen.

In addition to this contribution of $5,000 in gold, which was intended to be spent for arms, the county commissioners on August 21, 1861, appropriated a further sum of $700 "to furnish knives for the citizens of this county who may join the Colonel B. Stover regiment (of Confederate volunteers) now being raised," and it was further specified that each knife should have "a steel blade 16 inches long and two inches wide, with wood-riveted handle, iron guard, and the point two-edged for about three inches," the cost of each weapon not to exceed $3 for knife and tin scabbard.

In December, 1861, a convoy of Mexican carts from San Antonio hauled off 100,000 pounds of flour for the use of the army, and later a quartermaster's headquarters was established at Dallas for the procurement of grain and other supplies from North Texas. A factory for the manufacture of small arms and ammunition was opened in 1862 at Lancaster in Dallas County by Joseph H. Sherrard, William L. Killem, Pleasant Taylor, and John M. Crockett. This may have been the object of the spy activities against which the *Herald* warned its readers on May 10, 1862.

Numerous benefits and entertainments were given in the town throughout the war for the relief of soldiers in the field and their families at home. There were some people of Texas who were not above war profiteering; according to the *Herald*, Confederate soldiers were often forced to pay a month's wages as the price of a single night's food and lodging, and that "sometimes grudgingly bestowed." To relieve this condition the paper proposed in August, 1864, a soldier's home similar to those which had been set up in South Texas, to be established in Dallas. Toward this cause John B. Floyd offered to contribute $100 annually, and a short time later "Messrs. Walter and Floey, late of the Houston Dramatic Association," gave a "dramatic entertainment" in the courthouse to raise funds. By December the home was established with A. Burtle in charge.

As elsewhere in the almost purely agrarian South, the people of Dallas suffered severely during the war from an acute shortage of many of the necessities of life. As early as 1861 an announcement by a local merchant, J. Sherwood, discontinuing all future credit business betokened the onset of hard times. As the war advanced and drained the country of more and more of its resources to support the hard-pressed Southern armies in the field, prices rose sharply. Quotations in the *Dallas Herald* in June, 1861, showed hams at sixteen to eighteen cents a pound, wheat at sixty cents a bushel, and oats at twenty to forty cents a bushel. By September, 1863, hams were selling at thirty-five cents a pound, wheat at $2.50 a bushel, and oats at $1.50 a bushel. A shortage of paper compelled the *Herald* to suspend publication from September 30, 1863, to July 2, 1864, the editor apologizing to his readers later for the poor quality of newsprint he was able to obtain. It was "thin, dark, and rather small," he said.

Seize Cotton for Clothing

Nor was the clothing situation better, despite Dallas' location in a cotton-growing region, and frontier skill in home weaving. Toward the end of the war the people of North Texas were literally in rags. In the fall of 1864 General Banks of the Union army undertook to fight his way through Louisiana to Texas in a gigantic cattle raid on the chief source of the Southern beef supply. The Confederates withdrew before him, and Louisiana cotton growers began to move as much of their cotton as possible to places of safety in northern Louisiana, northern Arkansas, and East Texas. Long wagon trains began to roll into Dallas laden with cotton, which was dumped near the present site of the State Fair Grounds. Some of the women of the community—desperate for clothing for themselves and their children—staged a daring holdup of one of these cotton wagons, and pretending to be armed, seized a bale of cotton, burst it open, and divided it among themselves on the spot, carrying it off to weave into homespun garments. Some of the cotton was boldly carried off after it was stored at the Fair Grounds by persons who, according to the *Herald*, represented "their necessities as an excuse for the act." Respect for property was strong in the community, however, and such acts were not condoned, the town newspaper strongly reprehending the guilty parties irrespective of their need.

Great as were the hardships of wartime, the trials of the Reconstruction period that followed were even greater. When the war ended the state government was temporarily taken over by Federal military authorities under the command of General J. J. Reynolds at San Antonio, and an appointed provisional government sat with A. J. Hamilton at its head. This regime appointed a full slate of both county and municipal officials for Dallas, with W. H. Hord as chief justice and John M. Crockett as mayor. Later another appointed board was headed by Ben Long as mayor. The mail service was completely disrupted, save for such mails as were carried by private contractors on their own responsibility, with regular service only north to Bonham and south to Waco and Houston. In December the *Herald* was still inquiring the whereabouts of the lately appointed Federal postmaster, Samuel Seaton.

Dallas Re-enters the Union

Following the conclusion of hostilities 1,260 Dallas citizens took the so-called amnesty oath, or oath of allegiance to the United States of America, and perforce took part in the several official movements incident to Reconstruction in the state. In 1866 Dallas sent James K. P. Record and Alexander Harwood to the convention called to draft a new state constitution, and later in 1868–69 A. ("Big A") Bledsoe represented Dallas in the Reconstruction convention dominated by military and Northern radicals. John Henry Brown was the town's delegate to the constitutional convention of 1875, which in April of the next year promulgated the still existent organic law of Texas.

While many incidents occurred to irritate the community in the period of readjustment after the war, the Negroes, generally the fulcrum of carpetbag rule in the South, did not constitute as serious a problem in Dallas as in many other places. Comparatively little difficulty was found in keeping them under control, though the community took cognizance of the problem as early as the spring of 1865 by the organization of police patrol precincts in the town and the adoption of "other measures conducive to the good order of our Negro population." Following the Texas emancipation proclamation on June 19, 1865, the freed slaves had formed a settlement of their own called Freedman's Town, about a mile east of the town, near the later site of the Houston & Texas Central railway terminal. This was the genesis of the Negro section now known as Deep Ellum, on Central Avenue between Elm Street and Ross Avenue. After the war Negroes from other points were attracted to Dallas in large numbers by the comparative prosperity of the community, and some alarm was felt at the possibility that, with the majority of white voters disfranchised, the county might become Africanized.

In the first elections held in Dallas County under Reconstruction in 1868, the radical registration board headed by Jesse Asbury and Melvin Wade, a Negro, rejected all white men who answered in the negative the question, "Are you in favor of Negro suffrage?" In the election that followed—held to decide for or against a convention to revise the state constitution—the issue was carried by the Negro votes, which numbered 521 out of a total of 904, most of the Negroes voting for the first time. Major M. J. Bonner relates that in this and subsequent elections in Dallas during Reconstruction times he and other white voters passed between two lines of Negro troops to cast their votes. But the fears of the white population proved largely groundless as far as any permanent effect on the political life of the community was concerned.

Ku Klux Klan Appears

The Ku Klux Klan appeared in Dallas in 1868. On April 11 the citizens were startled to find posted in conspicuous places about the town the following notice:

K. K. K.
　Demon's Den, Dark Day,
　Cloudy Moon, Time Out,
　Dumb Ferret

Shrouded Brothers, Dallas Division, No. 21:

　The Great Past Grand Giant commands you. The hour to act has come. The knife and pistol to use are given. The Foeman's chain must now be riven. On the eleventh of this mortal's month go forth to the harvest of Death. Come from the shadow of the grave and dye your hands red with the blood of your victims.
　D. C. U. L. A., Beware: The PIT yawns to receive you.
　By order of the GREAT GRAND CYCLOPS

The *Herald* branded the authors of this inflammatory manifesto as an organization composed of "ignorant and superstitious members threatening turbulence and revolution," and spoke contemptuously of their effort "to impose upon the superstitious fears of the Loyal League and frighten them into a temporary quiet, as the nursery tale of Jack the Giant Killer or Raw Head and Bloody Bones scares first into silence and then into repose the annoying and petulant child." The same paper also denied there were any Ku Klux Klansmen in the county in 1871.

Nevertheless the secret order of hooded night riders grew in power around Dallas in the early seventies, and came to number substantial citizens among its members. Its activities were directed chiefly against the Union Leagues, and were probably confined for the most part to frightening the Negroes. Major M. J. Bonner, a Ku Klux member, related that he and some of his brethren accomplished the latter on a certain occasion when he was tipped off to a meeting of bushwhackers held one night at the Duck Creek (present Garland) School. There was a ventriloquist in the party who was stationed in the schoolhouse chimney to throw his voice and present a "hideous and grotesque appearance." This he did so successfully that the Negroes were almost frightened out of their wits, and the meeting broke up in confusion.

Klansmen's acts were sometimes of a more serious nature, however, as indicated by the trial in December, 1874, of S. A. Prewitt and others before Commissioner Ben Long for "banding together and going in disguise to assault J. K. Beekman." Early in that year one hundred Klansmen from Dallas County, unmasked but armed, had marched on Austin to join five hundred or more others gathered there, to compel the seating of Governor-elect Richard Coke, whose election had been contested by E. J. Davis, carpetbagger incumbent. Dallas County had supported Coke by a vote of 2,032 to 336.

Hard Times Follow War

Times were hard immediately after the war, but economically Dallas suffered much less acutely than many communities in the Old South. There was little pauperism or bankruptcy and there are frequent references in the *Herald* files to new businesses established in 1865 and 1866. The statement made concerning this period by W. N. Coombes in *Parade of the Pioneers* is significant. He says:

> The only way the average man could get hold of a dollar after the Civil War was to haul freight. Every man who could get a wagon and team began hauling. Everything that came into Texas or that went out had to pass through Jefferson, then an important town, or through Houston. And it kept men busy hauling supplies into the little towns and crossroad stores.

Dallas indeed profited by the economic debacle that followed in the wake of war in the Old South. Many residents from these older sections of the Confederacy, ruined by the war and despoiled of their slaves, their plantations unworkable and their faith in cotton shaken, turned to the newer country west of the Mississippi to rebuild their fortunes. In this general westward movement of a shifting population, Dallas received and retained a large share of the immigrants to the Southwest. On December 1, 1866, the local paper noted: "Hardly a day passes that we do not see large numbers of emigrants passing through the town—all their noses pointing toward the sundown," and later in the same month observed:

> Continually—hourly—we see trains of emigrants coming into our town, some bound further west, some who have Dallas for their destination, some looking for a location for a new home. They come from all the older Southern and Northwestern states, but some of them we notice are from the cotton portions of our own state, seeking the fertile prairies where they can get wheat lands. Those from eastern Texas generally settle in this vicinity. Dallas has become the center of attraction for a large emigration, and we hear of considerable property hereabouts changing hands.

Traveling overland before and for perhaps a decade after the advent of the railroads, these men and women suffered a legion of ills while en route to their new homes, their hardships often only increasing after their arrival. A graphic picture of the difficulties of the immigrants is given by a contemporary writer:

> They invariably traveled during the coldest season of the year. They could not leave the old states until they had disposed of their crops, if they were fortunate enough to have crops, and had settled their affairs there. Then, it was necessary to make the trip to Texas, purchase land, build some kind of shelter to live under and plow enough new sod land for a crop by planting time. To miss a crop or to lose one would be disastrous. The great bulk of moving came between November and February. Nearly all of the immigrants were on the road for weeks, many of them for months. Northers and blizzards often caught those poorly equipped to stand the rigors of cold weather. . . . The roads were not improved and there were few bridges. High water might delay one for days or weeks. A snow or a driving rain might force an encampment under the most disagreeable circumstances. Not infrequently sickness developed in an immigrant family.

60

Flood Brings New Hardships

The great Trinity River flood in the spring of 1866, though coming later than the customary months for migration, drove many travel-worn family groups from newly plowed farms in the Dallas area. Swollen by heavy rains, the river began to rise early in May, covering all the bottom lands opposite the town. By May 12 it had reached a height it had never before attained at Dallas in the memory of the oldest inhabitants, though John Neely Bryan thought the river might have risen a few inches higher during the winter of 1842–43. He was uncertain, however, because of the great changes wrought in its banks during the intervening quarter of a century. It was generally conceded that the water level was several feet above the 1849 and 1854 floods. A rise of another six or seven feet would have put it well over the town square. At the ferry the Cockrell residence was covered to half its height by the water. The tributary streams were proportionately swollen, and Dallas Branch in North Dallas and Mill Creek in South Dallas inundated these sections. All communication between Dallas and the outside world was cut off for a week or more. By May 19 the waters had receded considerably but the bottoms remained covered.

The Dallas of the late sixties and early seventies was no longer the peaceful settlement of antebellum days but was a booming, roistering western frontier town—crowded, noisy, uncouth and disorderly, full of strangers and bustling confusion, its unpaved streets choked with pedestrians, horsemen and wagons, and with life as raw as the whisky sold in the barrooms that never closed their doors. There was a steady influx of people and a thriving trade with the north and northwest, conducted by regular wagon lines to Decatur and Weatherford. Herds of longhorn cattle being driven overland to Kansas forded the Trinity River near Dallas.

By 1869 the systematic mass extermination of the great buffalo herds on the western plains had begun, giving employment to hundreds of men and creating a steady demand for supplies. Bands of picked riflemen went ahead, leaving the slaughtered buffaloes where they fell—to be skinned by the corps of skinners who followed and removed the hides from carcasses by slitting them down the legs and pulling them off with horses. The hides, which brought a price of $2, and the dried tongues, which were in great demand locally and as delicacies in the East, were then hauled to market in wagons. The rest of the carcasses were left to rot or be devoured by the wolves. Dallas became a center of this buffalo trade, and began to boom as never before.

On Border of Wild West

The Crutchfield House, dispensing homespun hospitality at the rate of $21 a week in gold for board and room, had eight lodgers, four double beds, and one washbowl and towel to a room; it was still the leading hotel. From one of the cheapest towns in Texas the boom had made Dallas one of the most expensive. Other hotels were the William Tell House and the Union Hotel, later known as the St. Charles. There were four churches—Methodist, Cumberland Presbyterian, Christian, and Episcopalian—at least four times that many gambling houses, eight licensed dramshops, five or six billiard parlors, and one pistol or shooting gallery. Just outside the town the "Wild West"—that was still wild in North Texas at the end of the sixties—began. A contemporary visitor expressed it mildly when he said: "There are temptations to young men to throw their money away."

It is said that in the days following the Civil War, "houses could hardly be built fast enough for the growing saloons, gambling halls, and variety show business." Gambling halls and saloons solidly occupied the whole north side of Main Street from Houston to Austin Streets, and the southwestern part of the town was thickly dotted with dance halls. These rough emporiums of frontier vice never closed and the music in them never ceased, except when it was momentarily interrupted by an exchange of pistol shots. Fiddlers were in demand as never before and reaped a golden harvest. Among those who became famous was John Botto, an Italian born in the United States, who without musical education could play almost any tune by ear and in such a manner as to attract widespread attention as far away as Nashville, Tennessee. In the midst of the hectic days of 1869 a fire broke out on the north side of Main Street opposite the courthouse, and laid the block in ashes. A similar fate overtook the block to the east a short time later, consuming the flower of the saloons and gambling halls. This loss was quickly recouped, however, by new and better structures, chiefly along the south side of Main Street.

The Booming Seventies

The census of 1870 gave the town a population of only 3,000 inhabitants, but it was always full of transients, and unofficial estimates were much larger. Pictures taken at this period show unpaved business streets lined with frame buildings, their wooden awnings sheltering plank-floored porches, which for the most part served as sidewalks. Hitching posts were numerous along the streets that were channels of mud in wet weather and lanes of swirling dust in dry spells. Mud was from five inches to two feet deep on Elm Street east of Austin Street in the spring, according to the *Herald*. Signs proclaimed various sorts of merchandise for sale, and that buffalo hides, peltries, and farm products were bought by the merchants. In 1872 there were only a few brick buildings in the business district which was still concentrated around the square facing the courthouse, a small and unimpressive building.

A few newcomers had begun to locate on Elm Street, the first of these being W. A. Rogers, who erected a little hardware store, 25x100 feet, just east of Austin Street in what is now the Sanger Brothers' block. The City Hall was upstairs on the northeast corner of Commerce and Jefferson Streets in an old frame house, and the post office, shortly afterward moved to Camp and Lamar Streets, was in a little one-story room on Jefferson Street near Commerce Street. Of sanitary ordinances there were none. The *Herald* complained of an "unsightly and stinking mudhole" on Main Street opposite its office, in which hogs rooted and wallowed.

There were a few scattered houses as far east as the present Fair Grounds, but the principal streets of the town such as Elm, Main, and Commerce extended only as far as Murphy Street. Ross Avenue and Bryan Street were only country lanes. Ervay Street was the Miller's Ferry Road; Swiss Avenue was Butcherpen Road; and the streets of Caruth's addition were bridle paths and cow trails. Later a fashionable residence section known as The Cedars grew up between Akard and Harwood Streets extending as far south as the present Sullivan Park.

Military Seek Mayor's Ouster

Though the town was showing great progress in its material development, as the decade opened it still was torn by the political dissension incident to Reconstruction, with military authority dominating civil administration. Perhaps most notable among the last episodes of this aftermath of war occurred in March of 1872 when Henry S. Ervay, mayor of the town, was imprisoned for contempt of court after he had refused to give up his office. Ervay had been appointed by the radical governor, E. J. Davis, but his loyalty to carpetbag rule was doubted by General Reynolds, head of the Federal military in the state, who ordered him removed, appointing Dr. J. W. Haynes in his place. Haynes sought the aid of Judge Hardin Hart in district court to oust Ervay who, on refusal to obey a writ, was temporarily jailed. He was released after a decision of the state supreme court denied the governor's right to remove him from office, and served out his term as mayor.

The attitude of the people of the community toward Federal military domination was reflected by the publication in the city directory of 1875 of the following reminiscent denunciation:

> The war ended, the people of this place passed through the annoyance and discomfiture of the petty tyrannies that were propagated by the official bummers who came to carry out the measure enacted by Congress for the reconstruction of the states. In doing so they were subjected to some rare indignities at the hands of the (Freedman's) Bureau agent, who will be long remembered in this community as a rich example of accomplished scoundrelism. Captain Horton of the United States Army is the gentleman referred to and for his withdrawal from this community public thanks are due Captain J. T. Carey and Judge J. J. Good.

During these earlier postwar days some of the wildest desperadoes of the West visited the town at the forks of the Trinity and declared "there was nothing in any mining camp to beat it." The cowboys who visited Dallas were as wild as the longhorns they drove. They would leave their herds to graze nearby, a resident of the period wrote:

> while they came back and pulled a stampede of their own by racing their horses up and down the town, yelling like Comanches as they fired their guns. Everybody knew that the cowboys meant no harm and that if anyone was hurt, it was an accident. Still the women would gather up their children and crouch with them in the houses until they left town.

In 1873 the "swellest saloon in town" was conducted by Julius Bogel, and Billy Henson had a row of resorts on the south side of Main Street between Austin and Market Streets. At the corner of Main and Houston Streets Johnnie Thompson ran a big variety show—the largest in the Southwest. The gambling fraternity were numerous, there being nearly one hundred professional gamblers in the town. The contention that closing the saloons and gambling halls would ruin business was a potent argument in a community as much given to hard drink and games of chance as Dallas in those days, and there was no attempt at outright suppression.

During this year, however, Mayor Ben Long attempted to secure some regulation. Though he demanded little more than a recognition of the existence of the city government, his interference was fiercely resented by the gambling house proprietors, who barricaded themselves in the second story of a downtown building and defied Long and his deputies for three days and nights. The siege ended in a compromise, celebrated by the smashing of many bottles, which defined the privileges of the municipality on one hand and of the gamblers on the other.

These lawless elements were not the only additions to Dallas' population during the period, however. Mayor Long, a Swiss by birth who had prospered in America, returned to his native country for a visit in 1870 and persuaded a group of his fellow countrymen from Zurich to return with him and settle in the growing town of Dallas. The first contingent of these Swiss settlers, numbering thirty-five, arrived in December, 1870, and the colony thus created quickly assumed an active part in the community life. From it have sprung many prominent latterday families, and two of the city's streets, Swiss Avenue and Germania Street (renamed Liberty during the World War), were named for it.

Railroads Bring New Boom

The advent of railroad transportation to Dallas in the early seventies lent a further impetus to the boom that was already under way, doing much to account for the phenomenal growth of the town during the ensuing decade. While efforts had been made to secure rail connections as early as 1848, it was not until July 16, 1872, that the first passenger train steamed in over the Houston & Texas Central Railroad. Less than a year later, February 22, 1873, the first train of the Texas & Pacific Railway steamed up Pacific Avenue. Further progress on this road to the westward was halted by the panic of 1873, and Dallas remained the end of the road for nearly three years.

Boasting, bombast, and reckless prophecy, soon to be surpassed in sober fact, were the order of the day. Dallas had become a typical example of the characteristic phenomenon of American economic life during the years of frenzied expansion that followed the end of the Civil War—as "end-of-the-tracks town." During the decade from 1870 to 1880, 20,174 people took up residence in Dallas County, as compared to 13,314 who had come during the period from 1841 to 1870. In the single year of 1873, 935 buildings were erected and the first city directory, December, 1873, recorded a population of 7,054 within the city limits. The *Herald* declared the population of the city and environs had reached 10,000 by May, 1874. Dallas became a concentration point for raw materials intended for shipment to the South and East, and an outfitting point for railroad passengers starting overland for the West. In one month in the autumn of 1874 business showed a three-quarters increase over the preceding month. The wagonyards were filled with emigrant wagons bound for West and Southwest Texas, and there were traffic jams on lower Commerce and Lamar Streets.

The *Herald* recorded that on October 15, 1874, "Elm Street was one snowwhite sea of cotton." A week earlier several carloads of the first cotton compressed in the city had been shipped to Fall River, Massachusetts. Immigrants arrived by every train, mostly from Kentucky, Maryland, Virginia, and Tennessee. In one day, on October 17, 1874, 220 arrived from Tennessee, most of them farmers intending to locate in Dallas, Tarrant, and Navarro counties. The city's infant industries began to boom. Orders were pouring into a local soap factory so fast that it was almost impossible to fill them. "Where is the man who says factories won't pay in Dallas?" crowed the *Herald* in proud rhetorical question.

Meanwhile the buffalo trade continued unabated, reaching its peak about 1875, when Dallas was the largest market in the world for buffalo hides. In this year, as a result of the buffalo market and railroad facilities, $6,000,000 was in circulation in Dallas' trade area. Outside capital began to be attracted to the city. Phil Chappell of Kansas City and Captain G. M. Swink of Dallas were granted a state banking charter, and established the Exchange Bank with a capitalization of $40,000. The first bank in the city, that of Gaston & Camp, had been established in 1868, and several others were opened during the following decade (*see BANKS AND BANKING: CAPITAL RESERVOIR*).

An outward sign of this new prosperity was the opening on October 7, 1875, of the three-story Le Grand Hotel, which at the time of its opening was advertised as "the most elegant hotel in the South." A chandelier thirty feet in circumference with seventy blazing gas jets in the main lobby, a fountain ornamented with a bronze figure of Neptune and surrounded by rare plants and flowers, electric "annunciators" or buzzers in every room, a telegraph office in the rotunda presided over by a "lady operator," and a parlor fitted out with a grand piano, a scarlet Brussels carpet, and lace curtains were among its featured luxuries. The Exchange Bank and an insurance agency occupied part of the first floor, with the west side taken up by Mr. Bogel's Saloon and Billiard Parlor, featuring frescoed walls, the latest in billiard tables, and a bar stocked with liquors and wines "unsurpassed in the city."

Nor was the dining room neglected. One of the hotel's early Christmas dinner menus offered over seventy different dishes to the gargantuan appetites of the period. In addition to the standard turkey and dressing, roast young pig, cranberry sauce, mince pie, and plum pudding, it included such exotic delicacies as oysters, sea turtle, capon, sweetbreads, truffles, ravioli, mushrooms, pate de foie gras, fresh lobster, olives, figs, pomegranate jelly, and imported cheeses. These were combined with incongruously homely frontier fare like pig jowls and kale greens and a bewildering variety of wild game—several species of duck, stuffed wild goose, broiled quail, saddle of venison, and roasted black bear. An added cosmopolitan touch was supplied by the French names given to many of the items on the bill of fare.

Tom Smith, a picturesque man about town, was the proprietor, and is quoted as having said when the hotel was opened that nothing in it was paid for.

The new hostelry (combined in 1879 with the Windsor to form the Grand Windsor) was completed just a few months too late for the reception of the city's most distinguished visitor of the year, Jefferson Davis, the still beloved and revered ex-president of the Confederacy, who spoke in Dallas on May 21, 1875. It was estimated that over a thousand nonresidents gathered in the city to hear and see the Southern statesman. A large crowd assembled to receive him and General Felix Robertson at the new Houston & Texas Central Station, where Davis was officially greeted by the mayor and a reception committee. From this point to Colonel John C. McCoy's grove where Davis spoke there was a parade through streets specially decorated for the occasion. At the grounds a crowd of from seven to ten thousand awaited the speaker. Colonel John J. Good delivered a welcoming address outlining Dallas' history and growth. Jefferson Davis spoke at length of his triumphal procession through Texas, touched briefly on the justice of the Southern cause, extolled the possibilities of Texas, and exhorted Texans to greater material and cultural achievements. He was followed by ex-Governor Frank Lubbock, Governor Throckmorton, Colonel Frank Sexton of Marshall, and others, including a number of officers and privates who had fought in the Confederate ranks. From Dallas Jefferson Davis returned to Houston, later visiting Marshall, Jefferson, Texarkana, and other towns in East Texas.

First Utilities Established

Other important developments of the middle seventies indicated Dallas' consciousness of the urban status which it had by this time attained. Among these were the attention given to an adequate water supply, the adoption of artificial gas for lighting, and the inauguration of commercial telegraph service in the city. A private water concern known as the Dallas Hydrant Company was chartered in 1873 to supply the city with water pumped in wooden mains from Browder Springs, in present Sullivan Park, to a water tower at Main and Harwood Streets *(see POINTS OF INTEREST: Sullivan Park)*. The service was far from comprehensive, however, as an item in the *Herald* dated June 10, 1874, reveals. At this time, the article stated, there were about twenty springs and "a respectable number of cisterns" in the city; nevertheless *aquadores* or water-carriers were doing a brisk business.

Cisterns under the sidewalks, filled by hand pumps with water from the Trinity River, afforded fire protection. Though the organization of a fire department had been agitated immediately after the fire of 1860, the Civil War intervened, and it was not until August 5, 1871, that a corps of amateur fire fighters called the Dallas Hook and Ladder Company, Number 1, was formed in the city. In 1873 it numbered fourteen men with W. C. Connor as chief; the engine house was on Austin Street. An anniversary celebration was held the following year, August 6, 1874. These pioneer firemen constituted little more than a bucket brigade, aided by volunteers, and when a blaze started in the small hours of the morning their uniforms often were only their nightshirts. The firemen were not lacking in resourcefulness, as was demonstrated on one winter night in 1877, when at a dance in a hall over Professor E. B. Lawrence's business college at 17 Main Street, the bunting decorations caught fire. The ensuing panic was heightened by the discovery that all the water had leaked from the cistern in the street below. Nothing daunted, the doughty firemen broached several barrels of wine belonging to L. Caperon, a Frenchman who operated a shop nearby, and with it proceeded to extinguish the blaze. By 1878 the Dallas Fire Department had a personnel of 168 men divided into four companies—two hook and ladder companies, a steam fire engine company, and a hose company.

The first telephone to be used in Dallas was installed in 1880 as an experiment. It connected the water plant at Browder Springs with the downtown office of the water company at Main and Harwood Streets, and with the fire station at Commerce and Lamar, and facilitated the handling of fires. This instrument is now in the Ford Museum at Dearborn, Michigan.

The Dallas City Gaslight Company was established in 1874 with offices in the Elm Street store of Schneider & Davis, wholesale grocers. Wooden mains carried the illuminant to the consumers, practically all of them in the business district, at a cost of $6 per 1,000 cubic feet—the lowest rate in the state, the *Herald* boasted. The installation of 102 gas lampposts for street lighting in the downtown area was approved by the city council June 18, 1874, and on June 22 the city was briefly illuminated for the first time with artificial gas. Regular service was inaugurated a few days later. Before this time kerosene lamps had been generally used for lighting. Gas did not begin to displace wood, coal, and coke for fuel purposes until much later.

Dallas acquired its first telegraph service with the coming of the railroads, the Houston & Texas Central bringing a line to the town in 1872, and the Texas & Pacific another line to the north in 1873. There was no regular commercial service until the fall of 1875, though the first commercial telegram was sent over railroad wires September 12, 1874, and the first commercial line into the city was opened from Fort Worth on September 13. The first telegram sent over this wire was a message of congratulation from the mayor of Fort Worth to the mayor of Dallas, sent by Operator Max Elser. The Western Union opened its first commercial office in the city October 1, 1875, in an upstairs room on the north side of Main Street near Poydras.

Belle Starr Comes to Town

With the acquisition of these modern conveniences Dallas felt it had definitely become a city. An eastern historian wrote: "It grows like an enchanted castle in a fairy tale." Nevertheless the lawlessness of the post-Civil War period and frontier boom days lingered on throughout the decade.

Some of the most sensational crimes of this period were committed by Belle Starr, known before her second marriage as Myra Reed. This notorious woman was the counterpart of the "gun molls" of the twentieth century, and worked with the James boys, the Younger brothers, William Clark Quantrell, and other well-known desperadoes of the time. She was born February 3, 1848, in Carthage, Missouri, where her father, John Shirley, a hotel proprietor, had moved from Virginia about 1842. When the Civil War broke out she became a rabid Confederate sympathizer and did scouting and messenger service for the Confederates early in 1863. In June, 1864, her twin brother, Edward Shirley, was shot and killed by Union soldiers, and Belle, strapping two revolvers around her waist, swore to avenge his death. That summer the Shirleys came to Texas and settled near Scyene in Dallas County to raise cattle—some accounts say to prevent Belle's marriage to Jim Reed, a horse thief and cattle rustler.

This young man followed the family to Texas and eloped with Belle in 1866, having won her hand by promising to help her avenge her brother's death. Her father tried to separate the couple by sending her away to an older brother's farm in Palo Pinto County, but Reed, kidnapping his bride, took her back to Missouri, where their child, Pearl, was born soon after. Here Reed killed a man in a quarrel over a horse race, and a feud developed which forced Reed and his wife to flee to the Indian Territory. There he was hidden by Tom Starr, a Cherokee Indian, one of whose sons Belle later married. After this they wandered all over the West, settling for a time as law-abiding citizens in Los Angeles, where their second child, Edward, was born. The couple returned to the Shirley farm in Dallas County in 1872, after reconciliation with Belle's father. Jim Reed was betrayed three years later in 1875 by his friend, John Morris, who shot him while they stopped to eat at a farmhouse near McKinney, Collin County.

After the death of her husband, Belle moved to Dallas and opened a livery stable somewhere near Camp Street where she dealt in stolen horses. She was involved in the crimes of the Younger brothers and was twice indicted by the Dallas County courts, once in April, 1875, for "willfully and feloniously with force and arms" burning the store of Nannie Alexander, and again in September of that year for the theft of a horse. For the first offense of arson she was acquitted; for the second offense of horse stealing she was confined in the county jail, whence she escaped while awaiting trial by inducing a sheriff's deputy to elope with her across the Red River into Indian Territory. Here she joined a band of bank robbers and cattle thieves, acting as a sort of treasurer for the gang.

She made frequent trips to Dallas and other larger towns for the fine clothing of which she was fond, and on one of these occasions a banker succumbed to her charms. Belle made a rendezvous with him at the bank after closing hours, and is said to have robbed him of $30,000 at the point of a pistol.

In 1878 she married Bruce Younger of Coffeyville, Kansas, whom she soon deserted for Sam Starr, the half-breed son of Tom Starr. At the time of her third marriage she was 32 and the groom 20, but they were happy and for a time Belle showed signs of a desire to reform. She was shot to death from ambush by an unknown assassin in February, 1889, near Eufala, in the then Indian Territory.

A host of legends have grown up about this daring woman outlaw of the seventies. Many of the accounts of her individual movements and exploits are confusing and contradictory. It is evident, however, that she was an attractive woman, gifted with unusual courage, intelligence, and resourcefulness. Almost all reports agree that, though a spitfire, she had a lively and pleasing personality as well as a ready sense of humor, and was capable of kind and generous acts. She was a crack shot and an expert horsewoman, and made a striking and picturesque figure in the black velvet riding habit—trimmed with fine leather straps and buckles—and the large plumed Stetson hat she affected.

During 1876, the year of the great "grasshopper storm" that is reputed to have stopped the trains between Dallas and Fort Worth, the city was meting out justice to malefactors according to the standards of the period. A Negro was hanged for rape from the Texas & Pacific Railroad bridge in the Trinity bottoms, and two young men were arrested and brought to trial for the daring theft of several horses from the very heart of the city. The horses were found hidden in the bottoms, and the *Herald* attributed the legal handling of the case to the good fortune of the pair in being apprehended in such a law-abiding county as Dallas. "For if they had been caught farther west," the paper remarked, "their doom would have been meted out in short order."

In the following year Dallas lost one of its leading citizens in a barroom shooting affray, when on June 29, 1877, former Mayor Ben Long was shot and mortally wounded by a shady character named Reynolds, said to be from Austin and San Antonio. The shooting occurred in a saloon at the corner of Austin and Wood Streets, kept by John Hausman, a Swiss. Ben Long intervened in behalf of the proprietor when Reynolds declared himself unable to pay for the beer he had drunk, and Reynolds, going out, returned with a pistol and shot both Long and Hausman. Hausman recovered, but Long died a few hours later. His assailant expired in the county jail the following day after having been shot in the manhunt that ensued.

Exploits of Sam Bass

Sam Bass' exploits, surpassing even those of Belle Starr, came later in 1878, when within a period of fifty days he and his gang held up and robbed four trains within a twenty-mile radius of Dallas. The outlaw "train crew" consisted of Sam Bass, the "conductor," who went through the train frisking the passengers, Frank Jackson, the "engineer," who took charge of the cab, and Seaborn Branes, Thomas Spotswood, Arkansas Johnson, Henry Underwood, Sam Pipes, and Albert Herndon. On February 22, 1878, this gang held up and robbed the Houston & Texas Central at Allen Station. A southbound train on the same road was treated likewise at Hutchins Station on March 18, the latter robbery netting the gang $400. They then retreated to a hideout in the Hickory Bottom thickets near Lewisville. Here the bandits lounged about, ate peaches, and discussed their next move. The lame Dallas & Wichita Railroad, which ran halfway to Dallas, was near at hand, but the redoubtable Sam Bass scorned to waste his talents on so feeble and probably unproductive a victim. He is reported to have said, "Ain't that a bonanza . . . the poor thing was bogged up in Elm Bottom, and I'd as soon hit a woman as tap it. Besides, if I had, I'd have had to rob the poor thing on credit, and that won't do in our business." Instead he decided to rob the westbound Texas & Pacific at the village of Eagle Ford, which he did without firing a shot on the night of April 4, escaping again to his hideout in Hickory Bottoms.

The express company had taken precautions against a possible holdup, however, and the third haul proved a lean one, netting the gang only about $50. The whole countryside was now aroused. The people of Dallas could talk of little else, and bankers and businessmen placed loaded shotguns within convenient reach. A posse had gone out from the town and found tracks leading toward Lewisville and the Hickory Bottoms, but no further trace of the robbers was discovered. Then on April 10 they struck again at Mesquite, in the eastern part of the county, looting the Texas & Pacific train of $150. This time the outlaws did not get off so lightly. They were met by a fusillade of gunfire from officials, express messengers, passengers, and a camp of convicts nearby, and several of the gang rode away with minor buckshot wounds that led to their later identification.

The big corporations, the railroads and express companies, and the United States mails, had been hit by the robberies. Newspaper men and detectives, including the famous Pinkertons, swarmed into Dallas and Denton counties. They made Dallas their headquarters. A Ranger detachment of thirty men was organized in the city, and June Peak, former deputy sheriff, placed in command. Peak's company arrested two of the principals in the Mesquite robbery, in Collins settlement near Denton, April 22. On June 12, together with a sheriff's posse, this company met Sam Bass' party on Salt Creek in Wise County, killing Arkansas Johnson, and capturing all the bandits' horses. Bass and the remainder of his men escaped, however, and after stealing new mounts made their way back into Denton County. Then began a manhunt which led finally to the arrest of some of the gang and the death of their leader at Round Rock in Central Texas, July 21, 1878.

Town Nears City Stature

By the end of the decade Dallas was laying claim to a population of 20,000 and boasting that it was second only to Galveston in wealth and power. The Federal census figures for 1880, however, gave the city a population of only 10,358. Dallas had attained a solid economic foundation. The tide of immigration continued to pour in from the North and East. Dallas had long been a grain and flour milling center; shipments of grain and cotton from the fertile and rapidly developing farming region of North Central Texas were increasing every year, and it was rapidly becoming a railroad distributing point with many branch houses established by large northern and eastern manufacturing firms.

The prevailing American, German, and French elements in the population had formed an industrious and enterprising blend of races with a strongly practical and utilitarian point of view, concerned with the "useful rather than the ornamental." They had streetcars, gas and water works, but as yet were unconcerned with fine architecture or an ostentatious display of wealth and "taste." The business blocks were plain, substantial brick and stone buildings, two and three stories high. A three-story distillery with a 230-foot front, costing $150,000, was probably the largest single establishment. Residences were comfortable, well-constructed frame cottages with no tendencies to grandeur. The courthouse was the only building, public or private, with any pretensions whatever—and it was a plain, solid stone structure that had cost something less than one hundred thousand dollars.

Hotels were always full of commercial travelers, and Dallas was beginning to be visited by some of the so-called big men of the time, among them Jay Gould, the railroad magnate, who came in 1880. Some of the simplicity, freedom, and informality of the frontier had begun to pass and Dallas citizens were paying the penalties of urban life. Even the servant problem had developed, as the establishment of a domestic employment agency in that year testifies.

City in the Making: 1880–1910

The 1880s opened with a rush and rumble of urban progress. During the next three decades Dallas gradually emerged from a sprawling, uncouth railroad boom town into a crowded, ornate city of the gilt and red plush era. This in turn began to be outgrown as the first decade of the new century drew to a close, and the way cleared for the planned city of today.

One of the first signs of transition was the introduction in Dallas of the electrical inventions that did so much to transform urban life in the last quarter of the nineteenth century. First came the telephone, then the electric light. The first telephone exchange was opened in May, 1881, by the Erie (later the Southwestern, now Southwestern Bell) Telephone Company, at 224 Elm Street. The first telephone pole stood on the spot occupied today by the southeast corner of the Slaughter Building. Judge John Bookhout was the first subscriber, and Miss Jennie E. Thompson the first operator. By September of the following year the telephone was "in use pretty much throughout the city, both in dwellings and nearly all business houses." In 1882 the company installed its first long distance line—to Lancaster—and later extended it to Waxahachie, Ennis, Waco, Denton, and Cleburne. By 1883 it had 259 city subscribers and its lines stretched out to Fort Worth, Terrell, Sherman, Gainesville, and McKinney.

There were also beginning to be proposals in 1881 that the city be illuminated by electricity. These suggestions the *Dallas Herald* condemned on the grounds that electric lighting had failed in London and had been temporarily abandoned in New York, not having by any means come up to expectations. "The truth is," this paper said, "that it does not give a regular, steady light. It suddenly flares up, burns evenly for a moment or two, and then depreciates in intensity."

Nevertheless an electric light plant was built by private capital under municipal grant in a small wooden building at the northwest corner of Carondelet (Ross Avenue) and Austin Streets in 1882, and was soon supplying the city with electricity. The first patrons of the company were the saloons. Mayer's Garden on the north side of Elm Street at Stone Street took five or six lights and became the most brilliantly illuminated place in town. The St. George Hotel had one light, the Grand Windsor two, and Sanger Brothers three. Though few and feeble, these first electric lights, all of the old arc-light type, were a source of pride to the young city, as indicated by the introduction to the city directory of 1883, which says:

A few months ago the electric light was introduced and now beautifully illuminates our grand hotels, merchant palaces, and streets in the heart of the town with its pale, ghostly, and weird rays.

The water problem became acute in the summer of 1881. A squabble over rates developed between the city and the Dallas Hydrant Company, which declined to furnish water for less than $62.50 a hydrant for one year and $50 a hydrant for a period of five years. As a result of this controversy the company shut off the water supply from the two fire engine houses, the police station, the city hospital, and the stock pound, and water had to be hauled to these places. The city thereupon resolved to build waterworks of its own. A special commission found what they believed to be an adequate source of supply in Bayard Springs, two miles east of the city, on the Lagow farm, which had a capacity of 3,000,000 gallons a day—about three times the requirements of Dallas at the time. The problem was solved temporarily the following year when the city bought the plant of the Dallas Hydrant Company for $65,000, including all mains and the equipment at Browder Springs and the standpipe at Main and Harwood Streets, on the site of the present City Hall.

Food prices were high in 1881, but local merchants were featuring the latest in clothing, including cabriolet bonnets, colored lace mitts, and white and red flannel shirts and drawers. Some of the more enterprising were taking advantage of the telephone to improve their service. By 1882 an opera house was being contemplated and $20,000 had been secured toward its erection. The Gulf, Colorado & Santa Fe Railroad had purchased ground for the construction of freight and passenger stations at Murphy and Commerce Streets, and the Texas & Pacific Railroad had decided to build a station at Lamar Street and Pacific Avenue.

Dallas Becomes a City

Dallas was beginning to assume the aspect of a city and had an estimated population of 25,000 in its metropolitan area. About 4,000 people resided in East Dallas, which had just been organized, and a large number in various other unincorporated suburbs. There were one hundred and eleven streets, "wide and crossing each other at right angles," in the city proper, with an aggregate length of ninety-eight miles. They were still unpaved, however, and in bad weather horses could hardly pull the vehicles through the mud. Three streetcar lines branching out from the square reached the principal parts of town.

The city had "one of the handsomest courthouses in north Texas," two pleasure parks, stores and residences "that would do credit to larger cities," two large hotels, a number of smaller ones, ninety to a hundred boarding houses, about twenty churches, and a free public school system supplemented by the Dallas Female College, Ursuline Academy, and two or three private boys' schools. Nor were places of entertainment lacking, among the chief being Mayer's Garden, which according to the *Dallas Sunday Mercury* afforded "ample room for evening strolls and rambles" with lemonade and ice cream as featured refreshments. In contrast to this gentle form of entertainment, the same paper in another issue remarked that "three hundred saloons every minute in the day pour their poisonous compounds down the gullets of their customers."

Dallas was still primarily a wholesale and retail center, catering to the varied wants of a population of some 60,000 living in a twelve- to fifteen-mile radius of the city. Between 1880 and 1882 its trade almost doubled. Local commerce was materially aided by the purchase in 1882 of the toll bridge across the Trinity, and its conversion into a free bridge by the county commissioners. There were five railroads in the county with 124.22 miles of tracks, valued at $627,400.

Industrial development was also evident. Dallas had nine saddle and harness establishments, at least four of them on a large scale. Other important establishments included plants for the manufacture of railroad cars, wagons, carriages, buggies, furniture, a foundry, two soap factories, a vinegar and cider factory, three flour mills, and numerous other small industries.

The March 19 issue of the *Dallas Sunday Mercury* headlined the tragic slaying on March 14 of Judge J. M. Thurmond, a prominent attorney and former mayor:

> On Tuesday about 1 p.m. the report came up the street that Judge J. M. Thurmond had been killed by Robert E. Cowart in the County Court room only a few moments before.

The slaying attracted much attention because of its background of city politics. Thurmond had been elected mayor in 1879 on an independent reform and morality ticket, but the following summer was removed because of his asserted inability to enact the promised reforms. This was the only ouster proceeding undertaken by the city government in its history, the city council at that time having authority under the charter to remove the mayor by a vote of lack of confidence. Cowart was one of the attorneys engaged to displace Thurmond. Later, Thurmond appealed to the people for reelection but Cowart took the stump against him and was generally credited with having defeated him. At his first trial Cowart was convicted of murder in the second degree and sentenced to seven years in the penitentiary. A second trial was granted a year later and this time he was acquitted.

Marriage Aid Organized

Another event of 1882 was the incorporation of the Texas Marriage Aid Association, "managed by a number of the leading citizens and business men of the city of Dallas." These included W. H. Lemmon, W. H. Thomas, W. H. Prather, C. M. Terry, A. C. Ardrey, F. M. Cockrell, J. B. Franklin, and T. S. Burnett. Such associations, a form of marriage insurance, were apparently common in Texas at the period. The advertised plan of operation of the Dallas Association was as follows:

> For five dollars, any unmarried white person of good character, or child, may become a certificate holder in this association, and will receive fifty cents a day on each five dollars invested, till marriage shall have occurred. And in case of failure to marry within two thousand days from the date of the certificate, each certificate held will draw one thousand dollars. No one person will be allowed to invest more than twenty-five dollars, and cannot, therefore, hold more than five shares.

In April the organization was pushing its work into all sections of the state, carrying advertisements in leading newspapers, and seeking agents. The total membership of the association by August 1 was 1,700, and a state convention was held in Dallas on October 18. Early in its existence it was paying benefits promptly, as the following newspaper item indicates:

> Chas. F. Bolanz of Dallas, a member 30 days paid into the association $30 and received $75 benefits. Miss Sallie E. Leonard of New Orleans, a member 33 days, paid into the association $30 and received $82.50 benefits. Fran Wright of Plano a member 13 days paid into the association $25 and received $52.50 benefits.

In 1883 freight service was tied up in Dallas as elsewhere by the nationwide railroad strike, which boomed the wagon trade and set saloon patrons to grumbling over the lack of ice for their beer. A site for the new Federal Building, 120x200 feet at Main and Ervay Streets, was bought for $11,000. Two handsome new streetcars with six seats each were received from St. Louis. The renowned Spanish Fort Band of New Orleans was secured at a cost of $6,000 to play for a State Saengerfest held in May, when the city was illuminated with electric lights. A destructive cotton compress fire in October, which destroyed the new electric light plant, called for the services of the Fort Worth Fire Department, and according to the *Sunday Mercury* "forty minutes from the time the dispatch was sent they had their engine and hose-cart at the scene of the fire, with firemen to manage it." A special train brought the equipment over the thirty-four miles separating Dallas from the adjacent city. Rivalry was already developing between Dallas and its neighbor to the west, which the *Daily Herald* a few years earlier had jocosely referred to as "that Micawber of the prairies." The Brown Stockings baseball team of Dallas beat the Haymakers of Fort Worth 23 to 1 in a matched game. During the year the town of East Dallas, by a vote of 288 to 17, decided against annexation to its big brother.

Still a Western Town

But Dallas was still a western town and North Central Texas still a part of the cattle country. Cattle stealing, according to the *Sunday Mercury* of October 13, 1883, was prevalent in the immediate vicinity of Dallas. The thieves would hide in the outskirts of town and in the river bottoms and watch for stock running at large, quietly killing yearlings and two-year-olds in the night and later selling their hides.

On February 9, 1883, the only case in the city court was "a poor specimen of humanity who was fined $1 for uttering an oath." Standards of morality in Dallas were not what they are today, however. Memories of the desperadoes of the frontier were still fresh. Frank James, brother of Jesse James, clerked in a Dallas shoe store for some time in the late eighties. A delegation of Dallas businessmen called on County Attorney Charles Clint on October 20, 1883, in an effort to dissuade him from running the professional gamblers out of town. Fort Worth was offering them free rent and $3,500 in cash to remove the seat of their operations to that city. The delegation pointed out to the county attorney that it would mean a serious loss of revenue to Dallas. The *Sunday Mercury* demanded that:

> The notorious localities in this city from which pistol shots are nightly heard to the great annoyance and danger of decent people living near should be looked after by the police and squelched. One is the notorious row of huts on the north side of the oil mills occupied alike by blacks and whites of both sexes, and the other "hell's half acre" on Pacific.

Wild game continued to be a common article of diet, with an abundance of wild turkeys, quail, deer, bears, antelopes, squirrels, opossums, and rabbits.

Memories of the sixties were fading from the public consciousness, but in 1884 Dallas was reminded briefly of the late conflict between the states. The *Daily Herald* of August 8 stated:

> On Monday morning a difficulty occurred between Col. J. S. Hammond and Mr. J. R. Shepherd, the former charging the latter with undue intimacy with his wife, who is better known as Belle Boyd, the Confederate spy. Mrs. Hammond denies the charge and says that she regards Shepherd as a boy.

A few days later Mrs. Hammond filed a petition in the district court for divorce from her husband, which was granted November 1. Meantime, in October, the same paper reported:

> Mrs. John Hammond, well known as Belle Boyd, the famous Confederate girl spy, shot a man in the arm at her home in The Cedars yesterday after she accused him of compromising her daughter.

In January of the following year Mrs. Hammond organized a dramatic troupe and announced her intention of making a tour of the states. Nothing further is recorded locally of this colorful Civil War personality who, for her participation as a spy in that conflict, gained the sobriquet of Siren of the Shenandoah.

New Newspapers Appear

A notable advance in 1884 was the paving of some of the streets of the city with bois d'arc blocks. City Engineer W. M. Johnson received a patent for this type of wooden paving in July, 1884, and generously gave the city the right to use it. Over the protests of some property owners, Main and Elm Streets were paved, and a few cross streets—Sycamore (Akard), Murphy, Poydras, Lamar, and Jefferson—received similar treatment. The new paving did not prove satisfactory, however, giving way in several places on August 4, 1884, when heavily loaded vehicles passed over it after a heavy rain. Johnson attributed failure of his invention to the fact that the blocks had not settled properly, and Dallas' streets continued to be paved with this material for many years. The first macadam paving, on Cedar Springs Road, was also laid in 1884. Brick and cement sidewalks came later, toward the end of the decade.

Headlined as "Delightful Dallas" by the *Weekly Herald* the town in 1884 was described as

> essentially a business city. Turn in whatever direction you may, you are sure to bring up against some building in the process of erection, whether it be the half-finished mansion of some merchant prince, or the massive walls of a trade emporium.

The same paper calls attention to the enforcement of the Sunday liquor law from 9 A.M. to 4 P.M., stating that "it required very fine maneuvering and a deal of rushing on the part of the thirsty to get their whistles moistened." That Dallas whistles were kept moderately moist is indicated by another excerpt: "Dallas drinks 52,000 kegs of beer annually."

In 1885 *The Dallas Morning News*, oldest and most influential of existing Dallas newspapers, made its first appearance on October 1. It was an offshoot of the *Galveston News*, established in 1842. Executives of the Galveston publication aspired to statewide circulation. To secure better coverage than was possible by train service, they resolved to establish a twin newspaper with an independent plant and staff in the rapidly developing North Texas area, and selected Dallas as the location.

Less than eight weeks later the *Dallas Herald*, which had been published continuously first as a weekly and then as a daily since 1849, was absorbed by *The Dallas Morning News*. The second of Dallas' present newspapers, the *Times Herald*, a merger of the *Dallas Times* and a second *Dallas Herald*, which existed only a few months, appeared the following year.

One of the last items of local interest published by the old *Dallas Herald* rejoices that:

At last the Union Depot (Houston & Texas Central), which has had a charmed life to the discomfort of all citizens of Dallas and all the public which has frozen within its walls in the winter and perished with thirst and heat in the summer, is to be renovated and made comfortable. . . . The railroad will put on new shingles, paint, weather boarding, etc., and it is hoped they will put new water in the bucket every week.

Items published by the *Morning News* during the first few months of its existence included one regarding the price of Dallas spot cotton, which was selling at 8.57 cents for middling. Others noted a new dress factory in the city; the inauguration of special delivery service by the post office; the death of Will Caruth, one of the oldest settlers; a visit of Governor John Ireland; a meeting of the Buckner Orphans' Home Society; a lecture appearance of the Southern novelist George W. Cable; the arrest of an outlaw who had held up a stage between Abilene and San Angelo a short time before; and a performance of Gilbert and Sullivan's newest opera *The Mikado*, under the auspices of John T. Ford, owner of the theater in Washington where Lincoln was assassinated.

In 1886 Dallas celebrated on San Jacinto Day the fiftieth anniversary of Texas Independence. Many of the veterans of San Jacinto were still alive, and there was a mighty display of bunting, Lone Star and San Jacinto flags. The occasion was celebrated with a parade and music but there was a notable absence of fireworks, an omission remarked upon by the *Dallas Mercury*.

Oak Cliff Is Laid Out

The suburb of Oak Cliff originated on December 15, 1886, when Thomas W. Field and Thomas L. Marsalis bought a farm of 320 acres on the west side of the Trinity for $8,000. The farm was cut up into twenty-acre blocks, and the plat of the new suburb made. There is some dispute about the origin of the name. One account says that Oak Cliff was so designated by Field after he had read the description of a beautiful suburban settlement of that name on the banks of the Hudson. The Dallas artist, J. D. Martin, claimed that it was named by Marsalis after the latter had seen a painting of Cedar Creek which Martin had done. According to a third witness, General Billy Patterson, Field asked him to name it, but he was able to offer no suggestions, whereupon Field himself pointed to the oaks and cliffs along present-day Ewing Avenue and said, "What about calling it 'Oak Cliff'?"

According to the first plat filed, the original township of Oak Cliff extended as far north as First Street, now Colorado Boulevard, just north of Lake Cliff, then known as Spring Lake, and as far south as a pavilion just south of Thirteenth Street, or about where the main entrance to Marsalis Park now is. It was bounded on the east by Miller Street, now Cliff Street, and on the west by Beckley Avenue. Jefferson Avenue was the route of a steam railroad, and the principal north and south thoroughfare was Marsalis Avenue, then called Grand Street.

Commenting on the social status of the city in 1886 the *Sunday Mercury* declared "Dallas can show as moral, cultivated and refined a population as any city on the continent." A revival conducted during March by Moody and Sankey, famed evangelists, may have contributed to this happy condition. Foreshadowing the present reputation of Dallas as a style center, fashions of the day were described by the same paper:

Gentlemen's gloves are heavily stitched and braided upon the back this winter. Pretty gloves of tan-colored undressed kid for women, stitched with brown braid upon the back.

Small animals, birds and reptiles appear upon the front of hosiery meant to wear with slippers, but, after all, ninety-nine times out of a hundred our women wear neat, plain dark hosiery of solid colors.

Dallas had reached an estimated population of 30,000 in 1887 and Jay Gould, railroad king, proved himself as canny at prophecy as in finance by predicting a population of a quarter of a million in the fifty years ahead. The town of East Dallas gained distinction by being chosen as the site of the consolidated Texas State Fair held that year *(see TEXAS STATE FAIR: EMPIRE ON PARADE)*.

In the city proper there were erected during the year seven hundred buildings, including a $60,000 city hall at the northwest corner of Commerce and Akard Streets, and the Cumberland Hill School. On November 1, $23,000 worth of lots were sold in the newly opened Marsalis Addition (Oak Cliff) before noon and on the following day ninety-one lots were sold for $38,113. "A grand beginning," remarked the *Daily Herald*, "of what will be the grandest suburban town in the South." Figures published later in November gave the new suburb a population of 500. The Oak Cliff Elevated Railway furnished the first transportation to Oak Cliff, using a small shuttle train pulled by a "dummy" engine. This steam railway was continued for many years for commuters and pleasure seekers. A fashionable hostelry at Jefferson Avenue and Crawford Street, now Forest Inn, featuring balls and music, with meals prepared by a New York chef, and Marsalis Park, then known as Oak Cliff Park, soon became popular as pleasure resorts. Comic operas were staged in the little opera house in the park and attracted large crowds from Dallas.

Pulling Out of the Mud

Signs of fast-gathering momentum toward a metropolitan city were evident in the events of 1888. Dallas was rapidly pulling itself out of the mud, there being at the time over twenty miles of paved streets, twenty-five miles of street railways, and a steam rapid transit line four miles long reaching to South Dallas and the Fair Grounds. Five newspapers chronicled the daily happenings. There were 1,242 separate business establishments, thirty-four churches, and twenty-eight schools manned by over a hundred teachers. In the first eight months of the year 800 new buildings were erected at an aggregate cost of $3,000,000, twice that of the preceding year. On December 10 the historic Crutchfield House burned the second time in a fire which destroyed much of the business district.

The North Texas city on the Trinity now also began to attract important gatherings and distinguished visitors. Among these were the famous actor, Thomas W. Keene, who was responsible for the organization of the first Lodge of Elks in the city; Henry W. Grady, the Georgia editor-orator, who addressed a crowd of 10,000 at the State Fair on October 27; and the theatrical star, Lily Langtry, known throughout the country as the Jersey Lily, who visited Dallas for the first time this year.

Sports of earlier frontier days, however, were still very much in vogue. Bears were still plentiful in the Trinity River bottoms and wolves furnished sport for huntsmen as well as opportunity to wipe out this menace to sheep. Plover hunts were numerous. The *Daily Times Herald* remarked editorially:

The game chicken fanciers say Dallas is the best town in the South. The race horse men say the same. In fact among thousands of people on the streets every day, there is not one among them who is not ready to swear that Dallas is the Cake-Taker.

76

Climaxing determined efforts on the part of civic leaders, the town of East Dallas was in 1889 annexed to Dallas by act of the Texas legislature, giving to the city a total of twelve wards and an increase in the membership of the city council from eighteen to twenty-four. Under the heading "Prosperous Dallas" the *Daily Times Herald* proudly noted, "After paying off all the city indebtedness, a balance of $240,000 was left on hand . . ." At that time the county of Dallas imposed a tax of fifty cents on $100 of valuation; its bonded debt was $54,000, and the total expense of the county government for the preceding year was $145,375. According to the Federal census of 1890 Dallas, with a population of 38,140, had become the second largest city in the state.

The new decade was ushered in by the destruction of the courthouse, which caught fire on the afternoon of February 15, apparently from a flaw in the newly installed heating apparatus. Most of the county records were preserved.

There was one of the periodic Trinity River floods during the spring of 1890 and later a plague of crickets. Of the latter the *Daily Times Herald* reported that:

> Four wagon loads were taken from the Union depot and the stench arising from the cricket stew was almost intolerable. Beneath the electric lights they were piled ankle deep.

Dallas witnessed in this year determined efforts to free the growing city of gamblers and notorious dives. There were five faro banks, four of them said to be within two blocks of the Windsor Hotel. On September 11 it was recorded that the notorious Black Elephant, a Negro dive, had ceased to exist, but that the dances still held there were a "disgrace to civilization and the doings of the black revelers and their talk would shock the worst tough on earth." There was a raid on September 22 of an opium den operated by one Charlie Chunn, who was fined $200 by the city judge.

Dallas' rapidly growing western suburb of Oak Cliff felt itself ready for existence as an independent entity by June 8, 1891, when a number of its leading citizens, including Colonel W. D. Wiley, T. L. Marsalis, and H. F. Ewing, met at Hodge's drugstore on Tenth Street to discuss problems of incorporation, which followed officially the next day. Two years later it was advertised as having acquired a public school system, girls' school, and a paper mill.

On July 14 the surviving members of the French colony of La Reunion with their descendants met on the original site of their colony four miles west of Dallas to celebrate Bastille Day. The talented utopians who had settled here thirty-six years before had long since abandoned their distinctive communal life to assume an active place in the trades and professions of the growing city but still remained loyal to their national traditions of "Liberte, Egalite, Fraternite."

The year 1891 is remembered in Dallas lodge annals for the eighteenth annual session of the Grand Lodge of the Knights of Pythias, which convened here for its state encampment. The 4,000 knights attending paraded the downtown streets in full panoply of their colorful uniforms and held a grand ball in the Music Hall of the Exposition Building at Fair Park. A new six-story Masonic Temple, to replace the old two-story brick lodge hall at the corner of Main and Austin Streets, was also proposed during the year and $50,000 placed to the credit of the building fund.

In September, 1892, Dallas businessmen organized into the Merchants' Cotton and Produce Association to promote the general trade interests of the city, and in particular to secure payment of the highest possible price for cotton which farmers brought to the city, with a view to making Dallas the dominant cotton center of North Texas. The establishment of a cotton exchange was also advocated. Leaders of the movement, which was apparently only partially successful judging from market prices of 7.25 and 7.35 cents a pound the following month, were Philip Sanger, George Holloway, J. H. Webster, B. R. Williams, J. F. Zang, and C. E. Gilbert.

Prosperity and Panic

Dallas greeted the New Year of 1893 with rosy visions of prosperity. The *Morning News* declared in a front page editorial that the farmers of Texas "were never before in such happy circumstances" as a result of bountiful crops and mounting prices. With the arrival of the steamer *H. A. Harvey* at the foot of Main Street in May *(see TRINITY NAVIGATION: EYES TOWARD THE SEA)* it was generally believed that Trinity River navigation was an assured fact. The whole community turned out to celebrate, and the *News* signalized the occasion with a special edition with alternate pages in red ink. The *Daily Times Herald* declared editorially on September 4 that Dallas was the second largest distribution point for farm machinery in the world and that the annual volume of business in this field had reached $10,000,000.

On October 9 the former glory of the Grand Windsor Hotel was eclipsed by the opening of the new Oriental Hotel at Commerce and Akard Streets, one of the showplaces of the South for a decade or more and far beyond the demands of Dallas at the time. Financed by Thomas Field, well-known capitalist, its note as a $500,000 building began to spread abroad even before it was completed. Work was commenced on it in 1889 but was interrupted by the panic of 1893.

The opening was marked by a grand reception, and visitors to the State Fair were awed by its magnificence. The hotel was a six-story red brick structure with a pointed minaret-like cupola at its main corner. Within, its appointments were the last word in luxury and refinement, and the delicate, easily swooning ladies of the period were particularly impressed by its modern ventilating system, by which the odors from the kitchen were diverted from the guests' bedrooms. Many of its public rooms, especially the Morrison Room, named for the Oriental's famed maitre d'hôtel, David Morrison, were showplaces in themselves and were scenes of many historic banquets and receptions. Noted statesmen, actors, actresses, and prizefighters were guests of the hotel during its heyday.

By the end of 1893, the city was beginning to feel the consequences of a nationwide financial panic—the most severe since the crash of 1873. On January 1, 1894, R. G. Dun & Company in a summary printed in the *Morning News* described the year just ended as "the worst in fifty." Prices were the lowest ever known and there were "millions of workers looking in vain for work . . . with charity laboring to keep back suffering and starvation in all our cities." Dallas on the whole survived these hard times better than many sister cities, though several banks failed and others had to be absorbed by stronger institutions to protect the depositors *(see BANKS AND BANKING: CAPITAL RESERVOIR.)* The *News* at first took the position that the depression was "a mere bank depositors' panic" which could not possibly touch the real wealth represented by real estate and other tangibles, but reluctantly came to the view that "some sort of government guaranteeism" of deposits was necessary.

During the year Dallas entertained the Democratic state convention which nominated Charles A. Culberson for governor, declaring unequivocally for "Cleveland

and sound money." Skating on the Trinity was a popular pastime for the last few days of December.

Early in 1894 a cyclone swept through Dallas from the Houston & Texas Central tracks in a northeasterly direction costing one life and leaving a path of destruction from fifty to a hundred yards wide with a property damage of $100,000. During the autumn of the same year Trinity navigation seemed a step nearer practical realization when a party of army engineers under Major Talfor began a 200-mile survey of the river in small boats. The survey began at Dallas and extended to Magnolia.

The big news of 1895 in Dallas was the proposed boxing match in the city between Jim Corbett and Bob Fitzsimmons for the world's heavyweight championship. Dallas was robbed of the pugilistic exhibition at the last minute by action of the state legislature at a special session called in response to a storm of protest by Texas' "young Christian governor," Charles A. Culberson *(see RECREATION: SPORTS OF A CENTURY)*.

Dallas Goes Republican

In 1896 the spotlight of local interest again shifted to politics, when William Jennings Bryan and the advocates of the free coinage of silver at a ratio of sixteen to one captured the National Democratic Convention held in Chicago in June. Pitchfork Ben Tillman and other free silver enthusiasts visited Dallas and a free silver rally was conducted on the night before the election. There were speeches by Martin W. Littleton of Beaumont, afterward a noted New York attorney, John H. Kirby of Houston, S. L. Daniels of Fort Worth, and W. C. Connor of Dallas. Thomas E. Watson of Georgia, Populist candidate for president, also spoke in Dallas. Dallas remained loyal to the gold standard, however, and on November 3 for the first time in its history gave a majority to a Republican candidate, the city going for McKinley by a majority of 244 votes. The Democrats carried the county, however.

Dallas had in 1896 reached an annual aggregate of $30,000,000 in its wholesale and jobbing trade. The year saw also the first golf game in Dallas, played over a six-hole course in Oak Lawn laid out by H. L. Edwards and R. E. Potter. Frances E. Willard, head of the Women's Christian Temperance Union, was a notable visitor on March 15. The cornerstone of the Confederate monument in City Park was laid during the Confederate State Reunion in June *(see POINTS OF INTEREST: SULLIVAN PARK)*. Twelve hundred delegates from the United States and Canada attended the convention of the Grand Lodge of Odd Fellows later in the year.

Early in 1897 Mrs. Isadore Minor, women's editor of the *Dallas News*—later the leader of a campaign for women's suffrage in Texas—remarked in the columns of the paper that "the blind unreasoning prejudice against the woman's movement has almost disappeared." And on February 3 there was an exhibition of Edison's newest invention, the vitascope. This first movie program in Dallas was noted editorially by the *News*, which called attention to the crusade already being conducted by Miss Frances Willard and other leaders of the Women's Christian Temperance Union against the lurid subject matter of the popular new fad—it was then regarded as little more.

The same year Dallas was horrified by the burning of Buckner Orphans Home, in which sixteen children perished, and laid the foundations for its first modern hospital—St. Paul's Sanitarium. The Dallas Commercial Club was notified on September 22 by a committee representing 100 farmers that they would take their trade elsewhere until Dallas gave them a better price for their cotton.

Dallas promptly "remembered the Maine" on the night of February 27, 1898, after the American battleship had been sunk in Havana harbor, when 1,000 indignant patriots gathered in the city auditorium and passed a resolution demanding war with Spain. Following the declaration of war in April and the call for 4,000 volunteers as Texas' quota of the 125,000 men requested by President McKinley, several companies were formed in Dallas. Among these were the Dallas Cavalry Company commanded by Captain John Hunter, the Dallas Zouaves commanded by Captain Joe R. Gunn, the Trezevant Rifles commanded by Captain Charles S. Mitchell, and a company of Civil War veterans, both Union and Confederate, formed by Major J. J. Miller, the youngest among them forty-eight, the oldest sixty. The first contingent of Dallas troops, 175 strong, left for service in Cuba on May 4. A little over two months later the war was over, and in October the victorious veterans of the brief conflict paraded through the city. Dallas County contributed at least one recruit to Theodore Roosevelt's famed Rough Riders—Wiley Skelton of Trinity Mills, whose mustering out was recorded by the *Times Herald*.

Colonel Robert G. Ingersoll, militant freethinker of the period, spoke in Dallas before the close of 1898, attracting a large crowd to the opera house with his celebrated lecture "Why I Am An Agnostic." On the occasion of his death the following year, July 23, 1899, Dallas freethinkers, organized into an association in 1894, expressed their regret at the passing of "the foremost thinker and bravest champion of human rights of the nineteenth century." It was the period of Texas' own W. C. Brann, "the Iconoclast," and this estimate is not altogether surprising.

Portents of Progress

The last year of the century, ushered in by the coldest weather in the history of Dallas with a temperature of 10° below zero on February 11, was full of portents of progress and a greater city to come. It was then that the first efforts at city planning were made when the Cleaner Dallas League was organized in May, 1899. Under its impetus a renewed attack on the water problem was made resulting in construction of the second of the surface water reservoirs, at Bachman's Dam. A tax-supported public library was urged in March, and on September 19, Mrs. Henry Exall, leader of the movement, announced a gift of $50,000 from Andrew Carnegie, to be matched by local donations and tax support. The question of annexation was raised in Oak Cliff, with annexationists and anti-annexationists waging a lively contest. Annexation was defeated by the close vote of 292 to 232 in an election of March 4. Democrats held a "dollar dinner" at which William Jennings Bryan was the principal guest.

When the Federal census of 1900 was taken, Dallas was surprised and rather hurt to find that it had a population of only 42,638. Unofficial advance estimates had been much larger. The panic of 1893 had retarded its growth, and during the preceding decade it had slipped back to third place among the cities of Texas, behind San Antonio and Houston. Early in the new year the flourishing suburb of Oak Cliff voted, 380 to 12, to join with greater Dallas. This election was nullified by court action, however. It was in 1900 that electric power was substituted for mules by the Dallas Street Railway Company, the transition having been started in the preceding year. On September 7 the company's service was blocked for a time by the hundreds of cotton wagons on downtown streets.

Dallas was now to be stirred deeply by events outside the city—the chief of which was the Galveston storm and tidal wave which struck September 8, 1900.

Cash and supplies were rushed to the stricken city, a number of Dallas men served with the troops sent to the island to preserve order and aid with rescue work, and thirty-six children orphaned by the storm were taken into Buckner Orphans Home. The city had earlier demonstrated its sympathy for the hard-pressed Boer Republic, doomed to extinction in its war with Great Britain, by holding a mass meeting. A woman was fined $5 in police court for appearing on the street in men's clothing. At the end of the year the city's wholesale trade was estimated at $50,000,000.

Early in the new century, April 25, 1901, the Dallas Opera House, one of the city's showplaces in the eighties and nineties, burned. There were two other destructive fires soon afterward—one destroyed the building and stock of the Rock Island Plow Company, the other burned two stores on lower Elm Street.

During this year Dallas came to the fore as a convention city. In April the newly organized State Federation of Women's Clubs met in Dallas, and on May 3 the Texas Association of Commercial Clubs was formed in the city.

The highlight of 1902 was the Confederate reunion held at the State Fair Grounds April 22–27. It was attended by some 3,000 veterans from all parts of the United States and, it was estimated, attracted over 100,000 visitors. The congestion which resulted from this sudden trebling of the population dramatized the need for city planning and led to the formation of a local branch of the American League for Civic Improvement.

Horseless Carriages Arrive

This year also made transportation history in Dallas. It was about this time the city began to become motor-minded. While Dallas had seen its first automobile, brought to Texas by Colonel E. H. R. Green some years earlier, it was in the autumn of 1902 that young Jesse Illingsworth drove another of Colonel Green's horseless carriages into Dallas, after a forty-mile run of three days and three nights from Terrell, leaving a trail of wreckage and damage suits in his wake—and this despite the precaution of two attendants who walked ahead of the machine to aid in holding horses that might try to run away. The daring driver, accoutered in cap, linen duster, gauntlets and goggles, his hip pockets bristling with tools, might have bettered this record if he had been able to travel at night, but his car had no lights. It entered the city limits at the reckless speed of twelve miles an hour.

Others soon followed this trailblazer with White Steamers and Pope-Toledos, the most popular automobiles of the day. Among the first automobile owners in Dallas were George Leachman, G. B. Murray, and J. C. Weaver. The first license in the city was issued to J. M. Oram. Henry Garrett, who was later joined by Jesse Illingsworth and had his garage where the Adolphus Annex now stands, was the first automobile agent in the city. James Roberts and a Mrs. Shuttles soon shattered Illingsworth's record by making the seventy-five mile run to Sherman in a little less than six hours, with only a few delays occasioned by frightened horses.

There was steam-driven automobile and motorcycle racing at the State Fair in October, 1902, and before the end of the year the *News* published a solemn dissertation on automobile etiquette. There were elaborate provisions for carrying a chauffeur, an indispensable necessity in the days when breakdowns were many and mechanics few. By rigidly following the rules it set forth, the article in question stated, the chances of accidents such as "unexpected bolting of the machine" would be reduced to a minimum.

There were other improvements in Dallas transportation, actual and projected, during 1902. In October the Federal government, which had appropriated $400,000 for the purpose, began the construction of locks and dams on the Trinity River just below Dallas, and it was sanguinely expected that by 1904 the river would be navigable from Galveston to Dallas for six months out of the year. On March 1 interurban electric service was inaugurated between Dallas and Fort Worth.

Prohibition an Issue

Prohibition was getting to be a highly charged political issue at this time, in Dallas as elsewhere. The Reverend Sam P. Jones attracted a crowd of about 8,000 people when, locked out of the Opera House on the grounds that he had rented it for a sermon and not a political meeting, he spoke from a buggy in the open air on St. Paul Street between Main and Commerce Streets.

By 1903—the year that the *Dallas News* editor telephoned Dayton, Ohio, for verification of the Wright brothers' first airplane flight—the new city directory gave Dallas a population of 75,415. The movement for the annexation of Oak Cliff, started in 1899 by J. F. Zang and others, bore fruit on May 16 when the citizens of the western suburb again indicated their desire to join greater Dallas by a vote of 201 to 183. There were still legal obstacles in the way, and Oak Cliff was not actually annexed until March 7 the following year.

Cotton sold for ten cents a pound in 1903 and late in the year the *Dallas News* reported that, "A conservative estimate of the number of out-of-town buyers, wholesale and retail, who were in Dallas Saturday on business, is placed at 5,000." During the winter season DeWolf Hopper and his company in *Mr. Pickwick*, "captured a generous portion of the best elements of the Dallas theatre-going public."

In 1904 Dallas had seventy-four miles of street railways, all electric, an assessed property valuation of $32,568,000, six national banks with combined individual deposits of $6,798,857, and 430 manufactories employing 5,278 persons. The Dallas Gas & Fuel Company was petitioning for a new franchise to extend its facilities to Oak Cliff, Oak Lawn, and other sections of the city not yet supplied. Many of the streets, which then bore odd names such as JZ, Matt, Milk, Veal, Quick, and Wolf Trail, were still mudholes in bad weather, and in February a fashionable young man of foresight starting out on a social engagement took a hired man along to carry him piggyback across the puddles. There were only some three-and-a-half miles of asphalt paving in the city.

Wireless messages were transmitted between Dallas and Fort Worth for the first time. The State Fair was reorganized and Fair Park became the property of the city. In this year Dallas was stirred by the brutal murder of a grocer named Sol Aronoff, in the presence of his wife and children by a white man and a Negro. Bloodhounds were put on the trail of the two, who were arrested and identified as Holly Vann and Burrell Oates. Holly Vann was found guilty on December 21 and received the death sentence, the first such sentence passed on a white man in Dallas County. The Negro was sentenced to death on December 24, but succeeded in gaining one reprieve and retrial after another until he was finally hanged at Waxahachie on the eighth anniversary of his crime, November 29, 1912, the execution following a trial on change of venue.

Carrie Nation, in her drive for prohibition, arrived in Dallas November 29, 1904, lectured in the County Criminal Courts Building, visited the saloons, harangued bartenders, and pinned her small hatchet emblems on hundreds. A city charter amendment of May 9, 1905, required saloons to close from 12 midnight to 6 o'clock in the morning.

Dallas was visited by a president of the United States for the first time when Theodore Roosevelt, en route to San Antonio to attend a reunion of his Rough Riders, stopped off in the city April 5, 1905. At a banquet held in his honor at the Oriental Hotel and attended by many notables, he referred to the project nearest to the hearts of his Dallas audience when he said, "I did my part a few weeks ago by signing a bill under which the Trinity River will be improved."

More Population Sought

The so-called Greater Dallas movement received a further impetus February 4, 1905, when the "150,000 Club" was organized with J. H. Ardrey as president.

The club's objective was to boost the population of Dallas to that figure by 1915. The new organization concerned itself with the raising of $66,000 for Trinity canalization and the erection of a downtown auditorium, toward which $15,000 was raised. This latter project was still to be realized in 1940. Concrete progress toward a greater city was made during the year 1905, however. Plans were under way for construction of the Scottish Rite Temple, the cornerstone of which was laid in 1907. City Building Inspector L. L. Bristol issued a building permit to the Order of Praetorians for the erection two years later of Dallas' first modern skyscraper, the fourteen-story steel, brick, and terra cotta Praetorian Building on the corner of Main and Stone Streets. The Young Men's Christian Association sought and raised by popular subscription $100,000 for a new headquarters building on the south side of Commerce Street near Harwood. The city acquired a modern theater with the opening of the Majestic vaudeville house on the corner of Commerce and St. Paul Streets.

On August 23, 1906, *The Dallas Morning News* announced:

Dallas is to have a new charter giving her the commission form of government. The charter is to be made up by a charter convention elected by the citizens. After having drafted the charter, the convention will submit it to the people for ratification.

Dallas was one of the first cities to follow Galveston's lead in adopting this form of municipal government. The new charter, providing for a mayor and four commissioners to be elected by a majority vote of the citizens, was approved by the legislature in April, 1907, and on May 21 a nonpartisan ticket headed by Stephen J. Hay for mayor was placed in office *(see GOVERNMENT: VILLAGE TO METROPOLIS)*.

The year 1907 was also notable for the opening of the restricted suburb of Highland Park, first planned city in the Southwest, developed largely through the efforts of J. S. Armstrong. During the year Dallas banks were forced to restrict withdrawals, but the financial panic did not materially retard local progress.

The Texas Local Option Association, represented by about one hundred delegates from all sections of Texas, met at the First Methodist Church in Dallas on January 16, 1908, and voted almost unanimously to launch a campaign for statewide prohibition. On January 20 the campaign was formally opened with a mass meeting attended by some 600 people, held at the Bush Temple and addressed by such famous prohibitionists as William D. Upshaw of Atlanta, Georgia, and Drs. George C. Rankin and B. F. Riley of Dallas. Rallies also were held at various churches.

Great Flood of 1908

The most memorable event of the year was the great Trinity River flood which the *Times Herald* on May 25 pronounced the worst in the history of the city. Summarizing the situation it said:

> People try to make comparisons between the present flood and those which Dallas has experienced in the past, that of 1890 and that of several years before that, back until the memory of man goes not, but from all indications there is nothing in the memory of people who have lived here for years and years, nor anything in the chronicles of past floods set down, that can equal that which has come with the present rise in the river.

The flood began in April and reached a height of 37.8 feet on April 21. Water covered the West Dallas pike, the Commerce Street bridge was closed to traffic, and there was widespread damage in North Dallas. Boats to rescue livestock and property were in great demand, and a steamboat, the *Nellie Maurine*, took sightseers up and down the river to view the flooded areas. There was a temporary recession; the crest of the flood came in May, when the river reached the unprecedented height of 51.3 feet. The Texas & Pacific Railroad trestle across the bottoms collapsed, drowning five men and leaving fifteen survivors clinging to the wreckage until they could be rescued in motor launches. Other railroad bridges spanning the bottoms were menaced.

By May 28 the Texas & Pacific and the Houston & Texas Central railroads were the only lines operating trains into the city. The only communication to the west was by boat. Dallas resembled a Mississippi River town, with craft plying between Oak Cliff and the city proper, discharging and taking on passengers at the foot of Commerce Street. Both the Dallas and Oak Cliff waterworks were shut down, as well as the electric light plants, leaving the city in darkness and without fire protection or drinking water. Business houses and other places of public resort were ordered closed at 7:30 each evening. Some sixty homes in South Dallas were submerged and many families in this section narrowly escaped drowning.

Four thousand people were rendered homeless; property damage estimated at $2,500,000 occurred. City and county officials worked in conjunction with government employees and the owners of boats to rescue refugees in the treetops, and $6,000 was raised by voluntary subscription for relief at a mass meeting on the afternoon of May 25. Two committees of ten were appointed to assist the mayor in finding needy families and furnishing them with food, clothing, and shelter. On May 29 and 30 the flood began to recede, and partial streetcar, water, and light service was restored. The shortage of drinking water continued acute in some sections, and sprinkling wagons were put to work hauling artesian water. Householders stopped the wagons as they proceeded through the streets, filling buckets and bottles, and long queues of people, vehicles, horses, cows, and livestock stood at the various artesian wells, the jam in front of the new Praetorian Building being so great as to block streetcars.

The ravages of the recently receded flood did not deter the city from putting on holiday dress to welcome the national reunion of the Benevolent and Protective Order of Elks in July. The downtown streets were lavishly decorated and at the corner of Main and Akard Streets rose a huge steel arch ablaze with purple and white electric lights and crowned with a great white elk facing the east. Avenues of specially erected lamp posts were erected on the intersecting streets approaching the arch, and fountains at the base of the four supporting columns sent up jets of vari-colored water. On July 16, as a climax to the reunion, thousands of Elks accompanied by bands and floats paraded down Main Street under the arch, while a crowd estimated at over 100,000 gathered along the line of march.

President William Howard Taft, returning from Juarez where he had exchanged greetings with President Diaz of Mexico on the new international bridge, visited Dallas October 22, 1909. He spoke at the Fair Grounds and was entertained with a reception and banquet at the Oriental Hotel, where the Reverend Alexander C. Garrett, Episcopal bishop of the northern diocese of Texas, delivered a toast to the president and an address on behalf of the people of Dallas and North Texas. The toast was drunk in grape juice, the committee on arrangements headed by G. B. Dealey having decided to set a new precedent by omitting the customary wines and other alcoholic beverages.

The decade closed with a new determination on the part of civic agencies to do something about the Trinity flood menace—a goal realized the following year in the first draft of the Kessler City Plan. In 1909 a new Chamber of Commerce was organized, Oak Lawn Park (now Robert E. Lee Park) was purchased, and a disastrous fire occurred in Oak Cliff, consuming fourteen blocks of residences, including the Briggs Sanatorium. On April 6, a bond issue was voted for the creation of an enlarged water supply and land aggregating 1,000 acres was bought on both sides of White Rock Creek preparatory to impounding its waters.

Seven League Strides: 1910–1940

The thirty-year period between 1910 and 1940 witnessed first a qualitative and then a quantitative change in the city of Dallas. The era was ushered in by George E. Kessler's blueprinted vision of a greater city to come, showing how Dallas, which already in 1910 had a population of 92,104, could best channel its growth over the next quarter of a century. Some of the developments envisaged by the original Kessler Plan, such as a union passenger terminal on the edge of the Trinity River bottoms, were inaugurated within a few years; others such as an eleven-mile boulevard encircling the city were not realized for two decades or more. But a decisive turning point in the city's expansion had been reached (*see THE DALLAS CITY PLAN: DESIGN FOR GROWTH*).

During the next decade and a half the crowded, rococo North Texas drummers' capital of 1900 gradually faded into the modern cosmopolitan city of soaring skyscrapers and far-reaching suburbs geared to the requirements of a fast-moving motor age and an interlocking world commerce in goods and ideas. After 1925 Dallas' growth was mainly quantitative but none the less noteworthy—a record of steady, planned expansion uninterrupted even by the great depression of the early 1930s.

In 1910 Dallas was fast acquiring the improved services of modern city life. The automobile was still a little suspect, as indicated by current city ordinances. Nevertheless, in January, 1910, the city moved forward to meet the imperious demands of the twentieth century by purchasing an automobile ambulance. The police patrol wagons and fire engines were motorized soon afterward. Householders received new house numbers during the year, natural gas replaced artificial gas in the mains on April 29, and improved telephone service came with the granting of a charter to the Dallas Automatic Telephone Company on November 16.

An acute water shortage during the early autumn, involving severe restrictions on residential users, led to a renewed attack on the problem of providing the city with adequate reservoirs. The use of city water for watering lawns and gardens was forbidden in September; first the Lemp and Blaylock wells and then the Wilson and Praetorian Building wells were tapped to supplement the dwindling water supply in the city mains. Forty wagons were put into service hauling water to distressed neighborhoods, and connections were cut off at the curb in residential sections in October as a precaution against fire hazards. Conditions were relieved by impounding the waters of various creeks in the vicinity of the city. The California Crossing dam was constructed in 1910 and the Carrollton dam in 1911. The White Rock Creek dam was begun late in 1910 and completed the following year, forming White Rock Lake, Dallas' principal reserve water supply until the creation of Lake Dallas (see POINTS OF INTEREST, White Rock Lake Park).

There were several sensational crimes during the year. The chief of these was the lynching on March 3 of Allen Brooks, a Negro who allegedly had criminally assaulted a two-and-a-half-year-old girl in the loft of a barn at her parents' home, where he was employed. A mob overpowered Sheriff A. L. Ledbetter, his deputies, and fifteen or twenty policemen to seize the Negro and throw him headfirst from a second story window of the Criminal Courts Building. He then had a rope placed around his neck and was dragged up Main Street to the ornate Elks' Arch at the intersection of Main and Akard Streets, where he was hanged from a telephone pole. The arch was dismantled soon afterward because of its association with this lynching incident. During the autumn there were several vendetta killings among the Italian colony in Dallas, attributed to the activities of the Mafia terrorists or "Black Hand" society.

One of the last important events of 1910 was the visit of William Jennings Bryan, who appeared for a lecture engagement at the Dallas Opera House on November 21. A crowd of 2,500 heard him speak, and 2,000 more ineffectually stormed the doors to hear the address of the eloquent Commoner.

Though Dallas had been the center of agitation for statewide prohibition in 1910 and prohibition forces had held their convention in the city, nominating A. J. Houston for governor, the city voted wet by 8,242 to 7,894 in the election of July 23, 1911. During the autumn of that year the city enthusiastically welcomed Woodrow Wilson, already a presidential possibility, when he made a speech at the State Fair. It was also in 1911 that Elm Street became a white way at night. Electric lamp posts, 110 in all, were installed from Market to Harwood Streets, and lights representing 220,000 candle power turned on September 11.

In the early months of 1912 the city fought desperately against the dread meningitis epidemic of that winter by fumigating streetcars, forbidding public funerals, and reserving Parkland Hospital exclusively for quarantine purposes. Even with these measures and a supply of Dr. Simon Flexner's newly discovered serum, the mortality rate ran as high as 45 percent.

Prewar Development

The year 1912 was marked by impressive monuments to the new metropolitan status that Dallas was beginning to attain. In February the Houston Street viaduct to Oak Cliff, the first of the city's modern trafficways across the Trinity bottoms, was accepted from the contractors (see VIADUCTS: TRAFFICWAYS FOR MILLIONS). The cost of new hotels and office buildings completed during the year totaled more than $5,000,000. Among these were the first unit of the Adolphus Hotel, 21 stories in height and costing $1,000,000. This hotel, one of the finest and most modern in the Southwest, entirely eclipsed the old Oriental Hotel and the Southland Hotel, built in 1907, which had previously shared the quality trade. The Commonwealth Bank Building, now the Fidelity Building, and the Southwestern Life Building were also erected in 1912.

Dallas, with 2,944 automobiles, ranked first among cities of its size in the number of motor cars on its streets. The Associated Advertising Leagues of the World, which met in Dallas in 1912, used automobiles exclusively in their parade, and Dallas County with 420 miles of improved roads claimed the finest highway system in the South.

In January, 1913, the old county jail on Houston Street at the eastern end of the new viaduct was bought by the recently organized Union Terminal Company for $150,000 and dismantled soon afterward. The site of the present Criminal Courts Building at Main and Houston Streets was bought the following month for $77,000. In May Dallas was selected by the Masonic Order of the Nobles of the Mystic Shrine for their national convention, which brought thousands of visitors to the city. The spirit of reform which was sweeping the country manifested itself in the suppression in November of Dallas' red light district, located north of McKinney Avenue in what is now Little Mexico, following a citywide crusade.

The year 1913 is also remembered for the most renowned unsolved crime in the history of Dallas, which originated in the brutal daylight slaying on July 28 of Florence Brown, 27-year-old stenographer, who was found with her throat cut in the offices of the real estate company where she was employed at 110 Field Street. Despite a statewide search, rewards as high as $1,000, and numerous "confessions," the slayer was never identified, and the story of the crime has been told times without number in "true detective" magazines and elsewhere, periodically reviving discussion of this unsolved mystery.

The following year saw the completion of the new City Hall at Main, Harwood, and Commerce Streets, begun early in 1913 *(see POINTS OF INTEREST, City Hall)*.

In April, the indefatigable efforts of local interests to secure one of the twelve regional banks created by the Federal Reserve Act of the previous year were rewarded by the selection of Dallas as a location for the Eleventh Federal Reserve District Bank *(see BANKS AND BANKING: CAPITAL RESERVOIR and POINTS OF INTEREST, Federal Reserve Bank)*. The outbreak of the World War found Texas with the second largest cotton crop in history. Prices broke disastrously, building operations were abruptly halted, and unemployment rose sharply. These conditions led to the Buy-a-Bale movement which swept the South, businessmen and employees of Dallas firms pledging themselves to buy a bale of cotton at approximately eight cents a pound to stimulate trade. Monetary uncertainty also temporarily interrupted the installation of underground utility wiring in the business district.

In 1915 the country was already drifting toward war. Representatives of the French government were in Dallas during the late summer buying horses for army service, and William Jennings Bryan, who had resigned his position as Secretary of State after the sinking of the *Lusitania* on May 7, spoke under the auspices of the Dallas Press Club October 2 on "The War in Europe and Its Lessons." In December George Wythe, a representative of *The Dallas Morning News*, accompanied the much-ridiculed Ford Peace Ship to Europe.

Locally, the most important development of the year not connected with the war was the opening of Southern Methodist University with a record-breaking initial enrollment of 700 students *(see POINTS OF INTEREST, Southern Methodist University)*. An amendment to the city charter was passed excluding Negroes from white neighborhoods but was later invalidated as unconstitutional.

In 1916 several years of negotiations among the railroads serving the city bore fruit in the completion of Dallas' $6,500,000 Union Terminal Passenger Station *(see POINTS OF INTEREST, Union Terminal Passenger Station)*. During the year the people of Dallas also demonstrated their approval of President Wilson's preparedness policies with a monster Preparedness Parade. Twenty thousand men and women were in the line of march.

On March 27, 1917, ex-President William Howard Taft visited Dallas a second time and predicted the outbreak of hostilities between the United States and the Central Powers within ten days. On April 6 his prophecy was fulfilled when President Wilson signed Congress' war resolution.

Dallas Does Its Bit

Dallas plunged into the task of winning the war with the same crusading spirit that distinguished the rest of the country. Before the end of 1917 Love Field had been opened as an important army aviation training field, and early in 1918 Fair Park was converted into Camp Dick, where men who had already earned their wings were taught the fundamentals of strategy and army discipline. The first officers' training camp at Leon Springs drew more than a hundred men from Dallas, with subsequent training camps also enlisting large numbers of candidates for commissions.

Out of a total of 15,037 who registered for the draft, about 8,000 citizens of Dallas served in the armed forces of the United States during the war. Prior to the war Dallas had been the home station of several units of the Texas National Guard, nearly all of which had seen service on the Mexican border during the Villa uprising of 1916, and when the Texas and Oklahoma National Guards were absorbed into the regular army, these became part of the historic 36th Division. Company B, Second Texas Infantry, recruited almost entirely from Western Union employees, logically became part of the 112th Field Signal Battalion; Company G, Fourth Texas Infantry, and Company E, Third Texas Infantry, were absorbed respectively by the 143rd and the 144th Infantry, which together made up the 72nd Infantry Brigade; the machine gunners of the Fourth Texas Infantry became part of the 131st Machine Gun Battalion; and the engineer company was taken into the 111th Engineers.

The historic Dallas Artillery Company, organized in 1879 as the Queen City Guards and famed in the 1880s and 1890s for its record in local, state, and interstate drill competitions, was mustered into service as Company A, 133rd Field Artillery, after the war losing its identity and becoming strictly a social organization.

The infantry and auxiliary units of the 36th Division fought in the Mont Blanc sector in France north of Somme Py and in the French offensive of October, 1918. Two other Dallas-recruited guard units saw more extensive combat service. These were Companies A and E of the 117th Supply Train, part of the 42nd (Rainbow) Division, made up of National Guard units from practically every state.

Dallas contributed heavily to both the commissioned and enlisted personnel of the 19th (National Army) Division of Texas, including the 411th Field Artillery and the 359th Infantry. In addition to these combat units Baylor Hospital also put into service a medical unit, creating for a time a severe shortage of doctors and nurses in the city.

No figures are available on Dallas casualties, but the city had its quota of gold stars. Ray E. Scott, first Dallas man to give his life in the war, was drowned at sea December 17, 1917. George Moreno and Patrick White, members of the crew of the torpedoed *Tuscania*, are also mentioned as being among the first casualties. John W. Low was the first Dallas soldier killed in action in France. His body was brought back to Dallas after the war and buried in Greenwood Cemetery, January 15, 1922, with military honors after lying in state in the city hall. The body was later removed to Forest Lawn Cemetery.

In the first Liberty Loan Drive the city's quota was $5,000,000 and $6,004,250 was subscribed. In the second drive its quota was $5,890,450. and $8,206,500 was subscribed. The Red Cross asked $150,000 during the summer of 1917 and received $175,000. The third Liberty Loan Drive in 1918 was also generously over-subscribed.

Dallas' "White Way" along Elm Street, as well as electric signs, the fronts of moving picture theaters, and all lights in mercantile establishments not absolutely necessary for police protection were darkened two nights a week to save coal. The city became accustomed to such wartime phenomena as soaring food prices, "victory bread" containing at least 20 percent substitution for wheat flour, war gardens, meatless days in the cafes, the collection of nutshells and fruit pits for gas masks, and the closing of the schools on exceptionally cold days to conserve fuel. In June, 1918, all business was halted at 11 A.M. for a daily minute of prayer and the citizens were adjusting themselves to the new daylight saving time, inaugurated in the cause of victory the previous April.

The steadily mounting tension of war broke when the siren on the Adolphus Hotel shrieked the news of the Armistice, November 11, 1918. The city went wild and November 14 there was one of the greatest parades in the history of the city— 25,000 in the line of march requiring two hours to pass, flags decking the buildings, banners and placards bearing appeals for the United War Work Fund, and United States flags carried net-fashion into which coins were tossed.

Scenes of almost equally wild enthusiasm greeted the returning troops in the spring of 1919. Fifteen hundred officers and men of the 133rd Field Artillery detrained at the East Dallas station and paraded through downtown streets March 29; the seasoned veterans of the 117th Supply Train of the Rainbow Division were welcomed home May 12; the 144th Infantry Regiment of the 36th Division, containing many Dallas boys, arrived June 16; and troops of the 90th Division, including the 345th Field Artillery and 35th Machine Gun Battalion returned on June 17.

As its final bit, Dallas outdistanced the other large cities in the South and was the first to reach its quota of $7,000,000 in the Victory Loan Drive. The city was again ready to turn to the tasks of peace.

Postwar Confusion

Other events of the war years of 1917 and 1918 were the local jitney war, prohibition, a firemen's strike, a carpenters' strike, a visit from the dynamic evangelist Billy Sunday, and the great influenza epidemic that swept the entire country in the autumn and winter of 1918. The jitney method of transportation, involving the packing of large numbers of passengers into private automobiles at a nickel a head, became widely prevalent in Dallas during the years immediately before the war, but after several ineffectual attempts at regulation the jitneys were run off the streets in July, 1918, by an ordinance requiring a $10,000 bond to operate. Dallas County voted for prohibition, 10,425 to 8,551, on September 11, 1917; it preceded the state as a whole, which went dry June 26, 1918—essentially a wartime measure dictated by the large number of training camps in Texas. In 1918 there was an effort to form a fireman's union, resulting in a strike. It was broken by the replacement of the striking firemen with a hastily organized corps of volunteers. During the summer of the same year work on several major downtown buildings was delayed by a strike of the carpenters demanding sharp wage increases.

The influenza epidemic began September 25, 1918, and a month later 5,647 cases had been reported, with 152 deaths. Hospital facilities were severely taxed and stringent quarantine regulations adopted. Influenza masks were issued in the training camps, Camp Dick was quarantined, theaters, churches, and schools were closed, and the hospitals set up additional beds in corridors and in tents on the lawns. St. Paul's Hospital was turned over to the military authorities, the streets were flushed nightly as a sanitary precaution, and circus performances were forbidden. In the wake of pestilence the threats of imminent hellfire that Billy Sunday poured on the heads of Dallas audiences when he spoke at the First Baptist Church in December had an added force.

Following the war, Dallas experienced further labor troubles, a construction boom, and fantastically high prices along with the rest of the country. In 1919 Dallas had the most serious labor disturbance in its history, when a widespread sympathy strike, first of the indoor electricians and then of all the building trades, supported by the garment workers, developed from a walkout of the linemen employed by the Dallas Power & Light Company *(see LABOR: ORGANIZATION AND STRUGGLES)*. Business and construction skyrocketed; building permits for 1919 topped $13,700,000 and bank clearings ran well over $1,600,000,000. The office buildings that had been the pride of prewar Dallas began to be dwarfed by the towering contemporary skyscrapers that shot up one after another in the downtown area. The American Exchange National (now First National) Bank Building was completed soon after the Armistice and the twenty-nine-story Magnolia Building, whose penthouse with its flying red horse sign is still, in 1940, the pinnacle of the city's skyline, was commenced about the same time. Profiteering reached such proportions that a board of three members was appointed to investigate complaints of overcharging in the city, and reduced the rents being charged by local landlords.

Mayor Frank Wozencraft, elected while still in army service, also appointed a committee of Dallas women to investigate local milk prices. During the summer of 1920 the retail price of ice soared to 80 cents per hundred pounds, and when District Attorney R. E. Taylor ordered manufacturers and distributors to reduce prices or face prosecution for conspiracy under the antitrust laws, two Dallas companies suspended delivery rather than comply. Gasoline was 32 cents a gallon about this time, and the people of Dallas even found themselves paying more to ride the streetcars, fares being hiked from five to six cents on June 27, 1920. A demand for further increase to seven cents followed almost immediately.

The voters of Dallas County ratified both the Eighteenth and Nineteenth Amendments to the Federal constitution by large majorities on May 24, 1919. National prohibition carried by a vote of 5,896 to 3,944, and women's suffrage by a majority of almost two to one—6,130 to 3,689. Mrs. A. B. Griffith of Highland Park was the first woman in Dallas County to cast a vote for president. She voted a straight Democratic ticket in the national election of 1920.

Early in 1920 a severe gas shortage gave rise to consumer agitation for more adequate mains. The Lone Star Gas Company and its subsidiary, the Dallas Gas Company, demanded increased rates, and were faced with a threat to revoke their state and city franchises. The controversy ended with the city's acceptance, on the recommendation of the Chamber of Commerce, of the Lone Star Gas Company's commitment to spend $1,500,000 on new pipelines and the drilling of new wells, guaranteed by the posting of a $200,000 bond in favor of the Dallas Gas Company. A compromise rate of 67 1/2 cents per 1,000 feet was agreed upon, effective on the completion of the pipeline to the West Texas gas fields, October 2, 1920.

Rising prices also precipitated sharp struggles with the other utility companies. The Dallas Power & Light Company was restrained by injunction, October 19, 1920, from disconnecting its power lines to Highland Park and charging more than six cents per kilowatt hour. The city likewise intervened in 1920 to prevent the collection of $4 and $10 a month rates by the Dallas Telephone Company, and a battle in the Federal courts ensued, ending in a compromise in November, 1921, based on party-line reductions and measured service.

On February 6, 1920, the city turned out almost en masse to welcome General John J. Pershing, victorious commander of the American Expeditionary Forces, at which time the five points where Commerce, Jackson, and Preston Streets intersect were christened Pershing Square. On April 18 Dallas entertained ex-President William Howard Taft for a third time. At the State Fair in the autumn the city played host to the president-elect of Mexico, General Alvaro Obregon.

The Fabulous Twenties

In 1920, also, the Dallas Little Theater was born, heralding a new era of cultural sophistication in the Southwest. The State Democratic Convention held in Dallas in May proved a prelude to the national defeat of the party the following autumn when the country repudiated Wilsonian wartime ideals for Warren G. Harding's program of "Back to Normalcy." On December 5 *The Dallas Morning News* reviewed Sinclair Lewis' *Main Street*—battle cry of postwar revolt. In 1921 Dallas acquired the Palace and new Majestic theaters, palatial movie and vaudeville houses featuring the elaborate combined stage and screen shows that became the standard theatrical entertainment of the period. The fabulous twenties had definitely begun.

One of the first manifestations of this topsy-turvy period was the political resurgence of the Ku Klux Klan after a lapse of fifty years. Dallas became one of the regional centers of the movement almost immediately, and the Klan was far more of a political power in the city during the early 1920s than it had ever been during Reconstruction. It emerged into the open in Dallas on April 1, 1921, when 800 masked and robed Klansmen paraded through the streets and branded the initials K. K. K. on the forehead of a Negro named Alex Johnson, after flogging him at a lonely spot near the Hutchins Road. On May 22, 1200 members of the Ku Klux Klan paraded silently in Indian file through the darkened streets of downtown Dallas carrying banners with words of ominous warning such as "Gamblers Go," "Thieves Go," "Parasites Go," "Grafters Go," "We stand for white supremacy," etc.

The Dallas Morning News spoke out boldly against these implied threats of terrorism under the headline "Dallas Disgraced," declaring "the only conditions which could be given to excuse the organization of such a body do not exist."

Other demonstrations followed and despite the denunciation of the press and official attempts to suppress the Klan's increasing political influence, it grew constantly bolder and more powerful during the following year. Several kidnappings and floggings were attributed to the Klan in the spring of 1922. The formation of a Black Ku Klux Klan, threatening reprisals, was rumored. An anti-Klan mass meeting, attended by some 2,000 people, was held April 5, and an official appeal was issued by Mayor Sawnie Aldredge for the Klan to disband. On the night of July 14, 1922, a public initiation ceremony in which 3,500 Klansmen participated was held in the stadium in Fair Park before 25,000 spectators, and in the election of August 27 the Klan candidates made a clean sweep in Dallas County. In 1923 influence of the Klan was at its peak, with its ranks swelled by the organization of a women's auxiliary. Under the eyes of Imperial Wizard Hiram W. Evans, 5,631 male candidates and 800 women were "naturalized" into the "Invisible Empire" before the grandstand at Fair Park with 25,000 onlookers on the night of October 25, 1923. Internal dissension developed between the Klan's founder, Colonel William J. Simmons of Georgia, and the newly elected Imperial Wizard, Hiram W. Evans of Dallas, and after unsuccessfully backing Dr. George C. Butte, Republican candidate for governor of Texas in his campaign against Mrs. Miriam A. (Ma) Ferguson in 1924, the Klan declined as a political force in Dallas.

The new forms of metropolitan postwar crime that arose to bedevil Dallas law enforcement authorities were another phenomenon of the early 1920s. On January 13, 1921, the Jackson Street postal substation was looted of $246,000 in cash and government bonds in broad daylight, the bandits escaping, to use a favorite journalistic cliché of the period, in "high-powered motor cars." Hardly a night passed without a case of safe-cracking or "knob-knocking" being reported somewhere in the city, many of the offenders being thrill-seeking youths in their teens. Representative of the criminal vagaries of the era was a kicking, biting, scratching, and hairpulling "duel" fought between two society women stripped to the waist before thirty or forty people in the glare of automobile headlights one June night in 1922.

A new movie-mad generation packed the Gardner Park Roller Rink in the spring of 1923 to watch Rudolph Valentino, reigning screen idol, and his bride dance the romantic Argentine tango he had popularized in the *Four Horsemen of the Apocalypse*. During the autumn of the same year Mrs. Carrie Chapman Catt, indefatigable worker in the cause of women's suffrage, addressed the recently enfranchised women voters of the city on their national and international responsibilities in a disordered postwar world.

These were hectic and turbulent years in Dallas as elsewhere, but the city, which in 1920 had a population of 158,976, continued to make rapid and solid progress. Prosperity was high, though paradoxically the only bank run in the city's history occurred during these years—a run on the Security National Bank, May 11, 1921 *(see BANKS AND BANKING: CAPITAL RESERVOIR)*. Constantly accelerated metropolitan development also created new and pressing problems which as the decade advanced the city moved to meet. The need for more efficient fire and police control led to the establishment in 1921 of WRR, first municipal broadcasting station in America *(see RADIO: 50 to 50,000 WATTS)*. The Metropolitan Development Association, formed by the Chamber of Commerce soon after the war, summoned

George E. Kessler to Dallas for consultation a second time. A zoning ordinance, later outlawed by the courts, was adopted on the last day of December, 1921, and during the early 1920s an extensive program of street widening, straightening, paving, and renaming was undertaken. A new downtown motor thoroughfare was created by the removal of the railroad tracks from Pacific Avenue in 1923. The same year saw the financial consolidation of the various relief and welfare agencies in the city through the creation of the Community Chest *(see SOCIAL SERVICE: SOUL OF A CITY)*.

Height of an Era

By 1925 Dallas had an estimated population in its metropolitan area of 264,534. It had become the largest spot cotton market in the world, and one of the six big insurance centers in the country. It also led the South in building permits and was becoming a really important industrial location, the manufacturing figures for the year showing a total of $128,695,421.

The years 1924, 1925, and 1926 saw the consolidation of Dallas' modern downtown skyscraper district and the erection of most of the large apartment hotels that dot the residential sections of the city. Among the structures completed in these years were several large factories, the Lone Star Gas Company Building, Republic Bank Building, Thomas Building, Cotton Exchange Building, Dallas Power & Light Company Building, Santa Fe Building, Dallas Athletic Club, Hilton Hotel, now White-Plaza Hotel, Maple Terrace, Stoneleigh Court, Melrose Court, the Auditorium at Fair Park, and the postal substation at Market, Wood, Young, and Austin Streets. The Medical Arts Building had been completed in 1923. Building permits during 1924 amounted to $30,650,000 and in 1925 soared to $34,849,558. Transformation of the city was also hastened by fire losses in 1925 of $2,431,206—the highest in history.

These years saw the passing of such historic landmarks as the renowned Oriental Hotel, which was closed in 1924 and replaced by the modern eighteen-story Baker Hotel; the old Opera House at the corner of Elm and St. Paul Streets, a site now occupied by Titche-Goettinger's department store; and the old Sanger residence at the corner of Ervay and Canton Streets, where the Sanger Hotel now stands. The old city of the 1890s had almost disappeared, but Dallas was not unmindful of its past, the memory of which it moved to conserve by the erection in 1924 of a granite marker on the site of the old French Colony west of the river and organization in 1925 of the Half-Century Club, composed of Dallas citizens who had lived in the city or county fifty years or more.

The long vexing problems of an adequate water supply, aggravated by numerous droughts about this time, was also finally solved by the construction of Garza Dam, begun in 1924 and completed in 1927 at a cost of $5,000,000. By impounding the waters of the Elm Fork of the Trinity River in Denton County, this dam created Lake Dallas, a 12,000-acre reservoir capable of supplying ample water for a city of a half million or more.

The so-called Jazz Era was at its height. The automobile and new modes in manners and morals, particularly among the younger generation, led in 1924 to a crusade against petting parties in parked cars on dark country roads and a series of gruesome holdup, murder, and rape cases in 1925. The most sensational of these crimes were committed by Frank and Lorenzo Noell, Negroes known as the Black Terrors, who during the month of April held up and butchered two couples in rapid succession. An attempt was made to lynch the pair, and they were finally sentenced to death in the electric chair.

Bootlegging, which began almost immediately after the passage of the Eighteenth Amendment, reached big business proportions by the middle of the decade. In 1925 there were in Dallas 3,136 arrests for drunkenness and a survey late in the year revealed the daily income of Dallas bootleggers to be around $36,000. Raids were frequent and stills and liquor caches were discovered in all sorts of unlikely places, one even being found hidden away in a South Dallas cemetery. Illicit traffic in narcotics flourished to a lesser extent, a probe in 1925 leading to the arrest of a number of drug peddlers and the seizure of $500,000 worth of narcotics smuggled into Texas from Europe.

The regulation of motor traffic had also become a serious problem in Dallas by the mid-twenties, and a number of death traps developed at congested points such as the three-way intersection at St. Paul and Live Oak Streets and Pacific Avenue, where an average of fifteen crashes a month occurred. During 1924 automobile accidents throughout the city took a toll of 41 lives. These conditions led to the introduction of automatic traffic control in 1924 and boulevard stop signs in 1926.

The year 1926 was notable for its conventions. In April there was a two-day convention of the Associated Traffic Clubs of America and a five-day session of the American Medical Association. In July 1500 delegates from all parts of the United States assembled for a three-day meeting of the American Institute of Banking. Dallas also made a name for itself in the baseball world by winning over New Orleans in the Dixie Series *(see RECREATION: SPORTS OF A CENTURY)*.

During the year the first air mail was flown from Dallas to New York. The following year Dallas acquired a municipal airport by the purchase of Love Field *(see AVIATION: OVERNIGHT TO EVERYWHERE)* and the city's importance was further enhanced by Dallas' designation as aviation control center for the Southwest. Colonel Charles A. Lindbergh received a tumultuous ovation from 10,000 admirers when he descended from the clouds at Love Field September 26, 1927, and on July 26 Captain Bill Erwin entered the spectacular air derby from Dallas to Hong Kong, in which he perished. The city acquired a second air field in 1928 when it bought Hensley Field, between Dallas and Fort Worth, for the use of the army air corps reserves.

The Ulrickson Plan

It was in 1927 and 1928 that the financial foundations were laid for the transformation of greater Dallas that has resulted from the rechanneling of the Trinity, the reclamation of the bottom lands between Dallas and Oak Cliff, and the construction of the elaborate system of viaducts that have bound the previously divided city into a planned whole. During the 1920s several severe floods had inundated low areas and menaced communications between Dallas and Oak Cliff. On July 26, 1926, the County Commissioners authorized the creation of the City and County of Dallas Levee Improvement District to replace old District 10 and appointed John J. Simmons, Leslie A. Stemmons, and W. J. Wyatt as a board of supervisors. From their efforts emerged a coordinated program that included the issue by property owners of the district of $6,500,000 bonds for constructing levees, straightening and moving the river channel, and other improvements; the provision by the county of $3,339,500 for viaducts and other improvements; the cooperation of the state to require the railroads and utilities to conform with the plan of the district as approved and filed with the State Reclamation Engineers an obligation on the part of the railroads and utilities to spend approximately $5,000,000 in the district; and the earmarking of $3,200,000 in bonds by the City of Dallas for expenditure in the district. The city responded on December 15, 1927, by voting the Ulrickson bond issue which included $3,500,000 for storm-water drainage, and the county on April 3, 1928, by approving the issue of $6,900,000 worth of bonds including the $3,339,500 that was to be its share of the improvements in the reclaimed area. On the same date the property owners voted the sum assigned to them as their part of the coordinated program.

The Ulrickson bond issue provided for much more than the city's contributions to the Trinity Reclamation project, covering a comprehensive nine-year program of varied civic improvements recommended by a committee appointed in 1925 by Mayor Louis Blaylock to make a study of the city's needs, and composed of Charles E. Ulrickson, Alex F. Weisberg, Frank L. McNeny, Leslie A. Stemmons, and Harry A. Olmstead. The committee's report was made public in October, 1927, and recommended the allocation of funds to public schools and other new buildings, street openings and widenings, parks and connecting boulevards, sanitary sewer improvements, storm-water drainage, street paving, a new central fire station, incinerators for better garbage disposal, an Institute of Fine Arts building, a municipal auditorium, additions to Parkland Hospital and other units of the city-county hospital system, and an improved water system (see CITY PLAN: DESIGN FOR GROWTH). The Ulrickson Plan and other contributions of Dallas to scientific city planning received nationwide recognition when the twentieth National Conference on City Planning met here in May, 1928.

The closing years of the decade were politically lively ones in Dallas marked by upsets, hoaxes, amusing incidents, and eccentric personalities. In the presidential election in November for a second time in its history Dallas broke with the political traditions of the Solid South and voted for Herbert Hoover over Alfred E. Smith by a majority of nearly 10,000. The election was also marked by a trumped-up case involving civil rights, when after the city commissioners had denied Communist candidates the right to speak in the city hall auditorium, Richard Potts organized the Royalist League of America, calling for the election of Bernard Shaw as king and Will Rogers as crown prince, and made similar application for use of the auditorium. J. Waddy Tate, blue-shirted Independent candidate for mayor and self-styled friend of the common man, battled his way to victory in the spring of 1929 with hot-dog parties, soapbox speeches, and a motto of the "Golden Rule and faith in the Lord." In this hotly contested mayoralty race there were over thirty entrants, nine of them representing one-man "parties." Tate's antics both before and after his election, the latter including the removal of "keep off the grass" signs from all city property and permission for "plain folks" to sleep in the parks, were the delight of local feature-story writers. He effected some genuine reforms in the city administration, particularly as regards the use of parks and playgrounds.

Despite the stock market crash in October, 1929, Dallas finished the year with confidence as indicated by a survey which showed $20,000,000 worth of construction work contemplated for 1930. Forty-eight big conventions had been held in the city during the year, and the convention of Rotary International late in May had attracted an estimated 10,500 visitors from all over the world. Further metropolitan growth was anticipated by the adoption of a second and more comprehensive zoning law dividing the city into six zones; it was contested like its predecessor but upheld by the courts.

The Federal census of 1930 gave Dallas a population of 260,397 showing a growth of 64 percent since 1920. Greater Dallas in 1930 had a population, computed on the basis of the city directory, of 308,030.

Despite the determined opposition of Mayor Tate, the council-city manager form of government was inaugurated in Dallas during 1930. Mayor Tate vetoed the charter election scheduled for April 1, but popular petition forced an election on October 10, when the citizens of Dallas voted overwhelmingly to adopt the new form of government providing for a city manager and a council of nine members.

Dallas gained steadily in prominence as an aviation center. By 1930 the city enjoyed overnight service to New York and Los Angeles, and during this year Captains Dieudonne Coste and Maurice Bellonte, after completing a nonstop flight from Paris to New York, continued nonstop to Dallas to win the purse of $25,000 posted by William E. Easterwood, Jr.

The Depression Years

Though Dallas did not feel the effects of the gradually spreading business and industrial depression as soon as many other cities, unemployment had begun to reach serious proportions by the end of 1930. The following year the number of jobless had grown to 18,500 and the emergency relief committee appointed by the Chamber of Commerce asked for $100,000 to relieve hunger and destitution in the city. Early in 1932 a program of work relief projects was drafted to provide employment for the jobless out of a special bond issue. The demands on the city's resources increased steadily as the year advanced and the Community Chest in its annual drive made a special appeal to big donors since those in the lower income brackets were no longer able to contribute as formerly. Discharge of married women from jobs, a five-day week in retail stores, the abandonment of modern machinery by state and county governments, a wholesale renovizing campaign, and all sorts of other desperate expedients for creating and spreading employment were agitated, and finally in September the distressed city and county authorities applied jointly through the Governor of Texas to the Reconstruction Finance Corporation for $450,000 for relief purposes. Home owners suffering from restricted credit were aided by the opening in Dallas on October 15 of a Federal Home Loan Bank.

During these trying early depression years Dallas, in addition to struggling valiantly to relieve the human misery resulting from mass unemployment, continued to build for the future, leading the state in building in July, 1932. Several of the trans-Trinity viaducts and underpasses were begun during these years, many streets were paved and widened, work was begun on the new Industrial Boulevard through the recently reclaimed Trinity bottoms, and improvements totaling $69,000 undertaken at the government airport at Hensley Field.

In the crucial election of November, 1932, Dallas concurred heartily in endorsing at the polls the New Deal promised by Franklin D. Roosevelt. The period between his election in November, 1932, and his inauguration in March, 1933, represented for Dallas the very bottom of the depression and was marked by a relief load of some 9,000 family heads. The city received a Reconstruction Finance Corporation loan in January; a city cannery where meat was put up to feed the unemployed was opened in February; work on the "Breadline Follies," a citywide charity benefit, was begun the same month; 1,379 families were issued clothing at the relief depot; self-help garden plots were urged; and swapping or barter ads appeared in the newspapers.

The bank holiday ordered by President Roosevelt as his first act after his inauguration was survived in Dallas with a minimum of inconvenience through the cooperation of local business houses, stores extending credit or accepting checks as necessary. The demand for small change was met by the banks setting up a change station in the old City National Bank, where businessmen were able to get bills changed into silver.

The nationwide recovery drive was on, and Dallas went over the top with a rush. Relief in the city was put on a more systematic basis with three more commissaries for the distribution of food and clothing, a better scale of pay for work relief, and county jobless camps where 1,560 men were put to work on Trinity River and other reclamation projects. On May 7 "Renovize Dallas" pledges totaled $3,318,392.

On June 14 the city, taking advantage of the new Federal funds available for public works, filed an application in Washington for $2,136,000 for city improvements, civic projects, storm sewers, and additions to the city-county hospital system. The Home Owners Loan Corporation opened offices in Dallas July 15; and in August the city matched Public Works Administration funds to the extent of $572,000. A report on October 1 showed 10,796 persons reemployed in Dallas as a result of the National Recovery Act, and a decline of 354 was noted in the caseload of the Dallas County Board of Welfare and Employment.

Sentiment in Dallas on the repeal of National prohibition was somewhat divided. However, in the election of August 27, in which Texas as a whole voted for repeal, Dallas went for repeal by a heavy majority, and on September 14 legal 3.2 beer flowed in the city amid general celebration and merrymaking.

The early months of 1934 were marked by agitation among the unemployed, organized by the Workers Cooperative League for rent, fuel, and clothes allowances in addition to groceries. The fight of local initiative against the depression continued unabated, resulting in the launching of an extensive public works program including the $1,000,000 Triple Underpass at the foot of Elm, Main, and Commerce Streets. By the end of the year the Works Progress Administration had also given employment to 3,000 workers in the city.

By 1935 Dallas showed definite signs of recovery from the depression. Local banks in January showed an increase in deposits of $3,500,000 over 1933, and a real estate survey revealed an acute shortage of dwellings, created by the many new arrivals in the city. A total of 609 new businesses located in Dallas during the first six months of the year, and a master plan was adopted for the beautification of the city's parks. Southern Methodist University won the Southwest Conference football championship for the third time in less than a decade and was invited to represent the East at the Rose Bowl game in California, January 1, 1936 *(see RECREATION: SPORTS OF A CENTURY)*.

Forward with Texas

The most important events of the mid-1930s were the Texas Centennial Exposition in 1936 and the Greater Texas and Pan-American Exposition in 1937. These two expositions involved a vast amount of construction work, attracted millions of visitors from all parts of the country, and completely transformed Fair Park, creating the spacious and beautiful Civic Center *(see POINTS OF INTEREST, Fair Park)*. On September 1, 1934, Dallas pledged the $4,000,000 plant of the State Fair and an additional $5,500,000 in cash for building purposes to secure the Texas Centennial Exposition and was designated as the central exposition city over the rival bids of Houston and San Antonio by the Centennial Commission meeting in Austin. The award was on the basis of competitive bids but the commission was also influenced by the fact that Dallas was the population center of the state and had had 46 years experience handling State Fair crowds.

Business in the city from 1934 on, particularly in the real estate and related fields, was sharply stimulated, and it is estimated the city alone employed 8,000 men on its share of the building and landscaping, in addition to those employed by the state, the Federal government, the Centennial Corporation, and the many exhibitors and concessionaires. At the same time Dallas was publicized from coast to coast through every advertising medium by the Centennial's promotional staff.

The Centennial Exposition, with Texas' progress and romantic history as its theme, was formally opened on June 6, 1936, by Secretary of Commerce Daniel C. Roper, was attended by many distinguished visitors including President Franklin D. Roosevelt, Vice President John Nance Garner, and sixteen state governors, and closed on November 1, 1936. The Greater Texas and Pan-American Exposition which ran from June to November, 1937, and which was really a continuation of the exposition of the preceding year, was even more ambitious in conception, stressing the ties binding Texas and the Southwest generally to Mexico and Central and South America. Invitations were extended to the Latin American Republics and the Dominion of Canada to participate, and at the close of the exposition parchment grand prize certificates were presented to the nations who had accepted, these including among others the Republics of Mexico and Chile. About 10,000,000 attended the Texas Centennial Exposition in 1936, and 2,384,830 the Pan-American Exposition in 1937. In 1938 the Texas State Fair, suspended in 1935, 1936, and 1937, was resumed on the greatly enlarged Fair Park grounds with a Golden Jubilee, commemorating the fifty state fairs held on this site since 1886.

By 1937 Dallas had attained the rank of third convention city in the United States and by the following year was surpassed only by Chicago. The general prosperity of the city also continued high. Dallas banks entered 1937 with the highest deposits and resources in their history. During the year building permits passed the $12,000,000 mark and 948 firms located in the city. In May, 1938, *The Dallas Morning News* declared the "recession" to be "only a rumor in Dallas," and the city gained the reputation as one of the "bright spots" in the nation on the basis of business reports in June which showed it to be the only key city in the country that had not suffered a decline in trade during the preceding twelve months.

The "recession" in Dallas was apparent only in a marked rise in the number of unemployed in the city and a relief crisis resulting from the reduction of the WPA rolls and the exhaustion of local funds necessary to care for unemployables. This crisis led to the appointment of a Citizens' Relief Committee late in 1937, and administrative changes in the set-up of the City-County Welfare Department.

Other events of 1937 and 1938 were a wave of mob violence and labor disorders in the summer of 1937 which culminated in the sending of Rangers to Dallas by Governor James V. Allred despite protests of local officials *(see LABOR: ORGANIZATION AND STRUGGLES)*; the plague of "Little Algae," as the local press humorously dubbed the harmless but offensive plant organism that polluted the water supply from Lake Dallas in the summer of 1937 and again in 1938; an investigation of alleged graft and corruption in the Park Board late in 1938; and the introduction of voting machines in Dallas during the sensational state election of August, 1938, when the city contributed to the landslide that placed W. Lee O'Daniel in the Governor's chair.

The early months of 1939 were marked by a visit on January 12 of Douglas (Wrong Way) Corrigan, hero of the recent freak trans-Atlantic flight in the fall of 1938. When the Allied Powers unexpectedly declared war on the German Third Reich September 3, many Dallas people were traveling in Europe, and a party of Texas schoolgirls, including several from Dallas, were on the ill-fated British steamer *Athenia* when it was torpedoed September 4. All were rescued, however, and received a rousing ovation when they arrived home several weeks later.

As the year drew to a close, citizens of Dallas were busy discussing the lively possibility of a city centennial celebration in 1941, inspired by a hundred years of growth, change, and progress since the visionary lawyer and Indian trader, John Neely Bryan, dismounted from his pony and pitched his first camp at the foot of the bluffs on the east bank of the Trinity River in 1841.

GOVERNMENT: VILLAGE TO METROPOLIS

In the 84 years of its existence as an organized community, Dallas has been governed under seven charters, ranging from the first granted the village in 1856 to the present council-city manager administration, generally accepted as the most efficient of all. In the interim the city has tried almost every form of municipal government known to America, and for a short time after the Civil War was under military rule, the civil government suspended.

The current form of government sprang directly from the people, since the election on a new charter was forced upon the old administration by popular petition, after submission of the issue had been denied by incumbent officials. The charter, drafted by a commission named under terms of the Texas home rule law for cities, while framed as amendments to the charter of 1907, is a complete revision of the original law. It was adopted by a majority of 3 to 1 on October 10, 1930, taking effect May 1 following.

At that time a council of nine men, three representing the city at large and six representing as many districts but all elected by the voters at large, succeeded a mayor and four commissioners, the last administration under the preceding charter, adopted in 1907. The council chose one of their number as mayor, and filled the administrative offices of city manager, city attorney, auditor, city secretary, corporation court officials, and supervisor of public utilities, together with a park board, all other positions being filled by appointment of the city manager.

Salient features of the charter include the initiative, referendum, and recall; civil service for all city workers except executive employees and common labor; indeterminate franchises for public utilities; the semiannual payment of taxes; and a modernized budgeting system.

Party or other group designations are not permitted in balloting for members of the city council, candidates being listed under numbers indicating their districts, 7, 8, and 9 representing the at-large places. Order of the names is determined by drawing. Voting machines are used in all elections, and while there are no primaries, a runoff election is required where any candidate fails to receive a majority of all votes cast.

100

T. L. Bradford was the first mayor under the new charter, and councilmen serving with him were E. R. Brown, Victor H. Hexter, T. M. Cullom, Joe C. Thompson, Charles E. Turner, Arthur B. Moore, H. C. Burroughs, and W. H. Painter. John N. Edy, former city manager at Berkeley, California, and Flint, Michigan, was the first city manager, serving four years under the first and the immediately succeeding councils. Hal Moseley was city manager from May 1, 1935, to July 1, 1939, when he was succeeded by James W. Aston.

While there is no detailed record of any form of communal government from the founding of the settlement in 1841 by John Neely Bryan until 1846, the village came under county administrative authority in that year, when Dallas County was organized by act of the legislature.

It was not until a decade later, in 1856, that a formal town government was set up, again by act of the legislature. On February 2 of that year the town's first election was held and Dr. Samuel B. Pryor was elected mayor. Less than 100 votes were cast. Councilmen named with Dr. Pryor were William Burtle, James W. Latimer, William J. Halsell, Burrell Wilkes, [a Mr.] Williams, and George M. Baird. Andrew M. Moore was the first city marshal, William L. Murphy the treasurer, and Samuel Jones the recorder.

Boundaries of the town under this government embraced the original Bryan survey of one-half a square mile. Poydras Street was the eastern limit; Water Street, facing the river, formed the western limit; paralleled between by Broadway, Houston, Jefferson, Market, Austin, and Lamar. East-west streets from the river to Poydras were Calhoun, Walnut, Carondelet, Burleson, Elm, Main, Commerce, Jackson, Wood, Polk, and Columbia, in order from north to south.

In April, 1857, John M. Crockett succeeded Dr. Pryor as mayor, serving until April, 1858, when Isaac Naylor was elected. In June of that year the citizens voted for a new charter, and in August following elected Dr. A. D. Rice as mayor. He served until August of 1859, when John M. Crockett was again made mayor. Crockett was reelected in 1860, but resigned to assume the duties of lieutenant-governor of the Confederate state of Texas, to which he was elected in 1861. His term was filled out by J. N. Smith, an alderman.

The record of town elections from 1861 until 1866 is obscure, the community, like others in Texas and the South, being more concerned with the Civil War than with local government. Available records do show that the Reverend Thomas E. Sherwood served as mayor from August, 1861, to August, 1862. A memorandum of ex-Mayor John M. Crockett shows that he temporarily resumed office from November, 1865, to April, 1866. In June, 1866, John W. Lane was elected mayor and served until September 4 the same year when he resigned to become private secretary of Governor Throckmorton. George W. Guess was elected to fill out his unexpired term.

It appears from such records as survive that Guess was supplanted by Benjamin Long, a native of Switzerland appointed by the Federal military (Reconstruction) government at San Antonio. Long served from September, 1868, until April 1, 1870. When he resigned, Henry S. Ervay was appointed in his stead by E. J. Davis, the Reconstruction governor. Ervay's conduct of the office did not please General J. J. Reynolds and in February, 1872, he was ordered removed and Dr. J. W. Haynes appointed in his stead. Ervay refused to give up the office and was jailed by Judge Hardin Hart for contempt, but was freed by the same court after a decision of the supreme court invalidating the power under which Ervay was ordered removed from the office. Ervay then completed his term, when Ben Long again became mayor, this time by an election supervised by Federal troops, the balloting continuing over a period of five days.

Meantime, on April 20, 1871, the town charter was abandoned and a city charter substituted by act of the legislature, providing for election of a mayor and eight aldermen representing as many wards. Corporate limits were enlarged from the original boundaries of a square half-mile to three times that area, the boundaries extending for a mile and a half along the Trinity River's eastern bank, north and south, and eastward a like distance to form the square of the area. Subsequently the charter was amended to provide for election of aldermen by the voters of their respective wards, instead of by popular citywide ballot.

Other new charters were adopted in 1875 and in 1876, a novel feature of the latter being a provision that council could by a vote of "lack of confidence" oust the mayor from office. This was done but once, in 1880, when J. M. Thurmond was removed and John J. Good named to succeed him. This charter provision was later repealed. Under all of these charters the voters elected all town officials, including marshal, recorder, treasurer, city attorney, tax officers, and even the superintendent of streets.

As population of the community increased it spread across the Trinity River to the western highlands and to the eastward adjoining the boundaries of the original incorporated area. This resulted in the incorporation of other municipalities, three of which have since been absorbed by Dallas. Residents of the western area incorporated the town of Oak Cliff June 9, 1891, by a vote of 271 to 19. H. F. Ewing was the first mayor. Oak Cliff was annexed to the city of Dallas April 6, 1903, under act of legislature authorizing a vote, but the annexation did not become effective until the autumn of 1904, due to contests in the courts.

To the east the town of East Dallas was incorporated September 9, 1882, with John L. Henry as the first mayor. This town embraced 1,425 acres of land in a region now within the central residential area of modern Dallas. East Dallas was annexed April 3, 1889, by act of the legislature. Last of the new towns annexed to Dallas was Lisbon, to the southwest of Oak Cliff, which was incorporated August 7, 1920, with P. G. Wilson as mayor, and which was brought into the central community on petition of its residents on July 29, 1929.

Remarkable growth of Dallas after 1900 imposed so many new burdens and problems upon the community that it became necessary to modernize the government, and this was done in 1907 when a new charter drawn locally was approved by the legislature, providing for the mayor-commission form of administration, patterned upon the emergency government adopted in Galveston after the great hurricane and tidal wave disaster of 1900. Stephen J. Hay was the first mayor under this charter, with William Doran, Dan F. Sullivan, Charles B. Gillespie, and Harry L. Seay as commissioners, these taking office May 1, 1907.

Under this setup the mayor exercised general supervisory authority over all departments of the city government, while each of the commissioners was assigned administration of certain major departments. The ward system was abolished, all of the elective officials being chosen by vote of the entire city, with all positions other than those of mayor and commissioners filled by appointment of the board of commissioners. Functioning admirably for a number of years, this type of government gradually deteriorated, and by the end of its twentieth year had precipitated a popular demand for still further modernization to secure greater efficiency in administration and a sound fiscal policy.

Mayors of Dallas

From the first incorporation of the town in 1856 to 1940 the following men have served as mayors of Dallas:

1856–1857—Dr. Samuel B. Pryor
1857–1858—John M. Crockett
1858　　　—Isaac Naylor
1858–1859—Dr. A. D. Rice
1859–1861—John M. Crockett
1861　　　—J. N. Smith
1861–1862—Rev. Thomas E. Sherwood
1865–1866—John M. Crockett
1866　　　—John W. Lane
1866–1867—George W. Guess
1868–1870—Benjamin Long
1870–1872—Henry S. Ervay
1872–1874—Benjamin Long
1874–1876—W. L. Cabell
1876–1877—John D. Kerfoot
1877–1879—W. L. Cabell
1879–1880—J. M. Thurmond *(Removed)*
1880–1881—John J. Good
1881　　　—John Stone *(Elected but could not qualify, not having resided in city limits for the required time)*
1881–1883—Dr. J. W. Crowdus
1883–1885—W. L. Cabell
1885–1887—John Henry Brown
1887–1894—W. C. Connor
1894–1895—Bryan T. Barry
1895–1897—Frank P. Holland
1897–1898—Bryan T. Barry
1898–1900—John H. Taylor
1900–1904—Ben C. Cabell
1904–1906—Bryan T. Barry
1906–1907—Curtis P. Smith
1907–1911—Stephen J. Hay
1911–1915—W. M. Holland
1915–1917—Henry D. Lindsley
1917–1919—Joe E. Lawther
1919–1921—Frank W. Wozencraft
1921–1923—Sawnie R. Aldredge
1923–1927—Louis Blaylock
1927–1929—R. E. Burt
1929–1931—J. Waddy Tate
1931–1932—T. L. Bradford
1932–1935—Charles E. Turner
1935–1937—George Sergeant
1937–1939—George A. Sprague
1939–1940—J. Woodall Rodgers

Suburban Cities

In addition to the three incorporated communities absorbed by Dallas, the city now is flanked by four self-governing towns. Highland Park and University Park, the first incorporated in 1913 and the latter in 1924, are the largest of these. Both are almost exclusively residential communities, separated from Dallas only by streets as boundaries, and with their residents engaged in business and the professions in the greater city.

On the southern edge of Dallas there is Fruitdale, a smaller community, incorporated April 17, 1937, while at the extreme north of the metropolitan area is Preston Hollow, a wholly residential town incorporated November 18, 1939.

With the exception of Fruitdale all of these towns receive water and sewage disposal facilities from the greater city, while education is provided by independent school districts.

RACIAL DISTRIBUTION:
95% AMERICAN

Dallas is primarily a city of American-born white people. With a population (1940) of approximately 350,000 in its metropolitan area, an estimated 43,000 Negroes make up the largest non-Anglo-Saxon group. The number of foreign-born, including those with one or both parents born abroad, is very small in comparison with the typical American city. In Dallas the total number is about 5 percent, whereas Carpenter in *The Sociology of City Life* (p. 169) shows that for the average city of between 100,000 and 500,000 the foreign element as thus defined amounts to 45.4 percent of the total population. In the United States as a whole the percentage is 10.9. Ratio of Negro to white population in Dallas in 1938 was 14.8 percent, as shown by a municipal survey.

The largest homogeneous foreign group is the Mexican, with a total of about 6,650. This element was one of the last to come to the city, and their language and customs are still largely those of their native country. In the foreign-born category, Germans rank second in number to the Mexicans, with Russians, English, Italians, and Poles following in the order given. Of this classification most of the Russian- and Polish-born are Jewish, contributing to an aggregate of approximately 8,000 of that race within the city. All of these ethnic groups are largely assimilated in the Anglo-Saxon element.

In a 1935 scholastic survey the question was asked in 53,000 homes whether any language other than English was spoken. The replies showed 72 homes using Italian, 24 using German, 24 using Yiddish, and 11 each speaking Greek and Bohemian. No other language was found to be spoken in as many as ten homes in the city.

Racial cleavages are fairly distinct in certain cases. Little Mexico, a near-slum area just north of the business district, and the Jewish and Italian group in Southeast and East Dallas comprise the bilingual areas.

The Mexican group, though the largest foreign-language element in the city, has had but slight effect on cultural and social Dallas. Principal reasons for the immigration to the city of these thousands of Mexicans were, first, that those coming believed work was to be had, or they had relatives already in the city; and second, the continual state of revolution in Mexico from 1910 to 1920, which impelled many natives to seek refuge in the United States. Later, chiefly between 1925 and 1930, these immigrants came in considerable numbers to Dallas. Little Mexico as a distinct racial area came into being in 1925, in what originally had been one of the best residential districts.

Movements inaugurated first in 1935 and again in 1938 to clear up this poverty-stricken district gained some momentum, but physical results were so meager as to preclude the gauging of effects upon the possible ultimate Americanization of the Mexican group in Dallas *(see LITTLE MEXICO: OUTPOST FOR MAÑANA)*.

The Jewish group has been largely Americanized, but continues to retain many elements of the original culture, especially the rich religious traditions of the race, which find expression in five synagogues, both orthodox and reformed, the latter representing the earliest Jewish migration to the region. In addition to a fairly definite cleavage from American racial stock, the Jews have their own differences, chiefly based on degree of religious conservatism and orthodoxy. The first immigration from Spain and Germany was succeeded by Russian and Polish Jews, and these have been only partly assimilated, clinging more closely to old-world customs.

Dallas Jewry has in the past grouped itself in definite neighborhoods. The first such district was near the present Parkland Hospital, and the second in South Dallas, about the intersection of Ervay and St. Louis Streets. The present Jewish center has moved eastward, being still in South Dallas, chiefly along South Boulevard and Park Row east of Ervay Street. The trend of the population today is toward general racial dispersion, the extent of the movement governed somewhat by economic conditions. Here, as elsewhere in America, Jews have contributed much to the cultural, social, and economic development of the community.

The Italian group in Dallas numbers perhaps 5,000, and though only a fraction of these are foreign-born, is recent enough to preserve considerable homogeneity. North and East Dallas have many Italian-speaking homes, and the race has its own newspaper, *La Tribuna Italiana*, one of two foreign-language news journals in the city. This element supplies small storekeepers and general laborers, with a growing number in the professions. The entire group is being rapidly assimilated.

Native German population in Dallas is small—a little more than 1,000—but the total German element numbers about 6,000, and is to be found throughout the city. The Germans came early, a group having settled near Garland in 1857. They landed in New Orleans and came directly to North Texas, bringing their established Lutheran religion. Location of the German colony in Dallas began along Swiss Avenue in 1879, by their first church, but aside from religion their native culture has been assimilated into the ideals of Americanism, though inherent social tendencies have survived to some extent, notably in the Sons of Hermann and Deutscher Clubs. Germans in Dallas are to be found in the professions and in all significant occupations, the whole constituting a solid, progressive, and prosperous economic bloc.

Approximately 300 Bohemian or Czechoslovakian families have come to Dallas since the beginning of the twentieth century, their immigration coinciding with the heaviest movement of this people to the United States. Their occupational grouping is diverse, with the bulk of the men in the trades and a number of the second generation following the professions, especially the law. Their homes are chiefly in North Dallas. The Bohemian influx is recent enough to make the members a somewhat distinct group within the city. The German and French languages are commonly spoken in these Czech homes in addition to English. "Sokol," the Czechoslovakian athletic club for men and women, is the social center for this nationality in Dallas. It is located at 3700 Carl Street.

Norwegians and Swedes, like the Germans, have become rapidly assimilated and a Scandinavian society which once aided in their unity has ceased to exist.

Greeks in Dallas, some 250 in number, live almost exclusively in the southern section of the city.

THE DALLAS CITY PLAN: DESIGN FOR GROWTH

In the first seventy years of its existence Dallas developed from a village of log cabins into a modern city without any attempt at planned growth. Typically the courthouse, near the river, was the center from which radiated the arteries of traffic.

The first town plat of 1844 provided blocks 300 feet square, bisected by streets 80 feet in width in the conventional rectangular manner, a practice abandoned when the first addition was laid out with 40-foot streets. The original streets paralleled the river north and south, and as early as 1872 extended eastward for a little more than a mile to the station of the town's first railroad, the Houston & Texas Central.

As the community grew to the north and south from the first three principal east and west streets, the new roadways followed existing country lanes, which had conformed to the meanderings of the Indian and buffalo trails leading from the east to the waters of the Trinity River. This created a permanent maze of crooked and in some instances very narrow thoroughfares.

When the second railway, the Texas & Pacific, came to Dallas on its way westward in 1873 it had to cross the Trinity here. It built its main line along a lane that was later to become a vital downtown street. This for years blocked any appreciable expansion of the business district to the north and forced it to spread along the streets eastward from the river to the railway terminals, and gradually beyond.

Unprecedented growth in population was rapidly rendering this situation intolerable when in 1909 the *Dallas News* initiated the movement for a city plan. A year later, January 25, 1910, the Chamber of Commerce endorsed the movement and there was organized the Dallas City Plan and Improvement League, which prevailed upon the city commissioners and the Park Board to employ the late George E. Kessler to prepare a plan.

While official status was not given to the resultant program until nearly a decade later, the citizens proceeded toward its realization with a degree of unity and vigor that brought about the building (1915–1916) of the Union railway passenger station, an item of Kessler's scheme, and initiation of the effort to remove railway tracks from Pacific Avenue. Then, in 1919, a city plan commission was appointed to devise ways and means of carrying into effect a complete program that would prevent Dallas from being choked to death commercially. In the same year the charter was amended to give the plan commission official status, and Mr. Kessler was brought back in 1920 to revise his plan to meet the needs of the larger city.

Major elements of the Kessler plan included, in addition to the unification of passenger terminals, the leveeing of the Trinity River for flood control, the widening and opening of a number of downtown streets, provision of parks and parkways, and final removal of the railway tracks from Pacific Avenue. The latter detail brought on prolonged litigation, and it was not until 1923, after the legal battle had been carried to the United States Supreme Court, that the tracks were removed. This enabled the city to make of the street a wide, paved traffic artery into and through the business district and remove the barrier to commercial expansion to the northward.

Supplementing the Union passenger terminal, a belt line railway was built removing the network of tracks from the downtown area and concentrating most of the freight terminals where they would interfere least with the flow of street traffic. Dead end streets were opened to through connections; north and south arteries were widened and opened, at a cost to the city and property owners that, between 1919 and 1939, aggregated approximately $65,000,000. The last of the major downtown street openings, that of Field Street, was completed during 1938 at a cost of about $1,000,000.

Through action of property owners $6,000,000 was expended in leveeing the Trinity River for eight miles through the city and pushing the stream one mile westward into a new and straightened channel, reclaiming 10,000 acres of land and preventing for all time a recurrence of the disastrous floods which had previously caused vast damage. After the levees were built, four new steel and concrete bridges were constructed to link the eastern and western parts of the city, with underpasses carrying the streets through the railroad yard district to connections with the bridges.

New bridges also were built by the railroads and the street railway company, and a wide paved highway was constructed along the eastern side of the levees to provide a north and south traffic route bypassing the congested downtown area, and giving connections to state and Federal highways both east and west of the Trinity River. Largest of the underpasses is a triple roadway linking Main, Commerce, and Elm Streets, principal business thoroughfares, with the western section of the city in a single route. This was opened in 1936, its building cost approximately $1,000,000.

While the Kessler city plan did not propose zoning as that term is now understood, the engineer did recommend the segregation of industries in adaptable districts to prevent blighting of residential areas by intrusion of factories. Dallas elaborated on this suggestion by securing the passage of state enabling acts permitting comprehensive zoning of land uses and carried test cases to successful conclusion in the state's highest court *(Lombardo vs. Dallas,* 124 Texas, P. 1; 73 SW II, p. 475). It is now the largest city in Texas operating strictly under comprehensive zoning regulations.

As early as 1925, effects of the city plan were visible in every section of Dallas. In addition to the downtown improvements and the beginnings of those which later revolutionized traffic across the Trinity, scenic driveways had been opened in two circles around Oak Cliff, western section of the city, and parkways and boulevards projected in some parts of the eastern area.

In 1927, on recommendation of a committee headed by the late Charles E. Ulrickson, the remainder of the Kessler plan was revised by Major E. A. Wood, then and again in 1939 city plan engineer, with the addition of other needed civic improvements. On December 15 of that year the people approved a bond issue of $23,900,000 for carrying out the enlarged program.

In 1939 practically all of the Kessler-Ulrickson program has been realized except the removal of railroad tracks from Central Avenue to create a great crosstown north and south boulevard, and negotiations are under way for the realization of this final phase of the original city plan.

Both of the adjoining suburban cities of Highland Park and University Park control their own development by plan and both have comprehensive zoning ordinances.

Skyline from Houston Street Viaduct

Downtown Dallas by Night, ca. 1930

Theater Row on Elm Street

Triple Underpass—Where Dallas Was Born

Peak Hour Shopping Crowds

Suburban Residential Street, ca. 1930

John Neely Bryan's Third Cabin

Delord House, Last of La Reunion

Main Street East from Scollard Alley, ca. 1887

Main Street East from Akard, ca. 1935

Commerce Street East from Lamar, ca. 1895

Commerce Street East from Lamar, ca. 1925

Economic
Development

COTTON:
BOUNTY OF THE BLACKLANDS

Where trade routes intersect, men inevitably meet to barter the products of the region. Dallas as a cotton market owes its inception and continuation to such an intersection, for it was the junction of two railroads here, coincidental with the development of North Texas blacklands for the production of cotton, that made the city a cotton concentration point more than sixty years ago. Today Dallas is the world's foremost spot cotton market. Perhaps one-third of the American production of the staple is grown within a radius of 300 miles of the city.

From Dallas this vital commodity moves into world consumption through Texas ports, approximately 2,500,000 bales being handled in a normal season by members of the Dallas Cotton Exchange, constituting a large portion of the southwestern production. The best staple in Texas is grown within 100 miles of Dallas, a hard, wiry type of blackland cotton famous with world spinners. The finest staples of the Red River valley north of Dallas are known universally to the trade and command special premiums.

Cotton first moved from Dallas into commercial channels in March, 1852, when J. W. Smith, pioneer merchant, started down the Trinity River with a flatboat laden with 22 bales for a Gulf port. The first gin in the county had been built in the preceding year, though cotton had been planted as early as 1846.

For the next two decades the commodity, grown in increasing quantities in the Dallas area, trickled into the market on oxcarts and below Dallas on steamboats, often to be taken in barter by merchants and traders, ultimately finding its way to the sea for export. In those days, before the exactitude of present grades and staples, most cotton was bought and sold on what was known as the "hog-round" basis—the buyer taking all of a grower's offering at an inclusive lot price on the basis of gross weight. Liverpool quotations, the price basis for the commodity, then were often more than a month in reaching Texas, and this forced the buyers to work on uncertain but wide margins.

When the first railroads came in 1872 and 1873, cotton buyers rushed to open offices in Dallas, then as now the hub of the rich blackland producing belt. Telegraph service followed with the world market quotations and enabled them to operate with greater facility and on smaller margins.

121

Lower Elm Street in another year or so became a curb cotton market. In the ginning season farmers' wagons jammed the section around Elm and Lamar for blocks. Most notable of the cotton transactions of this early period in the Dallas market was the sale in 1880 by Abe Schwartz, a 17-year-old operator, of 1,200 bales to Liverpool at 12 cents a pound.

In six months of the following year 50,000 bales of cotton were received in the town. When it is remembered that usually not more than three bales made a wagon load, it is not remarkable that merchants and citizens of downtown Dallas raised protests against converting the streets into market places. These complaints and the rapid growth of the business by 1884 prompted the erection of the Gaston Building at Commerce and Lamar Streets to house the cotton traders. These traders meantime had informally organized as an exchange, looking to concentration in one central location. Establishment of wagon and cotton yards near the Gaston Building relieved the congestion on the streets.

In the new central market the brokers and buyers received quotations by Western Union wire. This method of communication not only enabled operations on narrower margins but prompted "hedging" by spot buyers through the purchase of future delivery cotton on the New Orleans and New York futures exchanges. The first cotton exchange dissolved after 1894, when the town's first leased wire, installed by M. H. Thomas & Co., gave instant and direct connection with the world's markets, a facility soon duplicated by other brokers.

Speculative operations in futures in cotton and other commodities and in securities grew so rapidly through "wire houses" that in 1907 the Texas legislature enacted a drastic law against "bucket shops," forbidding telegraph companies to transmit futures quotations into or out of the state. This compelled the cotton operators to unite to protect their futures trading advantages. On April 11, 1907, the day after the new law became effective, the Dallas Cotton Exchange was organized and a few days later was granted a charter, with F. P. Webster as first president. Meeting at first in the offices of a member, the Exchange soon moved into the old Scollard Building on Main Street, which was utilized until 1912. Then a seven-story building was erected at Wood and Akard Streets for exclusive use of the cotton men.

Here the Exchange remained until 1926, when growth compelled another expansion. This resulted in the erection of the 17-story building at North St. Paul and San Jacinto Streets, the present home of the cotton trade in Dallas.

The Exchange Building is headquarters of approximately 35 exporting firms, numerous spot brokers, futures operators, insurance and railroad representatives of interior and port compresses. All of these are integral parts in the mechanism of merchandising raw cotton. British, German, Dutch, French, and Japanese brokers are among members of the Exchange. Buyers for domestic and foreign mills make their headquarters in the building. Cotton is shipped to every country in which there are facilities for its manufacture. Texas cotton is frequently shipped from Dallas to Bombay, where it is mixed with the Indian staple to improve its spinning qualities.

Purchases are concentrated and stored at Gulf ports where cotton may be loaded on ship the same day it is sold on the Dallas Exchange, so efficient is the service between those points.

Dallas being one of the ten designated spot cotton markets of America, the Exchange maintains a spot quotations committee to cooperate with the United States

Department of Agriculture in arriving at fair prices for the different qualities of cotton in relation to the quotations from the several futures markets. World prices and other information are broadcast daily from the floor of the Exchange over Radio Station WFAA. Producers and others interested in the market can thus know immediately the fluctuations in prices, assuring them of full value for their cotton.

The Dallas Cotton Exchange, during the growing season—April through August—gathers information regarding the development and condition of the crop in the various sections of Texas, Oklahoma, and Arkansas. More than one hundred correspondents, each familiar with conditions in their respective sections, make reports for this service. These reports are sent out by Exchange members to their clients in the various mill centers and domestic and foreign markets. The United States Weather Bureau, located in the Exchange Building, affords reliable and detailed information regarding atmospheric and climatic conditions affecting the crop in all producing sections of the region.

The rules of the Exchange are the guiding factor in all transactions in the market.

CITY OF MERCHANTS: 1842–1940

Mature in age and robust in stature now, commerce in Dallas grew out of a weak and lonely infancy. Its progenitor was the city's founder, John Neely Bryan, hardy Texas pioneer. From his arrival in November, 1841, until the late spring of 1842 Bryan was the sole inhabitant of the embryonic Dallas; his store, like his townsite plan, existed only in his imagination. Then in the spring of 1842 John Beeman came with his family in an ox-drawn covered wagon. Bryan forthwith borrowed the wagon outfit, proceeded to Preston Bend, on Red River, and bought a "stock of goods" for the store he had in mind for the site at the junction of the Elm Fork and West Fork of the Trinity River. What he bought for this first Dallas commercial enterprise was powder and lead, tobacco and whiskey, the whiskey to sell at 25 cents a quart. This limited stock was hardly sufficient even for the simple needs of the few families who settled in the county. The Billingsleys, who came in the fall of 1842, recounted having made the long trek to the Red River to trade their buffalo hides and buy their supplies.

It was two years later, in 1844, that one Lundy, pioneer blacksmith who also "kept store," diversified by displaying alongside his one barrel of whiskey the allurements of three bolts of calico, priced at 25 cents a yard. Two more years passed before James M. Patterson and John W. Smith opened in 1846 the first complete Dallas store. The stock of merchandise had cost $700, and required two wagons to haul it from Shreveport, the trip taking forty days, due to the need for building rafts to cross the rivers. The store was of logs, veneered with four-foot hand-hewn boards.

Adam Haught opened Dallas' first saloon the same year, his log structure being floored first with puncheon and later with the first sawn lumber known to the community, produced by hand with a ripsaw. In 1845 a trading post was established at Cedar Springs, three miles above Dallas, where buffalo hides were exchanged for ammunition and groceries. "There was nothing else to buy," a patron recorded.

In 1850 hoopskirts, silk stockings, bridal bouquets, Bibles, accordions, Mustang liniment, snake-root and castor oil were listed in the inventory of a deceased merchant. This advance in merchandising may be attributed to the establishment by that time of a gristmill to which farmers from many miles around brought their grain. Naturally they visited the stores to trade.

Although Dallas boasted but thirty-nine inhabitants in 1848, the census of 1850 showed a rapidly increasing settlement of the county, with a population of 2,743, and the town, already the temporary county seat, began to expand commercially. Between 1848 and 1851 the county filled up rapidly. Dry-goods and grocery stores were established in Dallas and a few in the county at different points. Merchants then had to ship their goods from Houston and Shreveport at a cost of $3 per hundred pounds, and residents paid 18½ to 20 cents a yard for calico and all other goods in proportion except groceries which were a little higher.

A cotton gin was built in 1851, and a bridge was constructed across the river in 1855. The village was now prepared not only to attract farmers, but to process their products and to sell them merchandise.

The town's population in 1858 had grown to 430 and Alex Simon was advertising "cheap prices for dry goods, groceries, hardware, ready-made clothing, paints and oils." The next year there were 775 persons in the town, and during the Civil War period, 1860–65, it was established there were 2,000. This growth naturally expanded retail trade, but no notable changes occurred until the coming of the first railroad in 1872. The town then saw the establishment of numerous retail stores by "terminal merchants."

A group of storekeepers and pack-peddlers had been following the northward progress of the Houston & Texas Central Railroad, building from Houston. Some of these had stopped in Corsicana, where it was expected a second railroad, the Memphis, El Paso & Pacific (Texas & Pacific) would cross the Central. On learning that Dallas would be the junction point they made plans to move here, and in one day purchased 70 lots on Elm Street for new business houses. These merchants thereby provided the nucleus of the city's present retail business. Among them were names to be found today in the Dallas shopping district—Sanger Bros., Padgitt Bros., Huey & Philp, The Schoellkopf Company, Linz Bros., and W. A. Green Company.

Of these concerns the story of Sanger Bros. is perhaps the most colorful. Five youthful Sanger brothers emigrated from Obernbreit, Germany, in the early fifties. Arriving in America they found employment with retail establishments in Eastern cities. Sometimes working for as little as $2.50 a month with room and board, they saved money and advanced in their positions. In 1872 two of the brothers, Philip and Alex Sanger, came with the railroad to Dallas, where they rented a store 30x70 feet on Main Street, opposite the courthouse. They sold plows, dress goods, hams, notions, and groceries—in short, anything and everything. Seeing possibilities for more business, they decided to build a store 50x80 feet, and by 1898 had department stores in Dallas, Fort Worth, and Waco, and employed 1,000 persons, with an annual sales volume of $3,000,000. Sanger Bros. today is a monument to the business acumen of the "terminal merchants."

As the century waned, department stores supplemented their stocks with more sophisticated merchandise than plows and hams, needles, pins, and calico. One advertisement of the "gay nineties" read: "200 derbies at $1.00 each; men's Chesterfield overcoats $9.50; suits $7.60."

In Dallas, retail trade has been from the beginning a principal factor in its business life. Today farmers, ranchers, and citizens from smaller communities of North, Central, and West Texas crowd its downtown shopping area. On Saturdays shoppers overflow into "Deep Ellum," marketplace of tenant farmers and others seeking less expensive merchandise. Department and variety stores and women's specialty shops are largely concentrated on Elm Street, while Main Street is the center for men's wear. Dallas is widely known as a retail market for diamonds and fine jewels, imported objects of art, exclusive gowns, fine furs, and high quality shoes. Several modern Dallas shops have attained national fame as purveyors of exclusive merchandise.

A Federal survey of 1935 showed 18,050 persons employed in Dallas retail establishments, an annual payroll amounting to $16,493,000 and a yearly sales volume of $130,532,000. National business publications estimate that in 1938 the sales volume was $150,584,000 and the number of persons employed 20,000. The peak in retail volume was reached in 1929 with a total of $178,927,224.

F. O. B. DALLAS: MARKET
OF MILLIONS

Due to soil and climatic conditions, North Texas from its earliest settlement was the major region of wheat production in the Republic of Texas. Establishment of a horsepower gristmill at Dallas in 1846, and later steam flour mills, made the town a central market in North Texas for breadstuffs. In the late forties farmers brought their wheat from twenty to sixty miles to Dallas to have it ground. The flour was bolted by hand. In 1859 a train of ox-drawn carts driven by Mexicans came from Brownsville to procure flour. The singular appearance of these vehicles, their high-wheeled bodies thatched with straw and the oxen attached by yokes on their horns rather than on their necks, and the strange musical cries of their drivers proved of unending interest to the townsfolk, according to the *Dallas Herald*. Other caravans followed until Dallas was supplying flour to a large section of northern Mexico.

At the outbreak of the Civil War Dallas was selected as one of the important foodstuff bases for the Confederate army. It was the center of a fertile farming area far removed from actual conflict and a divisional quartermaster's headquarters was established here for the supply of corn, wheat, oats, and meats for the army of the trans-Mississippi department.

Prior to the first railroad in 1872 Dallas was still just another prosperous agricultural town. Aside from the southern flour trade it served as a wholesale market for only the neighboring communities. Railroad transport at once created a new economic era. Business of North and Central Texas was diverted from Shreveport, Houston, and Galveston. Large wholesale concerns were established in Dallas. The growing city became the shipping point for raw materials from the regions north and west of it to the nation's larger consuming markets.

The slaughter of buffaloes on the western plains which had begun in 1869 reached its peak as Dallas became a rail terminus. From the West came long wagon trains with dried buffalo hides. They passed over the new iron bridge across the Trinity into the town, where their drivers sold their loads, purchased supplies, and returned to the plains. Thousands of these hides were shipped to the North, there to be tanned and made into sleigh robes, not always to cover the riders' knees but often to be thrown over the back of the seat, to be leaned against and stylishly float out behind.

Farmers in this period had a shipping point for a wide distribution of their products, and this brought about expansion in farms. Before the railroads came, 12 acres was an average for wheat grown on farms. In 1874 one Dallas County farmer harvested 800 acres. The increase in agricultural acreage and products favorably affected the wholesale trade of the city. From the manufacturing centers of the East came every type of commodity—hardware, building accessories, drugs, clothing, shoes, and novelties, a great part of which was shipped out by wagons to smaller towns, to farms and ranches. This wagon trade evidently was important to the wholesale business. When a cold snap struck the area in 1881, the editor of the *Herald* became worried and commented:

> Due to the cold snap wagon trade has been almost suspended . . . everybody is lying around the fires. They will not try to do anything until the winter breaks, the rains cease and the roads get dry.

Improved farm machinery began to flow into Texas. Eastern firms established warehouses in Dallas, the geographic center of the rich blackland belt. These concerns also handled wagons, buggies, surreys, and coaches. Their showrooms were as inviting and as important to the time as the automobile showrooms are today.

For many years the implement houses clustered on the west side of what was then the retail district, and their volume of trade helped to give the city its high rank as a wholesale market. For the most part the business was handled by regional branches of national manufacturers. In 1893 farm implement sales reached a total of $10,000,000. Since then the vast plains of West Texas have gone under the plow and today the annual volume is double that amount.

Twenty thousand pounds of candy was purchased in one order by a wholesaler in the early eighties. A carriage dealer shipped 170 buggies in a week. Ready-made houses were cut out and shipped to West Texas, every house in several villages of that section coming from Dallas. Lightning rods arrived by the carload and made many salesmen prosperous. A contraption called Jewett's Patent Horse Detacher was stocked by a Dallas wholesaler. This device allowed the driver of a buggy to pull a lever and free the horse in case of a runaway.

Shortly after 1872 Sanger Bros. went into the wholesale business and introduced an innovation to the trade. Salesmen with samples called on outlying retailers rather than waiting for the customers to come into town. Their first "drummer" drove a team of mules attached to a spring wagon with two spare mules hitched behind. When both teams became fagged the salesman returned with his orders and again went on the road with fresh mules and new samples. By 1880 three hundred "commercial drummers" were listed as living here. Five years later there were 875 traveling men working out of the city and the wholesale trade had reached $18,902,500. By 1900 this had increased to $54,055,000, by 1905 to $85,000,000, and in 1910 to $125,000,000.

With the development of the oil industry in Texas, Oklahoma, Kansas, Louisiana, and Arkansas, Dallas became the hub of the mid-continent area, not from a producing or refining standpoint but as a strategic financial and equipment center. Two hundred and eighty-six firms, including operators, lease brokers, royalty owners, geophysicists, machinery supply firms, and drilling contractors are locally listed as engaged in the oil industry in 1939.

In the early 1920s the wholesale merchants organized the semiannual Southwestern Style Shows, which now attract to the city twice a year 5,000 to 6,000 retailers who purchase seasonal merchandise for consumers of the trade area. Flour has long since ceased to be Dallas' principal product, but its distribution was the beginning of the city's wholesale trade, which now surpasses in volume any one division of business, extends into half a dozen states, supplying an area containing 14,000,000 people with manufactured and processed farm machinery, oil well equipment, dry goods, shoes, dresses, millinery, clothing, drugs, chemicals, cosmetics, leather goods, and almost every other commodity known to modern commerce and industry.

The all-time high wholesale business was reached in 1929 with a volume of $728,157,439. The Federal mercantile census report for 1935 listed the Dallas wholesale trade as employing 9,802 persons with an annual payroll of $16,184,000; nine hundred and three firms had an annual volume of $409,668,000. National trade publications estimated the volume in 1938 at $500,940,000.

MANUFACTURING: MADE IN DALLAS, U. S. A.

Maxime Guillot, a French carriagemaker, settled in Dallas in 1852 and opened a shop at Elm and Houston Streets for the manufacture of wagons and carriages. Guillot had arrived at New Orleans in 1848 and started the following year for California in the gold rush, but stopped in Texas at old Fort Belknap, in Young County, where he remained repairing wagons for the United States army until he moved to Dallas. In 1854 he visited his native France and returned with four skilled carriagemakers. Save for the gristmills, merely processing plants, Guillot's shop was the town's pioneer factory. Carriages were made entirely by hand and were sold over a radius of 350 miles. Some were elaborately designed and lined with imported French damask; some were plain buckboards for prairie travel, but all were famed for their fine craftsmanship.

During the Civil War Guillot closed his shop to become superintendent of a small-arms factory for the Confederacy at Lancaster. After the close of the war he again manufactured wagons and carriages. He retired in 1869 with a comfortable fortune but lost the greater part of it financing searches for Jean Lafitte's buried treasure.

Carriagemaking flourished and died, but the manufacture of another necessity in early travel, saddles, developed in the meantime and today still is an important Dallas industry. In 1867 John R. Tenison opened a small saddle factory, the first in the town. G. H. Schoellkopf came to Texas to buy buffalo hides and in 1869 established a small saddlery shop on the courthouse square. By 1886 this company had expanded to the extent that it employed fifty workmen and in later years its trade became worldwide. Trailing the construction of the railroad in the early seventies Jesse D. Padgitt, a saddlemaker, was making pistol holsters and cartridge belts. Upon arriving in Dallas in 1874 he found a booming town, established a shop, and was joined the following year by his brother, William Padgitt, in the manufacture of saddles and leather goods. This firm also attained a worldwide business.

Before modern machinery, that part of the saddle known as the "tree" was actually made from a tree. A fork was selected, cut off, soaked in hot water, and then shaped and carved to pattern. Today the saddle-tree is made in a few minutes by machinery. In the heyday of the cattle industry cowboys' saddles sold for from $65 to $500, depending on the amount of hand-tooled leather and silver trimmings employed.

Strange as it seems, with all the cattle in Texas then and now, good leather has always been imported from the East. It has never been definitely determined whether it is the water, the climate, or the cattle feed, but even with skilled tanners brought from Europe, the Dallas area has not been able to produce first-class leather commercially. But the consuming market, the basic incentive to all manufacturing, was here, and in 1902 Dallas led the world in output of saddles. They were sold in Texas, adjoining states, Mexico, Cuba, and Africa. Cuban and Mexican trade was lost through protective tariffs in those countries and gradually the demand for saddles lessened throughout the Southwest.

In the eighties and nineties local leather concerns also made harness in large quantities, some sets selling for as much as $250. The peak of leather manufacturing was reached during the World War when saddles, kits, packs, and belts were made and sold to the United States and British governments. While saddles still are manufactured, the bulk of the business has turned to trunks, bags, and automobile accessories.

The first brewery in Dallas was operated by M. Monduel of the La Reunion French colony, about 1857. In the late seventies the Dallas Brewery began operation and in 1885 the Wagenhauser Brewing Association erected a $200,000 plant with a daily capacity of 100 barrels. Inspired perhaps by the report in the *Herald* that the city in 1884 had consumed 52,000 kegs of beer, the Wagenhauser Company staged a grand opening and donated 400 barrels of beer to the public. As a local paper described the celebration at old Shady View park. ". . . legions of friends paraded proudly and quaffed the amber liquid amid martial strains, booming cannons and beer-born eloquence." One large brewery and a beer bottling plant provide the basic local beer supply today.

As tea is to the Englishman so are soft drinks to the Texan. Housewives carry them home from the grocery, the corner drugstore delivers them, and many a businessman quaffs them several times a day. Year by year national concerns have established regional bottling and syrup plants here, until there now are more than twenty in operation. The city is headquarters for the Dr. Pepper Company and one of its two syrup plants is located here.

Swann Bros. opened a repair shop for cotton gins at Young Street and the Santa Fe tracks in the early eighties and began manufacturing complete machines in 1884. The following year Robert S. Munger came to Dallas and formed a company for the manufacture of gins. As a young man he had made improvements on his father's ginning machinery on their plantation near Mexia. As these changes were perfected Munger had them patented. Until then few improvements had been made in the gin since its invention by Eli Whitney in 1793. Munger's patents revolutionized cotton ginning. These include a lint flue system and battery condenser, double revolving box presses, elevator and blower for seed, elevator system and belt distributor, and the self-tamp system. Plants were established by other concerns, and since 1900 the industry has won world prominence. Seven Dallas concerns now ship gins and accessories to every country in which cotton is grown.

For many years after the cotton gin came into use the cottonseed was thrown away. Then it was discovered, about 1872, that valuable by-products could be obtained from this waste. In 1873 the first cotton oil mill was erected in Texas. This industry rapidly spread throughout the state and by 1935 the value of products made from cottonseed in Dallas exceeded $10,000,000. Lower grades of this vegetable oil are used in the manufacture of soap, candles, linoleum, and phonograph records. The more highly refined oil is used in cooking and the manufacture of oleomargarine, shortening compounds, and salad dressing. Closely allied with the shortening industry is the local manufacture of 100-pound tin-coated sheet-iron containers, of which four to five carloads are produced daily.

The first cotton cloth mill was established here in 1888 and opened with 250 employees, fifty of whom were skilled operators imported from Georgia. One thousand bales of cotton goods were shipped to retailers throughout North Texas in a single day as early as 1895. More than 10,000,000 yards of fabrics now are produced annually and 700 workers are employed in the textile industry.

Red flannel underwear, shirts of red and white flannel, and other garments then in vogue were manufactured here in the early eighties. About the same time the manufacture of cotton garments began and increased throughout the latter part of the century until in 1900 this became another of the city's important industries. There are now more than thirty plants engaged in the production of wash dresses, the value of which exceeds $5,000,000 annually. Overalls, tents, awnings, mattresses, window curtains, neckwear, and uniforms are some of the many commodities also manufactured from cotton. Silk and wool clothing are produced in smaller quantities.

Manufacture of millinery began in 1919 and by 1928 had grown to large proportions. Twenty-two factories now operate exclusively on the production of women's hats. These plants employ about 500 people and their annual output is valued at $2,000,000. The manufacture of men's hats of all makes is almost equally important, the output of three factories, two in Dallas and one in the county town of Garland, amounting to 500,000 hats yearly.

Two industries, a piano factory and a shoe factory, flourished in the early eighties. A Houston dealer ordered 100 pianos at one shipment, and in less than three months the shoe factory produced 21,950 pairs of boots, but for unrecorded reasons both enterprises closed down in a few years. Today shoes are the only article of men's, women's, or children's clothing not manufactured in Dallas.

Flour milling, which constituted an important food processing industry in the early days, continued to prosper, and in 1885 two mills produced 800 barrels a day. Four concerns now are engaged in this business, with a daily capacity of 3,800 barrels.

Emil Remond, a former member of La Reunion French colony, began experimenting in the late eighties with the white rock lying along the west bank of the Trinity River. These experiments led to the establishment of a cement plant in 1901 and another in 1907. Now the production in Dallas is more than 3,000,000 barrels of cement annually.

An important and interesting plant in the Dallas industrial group is that of Sutton, Steele & Steele, Inc., at 1031 Haskell Avenue, manufacturers of a line of separator machines for international markets. The machines of this firm now grade, clean, and sort 38,000,000 tons of coal annually, having effected a practical revolution in coal handling methods. Starting in the late 1880s with a futile attempt in California to devise a machine that would separate gold from sand, the founders of the firm by accident hit upon a principle on which they built later in Dallas machines that separated given elements by specific gravity and also by electric forces. Today their machines are in use in various sections of the United States and in several foreign countries in separating weevil-infested peas from sound peas; buckhorn seed; nuts, teas, spices, tobacco; and the elements of drugs, bagasse, bone char, fuller's earth, and other substances. The firm's machines are used in far-off New Zealand to separate impurities from kouri gum, a product vital in the manufacture of linoleum. A medal was awarded the firm in 1931 by the Franklin Institute of Philadelphia, signifying the highest honor in the field of applied physical science.

Mannequin models for shop windows are fabricated by another Dallas concern. Its rooms are filled with composition female heads, busts, torsos, arms, legs, and hands. When assembled they reflect the sophistication and chic of the modern young woman and have superseded their older sisters, the stiff wax figures of past decades. Modeled by a skilled sculptor, these figures, for effect, are always taller than the average woman, have hair made of grass, wool, or seaweed, and hands cast from life by a patented process. They range in prices from $57.50 to $130 and the market is nationwide.

Handmade dog knives are manufactured here and sold throughout the world for trimming dogs' coats. Improved ice tongs and complete equipment for the iceman is the product of another successful firm. The trays that hang on the door of Dallas automobiles in curb service are local inventions and are manufactured by two firms. So-called ten-gallon hats are the product of one Dallas plant and wholesale for $72 per dozen, while another factory makes a patented self-conforming hat for men.

A machine that scientifically administers anaesthetics in surgical operations was invented and is manufactured here. One of the few successful mechanical cotton choppers is a Dallas product. Eighteen concerns manufacture cosmetics. Another firm makes athletic uniforms. Chili con carne, tamales, tortillas, black-eyed peas, barbecued meats, roasted coffee, pecans, and dairy products are among the foods produced and packaged in Dallas. Closely allied to these are barbecue sauce and liquid smoke for curing and flavoring meats. The tamale canning factory established in 1925 in South Dallas by F. L. White is particularly interesting. By means of machinery invented and patented by the owner the factory is completely mechanized and the tamales untouched by human hands in the process of mixing, wrapping, and canning.

Though it is an inland city Dallas has a boat building enterprise. The demand for small boats for hunting, fishing, and pleasure on the lakes and streams in the vicinity keeps the plant busy. Repairs and rehabilitation of old boats are a source of additional revenue. About 50 new boats, rowboats and outboards included, was the plant's production in 1938.

A Dallas manufacturing plant turns out a unique artificial lure for use in fresh and salt water fishing. It is a "bleeding" bait, in the form of a casting plug that leaves a trail of crimson when drawn through the water, the theory being that trout, bass, crappie, and other game fish will assume it to be wounded prey and pounce on it more readily than on bait which they might expect to be more active in attempting escape.

An automobile assembly plant employs 2,500 workmen and has a daily output of 400 cars. East Texas logs are shipped to Dallas and shaved into excelsior. Paints to the value of $2,250,000 are manufactured and distributed throughout the South, Southwest, and Middle West. There are twelve candy factories, one of which also makes cakes and crackers and employs 1,000 workers. A million and a half pairs of full-fashioned silk hose are woven each year by one Dallas plant. There are also several furniture manufacturing plants in the city, one of the largest, the Kroehler Manufacturing Company, opening a new $250,000 factory in the summer of 1939. Among other miscellaneous and widely diversified articles produced in Dallas are gaskets, directional drilling precision instruments and other oil field equipment, paper and paper products of various kinds, storage batteries, steel and wrought iron, coffins, baby buggies, soap, yeast, paints, and chemicals.

The 1935 Federal manufacturing report for Dallas showed 12,126 persons employed in 508 manufacturing plants. Wages were $11,078,681 and the value of products $112,255,891. In 1937 there were 562 manufacturing plants listed in the city employing 14,654 persons with aggregate payrolls of $14,210,497. The value of manufactured articles in the latter year was $140,626,858, approaching the 1929 peak year total of $142,512,320.

TRANSPORTATION: PACK-SADDLE TO AIRPLANE

Exactly three decades elapsed between the coming of the first wagon to what within the year became the village of Dallas and the arrival here of the first railroad train. These thirty years witnessed the growth of the community from the cedar-pole lean-to shelter of its founder to a flourishing town with a population of perhaps 1,000. John Neely Bryan, the first settler in 1841, brought his few possessions on the back of his pony, and the few men who first followed him had to do likewise. In April, 1842, John Beeman and his family came by wagon to join Bryan.

Then came other wagons; crude handmade vehicles of the frontier, with wooden axles and ironed spindles on which the wheels were held by linchpins. Every wagon had a bucket of tar for lubrication and a paddle for its spreading hung upon the coupling pole just behind the rear axle. Most of these wagons were covered with canvas sheets on wooden hoops; on the road life was lived in the wagon, and the sheets could be used for shelter tents when in camp.

There were no highways for these first wagons, drawn by plodding oxen, and blazing the route of immigration to the Peters Colony and the nearby hamlet on the Trinity. Their drivers followed Indian and buffalo trails, or found their own way across the open prairies, fording streams as they came to them or using the occasional ferries. In these wagons were hauled the household goods and much of the food and foodstuffs of the pioneers, together with tools and utensils for conquering the wilderness. For all of the years until iron rails were laid in from the south they provided the one means of transport of goods into Dallas and the moving to market of the products of the territory roundabout.

In 1845 the National Central Highway from Austin to the Red River, by way of the Trinity River crossing at Dallas, became something more real than the surveyor's projection begun six years earlier. A road also had been opened northward to Preston on the Red River, and it was possible in good weather to make a round trip by wagon from Dallas to Jefferson or Shreveport on the Red River to the east in four weeks.

Fort Worth was reached by crossing the Trinity, first by ford or ferry and after 1855 by bridge, and thence riding westward through Hord's Ridge, the Oak Cliff of today. Elm Street continued to the east as the road to Kaufman, and there was

135

another highway to the southeast to Houston and the Gulf coast, whence came much of the town's merchandise, and where Dallas County cotton went for export. Freight rates by wagon to and from Houston ranged from $3 to $6 per 100 pounds, with an average load of 6,000 pounds requiring five or six yokes of oxen. In summer, when the road was good, a round trip could be made in four weeks. Two-wheeled oxcarts were often used for short haulage before horses became numerous enough to supplant the slower animals.

The Trinity River, upon which Bryan had located because of its potential use as a transportation channel to the sea, was quickly found inadequate, though efforts to utilize it for navigation were begun as early as 1849.

An increasing volume of commerce in the early fifties brought the establishment of wagon freight lines with more or less regular routes and schedules. Upon the wagon freighter and his cargoes Dallas built its prosperity in the period before the Civil War, and upon these carriers the railroads depended for many years as feeders for their more rapid transport.

Passenger travel was even more difficult than the movement of freight. First settlers either brought their own wagons, oxen, and horses into Texas or outfitted themselves at the Red River, at Houston, Jefferson, or Shreveport. Individuals traveled on horseback until the advent of stage coaches, which came into Dallas in 1856, when the place had attained sufficient importance to warrant the service. Several short stage lines had by 1858 made Dallas either a breaking point or a terminus, extending its communication facilities in every direction. Within another year four of the state's thirty-one major stage routes entered the town.

One could go by United States mail stages to Fort Belknap, via Fort Worth and Weatherford, in three days, and to Palestine, via Kaufman and Athens, in the same time. Connections could be had with through stages from San Antonio to St. Louis via Little Rock, and at Sherman or Fort Belknap with the famed Butterfield Overland line from St. Louis to San Francisco. A week was required to go to Austin, the capital. Marshall could be reached in three days, at a fare of $21. It cost $7 to go by stage to Kaufman, and while all fares were not quoted, the average charge prior to the Civil War was 15 cents per mile. Payment was demanded in specie, with currency taken only at its exchange and not its face value.

Stage passengers often were required to get out and walk to lighten the load at bad places in the crude roads and sometimes to aid in pulling the vehicle out of the mud. Most of the lines operated on a thrice-weekly schedule. The stages did not travel at night; passengers lay over at designated points en route. Service at times was interrupted by stage robberies and again by the theft of horses by Indians. Travelers and townspeople alike deplored these hardships and prayed for a railroad.

The late 1840s had seen the first steps taken which were to lead ultimately to the securing of a railroad for Dallas. In 1848 the Galveston & Red River Railroad was incorporated, the name being changed in 1856, when but two miles of track had been built, to the Houston & Texas Central Railway, with Houston as its southern terminus. The road was not to reach Dallas for another sixteen years, despite continued effort by the town's business interests. Many delays occurred in construction. In 1860, when the road had reached Millican, about 80 miles from Houston, the Civil War halted all building operations. At the end of the conflict, the company was in such financial condition that the franchise and property were sold at sheriff's auction.

The Texas legislature in 1865 passed a law providing that all railroads in the state should receive sixteen sections of free land for each mile of railroad completed. Under these grants the Houston & Texas Central was enabled to continue construction and received altogether from the state 4,764,160 acres of land. The railroad also borrowed $450,000 from the state general school fund, the legislature having authorized a loan of $6,000 from that fund for each mile of line completed.

On a hot summer day, July 16, 1872, a small wood-burning locomotive, pulling a combination train of freight-laden box cars and a single wooden passenger coach, rolled into the new station of the Houston & Texas Central Railway at Dallas, cheered by 5,000 or more persons. It came to a standstill at the diminutive frame depot, a mile east of the town, on what later came to be known as Central Avenue. Colonel John Henry Brown was master of ceremonies and chief orator for the occasion. John Neely Bryan, founder of the town, had a seat of honor on the speakers' platform.

For many of the crowd, who had come from as far away as Indian Territory, it was the first sight of a railroad train, and the townsfolk had provided a feast of barbecued beef and mutton wherewith to feed the multitude. To secure the road, citizens had given $5,000 in cash, 115 acres of land, and a free right-of-way into the town.

Freight to Houston and the Gulf coast could be moved on the railroad at less than half what it had cost when carried by slow-moving oxwagons, while former minimum passenger rates of 10 cents a mile on the stage coaches were cut to five cents.

Yet the railroad was not altogether popular. It was charged that the line had been located a mile away from the center of the existing town so that its builders could profit by real estate development in the vicinity of the terminal. So numerous were fatal accidents on the road that it was dubbed "the angel maker," a term that clung to it for two decades. The Central road later was extended to Denison, connecting there with the Missouri, Kansas & Texas Railroad, giving Dallas direct rail service to St. Louis and points north and east.

The Texas & Pacific Railroad was the second to enter Dallas. It represented a merger of the Vicksburg & El Paso Railroad, started in 1852 and frequently referred to as the Texas Western, and the Memphis, El Paso & Pacific Railroad, started in 1853. First planned to follow the 32nd parallel, the road was rerouted by act of the legislature to extend west from Tyler to the Brazos River, varying not more than five miles from a straight line. This would have made the road miss Dallas by eight miles.

Dallas citizens, however, were determined that the new road must come to their town, to form a junction with the Houston & Texas Central. The new railroad simply had to be secured. It was secured by means of a legislative "joker." Representing Dallas in the legislature was John W. Lane, a former mayor. Through his efforts a law was enacted containing a provision that the new road must pass within one mile of Browder Springs. If any other legislator knew the location of the springs, he remained silent. They were in Dallas, in the present Sullivan Park, between South Ervay, Pocahontas, Gano Streets, and Park Avenue. The springs were the source of the city's first public water supply.

Thus the Texas & Pacific came to Dallas, passenger service being started in 1873. This railroad in a period of three years was extended first to Eagle Ford, then to Fort Worth, and ultimately to El Paso. It secured in all 5,167,300 acres of state land as a subsidy and borrowed $150,000 from the state school fund.

137

Sponsored by local businessmen, construction of a third railroad was started in 1872 from Dallas itself. Known as the Dallas & Wichita Railroad Company, it was incorporated in 1871, and authorized to construct a line from Dallas to El Paso by way of the Red River. Aided by a subsidy of land from the state (sixteen sections per mile of construction) as well as $100,000 in cash from Dallas citizens, the work of building was begun.

Physical and financial status of this road, typical of most of the locally projected lines, is illustrated by the refusal of Sam Bass, noted train robber, to molest what he called "the Dallas & Which-away." The outlaw is quoted by a biographer as having made this statement as to why he declined to follow the suggestion of a holdup, made by one of his men:

> Well, I would have pulled it, but the poor thing was bogged up in Elm Bottom, and I'd as soon hit a woman as to tap it. Besides, if I had, I'd have had to rob the sick thing on credit, and that won't do in our business.

The financial depression of 1873 delayed the work for four years, but during 1878 eighteen miles of track were laid. Then, funds exhausted, work ceased. In 1881, the Gould interests took over the railroad and completed it to Denton. This line is now the Dallas-Wichita Falls division of the M-K-T (Katy) Railroad.

In 1880 two other railroad construction projects were started from Dallas—the Texas Trunk Railroad and the Dallas & Cleburne Railroad. After two years of unsuccessful operation the latter was sold to the Gulf, Colorado & Santa Fe. Daily train service was established and the line extended northeast to Paris to connect with the St. Louis & San Francisco. The Texas Trunk, chartered in 1879, was built southeast from Dallas to Kaufman and Cedar. When 30 miles had been completed in 1883 it was sold by the Federal court for $162,500 to satisfy eastern bondholders and later passed into control of the Southern Pacific system. It was then merged with the Sabine & East Texas Railroad to form the Texas & New Orleans Railroad, a part of the present Southern Pacific lines, and extends from Dallas to Beaumont.

Dallas by 1885 had five railroads in operation with passenger and freight traffic increasing. A report of the last three days of August, 1887, gives the following concerning freight movement in carload lots; Receipts—merchandise 30, coal 11, lumber 21, wood 28, railroad ties 11, ice 5, wheat 16, oats 1, hay 2, produce 12, beer 3, whisky 1, machinery 1, hardware 1, oil 3, paper 1, miscellaneous 13. Shipments—general merchandise 51, hay 2, flour 5, bran 1, machinery 5, lumber 2, coal 2, miscellaneous 4.

Another railroad was added when in 1886 the Missouri, Kansas & Texas Railroad (Katy) completed its line from Greenville to Dallas.

In 1886, the state legislature passed an act which was to have a far-reaching effect upon the railroads as well as upon Dallas itself. This enactment, known as the Alien Land Law, was the result of a political crusade against the rail lines. Under its provisions suit could be brought against a railroad to recover any land given by the state under previous enactments. While ultimately held unconstitutional, the law while in force occasioned much trouble to innocent parties and retarded further railroad building.

A seventh rail line did not enter Dallas until August 1, 1898, when the first train of the St. Louis & Southwestern Railroad of Texas (Cotton Belt) arrived. For a time, trains of this road operated into Dallas over the Santa Fe tracks from Paris, but since 1910 have entered the city over the Rock Island tracks from Irving. Under the latter arrangement, 35 miles was cut off the previous route from Dallas to Texarkana and Memphis.

Continued efforts of Dallas citizens, supported by cash donations, within a few years brought three more railroads into the city. In 1903, having built into Dallas from Fort Worth, the Chicago, Rock Island & Gulf Railway's first train arrived, coming direct from Chicago. A year later, this road returned all public subscriptions, amounting to $62,000, saying the company preferred to pay its own way.

With the shortest route between Dallas and Houston as an inducement for patronage, the Trinity & Brazos Valley Railway opened service into Dallas in 1907. This road later secured trackage rights over the Southern Pacific as far as Galveston. In 1930, it became a part of the Burlington-Rock Island Railway and as such forms a portion of two other trunk lines.

Arrival on June 1, 1925, of the Fort Worth & Denver City Railway's first train in Dallas was made the occasion of a public celebration. Chartered in 1872, the railroad was constructed over a period of years from Fort Worth to Denver. Its extension to Dallas gave the city a direct rail route to the Colorado Rockies.

Freight service into and out of Dallas also is afforded by the Louisiana, Arkansas & Texas Railroad under trackage agreements.

Seven years after enactment of a law by the legislature requiring the several railroads entering Dallas to build a joint passenger terminal, Dallas' Union Station was opened in 1916. The new passenger terminal building and incidental facilities cost $5,500,000. Construction was begun in January, 1914, with Jarvis Hunt of Chicago as architect and C. H. Dana as chief engineer. Building of the Union Station climaxed several years of negotiations with the railroads by Dallas businessmen.

Previously five separate stations were used by the various lines. The Missouri, Kansas & Texas station was at Market Street and Pacific Avenue. That of the Houston & Texas Central and the Texas & New Orleans (Southern Pacific) was at Pacific and Central Avenues. The Gulf, Colorado & Santa Fe, the Chicago, Rock Island & Gulf, and the St. Louis & San Francisco utilized jointly a station on Commerce Street, on the site of the present Santa Fe Building. The Texas & Pacific station was on Pacific Avenue, between Lamar and Griffin Streets, while the present Greyhound Bus Terminal at Commerce and Lamar Streets had been used as a depot by the St. Louis-Southwestern and the Trinity & Brazos Valley. After the Union Station had been completed, the Texas & Pacific removed its tracks from Pacific Avenue.

Dallas today (1940) is served by eight trunk-line railroads, operating thirty-three passenger trains and numerous freight trains into and out of the city each 24 hours.

Streetcars were run in Dallas for the first time in the spring of 1873, following completion of tracks on Main Street from the courthouse to the Houston & Texas Central railway station, one and one-third miles eastward, at what is now Central Avenue. Service was inaugurated on February 7, after the facilities had been tried out by city and county officials during a celebration on the preceding night. Local businessmen had subscribed $10,000 to the capital of the Dallas City Railroad Company, the builders, of which G. M. Swink was president.

The cars, two in number, were but ten feet long, each drawn by two mules. Until the second railroad started operation only one car was used. The vehicles were named—one for Belle Swink, a daughter of the first president of the company, and the other for John Neely Bryan. One chivalrous driver carried a plank on the front

139

platform for use as a bridge between the car and the wooden sidewalks in bad weather as a convenience for women passengers. Length of the skirts of the period made this a very acceptable courtesy. Sometimes the mules were frightened and ran away, and one animal was killed when the car ran over him going down what then was a steep hill on Main Street just east of Akard Street. On another occasion, before final electrification of the lines in 1889, all of the street cars and their mule motors were impounded by writ in a suit of the city treasurer for taxes, payment of which later in the day relieved the traffic impasse.

A second line was constructed following the incorporation of the Dallas Street Railroad Company, August 2, 1875, extending two miles on Austin Street, Ross Avenue, and San Jacinto Street. A third line was built in 1876 by the Commerce & Ervay Street Railroad Company and, following the thoroughfares named, extended east and south a mile and a quarter.

The Dallas Belt Street Railway Company was formed March 19, 1884, beginning construction in May of that year on a line completed in August, extending from Ross Avenue and Lamar Street south on Lamar to Jackson, east to Akard, thence south to St. Louis, east to Harwood, north to McKinney, and southwest to Lamar, a distance in all of three and three-quarters miles. Its completion gave Dallas an aggregate of approximately eight miles of street railway. The four street railway companies were combined in 1887 into the Dallas Consolidated Street Railway Company.

Prior to electrification mules generally were utilized for power, although cars running to Oak Cliff, North Dallas, and an area known as the Colonial Hill section were drawn by small steam locomotives. Companies utilizing the latter mode of power were the Dallas & Oak Cliff Railroad Company (1887), the Dallas Rapid Transit Railroad Company (1888), and the North Dallas Circuit Railroad Company (1889).

By merger and purchase, the number of street railway companies had been reduced to four by 1910, all controlled by Stone & Webster of Boston. These were the Dallas Consolidated Electric Street Railway Company, the Metropolitan Street Railway Company (North Belt), the Rapid Transit Street Railway Company (South Belt), and the Northern Texas Traction Company.

The present company, operating all street railways in Dallas, is the Dallas Railway & Terminal Company. Incorporated September 22, 1917, it operates over more than 125 miles of trackage, with motor buses in many instances serving as auxiliaries to the electric cars.

Interurban electric lines touching Dallas have been in operation since 1902, the first (Dallas-Fort Worth) being constructed by the Northern Texas Traction Company. Operation was successful for a number of years, but the increase of automobiles and advent of motor bus service so reduced revenues that in 1935 it ceased operation, the road being dismantled.

The Texas Traction Company constructed the second interurban line, between Dallas and Sherman, in 1908. Other interurban lines were those of the Southern Traction Company from Dallas to Waco and to Corsicana (1912) and those of the Dallas Railway & Terminal Company from Dallas to Terrell (1923) and Dallas to Denton (1924), both abandoned in 1932.

During 1916 surviving roads were consolidated as the Texas Electric Railway, which operated them until 1931, when the company went into receivership. The Texas Electric Railway Company (1936) is successor to the Texas Electric Railway, and conducts both passenger and freight services north from Dallas to Denison, south to Corsicana and Waco.

Bus lines as organized companies date from June 1, 1928, when motor bus rules and regulations were adopted by the Railroad Commission of Texas. Prior to that time intercity buses and trucks were operated more or less haphazardly by individuals. With the promulgation of regulatory measures, franchises were awarded to the several bus and truck owners.

Gradual increase and systemization of the operation of motor buses and motor trucks has resulted (1932) in operation of 226 passenger schedules every 24 hours by seven motor bus lines through or into Dallas, the service either directly or through connecting lines extending to all sections of the country. Forty motor truck lines operate approximately 100 freight schedules each 24 hours.

Highways entering Dallas are US 67, 75, 77, 80, and 175, and State 1, 1-B, 6, 14, 15, 40, 68, 78, 114, 183, 197, and 246.

Finishing Felt Hats, Davis Hat Company

Knitting Silk Stockings, Baker-Moise Company

Setting Curls on Mannequins, Standard Fixture Company

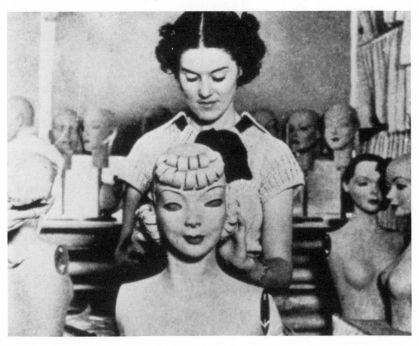

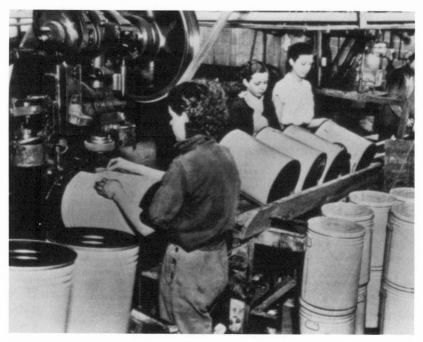

Labeling Cans, Proctor & Gamble Company

Assembly Line, Ford Motor Company

Workers at Loom

Market Room, Cotton Exchange

Sampling Cotton, Cotton Exchange

AVIATION: OVERNIGHT
TO EVERYWHERE

The "Aerial Queen," lighter-than-air dirigible with an under-carriage for passengers, was the first airship seen in Dallas. Brought to Oak Cliff by a carnival company, the "Aerial Queen" thrilled the populace with daily flights during a two-week period in April and May of 1908.

Previously Dallas' experience with navigation of the air had been confined to balloon ascensions, the first of which was made by a Professor Wallace April 16, 1861, when the local newspaper asserted that "this aerial navigator will furnish a through ticket to the other side of the Jordan to anyone who wishes to make the trip with him into parts unknown."

As early as 1893 Frank McCarroll of Dallas had been thought at least eccentric by his acquaintances because of his interest and faith in the possibility of man's flying. Experimenting, McCarroll used captive buzzards in his study of the air and the principles of aeronautics. In 1904 McCarroll built an airplane and it is claimed made one or more successful flights. He later built and flew several planes and received patents on retractable landing gear and other aids to air navigation.

General skepticism about heavier-than-air flying in Dallas was demonstrated by the editor of the city's largest newspaper when in 1903 the press wires brought the story of the Wright Brothers' successful flight at Kitty Hawk, North Carolina, and he telephoned to Dayton, Ohio, home of the inventors, for verification of their achievement.

Colonel E. H. R. Green, son of the famous Hetty Green, who was then residing in Dallas, purchased a Wright airplane for delivery in February of 1909. He was requested by the Dallas Fair authorities to have the ship here in time for the fall fair. The September 12 issue of a local paper carried an illustrated story on Colonel Green and his plane, wherein he asserted the machine was easy to fly, though it was not flown in Dallas. In October of the same year Frank Goodale circled the tallest buildings in town in a Stroebel dirigible and gave exhibitions at the State Fair.

All railroads made a special rate for an aviation meet in Dallas February 25–27, 1910. This meet was sponsored by the Dallas Chamber of Commerce and Louis

147

Paulhan, French aviator. Paulhan was prevented from flying by a Federal court injunction, but Otto Brodie demonstrated a Curtis biplane, described as 26 feet long, weighing 400 pounds, and powered by a four-cylinder gas engine, the whole mounted on three bicycle wheels. This was the first flight of a heavier-than-air machine in Dallas, and was the beginning of a series of meets at which the public was entertained by European aviators on tour.

Among the most notable of these were Roland Garros, Rene Simon, and John B. Moissant, all Frenchmen with international reputations as pioneers of the air. It was in Dallas January 9, 1911, that Garros, losing his way above the clouds, made a continuous flight of 45 miles. Moissant's metal plane, flown by Rene Barrier, two days earlier had attained an altitude of 4,420 feet over Fair Park, with 100,000 persons watching. Rules for this meet provided that, when air conditions prevented flying, spectators would be given "wind checks" good when the breezes had subsided. The Moissant International Aviators made an appearance in March, 1912, featuring Miss Mathilde Moissant, who at the time held the altitude record for women flyers.

During the crucial years in the history of flying from 1912 to 1918, Dallas kept constantly abreast of developments in the field. A Dallas-built flying machine, designed and constructed by Harry L. Peyton, a youth of nineteen, was successfully tried out near the city in March, 1912. Late in 1914 another youth educated in Dallas, Morris M. Titterington, who had graduated from the Bliss Electrical School in Washington, D.C., in 1913, was employed by the Sperry Gyroscope Company of Brooklyn, N.Y., in perfecting a stabilizer to prevent airplanes from turning over in the air, and on February 10, 1915, sailed for England to instruct English army pilots in the use of this device. Titterington invented the earth induction compass that made possible Colonel Lindbergh's trans-Atlantic flight and many other important safety devices. He was killed in 1928 in an airplane crash at Snyders, Pennsylvania. Later in the same year (1915) during the State Fair Art Smith, world famous aviator of the period, appeared in Dallas and thrilled thousands with his spectacular night flights and daring stunts in the face of adverse weather conditions. On January 8, 1917, Lestere Miller, a Dallas aviator, pioneered an air lane between Dallas and Fort Worth, making the initial flight in thirty-seven minutes.

Captain William Erwin of Dallas made aviation history in the American air force overseas during the World War and returned to become perhaps the most colorful character in the aviation annals of the city. Captain Erwin piloted the locally-sponsored "Spirit of Dallas," one of the three ill-fated planes which disappeared in the Dole $25,000 prize flight from San Francisco to Honolulu in 1927. Erwin left Oakland, California, August 19 with Alvin Eichwaldt, wireless operator, in one of the first planes equipped with radio for ocean flights and Eichwaldt's tragic "we are in a tailspin" was the last message from the Dallas man, once declared by General William Mitchell to be the most valuable American aviator in the World War.

May 12, 1926, Dallas folk celebrated the departure of the first air mail plane of National Air Transport for Chicago, a Curtis-Wright Carrier Pigeon, an open cockpit biplane piloted by Herbert L. Kindred. National Air Transport served Dallas eight years. After pioneering the Dallas-Kansas City-Chicago route, NAT was merged with other companies into United Air Lines. First passenger service was inaugurated in July, 1928, between Dallas and San Antonio and Houston by Texas Air Transport.

In the following half-dozen years numerous new air transportation companies were formed, and almost as rapidly disappeared in various mergers and eliminations incident to the hectic struggle for air mail contracts and the growing air passenger business. Dallas was served either as terminal or port of call by Texas Air Transport, Southwest Air Fast Express (Halliburton Lines), Crowell Airlines, Western Air Express, and Wedell-Williams lines during this period, with extension of routes to New York via Kansas City, St. Louis, and Chicago; to Los Angeles; Atlanta; and New Orleans; in Texas to San Antonio, Brownsville, Amarillo, Houston, and Galveston.

Stabilization of the air transport industry after the readjustment of air mail contracts in 1934 left Dallas with improved service afforded by American Airlines, Delta Air Lines, and Braniff Air Ways, which with their connections give the city practically overnight mail, passenger, and air express routes to both east and west coasts and to all larger points in Texas and the South and Southeast.

Dallas has been visited by many notable flyers. While here in 1910, Glen H. Curtis predicted that "airplanes will be of commercial value some day." Colonel Charles A. Lindbergh was a visitor September 26, 1927. Captains Dieudonne Coste and Maurice Bellonte in 1930 flew from Paris to Dallas with only a single stop in New York, to win a $25,000 prize offered by Colonel William E. Easterwood of Dallas, arriving here September 3. Douglas (Wrong Way) Corrigan was greeted by enthusiastic throngs in Dallas after his spectacular unannounced flight from New York to Ireland in 1938.

Love Field airport, municipally owned and operated, is located six miles from the central business district. This field was developed by Dallas businessmen and the first plane flight from it was made January 24, 1917. On November 5, 1917, Love Field was established as a United States army air training base. Training of hundreds of army aviators at Love Field made Dallas an air-minded city. In 1927 the City of Dallas purchased the major acreage of the field and in 1931 acquired additional land, making a total of 276 acres.

Beginning July 1, 1939, the United States government set up a school of instruction for army flyers at the Dallas Aviation School, at Love Field, with classes of sixty men given preliminary flight training.

Purchase of Hensley Field, 13½ miles southwest of the city, by the Dallas city government was made in 1928. This field is leased to the United States War Department for the use of government planes.

TRINITY NAVIGATION: EYES TOWARD THE SEA

For almost ninety years the people of Dallas have endeavored to make navigation of the Trinity River a reality. Inspired by the vision of a busy waterway between their city and the Gulf they long have pleaded with state and Federal governments to appropriate the funds necessary for its creation. They have contributed money for steamboats, locks, and dams. But each time, through no fault of their own, realization has been deferred. The story of Trinity River navigation is that after all these years Dallas is still endeavoring to become an inland port. It is a story of many failures, yet one of remarkable perseverance and tenacity of purpose.

Before the railroads came Texans turned to water transportation in preference to the slow and costly ox-drawn freight wagons. As early as 1836 steamboats plied the lower Trinity, penetrating as far north as Magnolia, a point 100 miles south of where John Neely Bryan was to establish Dallas five years later. These early boats carried cargoes of assorted merchandise which their masters traded along the route for farm products, returning to Galveston laden mainly with cotton. This was quite enough for the pioneer realty promoter W. S. Peters who, in advertising his colony, freely represented Dallas as an inland port, much to the disappointment of the colonists when they arrived.

When Dallas was less than a year old, at least one of its ten or twelve inhabitants believed in the possibility of downstream navigation to the Gulf Coast. John Billingsley, who arrived late in the fall of 1842, relates the incident as follows:

> One Smith, an old beggar, was lying around our camp begging for something to eat and none of us were stocked with provisions so he was advised to go where more people lived and provisions more plentiful so he concluded he would go to Houston and go by water. So he went to work and dug a canoe or rather a trough out of an old ash log and one day in the afternoon he launched his craft with a lot of sand in the bow on which he put some fire and a few pones of bread we got for him. He tooked [sic] his seat in the stern and shoved out into the main channel and straightening his bark with the current with a hunk of bread in one hand and a paddle in the other he disappeared around a point of land. That was the last seen of him.

150

Dallas citizens joined the movement for improving the Trinity as early as 1849, when John Neely Bryan, John M. Crockett, and the Reverend James A. Smith were chosen as delegates to a convention for that purpose, held in Huntsville.

The first attempt at navigation from Dallas was made in March, 1852, by J. W. Smith, a merchant, when he built a flatboat to carry his cotton downstream to market. Smith named the boat the *Dallas* and on March 2 with Adam Haught, the town's pioneer saloonkeeper, as captain, they started for Porter's Bluff, 40 miles from Dallas. The boat carried twenty bales of cotton and several bundles of cowhides.

After four months of tedious work with poles, oars, and axes they arrived at their destination. Here it was necessary to transfer the cargo to wagons to ensure it arriving in Houston before the next year's crop came on the market. Not long afterward the *Dallas* struck a snag and sank.

In 1853, the year after congress had authorized a survey of the river with a view to improving its navigation, army engineers reported: "The Trinity is the deepest and least obstructed river in the State of Texas." The following year the *Mary Clifton*, captained by Jack Swann, plied between Galveston and Porter's Bluff. It is estimated that as many as one hundred boats navigated the lower Trinity before the Civil War. But with the commencement of hostilities and for some years afterward river transportation became a negligible part of the commerce of Texas.

On May 5, 1868, Dallas for the first time heard the whistle of a steamboat and saw *Job Boat No. 1* tie up at the foot of Commerce Street. James McGarvey, captain and part owner, had built this sternwheeler at Galveston at a cost of $14,564. Sixty feet in length, the boat had a load capacity of 26 tons and was propelled by a 12-horsepower engine.

McGarvey had left Galveston just a year and four days previous to landing at Dallas. Along the route he had stopped for the usual trading and much of his time had been consumed in clearing the river of snags. The townspeople made a holiday of the event, feted the captain, presented him with deeds to several town lots and a purse of $5000 cash.

Financially the trip was a success for McGarvey, for besides his trading and bonuses he had a contract with Kaufman and Dallas counties to receive $15,000 if he landed his boat at Dallas. After a short stay he steamed back to Galveston, sold his half interest and placed his brother in command. *Job Boat No. 1* never reached Dallas again. On the second trip she sank near Porter's Bluff.

But the coming of the first steamboat so enthused the citizens that they built a boat of their own, launching it December 17, 1868. The steamer was christened the *Sallie Haynes*, in honor of the belle of the town, the daughter of Dr. J. W. Haynes. The people celebrated the launching and the town paper published this doggerel from the pen of a local poet:

Some people say it is all stuff,
It never will reach Porter's Bluff,
But if the captain don't run out of means,
He'll land her safe in New Orleans.

The *Sallie Haynes* was 87 feet long with a beam of 18 feet. Several trips were made as far as Magnolia but eventually the boat struck a snag and sank about 40 miles down the river.

In the next two years Lockridge's Bluff and Porter's Bluff were visited by steam-

151

boats during periods of high water. The Trinity River Navigation Company, with headquarters in Liberty, was incorporated in 1871, and in the next few years the river channels were cleared as far as Magnolia. Arrival of the first railroad in Dallas in 1872 completely diverted interest from river navigation.

During the 1880s several bills for making the Trinity navigable were introduced in the legislature. One bill, drawn by Colonel A. T. Raney of Anderson County, provided that any company that would clear the Trinity so as to make it navigable for a given number of miles would be given four sections of land for each mile cleared.

When the bill came before the House, the member from Brazos County created amusement by offering this amendment:

Provided, that one half of the land thus appropriated shall be used to bore artesian wells at the headwaters of the Trinity River to furnish the necessary water.

Immediately Colonel Raney wrote and offered an amendment to the amendment which read:

Provided, the other half shall be used to buy gimlets to bore the member from Brazos for the "simples."

This sarcasm defeated the bill, but the first suggestion might not have been so much a case of the "simples," for at the beginning of the century Captain C. H. Riche, an army engineer, reported that the use of dams and artesian wells would make the Trinity navigable.

In 1890 the movement for river navigation was revived by Dallas business leaders. Money was pledged and a new company formed and named the Trinity River Navigation and Improvement Company. In 1892 Congress was asked, but without success, for $500,000 to open the river. Still determined, the company built a boat named the *Dallas*, specially constructed to pull snags. This vessel cost $10,000 and 13,000 people attended its launching. A trial trip down the river was made and the *Dallas* returned with a load of cordwood. This was sold at auction, the first cord bringing $10 and some of the sticks fifty cents each as souvenirs.

The navigation company on March 8, 1893, bought the steamboat *H. A. Harvey, Jr.*, planning to run it between Galveston and Dallas. Built in New Orleans, it was 113 feet long with a beam of 19½ feet, of 100 horsepower. The tonnage was 59.96 and the cotton capacity 600 bales. Passenger capacity was listed at 150.

Piloted by Captain J. W. Rodgers the steamer left Galveston March 14 and after much difficulty from bridge spans arrived at the Oak Cliff bridge on May 20. Again the people of Dallas celebrated and again their hopes for river navigation soared. A temporary dam was built at McCommas' Bluff, 13 miles below Dallas. The *Harvey* and the *Dallas* made several pleasure trips in this locked section of the river. One trip was on June 17, 1895, when the *Harvey*, elaborately decorated, took fifty-six couples to Miller's Ferry for a dance at a newly constructed pavilion. Early in 1898, after being idle for a year, the *H. A. Harvey, Jr.* steamed downstream and away from the city of Dallas. It had been sold for use on the Calcasieu River in Louisiana. The same year the snagboat *Dallas* was dismantled and sold.

Notwithstanding these cumulative failures in the long effort to navigate the Trinity popular interest was not ended. Congress had made aggregate appropriations of $3,000 and $3,500, and again in 1899 appropriated $7,000 for a survey of the stream from Galveston to Dallas. Thus encouraged, the navigation company sent Commodore S. W. S. Duncan and Colonel Robert E. Cowart to Washington to seek more aid from the Federal government. Colonel Cowart represented the Trinity navigation movement in Washington for several years.

In 1902 Congress appropriated $400,000 and during the next twenty years spent several million dollars in constructing locks and dams on the river below Dallas.

In 1904 a congressional committee made an inspection trip in the steamer *Frank P. Holland*, named for a Dallas publisher and former mayor. Other boats in use on the river at this period included the *Commodore Duncan*, the *Nellie Maurine*, the *Katy Putnam*, and the *Charles T. Gray*.

Dallas citizens in 1905 contributed $66,000 with which to build a dam at Parsons' Slough, about 26 miles below the city. In this period nine locks were constructed but the World War halted the work. New navigation companies were formed in 1916 and in 1920, but the whole project was abandoned in 1921. The dams and locks which had cost millions of dollars were sold for trivial sums.

Becoming increasingly dissatisfied with rail freight rates the Fort Worth and Dallas Chambers of Commerce in 1930 formed the Trinity River Canal Association. This name was later changed to Trinity Improvement Association. A survey of the river was made by Colonel E. H. Marks in 1934, the work financed by a PWA grant of $93,000. By 1938 all the Federal agencies assigned to studies of improvement of the Trinity had made favorable reports in their preliminary findings. At that time the War Department and the Department of Agriculture were engaged in preparing a coordinated report which embraced all the phases of the project. Approximately $400,000 of government funds were set aside for this study, which was completed late in 1939, with a report to be made to Congress at its 1940 session.

VIADUCTS: TRAFFICWAYS FOR MILLIONS

Though a southwestern prairie city remote from the great waterways of the country, Dallas has always been in a peculiar sense a river town, conditioned by its situation on the banks of the Trinity. John Neely Bryan built his first rude lean-to at the foot of the bluffs along the river only to have it washed away a few months later by a swift and treacherous rise, and since that time the Trinity in its fickle moods has alternately tantalized the city with will-o'-the-wisp possibilities of inland navigation and ravaged its lower sections with sudden and unpredictable floods.

Chief among the problems of metropolitan development the river has raised for Dallas has been that of uninterrupted communication with its Oak Cliff section on the western bank. Normally the Trinity at Dallas is a sluggish creek meandering across the plains, but during the spring and fall rains it can become a churning, swirling sea of muddy debris-filled water, and with a mile-wide stretch of flat bottom land cutting the city almost squarely in half the problem of continuous intracity communication has been a pressing one almost from the beginning. How Dallas has solved this problem with a network of bridges and viaducts is in itself a major civic saga.

When Dallas was a village and for some years afterward a ferry provided the only communication between the eastern and western banks of the Trinity. The first permanent span across the river was a wooden toll bridge at the foot of Main Street built by Alexander Cockrell and the Dallas Bridge & Causeway Company in 1855. This stood on substantially the same site as the present Commerce Street viaduct. It was replaced in 1872 by an iron toll bridge, the profits from which are alleged to have run as high as 54 percent annually. In 1882 this bridge was purchased by the County of Dallas for $42,000, becoming the first free bridge across the Trinity. After a particularly destructive flood an attempt was made at permanent all-weather communication by the construction of a "long wooden bridge," the piers of which way still be seen in the bottoms near Cadiz Street in South Dallas. This bridge was made by sinking iron cylinders to bedrock, filling them with crushed rock, and then pouring cement over the whole to form the base for a wooden superstructure. It already had been condemned as unsafe when the great flood of 1908 swept it away.

154

This left the Zang Boulevard turnpike, an earthen fill with a single steel span across the river channel slightly to the north of the present Houston Street Viaduct, the only means of communication with Oak Cliff, and when there was even a moderate flood the commuters of those days had to take to boats. About this time G. B. Dealey, publisher of the *Morning News*, returned from a trip to Kansas City with the idea of securing for Dallas an intracity causeway similar to the one there. From his proposal sprung the Houston Street Viaduct, begun October 24, 1910, and opened to traffic February 22, 1912, with great fanfare and acclaim as the longest concrete bridge in the world. It was designed by County Engineer J. F. Witt, with I. G. Hedrick, designer of the Kansas City causeway, as consulting engineer, and was constructed at a total cost of $675,000.

The Houston Street Viaduct, though now only one of five similar structures, is still in use, and remains the most important artery of traffic between downtown Dallas and the older part of Oak Cliff. The concrete portion is 5,106 feet in length, supported by 51 concrete arches. Along each side of the central roadway are wide sidewalks protected with breast-high concrete copings, with concrete lamp posts set at regular intervals so that the viaduct, viewed after nightfall from any of Dallas' skyscrapers, is a beaded ribbon of light. A fine view may be obtained from the middle of this viaduct of the massed and pyramided downtown skyline of Dallas in one direction and of the wooded heights of Oak Cliff with its several tall buildings in the other.

Three of the other viaducts that link Oak Cliff and Dallas date from the early 1930s and the Ulrickson Plan bond issue, which made possible a fuller realization of the Kessler Plan that thirty years ago provided a blueprint for the future development of Dallas. All enter the city proper through underpasses tunneling the railroad yards that fringe the eastern edge of the bottoms, and the railroads shared the cost of their construction with the city and county. The Cadiz Street Viaduct, first in point of time to be completed, was finished in 1932, and the distribution of costs in its case may be taken as typical. On the underpass the city expended on construction and lighting $95,129 and the railroads involved contributed a total of $218,400. On the viaduct itself the county spent $474,000. The Corinth Street Viaduct, costing $745,500, was completed in 1933, and the Lamar-McKinney Viaduct, costing $614,769, was finished in 1934. Parts of the Commerce Street Viaduct were also completed during these years.

To the north of the city there is another concrete bridge over the Trinity channel connecting Industrial Boulevard with the Irving-Fort Worth Road. It is used chiefly by bus lines and was built by the county at a cost of $100,000 in 1930. The motorist may obtain a good idea of all of the viaducts as well as an excellent view of the Dallas skyline by turning onto Industrial Boulevard and proceeding south to the Corinth Street Viaduct. Another striking panorama of Dallas may be obtained from the Bonnie View Road, connecting with the Forest Avenue Bridge still farther south, which, along with the Holmes Street Bridge, constitutes an additional link between Dallas and Oak Cliff.

The triple underpass at the eastern end of the Commerce Street Viaduct was the last and crowning project to be completed. It was formally opened in May, 1936, and necessitated moving 19 railway tracks 125 feet westward to provide the proper grade for approaches. It cost the Federal government $500,000, the State Highway Department $132,000, and the City of Dallas $273,000, the railroads bearing the remainder of the expense necessary for its construction, in addition to that incident to the removal of their tracks. The Commerce Street Viaduct beyond, built by the county, cost $642,000, and can accommodate six lanes of traffic, three in each direction.

The triple underpass, a triumph of modern engineering skill with its electrically illuminated tunnels and maze of separate traffic lanes and signal lights scientifically guarding its approaches, constitutes a magnificent entrance to the heart of the city. Sweeping under the yards of the Union Terminal Passenger Station it emerges directly into the three principal east and west thoroughfares of downtown Dallas—Commerce, Main, and Elm Streets. Carrying these streets across the barrier of Union Station tracks to their original terminus of the east bank of the Trinity, it marks in Dallas the final triumph of man over nature and of civic planning and public enterprise over the accident of haphazard metropolitan development.

LABOR: ORGANIZATION AND STRUGGLES

Organized labor history in Dallas goes back for sixty years, almost to the beginning of local industrial development. Typographical Union No. 173, probably the oldest local in the city, obtained its charter on October 6, 1885. A carpenters' union was organized a year later. A few crafts in the city had before this been affiliated with the Knights of Labor, organized in April, 1882.

A composing room squabble at the plant of *Dallas Herald* in April, 1883, between union-minded printers and the foreman is the first recorded instance of a labor dispute in Dallas. The first real strike in which Dallas was involved was the railway walkout which occurred the following summer. The tie-up of freight trains, the local newspaper reported, forced the bringing into Dallas of large numbers of wagons for freighting. The next strike of local concern was that of 1886, involving about 3,700 employees of railways in Texas. On March 19 of that year, Jay Gould wrote to the Merchants' Exchange of Dallas (later the Chamber of Commerce) thanking that body for its support of the Missouri Pacific Railway, which had suffered a secondary strike, originally called on another railroad.

Among the early successful strikes in Dallas was that of the carpenters when they went out May 6, 1890, for a nine-hour working day. By 1896 there were twenty labor unions with an aggregate membership of about 2,000. On November 20, 1899, a charter was granted by the American Federation of Labor to the Trades Assembly of Dallas, the original central organization in the local labor movement. This assembly lasted until 1910, when on January 8 a charter was issued to the Central Labor Council, which still functions.

Some 5,000 building trades unionists went on strike in Dallas in 1903, and gained an advanced wage scale. In 1907 telegraph service in the city was briefly suspended when 135 telegraph operators, comprising the entire local force of the Western Union Telegraph Company, struck on August 10 in protest against the company's treatment of union members in other cities, and were followed on August 13 by the Associated Press and leased wire operators. The messenger boys were also involved and attempted forcibly to prevent the delivery of messages by deserters from their ranks. During the same month the United Textile Workers of

157

America in the Dallas Cotton Mills, about two-thirds of them women and girls, went on strike principally to secure union recognition. They were unsuccessful.

In the late spring of 1911 dissatisfaction among streetcar employees developed over alleged discrimination against one of their number who had become embroiled in a fight at the Elm and Peak car barns with Superintendent of Transportation H. L. Harris. Streetcar service was suspended and hundreds walked to work on the morning of May 27, while a temporary settlement was negotiated based on the resignation of Superintendent Harris. More employees were discharged and the men's grievances crystallized a few days later in the formation of a union with the general support of organized labor in the city. A strike was called and service was partially disrupted. A downtown demonstration occurred on the night of June 5, following a mass meeting in City Park, in which streetcars were attacked and four men injured. The strike failed.

In November, 1912, an inter-union controversy involving the refusal of the Plasterers' Union to recognize the International Hod Carriers, a Negro union, resulted in a stoppage of work on ten large buildings. Fourteen organizations affiliated with the Dallas Building Trades Council were concerned in the tie-up.

During the World War and the immediate postwar Dallas experienced its share of the wave of unrest and labor struggles which swept the country. In January, 1918, a four-day walkout of the city firemen necessitated the formation of a corps of volunteer firemen built around the Dallas Home Guard, who broke the strike. Some of the old men returned to work and a permanent new department was organized. The firemen of the city again organized a union in 1939, but abandoned it when faced with a long-extant city ordinance forbidding their membership in such an organization.

One of the most widespread and bitterly contested labor disputes in the history of the city was precipitated in the spring of 1919 when the linemen's union struck against the Dallas Power & Light Company. They were followed after a nine-week struggle by the inside electricians, who refused to work in any building served by the company. Fifteen large electrical contracting firms were affected and the strike spread to Fort Worth and other North Texas cities served by the affiliated Texas Power & Light Company. Three thousand members of the building crafts also came out on a sympathy strike and were joined by the Dallas women garment workers. Violence flared between union and nonunion workers, and a board of arbitration and conciliation assembled by Mayor Frank W. Wozencraft recommended an eight-hour day and a wage of not less than $6.50 per day, without taking a stand on the "open shop" question. State Labor Commissioner T. C. Jennings and Deputy State Labor Commissioner Thomas Ball also attempted, without success, to secure a settlement by arbitration, officials of the companies involved declaring there was nothing to arbitrate. On Saturday, June 2, a mass meeting of Dallas club women, held at the request of the strikers to urge arbitration, asked Dallas pastors to preach on the situation, which several did on Sunday, June 8. On June 11 a pitched battle with clubs and shotguns occurred at Routh Street and Cedar Springs Road, in which A. J. Fisher, a former deputy sheriff employed as a guard for a crew of nonunion workmen, was killed and four men wounded, three of them strikers. Seven union members were arrested and on June 24 the grand jury returned indictments for murder against four, Al Shrum, W. T. Butcher, Robert Roy, and W. F. Bohannon. Al Shrum was convicted of manslaughter October 27 and sentenced to three years imprisonment. Following the riot, the members of the craft unions returned to work, and the strike of the linemen remained purely a nominal one involving 27 of the original strikers. These were replaced with other men by the power company and most of them found jobs elsewhere.

There were three strikes in rapid succession in 1920. A chauffeurs' strike in January resulted in a fatal shooting between two employees of auto rent companies in the city; the boot and shoe workers struck in February for an eight-hour day and a closed shop; four hundred leather workers went on strike in April when the employers refused to grant their demand for a twenty-five cent an hour increase in wages. None of these strikes was successful.

In 1921 union printers in commercial shops struck to secure adoption of the 44-hour week. Comparatively few men were involved, and most of the city's larger printing establishments remain now on the open-shop or nonunion basis. The newspapers employ only union mechanical workers.

Dallas was but little involved directly in the railway shopcrafts strike of 1922, but suffered some inconvenience in secondary results of the walkout in nearby Southwestern cities.

The State Fair of Texas was embarrassed in 1924 when, in sympathy with building trades employees, union musicians boycotted the fair, causing the cancellation of theatrical productions and depriving the annual show of band music. This controversy was ironed out, and the Fair has since generally employed union labor and musicians affiliated with the American Federation of Musicians. In 1936 when intensive preparation was being made for the Texas Centennial Exposition a labor controversy arose in the construction of one of the major buildings, but was settled within a short time.

The 1930s have been marked by sporadic unemployed demonstrations and several major strikes. The most serious of recent labor struggles was the strike of members of the International Ladies Garment Workers' Union, called early in 1935, which brought several hundred women out of the city's dress manufactories. Increased wages and improved working conditions were the issue involved in this strike, which dragged out for many months. Minor violence marked the contest at frequent intervals and some of the incidents received national publicity. Efforts of a special committee named by the governor of the state failed to settle the issue and the strike was abandoned in January, 1936. The women garment workers called a strike on another shop the following August, which they won.

Organized butcher-workmen of the city walked out in more than fifty stores in November, 1935, but in all except two cases returned to work at advanced wages the next day. While all of the chain groceries and markets employ organized meat-cutters, it is not uncommon for independent groceries and markets to be picketed by members of the butcher-workmen's union.

A wave of violence swept the city in the summer of 1937 when a strike of the Hat, Cap, and Millinery Workers coincided with the appearance of CIO organizers bent on the organization of the Ford assembly plant. Several union members, labor attorneys, and sympathizers were severely beaten in the vicinity of the Ford plant and on downtown streets in daylight, and George Baer, international vice president of the Hat, Cap, and Millinery Workers, was kidnapped, beaten, and left in the river bottoms, later losing his sight in one eye. Climaxing these disorders, Herbert Harris, a socialist who attempted to show a labor film in one of the parks, had his projection machine and sound truck smashed and was carried off to be tarred and feathered by a mob. A mass protest meeting was held in the City Hall, and editorials appeared in the newspapers calling for a stricter enforcement of civil rights. Order was finally restored when Governor James Y. Allred dispatched a detail of Rangers to the city to make an investigation. Another brief strike marked by minor violence was called by the Hat, Cap, and Millinery Workers at the Garland plant of the Byer-Rolnick Company in July, 1939. It was referred to the National Labor Relations Board.

In 1940 there are no closed shops in the clothing manufactories in Dallas. The needle trades industry is represented by four union locals, the United Garment Workers of America and the Hat, Cap, and Millinery Workers, affiliates of the American Federation of Labor; the International Ladies Garment Workers' Union, independent union; and the Amalgamated Clothing Workers, associated with the Congress for Industrial Organization.

Near the end of 1939 all of the larger bakery establishments of the city signed closed-shop union contracts for a term of three years, affecting 400 workers, and carrying wage increases of from $2 to $8 a week. The baking industry had operated previously on an open-shop basis since a strike in 1932.

Fifty-two local unions in Dallas are affiliated with the American Federation of Labor, of which the most recent is that of the International Brotherhood of Teamsters, Chauffeurs, Stablemen, and Helpers. The Dallas Central Labor Council is made up of representatives from each AFL local. The Dallas Building and Construction Trades Council is composed of delegates from the AFL building trades unions.

The American Federation of Labor unions are housed in the Labor Temple, a four-story-and-basement structure at Young and St. Paul Streets, downtown, built at a cost for land and structure of $130,000. It was formally dedicated by Governor James E. Ferguson January 8, 1916.

Three hundred Mexican craft and industrial workers are banded together in the Dallas unit of the Mexican Confederation of Workers.

The Dallas Open Shop Association, in existence since 1918, has in its membership most of the leading industrial concerns of the city. Unorganized workers on municipal projects in Dallas are required by the city charter to receive the prevailing wage scale, and are limited to an eight-hour day. In the printing and some other industries the prevailing union wage is paid generally, with a work week of 40 or 44 hours.

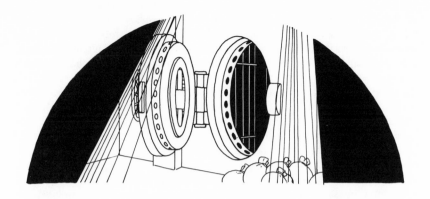

BANKS AND BANKING: CAPITAL RESERVOIR

"What to use for money" was more than a slangy metaphor among the early inhabitants of Dallas. It was a very real problem, which they solved by using almost anything that had any value in the community. In general, conditions duplicated those on each successive American frontier—a strong preference for specie or "hard money," but an unavoidable dependence in practice on shaky paper currency, foreign coins, drafts on distant banks, credit extended on a basis of personal good faith and community standing, and plain out-and-out barter.

Buffalo hides and other commonly accepted items of prairie commerce, along with the produce of the scattered farms, were exchanged at the village stores for manufactured goods; wheat and corn were traded to the miller for flour and meal. Honey and beeswax, wool, lard, peltries and hides and tallow all freely circulated in local trade.

In addition to the characteristic frontier scarcity of money, the succession of political changes, peaceful and violent, that occurred in Texas during the first quarter century of Dallas' existence also contributed to the early settler's currency problems. The "red back" currency and the later exchequer bills issued by the Republic went out of circulation with the annexation of Texas to the United States, and for a time such paper as was in use had no standard value. Both Louisiana and Mississippi banknotes were used to some extent, but the latter were acceptable only when endorsed by a reputable Texas business establishment. Mexican silver dollars were also in general circulation, supplementing what little United States specie the pioneers brought with them. Currency was accepted only at an agreed rate of exchange value in "hard money."

When Texas seceded from the Union and joined the Confederacy in 1861, Confederate currency came into universal circulation as legal tender, but when the fortunes of war began to go against the South, some foresighted individuals began to convert it into gold, or United States currency, which took its place alongside the deflated Confederate paper money, and became almost equally worthless, causing much hardship. Cash of any kind was very scarce in Dallas during this period, according to pioneer writers.

161

Until after the Civil War there were no banks, properly speaking, in Dallas, though as early as 1850 John Beeman conducted a small money-lending business, which made it possible to secure money in small lots at interest of five percent, which rose after the panic of 1857 to twelve percent. The political temper of Texas, both as a Republic and during its early *ante bellum* period of statehood, was generally opposed to the chartering of banks. For the most part merchants acted as bankers, leaving larger transactions to be handled directly by individuals.

The expansion of commerce and appearance of manufacturing in North Texas were beginning to demand better monetary facilities, and in 1858 the law firm of J. W. Ferris and E. R. Nicholson added the handling of exchange to their activities and opened offices for this service at Dallas and Waxahachie.

The real history of banking in Dallas begins with the establishment of private banks in the city during the Reconstruction period in the late sixties. From this point on it is possible to plot a continuous curve of development. The first banking house in the city was organized by T. C. Jordan and E. G. Mays some time previous to 1868 with an original capital of $20,000 in gold. Though Mays contributed the entire capital for the venture, the partners took the firm name of T. C. Jordan & Company. This pioneer bank had its quarters on the west side of the courthouse square, and charged an interest rate as high as five percent, or two percent on gilt-edge securities. The later City Bank of Dallas, also a private bank, organized in 1873 with a capital of $50,000 by Colonel C. C. Slaughter with W. E. Hughes as president, was an outgrowth of T. C. Jordan & Company. The City Bank was first located at Commerce and Market Streets and later moved to a site on lower Elm Street. In 1880 it was reorganized by Colonel Hughes and became the City National Bank with a capital of $100,000. It continued under this name down to 1929, successively absorbing Gannon Brothers' private bank (1881), the Dallas National Bank (1886), the State National Bank (itself a successor to Oliver & Griggs and the Fourth National Bank, 1894), the Trinity National Bank (1909), and the Tenison National Bank (1920). In 1929 it merged with the American Exchange National Bank to form the present First National Bank of Dallas.

Established soon after T. C. Jordan & Company was the bank of Gaston & Camp. It was organized in 1868 by Captain W. H. Gaston and A. C. Camp with $40,000 capital, a dry goods box as a counter, and their pockets as safe deposit vaults. Later W. H. Thomas was taken into the firm and its name changed to Gaston, Camp & Thomas. In 1873 Thomas took over Camp's share of the partnership, and the firm became Gaston & Thomas, to be merged in 1881 with the Exchange Bank, which had been organized as a state bank in 1875 with a capital of $60,000. The Exchange Bank in 1887 became the National Exchange Bank, which after absorbing the Mercantile National Bank in 1897 and the National Bank of Dallas in 1900, merged with the American National Bank in 1905. This last institution, as previously mentioned, merged with the City National Bank to form the First National Bank of Dallas. Thus the first two banks established in Dallas, through a complicated but directly traceable line of descent, still live in a single institution, which today is the largest bank in the Southwest.

Amid the many ramifications of the First National Bank's history, the career of Nathan Adams, its president in 1939, supplies a remarkable measure of continuity. Mr. Adams came to Dallas in 1889 to assume a minor clerical post in the old National Exchange Bank, and has remained with the bank through all its institutional metamorphoses. This fact made the Golden Jubilee Banquet April 13, 1939, at which financial dignitaries from all parts of the country gathered in Dallas to celebrate his fifty years of service in the banking world, almost equally a celebration of the conspicuous role played by the First National Bank and its predecessors in the growth of Dallas.

With the coming of the railroads in 1872–73, and the consequent rapid growth in population, commerce, and industry, the boom era began that within a few short years transformed Dallas from a struggling frontier town to a nascent city. At the beginning of the seventies it still was the center of the buffalo trade, then at its height, and its mills were selling flour to a wide surrounding area, even in Mexico. Eastern manufacturing concerns were also beginning to sense its possibilities as a market and distributing point and to establish sales offices in the city. Even the great financial panic of 1873 aided rather than retarded Dallas' growth, halting temporarily the construction of the Texas & Pacific Railroad, and making Dallas the western terminus of the road for two years or more.

This swift economic expansion made better banking facilities imperative and the banks in the city multiplied rapidly from 1870 to 1880. Among the private banks which opened during this decade were those of Bryan & Blake (1873), Adams & Leonard (1874), Flippen, Adoue & Lobit (1878), and Gannon Bros. (1879). The first state and national banks were also chartered during this period.

The first state charter granted to a Dallas bank under the banking act of December 2, 1871, was issued to the Dallas County Bank, organized June 4, 1873. This bank, which had a capital of $100,000, was located on the southwest corner of Main and Lamar Streets. John Kerr was president and E. H. Gruber cashier. The First National Bank was an outgrowth of the Dallas County Bank and was federally chartered July 16, 1874. John Kerr continued as president and W. J. Clark was named cashier. It was incorporated with the then impressive capital of $500,000, but proved short lived, surviving only until 1878. Its demise marked the first and only bank failure in the history of Dallas up until 1888, when the private bank of Adams & Leonard was liquidated.

The growth of Dallas as a banking center continued during the eighties, and in 1885 there were in the city six banks: the American National Bank, the City National Bank, the Dallas National Bank, the Exchange Bank, Adams & Leonard, and Oliver & Griggs. The banks of this period were for the most part located at or west of Lamar Street. Oliver & Griggs' bank was located farther east on Elm Street. Later in the decade there was also a bank in East Dallas, then a separate municipality. This bank, organized in 1887, was absorbed by the Central National Bank in 1890.

At the very end of the decade, in 1889, the National Bank of Commerce was organized with a capital of $100,000. This bank—a controlling share of its stock purchased in 1891 by J. B. Adoue of Flippen, Adoue & Lobit—has the distinction of being the only bank in Dallas that has retained its identity under the same name from its first establishment to the present.

Dallas, riding the wave of its previous boom years, did not feel the full impact of the panic of 1893, but several of its ten banks succumbed. The North Texas National Bank, organized in 1888, was liquidated to protect its depositors in July, 1893; the Central National Bank, organized in 1889, went into voluntary receivership in August; and the Bankers & Merchants National Bank, organized in 1890, followed it into receivership later in the year. The State National Bank, organized in 1887, was taken over by the City National Bank in 1894 to save its depositors, and the Ninth National Bank was finally liquidated during the same year. The latter bank had gone into receivership as early as 1891, and there were no more failures of Dallas banks until the depression of 1907, when the Western Bank & Trust Company, a state bank established in 1902, went under. The only other casualty recorded is the Farmers & Merchants Exchange Bank, a private institution which lasted only one year, from 1905 to 1906. It is noteworthy that withdrawals from Dallas banks were not limited, during the 1907 panic, until November.

The first bank to be established in Dallas under the state banking system adopted by the legislature in 1905, providing for guaranty of deposits, was the First State Bank, organized August 15, 1905, with a capital of $100,000. Judge George W. Riddle was its first president, and A. Ragland, Henry Dorsey, and J. W. Sparks among the original directors. In 1906 it absorbed the Riddle Exchange Bank, and in 1911 the Traders' Bank and Trust Company, a state bank organized in 1908. In 1919 it was itself absorbed by the Security National Bank, which had been formed by a merger of the Commonwealth National Bank and the Guaranty State Bank & Trust Company, both established in 1908. The Security National Bank, which became successively the Southwest National Bank in 1921 and the North Texas National Bank in 1925, merged in 1929 with the Republic National Bank & Trust Company, organized the previous year. The Republic National Bank & Trust Company continued under this name until 1937, when it became the present Republic National Bank of Dallas. The Republic National Bank & Trust Company was an outgrowth of the Guaranty Bank & Trust Company, originally established in 1920 and sometimes called the "Day & Night Bank," since it remained open until 8 p.m. for the convenience of late depositors.

Dallas had been designated in 1902 as a reserve center, despite the fact that in that year it had a population of only about 50,000, and in 1905 it had six national banks, two state banks, two private banks, and one trust bank. During the subsequent years of the present century, as has been illustrated in the case of the Republic National Bank and the First National Bank, the history of banking in the city has been largely a story of successive mergers and absorptions of smaller by larger institutions. The Mercantile National Bank, dating as such from 1933, has been an outgrowth in turn of Stiles, Thornton & Lund (1916), the Dallas County State Bank (1917), the Mercantile Bank & Trust Company (1923), the Mercantile National Bank of Dallas (1925), and the Mercantile Bank & Trust Company of Texas (1929). During its history it has absorbed the Commonwealth State Bank, organized in 1923, and the Mercantile Trust & Savings Bank, organized in 1925.

The Dallas National Bank originated in the Trust Company of Dallas, established as a state bank in 1903. It became the Dallas Trust & Savings Bank in 1907 and the Dallas Bank & Trust Company in 1930. This same year it absorbed the Dallas National Bank, organized in 1920, and was incorporated under its present name in 1937.

The present Liberty State Bank was established as the Liberty State Bank of Dallas in 1920, and Dallas' other smaller, specialized and neighborhood banks are all of recent lineage, none of them antedating the World War except the Oak Cliff Bank & Trust Company, which was established as the Oak Cliff State Bank & Trust Company in 1911.

The year 1914 represents a high point in the history of banking in Dallas, as in this year the city was awarded one of the twelve regional Federal Reserve Banks created by the Federal Reserve Act of 1913. Immediately after the passage of the act business and financial leaders undertook a strenuous campaign to have the southwestern bank located in Dallas. A mass meeting was held on January 16, 1914, and a committee chosen to urge Dallas' claims over those of the rival cities of Fort Worth, Houston, San Antonio, Oklahoma City, and El Paso, which was done at a special hearing held by Secretary of the Treasury William G. McAdoo and Secretary of Agriculture David F. Houston in Austin on February 14. After the hearing Dallas continued its efforts through Colonel E. M. House and Postmaster General Albert S. Burleson, and finally on April 2, 1914, was awarded the Federal Reserve Bank for the Eleventh District.

The bank opened for business on November 16 of the same year. Five hundred and seventy-nine member banks contributed to its organization capital stock of $937,000. The territory served was the entire state of Texas, northern Louisiana, a section of southeast Oklahoma, the southern half of New Mexico, and the southeastern part of Arizona. Branches of the Dallas bank were established at El Paso June 17, 1918, at Houston August 14, 1919, and at San Antonio July 5, 1927. Oscar Wells was the first governor of the bank.

There are today 546 institutions affiliated with the Dallas Federal Reserve Bank. Its total assets as of December 31, 1939, were $379,512,147.48. Its paid-in capital as of this date was $4,065,950 with aggregate surpluses of $5,240,504.97. Its present officers are: R. R. Gilbert, president; E. B. Stroud, first vice-president; W. O. Ford, cashier; R. B. Coleman, vice-president; Mac C. Smyth, assistant cashier; W. J. Evans, vice-president and secretary of the board; L. G. Pondrom, assistant cashier; R. O. Webb, assistant cashier; and E. B. Austin, assistant cashier.

The hectically prosperous twenties were marked, curiously enough, by the only "run" in the history of Dallas banking. On May 11, 1921, withdrawals by a large number of depositors in the Security National Bank caused a flurry in the community. The Dallas Clearing House, the Federal Reserve Bank, and many leading business houses promptly rallied to the support of the threatened institution, and though it remained open long after regular hours to pay all depositors desiring to withdraw their funds, it was enabled to close the day's business with ample cash on hand. Most of the depositors restored their accounts the next day. The late Colonel E. H. R. Green, then active in Texas railroad and business affairs, assisted the bank to weather this brief storm by depositing $100,000 during the one-day run.

The Dallas Clearing House, to which at present eleven banks belong, was not incorporated until October 6, 1927, but has been functioning since before the beginning of the century, rendering valuable service to the Dallas banks in the panic of 1893 and again in 1907. Its clearings offer a significant index to the growth of banking in Dallas. The clearings for the calendar year 1915 were $365,300,000; for 1939 they were $2,789,442,877.45, almost equaling the 1929 peak year total of $2,881,787,579.41.

The solvency of Dallas banks has on the whole been exceptional, as was demonstrated again in the severe and prolonged crisis which followed the Wall Street crash in 1929. Eleven bank failures were recorded by the Dallas Federal Reserve Bank in the early 1930s. Of these only one was in the city of Dallas. This was the State Trust & Savings Bank, which was liquidated in 1933.

Of the eleven commercial banks in Dallas in 1940 five operate under national and six under state charters. In the first category are the First National Bank, with $128,981,419 of deposits and the Republic National Bank, with $89,215,856 of deposits, the two being listed by the *American Banker* (January, 1940) as the largest banks in Texas or the Southwest. The First National Bank of Dallas is given sixtieth place among all banks of the country, and the Republic National of Dallas eighty-seventh place. A third Dallas bank, the Mercantile National, was ranked tenth among banks in Texas.

Other banks in Dallas are the Dallas National Bank, National Bank of Commerce, Liberty State Bank, Oak Cliff Bank & Trust Company, Texas Bank & Trust Company, Hillcrest State Bank, Grand Avenue State Bank, Highland Park State Bank, and the Dallas Morris Plan Bank. As of January 3, 1940, all Dallas banks had aggregate deposits of $305,667,618, and aggregate resources of $337,036,381.

INSURANCE: FOURTH IN AMERICA

Ranking fourth among American cities in volume of life insurance handled by its companies, Dallas has a history as an insurance center of more than sixty years. As early as 1876 a "Southwestern Life Insurance Company" with a capital of $250,000 offering "Cheap Rates, Definite Contracts, No Travel Restrictions, and No Dividend Delusions," had its home offices in the city and was apparently engaged in a state-wide business, since it had a local agent in Austin and inserted an advertisement in the *Austin Weekly Democratic Statesman* on May 4 of that year. *The Dallas Morning News* also records that Dargan & Trezevant, prominent among Dallas insurance agents when the *News* began publication in 1885, was established in 1876. Sam P. Cochran, who later joined the firm of Dargan & Trezevant, was a fire insurance agent in Dallas even before this date—about 1873—and presumably there were others.

In 1886 there were fourteen agents and agencies operating in the city including Dargan & Trezevant, George J. Dexter & Company, John S. Aldehoff, Edward R. Archinard, H. C. Dunn, M. W. Early, H. F. Ewing and William I. Addison, J. B. T. Hall, John B. Hereford and Paul Furst, T. A. Manning, T. Hudson Smith and Louis A. Bryan, O. Sondheim, J. M. Reagan, and Frank Wheat. Of these Dargan & Cochran was destined to become the most prominent. Sam P. Cochran bought out Dargan's interest in 1888 and the firm name was changed to Trezevant & Cochran. Twenty-eight years later, in 1916, its annual premiums had passed the $2,000,000 mark.

During this early period, when there was little or no state regulation, reputable insurance companies had to compete with fly-by-night concerns which disappeared or were found to be insolvent when claims were presented. This was particularly true in the field of fire insurance. For many years the premiums of fire insurance were also inordinately high in Dallas for a variety of reasons, including a bad record for arson, hasty and flimsy house construction, an inadequate water supply, and antiquated fire-fighting apparatus.

In 1899 the Modern Order of Praetorians, a fraternal organization with home offices in Dallas, was chartered to do a life insurance business. Other insurance companies with home offices in the city were also formed early in the new century. Among the first of these was the Southwestern Life Insurance Company, organized in 1903 (not to be confused with the earlier organization of the same name referred to as existing in 1876). The Sam Houston Life Insurance Company and the Southland Life Insurance Company, both organized in 1909, followed. These two companies merged in 1915 and operate today under the latter name.

The Praetorians and the Southland Life Insurance Company both have enriched the Dallas skyline by the construction of modern office buildings as their headquarters. The Praetorians built the first skyscraper in the city in 1907, located at Main and Stone Streets. After 1910 the Southland Life Insurance Company erected the Southland Life Building at the southwest corner of Commerce and Browder Streets, and in 1912 the Southwestern raised its 16-story building at the southeast corner of Main and Akard Streets. Other buildings also testify to Dallas' importance as an insurance center. The Southland Life Annex, formerly the Insurance Building, at the northwest corner of Browder and Jackson Streets, built by Gross R. Scruggs, houses several companies. The Texas & Pacific Building at the northwest corner of Elm and Griffin Streets is owned by the United Fidelity Insurance Company, and the old Marvin Building on Akard Street between Main and Elm Streets was remodeled and renamed the Gulf States Building in 1935 when the Trinity Life Insurance Company of Fort Worth merged with the Gulf States Security Life Insurance Company of Dallas under the latter title in 1935. The Gulf States Company merged with the Southland Life March 6, 1938.

Dallas is notable for the number of Texas companies having their home offices in the city. Out of 110 companies operating in 1936 in Texas, 42 had their home offices in Dallas. The activity of these Texas companies dates largely from the passage of the Robertson Law in 1907, requiring all life insurance companies doing business in the state to keep invested in Texas securities or real estate 75 percent of their legal reserves on Texas policies, and the heavy occupational tax levied two years later on all outside insurance companies. Many of the largest insurance companies regarded these measures as discriminatory legislation and withdrew from the state altogether.

At the time this wholesale withdrawal was a severe blow to the insurance business in Dallas, but it has proved an ultimate advantage since it has stimulated the formation of numerous fire, life, and casualty companies in the city. The large volume of business available in Texas has also induced many of the major companies to return to the state during recent years and to establish regional headquarters in Dallas. Of the 503 outside companies doing business in 1936 in Texas, 255 had their state headquarters in Dallas.

During the course of the development of the insurance business in Dallas, professional associations of insurance agents have done much to elevate standards of practice and to acquaint the people of the city with insurance trends. The Dallas Association of Life Underwriters was formed in March, 1910, with Orville Thorp as its first president. It had a membership of 200 in 1936. The Dallas Insurance Agents' Association, composed of fire and casualty agents, was formed in 1930 with R. W. Thompson as its first president and a membership of 23. In 1939 its membership numbered 96.

At present the number of insurance agents and agencies in Dallas runs into hundreds, and more than 3,000 persons are employed in the home offices or agencies of stock companies alone. All classes of the insurance business are abundantly represented. The Board of Insurance Commissioners, 1938, listed nine fire insurance companies, thirty-three life insurance companies, two fidelity, surety and guaranty companies, ten mutual assessment companies, six mutual aid associations, seven reciprocal associations, and five exempt associations authorized to transact business.

A survey of the ten most important types of insurance companies based on the annual report of the State Board of Insurance Commissioners for the fiscal year 1937–38 showed that during this year companies with their headquarters in Dallas collected $47,871,074.22 in premiums and from other income sources. This represented 43 percent of the total income of all Texas companies in these ten fields, and clearly demonstrated Dallas' preeminence as an insurance center over all other cities in the state.

Federal Reserve Bank, Eleventh District

Cultural
Development

RELIGION: BRUSH ARBOR
TO TEMPLE

Local church history has it that the first sermon preached in the Dallas area was by Thomas Brown, an itinerant Methodist minister, who on March 19, 1844, held services at the home of William Cochran at Farmers Branch, and that the establishment of a church by this denomination the next year was followed by the organization of the Christian and Baptist sects in 1845 and 1846.

These congregations and that of the Episcopalians, organized a decade later, gave to the Protestant faiths here the pioneer influence achieved by the Catholics in other of the earlier Texas settlements. Almost from the founding of the town of Dallas periodic camp meetings held at White Rock Creek attracted people from the whole region, regardless of denomination.

In his colorful journal of life about Dallas in the forties, John B. Billingsley thus describes these religious gatherings:

> When preachers first came to the border line of Texas we had no houses for them to preach in, only the houses we lived in. They were gladly received . . . and went from house to house preaching. . . . When we wanted camp meetings or protracted meetings we would go to some nice grove of trees and if the shade was not sufficient a brush arbor was built, grounds cleared off, seats prepared, and if it was to be a camp meeting camp-houses were built forming a square around the arbor and when the time came for the meeting all hands moved to the grounds with their provisions. . . . People sometimes come fifty or sixty miles on horseback and in wagons. . . . All were welcome. . . . All denominations, preachers, and people would come together to worship.

The same writer gives this portrait of a frontier preacher who held services in the Sam Billingsley home:

> The preacher's name was Welch and had but one eye but that was his shooting eye and it was a good one. He was dressed in buckskin and brought his gun with him. We all carried our guns everywhere we went Sunday and every other day, for we never knew when we would need them.

On call of a circuit rider named Daniel Shook the little group of men and women who heard Thomas Brown's exegesis of Romans 1:16 met again in May of 1845 at the home of Isaac Webb and organized the first church, and that autumn held their first revival or camp meeting. In the spring of 1846 the first church structure was built, a log house 18x18 feet, known as Webb's Chapel. A historical marker today indicates the site, 1.9 miles east of Farmers Branch. Later a part of this congregation merged with a church at Cedar Springs to found Cochran's Chapel, which was the parent of all later Methodism in and about Dallas.

In 1846 the Reverend Orin Hatch became pastor of the Dallas Mission, which served most of Dallas and Collin counties. From this developed the First Methodist Church, South, originally known as the Lamar Street Methodist Church. The first building for this church was erected in 1868 at the northeast corner of Commerce and Lamar Streets. The Reverend W. C. Young, a circuit rider, served as pastor.

The first congregation of Methodists affiliated with the northern branch of the church was established in 1874 as the First Methodist Episcopal Church, worshiping in a frame building on Pacific Avenue near Akard Street. German and Swedish Methodist groups, originally separately organized, were absorbed into this congregation, which came into the merged Methodist Church in 1938 as the First Methodist Church, with its building at McKinney Avenue and Pearl Street.

Today there are thirty-five Methodist churches in Dallas. The city is southwestern headquarters for the publishing house of the church, and the denomination sponsors Methodist Hospital, at 301 West Colorado, Oak Cliff.

Like the Methodists, the Baptists had their beginnings outside the village of Dallas. A congregation of eight members was formed at the home of Franklin Bowles, near Farmers Branch, May 10, 1846, and known as Union Church, erecting their first house of worship a year later on the farm of Thomas Keenan at Farmers Branch. The organizer and first pastor was the Reverend David Meyers, who preached throughout the surrounding country, using any convenient place as a chapel. He exhorted under trees, in farm houses, and in brush arbors. Tradition says that once while he was preaching in a woodland near Grapevine Springs a dove flew down and perched upon his shoulder. This was taken by his hearers as an omen from heaven, whereupon they organized a congregation as the Church of the Lonesome Dove.

The First Baptist Church in Dallas houses the oldest of the city's congregations of that faith, organized by the Reverend W. W. Harris, and its original structure was erected in 1868 near the site of the present edifice at Patterson and Ervay Streets. This congregation is the largest in the Southern Baptist Convention. Its pastor, Dr. George W. Truett, who has served this flock more than 40 years, is internationally known as president of the Baptist World Alliance. He has preached to members of the faith in many parts of the world.

Baylor Hospital in Dallas, one of the largest institutions of its kind in the Southwest, was founded and is sponsored by the Baptist Convention of Texas, as are the medical and dental schools affiliated with the hospital.

There are now 49 Baptist churches in Dallas affiliated with the Southern Convention, and 27 nonaffiliated.

Bishop James Alexander Gregg of Austin, first directing prelate of the Episcopal church in Texas, organized the parish of St. Matthew in Dallas in 1856, with the Reverend George Rottenstein as rector. Early services of the parish were held in the courthouse during the summer and in the winter in a better heated storeroom at the southeast corner of Commerce and Jefferson Streets.

In 1860 after the Reverend Silas D. Davenport, a missionary from New York, had become rector, a group of leading gamblers of the community who boarded at the hotel where the rector was a guest presented him with a bag of gold and silver coins, enabling him to begin construction of the first Episcopal church in the town, at the corner of Elm and Lamar Streets, a block from the court square.

Describing this incident and her part in it, Mrs. Kate M. Bryan (nee Keaton), daughter of the proprietor of the hotel, records that she was practicing her music scales at the parlor piano when the delegation of gamblers came in and asked her to "go for the parson." When he appeared the following presentation speech was quoted by Mrs. Bryan from memory:

> Parson, we heard that you was figgerin' on puttin' up a meetin'-house, and we figgered too that you was having an uphill pull, and as you've treated us like we was more or less human we thought we'd help you out a little, so we just passed the bag around among the boys and packed it to you without delay, and we want you to take it and buy lumber and start your meetin'-house.

Commenting on the occurrence, Mrs. Bryan wrote:

> Although Dallas was a wild frontier town in the sixties and early seventies, it was in many ways a more moral town than the present great city. There were saloons in plenty, and gambling houses, too, but they felt no need to hide their character. . . . There are gamblers and gamblers and the majority of those living here during that transition period must have belonged to the "and gamblers" class. . . . At all events, they were neither thugs, thieves, nor despoilers of women and children, and lived not by trickery but by matching their skill against that of their opponents.

In 1873, Bishop Alexander C. Garrett arrived in Dallas to take charge of the North Texas Episcopal diocese with its aggregate of less than 500 communicants scattered from Dallas to Weatherford on the west and to Texarkana on the northeast. Arriving on December 31, the first duty of the bishop was performed on New Year's Day, 1874, when he conducted funeral services for a citizen who had been shot to death during the festivities of the evening before. Thereafter for a half a century the history of the Episcopal church in North Texas became the biography of Bishop Garrett.

According to the churchman's own memoirs, his parishioners in the early days entertained rather unorthodox ideas as to behavior during church services. Frequently he was obliged to interrupt his sermons to remonstrate with the congregation for stamping their feet, and for what he seems to have regarded as an even more reprehensible habit, the spitting of tobacco juice on the floor and walls of the church. On one occasion, however, the bishop was able to bestow praise upon his unruly flock. In an outburst of zeal they had voluntarily built a fence about the church to prevent the intrusion of hogs on divine services.

Bishop Alexander Garrett died February 18, 1924, leaving the impress of fifty years of service upon the religious and social life of the community. He was succeeded by the Reverend Harry Tunis Moore as bishop of the diocese of Dallas. The Episcopal church has about 4,000 communicants in the city, comprising six congregations in as many churches, one of these for Negroes.

Franciscan Catholic missionaries who played such an important part in the early history of the state in general do not appear to have visited the Dallas area, though records show that the Spanish expeditions of Luis Moscoso, Fr. Juan de Padilla, and others must have passed close to the vicinity in their early explorations.

It was not until the summer of 1859 that the first Catholic service was held. The pioneer priest was the Reverend Sebastian Augagneur, who came from Nacogdoches to visit Maxime Guillot, in whose home he celebrated mass. A Frenchman, Fr. Augagneur was much beloved by the French and Belgian colonists at La Reunion, and he came twice yearly from Nacogdoches to minister to the needs of these settlers from Europe.

Prior to 1872 other missionary priests visited the Dallas region, sent by Bishop Jean Marie Odin of the Galveston diocese. In that year the Reverend M. Perrier was sent to the community to establish the first Catholic parish. He came by wagon from San Angelo, stopping at several military posts and at Fort Worth en route. An obese man, Fr. Perrier could not ride horseback, so he made the entire journey in a springless wagon. He first held services in the Odd Fellows' Hall, near what is now Pacific Avenue and Austin Street. The Reverend Joseph Martiniere was placed in charge of the new parish, and it was he who brought the Ursuline nuns to Dallas from Galveston, establishing in 1874 what later became Ursuline Academy, for more than sixty years one of the city's foremost educational institutions.

A decade later the Reverend Fr. Vital Quinon, who organized the second parish in Dallas, a priest whose veins were as full of red blood as his heart with charity, was held up by two ruffians at the point of a gun, and forced to kneel and pray. A few days later the priest encountered one of the men in a lonely spot, pulled his gun and ordered the bad man to pray. The man whined that he knew no prayers, so the valiant father forced him to kneel and taught him a prayer in which he became letter perfect before the priest would allow him to rise and depart.

Dallas was made the seat of the Catholic bishopric in 1891, with Bishop Thomas F. Brennan the first incumbent. The Reverend E. J. Dunne of Chicago succeeded in 1894 and it was under his regime that the beautiful Cathedral of the Sacred Heart (2215 Ross Avenue) was built. On the death of Bishop Dunne in 1910 the Very Reverend Joseph P. Lynch was made bishop.

Several institutions are operated under auspices of the Catholic church, chief of these being St. Paul's Hospital at 3121 Bryan Street. The Dunne Memorial Home for Boys is situated at the old home of Bishop Dunne, 1825 West Davis Street, Oak Cliff, St. Joseph's Home for Girls at 3812 Oak Lawn Avenue, and the Convent of Our Lady of Charity at 4500 West Davis Street.

Of the seventeen Roman Catholic churches in the city, three are for Mexicans and two for Negroes.

Elder Amon McCommas, who had come to Texas from Kentucky, preached the first sermon on behalf of the Christian church in Dallas County in 1845, and the first church of that sect in the town of Dallas was founded with twelve members in 1852. This congregation grew steadily and by 1873 was divided, one group becoming the Pearl and Main Church of Christ, and the other in time becoming the Central Christian Church.

In 1903 the East Dallas Christian Church was organized and in 1925 erected the structure at Peak and Junius Streets. There are now fifteen churches of this faith in the city.

Presbyterianism was introduced into Dallas as early as 1847, when the Reverend Daniel Gideon Malloy preached in the log courthouse. In 1850 a mission of the denomination was started and in 1853 services were held in a saloon owned by a Frenchman, who removed temporarily as much of his stock as possible. It was not until a decade later, in 1867, that the first congregation was organized into a church, the First Cumberland Presbyterian, the mother church of the now City Temple and the First Cumberland Presbyterian Church. Under the guidance of the Reverend F. H. Bone as pastor, a church building was erected in 1869 on a site near the Trinity River, now occupied by railway terminals.

City Temple Presbyterian Church, U.S.A., North Akard Street and Patterson Avenue, is the oldest Presbyterian church in the city, the congregation having been organized in the late 1860s by the Reverend Jack Hayes. This church has a membership of nearly 1,500, maintains a children's church and an orphanage, and teaches a course in art.

The First Presbyterian Church, U.S.A., housed at Harwood and Wood Streets, is the largest of that faith in Dallas. It was organized in 1868 by the Reverend Samuel A. King of Waco. For a time services were held in a blacksmith shop. The first building of the congregation, erected in 1871 at the corner of Elm and Ervay Streets, still left much to be desired, since it is shown in the records that elders kept long poles about the premises wherewith to drive hogs from their beds underneath the church while worship was in progress. First regular pastor was the Reverend A. P. Smith, who served from 1873 until 1894. Dr. William M. Anderson succeeded and served until 1901 when he retired, but later returned for another service of fourteen years until his death in 1924, when his son, the Reverend William M. Anderson, Jr., who had assisted his father since the latter's health failed in 1916, became pastor, holding the place until his death in 1936. The present church building was erected in 1912. The Freeman Memorial Clinic for Children, 3617 Maple Avenue, is sponsored and in part supported by the twenty local Presbyterian churches.

Followers of the mother church of the First Church of Christ, Scientist, in Boston found their way into Dallas as early as 1894, the First Church of Christ, Scientist in this city being located at Browder and Cadiz Streets. The church was organized at a meeting in the Cockrell Building at Commerce and Field Streets, the early members including Sam P. Cochran, Mrs. John Aldehoff, Mrs. W. W. Leake, Mrs. Cora B. Alexander, Mrs. A. D. Clark, Miss Sarah Clark, and Mr. and Mrs. Fred Moseley. The first church building was ready for occupancy on May 28, 1899. From this church there have sprung two other Christian Science churches, the Second Church of Christ, Scientist at 115 South Storey Street, and the Third Church of Christ, Scientist, the largest of the group, at 4419 Oak Lawn. The Third Church of Christ, Scientist, which was organized in 1923, completed its church building in 1931.

During the late seventies and the eighties Dallas witnessed many evangelistic meetings and revivals. There were many churches, described by a contemporary historian as "humble frame buildings, wanting in paint, in comfort, and having but one thing in abundance—religion." The same writer notes that "there was not a continuous sidewalk to a single church in the city. In rainy weather the mud, black, waxy and sticky, would pull your shoes off."

Dwight L. Moody drew capacity audiences at a revival in the old iron skating rink at Elm and Pearl Streets in 1888, but when Henry Ward Beecher lectured there he had but a scant audience, the still smoldering antiabolitionist sentiment outweighing his fame as a preacher. T. DeWitt Talmadge, noted pastor of the Brooklyn Tabernacle (Central Presbyterian Church), whose sermons for years were to be read in the weekly newspapers, filled the place to capacity despite a torrential downpour of rain.

"Dixie" Williams, fiery exhorter, and "Weeping Joe" Harding found fervent response at their revivals in the late eighties. Sam P. Jones, Georgia crusader against sin, conducted services here in 1902, and earlier the Reverend W. H. ("Wild Bill") Evans of Tennessee had preached to Dallas Methodists, later making the city his home. The noted Dr. Charles H. Spurgeon of London lectured at the Gaston Avenue Baptist Church in 1905, and Gypsy Smith, the English revivalist, preached to 16,000 at Fair Park in 1912. Billy Sunday, sensational evangelist of the postwar period, spoke at the Baptist General Convention of Texas at the First Baptist Church December 7, 1918. Aimee Semple McPherson drew large audiences on two appearances in the city. "Sin Killer" Griffin long held periodic sway among the Negroes, despite opposition he claimed was inspired by Satan, which on one occasion took the form of shotgun blasts fired into his tent.

Dallas' first Jewish congregation, Emanu-El, South Boulevard and Harwood Street, was organized July 1, 1872, as the outgrowth of a Hebrew Benevolent Association. Moses Ullman was the first president and Alex Sanger vice-president. Congregation Emanu-El was chartered as a Reformed Jewish congregation in 1874. Rabbi A. Suhler of Akron, Ohio, was made the first permanent rabbi in 1875, and the first synagogue was built a year later at Commerce and Field Streets, now in the heart of the business district. A school was conducted in connection with the temple, where children of all denominations could receive education prior to the organization of public schools.

Three years after the opening of the temple a group of members withdrew and organized a new congregation called Ahavas Shalom. This breach was healed in 1884 and the congregations again were united. In November of 1899, a new temple was dedicated at the corner of South Ervay and St. Louis Streets, with Dr. George A. Kohut as rabbi. Fourteen years later this building was found inadequate and was sold to the Unitarian congregation. In 1915 a new temple and annex was dedicated, the present Emanu-El. Dr. David Lefkowitz was made rabbi in 1920, and has been voted life tenure by the congregation. Membership comprises more than 600 families.

Second oldest Jewish congregation in Dallas is Shearith Israel, at 1324 Park Avenue, an orthodox congregation organized in 1884 by J. Emin and M. Wasserman. Until that time orthodox Jewry in the community had observed only holy days. First officers of Shearith Israel were Samuel Iralson, president; L. Levy, vice-president; M. Wasserman, treasurer; W. Lonberg, secretary; J. Gradwohl, J. Emin, and M. Goldberg, trustees.

Temple Shearith Israel successively occupied Turner Hall at Harwood and Commerce Streets, and Phoenix Hall on Jackson Street near Browder, until 1892 when a synagogue was erected on Jackson Street between Pearl and Preston Streets. The present synagogue was erected in 1920.

March 15, 1890, Congregation Tiferet Israel, now at 2312 Grand Avenue, was founded to accommodate the Jews of North Dallas, but in 1906 a group of members became dissatisfied with the ritual and organized the Rumanian-Austrian Benevolent Association, which later became the First Rumanian-Austrian Congregation. The latter group, known as Congregation Anshe Sphard, has a temple building at 1922 Park Row, South Dallas.

As the center of Jewish population moved further into South Dallas it became necessary to establish an orthodox congregation in that section of the city, and in 1926 a building was erected at 1722 Forest Avenue, at Wendelkin, to house Congregation Agudas Achim. This congregation conducts a Hebrew school five afternoons a week and religious school each Sabbath. Rabbi J. Abramowitz has served the congregation since 1925.

Among other comparatively early religious organizations established in Dallas were the Congregationalists, who organized a church of ten members in 1875; the Seventh Day Adventists, who held services in a grove on Swiss Avenue just east of the H&TC Railroad as early as 1876 and later at old Shady View Park; the Lutherans, 1878; the Unitarians, 1889; and the Mormons, 1897. The Salvation Army was established here in 1889 by A. E. Janelli of San Antonio, and while reported in the *Times Herald* as "not well received" at the time, has since become one of the most influential and helpful of the community's social agencies.

In 1940 there was an aggregate of 292 churches in Dallas for white worshipers, of which 188 were of the older Protestant faiths. Twenty-five churches were listed as nondenominational. In addition to the twelve Roman Catholic churches, there were three National Mexican Catholic, one Greek Orthodox, three Mormon, and two Spiritualist. There also are six public chapels maintained by the Roman Catholic Church. Miscellaneous sects represented in the city with one or more congregations include the Apostolic church, Evangelical church, Holiness church, Nazarene church, and Pentecostal church.

Negroes in Dallas as elsewhere in the South have for the most part followed the religious bent of their white neighbors. There were in 1940 140 Protestant churches and two Catholic parishes for Negroes. Baptists are more numerous than any other sect among the race, with Methodist next, while there are numerous groups of followers of miscellaneous creeds of the more emotional type.

EDUCATION: THESIS FOR 95 YEARS

Seven daughters of William and Alcy Hughes of Tennessee married men who were among the earliest migrants of the 1840s to what later became Dallas County. Several settled around Mustang Branch, soon renamed Farmers Branch. The Hughes sisters were all unusually well educated and the seven families were of the Methodist faith, which probably accounts for the fact that they established schools and churches almost simultaneously.

Isaac B. Webb was the first of the seven brothers-in-law to arrive here, first coming in the fall of 1842, and bringing his family in 1844. William M. Cochran, the second brother-in-law, came with his family in March of 1843. It was in the Webb house that Thomas C. Williams, a third brother-in-law, who had attended Dixon Academy at Shelbyville, Tennessee, conducted the first school in the present county in February, March, and April of 1845.

Later in 1845 these families, with the few other early settlers in the neighborhood, built the first school and church in Dallas County. This log structure was erected on the north side of Mustang Branch, about 500 yards from the Webb residence. Thomas C. Williams' wife Sarah, who had attended Columbia Female College in Maury County, Tennessee, taught here. She was the first woman to teach school in the vicinity of Dallas. Families with children living in this area were the Keenans, Cochrans, Fortners, Merrills, and Webbs.

Mrs. R. J. West (Mary Ann Ryland), who had taught in Washington County, Tennessee, before coming to Texas in 1845, taught the first school at her home in the village of Dallas in the winter and spring of 1846, using books she had brought with her. Later a separate log building with puncheon floor and wooden shutters was built one-half mile west of her home site near the present triple underpass, where Mrs. West taught until her death in 1850. Children used slates for writing, examinations were given orally, and the best pupils received, as rewards for merit, cards painted by their teacher.

As the first school house on Mustang Branch was not in a central location, a second was built about a mile northwest of the first one on Rawhide Branch, in which A. J. Downing taught a three-month school. The Reverend William K. Masten also taught in this school. It is recorded that several students came from a distance and boarded in nearby homes. John H. Cochran, who attended the school, described it thus:

> The textbooks used were Samuel Griswold Goodrich's *Peter Parley's History of China*, giving a full description of the Chinese Wall; Webster's old blue-back speller, *McGuffey's Reader*, *Smith's Grammar*, and *Smiley's Arithmetic*. Our benches were split logs, hewn smooth on one side. William K. Masten taught penmanship, which was the first penmanship taught in Farmers Branch schools, using pens made of goose quills with a sharp penknife. These were made by the teacher. Our writing desks were made by splitting large logs into slabs, hewn smooth similar to benches, and fastened to the inside wall around the school room at the proper height from the floor.

In 1846 Obadiah W. Knight, who had married one of the Tennessee Hughes sisters, reached Dallas and established a little trading post where Cedar Springs Avenue now joins Oak Lawn Avenue. He built a small church and another building which is credited with being the first public school in Dallas County. He hauled the timber for the building from the piney woods with his oxen and Negro slaves, and the venture cost him $300 in gold.

It may have been this school that George Jackson referred to in his *Sixty Years in Texas* when, as a former resident of the Peters Colony having immigrated here in 1848, he wrote:

> I went to school five or six months in an old log cabin—the first built in the north part of the county. The schoolhouse was known as the "Bark Log College" and the school was known as the "Blab" school.

Until 1867, when Obadiah Knight gave three acres of land for school purposes and deeded it to T. C. Williams, John Howell, George W. Record (another brother-in-law), and Obadiah W. Knight as trustees, no deeds on the lands on which schools were built had been given.

William B. Miller, a native of Kentucky, came to Dallas from Missouri in 1846 and ten years later bought a large tract of land and built a spacious home of red cedar logs, cut on the place. Mr. Miller's wife died in 1855 and left him with five daughters, four of whom were of school age. He sent to Kentucky for a teacher, Mrs. Sara B. Gray, and invited the girls of the county to come and study with his daughters. No other teacher being available, Mr. Miller himself taught dancing. Classes in 1855 began with twelve girls, all of whom resided at the Miller house. A Mrs. Sarah Jennings of Virginia came to conduct this school in 1856. The school existed for four years.

What developed into perhaps the largest of the earlier schools, advertised as a "public school," was conducted on the ground floor of the Masonic lodge building north of the courthouse square, where the MKT freight depot now stands. O. W. Grove was the first teacher, in 1854; Mrs. Sara B. Gray followed in 1856; Captain H. W. Coit opened his school there on Monday, June 5, 1859; Miss Jennie Waldron opened a school in 1861; Mrs. J. E. Farnsworth conducted a "female school" here in 1862; the Reverend Charles Carleton opened a ten-month male and female school in this building in September, 1862, which he said would close by a public examination. Mr. Carleton continued here for several years. A. Kissam became principal in 1863; J. T. Turner opened a ten-month male school in the hall Monday, June 26, 1865; Mrs. E. Helena Winn (daughter of R. J. West) taught through the years 1866 and 1867; the Reverend W. H. Scales began teaching a "French Seminary" in the lodge hall in 1869 and continued through 1871; M. W. Martin taught a free school here in 1872 under the state law of 1858. Other teachers who conducted schools in the Tannehill lodge quarters were Miss Mary A. Mullins, Miss S. J. W. Shepherd, W. R. Messick, Miss J. E. Wilcox, Miss Kate Smart, S. C. McCormick, and finally in 1875 J. P. Parsons, assisted by W. H. Littel, opened a school here in which his wife and daughters, Misses Cora and Porter Parsons, taught. This school had its last year of existence in 1876. The location is described by a writer of the period as "knee-deep in sand, full of fleas and with cattle browsing about outside." Trustees were: G. W. Guess, A. M. Moore, John W. Smith, Dr. S. B. Pryor, G. W. Baird, and A. W. Morton.

Mrs. Sara B. Gray, assisted by Miss M. Greenleaf, opened a private school in 1858 opposite the J. M. Patterson residence at the northwest corner of Sycamore (Akard) Street and Patterson Avenue. The *Dallas Herald* of June 8, 1859, carried advertisements of seven local schools. The tuition in these schools ranged from $1.60 a month for the primary department to $2.50 for higher English and $3.00 for instruction in languages.

Captain Coit wrote from Dallas to a brother on June 10, 1859:

I opened my school Monday by ringing the bell at "the Hall." The first day I had three scholars, my number increased during the week to eight and for next Monday I have the promise of twelve new ones and at least I hope to number twenty-five by the close of the week. I have been told that Mr. Morgan's school has dwindled down to twelve or fifteen. I have been examining the school law of 1858 and I find that the State pays a tuition allowance of ten cents a day. This, you see, is two dollars a month for each scholar, but nearly all of my scholars will be paying pupils. Many will pay more than this. . . . Everyone seems pleased with the idea of having a high school on the place and all that is necessary is for me to show them that I am the right man.

On September 8, 1859, Captain Coit again advised his kinsman:

When I wrote you last I felt sanguine of getting a good school but to my surprise I found a day or two after my school was opened that Mr. — had been among the parents and had secured twenty-seven pupils on his subscription list. His school house is on the edge of town. This man is well known and is a popular teacher when he is sober but unfortunately this is only a part of the time. . . . I have been teaching school four days and have only seven scholars. Five or six, however, have been speaking of coming. I do not know how many scholars to calculate upon for I have not been among the parents to inquire. My number can not be many for Mr. — and Miss Miller have already secured a good portion of the entire number of children in town.

J. Myers and Mrs. M. B. Myers opened the Dallas Collegiate Institute with separate male and female departments on the first Monday in September of 1858. The scholastic year was divided into two terms of five months each and the curriculum included literary education with tuition from $10 to $20; piano with use of instrument $25; modern language, embroidery, and drawing were an extra charge. An incidental tax of $1 was charged for wood, etc. The Myers' advertised that "board can be obtained in the place on the most reasonable terms."

J. H. Bishop on June 21, 1862, advertised the opening of this school:

ENGLISH, CLASSICAL & MATHEMATICAL SCHOOL

There will be a school opened on the first Monday in September, 1862, in the house known as the Cedar Springs Institute, upon the following terms, viz: Orthography, Reading and Writing, per month—$2.00. English Grammar, Arithmetic, Geography, Philosophy, &c—$3. Algebra & Higher Mathematics, Latin, and Greek—$4.00.

Not withstanding the pressure of the times, this school will commence its first session, with prospects in many respects highly flattering. It is the design of the undersigned to make it a permanent school, worthy of the confidence of the patrons. If sufficient patronage be obtained, there will be an associate teacher employed in the female department.

The location of the school, about four miles northward from Dallas, is healthy and in every way suited to such an enterprise. Boarding can be obtained at distances convenient to the Institute, for $10 per month, washing and lights included.

R. D. Coughanour, a lawyer who came with his wife from Kentucky in 1861, taught for several years before resuming his profession, in a small two-story brick building at Main and Lamar Streets. His wife, Mrs. Lou Coughanour, opened a female school in a dwelling previously occupied by a Mrs. Halleck on Monday, September 4, 1865. On Monday, September 7, 1868, she began her seventh session in the Main and Lamar building. The *Herald* of October 4, 1876, describes the new building on the corner of Still and Griffith Streets in which Mrs. Coughanour conducted her school as an "architectural conceit, very chaste and charming . . . erected at a cost of five hundred dollars." Miss Mary McOwen assisted Mrs. Coughanour as music instructor. Tuition ranged from $30 to $50 a year, and the city directory for 1878–79 indicated the school had forty pupils.

Another famous early day educational institution was the school on James Barton's farm (now in Lakewood Addition) started near the inception of the Civil War and lasting until 1869. One of the later teachers in this institution was Captain John Hanna, a veteran of the war, who was described by Victor Peak as "accustomed to dealing with men and who took a delight in what we now call 'rough stuff.'"

Mrs. Helena Winn in the *Herald* of August 19, 1865, "respectfully gives notice to the citizens of Dallas and vicinity, that she will open a Female School, in the room near Judge Patterson's residence, on the first Monday in September next." In the same issue J. Henry Chambers announces that "at the solicitation of many persons" he would give twenty more lessons in penmanship "commencing Monday 21st. inst."

Dallas Male and Female College was organized in the spring of 1863 with a board of trustees and given legal status as a corporation. Section 1 provided separate departments for boys and girls and that "Nothing denominational as far as religion is concerned is to be taught." Section 2 provided a "Course of study to be the same as similar institutions, with the science of war added." The Reverend Charles Carleton, A. M., opened the first session of the college the year of its organization and was followed by John Hanna as principal in 1869, when classes were held in the Christian church building. B. A. Landrum announced through the press that on Monday, October 31, 1870, he would open the school as the new principal, and that the course of study would embrace a complete course in mathematics, bookkeeping, the natural sciences, French, Italian, Latin, and Greek.

The college in December of 1873 listed its faculty as Professor H. W. Aldehoff, president; Professor George A. Calhoun and Miss Alice E. Aldehoff as assistants. In the same year Dr. F. E. Hughes, Jacob Nussbaumer, Henry Boll, and other prominent citizens contracted for the construction of a two-story school building of native white rock 25x50 feet at the corner of Cantegral and Live Oak Streets. The Reverend Archibald C. Allen, a retired Methodist circuit rider from Mississippi, succeeded Dr. Aldehoff as principal in 1874. His sons, William H. Allen and John R. Allen, were connected with the institute for several years. When the school was housed in the new building it was popularly called Rock College. In 1877 when the educational board divided the town into wards in order that the state school fund could be apportioned according to the number of children attending school in each district, this school became the Third Ward School. Students were allowed to attend free until the apportionment was used up, when for the remainder of the year tuition was charged.

The *Herald* of September 6, 1877, carried the following notice in regard to this college:

> For the convenience of their downtown patrons Dallas College will during the next year run an elegant school wagon to convey only girls and young ladies (women) to and from school each day. Wagon fee, only thirty cents per month. Apply at once, as the number will be limited.

November 18, 1865, the *Herald* published a request for a convention of Dallas County teachers "both male and female" for the second Saturday in December, for the "purpose of adopting as near as possible the kind of books best suited for the schools of the county, and for the purpose of agreeing upon some plan to advance the cause of education." The notice is signed "Many teachers."

September 25, 1869, John W. Smith and his wife Lucinda conveyed to the directors for Dallas Female College in consideration of $945 specie, property on the north side of Elm Street containing 75,000 square feet. This property ran 200 feet on Elm and 425 feet northwest to the Smith homestead (from Main and Poydras to Murphy and Elm) on the east.

In June of 1870 contract for the erection of a brick college building on this site, 35x63 feet, two stories high, the first story 13 feet and the second 11 feet from floor to ceiling, was let by the Trinity Conference of the M. E. Church, South. The building had a flat roof covered with metal, and an embattled parapet wall rising two feet above the roof, with one large room on the first floor and four rooms above. Donations for this building are recorded as: William J. Clark, $500; John Neely Bryan, $300; W. H. Scales, Mrs. Sarah Cockrell, and J. W. Crowdus, each $200; and others in varying smaller amounts. Work on the building was halted in the latter part of January, 1871, for want of funds, was resumed in July, and completed in the following September.

The Reverend W. H. Scales was designated to head the institute. In 1874 he led the movement to reorganize the institute because 100 feet right of way across the campus had been given the Texas & Pacific Railroad and its property values had increased. Three acres of ground, extending from Live Oak to Bryan Streets (location of present Technical High School), were purchased on which to erect a new building. In 1876 the institution, still housed at the first location, numbered 100 students of both sexes, ranging in age from eight to eighteen. Classes in the new building were opened on September 23, 1877, and the trustees announced that arrangements had been made with the streetcar company to give the children rates of twenty-five cents per week and that a plank walk had been constructed from the car tracks to the school. At one time fifty students from out of town, some of them from other states, attended school in this building. W. K. Jones, who became principal of the school in September, 1878, the Reverend Mr. Scales having died in April, 1877, and the Reverend M. H. Neely acting as president that year, purchased the building from the Methodists for $10,000 and operated it for a short while as a private school. In May, 1886, he sold the property to the city for $30,000.

E. B. Lawrence opened the Commonwealth Commercial College in January of 1874 at No. 317 Main Street and advertised, "The counting rooms of this institution are open day and evening for the reception and instruction of all who desire to gain financial prosperity, success and business honors." In 1876 telegraphy was added to the curriculum and instruction in music was included in 1877.

Other schools known to have existed in the seventies were Leonard Street School, between Bryan and San Jacinto, O. W. Grove, principal; Mrs. J. L. W. Phares' Private School for Girls (small boys admitted) in the grove between the Texas & Pacific depot and the Baptist Church; Cherry Hill Academy, for boys and girls, at the intersection of Live Oak and Leonard Streets; Mrs. L. M. Drake's school, held in the building on the east side of the Methodist Tabernacle on Elm Street; Mrs. Lilly's Private Primary School on Ervay Street; Swiss Street School, John Tooley, principal; Houston Street School for Boys, Reuben S. Parker, principal; Professor Giles' School, for both sexes, on Young Street; Sacred Heart School for Boys in the extreme northeastern part of the city, under direction of a Mr. Cremen; A. G. McCorkle's Select School for Boys in the residence of Mrs. Fox, on the McKinney road, one mile from the courthouse.

Dallas Springs Seminary, conducted by a Mrs. Miller, a graduate of Madison College, Pennsylvania, occupied a large building on Cumberland Hill with spacious grounds. In 1876 the attendance was eighty-five pupils.

Riverside Institute, seven miles south of Dallas, in charge of Elder Jas. R. Malone, had an appeal to Dallas students. This institute always advertised that "Ardent spirits cannot be sold within two miles of it."

The *Herald* of June 21, 1876, carries the editorial comment:

The number and attendance, as well as the grade of our schools has greatly improved within a few years. There are about fifteen hundred or two thousand children attending school now in this city and about that number, however, who are not.

Mother Joseph Holly, Superior, and Mother Paul Kauffmann, treasurer, with four other sisters of the Ursuline Order, left their convent in Galveston on January 27, 1874, to come to Dallas at the suggestion of Bishop Dubuis of this diocese, to establish Roman Catholic education here. On the tract of land where the Federal Building now stands these sisters began teaching on February 2, 1874, in a four-room house overcrowded with pupils. Before the end of the term the number of pupils had increased to fifty. In less than two years after its inception a much larger two-story building, to accommodate the increasing students, was begun. In 1878 the school was chartered by the legislature as the Ursuline Academy of Dallas. On August 15, 1882, the foundation of the present main building at St. Joseph and Live Oak was laid. In September, 1890, a day school was opened in connection with the boarding school and since that time the increase in students has necessitated additional buildings.

Rabbi Aaron Shuler in 1874 started holding classes in the School of Congregation Emanu-El above a furniture store on the Main Street side of what is now the Sanger block. It was open to Gentiles as well as Jews, and children of parents who were unable to pay tuition were taught free, regardless of creed. The school moved to the first floor of a frame building on what is now North Akard Street, just back of the present site of the Queen Theater. In 1876 on the completion of the new Temple on Commerce Street at the head of Field Street the school was moved into the new building. Several Gentile teachers served in this early Hebrew school and two Gentile principals headed the school in the last years of its existence. The first of these was Mrs. Laura M. Dake who became principal in 1880 and served five years. In 1885 A. P. Foster became principal and in that year the school reported an enrollment of sixty boys and seventy girls. In 1886 the school was discontinued because of the increased facilities for public schools.

On the night of August 5, 1876, a committee of Dallas citizens was formed to examine the law under which the city could act to provide Dallas with a system of public schools, and to ascertain what funds its scholastic roll would entitle it to receive from the state, in order to estimate what additional amount would need to be raised by taxation on city property.

An editorial of the next day summed up the situation as involving 1,200 school children who needed nine months of schooling each year at a cost of $16 per capita, a total of $19,200; and a city census of 17,000 inhabitants with $4,000,000 in property. The editor pointed out that one primary school house in each of the four wards would total $2,000; one girls' high school house $4,000 which added to the original per capita cost made an immediate need of $25,000.

In 1877 a city school district was formed and authority over the schools was transferred from the city council to a board of school directors, but the voters turned down the proposal for a local school tax. It was not until May, 1881, that the tax levy passed. In the following September the city appropriated money for the construction of four frame school houses, each to cost $1,960, in the four wards into which the city had been divided in 1873.

John Wesley Dixon wrote of the situation:

> In the spring of 1877 I took charge of the Fourth Ward School. At that time there was a school in each of the four wards. . . . John Tooley taught the second ward school, Mrs. Miller the third and James Giles the first. The school fund (State) was so small that it maintained the schools only three or four months out of the year. When the funds ran out each of the teachers continued the session as private schools. . . . The enrollment in the fourth ward school in those days was about forty. . . . In early days there was no prescribed uniform course of instruction in the public schools. Each teacher was at liberty to proceed as he thought best. . . .
>
> We taught the old-style English grammar, with *Spencer's Grammar* as text. . . . The geography taught was very meager in comparison with present-day geography. Many regions on the maps were marked unexplored. Davies' series of textbooks was used in teaching mathematics. We taught arithmetic, a little algebra and less geometry. . . . The instruction in history did not extend beyond the United States. The textbook used in 1877 was Barnes' which was very unsatisfactory, because the author was bitterly opposed to anything Southern. Up to that time no one had written a history which gave an impartial account of the Civil War, and it was the business of the teacher to correct Barnes on all points pertaining to the war. If the pupil questioned the propriety of departing from the text, the teacher always told him to ask his father, his uncle, or any other relative old enough to have been in the war and I, for one, can say that I never lost a case thus appealed.

Public schools did not take over education as easily as might be supposed, as many families regarded public schools as charity, and Dallas lagged behind many smaller Southwestern cities in her public school system. Several private schools flourished during the eighties. The most famous of these were O. W. Grove's school on the northwest corner of Main and Harwood Streets (present site of White Plaza Hotel), opened in 1880; Dallas Academy, at Jackson and Pearl Streets, opened in

1885 with Mrs. C. T. Dickinson as principal; Central Academy, maintained by Waldemar Malcolmson at the northwest corner of Harwood and Live Oak Streets and later moved to San Jacinto Street; Mrs. T. M. Miers' Select School of the Cedars, 324 Corsicana Street; two schools for children of German descent, one on Live Oak Street and one on Commerce Street; and the Misses Collier's Primary School, maintained by Miss Lucy A. Collier and Miss Bettie G. Collier at Browder and Marilla Streets.

Highlights on the public school system in Dallas were reflected in the editorial and news items of the *Herald* in the eighties:

> *October 26, 1881,* "The principals of the public schools complain that there is such a limited attendance upon their monthly examinations."
>
> *August 7, 1885,* "The Dallas board of school directors have rented the office at Elm and Sycamore (Akard) Streets and have bought 100 first-class desks and will fit it up as a high school. The public schools have eight grades and it is the purpose of the board to select 100 of the most advanced pupils and place them in the building."
>
> *January 7, 1889,* "The attendance upon the city public schools approximates 2,800 pupils, which Superintendent Hand thinks will be increased to 3,000 in the next two months. The city has put nearly $70,000 within the past year into brick and mortar and grounds for increasing public school facilities."

The city's first public schools for Negroes were built in 1882, the first building being on South Lamar Street and known as the Cedars school. By August of 1882 the *Mercury* reported that there were three Negro schools, the teachers being A. H. Jones, North Dallas; S. H. Smothers, East Dallas; and H. S. Howell, the Cedars.

Shortly after Bishop Alexander Charles Garrett came to Dallas on December 31, 1873, he began a movement for raising funds to establish an Episcopal college in Dallas that interested Episcopalians all over the United States. He traveled in the North and East making speeches on the subject. Some Boston women started a chain letter asking for contributions in stamps. W. C. Connor, mayor of Dallas, was notified by postal authorities of New York City, where it was alleged the post office was flooded with chain letters. The mayor discussed the matter with Bishop Garrett, who told him the funds were for Christian education. It was claimed that $6,000 was raised in this manner. On September 10, 1889, St. Mary's College, corner of Garrett and Ross Avenues, opened with twenty-four students. In 1903 the institute was incorporated and was authorized to confer degrees. In 1930 the college and preparatory departments were discontinued and the music schools were continued one year longer.

Other Episcopal schools were St. Andrew's Mission, a small free night school, opened on South Ervay Street by the Reverend Hudson Stuck and continued until after 1900, and St. Matthew's School for Boys with Frank E. Shoup as headmaster, established in 1899 and discontinued in 1909.

During the 1890s several private institutions were established, especially in the growing city of Oak Cliff. In 1893 Oak Cliff College for Young Ladies was opened in a four-story building at the corner of Crawford Street and Jefferson Avenue, built two years earlier for use as a hotel. Later this school was known as Eminence College for Young Ladies. Patton Seminary, at the northwest corner of Lancaster Avenue and Ninth Street, was next opened.

The University School of Oak Cliff was organized in 1899 and offered literary, commercial, and military courses at the southeast corner of Beckley and Jefferson Avenues.

187

Since 1900 many private, parochial, and commercial schools have existed. The Terrill Preparatory School for Boys was established at Swiss Avenue and Peak Street in 1906 by Professor M. B. Terrill. In 1930 the school moved to its present twelve-acre campus on Ross Avenue. A junior college was added in 1932 and the name changed to Terrill Preparatory School and Junior College. A group of businessmen in 1913 established the Miss Hockaday School for Girls, with Miss Ela Hockaday at its head, at 1206 North Haskell Avenue, the present site of Proctor Hall of the YWCA. Starting with ten students the school rapidly outgrew its quarters and moved to its present nine-acre campus at 2407 Greenville Avenue. The school offers training for girls from kindergarten through junior college. The Hockaday Junior College, opened in 1931, is on the approved list of the Texas Association of Colleges.

Southern Methodist University was established in Dallas by an educational commission appointed by the five annual conferences of the Methodist Episcopal Church, South, in Texas, and in 1914 it was made the connectional institution for all the conferences west of the Mississippi River. Located on a 133-acre campus on Hillcrest Avenue on the edge of the residential town of University Park, it opened its door September 22, 1915.

Today the university consists of nine schools, the College of Arts and Science, the Graduate School, the School of Theology, the School of Music, the School of Engineering, School of Law, School of Education, Arnold School of Government, Dallas School of Commerce, and Dallas College of Southern Methodist University, including an extension division and correspondence study. A summer session is maintained and courses given at a downtown branch located in the Central YMCA. The university helps support the Methodist missionary college of Porte Alegre in Brasil.

The university's original endowment was $279,178.62 supplemented by gifts of land from Dallas citizens, of which the largest was the donation by Mr. and Mrs. J. S. Armstrong of the 133 acres constituting the present campus. In 1939 the total value of its endowment and plant equipment amounted to $6,121,672.55.

In 1909 Baylor University of Waco took over financial responsibility for the school of medicine and pharmacy that had been established for the proposed University of Dallas. It also absorbed the Dallas Medical College department of Trinity University. In 1918 it merged with the Fort Worth School of Medicine and in the same year took over the State Dental College which had been organized here in 1904. Baylor Dental School is located at 420 Hall Street, and the Medical School at 810 College Avenue.

Evangelical Theological College opened here in 1924, holding its first classes in rented quarters on Hughes Circle, with nine men enrolled. A decade later the institution had eighty-six students and was housed in two modern buildings at 3909 Swiss Avenue. The institution is denominationally unrelated and was built largely with gifts from the Atlantic seaboard. The Administration Building, completed in 1927, was the gift of Adam H. Davidson, a Dallas businessman. The dormitory was added two years later.

In the spring of 1901 George Clifton Edwards, a young teacher in the Dallas high schools, opened a free night school in a small vacant building at the corner of Browder and Proctor Streets loaned for the purpose by the Episcopal church. The students were children who worked during the day in the nearby cotton mills. Unaided except for the loan of the building, Mr. Edwards carried on this project for one year, at which time he cited the success of the school before the Board of Education as proof that systematic night schooling was needed. As a result, public school evening classes were opened in 1902 in the Central High School. In 1929–30, with most of the classes held in Dallas Technical High School, the enrollment was 6,542. The evening schools now have more than sixty teachers and offer a variety of courses, embracing not only general high school subjects, but instruction in household, mechanical, artistic, and other vocational fields. For fifteen years the evening schools have held an open-house exhibit where tangible results of student training are placed on display.

The *Encyclopedia Britannica* refers to the Civic Federation of Dallas, founded in 1917 at 2419 Maple Avenue, as offering perhaps the best example in the country of a private educational venture for adults. Elmer Scott has been executive secretary and Miss Gaynell Hawkins educational director of the Federation from its beginning. Dr. Umphrey Lee has been its president since 1939. The Civic Federation has offered courses for adults in English, economics, religion, philosophy, and many other subjects. In recent years the Federation has held seminars in which series of lectures have been conducted by internationally known educators. Since 1919 the Federation has sponsored the Dallas Open Forum which brings to the city eminent lecturers in many fields. The Forum is supported by voluntary contributions. Among speakers to Forum audiences have been John Dewey, Will Durant, Alexander Meikeljohn, S. K. Ratcliffe, Sir Norman Angell, Bertrand Russell, Max Eastman, John T. Flynn, Dr. E. C. Lindeman, Dhan Gopal Mukerji, and Harry Elmer Barnes. The Belo Foundation, acting in cooperation with the Federation, has presented one or two speakers each year.

Education by radio was undertaken by the Civic Federation in 1930 in Sunday broadcasts over Station WFAA with the idea of stimulating reading interest in pertinent subjects and to encourage independence of thought. The New Era School was a project of the Civic Federation opened in 1934 to serve the high school graduates who were unable to enter college because of economic stress or other reasons. This plan is no longer in existence, but the institution at present seeks to induce a process of self education for adults by a program of home study and extracurricular work with high school students.

Recent additions to the Federation are a collection of symphony records and a film projection machine. Free musical programs are held regularly and among other films shown are many produced in foreign languages. Free public use of the Federation's library of 4,000 pamphlets has extended through Texas and into adjoining states.

The WPA Adult Education Program instituted in 1933 in cooperation with the county schools has maintained classes in adult education in centrally located buildings. Much progress in orientation of foreign language groups has been made through this program.

The City of Dallas maintains today seventy public schools, of which six are white high schools and two Negro high schools, the Lincoln High School on Oakland Avenue and Hatcher Street being completed in 1939; forty-six white elementary schools; two white junior high schools; and the evening school and printshop located in the Technical High School buildings. These schools represent an approximate investment of $13,500,000.

Cathedral of the Sacred Heart, Roman Catholic, 1911

First Methodist Church

190

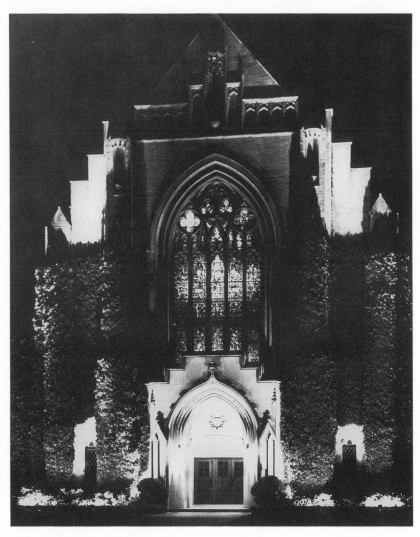

Highland Park Presbyterian Church

First Baptist Church

Third Church of Christ, Scientist

Temple Emanu-El, Reformed Jewish

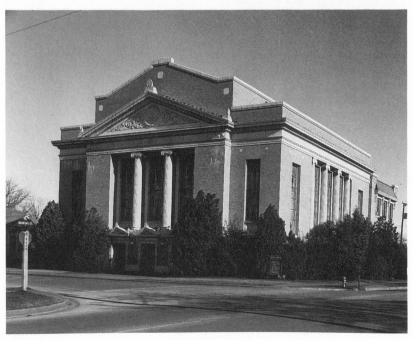

Woodrow Wilson High School

Southern Methodist University

Monterrey-type House

Cozy, Compact Cottage

Contemporary House.

Modern Functionalism

Breezy Southern Porches

Shrubbery and Shade

Munger Place Homes

ARCHITECTURE: LOG CABIN TO SKYSCRAPER

Since the first settler came to Dallas less than a hundred years ago, the early domestic architectural eras of the city did not include the beauty of the Georgian Colonial, the post-Colonial, or the Greek Revival that lent distinction to older cities of the nation. Instead the plain log cabins of the pioneers were soon replaced by the more comfortable but less artistic box houses of sawed planks.

With the coming of the railroads in the 1870s the city found itself in the midst of a boom where the main prerequisite in building was speed of construction. It was not until the eighties and nineties that fortunes began to be made and here again Dallas was handicapped in regard to beautiful architecture. The whole nation was in the throes of the Queen Anne or "gingerbread" period, and the pioneer builders followed suit.

The new century brought the bungalow, then called the "California bungalow," which with variations still is the most popular type of small house. Larger houses of today are comparable in architectural beauty to those of other cities in the same class. There is no one type of house which can be described as characteristic of Dallas or the region.

The log house of Dallas village was strong, rough, and plain, built for utility, not ornament. Its unaffected ruggedness indubitably reflected the character of its pioneer builders. In many cases the homesteader's first shelter was more or less temporary and required little skill to build. A small one-room hut of poles notched down into place, it resembled a type of corncrib found on many farms; but his second house was always substantially and skillfully constructed.

Long straight logs were selected, most often of cedar. These were hewn with a broadax, using a chalk line as a guide. Expert workmen shaped a squared timber with almost as much precision as though it had been planed by machinery. Finished logs were hauled to the building site and the neighbors invited to attend the houseraising. On such occasions a jug of whiskey often made the rounds, and as the logs were raised, fitted into place, and the cracks filled with clay, hilarity and good fellowship of the workers increased.

In making openings for doors and windows a peculiar method was followed. Instead of using short timbers the openings were sawed out of the solid walls which meant that much lifting, hewing, and careful selecting of timbers had been done for nothing. What few windows these houses had were usually near the chimney. Only hinged board shutters protected them since glass was practically unobtainable.

Doors were hung on homemade wooden hinges and fastened with wooden lever or bar latches, operated from the outside only when the latchstring hung out. The first floors were of puncheon—logs split, hewn smooth, and laid on the ground. Sawed plank, cut by hand with a ripsaw, was first used for flooring in the saloon of Adam Haught in 1846. Overhead ceilings were rare and the roof was more often of split or sawed boards than of drawn shingles. Chimneys and fireplaces as a rule were of the stick-and-dirt type. That is, sticks were built up in crib form and plastered heavily with clay. If an extra fine fireplace was desired the clay was faced with stone.

Two types of log houses were standard, the double-pen and the single cabin, the former being found more often on the farms than in town. Its distinguishing characteristics became clearly defined throughout North and East Texas as typical of the region and the period. The double-pen type might be described as two cabins under one roof, separated by a hall or "dog trot," eight or ten feet wide and often unfloored. This hall was seldom closed in the rear and never in front. A gallery about the same width extended across the front of the building. Shed rooms were attached to the rear of the houses, while closets and pantries bulged outward from these additions.

An example of this type of log home can be seen in the William H. Hord house at the southwest corner of Opera and Thirteenth Streets (Oak Cliff), erected about 1846. It does not afford an exact picture since the building has been modernized from time to time.

The smaller log house, or single cabin, consisted of one room with rear shed attached. The larger room was used for living purposes while the shed served as the kitchen. The John Neely Bryan cabin, restored and now standing on the courthouse lawn, is of this type, although after much moving from place to place and even dismantling, it differs greatly from the original.

While the furnishings of these early Texas houses varied greatly, there were two items found in all of them. One was the pegs above the fireplace for drying wild game, and the other the gun rack over the front door. The gun was always hung in this spot so it could be quickly reached when the door was opened and yet would be out of the children's reach.

There is no exact record as to when the first house of sawed lumber was built in Dallas. Presumably it was about 1850, for in the following year John W. Swindells came to Dallas and moved into a frame house on lower McKinney Avenue. Swindells' house, which was torn down only a few years ago, was built of planks faced with thin boards inside and out. It was the box type, square and high, one-and-a-half stories, with the usual shed room in the rear. Devoid of any beauty or grace, this typical house of early Dallas belonged to no architectural era and no term could be applied to it other than "box."

Bricks were first manufactured on a commercial scale in Dallas in 1853 but it was not until 1858 that the first brick home was built by W. W. Peak at what is now about the corner of Peak and Worth Streets.

No distinctive architecture appeared during the sixties and seventies. As the town emerged from its pioneer days into a somewhat settled condition the only changes that occurred in the domestic buildings were the inclusion of more conveniences, better craftsmanship, and more and larger rooms. Wings were added, cupolas erected, and galleries constructed. Inside, hardwood was used for trim. Solid walnut doors and mantels lent an air of permanence and affluence. But during the later seventies, when the boom was in full swing, in the majority of houses builders reverted to the old box type and cheap construction.

Two of the better constructed houses of this period are still standing. One is the Alexander Harwood house at 4117 Swiss Avenue. Built in 1875, it later became the property of United States Senator Horace Chilton and is now occupied by his daughter, Mrs. S. H. Boren. Originally this house had a separate kitchen in the rear. A cupola surrounded by an iron rail surmounts the old residence. Windows extend to the floor and inside are a solid walnut stairway, a walnut mantel and trim, although the latter has been painted white.

Another old house stands on Caruth Hill north of Southern Methodist University. Built in 1875 by William Caruth, it is now occupied by one of his descendants. The lumber for this structure was hauled from East Texas by ox teams and put together with square handmade nails. The floor boards are wide and the woodwork and mantels are handmade. A fireplace is in every room. There are two kitchens, one with a fireplace for cooking and one with a stove. Years ago this house was a popular resting place for passing travelers.

During the eighties and nineties Dallas ceased to be a temporary railroad terminal town. Many of its citizens were accumulating substantial fortunes through permanent commercial and industrial enterprises. They erected pretentious houses, some containing fifteen or more rooms, and costing $20,000 and upward. Builders vied in elaborate but often incongruous design. Towers, turrets, wings, dormers, and stained glass windows made up the style of architecture technically termed Queen Anne but more fittingly described as "gingerbread." Mansard roofs were topped off with weathervanes and lightning rods. On the lawns stood iron animals and at the curb an iron Negro boy with outstretched hand served as a hitching post. Beside him was the inevitable horse block.

Of this type of residential design and the current trend in architecture of public buildings, James Wahrenberger of San Antonio, president of the State Association of Architects, speaking in Dallas in 1890, said scathingly:

It appears absurd to me that in this age of steam cars [and] electricity . . . public buildings should be of such antique architectural styles as to remind one of the dark days of the Inquisition and the carrier pigeon. . . . Of that hideous nightmare, the so-called modern Queen Anne residence, perhaps the least said the better. Also of the peculiar misapplications of the misunderstood Byzantine and Mooresque forms, in which some of the younger brethren of the profession seem to take special delight to show their ignorance of architecture and esthetics—which in a great degree may account for the depraved taste displayed in much of our modern architecture.

The trend of the best residential districts in Dallas has in the main been to the north and east. In the early days fashionable additions were opened in what is now lower McKinney Avenue, then switched to the "Cedars," around Ervay and Canton Streets in South Dallas. For many years this section was the home of the citizens of wealth but when, with the coming of the railroads, the city grew with tremendous strides, more room was needed for finer homes. Westward movement was blocked by the Trinity River, farther south by low land, and although the railroad embankment on Pacific Avenue acted as a barrier for a time, Swiss and Ross Avenues finally became the location for fine residences during the eighties and nineties. The grading and graveling of these streets hastened this movement eastward. In the eighties Dallas had grown northward to meet Cedar Springs and here another splendid residential area, Oak Lawn, was opened.

At the beginning of the century fine houses had been built along Gaston, Swiss, and Ross Avenues to the farther outskirts of East Dallas. Munger Place addition was opened in 1905 as the first restricted residential section in the city. Today Swiss and Gaston Avenues, in Munger Place and east of it, still are sections of beautiful and costly houses. Following Munger Place, Highland Park and University Park were developed. Now the finest residences, beautifully landscaped, many enhanced by picturesque Turtle Creek and its abutting parkways, make Highland Park the more fashionable section of Dallas. West of the river (Oak Cliff) Kessler Park and Stevens Park, while not so large, compare favorably with Highland Park. Preston Hollow, newest suburban town abutting University Park to the northwest, is notable for homes developed as country estates.

Although there is no one type of house that can be said to be characteristic of the region, the Elbert Williams residence, 3805 McFarlin Boulevard, University Park, is a fine example of indigenous Texas architecture and material. Here several types, mostly found in Central and Southern Texas, have been blended and adapted to the modern mode of living, the environment, and the climate. This house was designed by David R. Williams, the architect who has probably done more to further an indigenous Texas architecture than any of his confreres.

One of the first sawed plank structures was the original courthouse, erected in 1850. This was 16x32 feet, and in planning it the court authorized John M. Crockett "to contract for the building of a good stick-and-dirt chimney." Evidently everyone at this time was not convinced of the value of planks in external construction, for two years later in 1852 the Crutchfield House was erected as the town's leading hotel, and it was built of logs.

Like the homes of the pioneers the earlier commercial buildings in Dallas were of logs. In 1846 the first exclusive store building was erected in the town, the owners elaborating the limitation of design by veneering the structure with four-foot hand-hewn boards. The following year the town's first hotel, the Dallas Tavern, was built, also of logs.

In the latter part of the 1850s frame structures for commercial purposes predominated. They were of the crossroads store type with a false front extending high enough to bear the establishment's name in blatant lettering. The floor level was several feet above ground and at the same level a covered porch extended across the front, allowing occupants of wagons and buggies to drive directly up to the store and alight. Rather than wade through the mud of the unpaved streets pedestrians used these porches as sidewalks, climbing and descending the steps at each end. Brick buildings followed the frame structures in style and it was not until the late eighties, when the town had passed from the haste of the boom to the permanence of a well-established city, that commercial architecture could be designated as anything but "flimsy."

The next type of brick building was generally of two stories, the first being of wood and glass, doors and windows filling in the space between heavy cast iron columns supporting the second story. Windows in the second story were long and narrow, and the building was capped by an elaborate cornice of sheet iron, in which almost invariably was the owner's name or the date of erection.

Four-story buildings of brownstone or brick were later constructed in a style described as thrice-removed Romanesque, popularized by H. H. Richardson. Carved ornamentation was often excellent. In 1888 the North Texas Building was erected at 905 Main Street. This was six stories of Romanesque architecture, and was the city's first real office building. It is still so used. Other examples of the eighties are the old county clerk's office at the southeast corner of Commerce and Jefferson Streets and the older Sanger Building at the northeast corner of Main and Austin Streets.

When railroads came, business in the little town moved eastward on Commerce, Main, and Elm Streets, toward the stations. Blocked by the Trinity to the west, downtown Dallas continued to expand eastward as the city rapidly grew during the nineties.

Dallas' first big step forward in an architectural way came in 1898 with the erection of the Linz Building at the southeast corner of Main and Martin Streets. This was six stories and was the first wholly fireproof building in Texas. In 1903 the Wilson Building was erected at the corner of Main, Ervay, and Elm Streets. It was the first eight-story structure in the state and was followed in 1907 by the Praetorian Building of fifteen stories, the first skyscraper in Texas.

With the skyscraper came a new type of construction, the steel cage. The heavy masonry effect of the Richardson Romanesque architecture was abandoned and the picture of downtown Dallas began to shape itself toward that of today. With approximately 150 buildings ranging in height from six to twenty-nine stories the city has been termed the "skyscraper center of the southwest."

While a few of the major structures of today were built in the period between the completion of the Praetorian Building and that of the original unit of the Adolphus Hotel (1912), it was not until after the World War armistice in 1918 that the real boom in skyscraper construction in Dallas began. This was accentuated from year to year thereafter until in 1925 the peak was reached with building permit totals of $35,149,558. Skyscraper design in Dallas has varied in detail, but it may be for the most part termed modern American, with increasing success in making these structures attractive to the eye in spite of the difficulties of scale.

Three Dallas buildings have long stood out as splendid examples of modern commercial architecture. The first unit of the Adolphus Hotel, French Renaissance, designed by Tom P. Barnett of St. Louis, the Medical Arts Building, modern office skyscraper, designed by F. C. Dale and H. C. Barglebaugh, and the Santa Fe Building, purely modern vertical setback type, designed by L. R. Whitson and F. C. Dale, are these outstanding structures.

Most noteworthy among public structures from an architectural standpoint is the Dallas Municipal Building, its design representative of the classic period of the French Renaissance—a simple rectangle with pavilions at either end and on the main facade, with Corinthian columns between, the whole topped by a mansard roof. C. D. Hill & Co. of Dallas were the architects.

The old County Courthouse, built in 1890, is in the Romanesque style, faced with gray granite on the first floor, red limestone above with granite trim. A steeply pitched roof of red slate and turreted towers at the corners confirm the period. Across the street from this building are the Criminal Courts Building and the

County Hall of Records. The first is the neo-Colonial style, its steel frame faced with terra cotta and red brick. The Hall of Records, newest of the courthouse group, is designed in the modified Gothic style, in one rectangular block, faced with Indiana limestone. H. A. Overbeck was architect on the courts building; Lang & Witchell for the Hall of Records.

Dallas' Federal Building is in the modern Italian style, faced with Indiana limestone, the first story rusticated and the four upper floors plain. Ornamental entrance doorways occur on the street fronts, while a colored stone cornice surrounds the upper part of the building, and an ornamental colored band or belt course occurs in the middle of the main shaft of the building. Picture spandrels in color occur between the upper story windows.

In religious edifices the city has had a late accession of architectural ambition. There was certainly no beauty to be found in the churches erected in the half century between 1880 and 1930. Three churches of recent years are notable architecturally: the Third Church of Christ, Scientist, in the Oak Lawn district, by Mark Lemmon; the Highland Park Methodist Church on Mockingbird Lane, by Dewitt and Lemmon; and the Highland Park Presbyterian Church on McFarlin Boulevard, by Mark Lemmon. The first of these is pure Italian Romanesque, the other two Gothic.

MUSIC: FOLKSONG TO GRAND OPERA

Soon after Spain had opened the province of Texas to foreign colonization, in the 1820s, Anglo-Americans brought the culture that, later transplanted to the present northern area of the state, has predominated throughout the history of Dallas. At first the crude, scattered, primitive life of the frontier offered little musical outlet. The Spanish custom of helping to attract American aborigines into the missions through the Indians' love of music had little demonstration in the region of modern Dallas, the early dominance of the French in this section having caused the Spaniards and Indians to move westward. Thus the locale of Dallas missed the high crest of romantic Spanish music so prevalent elsewhere in pioneer Texas.

Early Protestant churches in the Dallas area regarded the violin as an "instrument of the devil," the singing of other than sacred songs as profanation. The outgrowth of camp meetings in the 1840s was but a projection of the old singing conventions of the East, and play-parties furnished a singsong type of melody for the less religious. From these parties grew an indigenous music in the strange, haunting, melodic ballads sung in the pentationic scale.

Central and Southwest Texas were influenced by the immigration of the Germans with their trained musicians, instrument makers, and their Saengerbunds; East Texas felt the invasion of Louisiana's Creole music with its French gaiety and Spanish intensity, but Dallas long was isolated from both of these influences.

In 1854 when Victor Considerant brought his La Reunion colony of French and Belgian settlers to Dallas, Madame Clarice Vigoureux, an accomplished musician, was in the group. Also, there were Allyre Bureau, former musical director of the Paris Odeon; Abel Daelly, flautist; and Charles Capy, who organized a singing society. In the singing classes figures were used rather than notes in the written music. The colonists brought with them from Europe an organ, a piano, flutes, and violins, and twice weekly met in their communal hall for singing. While in the colony Allyre Bureau composed the peace song, *Clang, Clang, Clang*, and another vocal composition, *Choosing a Flower*, both included in the *Progressive Music Series*, and still sung by school children over the United States.

Though there was a cultural hiatus during and after the Civil War, Dallas felt the influence of this Old World music, and small singing groups began to appear. In 1868 when the town had only 2,000 persons the Dallas Glee Club gave a program for the purpose of raising funds for a new Methodist church. In the same year Judson B. Steffee, a music teacher, ordered instruments for a band. In 1874 a group of newly arrived immigrants organized the Swiss Glee Club and the Froh Sinn singing society. The Swiss Bell Ringers were presented in Dallas in that year. The Turnverein, German singing society, obtained a charter in 1875 and met at Turner Hall, then at 716 Commerce Street. The Maifest, or spring music festival, was inaugurated in Dallas in this period, sponsored by the Froh Sinn and Arian societies. These events, held biennially, did much to popularize German and French music, and were participated in by musicians from many sections of the state.

In 1875 Professor Bauer, teacher and composer, presented at the Episcopal Church a Christmas Anthem in which all the good voices of the city had parts. A typical Turner concert in this year included such numbers as the overture to *Tancredi*; the aria for tenor from *Der Freischutz*; Reichardts' *Das Build der Rose* as a chorus with a tenor solo; and Kuntze's *Weingalopp* by the chorus. The Dallas Musical Society was organized in 1876.

More removed from traveling musicians than many other Texas cities, Dallas in its early days had to depend on local talent. *Martha*, directed by Professor Otten at Field's Theater on February 12, 1875, was Dallas' first opera to be presented with an orchestra.

Tagliapetri, the great tenor, appeared at the Craddock Opera House in 1879 and was probably the first noted artist to sing in Dallas. Gustavus Gurstenburger, political refugee from Saxony, was the first professional organist in the town; in this year he played on Dallas' only pipe organ, a pedal instrument in St. Matthews Cathedral.

The *Mikado*, an amateur production directed by Henry J. Frees, was given in one performance at the Windsor Hotel ballroom in 1883. A state Saengerfest biennial festival was held in this year in Dallas, with the opening of the first local opera house. The Spanish Fort Band of New Orleans was hired at a cost of $6,000 for the "grand opening" performance, *Rose Maiden*; the seating capacity of 1,200 was taxed. For the first time in the history of this region there was a representative gathering here of Texas musicians, and Dallas emerged as a music center.

Mayer's Beer Garden on Elm and Stone Streets was a favorite place of entertainment of the more convivial in the 1880s. A five-cent cover charge entitled the guest to one glass of beer and the music of the Germania Brass Band and Orchestra, of which J. Parker was the leader. It was in Mayer's Garden in August of 1883 that the saxophone, "an instrument which gave forth exquisite music like the human voice," was first heard in Dallas. The player was one of a group of six Tyrolean Singers.

An advertisement in the *Dallas Herald* October 16, 1884, is typical of Mayer's guest artist entertainment:

The silver double-voiced English nightingale and Colorado thrush, Miss Carlotta Pearl, will give the citizens of Dallas an opportunity of hearing her Saturday and Sunday at Mayer's Garden.

Will A. Watkin, who established a local music house in 1882, directed a religious cantata, *Queen Esther*, with amateur performers which was presented in both

Dallas and Fort Worth. In 1886 the opera *Maritana* was produced under management of the Ladies Aid Society of the Presbyterian church. W. H. Bowyer was the director.

Emma Abbott came with her opera company in 1888, and at the Windsor Hotel ballroom, gave three performances, including *Il Trovatore* and *Norma*. In 1890–91 Emma Juch gave *Carmen* and *Faust*, with a "magnificent company." The French Opera Company in 1898 presented *La Juive*, which created a sensation because it was the first time many residents of Dallas had seen the ballet.

Realizing the city's need for yearly musical programs, a group headed by Mrs. Jules D. Roberts in 1895 organized the St. Cecelia Club, which for a decade pioneered in the cause of music for Texas and laid the foundation of a discriminating tradition in this field for Dallas. The first season sponsored by this club presented Maurice Aronson, who later became assistant to Godowsky of the Chicago Musical College. Each patron was assessed forty cents for this season, and the proceeds were used for the rent of the hall and piano.

Other great artists who have appeared in Dallas under the auspices of the St. Cecelia Club included Fannie Bloomfield Zeisler, 1899; and in the 1906–07 seasons, Schumann-Heink, Johanna Gadski, Teresa Carrero, Petschinkoff, the Russian violinist, Theodore Thomas, Melba, Harold Bauer, Edward McDowell, and Julie Rive-King, pianist and pupil of Liszt, who included in her concert Rachmaninoff's *Prelude in C-Sharp Minor*. Although the great Lillian Nordica required a guarantee of $2,000 and twenty-five percent of the gross over that sum, the St. Cecelia Club netted $25 on her appearance.

Because of that club, Dallas also had the opportunity to hear the Faust Opera Company and Campanini's company. The Boston Company presented *Faust*, *Iris*, and *Aida*; Scotti gave *Cavalleria* and *L'Oraculo*. Notable offerings from traveling companies were Handel's *Messiah*, Verdi's *Requiem*, Rossini's *Stabat Mater*, Saint Saens' *Samson and Delilah*, and Gounod's *Saint Cecelia Mass*. When the song cycle *Within a Persian Garden* was presented the audience expected to see a real Persian garden setting. But the troupe's baggage did not arrive, and the artists sang their roles in traveling clothes.

Fifteen days before Paderewski was scheduled to give a concert at Fair Park Auditorium in 1902 the roof of the building then under construction collapsed. The damage was repaired and Paderewski appeared to a record audience on April 20. Sousa and his band played at the new Opera House on February 26. Dallas folk were greatly disappointed when Madame Adelina Patti in 1904 canceled her engagement after practically all seats were sold.

The twenty-fifth Jubilee Saengerfest was held in Dallas in 1904, with Madame Marcella Sembrich and the Chicago Symphony Orchestra, and a chorus of 1,600 voices participating. Railroads offered special rates. Madame Sembrich was subsequently engaged for the next two State Fair performances.

In 1905 for the first time the Metropolitan Grand Opera Company came to Dallas and gave Wagner's *Parsifal*, an event which remained for many years the classical high spot in local musical entertainment. The May festival held at Fair Park in 1905 also brought a variety of distinguished musical talent to Dallas, including the Pittsburg Symphony Orchestra; Eugene Ysaye, violinist; Madame Ragna Linne, Norwegian singer; and Holmes Cowper, American tenor.

At the close of the 1906 season the St. Cecelia Club disbanded, with the claim that through the eleven years of its existence the expenses of the organization had totaled $29,999.

In the season of 1907–08 Mrs. Roberts, undaunted by the record of the St. Cecelia experiment, presented a concert course including Rudolph Ganz; David Bispham; Tirendelli, the violinist; Marcella Sembrich and Walter Damrosch with the New York Symphony.

Sembrich had a guarantee of $2,000 for this engagement and at 7:30 p.m., half an hour before the concert was to begin, only $1,200 had been collected from patrons. The diva sat in her dressing room at the Dallas Opera House and resolutely refused to go on the stage until the last penny due was in her hands. The curtain was held, the money gathered from the box office and counted, until finally at 8:30 p.m. the last ticket purchaser had arrived and there remained a deficit of $26.89. The singer agreed to accept Mrs. Roberts' personal check, provided it was certified by a banker. By this method the audience was not disappointed.

The Adolphus Palm Garden musicales were an experiment of the 1912–13 season. Lillian Nordica was heard here a second time shortly before her death, Frances Alda paid her first visit to Dallas, and the famous chamber music organization, the Kneisel Quartet, was heard.

A grand opera committee formed in 1913 brought the Chicago-Philadelphia Opera Company for a presentation of *Haensel und Gretel* and *I Pagliacci* on the afternoon of February 28; that evening Mary Garden sang the title role of Massenet's *Thais*, with Cleofonte Campanini in the pit. The next afternoon brought Wagner's *Die Walkure*, Dallas' first opportunity to hear this opera. The climax and the season's finale was on the evening of March 2 when Luisa Tetrazzini, famed coloratura, produced audience hysteria by her singing of the mad scene in Donizetti's *Lucia di Lammermoor*.

The second visit of the Chicago-Philadelphia Opera Company, March 4–17, 1914, brought Alice Zepilli singing Mime in *La Boheme* and the title role of *Tosca*. Tita Ruffo was the star of the season in Verdi's *Rigoletto*. The National Opera Company of Canada also came to Dallas in April of this year, opening with a presentation of *Gioconda*, February 11. Marie Rappold, Martino, Roas Olitzka, Marie Claenseno, Jose Segura-Tallien, and the dancer Pavlowa appeared in the company.

Marguerite Matzenauer, contralto, and Josef Hoffmann visited Dallas in 1916 but had very small attendance at their concerts. Other artists who appeared in this period were Kitty Cheathem, Esther Plum, Charles Wakefield Cadman (the latter in a program of his own music), Victor Herbert, Sarah Anderson, Nevada Vander Veer, Reed Miller, and Mark Kellerman. Somewhat later, just after the War, Amelita Galli-Curci delighted an audience of 4,500 with her rendering of popular operatic arias.

The World War period constitutes a colorful chapter in the history of folk music in Dallas. Some time shortly after 1916 Huddie Ledbetter, better known as "Leadbelly," self-styled Negro king of the twelve-string guitar players of the world, came to Dallas. Here he met "Blind Lemon" Jefferson, who played a Hawaiian guitar and sang ballads, and they combined forces to sing on the streets. Some of Leadbelly's versions of ballads influenced by his years in Dallas are to be found in the collections of John A. Lomax. *Fort Worth and Dallas Blues* is the prototype of thousands of blues tunes and begins, "Got the Fort Worth blues and the Dallas heart disease." Another ballad of Leadbelly's was claimed to have been made up by him about the life of Blind Lemon. Leadbelly says that not long before he moved to Dallas, Bill Martin shot down Ella Speed in the street and that along with other musicians of this area he composed the ballad *Ella Speed*. Lomax states that of all the guitarists' repertoire it is the finest combination of simple ballad style, unsophisticated folk melody, and fitting accompaniment. This ballad is found in several anthologies. In indigenous tradition Leadbelly made another version from an old melody and old theme, that of the drug addict, in which he uses the streets of Dallas:

> Walked up Ellum an' I come down Main,
> Tryin' to bum a nickel jes' to buy cocaine.
> Ho, Ho, baby, take a whiff on me.

"Iron Head," another Negro street singer, an habitual criminal and admittedly the "roughest nigger that ever walked the streets of Dallas," adapted and modified ballads to a Dallas locale.

The city's orchestral history dates back to 1901 when Hans Kreissig, who came to Dallas in the 1880s, organized string ensembles. Walter J. Fried, a young violinist who had studied conducting in Germany, came to make his home in Dallas in 1908. Immediately he began to promote a symphony, and in 1911 the Beethoven Symphony Orchestra was organized with forty players. Following the impetus given local musical movements by that event, Harold J. Abrams, Dallas businessman and violinist with this group, created a complete orchestra. Carl Venth, onetime master of the Flemish Opera in Brussels, once concert master of the Metropolitan Opera Orchestra and founder of the Brooklyn Symphony, was engaged as conductor until 1914, when Fried was appointed to that position.

The Dallas Symphony Orchestra of 1912 offered an expensive and heavy musical bill of fare. The sponsors, many of whom were members of the Dallas Symphony Society of 1940, attempted to have a second season in 1913–14; but a meningitis epidemic furnished a good excuse for concluding the venture.

In 1913 Fried resumed the symphony experiment of 1911. A new orchestra with forty members became officially known as the Dallas Symphony, and inaugurated a series of concerts for the city hall auditorium. Many local vocalists and instrumentalists appeared as soloists. A publicity campaign drew an audience of 3,000 persons to a concert given at very low admission prices in the Fair Park Coliseum. The orchestra thereafter conducted its programs in the City Hall to audiences averaging 500 persons.

Between 1918 and 1924 the Dallas Symphony was a half-professional, half-student group, and Fried had the hope of organizing a full-fledged professional orchestra. There was no offering by the Dallas Symphony in the 1924–25 season; Fried continued with his plans but died in the summer of 1925 before he could put them into effect.

Arthur L. Kramer, succeeding Fried as head of the association, decided to carry out the late conductor's plans for the symphony. Dr. Paul Van Katwijk, dean of music at Southern Methodist University, was chosen director of the rejuvenated enterprise. The first concert was given in December, 1925, at the Circle Theater, which has a seating capacity of 1,000; nearly 1,600 persons were crowded into the theater for the first performance and more than 1,000 turned away. The second concert was underwritten by the Dallas press and offered free to 6,200 listeners in the State Fair Auditorium. Thereafter the symphony played to almost capacity audiences of an average of 4,400 persons.

There have been minor crises since 1925 but the symphony has enjoyed continual existence since that time. Today it has a mature status as an all-professional salaried organization assembling from seventy to eighty pieces. The orchestra does not claim the smooth and finished symphonic readings of the New York, Philadelphia, Boston, and St. Louis organizations, but it strives for a conscientious, academic job of bringing to the music audiences of Dallas as wide a repertoire as a season of six concerts can afford. The Dallas Symphony receives few large subscriptions; the financial needs of the project are cared for by the sale of tickets *en bloc*.

Twenty-six-year-old Jacques Singer, who received his training under Stokowski in the Philadelphia Symphony Orchestra, became conductor of the Dallas Symphony in December of the 1937–38 season. He also served during the 1938–39 season and is under contract for two more seasons. A serious financial crisis developed in July, 1939, threatening to result in Mr. Singer's resignation, but concerts were successfully resumed in the autumn.

Many musical groups, both vocal and instrumental, have developed in Dallas public schools, colleges, and fraternal organizations. The Negroes of the city under the leadership of Professor A. S. Jackson and Fanny Gibson have made an organized effort toward the preservation of spirituals and the study of serious music. The A Capella Choir, made up of fifty Negro high school students, was featured at the Texas Centennial Exposition in 1936. The Civic Music Guild, a Negro organization, functions in cooperation with other clubs and presents Negro musicians of repute to Dallas audiences. Madame Lillian Evanti was presented by this group in 1936.

The Work Projects Administration Musical Project has since 1935 developed an orchestra which plays in public centers without an admission charge.

The Civic Music Association, founded in 1903, is a nonprofit organization that sponsors a season of music in Dallas from October through March. No donations are accepted, but a membership campaign is conducted for one week each spring. Each member is assessed a fee of $5 ($2.50 for students) which admits him to all the season's offerings. Invariably there is a long waiting list of prospective members. The concerts are usually held each month in McFarlin Auditorium on the campus of Southern Methodist University. Among the artists who have appeared on these programs are Lauritz Melchior, Kirstin Flagstad, Yehudi Menuhin, Marian Anderson, John Charles Thomas, Beniamino Gigli, Mischa Elman, Lina Pagliughi, Alexander Brailowsky, La Argentina, and the St. Louis Symphony Orchestra. Jan Ignace Paderewski played to a capacity house on April 19, 1939, thirty-seven years after his first appearance here.

Audiences were enthusiastic when the Dallas Grand Opera Association brought the Metropolitan Grand Opera Company on April 10-11-12, 1939. *Manon*, with Ezio Pinza, Grace Moore, and Jan Kiepura, was presented the first evening. Lawrence Tibbett, Giovanni Martinelli, and Irene Jessner broke all operatic box-office records of Dallas in *Otello* on the night of the eleventh, only to give way the following evening when *La Boheme* was sung by Grace Moore, Ezio Pinza, Charles Kullman, and John Brownlee. A matinee performance on the twelfth starred Lauritz Melchior, Elizabeth Rethberg, Kerstin Thorborg, and Herbert Janssen.

Following this successful season, the Metropolitan Opera Company returned to Dallas in the spring of 1940 bringing back several of the stars who had sung the previous year. A performance of *Lakme* with Lily Pons, Armand Tokatyan, and Ezio Pinza was given on April 15; *Die Walkure* with Lotte Lehmann, Marjorie Lawrence,

Lauritz Melchior, and Kerstin Thorborg on April 16; *Faust* with Grace Moore, Richard Crooks, John Brownlee, and Ezio Pinza on the afternoon of April 17; and *La Traviata* with Helen Jepson, Nino Martini, and Lawrence Tibbett that evening. *Lakme*, *Faust*, and *La Traviata* were accompanied with ballet arrangements.

Leonora Corona, native of Dallas and a successful concert pianist in this city, at fourteen decided to follow an operatic career. Following her debut in *Mefistofele* at La Scala in Milan she sang frequently under Toscanini, and created the role of Beauty in *Beauty and the Beast*. She made her debut at the Metropolitan in 1927 in *Il Trovatore* and has since sung leading roles in that house. She came to Texas State Teachers' College in Denton to sing the title role in Julia Smith's opera *Cynthia Parker* for its premiere performance.

David Wendel Fentress Guion, nationally known pianist, composer, and adapter of Negro spirituals, cowboy ballads, Indian and Mexican songs, and old fiddle tunes, was born in Ballinger, in the midst of the West Texas cattle country. Now a resident of New York, he was a familiar figure in Dallas musical circles throughout the 1920s and did some of his most distinguished work here. Mr. Guion came to Dallas from Brownwood soon after the World War and taught at Southern Methodist University, Fairmount Conservatory, and the Southwestern School of Fine Arts. His Negro ballet, *Shingandi*, produced at the New York Radio City Music Hall in October, 1935, had its premiere at the Dallas Little Theater several years earlier, and he briefly revisited Dallas in the spring of 1936 to confer with Jan Isbell Fortune, author of the *Cavalcade of Texas*, for which his *Cowboy Love Song* was used as a theme.

David Guion's better known compositions, many of which are popular on radio programs and "combine strong racial and local characteristics with remarkable formal . . . subtleties of workmanship," include a group of Negro spirituals published in 1918; *Turkey in the Straw*, first old fiddle tune to be arranged as solo by any composer; *Hopi Indian Love Song, Sheep and Goat Walking to Pasture, Arkansas Traveler, The Bold Vaquero, Bury Me Not on the Lone Prairie*, a suite of original piano numbers called *Alley Tunes*; *Mother Goose Ballet*; *Five Imaginary Early Louisiana Songs*; *Sail Away to the Rio Grande*, a sea chantey; and *Home on the Range*, probably the most beloved of all the composer's works and declared by President Roosevelt to be his favorite piece of music.

LITERATURE: VOICES OF THE SOUTHWEST

As one of the last American frontiers Dallas and its region repeated in its literature the pattern of all frontiers, modified by the former environment of its Anglo-American settlers and the spirit of the era. In its first decade of settlement it produced neither such purposeful chroniclers as the New England Puritans nor such glorifiers of colorful pioneer existence as those who painted the California of the gold rush. The majority of the settlers came from the South, where expression in that day centered on oratory rather than writing.

Unwitting heroes of an American epic, there was little of the consciously poetic in the Dallas settlers, if their latterday memoirs are to be taken as criteria. It was long after the rigors of establishing a community were over that a later generation pictured in song, poetry, and prose the trees and flowers, the animal life, and the grandeur of space on the open prairies.

First writings in Dallas other than personal letters were political and editorial articles concerned first with local and then with state affairs. Since the people of Dallas had not participated in Texas' struggle for independence they could contribute little to the heroic chronology of that conquest.

There are few records concerning early exploration in the Dallas area. Historians claim that Luis Moscoso penetrated as far east as Dallas County in 1542. Herbert E. Bolton, who wrote of the wanderings of Athanase de Mezieres, mentions places located in Dallas County. Edward Smith, an Englishman who had visited in Dallas, published in 1849 *An Account of a Journey Through Northeastern Texas for Purposes of Emigration* in which he included the story of Dr. W. W. Conover's five-year experience in Dallas, as told to him by the physician. Smith's description of a tree in Dallas County one hundred feet tall inclines the reader to believe he was somewhat given to exaggeration.

In the handwriting of the county clerk on the flyleaf of a criminal docket record for 1848–1852 is a parody on the song *O No, We Never Mention Him*. It is a lament on taking the temperance pledge.

Harry Peak was recorded as a poet in the fifties according to Henry Coit, who sent a *Herald* clipping of one of his poems to a brother in the East on September 8, 1859.

211

Dr. Eugene Savardan, who had come with the French La Reunion colonists in 1855, almost immediately wrote an article published in December of that year in the *Journal L'ani des Sciences* in Paris concerning what he considered an unusual local phenomenon—the Texas tumblebug. Dr. Savardan's book *Un Naufrage au Texas*, published on his return to France, recounts the history of La Reunion colony. His observations on the Dallas region, from the viewpoint of one unfamiliar with the culture of frontier people, recorded that the settlers failed to cultivate vegetable gardens, had a habit of sitting with their feet elevated, exhibited what to him was the peculiarity of rocking in chairs, and that the men had a gallant attitude toward women.

Dallas made its first contribution to Texas immigration propaganda when James Wellington Latimer in 1857 began writing for Willard Richardson's *Texas Almanac and Immigrants' Guide*. Because the farmer-homesteader was most needed and desired these articles were accounts of the agrarian possibilities of Dallas County, with advice as to what the immigrant should bring with him into the new country.

Local and state issues in journalism and immigration propaganda continued as the chief literary motifs until the approach of the Civil War, when the conflict of systems produced a new awareness of cultural patterns. This prompted editorial political discussions on a wider scale, some colorful and vitriolic polemics, and a few studied evaluations of regional ways of life.

Reconstruction was a period of reconciliation of the frontiersman's Jacksonian philosophy of democracy with the violent political upheaval through the South, and neither side was articulate. Men spoke and acted in terms of prejudices without reflection. Power of the victor needed no justification; the vanquished, surrounded by those of like faith and fortune, felt no need of the written word to defend his cause. But when John Henry Brown, well-known Texas journalist, historian, lecturer, and Confederate soldier, took direction of the *Dallas Herald* in 1873, he began a series of editorials dealing with Reconstruction in Texas that has remained one of the most scholarly collections on this era.

Mary Hunt McCaleb moved to Dallas in 1873 when her husband, D. McCaleb, became editor of the *Herald*. Mrs. McCaleb wrote first under the name of "L'Eclair" in 1870 and her poems "Lenare," "The Picture on the Wall," and "Little Relics" were widely read. After Mrs. McCaleb no longer resided in the city her poems were published in book form by G. P. Putman's Sons. Mrs. M. Josephine Williams lived in Dallas and wrote for the press some time during the seventies. "A Home Scene" is recorded in Sam H. Dixon's *Poets and Poetry of Texas* (1883).

In this decade, influenced by retrospective Southern writers who painted word pictures of a beautiful and gallant if faded feudal system, so elegant that it was far removed from possible reality, and by the works of the metaphysical authors, especially Emerson, more Dallas citizens began to write, usually choosing for their backgrounds the 1850s and 1860s, with scant reference to the hard-bitten forties. They portrayed a family life having somewhat vague roots in old Southern culture, which with militant spirit, optimism, and hard work conquered yielding nature. Many of them actual participants in frontier adventures beyond the probability of fiction, they wrote for newspapers success stories as obviously moralizing as a Horatio Alger, or they romanced over plantations, listlessly lovely girls, and faithful slaves.

If John Neely Bryan, Dallas' own rugged frontiersman-scout, and his counterparts did not stimulate the imagination of the Dallas writer and teller of tales until a much later date, such is not true of this region's one claim to an epic hero. Sam Bass, the Indiana youth who in the 1870s came down into the Southwest to become a highwayman and trainrobber, chose Dallas and its adjacent region for some of his most notorious deeds, and became in legend another Robin Hood, while Jim Murphy, the man who killed him, earned only popular contempt as "a six-gun Judas." Never-confirmed exploits of this bandit persist until today in the stories of the oldtimers. *The Life and Adventures of Sam Bass* was published anonymously in 1878 and Charles Lee Martin's *A Sketch of Sam Bass, the Bandit* in 1880.

The concluding paragraph of *The Life and Adventures of Sam Bass* contains this query and answer:

> Sam Bass was true to his friends and his convictions, but what of Jim Murphy? That man hated of all men, despised even by the rangers whom he had served, returned to Denton. Words cannot express the supreme contempt and hatred for the man (used for classification only) who, like a rattlesnake, turned and bit the one who befriended him.

Helena Webb Gillespie lived in Dallas County from childhood until her death in 1882. She was a school teacher and a writer of both prose and poetry. Her poem "Tennyson's Picture" was published in *Amaranth*, a monthly literary magazine that was for a short time issued in Dallas, and it was claimed that Tennyson wrote Mrs. Gillespie an autographed letter of thanks. "A Dress to Make," another poem by Mrs. Gillespie, gives a hint of the feminist. The poem closes:

> I knelt and prayed me, for a time
> When women frail should learn a trade
> And buy their dresses ready made.

Ammon Burr, who had a nursery in Dallas, was a contributor to *Burke's Texas Almanac and Immigrant's Hand Book* and prepared a Garden Calendar for the 1882 edition. In this calendar he says:

> It is strange to see a fruit tree or rosebush worth 50¢ or $1 neglected, while a cotton stalk, worth 4¢, receives the greatest care. Such cases are too common, and our climate receives unreasonable blame for failure.

Thomas Sloss Turner came as a child with his parents to live near Dallas in 1877. A volume of his verse was published in 1883 under the simple title *Poems*.

May Eugenia Guillot, born in Dallas in 1865, began to write poetry in the eighties. She wrote "Venice" and "Origin of the Willow Tree," and edited *Dixieland*, a volume of verse. Willie Blanche Robinson, descendant of John Marshall, United States Chief Justice, and a teacher in Cumberland Hill Public School, wrote "Texas to Jefferson Davis" and other poems under the pen name "Persia." Miss Robinson came to Dallas in 1873 from Kansas, and the poem was inspired by Davis' visit in 1875.

Elmore L. Forshey, railroad man and newspaper reporter, had several works published in pamphlet form before the year 1885. Among these were *My Heart's Lost Love*, a collection of verses; *Fashion's Fallacies*; *The Modern Ship*; and *A Mast Incident*. These were published under the pen name "Feromall."

John Henry Brown wrote the first chronological history of the county. His *History of Dallas County, Texas, 1837–1887*, published by Milligan, Cornett & Farnham of Dallas in 1887, deals with records, county officers, and important local events. He quotes from an address he had made on the adventures of Captain M.

Eastland's company of about fifty men who went on an expedition against the Indians in 1839:

> Through the shelter of the night they reached the river bottom, and along its serpentine banks they were harassed during the succeeding day, but their unerring rifles finally compelled their pursuers to abandon the conflict with a severe loss. For five days they followed the river down its meanders till they reached the junction of the Main and Elm forks, three miles above the city. On the sixth day they crossed to the east side at the mouth of Turtle Creek, and, a mile and a half below, came to the bluff, rising above overflow, where the village of Dallas was founded or first settled four years later. Some suffering with wounds, all well-nigh denuded of clothing and their flesh torn with thorns, they resolved to halt for repose. With mud and oak ooze their wounds were poulticed, buffaloes were killed for meat, their hides converted into moccasins and "leggins" and after three or four days thus spent at the spring near where Jackson Street crosses the town branch, they recrossed the river and traveled south along the prairie, but always near the timber for protection, if attacked, and finally reached the border settlements in the lower country.

John Henry Brown also wrote *The Indian Wars and Pioneers of Texas, Encyclopedia of the New West* (1881), *The Life and Times of Henry Smith* (1887), *The History of Texas* (1892), and *Two Years in Mexico*.

James Thomas DeShields, who has made his home in Dallas for many years, wrote the tragic story of Cynthia Ann Parker, published in book form in 1883. He also contributed largely to Wilbarger's *Indian Depredations in Texas*, asserted by him to have been illustrated by O. Henry (William Sidney Porter), and published in 1886. Other volumes by DeShields are *Border Wars of Texas* (1912) and *Tall Men with Long Rifles* (1935).

Several books dealing with the cattle industry include the story of Colonel C. C. Slaughter, mighty cattle king who came to live in Dallas in the early 1870s.

In the 1880s, with the growth of reading and study clubs, the women of Dallas began to write verse, some of which occasionally appeared in the local papers. Themes of these efforts usually were the death of a loved one, beautiful love affairs never reaching fruition, tributes to family relationships and friendships, the beauties of nature, and religious resignation. The men wrote to a lesser extent, and for the most part in the James Whitcomb Riley style of homespun sentiment.

Reminiscences of the pioneers sometimes appeared in the newspapers. These stories were without narrative pattern and portrayed no archetype of pioneer. The majority were from men who had become prominent, and were largely the expressions of the personal philosophy of the writers.

With the growth of the publishing business in the eighties and nineties Dallas became a center for religious publications, and several prolific writers developed a popularity through this medium which, while transient, spread over a wide area.

Colonel John F. Elliott, distinguished journalist, came to Dallas in 1878. He was a consistent contributor of articles on finance, politics, and social subjects to periodicals and magazines. He was the author of a volume, *All About Texas* (1888), "Avenged," a poem, and *Translations from the French*.

Mrs. S. E. Buchanan became active in the editorial department of *Farm and Ranch* in the eighties and wrote under the pen name "Aunt Sally" for that publication for more than fifty years. Death ended her editorial activity in 1939 when she was ninety-eight years old.

William Isaac Yopp came to Texas from Tennessee in 1893 and was a resident of

Dallas for several years. He wrote *Yopp's Cipher Code*, in its sixth edition in 1913, and a novel, *A Dual Role*.

Sam H. Dixon, prolific journalist and writer of the Texas scene, lived in Dallas for a number of years following 1889. His *Warren of Texas, The Texan Refugee: Thrilling Story of Field and Camp Life During the Late Civil War* was published anonymously by Jno. E. Potter, Philadelphia, 1890. While here he wrote *Dixonia: or Life on the Farm*, the story of the life of his father.

George McCalla Spears came to Texas in 1890, the same year in which his *Dear Old Kentucky* was published. His short stories and verse have appeared regularly since that time in Dallas newspapers and in Kentucky periodicals. His verse is included in several anthologies.

Dudley Goodall Wooten, Dallas attorney, compiled *A Comprehensive History of Texas, 1865–1897*, which was published in Dallas in 1898. This work, largely a reprint of the text of Yoakum's *History of Texas* with additional footnotes and contributions of essays from various persons, including two by the compiler, is in two volumes, containing 2,000 pages and many illustrations. The Lewis Publishing Company of Chicago published Philip Lindsley's *A History of Greater Dallas and Vicinity* in two volumes in 1909. It is largely a repetition of an earlier venture in vanity publishing brought out by the same company in 1893 but contains some bona fide historical material. Lindsley came to Dallas in 1875 and was a frequent contributor of articles and verse to the local press and other periodicals.

Eugene P. Lyle, Jr., who was born in Dallas in 1873, was still a child when his family moved to Kansas City, but visited in Texas at frequent intervals for many years and among his writings was *The Lone Star*, a historical book for children filled with Texas heroes in stirring adventures.

Sixty Years in Texas (1908) by George Jackson recounts "the experiences of John and Mary Jackson that emigrated from Devonshire, England, in the year 1848, to Texas." The author, who came with his parents when a young boy, fills his book with verse, data, and amusing incidents of pioneer existence. He contrasts life as his parents knew it in an English town with what they found on the frontier and the volume is a valuable source for a picture of social life and folkways.

Eliza Calvert Hall Obenchain, born in Kentucky but a resident of Dallas for many years, has written fiction, verse, and articles on arts and crafts. Her novels include *Aunt Jame of Kentucky* (1907), *Sally Ann's Experience* (1910), and *A Book of Handwoven Coverlets* (1912).

Other Dallas writers notable in the early years of the century were Harry Lee Marriner, whose verse appeared regularly in the *Dallas News* and later was published in three volumes, *Joyous Days Then and Now* (1910), *When You and I Were Kids* (1911), and *Mirthful Knights in Modern Days* (1911); Mrs. Isadore Miner, who wrote books for children, *In Every Land, Cats and Dogs, All Sorts of Children*; Mrs. Mary Winn Smoots, creator of the character "Aunt Lucindy"; Harry Hampton Williams, writer of humorous verse; and Jacob Hayne Harrison, poet, frequent contributor to state periodicals on education, and the author of several textbooks.

The study clubs which began in the 1880s evolved into more specialized groups. Among those clubs which today sponsor contests and definite literary projects are the Barrington Fiction Club, the Dallas Writers' Club, the Dallas Pen Women, and the Dallas Branch, League of American Pen Women.

Southwest Review, published in Dallas since 1924 and edited by John H.

McGinnis, is issued as a quarterly and gives most of its space to prose, short stories, sketches, and some verse reflecting the regional background. It has influenced research and the growth of indigenous literature and has maintained a high standard for inclusion. The *Bard* (1920–22), established by C. O. Gill, was claimed to be the first all-poetry magazine in the South. *The Kaleidograph*, a monthly poetry magazine established in May, 1929, has encouraged Dallas poets; five collections of poetry printed in this magazine have been issued in anthology form.

Many present-day Dallas writers have expressed themselves in verse. Grace Noll (Mrs. Norman H.) Crowell's poems have a strong popular appeal to home lovers, nature lovers, and the religious, in both America and England. Her collection *White Fire* (1925) won the first annual book contest of the Poetry Society of Texas. Other volumes are *Silver in the Sun* (1928), *Miss Humpety Comes to Tea* (1929), *Flame in the Wind* (1930), *Songs for Courage* (1930), and *The Light of Years* (1936).

Hilton Ross Greer, journalist by profession, has been the moving spirit of the Texas Poetry Society. Born in 1878 in Hawkins, Texas, he has written lyrical verse that reflects an unusual ear for word music, three volumes of which have been published: *Sun-Gleams and Gossamers* (1903), *The Spiders and Other Poems* (1906), and *A Prairie Flower and Other Poems* (1912). He edited *Voices of the Southwest* (1924), and in collaboration with Dr. Florence E. Barns edited *New Voices of the Southwest* (1934).

Margaret Belle Houston, granddaughter of General Sam Houston, makes her home in Dallas and in New York. Besides five volumes of fiction, *The Little Straw Wife* (1914), *The Witch Man* (1923), *Moon of Delight* (1931), *Hurdy Gurdy* (1933), and *Magic Valley* (1934), she has published her poems in *Prairie Flowers* (1907), *The Singing Heart* (1926), and *Lanterns in the Dusk* (1930).

Whitney Montgomery, called the pastoral poet of Texas, published his first poem in 1897, since which time several hundred of his poems have appeared in numerous periodicals. He is the author of *Crown Silks and Cotton Blossoms* (1928), *Brown Fields and Bright Lights* (1930), and (with his wife, Vaida Stewart Montgomery) *Locoed and Other Poems* (1930). He edited *Bright Excalibur* (1933), a collection of poems from *Kaleidograph*.

The Barrington Fiction Club issued *Fountain Unsealed*, a collection of poems written by their members in 1931.

Dallas poets whose verse has been printed in volume form or who have made notable contributions in their fields are Clyde Walton Hill, "The Little Towns of Texas;" Sharlie Fain Acree, eight times winner of the Hughes medal annually offered by the Texas Federation of Women's Clubs for the best poem; Merle Hayes Ponder, *Deep O' My Heart* (1916); Claude Harrison Thurman, *Sea Pictures* (1921); William Russel Clark, founder and editor of *The Buccaneer* (1923-25), a magazine of verse; Jan Isbelle Fortune, *Black Poppies* (1929); Cora Pritchard Dines, *White Moonlight* (1930), *Scrappy* (1934); Inez Baker Howell, *Life is Like a Flower* (1931); Ada Smith Evans, *Little Histories in Poems* (1931); Martha Lavinia Hunter, *Far Places* (1931); Florence Young Griswold, *Trees and Heart Strings* (1932); Goldie Capers Smith, *Swords of Laughter* (1932); Jesse Edmonstron, *Star-Dust* (1932); Pauline Bennett Saline, *Random Rhymes* (1933); Siddie Joe Johnson, *Agarita Berry* (1933); Walter Henry Cousins, *Cuz* (1922) and *Chuck Wagon Windies* (1934); George D. Bond, Jr., "Sketches of the Texas Prairie"; Nancy Richey Ranson, *The Bucking Burro* (1932), *Texas Evening* (1936), *My Neighbor's Garden—And*

Mine (1939); Clare McDermott, *There Shall be Twilights* (1935); and Frances Florenz Planisheck, editor of *The Caged Poets*, an anthology of verses by prison inmates.

Mary B. Ferris, writer of stories for children, wrote *The Doodle-Bug Book of Songs* (1926), in which she composed both the words and music. Cora E. Behrends, Julia Duggan Hart, and Lois Lucile Lasater have written lyrics set to music. Martha Lavinia Hunter wrote a hymn, "God Grant Us Peace," which sold extensively in the years following the World War. William Allen War, newspaperman who was born in Corsicana and came to Dallas in 1920, has had hundreds of poems and short stories published in American and foreign magazines, a volume of verse, *Stars and Cacti* (1936), and a novel, *The Homesteader* (1931).

Notable fiction has been written by Dallas residents, and with a Dallas background by authors from elsewhere who gathered material here.

George Patullo was born and educated in Canada, and worked on newspapers there, in London, and in Boston, with an interim spent in the ranch country of West Texas. Later he married Lucile Wilson of Dallas, and lived for some time in this city. He became a highly paid and popular writer of fiction, much of which appeared in the *Saturday Evening Post*, and was special correspondent for that periodical with the American Expeditionary Force during the World War. He has often written of the Texas scene. Two volumes, *Untamed* (1911) and *The Sheriff of Badger, a Tale of the Southwest Border Land* (1912), have a western background. His "Corazon" has been called by some critics the best short story ever written about a horse.

Norma Patterson, native Texan, has had hundreds of short stories published in national magazines. Her novels include: *Jenny* (1930), *The Sun Shines Bright* (1932), and *Drums of the Night* (1935). She has collaborated with her husband, Crate Dalton, on other stories.

Helen Topping Miller, author of many short stories and novels, has made Dallas her home since 1935. Her books include *The Flaming Gahagans* (1933), *Splendor of Eagles* (1936), *Love Comes Last* (1935), *Let Me Die Tuesday* (1936), *Storm Over Eden* (1937), *Hawk in the Wind* (1938), and *Never Another Moon* (1938).

George W. Barrington, former reporter and editorial writer, turned to fiction in 1924 and has been very prolific. Among his volumes are *Outlaws of Badger Hollow*, *Bandits of Bald Hill*, *Red of the Circle-G*, and *Blondy of the Double Star*. His serial *Swords*, an adventure-romance of old Mexico, appeared in book form in 1935 and his *Back from Goliad* (1935) was placed on the preferred list of the American Book Guild.

Westmoreland Gray, native Texan, has written more than fifty serials, novels, and novelettes. His novels include *Rolling Stone* (1932), *Danger Range* (1933), *Hostile Plains* (1934), and *Manhunt Trail* (1934).

Dr. Anthony Paul Perella, who sold his first fiction to the *Saturday Evening Post*, wrote *The Black Twin* (1927) and *The Angel and the Eskimo* (1928).

Malcolm Ross, formerly of Dallas, wrote *Deep Enough* (1927), a novel dealing with Texas. Allena Joyce Webb's *Lure of the Land* (1934) has been recommended for use in the public schools of Louisiana. Janice Longley wrote *Courage in Her Pocket* (1934). *Two on an Island* (1931) was written by Stella Hutchinson Dabney. Sigman Byrd wrote *Tall Grew the Pines* (1936) and *The Redlander* (1939), novels of East Texas.

Barry Benefield, native Texas novelist now living in New York, worked at one time on Dallas newspapers, and his novel *The Chicken-Wagon Family* (1925) has scenes in a Dallas hotel and in the Trinity River bottoms. Dallas scenes occur in Margaret Belle Houston's *Magic Valley* (1934).

Flowing Gold (1922), Rex Beach's stirring and popular novel of Texas oil fields, was partly written in Dallas. *The Stricklands* (1939) by Edwin Lanham, a vigorous novel of Oklahoma tenant farmers, includes an episode in the Dallas jail. *Hilltop* (1931), by Evelyn Miller Pierce, has its entire action in Dallas. *Yonder Lies Jericho* (1933) by S. B. Harrison is a story of a Dallas merchandising family.

William Hazlitt Upson, creator of the famous Earthworm Tractor stories, wrote the first of this series, "An Old Guy with Whiskers," in November, 1923, while in charge of the spare parts department of a tractor company in Dallas. Since leaving Dallas Upson has often used the Texas background in other tractor stories.

Andrew W. Somerville's "Transportation" appeared in the *Saturday Evening Post* in 1927, since which time many of his fiction stories of railroading have been printed. Kenneth Foree, Jr., has specialized in stories based on his experience in the cotton business.

Violet Short is the author of *Tintype Types* (1930). Winifred Sanford has had many stories in national magazines. "Windfall" (1928) was reprinted in *Best Short Stories of the Southwest*. Paul Leonard Heard, poet and author of "Arizona Love," compiled the material for the anthology *Love Stories of the Southwest* (1934). Howard Farrens won first prize in the Story Book contest of 1934 with "Moon Enchantment." Horace McCoy of Dallas and Hollywood writes stories largely concerned with themes of war and the West.

Angie Ousley Rosser, born in Dallas in 1890, is a writer of feature articles and verse, but is best known for her short stories, one of which, "Probation Wife," was made into a motion picture starring Norma Talmadge. Her textbook *Uncle Jim, the Fire Chief* (1935) at one time was in use in nine states.

Thelma Maxey, born and reared in Texas, maintains residence in Dallas. A group of twenty-five of her stories on China was published in France, England, and America under the title *The Crowing Hen*. Another group of stories from Indochina was published under the title *Goddess of Opium*. Miss Maxey wrote *Tote-Road*, a novel of her childhood in the Texas cotton fields.

Meigs Oliver Frost, prolific author of popular stories, lived in Dallas from 1908–1915. John E. Rosser writes short stories, humor, and verse. His volume *Mirrors of Selling Street* (1923) is a collection of humorous sketches on salesmanship. Mary Innes and Irene Freeman wrote a collection of stories, *Tales for Tiny Tots* (1930). Mary Innes also edited *Schools of Painting* (1911).

Arthur L. Kramer's *Motoring Through Spain* (1928) was a valuable work in its field. Eugene Debogory told of travel and adventure in South Africa in his *Roaring Dusk* (1928). Cosette Faust-Newton wrote *The Rainbow-hued Trail Around the World* (1923).

Frank Norfleet's *Norfleet*(1924) recounted the author's 30,000 mile pursuit of five confidence men who had swindled him. Its principal scenes were laid in Dallas.

Work of distinction has been done by Dallas playwrights *(see THEATER: TENT TROUPERS TO TORCHBEARERS)*. A valuable contribution to folklore is *The Texas Wild Flower Legends* (1933) by Nancy Richey Ranson.

The city's writers of biography and history number several whose work has been notable.

Sam Hanna Acheson, born in Dallas in 1900, wrote *Joe Bailey, the Last Demo-*

crat (1932), a biographical and critical story, and *35,000 Days in Texas* (1938), the history of *The Dallas Morning News*. Peter Molyneaux is the author of *The Romantic Story of Texas* (1937).

Herbert Pickens Gambrell is the author of *Mirabeau Bonaparte Lamar, Troubadour and Crusader* (1934), the coauthor (with L. W. Newton) of *A Social and Political History of Texas* (1932), and has contributed historical articles to periodicals and surveys.

Charles Shirley Potts was coauthor (with professors E. C. Barker and C. W. Ramsdell) of *A School History of Texas* (1912) and has written many articles and bulletins.

Samuel Wood Geiser, while primarily a writer of textbooks and articles on general biology, has written a volume, *Naturalists of the Frontier* (1937), that has proved popular.

Charles Clinton Walsh is the author of *The Student's Quiz Book*, in three volumes (1893–1896); *Early Days on the Western Plains* (1917); *The Old Quartette* (1923); *Passing of the Years* (1928); and *Memories of '93* (1928).

Other historical writing has been done by: Melissa Allen Castle, *Texas' Bloodless Revolution* (1934); Wayne Gard, *Sam Bass* (1936); Mamie Wynne Cox, *Historic Huntsville Through a Camera—Twenty Years of the Sam Houston Normal Institute* (1899) and *Romantic Flags of Texas* (1936); Laura Alline Hobby, *Washington the Lover* (1932); Frances Florenz Planisheck, more than six thousand biographies for the five volumes of *New Texas Encyclopedia*; Goldie Capers Smith, *The Creative Arts in Texas* (1926); Estelle Hudson (in collaboration with Dr. Henry Maresh), *Czech Pioneers of the Southwest* (1934); John Rosenfield, *Texas Historical Movies* (1935); Claud Andrew Nichols, *Moral Education Among North American Indians* (1930); Harrison Anthony Trexler, *Slavery in Missouri, 1804–1865*; Justin F. Kimball, *Our City Dallas* (1927), a study in community civics; William Brush Ruggles, *History of the Texas Baseball League, 1889–1923*; Jan Isbelle Fortune, *Fugitives, The Story of Clyde Barrow and Bonnie Parker* (1934); and Elaine Boylan (with Mary Hays Marable), *A Handbook of Oklahoma Writers* (1939).

J. Mason Brewer, Negro born in Goliad, Texas, in 1896 but long resident in Dallas, has written along several lines. His *Negro Legislators and Their Descendants* (1935) is history and biography. The folkways of his people are in his "Juneteenth" (1932) and "Old Time Negro Proverbs" (1933). His *Negrito* (1933) is a volume of Negro dialect poems of the Southwest.

Writers on religious subjects in Dallas have been prolific. James Britton Cranfill, founder and for many years editor and publisher of *The Baptist Standard* (1892–1904), put in volume form many of his writings from this periodical: *Courage and Comfort* (1895), *Cranfill's Heart Talks* (1906), and *From Nature to Grace* (1925).

Leon Decatur Young, Presbyterian clergyman of Dallas who has contributed many religious and educational articles to periodicals, is the author of the *Know Your Bible* series of essays. Albert Clay Zumbrunner wrote *The Community Church* (1922), published by the University of Chicago Press. Dr. Umphrey Lee, president of Southern Methodist University, is author of *The Lord's Horseman* (1928), a study of the life of John Wesley, and *The Historical Background of Early Methodist Enthusiasm* (1931). Franz Marshall McConnell, editor of *The Baptist Standard*, is author of *The Triple Appeal, Church Manual, Winning Souls and Strengthening Churches* (1913); and *The Deacon's Daughter* (1918). Dewitt McMurray wrote *The Religion of a Newspaper Man* (1916). John Monroe Moore has written many articles on religious and mission subjects, and is the author of *Etchings of the East* (1909), *The South Today* (1916), *Brazil—An Introductory Study* (1920), and *Making the World Christian* (1922). Bishop Charles Claude Selecman, former president of Southern Methodist University (1923–38), is the author of *Christ or Chaos* (1923). Claude Harrison Thurman, in collaboration with John W. Bowyer, wrote *The Annals of Elder Horn* (1929). Charles McTyeire Bishop, a contributor to many religious publications, is the author of *Jesus the Worker* (1910), and *Characteristics of the Christian Life* (1925). Thomas C. Gardner has written extensively on B.Y.P.U. work. Atticus Webb is a frequent contributor to Sunday school and church magazines and author of *Crime, Our National Shame* (1924); *Face the Facts* (1927); and *Dry America* (1931).

Among Dallas writers who specialize in feature articles are Arthur Coleman, whose articles on questions peculiar to the South have been widely read; Marie Calcot Harris, who while a prolific writer in many fields is best known for her articles on civic affairs; Z. Starr Armstrong, who has published feature stories on travel, agriculture, and Mexico; Stuart McGregor, writer on industrial and commercial affairs; Dr. Joseph Ussery Yarborough, who writes on psychology; Jerry Bywaters, author of articles on art and regional architecture; Roscoe Plimpton Dewitt, writer on architecture; Katharine T. Stout, contributor of many articles on art in the schools to educational magazines; Margaret Ann Scruggs, authority on early Virginia family history; and Marian Price Scruggs, author of *Gardening in the Southwest* (1932) and writer of horticultural articles.

Clyde Eagleton, professor for some time at Southern Methodist University and author of *The Responsibility of States in International Law* (1928), has written many articles published in national magazines.

Victor H. Schoffelmayer, specialist in the field of agricultural economics and industrial statistics, wrote *Texas at the Cross Roads* (1935). Ellis W. Shuler has written technical articles in the field of archaeology and paleontology, including "Collecting Fossil Elephants at Dallas, Texas." Samuel Dale Myres, Jr., is the author of monographs on government, editor of the Arnold Foundation Studies in Public Affairs and editor of *The Government of Texas—a Survey* (1923). George Waverley Briggs has produced works on the Texas penitentiaries and Texas housing problems, and compiled *Digest of Insurance Laws of Texas* (1920) and *Digest of Banking Law of Texas* (1920). John O. Beaty (with Jay B. Hubbell) wrote *An Introduction to Poetry* (1922), *An Introduction to Drama* (1927), and *John Esten Cooke, Virginian* (1922).

Robert T. Hill came to Texas in 1873 and four important books from his pen are *The Geological History of the Isthmus of Panama and Portions of Costa Rica, Geology of Jamaica, Cuba and Porto Rico, Southern California Geology*, and *Los Angeles Earthquakes* (1928).

James Quayle Dealey is the author of *Textbook of Sociology* (with Dr. Lester F. Ward, 1905), *Our State Constitutions* (1907), *Ethical and Religious Significance of the State* (1910), *The Family in Its Sociological Aspects* (1912), *State and Government* (1921), *Foreign Policies of the United States* (1927), *Political Situations in Rhode Island* (1928), and several other volumes.

Dr. William E. Howard is the author of "The Eye in Epidemic Cerebro-Spinal Meningitis" (he reported 150 cases under his observation during the cerebrospinal meningitis epidemic in Dallas); "Evaluation of the Economic Loss of Vision in Workmen's Compensation Insurance," a report of 300 submucous resections of the nasal septum; and has written various articles on Texas history and Texas folklore. Dr. Howard is nationally known as a collector of Texas and Mexican historical material.

Anderson M. Baten is the author of *Slang from Shakespeare* (1931), *Philosophy of Shakespeare* (1937), and has *A Dictionary of Shakespeare* in manuscript form.

Ernest E. Leisy wrote *The American Historical Novel Before 1860* (1923), *American Literature: an Interpretative Survey* (1929), and edited, with Howard Mumford Jones, *Main Figures in American Literature* (1935).

Charles Franklyn Zeek has written French textbooks, Lucile Blake Gardner primary works, Dodie Hooe arithmetic practices, Roberta Walton King Spanish textbooks, Daisy Armstrong Shaw Spanish textbooks, William Porter Matheny civics texts, and Bernard Paul Reinsch has written mathematical texts and articles on technical subjects and mathematics.

Dallas has steadily developed as a publishing center, and to a large degree the companies have given favorable consideration to regional writers and writings. Southern Methodist University maintains a noncommercial press, established in 1937.

The Little Theater of Dallas

presents

THE 1924 BELASCO CUP PRIZE PLAY

"Judge Lynch"

By J. W. Rogers, Jr.

With the Original Cast.

MRS. JOPLIN	Julia Hogan
ELLA, *her daughter-in-law*	Louise Bond
STRANGER	Joe Peel
ED JOPLIN, *Ella's husband*	Louis Quince

TIME—The Present.

SCENE—Somewhere in the South

The Play directed by Oliver Hinsdell.
The scenery designed by Olin Travis.
Built by Ben Smith and Circle Theatre.

NOTE—The prize production of "Judge Lynch," which the LITTLE THEATRE is presenting this week, was originally intended for season ticket holders only. Friends of the LITTLE THEATRE have shown so much interest in it, however, that it was decided to throw the performances open to the public as well as subscribers.

Due to the uncertainty of the hot weather at this time of year, it seemed wiser not to prolong the evening into a full bill of one-act plays. Friends of the LITTLE THEATRE who are visiting it for the first time are asked to bear in mind that this is not a production of the regular LITTLE THEATRE season, and that all productions of the regular season are the ordinary professional theatre length.

"Judge Lynch"—Belasco Cup Winning Play

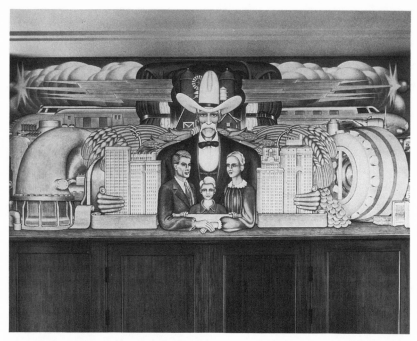

"Old Man Texas"—Mural in Hall of State

Statue of Robert E. Lee, Lee Park

Confederate Monument, Sullivan Park

Texas Immortals in Bronze, Hall of State

Fair Park Auditorium

Sydney Smith Memorial Fountain, Fair Park

The Dallas Public Library

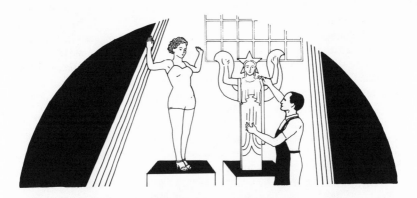

PAINTING AND SCULPTURE: ESTHETIC ASSETS

The early history of art in Dallas follows practically the same pattern as that of other Southwestern cities. As a pioneer community Dallas was filled with a populace busy making a living and accumulating property of a somewhat less abstract nature than art. Itinerant artists here as elsewhere drew crude likenesses of persons who could pose and pay for a portrait.

Graphic art in general was left to a few "foreigners" who visited in the region, painting heroic scenes of Texas' struggle for independence. "Siege of the Alamo" by Professor L. R. Bromley was exhibited at the Star Art Gallery in May, 1884. In September of the same year Professor Wears gave a series of lectures on "the theory and practice of art and art criticism."

In 1887 Professor Richard Lentz, at that time dean of Dallas artists, traded a painting, "View of Dallas from Oak Cliff," for a town lot. Professor Lentz, a German painter of the Munich school, was an instructor of art in Dallas for a time.

As an increasing number of Dallas families accumulated property some gesture towards art and art collecting naturally evolved as a part of the general scheme of culture then being acquired. Before the 1900s this phase was well under way. The movement was without direction and as there was no American art, Dallas, like all of America, gave obeisance to the established forms of European art. While collectors of Dallas were sometimes misled by their agents, they were sincere in their efforts to refine the citizenry by bringing esthetic appreciation of art and were busy trying to import European and American artists who bowed before traditional forms.

The young of the region bent upon art as a career went to the Eastern cities for technical training. Some few won scholarships in Europe and others went abroad under the general conception that Europe was the center of technical training and even of subject material. Those who studied in Paris in the Left Bank art colonies picked up the vernacular and methods of the French Impressionists.

Usually when they completed their studies they remained in Europe or returned to Eastern American cities for their subject material. Artists stayed away from what they regarded as the philistinism of Dallas. Those with original tendencies remained in sections where newer forms were recognized, largely ignoring Texas as subject material.

R. J. Onderdonk was perhaps the most competent teacher and artist in Dallas after the frontier period. He was not a native Texan and was trained in the European tradition of figure painting. He preserved the faces of many of the wealthy and politically prominent in the established manner of English historical painting. His painting "Roses and Mahogany," which caused a mild sensation when exhibited in 1902, may still be seen in the Art Museum.

The annual State Fair of Texas afforded exhibitions for local artists and the stimulus of competitive prizes. Frank Reaugh, the leading Dallas artist, was influential in obtaining paintings for the early fair exhibits. Reaugh came to Texas from Illinois in 1876 at the impressionable age of fifteen. He went to France, Belgium, and Holland to study. When he returned he translated on canvas in an Impressionist technique much of the Texas scene. He found in the ranch life of her plains and cattle herds motifs for his European training. By 1900 his work had won recognition in St. Louis, Kansas City, and Eastern centers.

In 1900 a public library was given to Dallas by Andrew Carnegie and through the efforts of Reaugh and the library association a specially lighted art exhibit room was included in the building. This room was the scene of Dallas' first art exhibition in October, 1901. Proceeds went into the purchase of two paintings, "Gondolier's Kitchen" by Robert W. Faulkner and "September Moonrise" by Childe Hassam.

In April, 1902, *The Dallas Morning News* published an article tracing the development of art in Dallas. The article asserted there were "a dozen or more professional artists of fine ability who conduct paying studios in the community, to say nothing of the many who pursue art to gratify their personal tastes." Among the artists listed as being especially successful at that time were Frank Reaugh, Eva Fowler, Charles Kent Owens, F. H. Morse, Cordie Hearne, and Lulu Rippey. Miss Clyde Chandler, a girl in her teens, was listed as the only sculptor.

In 1902 there was only one private studio built especially for art purposes, that of Mrs. W. L. Crawford, which was chiefly adorned by the owner's own work. Mrs. E. J. Kiest also had equipped a studio for china painting, at that time one of the most popular pastimes for women. Eva Fowler of Dallas had won a prize in this field at the Chicago World's Fair in 1893. The first art school in Dallas was established in 1902 by Vivian Aunspaugh—the first complete art school in Texas. The Aunspaugh School of Art is still in existence.

In January, 1903, the Dallas Art Association was founded by fifty members with Mrs. Charles L. Dextor president. From this beginning there came an organized movement for making Dallas an art center. The Fine Arts Building in Fair Park was completed in 1909 when the art collection of the association was placed on exhibition in this building and formally presented to the city. In 1913 a charter was obtained for the association.

Mrs. George K. Meyer had become the president of the Art Association in 1909 and held that office until 1927. During the years of her presidency the exhibitions were for the most part representative of the work done in the East by artists at their peak.

For several years the Dallas Art Association took on the Herculean task of carrying the burden of art in the community. Some public and a few private buildings acquired paintings, but the mass of people either did not understand art, looking on it as inapprehensible, or merely did not care about it. Barring rare exceptions it remained the pleasure of the privileged few. Art still belonged to Culture with a capital C. There remained at this time no regional or American scheme or manner for Americans as subject matter. The savage beauty of Texas and the Southwest scene was yet to be interpreted by individual or regional technique.

In order to provide local artists with an opportunity for exhibition, Mrs. A. H. Bailey in January, 1924, organized the Highland Park Society of Arts. In October of the preceding year the first exhibition of art in the Highland Park Art Gallery had been held, but it included no local work.

However, with the formal organization of the society local artists were given recognition, and it was in the Highland Park gallery that E. G. Eisenlohr and Frank Reaugh, long recognized as the two most renowned artists of the city, were given their first one-man shows in Dallas. The artists and patrons of Dallas were becoming aware of the scientific spirit of the twentieth century. There was evidence of a new impetus of art developing nearer to contemporary scene and thought.

Julian Onderdonk, E. G. Eisenlohr, Frank Reaugh, and the younger artists, Olin Travis and Reveau Bassett, are some of the Dallas painters who used a modified Impressionism depicting life in Texas and in the Southwest. Onderdonk, usually thought of as a San Antonio artist but who made his home here for several years around the turn of the century, was the first to use the Texas bluebonnet en masse. Reaugh dedicated a lifetime to preserving the Texas longhorn on canvas. Olin Travis painted many Texas rural types. Reveau Bassett took the local landscape and its bird life for his theme. These artists insisted there was a Texas scene worthy of attention. The landscapes of Texas with their purple hazes and misty vastnesses lent themselves well to the medium of Impressionism.

Of more importance to local artists was the annual exhibition sponsored by the Dallas Woman's Forum. The first exhibit was held in 1911 at the Methodist Publishing House. Texas-born artists or those making their homes in Texas were eligible for entry. Under the leadership of Vivian L. Aunspaugh those exhibits continued until the trough of the depression ended such activities. Many competent Texas artists began their careers through these exhibitions. When America as a whole was feeling the growing pains incident to the development of a truly native art that also was penetrating Dallas, the World War made all art movements suddenly unimportant.

Joseph Sartor opened the Sartor Galleries Inc. in 1921 but a difference in policy caused a break between Mr. Sartor and his associates and in 1926, after having been awarded in court the use of his name, he established the Joseph Sartor Galleries at 3017 Knox Street, their present location, where local artists were given recognition and exhibitions. The Lawrence Gallery opened one year later at 1904 Pacific Avenue, and dealt in photography as well as art but now handles only art work.

Following the immediate postwar period the confidence of young Dallas art students was strengthened by the success of regional literature in America. Many artists were influenced in their student days by the rebellion and daring appeal of post-Impressionism and the moderns of Paris. This phase produced little effect on actual work produced. The Dallas artists came to see the fallacy of allowing European methods of approach to dominate and mold the local scene.

In 1926 Olin Travis and James A. Waddell started the Art Institute of Dallas. Reveau Bassett, associate artist, aided materially in the development of this school and art education in the city. The Art Institute now is a civic organization governed by a board of trustees. This school enrolls 200 students. Southern Methodist University and Hockaday School for Girls have art departments. The Dallas School of Creative Arts teaches metal and jewelry working and other crafts.

Dallas acquired two valuable pieces of art in the Busch Loan Paintings, which hang in the main lobby of the Adolphus Hotel, and which were loaned to the hotel in 1927 for an indefinite period by their owner, August A. Busch. Probably the more interesting of the two is the Belgian masterpiece by Edouard Farazyn, "Les Emigrants," that hangs behind the flower desk in the east wing of the lobby. The scene it portrays of a crowd of emigrants huddled with their belongings on the docks preparatory to their departure for a new land is full of human interest and shows among the group Farazyn himself (the standing figure in the center with a long blond beard) along with several other contemporary painters. It was for a long time a center of attraction at the St. Louis Art Museum and some years ago was sent by its owner on an extensive exhibition tour throughout the United States.

The other painting, a vivid and spirited landscape glowing with color entitled "The Forest Fire," hangs on the opposite side of the lobby and is the work of the Russian artist Denizoff-Uralsky. Its realism is such that it is commonly said that the observer cannot stand too close because of the heat from the painted flames. It was first exhibited in this country as part of the Russian Section at the Louisiana Purchase Exposition in St. Louis in 1904, and was later bought by the late Adolphus Busch. These paintings, valued at $50,000 each, are effectively displayed with skillful gallery lighting in a setting of rich carpets and hangings and expensive bric-a-brac in the main lobby of the hotel. Surrounding these are other excellent paintings and several striking photographic studies.

As added emphasis to art stimulation in Dallas by artists and the civic-minded, a home for art has been prepared in the $500,000 Museum of Fine Arts. This building is located in Fair Park and was built in 1936 under the Texas Centennial Exposition program, the money being derived from a municipal bond issue voted in 1927. The structure is an adaptation of Greek architecture and is open to the public from 8 a.m. to 5 p.m. except on Sunday, when hours are from 2 to 7 p.m.

The museum is operated by the Dallas Art Association which opened the Centennial Exposition exhibition (June 6-November 29, 1936) with a collection assembled by Robert B. Harshe and John Catton Rich of the Art Institute of Chicago. The assembled pictures gave spectators opportunity to view art from the Primitives through the Renaissance, American Retrospective artists, various phases and schools of art, to the works of local artists. Sculpture, tapestries, and other art forms were shown.

The exhibition of the Greater Texas and Pan-American Exposition in 1937 included collections of art from the Mayan to the moderns of the Latin Americas. Contemporary American art was given emphasis. An estimated 160,000 persons visited the 1936–37 exhibitions. The director of the museum says that between 10,000 and 12,000 persons visited the museum during the 1937–38 winter after the exposition closed.

Following the exposition the twenty-one members of the Art Association's governing body projected a program of evening lectures, study courses, and special exhibits in the museum. Activities include children's classes. The Art Institute of Dallas moved from its former headquarters on McKinney Avenue into the classrooms of the museum. The art schools and Dallas public schools find in the museum a center they are making of continued use. Visits to the museum are part of the public education system's extracurricular activity program.

Karl Hoblitzelle, Dallas theater magnate, loaned a group of forty-three pictures to the museum which his brother Clarence Hoblitzelle acquired from the Marquis de Torre Teglia. Research shows this group includes a number of old masters of considerable value. Eight of the paintings have undergone restoration and have been identified. The remainder are in process of restoration, which will take several years to complete.

Dallas was selected in 1939 as one of eight American cities to receive a Kress Foundation painting gift. The painting awarded to Dallas is the "Madonna and Child with St. Jerome," an Italian Renaissance painting spoken of as "an example of the gifted Ferrarese master, Garofalo, at his best." The works of local artists chosen for exhibition in the Dallas Museum were selected by judges from other sections of the United States.

The young contemporary artists of Dallas comprise a group of about one hundred men and women. The most prominent of these are Reveau Bassett, Olin Travis, Everett Spruce, William Lester, Otis Dozier, Alexandre Hogue, Charles T. Bowling, H. O. Robertson, Jerry Bywaters, Arthur Niendorff, Thomas M. Stell, Harry Carnohan, Perry Nichols, Dan Dial, Jessie Jo Eckford, and John Douglass, all painters. Among the sculptors are Dorothy Austin, Allie V. Tennant, and Mike Owen. Many competent artists of Dallas find it necessary to combine their painting with other employment. Alexandre Hogue, head of the Hockaday art department, has won wide recognition for his series of paintings depicting the middle-western droughts. The Jeu de Paume, noted museum of Paris, France, purchased "Drought Survivors," one of the few American works acquired toward establishing an American wing to the building.

Within recent years the Negroes of Dallas have made organized movements in the development of their race's art and handicraft. This plan has been in existence since 1931 and the functions are held either in the Moorland Branch of the YMCA or the Maria Morgan Branch of the YWCA.

Sixteen Negro women form the Royal Art Club and meet weekly to work together on plaques and pictures for decoration. They hold an exhibit each Spring in the home of some member.

O. W. Johnson, William Bryant, Henry Howard, and Ethel Davis do paintings, drawings, and sketches. Thurmond Townsend in 1938 did his first art work in modeling a life-size head of his wife from clay obtained in his backyard. The Dallas Art Institute proclaimed it a remarkable piece of modeling and the head was established in the Paul Laurence Dunbar library of Dallas. Encouraged by the reception of his work Townsend has turned to painting and has gained recognition in the local art columns. The Negro artists of Dallas are with one exception untrained.

Mural art is comparatively new to Dallas. In 1934 the Public Works Administration Art Project employed Dallas artists to paint murals in the schools and public buildings of the city. The project resulted in some heroic historical and contemporary scenes. In the City Hall Alexandre Hogue and Jerry Bywaters, assisted by Rus-

233

sell O. Bailey, painted "Development of Dallas." Adele L. Brunet painted "Nursery Rhymes" in Parkland City-County Hospital. "Rural Workers" and "Industrial or City Workers" by Harry Carnohan decorated Oak Cliff High School. North Dallas High School has "Historical Development of Educational Institutions in Texas," by John E. Douglass. Douglass also painted for the Dallas County Criminal Courts building the mural, "Two Phases of Crime Control in Texas." Otis Dozier did the murals "Cotton" and "Oil" for the Forest Avenue High School. Frank Klepper painted one panel, "McKinney Post Office," and William Lester painted "Development of American Industry" at Woodrow Wilson High School. Lester also decorated Boude Storey Junior High School with "Agriculture," "Electricity," and "Arts of Building." "Mechanics and Machinery" and "Radio and Electricity" by Perry Nichols are the murals in Dallas Technical High School. Thomas M. Stell's "Surrender of Santa Anna" is in Forest Avenue High School. Highland Park Town Hall has "Early Texas Life" and "Perils of the Trail" by Ruby Stone, and "The Eagle Dance" by Maude S. West. Granville Bruce painted "Landing of Pioneers" in Sunset High School. Olin Travis painted "Man's Interdependence" in J. L. Long Junior High School.

The Hall of State, opened in Fair Park September 5, 1936 *(see POINTS OF INTEREST, Hall of State)*, has an enormous gold medallion centering its interior main chamber. A gold star in bas relief painted by Joseph C. Renier centers the medallion.

In the large chamber Eugene Savage, New York artist, assisted by Reveau Bassett, James Buchanan Winn, Jr., William Smith, and Lennie Lyons painted murals depicting scenes from Texas history. These murals are 80x30 feet, in a modified Byzantine style—as Savage said, "the largest of which I know at present."

Arthur Niendorff painted the mural scenes in the North Texas room; J. O. Mahoney those in the South Texas room; Olin Travis in the East Texas room; and Tom Lea those in the West Texas room. These regional murals depict the development of Texas.

The Hall of Heroes contains bronze statues of Texas men of history. Stephen F. Austin and Sam Houston hold the commanding positions at the entrance to the Hall of State. The other statues are Mirabeau B. Lamar, James Walker Fannin, Thomas J. Rusk, and William Barrett Travis. Pompeo Coppini, resident of San Antonio from 1901 to 1916, was the sculptor. Several friezes in bronze letters recall outstanding Texas events.

It may be said that in Dallas there is a regional school of art. Dallas artists in their evolution have moved out of the ivory tower and many of them now use their craftsmanship in portraying their native environment. It is the consensus of artists and instructors that a vigorous, individual, indigenous art is growing here.

In part this has been a reflection of a national trend—the rejection of pure esthetics and the rediscovery of contemporary America by American artists in terms of forthright social and geographical commentary. Significant of this new orientation and appropriately closing the decade from 1930 to 1940, an exhibit of twenty-five selected paintings, representative of nine states and produced under the sponsorship of the Work Projects Administration Art Program, opened at the Museum of Fine Arts January 1, 1940. The paintings were chosen from the Frontiers of America Art exhibit, which was one of the principal attractions at the Golden Gate Exposition in San Francisco, and sharply mirrored various facets of the American scene in studies as diverse as Aaron Bohrod's "Slag Heaps," Joseph Hirsch's scene of homeless men wandering the streets, Paul Clement's two pictures of Casey at the Bat, Yvonne Twining's precisely realistic representation of the Boston tenement district, Loren MacIver's fanciful cityscape, and the contrasting Californian, Alaskan, and Michigan landscapes of Paul Julian, Edwin Boyd, and Norman MacLeish.

THEATER: TENT TROUPERS TO TORCHBEARERS

Tent shows, traveling by wagon, brought the first dramatic attractions to Dallas soon after the Civil War. "Queer, quaint and quizzical," according to the advertisements, were the presentations of the Bailey Dramatic Troupe, showing in a tent in the summer of 1869. Entertainment offered by this aggregation combined, its billing asserted, "harmony, mirth, wit, humor, pathos; musical, farcical, intellectual, fantastical, tragical, vocal, instrumental, lyrical, moral and laughable eccentricities and peculiarities," all for an admission fee of fifty cents in specie—hard money. In the same year the Crisp Troupe, playing in the new Camp & Gaston Building, "won golden opinions from all sorts of people," the *Herald* reviewer conceded, in its presentations of *Romeo and Juliet* and *Pocahontas*.

First theaters in Dallas hardly deserved the name. Having their inception in the late sixties and early seventies when the town still was the center of the buffalo-hide and flour trade, these places of entertainment were for the most part located in the restricted district of "sporting houses," then centered about Camp and Griffin Streets. Known as variety theaters, they actually were typical forerunners of the honky-tonks of a later day. The variety consisted of drink, food, and more or less bawdy diversion ranging from burlesque to crude dramatics.

Resentment of many of the townspeople against these so-called theaters, culminating in the burning of several of them, is thus explained by a writer of the period:

> These places were the resorts of the most depraved characters in the country, whose carryings-on would now and then reach such a scandalous pitch that the better class of people considered it an act of patriotic vandalism to bribe some good man to set fire to the theaters. Such fires usually occurred between 1 and 2 o'clock in the morning.

John W. Thompson, who in 1872 opened Thompson's Variety Theater at 444 South Jefferson Street, on the site of the old post office, later removing to 718–20 Main Street, at Martin, is generally credited with being the father of the theater in Dallas. An advertisement of September 4, 1873, reads "Johnnie Thompson's Varieties, Open Every Night, Songs, Dances, Jigs, Farces, Etc., Best of Wines and Liquors Always on Hand." With the coming of a second railroad in 1873 there was marked growth in the number and type of theaters. The Alhambra, opposite the famed old Crutchfield House, dealt in food, drink, and entertainment in 1873, and William Womble was proprietor of a variety establishment at 314 South Jefferson Street in the same year. F. Debecque's Mascotte Theater at 831 Main Street thrived for a time, and the Joe Mills and Gus Woods houses on Camp Street were known as lively places in later years. Ben Loeb was the proprietor of another of the popular early variety theaters, and Hanlon's Varieties at 716 Main Street and the Pavillion at 821–27 Commerce Street, near Field, drew large audiences.

The Colosseum Variety Theater's actors decided in the summer of 1885 that their talents were wasted in Dallas and began rehearsals on an opera. This organization was headed by Mrs. Isabelle Hammond, better known as Belle Boyd, famous Confederate spy. They left on tour on October 13, but the trip was tragically short-lived and the cast was never reassembled in Dallas.

A notorious Negro variety theater that existed through the late eighties was the Black Elephant, owned by Sanford & Jones, and located first at 716 Commerce Street and later at Young Street and Central Avenue. An ordinance passed by the city council in October, 1890, banned the operation of all variety theaters.

J. Y. and Thomas Field built the Field Opera House on the south side of Main Street between Austin and Lamar Streets in 1873 and leased it to Captain William H. Crisp for twelve months. The Crisp sisters, Misses Jessie and Cecelia, opened the house with Bulwer Lytton's *Richelieu*, on September 30, and again won popular acclaim. *Under the Gaslight* was a "great sensational drama," given by "those deserving artists, Jessie and Cecelia Crisp" on December 18, 1873. Henry Greenwall of the Tremont Opera House in Galveston brought the Greenwall Dramatic Company to the Field for a week's engagement in *The New Magdalen*, opening January 12, 1874, with Miss Ada Gray in the title role.

As the town's first legitimate theater, the Field has been memorialized by the late Frederick Warde in his *Fifty Years of Make-Believe*. The house had no dressing rooms. Therefore Mr. Warde dressed in the old Le Grand unit of the Grand Windsor Hotel, at the southwest corner of Main and Sutin Streets, and crossed Austin Street by a diagonal covered bridge to the hotel's other unit at the northeast corner of Commerce and Austin. The actor then climbed out of a window, crossed the roof and entered the opera house by another window that opened onto the back of the stage. This procedure had to be followed for each change of costume. The Field passed to the management of Max Elkins in 1876.

Through the 1870s Dallas was the scene of many one-night stands and of some long-run plays. On May 30, 1873, the Lone Star Minstrels played Dallas with Milton Barlow giving impersonations of Stephen Foster's song character "Old Black Joe." Pat Parker, who died at the Dallas County poor farm in 1885 at the claimed age of 125 years, was the reputed original "Old Black Joe" as interpreted by Barlow. The Marinetti-Ravel Troupe, "The Great, Original Pantomime & Ballet Troupe," entertained at the Odd Fellows' Hall on Monday and Tuesday evenings, June 9 and 10, 1873, with "Grand change of Bill Tuesday Night," at admission prices of $1.00, children 50 cents.

William H. Leake, the tragedian, and Annie Waite brought their organization to Field's Theater on February 19, 1876, opening with *The Female Gambler*. Leake played *Hamlet* on the night of the 20th and the Simmons Comedy Company took over on the 21st, participating in a Mardi Gras celebration that was being held. *The Lady of Lyons* was given as a matinee performance on February 24. Saturday, February 29, *The Merchant of Venice* was the attraction, followed by *Oliver Twist* on

March 2. The "Oriental Japanese" acrobatic troupe was heralded a week before their "exhibition of dexterity" on April 12. In the middle of May, 1876, the Simmons Comedy Company and William H. Leake and Annie Waite combined troupes to give the town "dramatic representations." Starting on November 21 Kiralfy's Pantomime and Burlesque Troupe played for five nights.

The next year was no less important to theatergoers, for on March 4 and 5, 1877, Mary Anderson, "the rising young tragedienne," who already at the age of 27 had attained international fame, gave Dallas her performance of Pauline in *The Lady of Lyons*. She followed Frank Chanfrau in *Kit the Arkansas Traveler*, and Lewis Morrison and Rose Wood, who had begun the year at the Field Theater.

The *Dallas Herald* of September 1, 1877, recorded that:

Tonight is the last night of Mark Grayson's drama of *Daisy Dell* at the Thompson Theater. Next week will be the seventh week he has produced a drama of his own authorship. Monday his new drama *Neptune* will be presented.

In 1879 L. Craddock erected a building on the northwest corner of Main and Austin Streets, the lower floor of which was a wholesale liquor establishment and the second floor an opera house seating 430 persons, with a stairway entrance on Main Street. Ordinary straight chairs were placed flat on the floor, marked into aisles and sections by huge white symbols painted on the walls. A stage 18x48 feet, a dressing room 6x6 feet and scenery and properties purchased from the earlier Field's Opera House completed the equipment for performances. George Robinson, stage manager, press agent and billposter, kept a check of advance reservations on the back of a railroad timecard. Cardboard signs with the word "Taken" were dropped on the seats as they were sold.

John A. Moniger, lessee and manager of the Craddock, went to New York each year and arranged for the coming season's attractions. Such Broadway notables as Fanny Davenport, Alice Oates, Emma Abbott, Edwin Booth, Lawrence Barrett, John Templeton, John McCullough, Frederick Warde, Maurice Barrymore, and Milton and Dolly Nobles played in the Craddock. Haverly's Minstrels played the house in 1881, on the eve of their tour of Europe.

A top price of $1.50 was readily obtained, and a full house was the rule. When John McCullough appeared, seats sold at $5 and there was a standing room house. Even *Uncle Tom's Cabin* was presented, complete with hounds. On the day following the performance of *Olivette*, in which John Templeton appeared, the Ladies' Sewing Circle unqualifiedly condemned not only the play but all persons "who would sit and watch girls in scanty clothing behave in such an undignified manner."

The old Field and Craddock Theaters passed into history with the opening in 1883 of the first Dallas Opera House, at the southwest corner of Commerce and Austin Streets, seating 1,200 persons and with a parterre and galleries. The Dallas Opera House Association, composed of twenty-two members with A. Davis as the first president, owned the building, erected and furnished at a cost of $43,000. It was leased to Mrs. Charles Benton of California, who had staged a home-talent production of *Cinderella* at the Craddock Theater. J. T. Trezevant followed Mrs. Benton as manager of the house. For two years this theater crowded two seasons of entertainment into one. Clara Morris, then in her heyday, received $1,000 each night of her two appearances in *The Lady of Lyons* in November of 1884.

Chain theater for Dallas arrived in 1885 when the Greenwall brothers of New

Orleans, who controlled theaters in Galveston and Houston, took over the management of the Opera House, making George W. Anzy the manager. The first performance was *Fortune's Fool*, with Louise Rial and Will Marion and the Rial-Bigger Troupe, on October 7, and a matinee and night performance on the 8th of the *The Black Flag* with Harry Woodruff and L. R. Willard; Lizzie May Ulmer in *Dad's Girl* followed. Myra Goodwin fell and injured herself slightly when she opened October 9 for two performances in *Sis! Sis! Sis!* but was able to go on with the show. On October 18, J. G. Barrows played the lead in *The Professor*, and a troupe whose name is lost to record brought *Mountain Pink* on the 24th. Belle Moore completed October's offerings with *The Danites* on the 25th. The Opera House celebrated New Year's Eve in 1885 by presenting Emma Abbott in *Il Trovatore*.

The Ford-O'Jera Company opened on January 5, 1886, with *The Black Crook*, and presented Gilbert and Sullivan's *The Mikado* on the 6th. Several other plays were given from their repertoire and John T. Ford, manager of the company, gave the local newspaper reporters an interview on Lincoln's assassination, which had occurred in his Washington theater. Frederick Warde gave *Galba, the Gladiator, Virginius*, and *Richelieu* on January 7, 8, and 9. Dallas thrilled to the genius of James O'Neill in *The Count of Monte Cristo* on January 11 and 13, and laughed with Roland Reed in *The Humbug* and *Peck's Bad Boy* on January 21. The famous Annie Pixley made her debut in Dallas with *M'Liss, Zara*, and *Michael Strogoff* on February 20, 21, and 23. Lawrence Barrett gave matinee and night performances of *Hernani* and *Francesca da Rimini* on April 16.

The local Turnverein, German and Swiss singing society, with headquarters in Turner Hall, 716 Commerce Street, in 1886 brought a paid director from Europe for amateur theatrical productions. The director's wife, a former actress, brought several trunks of costumes for which amateurs found frequent use. This project, modeled on the traditional German folk theater, continued for six years.

The Dallas Opera House thrived from 1883 to 1901, with many of the greatest names in the theater world adorning its boards, including those of Edwin Booth, F. S. Chanfrau, C. B. Bishop, John A. Hearne, John T. Raymond, Oliver Dowd Byron, Sarah Bernhardt, and Lily Langtry. The opera house was sold out a week in advance of Edwin Booth's *Hamlet* on February 24, 1887, despite a charge of $15 per seat, with several hundred members of the audience coming from out of town. The impact of Bartley Campbell's declamations in *The White Slave* was felt by Dallas in 1888, while in the same year Thomas W. Keene on tour stopped over in Dallas long enough to organize a local lodge of the Benevolent and Protective Order of Elks on January 28. "By special arrangement there will be no advance seats on sale," was the announcement of a local paper concerning the presentation of Alexander Salvini, supported by Selena Fetter, on December 7 and 8, 1891, in *Don Caesar De Bazan* and *The Three Guardsmen*.

Lily Langtry failed to impress the reviewer of the *News*, who complained on her appearance in 1888:

> As an actress Mrs. Langtry does not rank very high. Her personal charm seems to be the secret of her popularity. She certainly has a magnificent physique of the tall, queenly type, and an exceedingly attractive face. Mrs. Langtry's bust is a model. Her support, like the play, is light.

By 1890 the town had become so theater-conscious that stock companies were initiated, one of the enterprises established in this period being the Cycle Park open-air theater on Second Avenue near the Fair Grounds, opening in June of 1890, which continued with varying success for more than two decades. A later development was the Happy Hour Theater on Main Street at the intersection of Stone Street wherein played at one time or another most of the burlesque troupers of the country, at an admission price of 10, 20, and 30 cents. The Bush & Gerts Music House, 1311–13 Elm Street, had an auditorium on the second floor where road shows and stock productions were given from time to time. Harry Corson Clark, who appeared there variously in light comedy roles, became a favorite in Dallas.

On April 25, 1901, the Opera House burned in the middle of the night. Manager Anzy, having fallen asleep in the dressing room of Knowles the hypnotist, who had given a performance that evening, barely escaped burning to death. Dallas was without a theater until the second and last Dallas Opera House was opened November 29, 1901, by Stuart Robson in *The Henrietta*. The new show house, at the northeast corner of Main and St. Paul Streets, was an imposing affair decorated in gold, ivory, and plush, with two balconies and a seating capacity of 1,700. The building boasted 1,464 electric lights, 500 of which were to illuminate the stage. Footlights were of red, white, and blue. Gas lights were installed as auxiliaries and scenic equipment comprised twenty-two sets. Road shows from New York were presented here for fifteen years until the cinema began to take over public amusement.

Every effort was made by the Dallas Opera House to meet the cultural and entertainment needs of the growing city, and its presentations ran the histrionic gamut from Shakespearean tragedy, contemporary melodrama, and musical comedy to Wagnerian opera. Melodrama of the period was of the old direct school in which heroes and heroines were altogether noble and villains and adventuresses were wholly despicable. The Earl Burgess Stock Company in March of 1908 gave six matinees and six night performances of such productions without repeating, the week's offerings including: *Tracked Around the World*, *Queen of the White Slaves*, *For His Sister's Honor*, *Her Fatal Likeness*, *How Hearts Are Broken*, *Dangers of Working Girls*, *No Mother to Guide Her*, and *The Whole Damn Family*. Lincoln J. Carter's *The Fast Mail* was a surefire house-filler in Dallas and played as early as December 1, 1903, at 25, 50, and 75 cents admission.

Fifteen minstrel companies played Dallas regularly from 1900 through the next ten years. Most popular of these was the Black Patti Troubadours, who appeared as often as twice in one season and never missed a year. The Swor brothers, Johnnie, Will, and Bert, and Leroy (Lasses) White, Dallas' own minstrels, were notable among endmen of the day. Dallas earlier had contributed John King, Jack Baxley and wife (Baxley and Porter), and Tom Beeson and wife (Mamie Merritt) and their daughter Lula Beeson, famous as a buck-and-wing dancer, to minstrelsy. The Primrose & West Minstrels, Richards & Pringles' and Al. G. Field's Greater Minstrels were well known to theatergoers of Dallas.

Usually there were three to seven Shakespearean plays each season. Mme. Helena Modjeska starred in *Henry VIII* on December 2, 1901, and gave *The Merchant of Venice* and *Macbeth* in matinee and night performances the next day. Richard Mansfield's *Richard III* received a large audience on December 21, 1905; Robert Mantell presented *Richard III*, *King Lear*, *Hamlet*, and *Othello* from his Shakespearean repertoire on January 2, 3, and 4, 1908. E. H. Sothern and Julia Marlowe, at the height of their fame, appeared on December 18 and 19 of 1913 in *The Taming of the Shrew* and *The Merchant of Venice*.

In the realm of opera, Verdi and Wagner shared honors with Bizet and Gounod. Entertainment in Dallas reached a classical high when the Metropolitan Grand Opera Company gave Wagner's *Parsifal* in 1905. Light opera and musical comedy productions were not presented as often as other types of entertainment, but were always popular and had longer runs. Their featured players included Lillian Russell, Fritzi Scheff, Anna Held, Marie Cahill, Florence Webber, Jefferson DeAngelis, DeWolf Hopper, Raymond Hitchcock, George M. Cohan, George Sidney, Murray and Mack, Frank Daniels, Eddie Foy, and Julian Eltinge.

Bernard Shaw's plays were well known to Dallas audiences in the early years after 1900, while Ibsen was the most popular of the newer dramatists. Mme. Alla Nazimova played here to a large audience in one of Ibsen's less-known works, *Little Eyolf*, on February 8, 1911. Others of the favorite playwrights were Pinero, Rachel Crothers, and Sir James Barrie.

Immortalized in the memory of elderly Dallas drama-lovers are many stars and the roles they made famous. Viola Allen made her bow to Dallas in *The Palace of the King* on January 25, 1902, and appeared again in *The White Sister* on November 29 and 30, 1910. Richard Mansfield played in Booth Tarkington's *Monsieur Beaucaire* on February 15, 1902, traveling on a special train which had right of way over all traffic except mail trains on every line on which it traveled. Kate Claxton appeared in *The Two Orphans* January 2, 1903, and was followed the next night by Joseph Jefferson in *Rip Van Winkle*. Jefferson brought this play to Dallas several times. William Gillette, creator of the role of *Sherlock Holmes*, first appeared in Dallas in that play on February 3 and 4, 1903, and reappeared in the same role and in a revival of his *Secret Service* during the next few years.

The Virginian was made memorable to a Dallas audience by Dustin Farnum on December 19, 1904. The year 1908 saw the appearance of Mrs. Leslie Carter in *Du Barry* and *Zaza* on the evenings of April 20 and 21. Minnie Maddern Fiske was hailed in *Salvation Nell* for two nights, December 27 and 28, 1909, and was last seen in Dallas in *The High Road*, January 9 and 10, 1914. *The Servant in the House*, with Henry B. Miller, played January 13 and 14, 1910. Dallas saw Maude Adams as *Peter Pan*, November 1 and 2, 1912. The daily press acclaimed Otis Skinner as an old favorite when he appeared in *Kismet* March 27 and 28, 1914. The farewell American tour of Sir Johnston Forbes-Robertson in 1914 brought him to Dallas in *Hamlet* on the night of November 24, followed by *The Passing of the Third Floor Back* the next night.

Less than ten lines in the press announced the coming of Anna Pavlova and M. Mikhail Mordkin with the Imperial Russian Ballet on February 7, 1911, but a large audience greeted the world-famed dancers, who arranged their program to include an Oriental choreographic adaptation from *The Arabian Nights*, *The Swan*, *The Fire Bird*, and *The Bacchanale*.

Many plays in Dallas had runs out of proportion to the city's population. From November 15, 1902, to March 15, 1903, there were seventy-four theatrical nights during which time sixty-five different performances were given. Two years later during a four-month season, sixty-seven shows were given in ninety-six nights. In 1909–10 the theater was open ninety-eight nights for only fifty-two plays.

During Dallas' brief period without an opera house a large tent was raised on Commerce Street at Browder, where *The Burgomaster* and Billy Kersand's minstrels were among productions shown. Sarah Bernhardt, who at the time was quarreling with theater managers over financial adjustments, played *Camille* in a tent near Fair Park on her second visit to Dallas in 1906. Bernhardt was last seen here in 1910.

Lake Cliff Casino, built in the present Lake Cliff Park at a cost of $50,000 with a seating capacity of 1,900, and the nearby Garden Theater were the last of the large stock houses in Dallas. The Casino was opened in 1907 and continued until 1914. Young Richard Dix, then playing juvenile leads, drew crowds to the Garden Theater and in turn Blanche Yurka or Tyrone Power, Sr. filled the Casino. Ada Meade, who played light opera leads in the seasons of 1908–9 and 1909–10 at the Casino, is still recalled for her *Madame Sherry* and *The Fortune Teller*. Lily Cahill and Boyd Nolan were also Casino favorites.

The stock company headed by Gene Lewis and Olga Worth came to Dallas in 1916 and played for several years at Cycle Park. In 1921 the Capitol Theater—the old Opera House—opened for legitimate drama, but burned December 27 the same year. The Circle Theater was built on North St. Paul Street, and opened on Christmas night of 1923 with Leona Powers, who had been playing at the Capitol when it burned, in *Why Men Leave Home*. The Gene Lewis stock company played there for a time. A road show production of *White Cargo* in 1926 brought a storm of criticism of an allegedly decadent theater and started discussion in the Dallas press that lasted for weeks, and from that year to 1931 one stock or road venture after another was tried at the Circle with small success. The last stock company to play the Circle was the Haydens, in October of 1931. They renamed the theater the Playhouse and planned a thirty-week run, but closed within a few weeks. Hayden's Stock had played Dallas for a decade and Lyle Talbot, their leading man, had become familiar to Dallas stock audiences.

The Jefferson Theater, 1521 Elm Street, first known as the Garden Theater, a stock house, came into the possession of Ray Stinnett and Si Charninsky in 1921 when it booked Pantage's Vaudeville. In 1922 they instituted a form of entertainment termed musical tabloid, starring Pete Pate and Bud Morgan. The Lasky Brothers bought the Jefferson and continued the program until it became a motion picture house, rebuilt as the Mirror.

An exhibition of "Edison's newest invention, the Vitascope," at the Dallas Opera House February 3, 1897, revealed scenes of a Mexican duel, a lynching, a fire rescue, and Niagara Falls. This was the first motion picture seen in Dallas. Later in the same year Henry Putz opened the first moving picture theater in a room over Bumpas & Kirby's drugstore at Main and Lamar Streets, using a bed sheet for a screen. In August, 1911, colored motion pictures of the coronation of King George V showed for one week. Mme. Bernhardt's film of *Camille* was exhibited in 1912 and *The Birth of a Nation* on its first Dallas engagement, October 4, 1915, ran for two weeks as a road show at top prices.

By the end of the decade between 1910 and 1920 it was apparent that the little motion picture houses along Elm Street from Lamar to Ervay, with their admission fees of 5 cents, 10 cents, and occasionally 25 cents, were too much competition for the Dallas Opera House. Legitimate players at this period were no longer touring. Bigger and better houses were built to bring Hollywood drama to Dallas.

Footlight performances were scarce in Dallas from 1920 until 1925, when Fair Park Auditorium was opened. Built at a cost of $500,000, with seating capacity of 4,400, it was admirably adapted to large musical shows, and at it were successfully presented such productions as Sigmund Romberg's *The Student Prince, The Des-*

ert Song, Billy Rose's *Crazy Quilt*, and the Winter Garden's *A Night in Spain*. But for legitimate theater it was too large to be satisfactory. After seeing the vast expanse of seats Ethel Barrymore instructed her actors to forget the finesse of *The Love Duel*, and to shout their lines. Maude Adams, Jane Cowl, Billie Burke, Evelyn Herbert, Otis Skinner, Lou Tellegen, Fritz Lieber, and Howard Marsh were among those who attempted with only moderate success to make themselves heard.

Vaudeville was known in Dallas as a form of diversion as early as 1873. The *Herald* of October 2 noted that "another packed house greeted the vaudeville combination last night" and that "they play every night during the week." Specialty acts of the stock companies around the turn of the century were a form of vaudeville. Charles A. Mangold, owner of the Casino, booked vaudeville talent in 1910, bringing here such celebrities as Al Jolson, Marshall Montgomery the ventriloquist, Havel and O'Brien, Williams and Wolfus, Mr. and Mrs. Jack McGreevey, and Charlotte Greenwood. When the Majestic Theater was built at the northeast corner of Commerce and St. Paul Streets by Karl Hoblitzelle in 1905, with a seating capacity of 800, he imported the established talent of the B. F. Keith and Orpheum circuits. Two shows a day with a 75-cent admission brought such variety artists as Sophie Tucker, Eddie Cantor, Al Jolson, Olga Petrova, Anne Codee, Phil Baker, Grace Hayes, Irene Franklin, Eva Tanguay, Ben Bernie, and many others over a period of nearly twenty years. The present Majestic Theater, 1921 Elm Street, was built in 1921 with a seating capacity of 2,500 and in 1925 the management instituted a summer policy of five acts of vaudeville combined with motion pictures. This venture proved so profitable that the two-a-day vaudeville was increased to three-a-day and later four-a-day, combined with pictures. The depression in the early 1930s ended this program as a definite policy.

Motion picture chain ascendancy collapsed in Dallas in 1933 and there were many changes and reorganizations. First-run theaters of Elm Street again came under control of Karl Hoblitzelle, who had built the first Majestic Theater in 1905. These houses were no longer held sacrosanct for motion pictures but were committed to anything Dallas audiences might find entertaining.

Again the stars of Broadway who took their plays on tour were available for Dallas audiences. Marilyn Miller, Helen Hayes, Eva LeGalliene, Katherine Cornell, Blanche Yurka, Eugenie Leontovitch, Alla Nazimova, Lynn Fontanne and Alfred Lunt, and other stars famous in the Broadway firmament have been presented here in more recent years. Robert Mantell closed an engagement in Dallas in 1927 with an exhibition of *Hamlet* in modern dress. An expurgated version of the *Folies Bergere* was presented for a week's run in 1928 and was seen again in a fifteen-day run during the State Fair of 1939. Fannie Brice in Billy Rose's *Crazy Quilt* in 1935 pleased a Dallas audience. Among the road show attractions which played in Dallas during the 1939–40 season were *The Moulin Rouge, I Married an Angel*, Clifford Odets' *Golden Boy*, Alfred Lunt and Lynn Fontanne's *Taming of the Shrew*, Sophie Tucker in *Leave It to Me*, Katherine Cornell in *No Time for Comedy*, Martha Graham's ballet, and the Ballet Russe De Monte Carlo.

Success of *The Drunkard* as an amusement feature during the Texas Centennial Exposition resulted in a revival of "nineties" melodramatic entertainment and 1938–39 witnessed such plays as *The Drunkard's Daughter, He Ain't Done Right By Our Nell*, and *Ten Nights in a Bar-room*, put on for beer-drinking audiences in theaters in Fair Park.

The Federal Theater's all-Negro production of *Macbeth*, in a Haitian setting, ran

243

for a week in Fair Park amphitheater in the summer of 1936. Among other centennial year offerings, *The Freiburg Passion Play* and *The Miracle* were the more popular.

Although born in San Antonio and reared in Texarkana, Macklyn Arbuckle, famous to an earlier generation especially for *The County Chairman* and *The Roundup*, practiced law here before he chose the theater as a career. Hope Hampton, Bebe Daniels, and Mary Brian claim this city as the home of their childhood. Hope Drive is named in honor of Miss Hampton and the Melba Theater was originally opened as the Hope Theater. Ginger Rogers, a Fort Worth girl, began her stage career as a Charleston dancer in Dallas in the middle 1920s.

Jan Duggan of the stage and motion pictures and Margaret Douglas and Ben Smith of legitimate theater secured their early training in the Dallas Little Theater. Peggy Fears, Ziegfeld Follies beauty and later of motion picture note, was born and grew up here. Ann Shirley, a native of Dallas, is a popular ingenue in motion pictures. George Robert Phillips (Spanky McFarland of "Our Gang" comedy fame) was born in Dallas. Robert Gottshall, generally known under his screen name of Shaw, is another currently featured player hailing from Dallas.

Margaret Tallichet, Constance Moore, and Monetta Darnell are the most recent of the native daughters to gain national publicity and a chance in the Hollywood game of fortune in motion pictures.

Ann Sheridan, the much publicized "oomph girl," was first discovered by Hollywood talent scouts in Dallas during the Search for Beauty screen tests conducted here about 1934. She was born in Denton and was a coed at North Texas State Teachers College at the time. Her success on the screen was almost instantaneous.

The Dallas Little Theater

The Little Theater in Dallas, which became nationally famous, had its actual inception when in 1920 the Dallas Woman's Forum created a dramatic department within its organization and secured H. T. Pearson, who had worked in amateur dramatics in his home town of Liverpool, England, as director. *Between the Soup and the Savory*, a play in one act by Gertrude Jennings, was the first production, given at an open meeting of the Forum in the Palm Room of the Adolphus Hotel. *The Magistrate*, Pinero's three-act play, was produced on December 20, 1920, at the Scottish Rite Temple.

The consequent highly favorable newspaper comment and awakened public interest convinced the dramatic department that the time was ripe for the formation of a Little Theater. Six members applied for a state charter for the Little Theater of Dallas which was granted on January 7, 1921. The season of 1921–22 found the board of directors increased from six to twenty-four members. During these first two seasons a part of the presentation was music between acts, furnished by well-known vocalists, violinists, and pianists of Dallas.

Alexander Dean, a graduate of the English Workshop at Harvard University, was appointed the first full-time director in 1922. Oliver Hinsdell, nationally known through his connection with Le Petit Theatre Du Vieux Carre at New Orleans, came to take charge of the organization at the beginning of the 1923–24 season.

The increasing audience appeal of the Dallas Little Theater brought about the construction of its first home, a frame building on Olive Street between Live Oak and Cochran Streets, costing $25,000. This house had a seating capacity of 242, a 22-foot stage and four dressing rooms.

The Dallas theater won the Belasco Cup in the New York Little Theater competition in 1924 with John William Rogers' *Judge Lynch*, in 1925 with Paul Green's *The No 'Count Boy*, and in 1926 with Margaret Larkin's *El Cristo*. *The No 'Count Boy* played by the Dallas Little Theater was the first Paul Green show to reach Broadway.

Mr. Hinsdell conceived the idea of a Texas Little Theater tournament and in 1926 the Dallas group sponsored the contest. The same season the Olive Street house was redecorated, but the Little Theater of Dallas had outgrown it. In 1928 the Maple Avenue home of the theater was opened. Of modified Spanish architecture, designed by Henry Coke Knight and Arthur E. Thomas, Dallas architects, it is a two-story structure of cream-colored brick. It has a seating capacity of 650, four dressing rooms, and modern mechanical equipment. Entrance is through a spacious lobby with a second floor housing a lounge and theatrical library. In the lounge are maintained from time to time exhibitions of the work of local artists. The structure cost $125,000. A school of the theater was inaugurated in 1935.

The Little Theater of Dallas came in the boom years and expanded rapidly in its early seasons. Patrons were not difficult to find and it was the special cultural pride of the city. Actors and actresses attained a status of unusual amateur proficiency, several of them being absorbed by Broadway.

Charles Meredith followed Oliver Hinsdell as director in 1931. A large overhead and debts from expansion made survival difficult through the depression. The Maple Avenue theater was lost to the organization in 1937 and the following season's offerings were given in the old Circle Theater downtown. The Little Theater of Dallas underwent financial reorganization in 1938 and regained control of the building on Maple Avenue. Edward Crowley took over the directorship and opened the 1938–39 season.

Other Amateur Groups

The Civic Theater of Dallas was organized in 1937 under the directorship of Paul Moore and took over the Globe Theater in Fair Park, a replica of the famed old London house constructed for the presentation of Elizabethan drama during the Texas Centennial Exposition of 1936. Among their major productions were *Russet Mantle* by Lynn Riggs and *The Pursuit of Happiness* by Lawrence Langer. It disbanded in 1939 and the Globe Theater was offered for sale.

The Arden Club, an amateur group, was organized in the fall of 1916 by the students in the Speech Arts Department of Southern Methodist University. Seven plays, including a Shakespearean drama, are presented each season under the direction of instructors in the drama department.

The New Theater League of Dallas, organized in 1938 as a socially conscious dramatic group, opened the season in the Civic Federation Auditorium with *Sticks and Stones*, a play written about local housing conditions with script and music by local women. The 1939 season was opened with selections from *Pins and Needles*, followed by Irwin Shaw's peace play *Bury the Dead*. This theater, besides working on major productions, maintains a theater workshop which takes one-act plays and skits to ready-made audiences. Educational projects are also maintained.

In the late summer of 1939 William S. Ulrich, formerly associated with the Hedgerow Theater, after a survey of various possible locations throughout the country, decided on Dallas for the organization of a semiprofessional cooperative repertory theater along the same lines as the parent theater in Pennsylvania. For this purpose he rented the old Oak Cliff Little Theater building on North Crawford Street and opened there on September 18, 1939, with Piscator's version of Theodore Dreiser's *An American Tragedy*, announcing an all-year-round repertory policy with a weekly rotation of eight or ten significant contemporary and classical plays chosen by the group. Mr. Ulrich's eventual goal is the establishment of a permanent resident company of a dozen or so people who will live, work, and study together on the same communal basis as the original Hedgerow players.

Dallas Playwrights

Play writing in Dallas has more or less paralleled the rise of the amateur theater. Mollie Moore Godbold, niece of the gifted Mollie Moore Davis, wrote her first play, *The Microbe of Love*, in 1909 but it was in 1920 that the comedy achieved success. Other plays of Mrs. Godbold's are *Polly Tikks, Flapper Grandmother* (in collaboration with Hettie Jane Dunaway in 1924); *Help Yourself*, a three-act comedy with musical numbers; *The Love Cure* (1926), a one-act comedy that has had performances in Canada and in Kingston, Jamaica, as well as in the United States; and *The Love Bug* (1930). *Gun Shy* (1930) has a Texas setting. Her play *Raw Edges*, a drama in three acts and a prologue, was produced in Dallas by a stock company for a period of one week in April, 1934.

John William Rogers, born in Dallas in 1894, has divided his time between this city and New York. Mr. Rogers has written ten one-act plays which have been published and acted throughout the United States and Canada and included in numerous anthologies. His play *Judge Lynch* (1923) won the Belasco Cup in the National Theater Tournament. Other one-act plays are *Saved, Bumble-Puppy, The Rescue of Cynthia Ann, Women Folks, Mary Means What She Says, Ringleader, Wedding Presents*, and *Westward People*, dealing with Mary Austin Holley's first visit to Texas. He has written two full-length plays: *Roam Though I May* (1933) and *Angel in the Parlor* (1934).

Jan Isbelle Fortune is the author of fifty-two Texas history plays broadcast from station WFAA; *Flammule*, a comedy of the Southwest; *Abbie Carter's Honor*, a drama of the traditions in the South in 1890; and *Roman Holiday*, a satire on Nero. She was the author of the *Cavalcade of Texas*, the historical pageant of Texas which showed two performances daily at the Texas Centennial Exposition here in 1936 and the *Cavalcade of the Americas*, a pageant of unfolding democracy in the Western Hemisphere which played at the Pan-American Exposition in 1937. She is now employed as a writer by Metro-Goldwyn-Mayer Studios in Hollywood.

Other Dallas playwrights include: Jane Bailey Fitzgerald, *The Broken Rosary* and *The Youth of the Virgin Mary*; Mamie Folsom Wynne, *The American Girl* and *Wartime Wedding*; Kathleen Witherspoon, *Jute* (1931); Leah Zeve, *Where Are the Tangles?*; and Dorothy Rosenbaum, *Sticks and Stones* (1938).

Oliver Hinsdell, one-time director of the Dallas Little Theater, wrote *Making the Theater Pay* (1925), the history of this city's Little Theater movement.

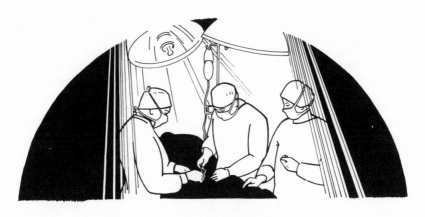

MEDICAL CENTER:
THE HEALING ARTS

The position of Dallas as a distributing point for services as well as goods has for fifty years made it an important medical center and has created extensive facilities for study, research, and practice, including a first-class medical and dental college; several nurses' training schools; a modern city-county hospital system and public health service; twenty-nine private hospitals, clinics, and convalescent homes; and a nineteen-story skyscraper especially constructed and equipped for the exclusive use of the medical and dental professions. Many important professional gatherings have been held in Dallas and patients come from all parts of the Southwest for treatment. There are in 1939 more than five hundred physicians and about six hundred graduate nurses registered in the city.

Skilled physicians and surgeons have been attracted to Dallas from pioneer days. Dr. John Cole, who settled in 1843 on a 640-acre tract covering parts of what are now Oak Lawn, North Dallas, and Highland Park, was probably the first, though Dr. W. W. Conover settled at Cedar Springs at about the same time. Dr. Jonathan L. Samson, known as "the hot water and steam doctor," also practiced in Dallas from about 1845 to 1849, when he went to California to seek gold. When the town of Dallas was incorporated in 1856 two physicians, Dr. Samuel B. Pryor and Dr. A. D. Rice, offered themselves for the position of mayor, the former being elected. Like their contemporaries, the circuit-riding preachers, these pioneer doctors of medicine made their rounds on horseback carrying the tools of their trade in saddlebags, and stood ready to minister to the sick and dying at all hours and in all weathers. Surgery was generally limited to the amputation of mangled limbs and the treatment of wounds.

A Dallas County Medical Society was in existence as early as 1871, an annual meeting being recorded on November 13 of that year at which Dr. L. Elliott was elected president, Dr. J. W. Crowdus and Dr. R. C. Campbell vice presidents, Dr. R. O. Purviance and Dr. A. A. Johnson secretaries, and Dr. J. T. Turner treasurer. Dr. S. D. Thruston was a moving spirit in this early organization, which was succeeded in 1876 by the Dallas County Medical and Surgical Association. Dr. H. K. Leake, who in later years maintained a private hospital in East Dallas, was first president of the latter, and the two organizations apparently existed concurrently for a time.

247

About this period, in the early seventies, Dallas also acquired its first permanent hospital, though it would seem that there was some kind of military hospital in the vicinity during the Civil War period, as there is an appeal in the *Dallas Herald* under date of February 2, 1865, for old linens to be used as bandages by the post surgeon. The first hospital of which there is any record was a two-room, frame shack at Wood and Houston Streets, near the present Union Terminal, where the indigent sick were treated free of cost by the city physician. Though at the time there was no other hospital nearer than the one attached to the State Medical College at Galveston, the hospital in Dallas was considered fit only for down-and-outers, the friendless, and emergency cases, who were transported to it in the police patrol.

An investigation in 1876 revealed it to be clean and the patients reasonably well cared for, but the building in a bad state of repair and grossly overcrowded, 169 patients having been treated there from April, 1875, to April, 1876. It was also located in an inconvenient and unsavory neighborhood, in the midst of the town's red light district, attending physicians taking care to display their medicals and other badges of their profession to protect their reputations when they called on patients.

These meager hospital facilities were supplemented for the poor of the community by free clinics conducted by private physicians. Such service was available as early as 1875, Drs. Hughes, Leake, Munday, and Peyton advertising in this year daily clinics from 9 a.m. to 10 p.m. with consultations, and medicines, furnished free of charge.

For a time in the late seventies and early eighties there was no permanent organization of the medical profession in the city, but in 1884 the present Dallas County Medical Society was formed, the organizational meeting being held April 3 in the office of Drs. Chilton and Smith on the north side of Main Street near Akard Street. A general call was issued to the physicians of city and county and a second meeting held April 12, at which Dr. John Morton was elected first president and Dr. H. K. Leake vice president.

The frame shack on South Jefferson Street continued to serve the city as a hospital until 1885, when a two-story Negro school building, originally costing about $1,500, was removed from Market Street to a site on Lamar Street between Wood and Young Streets and remodeled for use as a hospital. It was divided into two wards, each about 25x60 feet in size with a combined capacity of twenty-five beds, and a small cottage on the lot was made to serve as a kitchen. The building was whitewashed and renovated by Dr. J. L. Carter, city health officer, early in the year, and to it the patients in the old city hospital were transferred May 27, 1885.

By 1885 there were sixty-five physicians and surgeons practicing in Dallas, the more prominent including Dr. H. K. Leake, Dr. S. D. Thruston, Dr. Jesse D. Pace, Dr. Ewing L. Thompson, Dr. G. E. Peters, Dr. John Morton, Dr. Samson Eagan, Dr. I. A. McCarthy, Dr. David Mackay, Dr. J. L. Carter, Dr. H. I. McLaurin, Dr. H. A. Moseley, Dr. F. S. Davis, Dr. W. S. Lee, Dr. W. R. Wilson, and Dr. A. A. Johnson.

The healing art was still in a primitive stage in Texas. The germ theory of disease was not universally accepted and asepsis frequently ignored in operations. Many erroneous theories were also still current such as that of "laudable pus" and the danger of performing operations in hot weather. Chloroform was the anesthetic generally used. Plaster of paris for setting broken limbs had just been introduced, rude splints having previously been used, and a broken leg usually meant a permanent limp.

Following the establishment of a medical college in the city and the opening of the first modern hospitals about the turn of the century, Dallas forged rapidly to the front as one of the leading medical centers of the Southwest. In 1903 Dr. Adolphe Lorenz, world famous orthopedic surgeon of Vienna, held a widely attended clinic in the city, refusing all fees and operating with bloodless surgery on fifteen children. About 1905 a great improvement in medical service was achieved by the establishment of the Dallas County Physicians, Surgeons, and Nurses Registry, making it possible to locate practically any doctor or nurse in the city at any time of the day or night.

In January, 1912, Dr. Abraham Sophian brought to Dallas the newly discovered meningitis serum of his associate Dr. Simon Flexner, and led the fight against the disease here throughout the epidemic, which had begun in the late autumn of 1911, refusing to leave even when his mother was dying in New York.

In 1915 the Southern Medical Association chose the city for its ninth annual convention, 1,500 physicians from all parts of the South assembling for its opening November 9. In 1923 Dallas made a significant contribution to organized modern medicine by the erection of the Medical Arts Building, the first structure of its kind in the world to be devoted exclusively to the medical profession, and the prototype of many similar buildings in other cities *(see POINTS OF INTEREST, Medical Arts Building)*.

In 1926 the American Medical Association met in Dallas and elected a Dallas doctor, Dr. E. H. Cary, as their national president; and in 1934 another Dallas doctor, Dr. John O. McReynolds, was honored by being elected president of the Pan-American Medical Association, an international body which had met in the city the previous year. The Dallas County Medical Society, which on January 1, 1940, had an active membership of 494, has attained national prominence, and the Southern Clinical Society meets annually in Dallas, every year bringing distinguished figures in the world of medicine to the city for special lectures. The meeting in March, 1940, was attended by 600 physicians.

The latest important medical gathering in the city was the forty-third annual convention of the American Osteopathic Association, held in June, 1939. Over two thousand osteopathic physicians from all parts of the United States and Canada assembled in Dallas for a week of discussion and clinical demonstrations of new techniques in various fields of osteopathy. Preceding the convention the American Osteopathic Society of Ophthalmology and Otolaryngology, an associated body, held an eye, ear, nose, and throat clinic, performing many difficult and delicate operations including the removal of a cataract from the eye by means of a vacuum cup.

Training facilities in Dallas comprise the fully accredited Baylor University College of Medicine, College of Dentistry, and School of Nursing, which together with Baylor University Hospital constitutes a complete medical center. There are also opportunities for intern work and training in nursing at St. Paul's Hospital, the Dallas Methodist Hospital, and Parkland Hospital. The Baylor University College of Medicine was organized in 1900 as the medical department of the University of Dallas, and was taken over by Baylor University in 1903 under a special arrangement whereby the College of Medicine governed the finances.

This arrangement continued until 1909 when the College of Medicine became an integral part of the university. The College of Dentistry was originally the State Dental College, organized in Dallas in 1904, and was taken over by Baylor University in 1918. The School of Nursing was incorporated as a branch of the university when the College of Medicine and the College of Dentistry were consolidated with Baylor Hospital under a single board in 1921–22. In 1939–40 the College of Medicine had an enrollment of 305; the College of Dentistry an enrollment of 151; and the School of Nursing an enrollment of 165. All of these associated schools use the clinical facilities of the Baylor University Hospital, and the students of the College of Medicine also have access to Parkland Hospital, Woodlawn Hospital, the Bradford Memorial Hospital, and the Scottish Rite Hospital for Crippled Children.

The first training school for professional nurses to be incorporated in Texas was instituted at St. Paul's Sanitarium in September, 1906, and Dallas today graduates more nurses than any other district in the state. The Texas Graduate Nurses Association, organized in El Paso in 1933, maintains district headquarters in the Medical Arts Building and has its own registration bureau where nurses can receive professional calls day or night. The Dallas branch of this organization has over 400 members and is the largest in the state.

Parkland Hospital, maintained by the city and county and located at Maple and Oak Lawn Avenues, is the oldest hospital in the city, originating in a letter written by John E. Owens to *The Dallas Morning News* in 1890, calling attention to conditions at the City Hospital on Lamar Street, including lack of proper sanitation, trained nurses, and ambulance service, and the performance of operations under a small hanging lamp in the presence of other patients. As a result of the ensuing agitation a seventeen-acre wooded tract called Parkland, on what was then the northern edge of the city, was bought and the hospital, originally consisting of a group of wooden structures built on the pavilion plan in the manner of an army cantonment, opened May 19, 1894. The meningitis epidemic of 1911 dramatized the need for enlarged and improved hospital facilities, and the first unit of the present brick hospital was constructed in 1913, the year the city-county hospital system was inaugurated. A nursing school was also established in 1914. Additional units, including a nurses' home, were built in 1922 and 1930, and since 1934 an extensive program of improvements financed by a city-county appropriation of $341,256 and a Federal grant of $223,591 has been carried out. These improvements have included the addition of one floor to the nurses' home, two wings to the main hospital, provision for contagious cases previously handled at the old Union Hospital, 40 additional beds for Negroes, interns' quarters, and additional space for operating rooms, kitchen, laundry, and delivery rooms.

Parkland Hospital in 1940 has a capacity of 400 beds and is equipped with a clinical laboratory, operating rooms, a maternity department, and apparatus for electro-therapy. Particularly worthy of note is the free venereal clinic for both male and female patients, one of the largest in the country, opened in 1937 under the supervision of Dr. J. W. Bass, Dallas director of public health. It was made possible by the National Social Security Act authorizing the appropriation of $8,000,000 per annum for allocation to state and local health departments for the establishment and maintenance of more adequate public health services. The clinic is under the direction of Dr. Arthur Schoch and Dr. R. W. Maner, both of whom give their services without pay, and after the first thirty days it was open, was handling over

250

seven hundred cases a week. During the fiscal year 1938–39 110,000 visits to the clinic were recorded.

Prior to 1922 Parkland Hospital admitted only charity cases; since then it has admitted both charity patients and those able, in varying degrees, to pay, but with preference given to the former. During 1938–39 the hospital handled 11,000 bed patients, 24,000 emergency cases, and 100,000 out-patient visits. This hospital is the center of the entire city-county system and maintains a large staff consisting of superintendent, several physicians engaged in continuous clinical and laboratory work, laboratory technicians, graduate nurses, student nurses, two social service workers, a small office force, and two visiting physicians who make free house calls. These visiting physicians made more than 10,000 calls during 1938–39. Other medical service is provided by a departmentalized staff of 145 physicians, all having teaching affiliations with Baylor Medical College; these physicians serve without remuneration.

St. Paul's Hospital, at Bryan and Hall Streets, is the oldest privately supported hospital in the city. In the middle nineties a group of Dallas physicians, including Dr. Joseph Letcher, Dr. C. M. Rosser, and Dr. W. R. Wilson, inspired by Dr. John Wyeth of the New York Polyclinic Hospital who had lectured in Dallas a short time previously, became convinced of the need of better hospital facilities in the city and approached the Right Reverend Edward Joseph Dunne, then bishop of the Roman Catholic diocese of Dallas, on the subject, later going to New Orleans to confer with church officials there. As a result of these negotiations the Sisters of St. Vincent and St. Paul agreed to operate a hospital in Dallas, and Sister Mary Bernard came to the city in 1896 to participate in the raising of funds for its erection. Dallas citizens subscribed $10,000 and ground was bought at Hall and Bryan Streets. Ground was broken November 13, 1896. Two weeks later a temporary baby hospital was opened on Hall Street; and on May 18, 1897, the cornerstone of the institution was laid with Bishop Dunne officiating. St. Paul's Sanitarium, a large three-story brick building in the Romanesque style, was opened in June, 1898, several thousand people attending the opening reception, presided over by Sister Mary Bernard, who remained head of the institution until 1905, later establishing hospitals at Sherman, Austin, and Mobile, Alabama. A nurses' training school was established in 1900 and registered in 1906. A large annex was built in 1920, and the name of the institution changed to St. Paul's Hospital in 1927. The hospital, which has accommodations for 300 patients, is equipped with X-ray and operating rooms and maintains, in addition to a regular clinic for charity patients, a special clinic for Mexicans.

Baylor University Hospital, located at Junius, Adair, and College Streets and Gaston Avenue, is the largest of the city's hospitals and was opened as the Texas Baptist Memorial Sanitarium in October, 1909. Dr. Edward H. Cary, dean of the Baylor University College of Medicine, and Dr. C. M. Rosser, professor of surgery, who saw the need of hospital affiliations to provide the necessary clinical material for the medical college, were principally responsible for interesting prominent Texas Baptists in its erection. A financial campaign extending over several years was carried on, Colonel C. C. Slaughter, wealthy cattleman, contributing liberally; and ground was first broken in 1904, though the hospital's large, fireproof brick building was not completed until 1909.

At first the College of Medicine had access to the hospital but no distinct affiliation. In 1912 closer affiliation was achieved by the formation of an executive staff selected from the faculty of the college. In 1920 the Texas Baptist Convention voted to consolidate the College of Medicine and the hospital under the board of trustees of Baylor University, and in 1921–22 the institution became the Baylor University Hospital and its training school for nurses the Baylor University School of Nursing. In 1923 the Baylor Hospital for Women and Children, a very modern five-story building, was completed. This building, connected with the main hospital, added to its capacity by 150 beds, and also provided modernly equipped operating rooms, amphitheater operating room, the hospital clinical laboratory, the X-ray department, and the autopsy room. The Florence Nightingale Hospital, a block away from the main hospital on the corner of Gaston Avenue and Adair Street, devoted exclusively to maternity cases, was a gift from Mr. and Mrs. Edward Rolfe Brown of Dallas and was finished in 1937. It is a light, airy, two-story building of cream-colored brick, air conditioned throughout and connected with underground passageways with the other hospital buildings. It contains beds for sixty mothers and ample nursery space and isolation room for a like number of infants.

Baylor University Hospital, approved by the American College of Surgeons and American Medical Association, is a general hospital with a total capacity of 385 beds and cares for all types of patients except those suffering from contagious and mental diseases. During 1938–39 it admitted 15,343 patients to the hospital and treated 3,523 in its out-patient department. It maintains a free general clinic for charity cases, a dental clinic, and a tumor clinic. The dispensary occupies two floors of the annex and its numerous departments cover a wide field of medicine. These services are all conducted in connection with the work of the Baylor University College of Medicine and College of Dentistry.

The Medical Arts Hospital, which occupies the seventeenth and eighteenth floors of the Medical Arts Building annex at Pacific Avenue and St. Paul Street, is operated by Dr. and Mrs. E. H. Cary largely for the convenience of the physicians and dentists who occupy offices in the building. It has a capacity of 86 patients with four operating rooms, X-ray laboratories, and other facilities. It is used principally for diagnostic purposes and to take care of minor operations and office emergencies.

The Dallas Methodist Hospital, located on a landscaped knoll at Bishop and Ballard Avenues and Colorado Street in Oak Cliff, is the newest of the general hospitals in the city. It is located on historic ground, its site once forming part of a 200-acre plot granted by Governor Elisha M. Pease to Colonel John M. Crockett, an early lieutenant-governor of Texas and colonel in the Confederate army. Here Colonel Crockett built in 1855 what was said to be the first two-story house in Dallas County, and here somewhat later Dr. Samuel B. Pryor, first mayor of Dallas, made his home. The movement for a Methodist hospital in Dallas, which was initiated by the Reverends George M. Gibson and R. F. Bryant, two Oak Cliff pastors, was begun in 1920. The site of the hospital was bought for $50,000 in 1922 and ground broken February 21, 1923, three bishops of the Methodist Episcopal Church, South, officiating at the ceremonies. The seven-story, fireproof building, one of the tallest in Oak Cliff, was completed late in 1927 and was formally opened on December 27. The hospital has a capacity of one hundred patients and the latest equipment, including telephone connections to every room, a sunroom on each floor, modern refrigeration and fan ventilation from every part of the building, a complete X-ray department, two general operating rooms, an emergency operating room, a maternity room, an eye, ear, nose, and throat room, and a plaster room. It has main-

252

tained a school of nursing since it first opened, and also operates a free clinic which performs a large amount of charity work.

In addition to these general hospitals Dallas also has several specialized hospitals and clinics which are worthy of note for their high professional standing. One of these, Woodlawn Hospital, on Lucas Drive one mile north of Parkland Hospital, is operated for tubercular patients as part of the city-county hospital system. It was originally established in 1913 and averages about a hundred patients, treating all types of tuberculosis with the latest methods. Union Hospital, adjacent to it, was formerly used by the city and county for the isolation and treatment of contagious diseases, but is now closed. The Freeman Memorial Clinic, 3617 Maple Avenue, was originally known as the Presbyterian Clinic and was first projected in 1921 by the Reverend William M. Anderson, pastor of the First Presbyterian Church. The building, costing $72,000, along with the ground on which it stands, was donated by Mr. and Mrs. Percy R. Freeman as a memorial to their son, Percy Richmond Freeman, Jr., and Mr. Freeman further endowed the clinic with $200,000 in money and property on the death of his wife in 1923. It is operated for the benefit of boys under fifteen and girls under eleven whose parents are unable to pay for medical attention and some fifty doctors serve without pay on its staff.

The Bradford Memorial Hospital for Babies, 3512 Maple Avenue, was opened in 1929 and was built at a cost of $100,000 by Mayor T. L. Bradford as a memorial to his wife and their daughter, Mrs. Elizabeth B. May. The hospital, which is in part an outgrowth of the Dallas Baby Camp established by the Graduate Nurses' Association in 1913, is devoted mainly to charity cases. Its equipment includes sixty beds, five electrical incubators, an operating room, an X-ray department, an electric sterilizer, an electric ventilating system, a violet ray room, and an amphitheater where nurses and mothers may listen to lectures.

The Texas Scottish Rite Hospital for Crippled Children, 2201 Welborn Street, is probably the most distinctive institution in the city, being the only charity hospital in Texas devoted exclusively to the treatment of crippled children. It had its origin in 1920 when a children's clinic operated by Dr. W. B. Carrell, now chief surgeon of the hospital, backed by a group of local citizens, was opened in East Dallas on Worth Street. Dallas Shriners, impressed by the number of crippled children needing medical attention, decided to establish a hospital for them and broke ground on the Welborn Avenue site in 1921. The hospital was opened as the Shriner's Hospital for Crippled Children in November, 1923. Its ownership and operation was transferred to the Scottish Rite bodies of Texas May 1, 1926, at which the name was changed. Since its opening 17,000 children from all parts of Texas, only about one hundred of them from the homes of Masons, have been treated at the hospital, which specializes in the treatment of deformities resulting from infantile paralysis. Men of national and international repute in this field head its staff, and a special brace-making department is maintained where shoes and braces are made to measure for children entering the hospital.

Climaxing efforts extending over ten years, contracts were awarded in July, 1939, for construction of the first units of the Texas Children's Hospital in Dallas, which will afford statewide service for the treatment of diseases of children. The new institution is located on a site adjoining the Freeman Memorial Clinic for Children, the land given by Percy R. Freeman, founder of the Freeman Clinic. It is across Welborn Street from the Scottish Rite Hospital for Crippled Children and Hope Cottage, a foundling hospital, and within a short distance of Parkland City-

253

County Hospital. The first units will cost about $140,000, the costs of construction and maintenance provided for by public contributions and endowments. The first unit will care for fifty patients, and will be opened in the summer of 1940.

Group hospitalization has met with widespread favor in Dallas. Baylor Hospital pioneered in this field in 1929 and St. Paul's Hospital and the Dallas Methodist Hospital adopted similar plans later. The groups at all three hospitals are now organized under the National Hospitalization Systems, Inc., which supply the necessary clerical and organizational activities.

The hospitals of Dallas were collectively honored at the convention of the American Hospital Association in Toronto in 1939 by the award of a trophy for outstanding work in educating the public in the appreciation and use of the city's hospital facilities.

PUBLIC HEALTH: FIRST LINE OF DEFENSE

Public health service became a part of the official government machinery of Dallas in 1872, when Dr. Matthew Cornelius was made city physician. It has developed consistently in scope and importance with the growth of the community from the 3,000 of that day to the present metropolitan population.

While Dallas has never had a major epidemic its earlier years were marked by prevalence of many ills among the population, including a few cases of cholera in 1873. Impure water was a factor in spreading typhoid, while recurrent floods in the Trinity River and tributary creeks left ample breeding ground for mosquito carriers of malarial and yellow fevers. The latter scourge appeared only once in Dallas, when six cases were reported in 1874, though there were annual fever scares until the late 1880s, armed men often quarantining the town against travelers from infected regions. On one occasion all railway passengers from the south were turned back at Mesquite, a few miles away in the county. The city suffered a severe outbreak of meningitis in 1912, and had many cases of influenza in 1918.

As early as 1873 Dr. F. E. Hughes, a local physician, was urging the use of cistern water as a preventive of yellow fever, and inveighing against a plan of the city council to turn hogs loose in the streets as scavengers. When this ordinance finally was passed in 1876 the local newspaper commented that "the hogs who have taken the contract to scavenge the streets have their mouths full." Health officers of the earlier years actively directed and often personally performed the police work of quarantining the community against potential epidemics.

Municipal inspection of the milk supply had its beginning in 1880, when the milk sellers themselves petitioned the city council for inspection of their products for protection of the public. It was not until nearly three decades later that milk and meat were brought completely under control of the health department.

Today the city maintains an efficient and well-equipped health and sanitation staff. It has an emergency hospital with 24-hour service, located in the City Hall Annex in the heart of the city. Health centers are situated in eight separated sections, under direction of visiting physicians and nurses, where weekly clinics are held, and a complete inspection division is headed by a veterinary surgeon and a

255

sanitary engineer. Citizens of Dallas have access to a modern general city-county hospital in addition to numerous private hospitals. In 1936 the city, in cooperation with the Federal government, established at this hospital a free clinic for the treatment of venereal diseases. A psychopathic division is also provided.

Care for indigent tuberculars is afforded at a modern city-county institution, Woodlawn Hospital, while the Convalescent Home at Hutchins, in the county, furnishes a comfortable retreat for the aged who are unable to maintain themselves.

In addition to the director of public health the city employs four full-time physicians in the public health work, with six graduate nurses and two intern physicians. Five of the nurses are on full-time visiting duty. Special attention is given to prenatal work and to diphtheria control.

Activities of the inspection division include constant supervision of the city water supply, milk, meat, foodstuffs, drugs, all food-handling establishments, and direction of malaria control, with a completely equipped and adequately staffed laboratory in connection. Every person engaged in the handling of foodstuffs must have a certificate of health, renewed periodically, and every food-handling establishment must have a permit from the department for its operation.

Despite lower per capita expenditures than any of the competing cities in its population class (250,000–500,000), Dallas in 1937 was awarded first place on its record for the preceding year in the annual inter-city health contest conducted by the United States Chamber of Commerce in cooperation with the American Public Health Association. The city had received honorable mention for three years and was in third place in the 1936 awards. In achieving the distinction of first place Dallas showed a per capita expenditure for public health purposes of 57 cents, while the per capita average for other competing cities in the same group was $1.30.

Again in 1938 Dallas, being ineligible to receive first award a second consecutive time, was given a certificate of special merit for the period covered by the 1937 contest, while two other cities in the same population class were tied for first place. The city was given fourth place for its 1938 health work, and received an award of merit in the 1939 contest.

Factors governing the contest include purity of water and milk supplies; environment sanitation; preventive work, especially in inoculation against diphtheria; home educational promotion of health; and the degree of support given to various local activities sponsored by organized groups. The Dallas milk supply has been each year since 1932 on the honor roll of the United States Public Health Service. It is the only large city in the Southwest to have won the inter-city contest or to receive honorable mention in the second population group.

Dr. J. W. Bass has been director of public health since 1931. His predecessors in the office, earlier known as health officers, were:

1872–1878	Dr. Matthew Cornelius
1879–1880	Dr. J. L. Carter
1881	Dr. Sam Fields
1882–1883	Dr. M. M. Newsom
1884–1890	Dr. J. L. Carter
1891	Dr. W. R. Wilson
1892	Dr. C. M. Rosser
1893–1898	Dr. V. P. Armstrong
1899–1901	Dr. J. H. Florence
1902–1905	Dr. J. H. Smart

1906–1910	Dr. T. B. Fisher
1911–1914	Dr. A. W. Nash
1915–1917	Chas. Savill, Director (by ordinance)
	Dr. Edgar Loomis, Health Officer
1917–1918	Dr. A. W. Carnes
1919–1920	Leslie C. Frank, Director (by ordinance)
	Dr. Lane B. Cooke, Health Officer
1921–1922	Col. William P. Davidson
1923	Dr. Lane B. Cooke
1924–1927	Dr. N. W. Andrews
1927	Dr. J. W. Bass
1927–1929	Dr. M. M. Carrick
1929–1931	Dr. Lane B. Cooke

NEWSPAPERS: CHRONICLERS
AND BUILDERS

In 1848 James Wellington (Weck) Latimer, printer and lawyer, publisher of the *Western Star* in Paris, Texas—a son of Albert H. Latimer, a signer of the Texas Declaration of Independence—decided that Dallas held better prospects for growth because of the possibility of navigation of the Trinity River. In the spring of 1849 he loaded his Washington hand press and cases of type into an ox-drawn wagon and set out for the new town. Among a clump of cedars where Commerce and Houston Streets now meet he erected a 12x14 foot building of cedar logs covered with clapboards, with a stick-and-mud chimney and a single door on wooden hinges. This on completion was the best building in Dallas. The structure fronted on Commerce Street and had a log cut out to admit light on the present Jefferson Street side. Here on April 6, 1849, was printed the first issue of Dallas' earliest newspaper—then and for a dozen subsequent issues titled the *Cedar Snag*.

The printing press, crude though it was, created a mild sensation, and people came from miles around to see it in operation. There was no hand roller; a ball-like leather-covered pad was spread with ink and applied until the pages of type were well covered. By this process Latimer issued his small weekly sheet every Saturday for residents of Dallas and approximately 200 widely scattered subscribing families in the countryside. Such news as reached the editor came by two weekly mails, one from Mount Pleasant and the other from Bonham by way of Dallas to San Antonio.

It was a day of personal journalism and editorial invective and Latimer, a Democrat of positive opinions, set about the task of reformation in keeping with his personal views. He soon decided that the title of the newspaper smacked too much of levity for its serious purposes, and asked suggestions for a new name. Acceding to a majority vote of the readers, Latimer renamed the publication the *Dallas Herald*.

On one occasion in 1850 the *Herald* published an especially derogatory editorial about two abolitionists; although no names were mentioned the inference was strong enough in a small community to readily identify the men in question. The following day William M. Wallis called upon Latimer and demanded that the editor retract the statements that had been made, and apologize. Latimer informed Wallis that he could obtain satisfaction in the traditional manner of a gentleman but that the *Herald* would never retract an editorial expression. The outcome was that the men retired to the rear of the building to settle the issue with their fists.

Victorious in the combat, Latimer wrote a column in his next issue conceding that, while Wallis unfortunately was wrong in his political affiliations, he nevertheless was a gentleman and should be respected as such by the community. In 1851 Wallis became associated with Latimer in publishing the *Herald*.

What became of Wallis is not recorded, but in 1853 Latimer acquired J. W. Swindells as a partner. Swindells was a native of New York and a practical printer; the partnership lasted until the death of Latimer on April 6, 1859. Throughout the fifties the *Dallas Herald* did much to publicize not only Dallas County but all of North Texas. When Willard Richardson, editor of the *Galveston News*, began publication of the *Texas Almanac and Immigrants' Guide* in 1857, Latimer was one of the first asked to contribute to its pages.

After Latimer's death Dr. Charles R. Pryor of Virginia was employed as editor by Swindells. It was Pryor who sent the mail dispatch telling of the big Dallas fire of 1860 by a four-day stagecoach to Houston, where an extra was issued by the *Telegraph*. The *Herald* plant was completely destroyed, but within a few months new machinery was received. Junius Hutchins succeeded as editor in 1861 when Pryor became secretary of state of Texas.

When Fort Sumter surrendered in 1861 the *Herald*, strongly Southern in sympathy, commented that "The war will be prosecuted with vigor." But while commodities were being sold in Dallas at boom prices for use by the Confederate armies, the *Herald* could not ride the high tide of business prosperity because of a scarcity of paper. By midsummer of 1861 the newspaper's size was necessarily reduced from four pages to two. On December 11 it had diminished to five columns, folio. At about this time the pages became dim, probably because of dilution of the ink. In January, 1862, Swindells announced that he would soon suspend publication, not only due to the lack of paper but because his office force from the editor down had decided to join the Confederate army. On February 5 the paper was issued as a two-column handbill, and four days later publication was suspended entirely.

The *Herald* appeared again on April 19, 1862, and continued to be published on schedule until March 11, 1863, when with white paper no longer available, it was printed on butcher's brown paper. The issue of March 18 was on crimson paper. On September 30, 1863, the owners were forced to suspend publication because no paper of any color was available. The editor then informed the public that he had kept money on deposit in Houston for four months past with which to buy paper, but none could be had.

The *Herald* would not die. It valiantly appeared again on July 2, 1864, printed on one side of flimsy tissue paper.

John W. Lane, of moderate Republican political persuasion, became connected with the *Herald* in the first year of Reconstruction. He was elected mayor of Dallas in 1866, going from that office to the Texas legislature. There was smooth sailing for the *Herald* in this troubled period, largely due to Lane's influence. In 1872–73, with the coming of the railroads, Dallas was connected with the outside world by telegraph wires.

John Henry Brown, well known journalist of South Texas, historian, lecturer, politician, and Confederate soldier, assumed editorial direction of the *Herald* in October, 1873, and immediately opened an editorial attack on the legality of the acts of Reconstruction Governor Edmund J. Davis. Davis ultimately resigned, and the Dallas newspaper's editorial arguments were often afterward cited.

With wire service and a commercial boom, in 1874 Swindells felt justified in converting the weekly into a daily. Swindells ended his connection with the *Herald* in 1876 when he went to Austin to become private secretary to Governor R. B. Hubbard. It was in this year that the *Herald* began using dispatches of the Associated Press and moved to a new plant on Main Street, between Lamar and Austin Streets. Ownership of the paper passed to Samuel J. Adams, Dallas banker, who sold it several times in the following two years, only to have it revert to him after each sale.

In the winter of 1878 Adams sold the *Herald* to P. S. Pfouts, a native of New York and a practical newspaperman who had come to Dallas in 1877. Colonel John F. Elliott joined the staff the following February as part owner and business manager. The local newspaper field then included the *Morning Call*, published by J. E. Roberts and Charles L. Martin, and the *Intelligencer*, published by Judge A. M. Norton, a Republican. On June 5, 1884, the *Herald* published this dispatch from Chicago:

> A wealthy rancher, a man who by his Rip Van Winkle appearance is attracting very general attention here, is Judge A. M. Norton, editor of the *Intelligencer* of Dallas, Texas. He made a vow in the dim, distant past to let neither shears nor razor come near his hirsute excrescences 'till Henry Clay had been elected President. That event not coming to pass, his hair and beard look very odd, to say the least.

Other newspapers printed in the city in 1880 were the *Volksblatt*, a German semiweekly, the *Christian Preacher*, and the *Texas Baptist*. The Negro Baptists also had a weekly publication. Captain E. G. Rust printed the first *Sunday Mercury* on January 1, 1881, in which he opened fire on what he called the prevailing immoralities in Dallas—the gambling dens, variety theaters, and general rowdyism of the city, as well as alleged corruption in municipal politics. Within eighteen months the paper was firmly entrenched and enlarged to a six-column quarto. Its exclusively Sunday features were dropped and the name changed to *Dallas Mercury*. The Farmers Alliance adopted the *Mercury* in 1886 as its official organ; in 1887 the name was again changed, this time to *Southern Mercury*. In 1894 this newspaper claimed a circulation of 40,000 throughout the South. In that year Milton Park, who had become manager in 1890, purchased the company and converted the *Southern Mercury* into a Populist party organ.

The *Dallas Daily Gazette*, a newspaper whose editors were strongly Republican, and the *Evening Blade* began publication in 1881. Their existence was brief. *Farm and Ranch*, a monthly, was first published in Austin on April 1, 1883, but moved to Dallas in 1885 and has since appeared continuously as a semimonthly.

In 1876 the *Times*, an evening paper edited by the Reverend J. A. Adams and later by Mose C. Harris, appeared. The *Times* had no telegraph service but its editor, assisted by Jim Roberts, the sole reporter, filled its columns with sensational news. The *Times* was later sold to E. C. McClure. In this period the *Daily Commercial*, a morning newspaper established in July, 1874, and published by W. L. Hall, attained a circulation of 3,400 and was a formidable competitor of the *Herald*.

On a dull night in 1880 when there was a lack of headline news for the next morning's paper the *Herald* staff hit upon a scheme of creating some news to scoop their rivals on the staff of the *Commercial*. They sent the printer's devil to the slaughterhouse for a bucket of blood, which was liberally sprinkled on the bridge over the Trinity at the foot of Commerce Street. A note was placed by a pool of blood, declaring the intention of suicide by an imaginary person who, being jilted in love, was making doubly sure of death by cutting his throat and then jumping into the Trinity.

The *Herald* next morning carried a two-column story of the suicide. The *Commercial* reporter was dismissed for missing the story. He sensed a hoax, plied a loquacious *Herald* printer with drink and secured the story of a faked suicide. Publisher Hall of the *Commercial* was on the verge of exposing the *Herald* when Pfouts, still one of the owners of the latter newspaper, persuaded him that a merger was preferable to prolonging the fight.

A new publication in Dallas was thus described by the *Herald* on March 19, 1880:

A newspaper edited by H. T. Halverson of Dallas is the latest fashion in the newspaper world. It is a small paper, 14x20, and semi-monthly. Each page forms a separate department, which are—first page, critical economy; second page, social economy; third page, local economy; and fourth page, celestial economy.

A number of short-lived publications reflecting the personal journalism of the period evidently existed during the early eighties, the *Dallas Sunday Mercury* of June 18, 1882, mentioning three new papers that had appeared within ten days. One of them, a comic, was *Texas Oddities*, published by J. L. Lord.

On October 1, 1885, the first edition of *The Dallas Morning News* published by the proprietors of the *Galveston News*, appeared. The morning designation was used to distinguish the new paper from an earlier *Evening News*, which had expired after a brief career. *The Dallas Morning News* was provided with all the equipment of a first-class newspaper of the day; no expense was spared in mechanical outfitting and the provision of an ample and able editorial corps. It also had the advantage of the membership of the *Galveston News* in the New York Associated Press, together with the parent newspaper's wide and highly perfected system of agencies and correspondents throughout Texas. Colonel A. H. Belo, a native of Salem, North Carolina, and a Confederate veteran who in 1866 had become a partner of Willard Richardson in publishing the *Galveston News*, moved to Dallas in 1885. As president of the publishing firm he directed *The Dallas Morning News* until his death in 1901.

James Melvin Lee, historian of the newspaper business, in writing of the growth of "chain journalism" credited the *Galveston News'* virtual duplication in *The Dallas Morning News* as the first example of "co-operative journalism" in America.

The struggle between *The Dallas Morning News* and the *Herald* was interesting but terminated shortly. Within two months it was readily apparent that a city of less than 25,000 could not maintain two large morning newspapers. On November 30, 1885, *The Dallas Morning News* gave notice of the purchase of the *Herald*, and that paper issued a farewell statement to the city it had served for thirty-six years—from its infancy through war, to peace, a bitter Reconstruction, and the dawn of an era of phenomenal prosperity.

William Greene Sterett (1847–1924), a young lawyer of the city who had bought the *Evening Times* from E. C. McClure on May 16, 1880, and had gained recognition over Texas for witticisms in his columns, was now hired by *The Dallas Morning News*. Colonel Sterett—a title he later had—was the first correspondent to represent directly a Texas newspaper in Washington, when in 1889 he went to the capital for *The Dallas Morning News*. He became the close friend of many men high in political circles, including Grover Cleveland, Theodore Roosevelt, and William Jennings Bryan, as well as a host of the great and near-great in other fields. Through the years of his association with the *News*, Colonel Sterett became well known throughout the United States as a journalist, sage, raconteur, and home-spun philosopher. It was said of Colonel Sterett that every cattle king, ward boss, preacher, gambler, outlaw, and society man in Texas knew him or knew of him.

One of the most notable beats by the *News* was effected by Colonel Sterett in 1897 when he secured a decision of the United States Supreme Court upholding the constitutionality of the Texas Railroad Commission, and telegraphed the complete text of 22,000 words to *The Dallas Morning News*.

When the Democratic Governor William Goebel was assassinated in Frankfort, Kentucky, on January 30, 1900, Sterett was sent by the *News* to cover the situation and the ensuing threatened reign of terror. His wire story of the funeral of Goebel was most unusual. He wrote a stirring narrative of the death and burial of Julius Caesar, showing the parallel political situation in the two tragedies, described the oration of Anthony, and pictured the effect of that celebrated death pageant upon the opinions and emotions of the Romans. The first mention of the Goebel obsequies came in the last paragraph:

> William Goebel, the Democratic Governor of Kentucky, was buried in the Frankfort cemetery today. Senator Joe Blackburn pronounced the funeral oration.

Colonel Sterett was the guest of honor at a dinner given at a Washington restaurant by the Snail Club newspapermen's organization in February of 1904. In a letter to his editors he admitted eating eleven snails, for which lapse from his "raising" he apologized to his Texas clientele, declaring that while his personal taste ran to "bacon and greens and other civilized provender" he was helpless in the circumstances. "The proprieties," he wrote, "would have required me to eat horse meat or barbecued rats, if served."

After the death of Colonel Belo in 1901 his son, Alfred H. Belo, became president of the *News*. Young Belo died in 1906 and the Colonel's widow, Mrs. Nettie Ennis Belo, became titular head of the publishing firm; with the aid of Caesar Maurice Lombardi, vice president, she directed the *News* until her death in 1913. Mr. Lombardi followed as president and held that position until his death in 1919. In that year G. B. Dealey became president, and in 1940 still occupied this office.

Born in Manchester, England, George Bannerman Dealey at the age of eleven came with his parents to Galveston. In 1874, at fifteen, he was employed as an office boy—at $3 a week—by the *Galveston News*. He became a staff representative, and was stationed in Waco, Dallas, and Houston. Impressed by Dallas when he was making a study of circulation and business prospects for the *Galveston News*, he was instrumental in establishing *The Dallas Morning News* and became its first business manager. In 1901 he became a director of the firm and in 1906 became vice president and general manager. He is chief owner of the *News*, which has been under his control since 1926.

Mrs. W. A. Callaway, the first women's editor of *The Dallas Morning News*, joined the staff on January 1, 1893, and was identified with the newspaper until her death in 1916. Mrs. Callaway was a pioneer advocate in Texas of equal suffrage, as well as the founder of both the Dallas and the Texas Federations of Women's Clubs. Through her columns, under the pseudonym of Pauline Periwinkle, she was instrumental in promoting child welfare projects, including playgrounds and free kindergartens, when those social agencies were new civic ideals. She crusaded for many progressive movements, among them the public library, the filtration of city water, and organized charities.

The period of the mid-eighties and early nineties was one of rapid growth for the local publishing business. Prominent among the publications of this era was the *Dallas County Daily Mercantile Report*. Among the weeklies were the *Dallas Weekly Record, Dallas Weekly Review, Oak Cliff Sunday Weekly, Weekly Express* (Negro), *Texas Christian Advocate, Texas Farmer, Texas Sandwich, Texas Stock and Farm Journal*, and the *Post*, a German language periodical.

The second Dallas publication to be called the *Herald* was an evening newspaper that had been established in 1886 by C. E. Gilbert and L. L. Foster. After Colonel Sterett had sold his interest in the *Evening Times* in 1888 there was a consolidation of these two newspapers. The *Times Herald* became the major evening paper of the city; among well known newspapermen connected with it were George M. Bailey, State Senator J. C. McNealus, William M. Reilly, W. M. C. Hill, and Hugh Nugent Fitzgerald.

Edwin J. Kiest, native of Cook County, Illinois, came to Dallas in 1891 as southwestern manager of the Western Newspaper Union, and in 1895 purchased the *Times Herald*. Kiest led the publication through a lean financial period and today directs the paper, with Tom C. Gooch as editor-in-chief, and maintains a large staff and one of the finest plants in the Southwest.

Alfred O. Andersson, native of Liverpool, England, who had come to this country at the age of fourteen and later entered the newspaper field in Kansas City, was sent to Dallas in 1906 to establish an evening paper for the Scripps-McRae organization. Thus the *Dallas Dispatch* came into being. Control of the paper later passed to Mrs. Josephine S. Scripps of the Scripps-Canfield organization, and still later to the Scripps League, but remained under Mr. Andersson's management until his retirement in 1937. The *Dispatch* was the first newspaper in Texas to sell on the streets for one cent a copy, although there are no penny papers in the city today.

In 1938 the *Dispatch* was sold to Karl Hoblitzelle and associates, who also bought the *Dallas Journal*—an evening paper launched in 1914 by the A. H. Belo Corporation, with Tom Finty, Jr. as editor-in-chief—which had been published in conjunction with *The Dallas Morning News*. The *Journal* was intended to meet the competition of local and Fort Worth evening newspapers, which had unusually wide coverage in North Texas territory. The *Dispatch* and the *Journal* were merged to form the *Dispatch Journal*, which was published as an evening newspaper from the plant of the former *Dispatch* until December 1, 1939. On this date the newspaper was bought by J. M. West and his associates and the name changed to the *Dallas Journal*. The policy and staff remained the same.

At present Dallas has three daily newspapers. The morning field has been occupied exclusively by *The Dallas Morning News* for many years, and the evening field is shared by the *Dallas Journal* and the *Daily Times Herald*, the latter also publishing a Sunday morning edition. The venerable and politically powerful *Dallas Morning News*, generally speaking, occupies an editorially dominant position in the city and has an extensive circulation throughout the state. It is unquestionably the most widely known of the city's three newspapers, but in matters of local leadership, advertising, and circulation, it has a keen and formidable rival in the *Daily Times Herald*. The *Dallas Journal* is popular for its distinctive makeup and numerous syndicated features. It also continues the traditions of the *Dallas Dispatch* and *Dispatch Journal* in its lively tone and emphasis on local feature items of a human interest nature.

There is no sharp political, religious, racial, economic, or other cleavage among Dallas' daily newspapers as regards either their circulation or their editorial policy. All three circulate equally among almost all classes and reflect editorially the civic progressiveness and political conservatism that distinguishes the homogeneous, business-dominated community they serve. Their respective official points of view on major issues are frequently almost identical. They tend to see eye to eye politically, and when one advocates a specific civic project or reform, the other dailies usually cooperate.

In addition to these three general dailies the city also has a number of well established specialized journals that serve definite racial, religious, and occupational groups. Most of these are weeklies, and at the beginning of 1940 included the *Baptist Progress*, *Baptist Standard*, *Daily Commercial Record*, *Dallas Craftsman* (official organ of the Dallas Central Labor Council), *Dallas Express* (Negro), *Dallas Gazette* (Negro), *Diversified Farming*, *Farm and Ranch*, *Jewish American*, *La Tribuna Italiana* (Italian), *Oak Cliff Tribune* (neighborhood), *Semi-Weekly Farm News*, *Southwestern Advocate* (Methodist), *Texas Weekly*, *Uncle Jake's Sport News*, and *La Variedad* (Spanish). There are also a large number of trade, professional, and technical journals published in Dallas, and several magazines, of which the oldest and best known is *Holland's Magazine*, a woman's magazine having a wide circulation throughout the South.

Among Dallas newspapermen are many whose work has brought them note outside of the local field. Stanley Walker, for several years city editor of the *New York Herald Tribune* and author of several books, is a Texan and one-time reporter on *The Dallas Morning News*. H. R. Knickerbocker and Clarence Dubose, former Dallas residents, are widely known as foreign news correspondents. Bill Cunningham and George Kirksey, nationally known sports writers, were *Dallas News* and *Journal* workers in their earlier years. Richard Owen Boyer, news writer and author, who covered the Seabury investigations for the *Herald-Tribune* in New York, went to the big town from the *Dallas News*. Albert D. Lasker, multimillionaire philanthropist and head of the advertising firm of Lord & Thomas, who served as a dollar-a-year man on the Shipping Board during the World War, began his career as a reporter on *The Dallas Morning News* in the late 1890s.

John Knott of the *News*, dean of Southwestern cartoonists, has a national reputation for his pictorial comments on world events. Ed Reed ("Off the Record"), Jack Patton ("The Easleys") and Edwin Cox ("Private Lives"), whose comic and feature cartoons are widely syndicated, all had their early training in Dallas, and Patton still works as staff cartoonist of the *Dallas Journal*. Frank Owen, originator of "Philbert" in *Collier's*, resides in New York.

Probably the most colorful figure produced by Dallas journalism was Wilford B. (Pitchfork) Smith, fighting owner and editor of the *Pitchfork*, apostrophized on the occasion of his death on July 10, 1939, by *Time* magazine in these words:

Prodigiously built (he was six feet four), prodigiously dressed (in black suit, broad black hat, and flowing black Windsor tie), a prodigious writer, talker, fighter, and drinker, Pitchfork Smith worshipped at the shrine of one man and one man only: William Cowper Brann (the *Iconoclast*).

Pitchfork Smith's career was cut to the pattern of his hero, on whose grave he was wont to pour out libations of whiskey. The son of a farmer who was also a part-time minister, he was born March 17, 1884, in Thackerville, in the then Indian Territory. On coming of age, he was successively barber, clerk, country school teacher, lawyer, and publisher. His first journalistic venture was a magazine published in Kansas City called *Plain Talk*, which was suppressed for inciting race hatred. He then established the *Pitchfork* (1907) "because the pitchfork is the poor man's implement; you can fight with it or you can work with it" and when he was finally ordered to leave Missouri he moved his editorial offices to Dallas, where for twenty-five years he played the role of local satirist, prophet, moral philosopher, reformer, and political gadfly. His private battles and oratorical eloquence became known throughout Texas. Many of his speeches, among them his street corner funeral oration over the bier of John Barleycorn on the night before national prohibition went into effect and his dissertation on immortality entitled *When You Die, Will You Live Again*, are still quoted. He was a vigorous supporter of James E. Ferguson in the latter's gubernatorial campaigns. As time passed Pitchfork Smith's political influence waned, but the stories of his personal eccentricities remained undimmed. In the latter field he maintained his reputation until the end. His funeral was conducted by the Elks Lodge, which he called "my church," and the Bill of Rights was read over his grave.

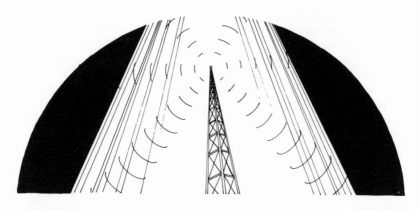

RADIO: FIFTY WATTS TO 50,000

A large fire in southern Dallas in 1920 demanded the service of the entire city fire department and meanwhile another fire broke out in the northern section of the city. Telephone lines had been destroyed by the flames and it was impossible to establish connection between the central station and the apparatus at the first fire. To avoid such a situation in the future Henry (Dad) Garrett, chief of the signal department, installed WRR, a 50-watt radio broadcasting station, in the fire department headquarters for transmission of alarms coming into the central station to receiving sets in radio-equipped cars sent to all fires. This and other electrical inventions of Garrett constitute important though disputed contributions of Dallas to the modern metropolitan problems of scientifically administered fire fighting, traffic control, and law enforcement.

After Garrett's system of transmitting fire alarms became firmly established in 1921, phonograph records were played between alarms to insure continuity of connection. Radio amateurs quickly began to pick up the phonograph music with crystal sets, and when improved mechanism made record playing unnecessary the fans demanded a return of the music. This resulted in the establishment in 1921 of the first municipally-owned broadcasting station in the country furnishing regular programs for entertainment. It was the second broadcasting station in America, being preceded only by KGKO, then of Pittsburgh. Made a commercial station in 1927, demands on WRR became so heavy that another station was established in 1931 to handle fire and police calls exclusively. This was first called 5-ZAQ and later the present KVP, operating on 1712 kilocycles. This station handles broadcasts for peace officers for all North Texas in emergency cases.

WRR operates a 500-watt station on 1280 kilocycles, with modern air conditioned studios in the former Chrysler Building in Fair Park. Its commercial programs cater only to local business enterprises. It is affiliated with the Mutual Broadcasting System. Revenue of the station is sufficient to maintain both WRR and KVP. Broadcasting hours are from 7 A.M. until 12:30 midnight.

The second broadcasting station to go on the air here was WFAA, which began operation in June, 1922. Owned by *The Dallas Morning News*, both studio and station were first located in the *News* building. Initial power used was 150 watts, on 360 kilocycles. This power was shortly increased to 500 watts and in 1929, when a new transmitting plant was built at Grapevine, 18.2 miles northwest of Dallas in Dallas County, it became a 5,000-watt station. The highest power permitted by the Federal Radio Commission, 50,000 watts, was installed in 1930. The station has applied to the Federal Communications Commission for a 100-watt facsimile transmitter which as an experimental project will transmit miniature newspapers over a twenty-five mile local area.

Broadcasts begin at 5:45 A.M. and continue until midnight weekdays, and from 7 A.M. until midnight on Sunday. The station's studios and offices are located in the Baker Hotel, but scheduled to move to the Santa Fe Building penthouse in September, 1940.

WBAP of Fort Worth broadcasts under contract from the Grapevine plant of WFAA, shares the same frequency, and alternates time throughout the broadcasting period. Both stations offer National Broadcasting Company programs on the Red Network.

KGKO, a Fort Worth station with its plant at Arlington, Texas, maintains studios in Dallas, operating on 570 kilocycles and 5,000 watts power. This station broadcasts Blue Network programs of the National Broadcasting Company.

Station KRLD, operated by KRLD Radio Corporation, a subsidiary of Times-Herald Printing Company, publishers of the *Dallas Times Herald*, went on the air in 1926 with 500 watts power. In November, 1928, power was increased to 10,000 watts and in 1939 to 50,000 watts. The broadcasting unit is located one mile south of Garland, Dallas County (US 67), with studios in the Adolphus Hotel. Broadcasting hours are from 6:30 A.M. to midnight, on a frequency of 1240 kilocycles. KRLD is the oldest and largest outlet in Texas for the Columbia Broadcasting System.

Amateur wireless experimentation began in Dallas as early as 1912 and today the Dallas Amateur Radio Club is made up of members who own and operate shortwave stations.

267

Social
Development

SOCIAL GROWTH: THE COMMUNITY PATTERN

The unremitting struggle to secure necessaries for life itself and such meager luxuries as candlelight by night in the lonely cabins of the pioneers made social life practically nonexistent in the first years of the embryo city of Dallas. Human relations, while kindly and neighborly, were confined chiefly to cooperation for economic survival and the sharing, out of common experience, of family crises of birth, sickness, and death.

What these emergencies meant under lonely frontier conditions and how much the sympathy and helping hands of a neighbor was appreciated may be imagined from the description of a pioneer burial in Dallas County witnessed by John Billingsley, who arrived as a child with his father Samuel Billingsley in the fall of 1842:

> The first person I saw buried was buried without a coffin. It was an old man McComace by name [Steve McCommas]; his grave was dug down to the white rock that formed the foundation of all portions of that country, a nice vault was cut in the rock, and he was wrapped in a sheet and layed in the solid rock, there to wait the summons where all, both small and great, rich and poor, will hear in that day. There was no lumber yard or furniture houses in the land.

Immigrants coming in growing numbers after 1842 into the area that is now Dallas were readily welcomed by the few who had preceded them. There was exchange of advice about land for gossip from the East; sometimes seed corn for a little of the same commodity liquefied, with which the immigrant had fortified himself against the cold and toil of the trek into the frontier country. The majority of the immigrants came between the period of harvesting one crop "back home" and spring planting in the new land. Earliest homes afforded but one room for sleeping, cooking, and eating. First additions to living quarters usually were either a lean-to for storeroom and kitchen or an upper-story room where the children might sleep. Several plantings and harvestings were necessary before houses could be afforded with room enough for social gatherings.

William H. Beeman, who settled on White Rock Creek in 1842, said:

. . . a part of the time we were in constant dread and fear and we invited immigration. We welcome the newcomer and divided what we had with him. We wanted him to increase our number and help keep back the Indians. . . . We lived peaceably and enjoyed ourselves those days. We had no trouble. Everybody was honest.

The testimony of John Billingsley is much the same:

We were a self-ruling, self-supporting, and self-protecting band. . . . We had no law but the law given to Moses on Mt. Sinai. . . . All was peace and quiet everywhere. . . . We knew everybody in twenty miles and called them neighbors. . . . A band of brothers and neighbors all along the border line and whenever one cried for help, his cry was heard and responded to, and if a stranger came among us, he was fed, lodged, if sick was nursed without pay. . . . We needed no law or officers of law to keep the peace. . . . Our motto was peace, friendship with everybody, and everybody was our friend.

In 1892 W. P. Overton, who had come to Dallas County in 1844, in a reminiscent interview recalled that, "When I first came to this country it was no more like it is now than chalk is like cheese. Men were not trying to swindle each other. I could go to Dallas and lie down with $100,000 and it would be there next morning. There was no stealing in those days and if you wanted to borrow $500 or such an amount you didn't have to give a mortgage to get it. I knew men to borrow $500 and never give a note." The majority of the Dallas pioneers who in riper years wrote their memoirs recalled the early days of communal development with poignant nostalgia.

First community gatherings were both religious and social in nature. Isaac B. Webb, who settled on Farmer's Branch in 1844, gathered those of his own Methodist faith together in his cabin and from this grew an informal society. The Baptists also congregated together in the days before their first church. From these gatherings evolved the camp meetings of 1848–49 that furnished for isolated families their only social contacts and vacations for many years.

Although the religious element was predominant in the camp meetings the social features played a large part in their popularity. Held in summer when the men were not needed in the fields, these gatherings lasted for two or three weeks. Entire families, many from a distance of forty miles, came in wagons bedded with straw, bringing chairs and bedclothes with them, usually for a week's stay. The wagons in the first years were drawn by oxen and a point on White Rock Creek, about ten miles northwest of the present White Rock Lake, was long a favored camping site. The best the homesteader could afford in foodstuffs was brought and cooked, at first over campfires and in later years on stoves set up in front of tents serving as commissaries.

Before the county fairs, which began in 1859, the camp meetings gave opportunity for the housewives to exhibit their pickles and preserves, handwoven cloth and home handicrafts. Preaching, usually in open woodland or under brush arbors, was held at midday and by torchlight at night. Pallets of straw and quilts were put on the ground and fretful babies and small children were hushed to sleep where the mothers could keep a watchful eye on them. The joy of community singing, for many years without instrumental accompaniment, the preaching, outdoor meals, the opportunity of friendly gossip for the lonely farm women, and of meetings and courtship for the young made the camp meetings the most vital source of fulfillment for esthetic, cultural, and gregarious as well as spiritual needs of the people. Here, between religious devotions, were discussed all current problems—the weather, crops, politics, commodity prices, and happenings in the remote outside world.

A vivid picture of the Dallas region and the economic and social status of its people was given by pioneer Josiah Pancoast when on February 4, 1847, he wrote to his sister, Miss Hannah C. Pancoast of Woodbury, New Jersey:

> We have no apples, peaches, or pears, no fruit of any kind, nor have I tasted a piece of wheat bread since I left home, but next year we shall have plenty of wheat. More than seven months out of the twelve last year I slept on the open prairie with nothing more than my blanket, but still I would rather be here 10-to-1, than in the East with all the luxuries of your great country.
>
> You have no such country as we have, you have not the freedom, you do not live in the harmony we do, for here we are all as a band of brothers. One could not live without the other and in times of peril and danger it binds men very close together. People here are so very free, open and kind, and a poor man, if honest is thought as much of as a rich man. It often makes me think of the times which I have heard my father talk about when a boy, and I think I am living those good old times over again.
>
> The girls are not afraid to go in the cowyard to milk, to the wheel to spin, nor to the loom to weave, nor are they ashamed to be seen in a nice jeans frock or in linsey with a nice collar for Sunday, and they will jump up on a horse behind a young man and canter off to meeting. The men are not afraid to go in their buckskins to see the girls nor to go to meeting with a good pair of jeans breeches that their mother has made for them and their sisters have spun and woven for them.

There were not more than one hundred settlers when in 1847 Henry Harter built the Dallas Tavern of logs with a puncheon floor, its upper surface smoothed with an ax. Here Christmas and New Year balls began in 1848 and continued for several seasons to be the principal social events of the year. Two Negro fiddlers played and the sets or figures were called for reels, cotillions, minuets, and square dances. Waltzes did not appear in the rural districts of the South until the mid-fifties.

Again Beeman may be quoted:

> Before we began to raise wheat, flour was a luxury but few could afford. Judge John Thomas, the first judge Dallas County had, was about the only man in the county who could afford to have flour and sugar. I went to a wedding at his house once and they had pound-cake. When we went to entertainments in those days we generally spent the night. We lived too far apart, usually, to go home in the dark. . . . We didn't dress as fine back in the forties as the present inhabitants of Dallas do. Deerskins were plentiful and I've dressed many a one. We made nearly all men's and boy's clothing out of buckskins, sewed with deer sinews. We wore coats, pants, and leggins of buckskins. Also we made moccasins of it for footwear. John Neely Bryan was very expert in making buckskin clothing and sewing with sinews. He once made himself a very warm coat out of a striped blanket. The stripes were deep red and dark blue, and upon special occasions I used to borrow it. I wore it to the wedding at Judge Thomas'.

John Jackson emigrated to Dallas County from England in 1848 and went through the usual pioneer struggle of building a house, fencing the land, and producing food and feed for his family and livestock. The family's first social contacts were at the camp meetings in 1849 and 1850. The older boys and girls of the family wanted to have a party in order to meet the children of other settlers and the par-

273

ents agreed to let them have a quilting bee. A son, George Jackson, in his *Sixty Years in Texas*, describes the function:

> We did not send out invitation cards, but Bill and John took turn about on our old white horse, going in different directions, inviting the young people to the quilting bee we were going to have. This was the first party in that part of the country and the young people came from far and near. We had to invite all, as it would not do to slight anyone. When the quilts were completed in the middle of the evening the young people engaged in games and singing. Some of them wanted to dance and some objected. Someone asked my father for his permission to dance and he gave it. A fiddler was secured and we joined the pretty girls in trying to keep time with the frisky fiddle, as the tall man in the corner kept playing fast and furious on the one old tune on his three-string fiddle.
>
> "Chicken in the bread tray, picking up the dough, Granny, will your dog bite? No, child, no."
>
> Dancing kept up all night and the fiddler stuck to the same tune, and when the gray streaks of dawn began to appear in the east the revellers began to take leave. Some went in ox-carts, some on horseback, with girls behind them. Other girls had their own horses and saddles, and most of the girls in those days were good horseback riders. So the first party in Dallas County was over.

Later in the morning, when John Jackson was looking over his place and noted that a horse had been fed in every fence corner, he announced that parties were far too expensive to be given often.

Gossip recorded in a Dallas girl's diary in 1857 tells of frequent visits of the "spend-the-day" or "spend-the-week" type in the community. She uses the term "by special invitation" in speaking of formal visits to distinguish them from those of the "drop-in-unexpectedly" nature. Several young men were named as having escorted her to meeting and she tells of being awakened at times in the summer by "the most beautiful serenades—the serenaders were unknown to us, but received our thanks just the same." On July 12, she notes that "this is Friday and the people are going crazy about the circus."

The play-party had a large place in the social development of frontier Dallas. The population being largely of Anglo-Saxon origin it evolved naturally that the old English contra dances (or longways dances) were the first to be enjoyed in remote Texas settlements. Conditions were unfavorable for any but the square dances because of rough floors and lack of space, and also because religious sentiment was opposed to more modern dancing. The general custom did not provide for direct invitation but word got about that a play-party was to be held at a certain home and those interested came. These events were usually given in the winter, and the largest room in the house was cleared of furniture and planks laid from chair to chair against the wall and covered with quilts to furnish seats for the company. The man who called the dance figures and movements of the games was an important member of the community. He usually began with something like, "All to your places and straighten up your faces," or "Every man to his puncheon!"

Often the only music was untrained voices singing out popular ballads of the time, accompanied by the rhythmic beat of the onlookers' feet, the shuffle of the dancers, and the clapping of hands. Dignified ballads when reduced to the folk-level of the community often assumed rare forms. For instance, the old ballad:

King William was King Jamie's son;
Upon the royal race he run.

He wore a star on his breast
Pointing to the East and West

had more meaning in this locality when sung:

King William was King Jamie's son;
Upon the royal race he run.
Upon his breast he wore a star
Pointing to the pickle jar.

If the frontiersman took liberties with the English folkdance tradition, what he did to useful words lifted bodily from the French language was even more surprising. The term *dosedo* or *do si do* when given as a command in the play-party meant back-to-back, even if the players were unaware of the Frenchman's *dos a dos*. The French quadrille command *chassez* or *chassee* evolved into "sashay" and "sashaway right," or "sashaway left." "Sashay" is in colloquial usage in Dallas today.

Although the majority of immigrants in Dallas County brought with them little other than their families and a will to work, and only one man in the county ever owned as many as twenty-five slaves, prodigality inspired by ownership of the land in large tracts and continuation of contacts with their native culture in the older sections of the country tended to create a society whose structure emulated the customs of the Old South, the East, and the Middle West.

Frank M. Cockrell, historian son of Dallas' first capitalist, explained the social evolution of this period thus:

The aristocratic ideas of these old Southern mothers were not forgotten in their struggles, but were inculcated in their children. Socially all on an equality. Merit the only distinction. Pioneer and border people are generally frank and friendly in manner, of simple life habits and moderate desires and of more than ordinary personal courage and honesty. Add to these qualities the adaptability and self-government of the Anglo-Saxon race, characteristic of the Southern people, and you have a very superior immigrant. The manners and conventions of the social scheme of that day did not provide for a chaperon. In private homes, at the first call of the gentleman, the father or the mother or both, were present, extended hospitable greetings and soon retired.

At social gatherings and balls (I do not refer to public balls where all attended) no chaperon was needed. The requirement for an introduction was proof enough that a man was a gentleman. There was no drinking at these social gatherings, nor rudeness of any kind. It was contrary to good breeding and good raising, in the presence of women. If there was an offender, he was barred. Nor did men smoke in the presence of women, except by concent. This was not provincialism but an inherited custom.

These were the only restrictions necessary for protection in vogue from the time of the first colonies in the South. There were chaperons, but not as in provincial New Orleans where it was extreme. From mother, daughter and granddaughter these social restrictions were enforced.

Dancing had early become a popular pastime in the town. M. Gougenant, a fellow countryman of Daguerre, the father of modern photography, in the late fifties opened a photograph gallery on the public square, converting the interior into what he called an art salon.

This was a popular place for social gatherings, music often being furnished by Albert G. Walker, the fiddler who in 1848 had defeated the noted John H. Reagan of Palestine for the state senate. Here the elite of the village danced to such breakdown tunes as "Sallie Goodin," "Blackjack Grove," and "Billie in the Low Ground," with the fiddler sometimes breaking into song as he played.

The opening ball of the St. Nicholas Hotel at Broadway and Commerce Streets was the biggest social event of the year 1859. When Sarah Cockrell, owner of the hotel, selected her manager she chose Nicholas H. Darnell, a man devoted to fraternal orders, and who had been an army officer and high in political circles. Darnell was noted for his taste no less than for his egotism, and he urged a grand opening ball for the establishment named in his honor. A contemporary writer thus described the affair:

The town was on the *qui vive*. The citizens vied with one another. It would be their first grand ball. It would give additional prestige. It would give political and social standing. They would reap much benefit. They looked forward to the event. Bright shone the lamps over a brilliant assembly of beauty and chivalry . . . large chandeliers hung from the ceiling and brackets on the wall, receptacles for oil lamps, sent forth a mellow, soft glow, reflected from a polished ceiling; an almost twilight effect. Tapestry of the old families from the Southland hung upon the walls, a half-circle balcony with balustrade, where were seated the invited guests, was decorated with the United States and Texas flags. Boughs of cedar, wreaths of evergreens and garlands of wild flowers draped the windows. The decorations ensembled a simple elegance.

The cultured and the elegant, fair women and gallant men, were there. The guests came from all over the State. The neighboring towns, villages, and counties vied one with another.

An orchestra, on a raised platform, was conducted by Mr. Leonard, a noted violinist. . . . After a musical prelude, led by Col. John C. McCoy, Nestor of the bar, with a beautiful young lady listless on his arm, gracious and smiling; a long train of handsomely gowned matrons and becomingly attired young women; debutantes too, with visions of happiness dancing o'er their minds, with debonair and faultlessly dressed escorts in evening dress of Prince Alberts, they circled the hall . . . flashing jewels and old lace—rare and costly heirlooms, adorned the many. . . .

The dances were the waltz, the schottische, the mazurka, the polka, lanciers, and the Virginia Reel, and the slow, stately and dignified dance, the minuet. Suddenly the bird-like flute filled the hall with its soft cooing call for the waltz. The orchestra played one of those tender, gentle Southern melodies. . . .

During the Christmas holiday season of 1861 the editor of the *Herald* recorded an entertainment of a different nature for the Negroes—the one people definitely on the other side of the social structure:

On Saturday night last, there was a regular old-fashioned "corn-shucking" at the huge corn pile of our enterprising countryman, T. C. Hawpe, Esq. The Negroes enjoyed themselves highly, singing, dancing and feasting to their hearts' content. The stillness of the night was broken by their musical voices as the whole party joined in the stirring chorus of "Round de Corn, Sally," "Jim Crack Corn," and "Nigger in the Woodpile." A corn-shucking in this part of Texas is quite an event and will have a very beneficial effect on the Negroes, all of whom are passionately fond of the amusement and do not object to the work.

At the end of this hilarious and innocent festival, they very respectfully entered the yard, according to custom immemorial, and serenaded the mistress of the mansion, called for the children, caressed them, danced and dispersed to their homes, singing the inevitable "Dixie," happier and better Negroes for the revival of an amusement and custom dearer to them than bullfights to the Spaniard, the prize ring to the Cockney, the opera to the French, cock-fighting to the Mexicans, or shooting with rifle whiskey to the American.

Soon after the first flush of excitement over the Civil War and the entertainments given for the boys donning gray uniforms, the people had to return to their earlier modes of life, wherein they produced practically all the things they used and social life ebbed, to come again into full tide only after the dark days of Reconstruction were over and the trade boom brought more money and new blood into Dallas.

During this period the usual amusements of picnics, serenades, pecan "hunting," strawberry festivals, and charivaris (mock serenades, particularly for newly-married couples, and in this region pronounced "shivaree") supplemented the play-parties and camp meetings. Another custom transplanted from the older Southern settlements was the procession of New Year's day calls. Younger bachelors of the town began early in the morning a round of visits from house to house where they were served refreshments common to the season by their friends.

The Christmas holidays of 1868 were recorded as having been "enjoyed to the full by our citizens, in a quiet sociable way. Numerous invitation and storm parties have taken place, at all of which gaiety and pleasure were the order."

The fancy dress ball at the City Hotel held on January 8, 1869, the town newspaper observed:

> heralded the return to elegance. The popular caterers, Messrs. Keaton & Johnson, proprietors of the hotel, in their arrangements betokened a familiarity with details highly creditable to themselves and agreeable to the company. The splendidly decorated saloons were thronged with the very flower of youth, beauty and grace, while the lights were refracted by the coruscant spangles and jewels worn by the gay and beautiful, and many of the belles of the city and county looked more like angels in a dream of Eden than beings we have been wont to meet in the dull walks of every-day. . . . But who will ever forget that quaint costume, gotten up at such great expenditure of time, taste, talent and "squidulums?"—when that of Di Verron, Fairy Queen and Gipsy, shall be forgotten, the dress of the proud chief of the Aborigines will rise like a bright pharos over the ocean of memory.

In the 1870s, when there was a steady influx of people and trade and Dallas had reached a boom that brought in many persons the older settlers considered undesirable from a social viewpoint, there began to emerge sharper lines of social distinction. While Dallas was never a center of the cattle industry, yet as a place of residence it attracted a number of the cattle barons of the state in the seventies. These men controlled more available wealth than earlier residents had ever possessed. Their influence was felt in the industrial and commercial growth of the community several years previous to their inclination toward the social world.

Small social groups began to develop in this era. The Eclectic Quartet was formed and made a custom of serenading the young ladies. The first social and dancing club was called the B. B. (Bully Boys) Club and the Willing Fellows were organized shortly thereafter, both made up of young male members of the established Dallas families. The Cedars was the fashionable residential section of that period, where garden parties and the Archery Club were popular. The women began forming reading circles, study clubs, and Shakespearean societies, while the newspapers began to use the words "select" and "elite," in fashion notes and more often. One such read: "Impressionable young gentlemen in Dallas have the monogram of their sweethearts embroidered in the corner of their handkerchiefs and for fear they may accidentally blow their noses on such a sacred spot, they pin that part in their pockets." A silk hat, Prince Albert coat, light-colored pantaloons, and kid gloves were by now the proper dress for the man who would be sartorially up to date.

An editor of that period seemingly thought it necessary to defend social life in Dallas and did so on April 4, 1873:

> Perhaps it will tax the credulity of some of our friends from the North when we say that society is good here. We know that the impression has been made upon many minds that this is a semibarbarous country, without morals and without education. And why should we not have good society here? Hundreds of the best families from other states have immigrated to this country. The once rich planter and "fine Southern gentleman" came here from the cotton growing states to get rid of Negro rule.

Turner Hall, opened on lower Commerce Street in 1874, became a place for prominent social gatherings. Other social resorts were Shady View Park at San Jacinto Street and Capitol Avenue, Meisterhan's Garden on Bryan Street between Pavillion and Field, and Long's Lake, in the rear of the present Parkland Hospital. Confederate reunions brought out large crowds, but there wealth and prestige were forgotten in the stronger bond between the defenders of the old order.

The growth of real estate values and business and industrial development following the first railroads in 1872–73 brought increasing wealth to Dallas and with it a gradual transition of social life into the more formal pattern of that in older cities. Pioneer George Jackson in writing of this era said: "Slowly but surely the wealthy of Dallas are forming a social circle where the common herd can never enter."

Sixteen socially popular sons of prominent families formed the German Club at the close of the 1870s for the purpose of giving germans twice monthly. The german consisted of a capriciously involved pattern of dance steps called by a leader, intermingled with waltzes. "The heel and toe, away we go" was one of the popular figures, as was the "basket." Most of these affairs were held in the homes of the well to do.

This group disbanded upon organization in 1884 of the Idlewild Club, which was the outcome of an informal Sunday afternoon gathering where it was decided by a group of young bachelors that a dancing club was needed to properly represent the city's Four Hundred. The first Idlewild grand ball was given October 13, 1884, in the Merchants' Exchange Building at Commerce and Lamar Streets. A program of this event numbers eighteen dances, including the lanciers, the schottische, heel-and-toe polka, the glide, the Newport, and the waltz. There was no actual formal presentation of debutantes at the first Idlewild balls, but attendance signified that this was the young ladies' first winter at home after attending finishing school.

Today the Idlewild Club remains one of the most distinguished and exclusive social clubs in the South, with a background antedated in Texas only by the Artillery Club of Galveston.

Throughout the eighties and nineties several other social groups were formally organized. Among these were the Chesterfield Club, Bachelors' Cotillion Club, Dallas Zouaves, Dallas Light Guard, Dallas Artillery Company, the Volunteer Firemen, the Elks Club, Avolonte Club, and La Fave Club. The Allegro Club was popular among the married set and the Merry Wives Club, formed in the middle 1890s by young matrons, is still in existence. The Merry Wives gathered to play the fashionable card game of euchre, later whist, then auction bridge, and now contract. The Standard Club, formed in 1886, went in for chamber music. The Dallas Chess and Checker Club, formed in 1887, later known as The Dallas Club, built a clubhouse at the northwest corner of Commerce and Poydras Streets at a cost of $80,000, which for years was the scene of notable social events. The Terpsichorean Club was organized in 1898 and today shares social distinction with the Idlewild.

The opera in Dallas served the same social function as in most other cities in the era around the turn of the century. The socially prominent could see and be seen, attired in what the latest dictates of Eastern designers declared modish. The society columns' list of who went where for supper after the opera established an individual's status in society. Leading dining places then were the Windsor and Le Grand Hotels and Delmonico's, Botto's, and Boedecker's restaurants, but few formal dinner parties were given in public places.

The Dallas Review, a society paper, in May, 1894, published "In Social Circles," a list of hostesses of which it was said: "Society people will find the following a valuable list as it gives the names and residences of those who are 'at home' to their friends. . . . We shall continue this list from month to month. . . ." *The Beau Monde* appeared in 1895 and continued for a decade as a society paper, giving intimate information about people, literature, and the arts. *Dallas Saturday Night* and the *Dallasite* existed for a short time after *Beau Monde* had ceased publication.

Social life among the early Jewish citizens, many of whom had come from large Eastern centers, was brilliant and many prominent persons from the large cities of the world were entertained in Dallas homes. Jewish social leaders have through the years made a large contribution to organizations sponsoring education, the fine arts, music, and the theater. The Columbian Club, still in existence, was organized in 1905 to present Jewish debutantes.

Existing today, and peculiar to this region, is an unusual version of the house-party custom. Invitation to be "in the house-party" for social gatherings such as teas and receptions lasting through the usual afternoon or evening hours means that the guest will come earlier, wear formal dress, be in the receiving line, and leave only after those not included in the house-party have gone. The usual society column write-up in the newspapers lists those included in the house-party as distinct from other guests.

Catering to what might be called the strictly social life of the city today are several organizations besides the Idlewild, Terpsichorean, and the Columbian Clubs. These are the Junior League, the Junior Dancing Club, the Calyx, the Hesitation, the Thalia, and the Slipper Clubs, all of which entertain with elaborate as well as less formal affairs in their clubhouses or the fashionable ballrooms and dine-and-dance places afforded by the city.

SOCIAL SERVICE: SOUL OF A CITY

Organized efforts in Dallas to care for the needy and unfortunate members of the community have varied with the volume and character of the need at different periods, with a definite and steady trend toward ever greater diversification of services, consolidation and improved coordination of agencies, and increasing public responsibility.

In frontier days there was more work than there were hands to do it; any able-bodied man could find a job, and for the sick and friendless stranger hospitality took the place of charity. Not until Dallas, along with the rest of the South, was confronted with the problem of caring for the Confederate soldiers returning hungry, ragged, and worn from the field after a disastrous war, was organized community effort necessary. December 6, 1864, the Ladies' Welfare Association of Dallas established a soldiers' home with money obtained from tableaux, concerts, plays, and box suppers. Three months later they made an appeal to the general public for funds to continue their work, announcing that they had during this period assisted 181 soldiers, serving 411 meals, and furnishing 200 lodgings, at a cost of $204.

Dallas citizens, quickened to wartime suffering, also contributed generously to the Society for the Relief of French Widows and Orphans after the Franco-Prussian War, the *Herald* for March 25, 1871, noting the receipt by the treasurer of the society of $360 from Dallas and vicinity.

Next to war, the greatest breeders of concentrated suffering in the seventies were the periodic epidemics of contagious diseases that swept the country, and the Howard Association, now dedicated to the rehabilitation of released convicts, was primarily concerned in Dallas in 1873 with the isolation and proper care of persons suffering with the dreaded Southern scourge of yellow fever, though the sufferers from this disease were never numerous in the Dallas area. In the *Herald* of October 3, 1873, John Henry Brown, temporary president, announced that a Howard Association, consisting of himself, J. F. Caldwell, Travis Hensley, D. McCaleb, Light Smith, Pierre Brown, G. B. Hughes, and others, had been formed in the city and that it would make its principal end the proper nursing of yellow fever victims by persons who had had the disease. All those immune were invited to volunteer for nursing, and others to contribute their advice and counsel. There were six cases of the fever in Dallas the next year.

Another problem in this same period, when Dallas was a rapidly growing and not very orderly frontier railroad town, was the providing of decent social life for large numbers of unattached men who crowded the hotels and lodging houses. To meet this problem efforts were made to organize a Young Men's Christian Association as early as 1873, and in 1875 the "Y" established a reading room where prayer meetings were conducted and homeless men could read and talk under what was regarded as proper supervision. The YMCA as a permanent organization dates only from 1885, and the YWCA did not come until much later, in 1908, when the emancipation of women and its economic and social effects began to be felt in the Southwest. Both the YMCA and YWCA now occupy handsome buildings of their own and carry on extensive and varied social service programs in the city.

In 1887 some little excitement was created by the arrival of another service organization interested in both material and spiritual welfare—the Salvation Army. In July of that year the *Herald* announced that "This band of peculiar worshippers will come in force and make a charge on the sinners of Dallas." The Salvation Army is now an important welfare agency in the city, maintaining their own headquarters building at 500 North Ervay Street, a recreational camp for mothers and children who can not afford a vacation, and a lodging house on North Akard Street providing temporary food and shelter for homeless men stranded in Dallas.

The late seventies and early eighties also saw the first organized public endeavor to meet routine need in the Dallas area. Before 1877 wards of the county were lodged in the jail, but in that year the county bought 339 acres for a poor farm 11.5 miles southeast of Dallas. The city also "took steps to alleviate hunger and other forms of suffering." Later, in 1881, Dr. W. H. Howell was accepted as county druggist, contracting to fill prescriptions for county cases at 14 cents each. In 1885, the city council authorized Mayor W. L. Cabell to buy ten cords of wood for the poor and later the same year the *Herald* editorialized on the fact that Mayor Cabell's successor, Mayor Brown, was keeping a list of indigent persons furnished with food, fuel, and other necessities.

By present-day standards the need continued small, the summer relief rolls numbering only eight or ten families, with a slightly higher number during the winter months. In November, 1886, Mayor Brown instituted the first recorded "economy in relief" measure by putting the occupants of the calaboose who were unable to pay their fines to cutting wood for the use of charity cases dependent on the city.

What developed into the United Charities, for four decades the chief social service agency in Dallas, had its origin in sporadic efforts at group charity in the early nineties, crystallized by the first major depression Dallas experienced under urban conditions.

In October, 1891, a local charity agency was formed, with Colonel Henry Exall as president, to aid the poor during the coming winter, and Mrs. Virginia K. Johnson had for some time previously devoted herself to collecting and distributing supplies for those in need, using her back porch as a place of storage. By the winter of 1893, when the panic began to make itself felt, sixty families were receiving city aid.

This number mounted sharply, and by the following winter, 1894–95, unemployment had become so widespread that the existing agencies were quite inadequate to cope with the crisis. A central place of distribution for food and clothing was consequently set up in Sanger Brothers' warehouse on the south side of Commerce Street, west of Akard Street, with the Reverend Harrison Bradford in charge of distribution. Captain J. Farley raised several hundred dollars from local business-men, and housewives of the city donated supplies. In May, 1895, a big charity cir-cus was held, with tent shows and a parade. In the fall of 1896 Captain Farley was asked to conduct another drive to raise funds for winter charity work, and he and several other businessmen proceeded to organize the United Charities, patterning the Dallas organization on similar agencies already existing in the large Eastern cities.

During 1896 G. B. Dealey arranged with J. L. Long, superintendent of Dallas schools, to have the school children make donations of food and clothing to the United Charities at Christmas—a plan which was continued through 1912. In the winter of 1897–98 the organization maintained an upstairs office at Main and Aus-tin Streets, and issued provisions to 338 persons, clothing to 136, and wood to 193. No case records were kept, and applicants were investigated by the police depart-ment. In 1899 begging on the streets was prohibited, and unemployed men were sent by the police to the United Charities where they received work relief.

In the early years of its existence the United Charities was active only during the winter months, but on September 16, 1908, it was reorganized on a permanent full-time basis. The following year, 1909, Miss Flora Saylor, secretary, declared the organization would require $18,000 to meet urgent needs of the community's indi-gent. In 1911 the United Charities took the lead in the movement which resulted in the establishment of Woodlawn Tuberculosis Hospital. On March 31, 1933, it was chartered by the state. About this time, when Federal relief became available, the organization began to abandon its relief functions, and today it is almost exclu-sively a social adjustment service. Since about 1937 it has been known as the Fam-ily Consultation Bureau and is supported by the Community Chest.

The Dallas County Red Cross, organized in June, 1905, was one of the first units west of the Mississippi, and was called the Texas Branch of the Red Cross until 1911 when it was chartered under its present name. It performed its first general emer-gency service in 1908 when in cooperation with the United Charities and a special citizens committee it temporarily housed and cared for 4,000 persons driven from their homes by the floodwaters of the Trinity. Normal membership in the Dallas unit averages about 25,000, and one of its major enterprises is caring for the blind and maintaining handicraft classes for them.

The City Welfare Department was established in 1915 under the administration of Mayor Henry D. Lindsley "for the purpose of coordinating the work of public and private agencies for charity and social service." Elmer Scott, now executive secre-tary of the Civic Federation of Dallas, one of whose functions has been the training of social service workers, was recalled from the East to take charge of the newly created department. In the years that followed the World War the department had a broad social welfare program, including the maintenance of homes for underpaid working girls and care for juvenile transients. Many of its former activities have now been delegated to other agencies, and the department at present maintains only a director, two case workers, an attorney, and one secretary.

The declared aim of the department is now to foster the development of welfare programs in public and private agencies and to cover a broad field of social service adequately to meet the needs of the community for each type of welfare service. It continues to furnish free legal aid through a special branch and to do a certain amount of emergency juvenile delinquency work. During the fiscal year 1937–38, 1,656 inquiries of all types were handled. It also licenses dance halls, and after proper investigation issues permits for the solicitation of funds for patriotic, religious, or philanthropic purposes. During 1937–38, 54 applications for such permits were made and 17 granted. Max L. McCullough is the present director.

One of the most outstanding contributions yet made to the efficiency of social service work in Dallas was the organization in 1923 of the Community Chest, formed by the Dallas Chamber of Commerce to relieve the city of constantly recurring financial drives to support various relief and welfare organizations. When granted a charter the Community Chest assumed financial responsibility for a large group of agencies, including in 1939 the Dallas Camp Fire Girls, Dallas League for the Hard of Hearing, Family Consultation Bureau, Girl Scouts, Goodwill Industries of Dallas, Social Service Exchange, Traveler's Aid Society, Volunteer Placement Bureau, West Dallas Social Center, Children's Bureau, Dallas Day Nursery and Infant Welfare Association, Dallas Big Brothers, Dean Memorial Home for Children, Bradford Memorial Hospital Clinic, Dallas Child Guidance Clinic, Dallas Tuberculosis Association, Dallas Visiting Nurses' Association, Children's Recreation Camp of Salesmanship Club, Salvation Army Lone Star Camp, Camp Sterling Price of Confederate Veterans, the annual Empty Stocking Crusade at Christmas, and Hope Cottage, where abandoned infants are cared for until such time as foster parents can be found for them. Barbara LaMarr, motion picture star, adopted a six-month-old boy from this home in 1924. The Community Chest makes one annual drive for funds to support all these various agencies, and then allocates the money raised according to a fixed budget determined by their respective needs and social usefulness.

Important social service agencies in the city not associated with the Community Chest are the Jewish Federation, affiliated with the Jewish Community Center; the Catholic charities, including the Catholic Women's League, the Dunne Memorial Home for Boys, and St. Joseph's Home for Girls; the C. C. Young Memorial Home for the Aged, supported by public subscription under the auspices of the Methodist Church; the Reynolds Presbyterian Home for Children; the Juliette Fowler Home for Orphans and Aged Women, founded by the Christian Church; Buckner Orphans' Home, founded in 1879 by the Baptist Church and maintained by voluntary contributions; the Scottish Rite Hospital for Crippled Children, the only orthopedic hospital in the state treating children exclusively, maintained principally by contributions from Masonic bodies; the Freeman Memorial Children's Clinic; the Boy Scouts; the Dallas County Humane Society; the YMCA; the YWCA; the Sunshine Society; the Neighborhood Councils, supported by the Rotary Club in the interest of delinquency prevention; and several veterans' societies with welfare functions.

Since 1932 the city and county have jointly maintained the City-County Boys' Industrial School for delinquent and dependent boys. This institution, located on a 125-acre tract of land near Hutchins, takes care of about 50 youngsters, furnishing schooling, vocational training, recreation, and wholesome outdoor environment. The boys stay at the school until they can be taken care of by their parents. Direction of the school is delegated to a board of managers appointed jointly by the city and county governing bodies. J. H. Arnspiger is the present superintendent. Annual budget of the school for the fiscal year 1938–39 was $17,000.

Financed wholly by the county is the Sunshine Home, 1545 South Ewing Street, an institution to which dependent and neglected children of both sexes between the ages of 4 and 14 are directed by the District Courts. The children are kept here until they are placed in suitable homes or their parents are able to care for them. Between 50 and 60 children are accommodated at this institution. They attend the city schools and at the home are under the supervision of the matron, who at present is Mrs. O. A. Teal.

As a result of a proposal by *The Dallas Morning News*, the *Times Herald*, the *Dallas Dispatch*, and the Dallas Chamber of Commerce, the Dallas Community Trust was formed June 25, 1929. This trust, composed of seven presidents of banks having trust powers, receives and administers through its board of governors funds willed or given to it, which are used primarily in local welfare work, though its constitution permits the organization to use the money for work outside of the county.

With the onset of the depression in 1929–30 Dallas, in common with the other large cities in the country, was confronted for the first time with mass unemployment, a condition which has persisted throughout the past decade, and which has resulted in the gradual replacement of private by public relief. By the winter of 1932–33 the United Charities and other private relief agencies in the city were completely swamped by the unprecedented demands on their steadily dwindling resources. There followed the period of wholesale Federal relief, direct and work, first through the RFC, located at 2016 Jackson Street, and later through the CWA, FERA, and WPA.

Shortly after the WPA was set up in September, 1935, the number of families on direct and work relief was 6,306, representing a total of 26,549 persons or about ten percent of the population of the city of Dallas proper. During this period, efforts were made not only to minister to the needs of residents but also to the large numbers of transients stranded in the city, the Texas Transient Bureau opening headquarters first at Fair Park on October 25, 1933, and later at 2012 Commerce Street. Two camps for transients also were established—Camp Dallas at Lake Dallas, which operated from February, 1935, until December, 1936, and Camp Hutchins, which operated from June, 1934, until February, 1936.

When direct relief was turned back to the state and local authorities July 1, 1936, the City-County Bureau of Public Aid, now known as the City-County Public Welfare Department, was set up at 1706 South Ervay Street in order that welfare might be administered on a countywide basis. This agency, supported jointly by city and county funds, for the first six months of its existence cared for over 600 cases, nearly all unemployables, who theretofore had been receiving direct aid through the Texas Relief Commission from Federal funds and from proceeds of the $20,000,000 "Bread Bond" issue voted by the state of Texas in 1933.

Widespread unemployment in the winter of 1937 caused an expansion of policies and by February, 1937, the caseload grew to approximately 1,400, many of these being employables awaiting assignment to WPA projects. Thereafter the relief load experienced sharp curtailment and rises, the amount of aid given being governed by available funds from city and county appropriations until, in the early part of 1939, both city and county officials agreed that only unemployables could be cared for, which policy is now being followed. Unemployability, in 1940, is determined by physical examinations at the Parkland free clinic.

Duplication with private agencies is avoided by consulting the files of the Social Service Exchange. The City-County Public Welfare Department also acts as a service agency, under the supervision of the Texas Relief Commission, for establishing eligibility for WPA employment and CCC appointment; and surplus commodities including food and clothing are distributed from the warehouse on South Poydras Street. As of April 30, 1939, the City-County Public Welfare Department had registered 1,925 active cases representing 5,836 persons. By September 20 the active cases had been reduced to 872. The total budget of the city and county for direct relief, exclusive of administrative costs, in 1937–38 was $212,103.44, representing an average cost per active case of about $14 a month. Campbell Loughmiller is the present director and Miss Ruth Boutwell casework supervisor.

Employable relief clients depend altogether on the WPA with headquarters in the Allen Building and County Records Building. At the beginning of May, 1939, there were 8,939 persons certified for employment, and 4,973 actually assigned to projects. According to a social service worker a large though undetermined number of individuals in varying degrees of need were thus left unprovided for by any existing agency, public or private.

In 1938 a Citizens' Committee was formed, headed by Holmes Green, at whose request the American Public Welfare Association made a survey of relief conditions in the city, expected to bring about remedial organizational changes, but this proposed program has not been put into effect.

LA REUNION: ADVENTURE IN UTOPIA

Conditions in Europe growing out of the French revolution, the ascendancy of Napoleon, and the consequent general economic debacle brought about the emigration to America eighty-five years ago of the men and women of La Reunion, a Franco-Belgian colony adjacent to what then was the village of Dallas. From these peace-seeking projectors of a novel social and economic philosophy the modern city drew much of its cultural development.

On June 16, 1855, the youthful settlement on the Trinity declared a holiday and turned out en masse to greet the expected but nonetheless strange little band of folk. They entered Dallas in foreign garb, the clatter of their wooden sabots on the boardwalks followed by slowly moving ox-carts laden with implements and household goods. It was journey's end after 26 days of travel overland from Houston for 200 weary men, women, and children who had come to America from Belgium, France, and Switzerland, actuated by a vision of utopia. Elation of the villagers and the immigrants was mutual. Culmination of the rendezvous with the advance agents of the colony who had come a year earlier and other smaller parties of immigrants who had preceded the main body during the spring of 1855 gave good reason for the name "La Reunion" for the settlement. These immigrants were disciples of Charles Francois Fourier, whose theory of socialism they had come to Texas to put into practice.

Victor Considerant, young Fourierist enthusiast, was exiled from France in 1851 and came from Belgium to America in 1852. In New York he met Albert Brisbane, Horace Greeley, James Russell Lowell, Charles A. Dana, and others who had been influenced by Fourier. Through Brisbane, Considerant met Major Merrill of the United States Army, who was stationed at Fort Worth, and on April 30, 1853, left the East to journey with the army officer to Texas.

During this trip Considerant sojourned briefly with a fellow countryman by the name of Gouhenans, who, he records, was the leader of the advance guard of the Icarians, another sect of utopian socialists who had come to Texas in 1848 for the purpose of establishing a colony about thirty miles north of Dallas under an ill-advised arrangement made by Etienne Cabet with the Peters Colony promoters.

The Icarians had withdrawn, disgruntled and disillusioned, to attempt another colony in the Middle West, but Gouhenans had remained behind, settling near the three forks of the Trinity in the vicinity of Dallas, where he was engaged in wine making when Considerant visited him. According to Dr. Eugene Savardan in his account of La Reunion, *Naufrage au Texas (Shipwreck in Texas)*, Considerant confided his project of establishing a Fourierist settlement to Gouhenans, and in Savardan's opinion was deliberately deceived by him. At least Considerant was not deterred by the experience of the Icarian colonists from advocating the abandonment of revolutionary struggle in Europe in favor of establishing a utopian commune in the Texas wilderness.

On his return to France, Considerant published a book, *Au Texas*, describing it as a country of ideal climate and fertile soil, suitable for raising tropical fruits. As a result of this publication a colonization company was formed in Paris with Francois Jean Cantagrel at its head. Among the stockholders were M. Buckly of the Swiss Congress and Marshal Francois Achille Bazaine, one-time imperial military commander of Mexico.

Cantagrel and Roger, another leader of the colony, carrying instructions from Considerant, came to Texas to purchase land. A tract in Tarrant County they had originally planned to buy was already appropriated by Considerant's erstwhile host, M. Gouhenans; so they purchased 2,000 acres at $7 per acre along the West Fork of the Trinity River, three miles west of Dallas. This appears an odd choice, as the land was of limestone formation and inferior to many available blackland tracts. The most tenable explanation is that the chalky bluffs resembled the vineyard country of France and hence had a nostalgic appeal to the newcomers, reinforced by Gouhenans' success in making wine that sold for $1 a bottle from the wild mustang grapes that grew in the Trinity bottoms. This choice of land perhaps doomed the colony as an agrarian project from its inception.

Maxime Guillot, French immigrant who had settled in Dallas in 1852, acted as interpreter between the villagers and the colonists. There was astonishingly little cultural conflict between the Dallas pioneers and the La Reunion residents. The foreigners were highly cultivated French, Belgian, and Swiss artisans, farmers, and professional men, but they were totally unfitted for the rigors of pioneer life. In every essential they had an inauspicious beginning.

The original intention was to navigate the Trinity from Houston to Dallas, but an extended drought had left the riverbed dry. Ox-cart drivers were hired to transport the goods of the colonists from Houston to Dallas, and those who could not buy horses walked the entire distance. There was lingual difficulty in purchasing foodstuffs on the way and the immigrants were frightened by anticipations of encountering the Indians of Cooper's tales.

One group of the settlers who walked the distance to Dallas from the Bayou City brought with them thirteen trunks, for which they paid 3¢ per pound for hauling. One old man in the party had slipped on the deck of the ship en route and had broken a leg. He was put into an ox-cart as freight and his transportation was paid for at the same rate as for the trunks.

Another detachment sent over by the European company arrived in 1856, and a party of the young men had to go ahead of the caravan to blaze a path through the underbrush. Cesarine Santerre, a seventeen-year-old girl, and her mother walked from Houston in their wooden shoes and took turns carrying two-year-old Raphael Santerre on their backs. There are today more than 150 living descendants of the

Santerre family in Dallas County. One night when the party was twenty-five miles from Anderson, Texas, a heavy rain came and washed away the rows of sabots under the wagon. This footgear had to be found before the journey could continue.

Considerant had set forth grandiose plans in his *Au Texas* for making La Reunion a center from which would radiate other settlements, and for making the Trinity River navigable. He began purchasing additional lands before La Reunion was firmly established.

Colonists who arrived in the first six months set to work with faith in the establishment of a phalanstery (the name given to any communal city designed by the Fourierist society). By April, 1856, the colony had platted a little city, built the president's office, a building for making soap and candles, a laundry, a building for offices, a kitchen, a grocery store, beehives, a chicken house, a smoke house, a forge, a cottage for the executive agent, and had begun the construction of two dormitories of eight apartments each to be given to two different households. The buildings were constructed of wood and native stone quarried on the site and were inadequately built for the rigorous northers that descended on the region.

When a sufficiently large group had settled at La Reunion the people formed the "Society of Reunion." The operating or social fund of the society was fixed at $600,000. The society put into cultivation 430 acres of land; purchased 500 head of cattle, some sheep, pigs, and fowls; dug wells; built a few short shallow canals; bought mowing, reaping, and threshing machines; and secured two additional half sections of land near the settlement. A very large garden was planted and developed along formal lines practiced in Europe.

There was a cooperative kitchen where the colonists had their meals. Some of the leaders in the colony were opposed to this form of food service and insisted upon a cafeteria plan, claiming the family style meals resulted in unequal distribution of the food. The cafeteria system finally was inaugurated but later dissolved into family group kitchens.

One Dallas writer in describing the store at Reunion said:

> We are indebted to the courteous and gentlemanly proprietors of the Reunion store for a lot of choice cigars and a jar of delicious brandy pears. They have at Reunion a well-selected stock of new and fashionable goods, which they are prepared to sell at unreasonably low prices.

The colonists, as was their native custom, gave parties on Sunday evenings. The people of Dallas were soon decidedly concerned over such conduct. When the colonists became aware that in the eyes of the villagers they were breaking a Sabbatic law they heatedly defended their dancing on the grounds that in Europe there was only one holiday; Sunday was spent both in worship and in pleasure, while in America the people had accustomed themselves to having also a half-holiday on Saturday. Bolder Dallasites began attending the Sunday parties and in consequence romances between the young of the colony and the village progressed with the aid of French and English dictionaries. An organ, a piano, flutes, and violins brought by the colonists were rare acquisitions to the community.

Dr. Savardan, a leader in La Reunion's development, wrote much concerning plant and animal life in the Dallas region. He tells of the grasshoppers, which the older people ate with gusty appetites, and for which they made various known or newly invented sauces. A letter which Dr. Savardan wrote to the publisher of the *Journal l' ani des Sciences* concerning what he termed *compagnons roulers*

(*Phanasus Carnifex*), or in plain Texas terminology tumblebugs, was published in that scholarly Paris magazine on December 2, 1855. The Texas community was greatly annoyed by other unfamiliar insects, especially centipedes, termites, tarantulas, and locusts, which they appropriately called stridents.

The colony never flourished. Considerant, the visionary, was not an executive. A land speculator and developer embezzled $10,000 from him in San Antonio. His bookkeeping, or lack of it, was never understandable to the colonists. He complained that the company in Europe sent colonists too soon and continued to send settlers who were not farmers.

Droughts, a plague of wheatbirds, lack of water, poor land, muddled land deeds, alleged misuse of funds by the directors, and impractical distribution of the work were prime factors in the failure of Reunion. There was failure on the part of Americans to participate in or encourage the colonists' efforts. Finally there was dissension in the colony over establishment of other colonies, and over the management of Reunion. The colony began to deviate from the original plan in 1857 and to dissolve by attrition.

John Goetsels, Belgian, came to Reunion in 1856 and later withdrew in supplies his investment in the colony and removed to Mountain Creek. Here he founded a rival colony for Belgians, which he called Louvain for the Belgian city of that name. After the disintegration of Reunion such families as the Bolls, Fricks, Frichots, and others moved into Goetsels' colony, which ultimately shared the fate of La Reunion. This settlement was sometimes referred to as Flanders Heights.

The Reunion colonists left Europe to get away from war and the majority of them made every attempt to escape being involved in the controversy which led to the American Civil War. When they expressed their views at all their sympathy was for emancipation. Once during the early days of the war an old colonist by the name of Girad was accosted by two Confederate sentries as he was walking toward Dallas. He did not comprehend an order to halt and was shot in the hip. He made his way back to La Reunion, where his compatriots took this as a sign of hostility and prepared to withstand a siege. The formal colony had been disbanded but a number of the colonists still remained on the site.

These improvised a fort from the old storehouse and barricaded the doors. When a detachment of Confederate soldiers was sent to draft the settlers into service Alexander La Notte, one of the few colonists who could speak English, was sent to talk with them. The officer explained that he had come to draft them and demanded that they come out at once. Mr. La Notte answered, "Mais non, Monsieurs, il faut que vous entrez." At this prearranged signal, every man and woman in the fort thrust out the windows all the firearms they had been able to muster. Thinking that there must be more than a hundred men inside, the detachment retreated. Later the Confederate soldiers came to get the weapons, but the French had anticipated the move and buried them. A few of the adventurous young men joined the Confederate Army and distinguished themselves in service. Among these was Emile Remond, who later was the first person to discover and develop the commercial value of Dallas County minerals in the making of cement. The governor of Texas finally gave exemption to the group.

Two men associated with La Reunion colony became internationally known and honored. One of these was Julien Reverchon, who came to the colony as a lad with his father Maximilien Reverchon, and who later attained fame as a botanist. The other was Jacob Boll, Swiss naturalist. Boll arrived in 1869, after dissolution of the colony, to join his brother Henry Boll, a La Reunion resident. Aided by Jacob Boll, who was engaged in making a botanical collection for Harvard University, Reverchon developed his inherent talents in the study of plant life. Among his achievements was the discovery and classification of many heretofore unknown Texas plants and flowers. Reverchon Park in Dallas was named in honor of Julien Reverchon.

Complete dissolution of La Reunion occurred in 1867. The remaining families moved into Dallas, where the men went into business. The first abattoir in Dallas was set up by Jacob Nussbaumer, Swiss colonist. Benjamin Long, who also had come from Switzerland, was twice elected mayor of Dallas. John B. Louckx, Belgian architect, was instrumental in inaugurating the Dallas public school system. The cultural contribution by those colonists who remained in Dallas is immeasurable and they left a traceable record of civic leadership.

Last of the original group of immigrants, Emanuel Santerre, who was five years old when he arrived from France, died on April 20, 1939, and was buried in the old French (Fishtrap) Cemetery, beside others of the colonists long preceding him. He had resided 84 years on the site of La Reunion.

THE NEGRO IN DALLAS:
75 YEARS AFTER

Dallas ranks twenty-second among American cities in Negro population (1938), with approximately 43,000 members of the race. These form the largest non-Anglo-Saxon group and comprise an important element in the economic life of the community.

Here as in other large American cities the existing Negro sections grew up through the natural tendency of these people to live among their kind. While there is no formal segregation, economic conditions and environment combine with racial affinity to clearly mark the areas of Negro occupancy from those of the white race.

From his advent in the community the chief contribution of the Negro to the economic life of Dallas has been labor. Slaves brought into the county when cotton became a principal crop in the early 1850s continued their functions as workers after emancipation, and their children and their children's children, though enjoying constantly increasing advantages of education and economic opportunity, for the most part still are manual workers.

Negro laborers who helped to build the first railroad into Dallas remained as citizens. Others came, following the white man westward in pursuit of livelihood in the new country of Texas. This last group of Negroes came principally from Louisiana, while others of today's Negro residents trace their ancestors to Mississippi, Alabama, Georgia, and a few to Tennessee and the Carolinas.

Today Negroes in Dallas find employment chiefly in industrial plants, in common labor, as chauffeurs, porters, janitors, household servants, waiters, and elevator operators. The professions are represented by physicians, dentists, lawyers, and teachers. Many Negroes are merchants, most of them engaged in the grocery trade; drugstores are operated by and for Negroes; a box factory and two cosmetic laboratories are operated by members of the race; and a number are engaged in funeral direction.

Negroes operate two old-line life insurance companies in the city, while a number of other insurance companies give employment to about 400 persons in clerical and sales work. Three medical and surgical clinics are staffed by Negroes, and the city supports three weekly Negro newspapers.

291

In social and cultural life the Negro has developed rapidly. From educational facilities which include two large, modern high schools has stemmed a growing cultural aspiration, reflected in social, musical, and literary organizations, several art clubs, and a Negro Little Theater which has produced such plays as *Jute* and *Porgy* with complete Negro casts. During the 1936 Texas Centennial Exposition in Dallas the WPA Federal Theater presented the road show *Macbeth* (modern version, the locale Haiti) with a complete cast of Negro players for a week's run in the amphitheater in the Centennial grounds. Three motion picture theaters are exclusively for Negroes. The well housed and well equipped Negro YMCA and YWCA are valuable adjuncts to the community social life.

A branch of the public library named for Paul Lawrence Dunbar, Negro poet, located at 2721 Thomas Avenue, serves a large clientele.

Recreational facilities for the race are provided in a number of parks, with a community house in the Hall Street Park serving the most congested district in the city. Here there is a swimming pool, with tennis courts and other recreational equipment, and from this headquarters is sponsored a mothers' club and a sewing circle for adolescent girls. Negro nurses of the city health department care for the indigent sick, and take health instructions into the homes through a visiting staff.

The Progressive Voters League of Dallas claims to be the first effective political organization of Negroes in the South. Aim of the leadership of the league, made up of men and women of the business and professional groups, is to attain political solidarity as a means of promoting welfare of the race.

Despite the fact that an estimated 25 percent of Negro residential tenants own or are buying their homes the racial group as a whole is poorly housed, though this condition gradually is being improved. In a municipal government housing survey in 1938 in which 2,037 Negro homes occupied by 3,270 families were investigated, 1,755 or 86 percent of the houses were found to be substandard. In the largest single Negro area of 191 acres, with a density of population of 36 to 40 persons per acre, housing was found to be 76 percent substandard. Economic conditions were in some degree reflected by the fact that of the group investigated only 187 Negro families were on direct relief, with 252 families dependent upon Federal or other relief employment. Welfare workers among the Negroes believe that the attention focused on the living conditions of the race during the peak of the depression has resulted in a definite betterment, with a constantly descending curve from the peak of 32 percent of unemployables early in 1937.

First concentration of Negroes in the town after the Civil War brought freedom was about the present Elm Street and Central Avenue. From that beginning naturally evolved the congested districts adjacent to "Deep Ellum," wherein are located most of the city's Negroes. This concentration of the race, including both business and residential areas, is on Thomas Avenue and Hall, Allen, Boll, San Jacinto, and Good Streets. It begins in the 2700 block of Thomas Avenue, extends to the 2700 block of Washington Avenue, and takes in Hall Street from Ross Avenue to State Street.

As a result of this municipal survey negotiations were completed early in 1939 for the Federal financing of a Negro slum clearance project in this congested district, to cost $3,503,000, and which will when completed provide modern housing for 626 Negro families. Existing buildings will be razed in much of the district about the Thomas Avenue-Hall Street intersection to make room for the new structures, and part of the land will be utilized for parks and playgrounds. Work on the project will be completed in 1940.

Wheatley Place in South Dallas, among the better of the Negro residential areas, was named for Phyllis Wheatley, a Negro poet of the eighteenth century. It contains a park and a cemetery. Queen City parallels Wheatley Place and extends southward to the Ideal and Lincoln Manor additions, in which many Negroes own their homes. Roosevelt addition is on Second Avenue in the extreme South Dallas suburban district. Mills City section, better known as the Wahoo Lake district, runs from Second Avenue to South Haskell, around Wahoo Lake. The West Oak Cliff section in Southwest Dallas is the most exclusive Negro area west of the Trinity River. North Park addition, better known as Elm Thicket, is a village of Negro residences and business enterprises in extreme North Dallas. Booker T. Washington addition also is in that section. It is estimated (1940) that 25 percent of the Negroes in the city reside in servants' houses on the premises of white employers.

DEEP ELLUM: HARLEM
IN MINIATURE

Down on "Deep Ellum" in Dallas, where Central avenue empties into Elm street is where
Ethiopia stretches forth her hands. It is the one spot in the city that needs no daylight
saving time because there is no bedtime, and working hours have no limits. The only place
recorded on earth where business, religion, hoodooism, gambling and stealing goes on at
the same time without friction. . . . Last Saturday a prophet held the best audience in this
"Madison Square Garden" in announcing that Jesus Christ would come to Dallas in person
in 1939. At the same time a pickpocket was lifting a week's wages from another guy's
pocket, who stood with open mouth to hear the prophecy. . . . J. H. Owens ("Old Iron-
sides"), columnist in *Dallas Gazette* (Negro weekly), July 3, 1937.

Deep Ellum is the colloquialism used by both Negroes and whites for the congested Negro shopping district and amusement center lying on both sides of Elm
Street between Preston and Good Streets, and the section about it for two or three
city blocks to the north and south, on the eastern fringe of the Dallas downtown
theater and shopping district. This Deep Ellum is the survival of the "Freedman's
Town" settlement of former slaves established after the emancipation proclamation
of June 19, 1865, growth and permanence of which was enhanced by the location
nearby of the terminals of the town's first railroad in 1872.

The police department regards the real Deep Ellum as that area between Central
Avenue, where run the all but abandoned railroad tracks, and Hawkins Street to
the east in the 2500 block. Though Deep Ellum by thinning extension along the
railroad tracks merges into the more pretentious Negro section on and about Hall
Street to the northward, it is not recognized by the educated Negroes as a part of
that more select purlieu.

Under the veneer of civilization and custom there runs in Deep Ellum the under-
current of jungle law; superstition, hatred, and passion. Here is the transplanted
farm Negro and the Negro reared in the city's alleys and shacks. It is a district
sleepily quiet or restlessly gay, but in either mood may be easily aroused to quick
violence, as corporation court records prove.

In Deep Ellum marts of forgotten things it is possible to buy anything from a
threadbare cloth-of-gold dress to a collapsible bathtub. Most of the cheap stores are
on the south side of the street. Hole-in-the-wall exchanges vie with more preten-

294

tious but oft-crowded stores. The passerby who gives more than a casual glance to the wares promiscuously displayed is urged to come in and make a bargain, usually at a loss to the proprietor if the latter is to be believed.

There are secondhand clothing stores, job-lot sales emporiums, gun and locksmith shops, pawnshops, tattoo studios, barber shops, drugstores. Sales here are not the matter-of-fact transactions of other retail districts, but negotiations involving critical examination, head shaking, and loud argument by both seller and buyer. It is a game they play in Deep Ellum and *lagniappe* (the small gift to make the bargain more attractive for which this New Orleans word is used in the same manner as is *pelon* in the Spanish-founded Texas cities) is often inducement of last resort. Pitchmen hawk their wares. Street evangelists exhort, their frenzied appeals often but little noticed.

An Indian herb store flourishes on the sale of a vermifuge made on the premises. This is not a place for the squeamish; the emporium's decorative motif is somewhat startling. A mangy bull-moose head towers amid stuffed coiled rattlesnakes, armadillos, a boa constrictor hide, and snarling bobcats. On a wall among Indian relics are some beautiful prints of tribal life. But the main attraction here is a collection of ex-stomach worms, neatly preserved to posterity in jars of alcohol. "Before and after" photographs, reinforced by a small pickled octopus, are potent factors in breaking down sales resistance. The alert proprietor declaims that a purchaser bringing him the worms will have the price of the palliative returned.

Clothing, like liquor and fighting equipment, is cheap in Deep Ellum. New clothing and foodstuffs, bought in job lots from unclaimed freight sales and bankrupt stocks, find their way to consumers at amazingly low prices. But the secondhand store is the backbone of the clothing business. Suits may be bought for $3. Battered hats and caps start at 15 cents; good overcoats sell from $4 up; the badly worn for much less. Shoes are to be had for 25 cents and 50 cents; new footwear from $1.25. Three pairs of men's socks are offered for 10 cents. Women's dresses start at 50 cents and $1; hats for the feminine head at 15 cents.

Convenient chattel loan offices, identified by the sign of the three balls, make it possible to exchange a day's luck for what it takes to get action in the cafe a door or two away. The transactions with the "Broker" are matter of fact, with wistfulness of present possession overcome by faith in the adventitious redemption of the morrow. Nickel-plated revolvers in a grimy window always draw admiring inspection.

Under the sign of hotel accommodations, walk-ups advertise rooms at 25 cents the night; clean beds at 15 cents. Most imposing edifice in the district is the Negro Knights of Pythias building on the north side of Elm. Also on this side of the street are found the automobile graveyards and parts stores. At Central Avenue is the Harlem movie house, flanked by beer joints, cafes, domino halls, and the Gypsy Tea Room. This is the gay white way of the Negro in Dallas.

Con men—"pigeon droppers"—the reefer man, the card sharp, the too-lucky craps shooter, and the dusky lilies of the field, faces powdered to a cadaverous blue dinginess, tight-fitting gowns supplemented by five-and-dime costume jewelry, hair groomed by the hot-iron straightening process, rub shoulders in the evenings with those innocently bent on spending their wages for a touch of night life.

Rumor holds that sweet dreams and cheap courage can be bought from the reefer man. Marijuana, the loco weed, lends itself to cultivation in Texas back yards and when smoked in cigarettes makes a cheap and powerful stimulant. Addicts are called muggle-smokers.

Night amusement resorts have lost their most notorious example since the quite recent abandonment of the Cotton Club, an erstwhile popular cabaret in this section which had entrance through two wooden tunnels, one for males and the other for females. Muscular attendants searched each guest for weapons, the management well aware that the exhilaration of the swing music, bright lights, and the contortions of truckin' and the Susie-Q do not tend to restrain boisterous conduct. On his departure the guest might retrieve any weapons save ice picks or razors, which were confiscated. White people visited this place only by appointment through the city's dance hall inspector.

Refreshments solid and liquid draw the Negroes to the cafes, beer saloons, and barbecue stands. Collard greens, chit'lin's, po'k chops, barbecued beef, and catfish—"cat" and "fish" are well-nigh synonymous to the Negro—combine to create a seventh heaven of hedonistic reality. Lights, food, and drink are conducive to conviviality and conversation waxes in a dialect both apt and earthy. Deep Ellum Negroes usually begin their verbal intercourse with a grunted "Er-uh" and on being directly addressed answer by "Suh?" or "Who, me?"

Police are "the law." A penniless person is the "ain't got a penny one." Riddance is a word unused in their vocabulary, rather do they speak of "getting shet" of something. "He sho' do go slick" refers to a well-dressed man. Willie is a favorite name among Negroes for both men and women. Call out "Willie!" in a group and the chances are there will be several responses. Nicknames are almost universal—such as Cootie Boo, Hookie Boo (Brother of Cootie), Snapbean, Wasp's Nest, Black Cat, Papa Dad, Bug-Eye, Eight Ball, Day Break and Trigger Leg.

From the jungle lore of Africa and the later environments of Southern swamps and fields the Negro has inherited a belief in the supernatural and love for black magic. Generations gone by brewed potions of love and hatred on moonless nights, with incantations to the rooster and the goat, and magic was made into *tobys* and *conjures* with patience and ceremony by *juju* doctors and *voodoo* names.

The wiser but no less wishful Deep Ellum Negro buys his philters, love potions, lucky numbers, and incense, wooing lady luck at a fixed cost even if vicariously. One concern, the Wish-I-Wish Company on Central Avenue, offers choice of a large stock of incense, powders, luck bags, and mystic oils. There is one for nearly every complication of life—love drops to attract the indifferent, magnetic lodestone for poker players, Van Van oil to shake a jinx, High John the Conqueror lucky number root for general success. New Orleans lucky bags are featured, as are similar charms believed effective for one year. The proprietor, a white man, is called "doctor" by his clients, some of whom credit him with power to read the more potent policy numbers in the smoke of incense.

Though the quarter is of, by, and for the Negro, even he knows that:

When you go down on Deep Ellum,
To have a little fun
Have your sixteen dollars ready
When that policeman comes.

Chorus

Oh, sweet mama, your daddy's got them
Deep Ellum Blues.
Oh, sweet mama, your daddy's got them
Deep Ellum Blues.

Once I knew a preacher,
Preached the Bible thru and thru.
Till he went down on Deep Ellum,
Now his preaching days are thru.

(Chorus)

When you go down on Deep Ellum,
Put your money in your socks,
'Cause them Women on Deep Ellum
Sho' will throw you on the rocks.

(Chorus)

Once I had a sweetheart,
And she meant the world to me
Till she hung around Deep Ellum,
Now she's not what she used to be.
                    —"Deep Ellum Blues"

Little Mexico, Skyscraper-shadowed Latin Slum

Cinco de Mayo Celebration, Little Mexico

Deep Ellum, Harlem in Dallas

Children at Play

Young Men's Christian Association

Shotgun House, the Tenement of the South

Cedar Springs Place, Federal Housing Project

Domino Players

Football at Cotton Bowl, Fair Park

303

Aquaplaning, White Rock Lake

Idlewild Debutantes, 1939–1940

Beauty in the Box, Softball League

LITTLE MEXICO: OUTPOST FOR MAÑANA

Little Mexico, an area covering about ten city blocks extending along both sides of McKinney Avenue from Akard Street to Griffin Street and thence to Standpipe Hill on the northwest and the city dump and the MKT Railroad tracks on the southwest, is one of the few slum areas in Dallas possessing individual character.

Though its Mexican residents are considerably Americanized and the colony is recent in its origin compared to the Mexican quarters in San Antonio and other South Texas cities it possesses sufficient color to attract the tourist, and its restaurants, curio shops, and motion picture theater are patronized by many non-Latin Dallas people as an aspect of the city's night life.

Surrounded by the huge warehouses and towering smokestacks of Dallas' wholesale district, Little Mexico is a close-packed mass of flimsy, tumbled-down frame shanties and "shotgun" houses threaded by narrow, twisting, unpaved streets, muddy or dusty according to the weather. Although Dallas' Mexican population is scattered throughout the poorer sections of the city and there are smaller colonies in West Dallas, Oak Cliff, and South Dallas, the great majority live in this congested wooden slum. Two and three families live in a single house with others sheltered in sheds and outhouses arranged around dirt courtyards at the rear, and even the most primitive sanitary conveniences are sometimes not provided. The dominant notes are poverty and squalor with a relatively high ratio of malnutrition, tuberculosis, syphilis, and other diseases, but the inhabitants appear to endure their lot with the patient resignation of their race, and crime, drunkenness, and disorder are rare.

Bright flowers and potted plants blossom in the narrow front yards; overalled men with bronze, prevailingly Indian features lounge, smoke, and chat in front of the corner groceries and native bakeries; women prematurely aged by hard work and much childbearing hold babies in their arms while they gossip volubly in Spanish around the doorways and stoops of their houses; barefooted, ragged children and yapping mongrel dogs overflow in cheerful and noisy confusion into the streets. McKinney Avenue, the main business thoroughfare of the quarter, is lined with shops bearing signs *Botica* (drugstore), *Barberia* (barber shop), *Ropas* (clothing), and *Abarrotes* (groceries), most of them appealing to their customers with the added legend, *Mas barata en la ciudad* (cheapest in the city). The aspect of this street is somewhat different from the rest of the quarter. Here there is an air of pseudo-American bustle; restaurants and night clubs proclaim with their sprucely modernistic fronts that they cater to the tourist trade and night life of the city; and members of the Mexican younger generation stroll along in cheap but garishly fashionable clothing.

Though Dallas' contacts with Mexico date back to 1886, when a Mexican military band was welcomed to the first State Fair by Mayor John Henry Brown, and the city is today Mexican consular headquarters for North Texas, Little Mexico did not begin to develop until about 1914. Previously the area it now occupies had been a rundown neighborhood that included, in the days of segregated prostitution, Dallas' "red light district." At first only a few Mexican families settled here, but the number increased rapidly, reaching a peak of 10,000 persons in 1920, the year that Mexico's President-elect Alvaro Obregon, his staff, and the Estado Mayor Band visited Dallas. Since then the Mexican population of the neighborhood has gradually declined to about 6,000 with some seasonal fluctuations. Further slight recession is anticipated in 1939 as a result of the present Mexican government's land settlement and repatriation policy, and the disqualification of aliens for WPA employment.

The Dallas colony is overwhelmingly working class in composition and normally finds employment as dishwashers, busboys, dining room foremen, gardeners and yardmen, tailors, ditchdiggers, and common laborers on construction projects. Many of them also find employment part of the year in pecan shelling, cotton picking, and other agricultural pursuits. Social, political, and cultural bonds with the Cardenas regime are generally close and present-day ideological trends in Mexico are strongly reflected in leading group organizations of the Dallas colony.

The most important centers of communal life in Little Mexico are the Cumberland Hill School, the various churches and missions in the quarter, the Cervantes Printing Company, and Pike Park Community Center. The Cumberland Hill School on North Akard Street, just outside the southern boundaries of the colony proper, has the reputation of being the scholastic melting pot of the city because of the number of races represented among its student body, but the Mexican pupils far outnumber all other nationalities, having constituted at times as high as 92 percent of the school's total enrollment. The school has amassed a large and varied collection of drawings, pottery, and woodwork in its art classes, attesting the Mexican tradition of skilled craftmanship among its pupils. Since the discontinuance of the seventh grade at this school in the early thirties, the William B. Travis School on McKinney Avenue considerably beyond the northern limits of the colony has also had a large Mexican enrollment, now over 10 percent. Most of the Mexican pupils who reach high school grades attend Dallas Technical High School, and though the percentage of those who complete the course is relatively low, some have graduated with honors. Many Mexican families also send their children to St. Ann Parochial School in preference to the public schools.

A majority of the Mexicans in Dallas are of the Roman Catholic faith, attending mass and other services at the Church of Our Lady of Guadalupe, although among the "intelligentsia" and militant labor groups a certain amount of anti-clericalism exists, especially evident since the rift between church and state in Mexico. Social work of value to the Mexicans is carried on by Methodist, Presbyterian, and Baptist missions.

The editorial offices of *La Variedad*, a monthly literary and commercial magazine in Spanish containing news of the Mexican colony in Dallas, are at the plant of the Cervantes Printing Company, 2702 North Harwood Street. Another monthly magazine in Spanish, *Cinemax*, is also published by this company. Some of the Dallas labor unions, notably the UCAPAWA, in which Mexicans predominate, mimeograph news of their organizations in Spanish and distribute it weekly among their members.

Pike Park Community Center, with its walled play park and Spanish style community house dominating, like a mansion of some colonial grandee, the huddled shacks of the quarter from a steep hill at Turney and North Akard Streets, plays a particularly significant role in the life of Little Mexico. Its swimming pool and play park, under the supervision of the city park department, attract the underprivileged children of the neighborhood by hundreds, particularly during the warm months, and the field house, with its large playroom on the first floor and auditorium on the second floor, is the scene of innumerable dances, plays, and other community affairs.

In this park the Mexican colony enjoys its two most important fiestas of the year—Mexican National Day, September 16, which celebrates Father Ignacio Hidalgo's proclamation of the revolution against Spain in 1810, and Cinco de Mayo (fifth of May), commemorating the victory of the Mexican forces over the French invaders of Puebla on that date in 1862. Pike Park, on September 15 and 16, is transformed into the plaza of the Mexican village, with gaily decorated stands indiscriminately dispensing Mexican and American foods, and strolling Mexican minstrels, many of them radio and restaurant entertainers. On the afternoon of the 15th programs of folk songs and native dances include *El Jarabe Tapatio*, *El Fado Elanquito*, and *La Sendunga*, with prizes for the most accomplished participants, and patriotic addresses are made by the Mexican consul and other prominent members of the colony. In the evening two dances are held, one in the community house and the other at the swimming pool, transformed into a pavilion for the occasion. The day of the 16th is devoted to athletic contests with special events for children; at night the men and women of the colony don traditional national dress, the *caballeros* in *sombreros* and *charro* suits and the *senoras* and *senoritas* in bright colored *china poblana* costumes, and participate in general festivities. Cinco de Mayo is celebrated in a similar but less elaborate manner.

A *tortilla* factory where *tortillas* are rolled by hand on the *metate* is located at 2209 Caroline Avenue, and visitors are welcome. The Colonia Theater on McKinney Avenue near Orange Street features Spanish-language pictures made in Mexico, with Mexican film stars in the leading roles.

There are several good restaurants along McKinney Avenue serving authentic Mexican dishes such as *tamales*, *tortillas*, *tacos*, and *enchiladas*, as well as the more familiar *chili*, which is a Texas rather than a true Mexican dish. El Fenix Cafe at 1608 McKinney Avenue and the Little Palace Cafe at 1403 McKinney Avenue are among the best known. El Fenix, which is one of the city's popular "night spots," features Mexican music and dancing, as well as native cuisine. Such places are operated by Mexicans but patronized almost exclusively by non-Latins. There are smaller and more obscure cafes, patronized principally by Mexicans, which will interest the tourist who is more insistent on authentic color than on sanitation.

RECREATION: SPORTS OF
A CENTURY

From its very beginning Dallas has been a sporty town but, save for brief and sur-
reptitious interludes, has never justified the appellation of wide-open as to those
diversions involving elements of chance. Poker players were arrested and fined as
early as 1848, when there were so few adult males in the place that the defendants
had to serve as jurors in the trials of each other. On another occasion a prominent
citizen, later for long years a county official, was fined $120 for having cut a deck of
cards in a saloon to determine who should pay for a round of drinks.

Dominant religious and fraternal influences in the formative years of community development impelled a degree of law enforcement in Dallas far from common
in the Southwest of the period.

Pastimes of the people, legal and illegal, were as rugged as the frontier country
itself. Even the relaxation of the gaming room was to be found only in an environment often fraught with physical dangers no less than those threatened by the law.
Chroniclers of the mid-fifties record that it was a shooting growing out of a poker
game that caused the businessmen to incorporate the town in order to secure
better police protection. But whatever the deterrents on gambling, legal sports and
recreations have flourished increasingly for ninety-two of the city's ninety-eight
years of existence.

Quarter-mile horse races were run at nearby Cedar Springs, now within the city,
as early as 1847, and open-air bowling alleys were set up in the village in the same
year. Jousting tournaments, in which mounted men tilted with wooden lances at
rings suspended from poles, also was an early diversion, in evident innocuous emulation of the knights of feudal Europe. But most popular and democratic of the
sports of the townspeople for the first half-century were cock-fighting, dog- and
badger-fighting, and rat-killing.

Cocking mains of interstate interest began in Dallas in 1883, the fights being
held in a pit at Main and Martin Streets. A six-day tournament in 1884 drew large
attendance and for some years after 1885 the Glen Lea cocking pit in the saloon of
that name at Main and Murphy Streets was a notable rendezvous for the sporting
element. Many breeders and cockers from other states came to Dallas in February,

1886, to attend a great main between Dallas and St. Louis. The event took on the aspects of a modern baseball or football championship contest. St. Louis and Chicago newspapers sent reporters to cover the story. Dallas won, the owners of the championship fowl receiving a purse of $2,500.

Advocates of this sport defended it by asserting that President Grover Cleveland had, while sheriff of Erie County, New York, been a devotee of cock-fighting. The last big main, an interstate event, was held in 1905, after which time the legislature outlawed the sport. It is, however, still carried on more or less furtively, with frequent mains on Sundays in the Trinity River bottoms.

In 1887 in the old Turner Hall, 716 Commerce Street, Dallas dog-fight fans matched animals with Fort Worth sports and lost considerable money when the visiting dogs, which according to a newspaper account had "physiognomies that would do credit to New York aldermen," won the match. Fights between dogs and badgers were held as late as 1899, when one local dog killed fifty badgers before he succumbed. Another dog killed eleven rats in 40 seconds. Greyhound coursing, now using mechanical rabbits, originally employed live animals, the first events of this kind being held at the State Fair in 1897. Dog races were held at Dallas tracks when pari-mutuel betting was temporarily legalized, 1933–37.

Dallas quickly succumbed to the cycling craze of the early 1880s. The first bicycle, brought to the town soon after the display of the vehicle at the Centennial Exposition at Philadelphia in 1876, had wooden wheels—a large single wheel in front, with a small trailer or guide-wheel behind—with iron tires. It was owned by Hugh Blakeney. In 1882 Gross R. Scruggs paid $162.50 for the first rubber-tired bicycle seen in Dallas. In 1886 the Dallas Wheel Club was formed with twenty-three members, and rival clubs quickly followed. Tom Monagac of Dallas became the state champion as a speedster, and races were run on a quarter-mile track at the State Fair grounds.

The first "century run" made in Texas on a bicycle was by C. T. Daughters of Dallas, who in 1891 pedaled 103 miles in 13 hours and 10 minutes. With the advent of the low-wheeled safety bicycle women took up riding, which reached its height in 1896. In this year Cycle Park was built at Exposition and Parry Avenues, with a half-mile board track, and was used for bicycle races until its conversion into an open-air theater.

At the height of the cycling craze Governor James S. Hogg of Texas predicted that "use of bicycles soon would have people running about on all fours, like monkeys. The boys," he said, "won't wear coats and the girls want to wear breeches all the time. Tell your folks not to learn to ride the things and thus avoid deformity."

Dallas people had their fling in the famed Louisiana Lottery while its operations still were legal, and in January of 1885 the winning by E. A. Hall, a clerk in Sanger Bros.' store, of $2,000 on a Louisiana ticket brought a host of ticket-buyers to the lottery, which advertised in the local newspapers. After the deaths of General P. G. T. Beauregard and General Jubal A. Early, the latter in 1894, each of whom had been an official of the lottery company, General W. L. Cabell, twice mayor of Dallas and known throughout the South as "Old Tige" because of his record for valor in the Civil War, succeeded as a betting commissioner for the Louisiana company, supervising the drawings at an initial salary of $6,000 a year. After a long contest the lottery, which meantime had moved its offices to Honduras, was completely banned from the United States in 1907.

Early indoor sports included roller skating, which in 1885 was housed in a building at Elm and Olive Streets with a seating capacity of 3,500 and long known, from its metal construction, as the iron skating rink. Here teams representing Dallas and Fort Worth played roller polo. In recent years skating has again won favor, with several rinks catering to a youthful clientele, and occasional professional matches held at the Fair Park livestock arena.

Another popular pastime of the town's earlier years was billiards. Louis L. Magnus was a notable local player and operated a billiard hall in connection with his saloon at Main and Austin Streets. The Coney Island and the old McLeod and Oriental Hotel poolrooms were highly popular. Billiards was one of the first masculine recreations to be shared by the women of the community. When Tom Smith, debonair boniface of the Grand Windsor Hotel, installed tables for women players in 1883 the local newspaper declared "There is no prettier sight than to see the ladies playing billiards." Pool and billiards are now by state law confined to private clubs.

Bowling has been a popular recreation in Dallas since the pioneers played on crudely equipped open-air alleys nearly a century ago. Today several modern air-conditioned plants provide facilities for players, both men and women, including a number of city leagues playing on regular schedules.

First recorded boxing matches in Dallas were held in the early eighties in a garden in the rear of Dick Flanagan's saloon at Main and Ervay Streets, and somewhat later "the Texas Rosebud," a Negro, attained local prestige in amateur bouts in a ring built on top of whiskey barrels at the Spring Palace Saloon at Commerce and Akard Streets. Jake Kilrain, fresh from his game but losing 75-round barefisted battle with John L. Sullivan at Richbourg, Mississippi, visited Dallas with a group of boxers in 1890. In an exhibition fight at the Opera House a local bricklayer was killed by a knockout by one of Kilrain's entourage, but the boxer was freed of a murder charge.

John L. Sullivan visited Dallas in March, 1884, and again, while still the champion, gave an exhibition at the Opera House in 1891. James J. Corbett was a Dallas visitor in 1894, after he had taken the championship from the mighty John L. In 1895 Dallas fight fans raised $41,000 to bring the heavyweight championship fight between Corbett and Bob Fitzsimmons to the city. A vast frame auditorium seating 53,000 and covering an entire block at Browder Field, Herschell Avenue and Armstrong Boulevard, was being built when, following protests by ministers and other citizens of Dallas and the state, Governor Charles A. Culberson called a special session of the legislature to outlaw boxing in Texas. The disappointed fans had to depend on telegraphic and newspaper accounts of the battle held nearly two years later at Carson City, Nevada.

Jack Johnson, Galveston Negro who in 1910 became the heavyweight champion, was for a time a dishwasher in John Delgado's restaurant at 248 Main Street in Dallas, and established his prowess as a boxer in local matches with fighters of his own race.

Since the restoration of boxing under regulation by act of the legislature June 13, 1933, ten-round matches are held frequently in Dallas.

Wrestling had its beginnings here in the nineties, matches being held in a hall on lower Commerce Street that had once been St. Matthews' Cathedral, and in the old City Hall auditorium. Visits to Dallas in 1934 and 1935 of Jim Londos, heavyweight champion, stimulated interest in wrestling which has been more popular than boxing, and weekly matches are held.

When the Texas Baseball League was organized in 1887 Dallas already was baseball conscious. Sandlot ball and semiprofessional games of local teams against visitors from as far away as St. Louis and Cincinnati had been played here years before.

Informality of the rules of early-day baseball is indicated by the scores in an interstate elimination tournament in Dallas on July 4, 1874, when the Trinity team beat the Dallas Mutuals 52 to 11 in a morning contest, and the R. E. Lees of Houston defeated the Shreveport (Louisiana) Southerners in the afternoon 48 to 45. Baseball was first given semipro standing in the community when on June 13, 1883, the Dallas Amateur Baseball Association was organized with three teams, the Trinities, the Blue Stockings, and the Red Stockings.

The Dallas entry in the new professional league was known as the Hams, the franchise owned by Leon H. Vendig, and despite its name claimed the unofficial pennant for 1888, winning 55 and losing 27 games in a season marked by many changes in member towns and teams.

Dallas has been represented in the Texas League through all its vicissitudes, the fans resisting a number of efforts in earlier years to put the city in the Southern Association. Local teams have won the pennant six times since the dubious victory of 1888, and tied for the honor with Houston in 1910. The Gonfalon came to Dallas in 1898 with John McCloskey as manager; in 1903 with Charles Moran; in 1917 with Ham Patterson; in 1918 with Walter Mattick; in 1926 with James P. (Snipe) Conley, who in 1917 had won nineteen consecutive games as a pitcher for Dallas; and in 1929 with Milton Stock. Dallas, representing the Texas League, won over New Orleans representing the Southern Association in the Dixie Series in 1926, winning 4 games, losing 2, and tying 1. A number of Dallas players have won places on major league teams.

Golf in Dallas had its inception in a cow pasture. This was in 1896, when a six-hole course was laid out at Haskell Avenue and Keating Street in Oak Lawn by H. L. Edwards and R. E. Potter, who had been introduced to the game while visiting England, their native land. Interest thus aroused led to the formation in 1900 of the Dallas Golf Club, with its first building erected at Argyle Street and Lemmon Avenue, which organization later became the Dallas Country Club, the city's first institution of its kind and presently the largest among numerous golf and country clubs. Its original clubhouse was destroyed by fire January 30, 1908, but another building was erected almost immediately. Mr. Edwards, father of golf in Dallas, in 1906 helped to organize and was the first president of the Texas Golf Association. Nearly 80,000 people played golf on the two municipally owned courses in 1938.

George N. Aldredge of Dallas won the city's first state championship in 1916, Louis Jacoby was the winner in 1920, and Reynolds Smith took the honor twice, in 1934 and 1936. Smith was a member of the United States Walker team in 1936 and 1938. Ralph Guldahl, runner-up in the National Open in 1933, won the championship in 1937 and repeated in 1938. Other Dallas golfers with noteworthy achievements to their credit include Charles L. Dexter, Jr., who has won Texas and Southern championships; David (Spec) Goldman, who went to the finals in the National Amateur in 1934; Gus Moreland, a Walker Cup player two years in a row; Jack Munger, Southern Amateur in 1937; and Don Schumaker, winner of the Trans-Mississippi in 1936 and Eastern Amateur in 1938. Harry Cooper of Dallas was the leading moneywinner among the pros in 1937. Harry Todd won the city championship in 1938 and Western Amateur championship in Oklahoma City in July, 1939. Earl Stewart, Jr., brought Dallas the state high school championship in 1937 and 1938.

Dallas women have not been slow in their emulation of masculine golfers. One of the best players to represent Dallas was Mrs. Clay C. Cary of Cedar Crest Country Club, winner of many tournaments before her removal to Denver. Mrs. Dan Chandler won the Texas Women's championship in 1932, and Betty Jameson, who after leaving Dallas, won the Trans-Mississippi in 1937, had attained the Southern Women's title at the age of 15, Mrs. E. H. Wohlfart was seven times city municipal champion and twice state muny champion, and Mrs. Johnny Parnell won the state municipal title for women in 1938.

"The excitement at times was so great that the audience rose to its feet and with cheers and show of handkerchiefs attested its appreciation," said the *Dallas News* of the first major football game played in the city. "A crowd estimated at 300, about one hundred of whom were ladies" witnessed the game, a contest between Dallas and Fort Worth teams at Oak Cliff Park in October, 1891. Dallas won, 24 to 11. This was Rugby football, which had been introduced in Dallas a short time before by Captain G. W. E. Merewether, a local mailcarrier of English parentage.

Two years later on Thanksgiving Day, playing the newer American version of football before a crowd of 1,000, the University of Texas team triumphed over a Dallas aggregation by a score of 18 to 16. By New Year's Day following, Dallas players had acquired enough skill at the game to defeat Galveston, 20 to 15, at Fair Park, where an estimated 2,500 persons saw the scrimmage. Top hats and Prince Albert coats identified the referees in these early games, and despite the roughness of the sport they managed to survive.

Local interest in football appears to have lapsed in the period between 1894 and 1908, when colleges generally began to adopt the game and new uniforms with protective features for the players were introduced. In the latter year Dallas saw its first high school football game between Bryan Street High and Oak Cliff High. In 1924 Oak Cliff High of Dallas defeated Waco for the state high school championship. When on October 7, 1930, North Dallas and Sunset High Schools played the first night game of football in Dallas, 46,000 spectators filled the Cotton Bowl at Fair Park to capacity. More than 250,000 persons attended high school games during the 1938 city season. A new $1,000,000 high school athletic field, opened in 1939, has a stadium seating capacity of 27,000. The state championship football game between Lubbock High School and Waco High School was scheduled to be played in this stadium in 1939 but was transferred at the last minute to the Cotton Bowl because of the condition of the streets in the vicinity of the new field.

Southern Methodist University initiated football in 1915, defeating Hendrix College of Conway, Arkansas, 13 to 2 in its first intercollegiate contest. The SMU Mustangs since have won the Southwest Conference championship four times—in 1923, 1926, 1931, and 1935, the latter victory bringing an invitation to the Rose Bowl in California as representatives of the East. Stanford defeated the Dallas entry on January 1, 1936, by 7 to 0. Ownby Stadium at SMU seats 20,000.

Dallas is and has been for a decade the scene of an annual football game between the University of Texas and the University of Oklahoma, played on the first or second Saturday in October during the State Fair of Texas, in the Cotton Bowl at Fair Park. Started in 1912 these games continued for five years and then lapsed until 1929 when they were resumed, and by contract between the two universities will continue at least until 1944. These colorful contests always draw large crowds.

Beginning in 1937 the Cotton Bowl, built in 1930, has had a gridiron contest on New Year's Day. In 1937 Texas Christian University, Southwest Conference winner, defeated Marquette 16 to 6. In 1938 35,000 persons saw Rice Institute, also Southwest champion, defeat the University of Colorado 28 to 14, and in 1939 St. Mary's of California played Texas Technological College before 42,000 people, winning 20 to 13. In 1940 a slightly smaller crowd witnessed the victory of Clemson College over Boston College by the narrow margin of 6 to 3.

David O'Brien, All-American quarterback in 1938, though playing with Texas Christian University resided in Dallas, as did I. B. Hale, 1938 captain and tackle of the Christians. Mortimer E. (Bud) Sprague of Dallas was captain and tackle for the Army in 1928, and Roy (Father) Lumpkin of Dallas played with Georgia Tech in the 1929 Rose Bowl contest.

Interest in horse racing in Dallas, fostered by pioneers of the region, when the present city was a village of log cabins, continued through the years, with the sport largely confined to the quarter-mile events. These developed the so-called quarter-horses in the period prior to 1870. Notable among animals of this type, adapted by breeding and training to short-distance racing, were Shiloh and Steel Shaft, each of which had a large following among early-day sportsmen. Racing at the rival Dallas fairs in 1868 created great enthusiasm for the sport.

The first Dallas Jockey Club was organized in 1869, holding its first meet in October of that year. This organization lasted only a short time, but a second Jockey Club was organized in 1877, under whose management racing was successfully handled for years. The first Texas Derby was run at the Fair Grounds track in 1890.

Many pacing, trotting, and running records were made on Dallas tracks, especially after 1893, when 15,000 people saw Lena Hill lower the world's pacing record for a 2-year-old. In the following year Lena Hill's mark was lowered here by Judge Hurt. Both these were Dallas horses bred and owned by M. C. Hill. Elrod, owned by Colonel Henry Exall of Dallas, broke the world yearling half-mile pacing record here in 1894.

Perhaps the most famous horse ever to appear in Dallas was Dan Patch. In 1904, after breaking the world pacing record at Memphis in the previous October by covering a mile in 1:56-1/4, Dan Patch set a track pacing record here by completing the course in 2:01-1/5.

In 1909 Texas religious forces, concerned over the prevalence of betting, obtained state legislation against racetrack gambling. This action proved an effective discouragement to horse racing in Texas for more than two decades. A changed attitude at Austin made possible the revival of racing at Arlington Downs, between Dallas and Fort Worth, in the fall of 1933 and at Fair Park in the spring of 1934, with betting permitted under the pari-mutuel system. The Forty-Fifth legislature, however, responding to a new crusade against racetrack betting, again outlawed the sport by an act passed June 27, 1937, becoming effective September 24 of that year. The Fair Park track which had been inactive during the Texas Centennial Exposition of 1936 remained closed, while the Arlington plant was partially dismantled and restored to use as a stock farm.

A lawn tennis club was organized in Dallas as early as 1882, of which both men and women were members. In 1888 the Surprise Tennis Club was organized, with courts at Wood and Browder Streets. In 1901 the Dallas Lawn Tennis Club was organized and is still in existence. Other clubs and numerous public and school courts afforded facilities for the present great number of players. Dallas has produced several state champions and nationally known players, both men and women, and a Southern Methodist University team won the Southwestern Conference tennis championship in 1927. J. B. Adoue, Jr., became Texas State Champion in both singles and doubles and was a member of the Southwestern championship team in doubles in 1913. In 1919 he was runner-up in the national senior championship tournament at Forest Hills, Long Island, and in 1931 he went to Mexico City as nonplaying captain of the United States Davis Cup team.

Harvey M. MacQuiston became Texas State champion in singles and doubles, Gulf States champion in singles and doubles, Southwestern champion in doubles, and Republic of Mexico champion in singles and doubles. Louis (Red) Thalheimer won the intercollegiate doubles championship twice in succession and later took the National clay court championship at Longwood Bowl. Daniel (Dock) Barr and Jimmy Quick won the state doubles title in 1935, while Barr also captured the singles crown.

Dub Boyer and Jimmie Griesenbeck won the state mixed doubles championship in 1934. Fred Royer in 1932 won the Missouri Valley singles and doubles with George Willett, and in 1937 with J. B. Adoue, Jr., won the state open doubles championship. Billy Wilkins and Philip Baird won the state municipal junior doubles in 1938. Gene Fason was winner of the State Veterans singles in 1938 and shared the doubles championship with W. T. Strange.

Dallas women tennis stars include Miss Charlotte MacQuiston, who took women's singles championships in Texas and Gulf States tournaments, and Miss Mary Zita McHale, who won more than fifty medals and cups before becoming Mrs. Oswald Jacoby and moving to New York. In singles she won Texas, Southwestern, National Municipal, and other women's championships. Paired together, she and Miss Mac-Quiston won Texas, Southwestern, National Municipal, and National Parks women's championships in doubles. Mildred Reddick and Bobby Keith were Women's State Municipal doubles champions in 1938.

Gun clubs existed in Dallas as far back as the seventies, there being a German "Schutzen-Verein" or gun club in 1875 which held meets at Lake Como northwest of the city. Skeet was introduced in Dallas in 1927, only a few months after its origin in New England, and immediately became popular, since it was an improvement over the earlier trapshooting and made up for the increasing lack of feathered game. By 1935 Texas led the country in skeet, with Dallas marksmen taking their full share of the achievement, maintaining the reputations made by members of earlier organizations such as the Clipper Gun Club, which held tournaments here in the 1890s.

Since the annual selection of an official all-American skeet team was started in 1930 Dallas has been the only city to place five men on these teams. N. T. MacCollom made the team in 1930. H. C. Sparkman, Dr. A. R. Beckman, and H. L. Weiland were picked in 1931. The next year N. T. MacCollom, H. C. Sparkman, and J. O. Bates were honored, and in 1934 J. O. Bates and H. L. Weiland made the team again.

Besides its individual stars, Dallas has made several bids for national team honors. In 1932 local gunners tied Houston for first place in the national telegraphic championship. Members of that team were J. O. Bates, Dr. A. R. Beckman, Charlie Pyle, H. C. Sparkman, and N. T. MacCollom. Roy Cherry of Dallas won the state championship in 1936, after winning the Southwestern the preceding year.

Several Dallas marksmen besides the skeeters have attained national renown in recent years. Phil Miller made the highest registered average over the traps in the United States in 1924. His mark stood for eleven years.

Mark Arie, Dallas resident in the early years of the present century, attained international fame as an all-around gunner. In 1934 he was one of only three American gunners who had broken more than 100 straight clay pigeons from twenty-five yards.

Thurman Randle, representative of the National Rifle Association in the Southwest, has been a member of United States teams in seventeen international rifle matches. He also has won Texas, Missouri, Southwestern, and many other championships in small-bore competitions, outstripping entrants from eight other states by winning eleven matches in the rifle and pistol shoot at Cheyenne, Wyoming, July 4, 1939. Three times he was runner-up in the small-bore national championship and in 1934 he set a new world record with a small-bore rifle by running 196 consecutive hits at 200 yards in a 7 1/5-inch bull's eye. R. C. Pope, another Dallas marksman, won a place on the winning American rifle team that competed successfully for the Pershing Trophy in the international match at Bisley, England, in July, 1939.

Basketball in Dallas is confined to the public schools; Southern Methodist University, which annually contests with teams of other universities in the Southwest Conference; and a large number of amateur teams, both men's and women's, which represent various clubs, churches, and commercial houses, and compete in intracity play.

There are numerous softball leagues playing in Fair Park and at Lions Field on Industrial Boulevard.

The Didrikson Saga

Dallas has won victories in many sports but the most conspicuous achievement of the city in the whole field of athletics probably has been the brilliant career of Miss Mildred (Babe) Didrikson, recognized today as perhaps the greatest all-around woman athlete in history.

Dallas sportsmen feel justified in claiming Miss Didrikson as a Dallas product athletically, although she was not born and reared here, because it was in Dallas that her meteoric career got its start.

Miss Didrikson came to Dallas in 1926 from Beaumont High School, where friends said the budding young athlete had frequently expressed her indignation to the faculty because she was not allowed to play on the school football team with the boys. In later years she justified this claim by donning full equipment several times and scrimmaging proficiently in practice with members of the Southern Methodist University varsity team.

Under the coaching of Major J. M. McCombs in Dallas Miss Didrikson rapidly won recognition for speed and accuracy in basketball, indoor baseball, track events, and golf. The Employers Casualty Company's Golden Cyclones girls' basketball team on which she played won the national championship in 1931. In 1932 at the National field and track meet in Chicago she won the individual field and track title as a one-"man" team, competing in eight events and accumulating a score of thirty-two points. At the Olympics in Los Angeles she won the 80-meter hurdles by surpassing the world record in 11:07, and also won the javelin throw, 143 feet, 4 inches; high jump, 5 feet, 5 1/4 inches; 100-yard dash, 10 8/10 seconds, the American record; 220-yard dash, 25 2/10 seconds, also the American record; shot-put, 39 feet, 6 3/4 inches; broad jump, 19 feet, 1 3/8 inches; baseball throw, 296 feet, 3 inches, a world record for women. In that same year Miss Didrikson

316

further proved her ability to cope with male athletes by knocking out a Beaumont boy in the fourth round of an exhibition boxing match in that city.

Miss Didrikson gradually turned to golf as she became more proficient at the sport, and in 1934 won the Texas Women's Golf championship at Houston. Shortly afterward she was declared a professional by the United States Golf Association and turned to the game for a livelihood. Her power in this field was demonstrated when she drove a golf ball 346 yards in Seattle, Washington, probably the longest drive ever made by a woman according to leading golfers.

She was one of the centers of attraction at the Texas Centennial Exposition in 1936 as a featured performer in the sports program.

In 1938 Miss Didrikson was married to George Zahairis, professional wrestler, and in 1939 the two toured Australia, Miss Didrikson playing exhibition golf matches and Zahairis wrestling.

STATE FAIR OF TEXAS: EMPIRE ON PARADE

Although Dallas in recent years has become an increasingly important convention center and the scene of intersectional football games and other events that normally draw thousands of out-of-town visitors, the State Fair of Texas, held at Fair Park for two weeks every October, outranks all other annual attractions on the city's calendar. It is one of the largest events of its kind in the world, in good seasons having a total attendance of over 1,000,000 visitors, and for these two weeks the city decks itself in gala attire. The hotel and amusement places provide special accommodations and programs to attract the tourist trade, downtown streets blossom with flags and bunting, holidays are granted school children and for one day, Dallas Day, the city's business houses close their doors in order to allow employees to attend the Fair.

Dallas' tradition as a fair center extends far back into pioneer days. In 1859, though at that time the population of Dallas numbered only about 175 people, James Wellington Latimer, editor of the *Dallas Herald*, made an eloquent plea for a local fair. As interest grew in his proposal he predicted that an annual fair would be a major factor in the future growth of Dallas, even forecasting the successful semicentennial fair of 1886 and the Centennial Exposition of 1936. This first fair, promoted by the editor of the *Herald*, was held under the auspices of the businessmen who composed the Dallas County Agricultural and Mechanical Association of which John M. Crockett, second mayor of Dallas, was secretary. It opened on Tuesday, October 25, 1859, and lasted for three days.

The fairgrounds were near the present intersection of Pacific and Central Avenues, not far from where the Houston & Texas Central's East Dallas station was later built. As might be expected in an undeveloped frontier farming community where manufacturing was as yet largely limited to household handicraft, the exhibits consisted of needlework, articles of domestic manufacture, flour, plows, vegetables, carpets, shawls, quilts, and the like. The four-day celebration was climaxed by an exhibition of driving and horsemanship, and drew a total attendance of about 2,000 persons.

By the following year the fair was being proclaimed as an institution, and elabo-

318

rate provisions were made for its orderly and dignified operation. Intoxicated and disorderly persons were barred from the enclosures, stock and vehicles were restricted to definite areas, marshals were stationed at various points on the grounds to maintain order and direct visitors, and a "cottage" was provided for the exclusive use and convenience of "the ladies," for whom special seats were reserved on the north side of the show-ring.

The fair was continued through the early 1860s and during this period Amon McCommas, president of the association in 1862, was a moving spirit. On the board of directors were John Jackson, W. H. Hord, and William McKamy. But as the Civil War progressed and more and more men were needed at the front, the fair fell into neglect and was not revived until Reconstruction days, when Captain W. H. Gaston assumed leadership and the exposition was reopened near the present site of Baylor Hospital on Junius Street.

Directors of the Dallas County Agricultural and Mechanical Association met on March 14, 1868, for the purpose of officially reestablishing a fair, and that October the first fair to be given after the Civil War was held. It featured fruits, vegetables, livestock, articles from "the handiwork and skill of the ladies," and "feats of equestrianism by ladies and gentlemen." The *Herald* of September 17, 1870, noted the approach of the fifth fair held under the auspices of the Association, and expressed the belief that it would be well attended. W. B. Miller was president in that year and George M. Swink and Ben F. Jones directors.

In 1872, when the first train steamed into Dallas over the newly laid tracks of the Houston & Texas Central Railroad, the fairground was the scene of a barbecue attended by 5,000 people. W. H. Gaston was president of the Fair Association, and Ed Bower was secretary. The fair, like other Dallas enterprises of the time, seemed about to enter on a new era of prosperity. But when the panic of 1873 struck, the directors were hard-pressed to keep it alive as an annual event.

In 1876 a major reorganization occurred and the Dallas fair for the first time began to assume a statewide or at least regional character. On July 29 of this year the North Texas Fair Association was formed for the purpose of "promoting the beautiful and useful and advancing the agricultural and industrial interest of Texas and the entire Southwest." In August 65 improved acres in East Dallas, with a good one-mile race track belonging to Captain Gaston and facing the Texas & Pacific Railway tracks, were purchased for $20,000. An additional $20,000 was expended for beautifying and equipping the grounds for exhibition purposes; and $7,000 in cash, besides medals of gold and silver and handsome diplomas, was offered for premiums.

The main exhibit hall was a two-story frame structure, 100x150 feet, in the form of a cross with a rotunda on the second floor. The exhibits were arranged in booths and showcases, with those of Sanger Brothers and J. R. Davis and Cobb, photographers, among the more outstanding.

When the fair opened on October 28 after a delay caused by unfavorable weather, it was a rousing success. Trains ran between the grounds and the city every thirty minutes, carrying passengers for the small sum of twenty-five cents a round trip. The secretary, Major Baskerville, and his assistants had difficulty accommodating all the exhibitors desiring space. When the fair closed on November 2, the *Denison News* congratulated Dallas on its success and called for its support as an annual event in North Texas, remarking that it equaled or surpassed the "so-called" state fairs previously held in Houston.

In 1886 prospects were bright for a really brilliant exposition on the occasion of the semicentennial anniversary of Texas independence. A schism developed, and C. A. Keating and a group composed largely of implement dealers declared the East Dallas site to be "the worst kind of hogwallow." With the backing of the Farmers' Alliance and the Knights of Labor they set up a rival exposition called Fairland, on a tract belonging to John R. (Jack) Cole in North Dallas east of Haskell Avenue, adjoining the Houston & Texas Central tracks.

The East Dallas Fair, headed by Colonel J. B. Simpson, Thomas Field, T. L. Marsalis, J. T. Trezevant, and W. H. Gaston, was held simultaneously at the present Fair Park site. The city of East Dallas extended Main Street and opened Exposition Avenue for the occasion, building a bridge across Mill Creek for the accommodation of traffic. A mule-car line was opened, supplementing the Texas & Pacific train service. The two fairs together cost $200,000, with premium lists totaling $60,000. Both were extraordinarily successful, and attendance ran as high as 38,000 a day.

Out of this rivalry grew the present-day State Fair of Texas, the two fairs consolidating the following year (1887) under the leadership of Major R. V. Tompkins, Jules E. Schneider, and James Moroney. The last of these was made president; the new board included Jules E. Schneider, C. A. Keating, W. H. Gaston, A. J. Porter, B. Blankenship, James Arbuckle, J. V. Hughes, T. L. Marsalis, F. M. Cockrell, A. B. Taber, and Alex Sanger. Captain Sydney Smith became secretary and served the Fair continuously until his death in 1912.

The costly fratricidal struggle of 1886 left the Fair Association with an indebtedness of $100,000 but the Fair of 1887, by far the most elaborate thus far to be held in the city, netted a sum of $96,182, all but wiping out the association's indebtedness. The Fair of 1888 was less successful; the first report of the secretary of the Texas State Fair and Dallas Exposition in January, 1889, showed receipts totaling $67,616. Expenses for buildings and improvements were $21,807; other expenses amounted to $53,980. This report showed the State Fair operating at a deficit, which it continued to do for a number of years, a succession of calamities overtaking it whenever it seemed about to become financially successful.

Among these were a fire in 1890 that destroyed the main exposition building, another fire in 1891 which consumed the racing stables, a collapse of the baseball stands which resulted in the injury of a number of persons and several costly suits, and the outlawing of horse racing in 1902, which eliminated one of the Fair's main sources of revenue. Only the timely financial assistance of Jules Schneider, W. H. Gaston, J. B. Wilson, and others in reducing or refunding the Fair's indebtedness at various crucial moments during these years saved it from complete bankruptcy.

An end to the Fair's misfortunes came in 1904 when the city of Dallas took over the grounds as a public park. This was known as the Reardon plan, from the name of the chairman of the committee which drafted it, E. M. Reardon, and from it dates the existence of the Dallas Park Board.

The old Coliseum, with a seating capacity of 8,000, was completed in 1910. Since that date the history of the State Fair of Texas has been one of almost continuous expansion. A livestock pavilion was erected soon after the completion of the Coliseum, and a banked auto racecourse was added in 1916. An automobile building was constructed in 1923, and the old exhibition hall remodeled in 1924. The present auditorium was built in that year, and the athletic stadium in 1930. During the war the grounds were turned into an Army training center, Camp Dick.

In 1935 the State Fair was suspended to make way for an extensive construction and landscaping program demanded by the Texas Centennial Central Exposition, which opened on June 6, 1936. The idea of such an exposition as a means of publicizing Texas' history, resources, and opportunities was officially launched in 1923 at the convention of Advertising Clubs of Texas in Corsicana, but it was after more than a decade of intensive promotional activity that this was finally consummated. The Centennial Exposition, as it was eventually developed, represented an investment of over $15,000,000, was advertised from coast to coast, and brought thousands of visitors to Dallas from all parts of the country. The state legislature appropriated $3,000,000 toward its costs late in 1934, to which a Federal appropriation of another $3,000,000 was added. To secure the exposition the city of Dallas pledged $9,500,000 in cash and property, including the $4,000,000 plant of the State Fair of Texas, which served as a nucleus for the exposition. The Texas Centennial Exposition has left as its legacy to the State Fair and the city of Dallas 21 magnificent permanent buildings on the grounds, and lagoons, gardens, and other landscaping that have made of Fair Park a beauty spot with few equals in the Southwest. The exposition was financially a failure.

But in Dallas' best tradition of snatching victory from defeat and following financial reverses with further expansion, it was decided to hold another major exposition in 1937. This resulted in the even more elaborate Greater Texas and Pan-American Exposition, dedicated to promoting friendly relations between the United States and the other republics of the Western Hemisphere, as well as publicizing Texas and the Southwest. The State Fair was resumed in 1938 with a Golden Jubilee celebrating the fiftieth anniversary of the Fair in Dallas.

Among the notables who have journeyed to Dallas during these fifty years to appear at the State Fair have been Henry W. Grady, famous Georgia orator and editor, in 1888; Governor David R. Francis, of Missouri, member of Cleveland's cabinet and later ambassador to Russia, in 1890; William Jennings Bryan and Champ Clark in 1899; Vice President Charles W. Fairbanks in 1907; President William Howard Taft in 1909; Woodrow Wilson, later to become president of the United States, in 1911; Jess Willard, heavyweight boxing champion of the world, in 1915; General Alvaro Obregon, president-elect of Mexico, in 1920; Luis M. Rubeclava, Mexico minister of industry, commerce, and labor, in 1921; and Sigmund Romberg, one of America's greatest composers, in 1926.

President Franklin D. Roosevelt and Vice President John N. Garner spoke at the Texas Centennial Exposition during the summer of 1936, and Secretary of Commerce Daniel C. Roper participated in the official opening ceremonies. The Centennial Exposition was visited by state governors from all parts of the Union and by a host of radio, movie, and stage stars. Among the visitors were two of the picturesque political figures of recent years—William Lemke, third party candidate in the 1936 presidential campaign, and Dr. Francis Townsend, proponent of the $200-a-month old age pension plan.

City
Addenda

STREET NAMES: LIVE ON, O PIONEERS!

Of the eighteen names utilized by John Neely Bryan to identify the streets of his new town on the first plat of Dallas, made in 1844 and officially recorded ten years later, only two were unfamiliar to the Anglo-Americans who had begun to populate the frontier village. There was obvious reason for such names as Houston, Lamar, Jefferson, Jackson, Polk, Columbia, Main, Commerce, and Market. Only Carondelet and Poydras did not belong, the latter being important chiefly because it was the eastern boundary line of the projected half-mile-square town.

There is no known explanation of the honor paid by Bryan and his confreres to the Baron Francisco Luis Hector Carondelet, French-born governor of Louisiana and West Florida in 1791. Nor is it recorded why a Dallas street should have been named for Julien de Lalande Poydras, a Frenchman who had come from Brittany to New Orleans in 1768 and thereafter acquired great wealth and note as a philanthropist.

It may have been that Bryan had heard of Carondelet or more probably of Poydras, who in the ramifications of his big business in Louisiana had engaged in trade with Texas. It is likely that the streets were so named because Bryan and his friend and fellow-villager Captain Mabel Gilbert, a steamboat master on the Mississippi before settling on the Trinity in 1842, retained pleasant memories of the gaieties of the older Carondelet and Poydras Streets in New Orleans. Dallas' Carondelet Street long ago was absorbed by the longer Ross Avenue, but Poydras remains, a vital but now pitifully narrow downtown traffic artery.

When the village burst its bounds to become the town, additional streets for the most part took the names of men prominent in community development or of landowners and promoters of residential additions, with an increasing perpetuation in their nomenclature of men or events notable in Texas history. John Neely Bryan did not name a street for himself but this was done after his death.

Of this secondary group of streets more than one hundred still bear their original names, though there were many changes from the plat of 1844 and subsequent early map designations. In the downtown district Sycamore was made Akard Street north of Commerce, the first Akard Street only extending southward from that point. Columbia, abandoned downtown, still is on the map, but now as an East

Dallas residential street. The downtown Polk Street of 1844 has disappeared, but the name remains in the Oak Cliff residential district. Site of old Water Street, on the banks of the Trinity, is now occupied by railway terminals, and the river itself has been moved a mile westward since Bryan and J. P. Dumas labored over the first city map.

In August, 1872, a mass meeting of older settlers in the community, presided over by John Henry Brown, street commissioner, recommended names for a number of the town's streets, which later were approved by ordinance. Among streets then named were Hord, Cochran, Harwood, Phelps, Patterson, Good, Burford, Crockett, Martin, Bryan, and Murphy.

More important of these older city thoroughfares and their name sources are:

Adolph—For Adolph Frick, one of the Swiss Colony.
Adair—For Dr. W. W. Adair, early physician and landowner.
Akard—For W. C. C. Akard, merchant (1864).
Alamo—For the Alamo at San Antonio.
Alderson—For the Reverend E. W. Alderson, early-day minister.
Allen—For Dr. R. W. Allen, early-day physician.
Annex Ave.—Boundary of old Fairfield Annex to East Dallas.
Ash Ln.—By Martha Ash in memory of William Ash, in 1895.
Austin—For Stephen F. Austin.
Barry—For Bryan T. Barry, twice mayor of Dallas.
Beaumont—For the Robert L. and Godfrey Beaumont families.
Beeman—For the John Beeman family, first settlers after Bryan (1842), etc.
Bell—For P. H. Bell, governor of Texas, 1849–53.
Bennett Ave.—For William H. Bennett, landowner (1856).
Blakeney—For J. C. Blakeney.
Blaylock Dr.—For Louis Blaylock, capitalist, mayor, 1923–27.
Bogel—For Julius C. Bogel, city tax collector (1890).
Boll—For Henry Boll, La Reunion French colonist (1855) and one-time city treasurer.
Bomar—By L. H. Bomar, in an addition opened in 1900.
Bookhout—For John Bookhout, lawyer, about 1890.
Bopp—For Jacob Bopp, Swiss colonist (1870), fruit raiser and winegrower, in 1889.
Bowen—For Ahab Bowen, early-day feed merchant.
Bowser Ave.—For O. P. Bowser, real estate dealer.
Bryan—For John Neely Bryan, founder of the city.
Browder—For Edward C. Browder, one-time district clerk.
Cabell Dr.—For General W. L. (Old Tige) Cabell, Confederate commander, mayor.
Camp—For A. C. Camp, early banker and city official.
Cantagrel—For Francois Jean Cantagrel, head of La Reunion Colony Company.
Caruth Blvd.—For Walter Watt Caruth, early settler.
Carroll Ave.—For Dr. Carroll Peak.
Cedar Springs Rd.—Original highway to springs and village of same name.
Central Ave.—Parallels route of Houston & Texas Central, first railroad to enter city.
Clark—For Edward Clark, governor of Texas, 1861–63.
Cochran—For William M. Cochran, first county clerk (1846).
Cockrell Ave.—For Alexander Cockrell, early capitalist.
Cole Ave.—For John Higgs (Uncle Jack) Cole, landowner in area (1843).
Commerce—Original principal business street, so named by John Neely Bryan.
Corinth—For the ancient Greek city of Corinth.
Corsicana—For Corsicana, Texas (Island of Corsica).
Crockett—For John M. Crockett, early-day lawyer (1848) and mayor in 1860.
Crowdus—For Dr. J. W. Crowdus, druggist and mayor in 1881–83.

Crutcher—For C. F. Crutcher, city secretary of town of East Dallas, later Dallas alderman (1885).

Davis—For A. E. Davis, developer of an addition in 1890.

Dickason—For Colonel M. L. Dickason, landowner.

Duncan—For S. W. S. Duncan, early-day engineer.

Eakins—For John J. Eakins, developer of an addition in 1878.

Elm—For grove of elm trees near Trinity River.

Ervay—For Henry S. Ervay, mayor in 1870–72. (First named Johnson for Negro carpetbagger; renamed to honor Ervay after released from jail during Reconstruction.)

Ewing Ave.—For H. F. Ewing, first mayor of Oak Cliff, 1891.

Exposition Ave.—Original street leading into State Fair grounds.

Field—For Tom W. Field, capitalist, landowner, builder.

Fitzhugh Ave.—For L. H. Fitzhugh, early settler and landowner.

Forney Ave.—Forney Pike—For John W. Forney, Philadelphia newspaperman; publicity agent for Texas & Pacific Railroad in 1872–73.

Forest—Believed to have been named originally for the Confederate General Nathan B. Forrest. Present spelling, adopted some time during the 1880s, suggested by the trees which lined the street.

Gano—For General R. M. Gano, rancher, physician, and noted Confederate soldier.

Garrett Ave.—For Bishop Alexander C. Garrett of the Episcopal diocese of Dallas.

Gaston Ave.—For Captain W. H. Gaston, early-day banker and developer. Originally Wallace Street, for Wallace W. Peak.

Gillespie—For Dr. John P. Gillespie, physician and landowner.

Good—For John J. Good, lawyer, landowner, mayor, 1880–81.

Gould—For Jay Gould, financier, builder Texas & Pacific Railroad.

Grand Ave.—Believed to have been so named because it long was used as concourse for informal horse racing.

Greenville Ave.—Original highway from Dallas to Greenville.

Grigsby—For C. Grigsby, early real estate developer.

Guillot—For pioneer family founded by Maxime Guillot, 1849.

Hall—For Peter Hall, early settler and landowner.

Harwood—For Alexander Harwood, county clerk, 1850–51, 1875–83.

Haskell Ave.—For Horatio Nelson Haskell, alderman of East Dallas in 1883.

Hawkins—For J. A. Hawkins, secretary, Dallas & Wichita Railroad, 1872.

Henry—For J. L. Henry, first mayor of East Dallas, 1885.

Holland Ave.—For Colonel Frank P. Holland, mayor, 1895–97.

Holmes—For Edmond E. and Martha J. Holmes, 1888.

Houston—For General Sam Houston, hero of San Jacinto; first president of the Republic of Texas.

Jackson—For U. S. President Andrew Jackson.

Jefferson Ave.—For U. S. President Thomas Jefferson.

Jordan—For William Jordan, realty developer.

Junius—For Junius Peak, landowner, Texas Ranger.

Keating Ave.—For C. A. Keating, pioneer farm implement dealer.

Knight—For G. A. (Dude) Knight, feed merchant.

Lagow—For Richard Lagow, early owner of 4,444 acres in the area.

Lamar—For Mirabeau B. Lamar, second president of the Republic of Texas.

Lancaster Ave.—Original road to Lancaster, Texas.

Lane—For John W. Lane, mayor, 1862–66.

Latimer—For J. W. Latimer, founder of the *Dallas Herald* in 1849.

Ledbetter Dr.—For W. H. (Uncle Peahull) Ledbetter, county commissioner, in 1932.

Lemmon Ave.—For W. H. Lemmon, realty developer.

Leonard—For J. L. Leonard, alderman, 1874.

Lewis—For Henry Lewis, sheriff, 1888–92.

327

Lindsley Ave.—For Henry D. Lindsley, capitalist, mayor, 1915–17. (Formerly Watts St.)

Loomis Ave.—For George Loomis, hotel operator.

Madison—For James Madison, U.S. president.

McCoy—For Colonel John C. McCoy, Dallas' first lawyer, who came here in 1845.

McKinney Ave.—Original road to town of McKinney. (For Collin McKinney.)

Magnolia—For trees growing along the street.

Main—By John Neely Bryan in town plat of 1844.

Market—By John Neely Bryan in town plat of 1844.

Marilla—For Mrs. Marilla Ingram Young, wife of Reverend William C. Young, about 1878.

Marsalis Ave.—For T. L. Marsalis, "father of Oak Cliff."

Martin—For Bennett H. Martin, district judge, 1848–50.

Masonic—Masonic-Odd Fellows Cemetery located thereon in 1857.

Milton Ave.—For Milton Paulins, real estate developer.

Nussbaumer—For Jacob Nussbaumer, one of La Reunion colony of 1855.

Oak Grove Ave.—By J. D. Cole, developer of Oak Grove addition, 1885.

Oram—For J. M. Oram, Dallas jeweler.

Overton Rd.—For W. P. Overton, pioneer landowner, builder of first gristmill in county (1846).

Pacific Ave.—By Texas & Pacific Railroad officials as right-of-way, 1873. (Previously Burleson St.)

Park Ave.—First named Portland St.; changed 1876 because of location hereon of city's first park.

Parry Ave.—For W. E. Parry, early resident of the section and city secretary, 1884–87.

Patterson Ave.—For J. M. Patterson, first general merchant (1846) and later county judge.

Peak—For Captain Jefferson Peak, early settler, landowner.

Polk—By John Neely Bryan for U. S. President James K. Polk.

Pollock Ave.—For Henry Pollock, landowner.

Prather—For W. H. Prather, city secretary in 1874.

Rawlins—For William Rawlins, landowner.

Reagan—For J. M. Reagan, landowner.

Reiger Ave.—For John F. Reiger, addition 1890.

Richardson Ave.—For S. Q. Richardson, ice manufacturer, 1878.

Roosevelt—For U. S. President Theodore Roosevelt.

Ross Ave.—For William W. and Andrew J. Ross, early owners of land which street bisects.

Routh—For the Reverend Jacob Routh, pioneer North Texas preacher.

Rusk—For Thomas J. Rusk, U. S. senator, 1846–57.

Sale—For Henry Sale, landowner.

Samuell Blvd. (formerly East Pike)—For Dr. W. W. Samuell, who in 1939 bequeathed $1,000,000 in cash and property to Dallas park system.

San Jacinto—For the historic battlefield where Texas Independence was won.

Seegar—For J. A. Seegar, developer, in 1885.

Simpson—For Colonel J. B. Simpson, capitalist, developer.

Stone—For Thomas Stone, landowner, in 1854.

Swiss Ave.—For Swiss Colony immigrants, who settled along this street in 1870.

Terry—For L. R. Terry, real estate developer.

Thomas Ave.—By J. Pinckney Thomas and M. H. Thomas, in 1890.

Travis Ave.—For William B. Travis, hero of the Alamo.

Trunk—Original right-of-way of Trunk Railroad. (Now Texas and New Orleans Railroad.)

Turtle Creek Blvd.—For stream upon which the parkway abuts.

Victor—For Victor Peak.

Water—First street east of Trinity River in town plat of 1844.

Washington—For George Washington.

Welborn—For Olin Welborn, congressman from Dallas district from March 4, 1879, to March 3, 1887.

Wendelkin—For J. M. Wendelkin, alderman, 1888.
West—For John R. West, county surveyor.
Wood—For George T. Wood, governor of Texas, 1847–49.
Word—For Jefferson Word, landowner, 1874.
Worth—For Worth Peak.
Young—For the Reverend William C. Young, district clerk, 1867–68.
Zang Blvd.—For J. F. Zang, Oak Cliff land developer, in 1900.

Dallas streets bear names of twenty-two states and one territory, a majority of these in Trinity Heights, an Oak Cliff residential area. They are Alabama, Alaska, Arizona, California, Colorado, Delaware, Georgia, Idaho, Illinois, Indiana, Iowa, Louisiana, Michigan, Missouri, Montana, Oregon, Ohio, Pennsylvania, Rhode Island, Tennessee, Utah, Vermont, and Virginia.

Eighteen streets have names of Indian derivation, though these are by no means confined to tribes once residing in the vicinity: Aztec, Brazos, Caddo, Cherokee, Chihuahua, Comal, Concho, Montezuma, Nakoma, Owega, Pocahontas, Powhattan, Sewannee, Swananoah, Taos, Tuskegee, Watauga, and Wichita.

Influence of the World War is shown by such street names as Versailles, Belleau, Argonne, Bordeaux, Lausanne, and oddly, Rhine. The former Germania Street became Liberty Street in 1917. Only one Dallas street name was surely taken from the Bible—Canaan. One other—Eli—may have had a direct scriptural genesis.

There is a street named for David G. Farragut, Civil War naval commander who opened the Mississippi for the Northern forces, and another for Colonel Charles A. Lindbergh, world-famed aviator. Finally there is a Joe Louis Street in an area inhabited by Negroes.

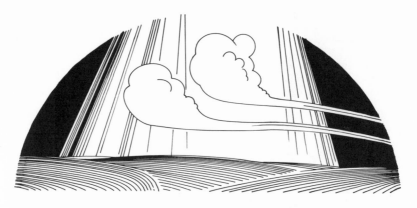

DALLAS WEATHER: WINDS OVER THE PRAIRIE

Though Dallas is subject to northers (sudden cold waves) in winter and prolonged periods of high temperatures during the summer months, winters are generally mild and the summer heat is tempered by breezes from the Gulf of Mexico accompanied by low humidity. The city is on the 45 degree normal January temperature line. The average wind velocity is 10.2 miles per hour, the average humidity at 12 noon 53 percent. Yearly sunshine hours average 3,142 or 69 percent of the possible maximum. The growing seasons—days between killing frosts—average 245. There are 87 days a year with .01 inches or more of precipitation, and the average snowfall is .113.

The winter season at times brings drops in temperature of from 20 to 40 degrees within two or three hours. These are sometimes called "blue northers," because the front edge of the approaching clouds and cold air takes on a blue tinge.

The coldest day in recorded weather history of Dallas was February 11, 1899, when the minimum temperature reading was 10 degrees below zero. At 2:30 A.M. the thermometer registered 5 degrees below, and continued to fall until 8 A.M. The frigid weather was prevalent throughout Texas and the South. One Dallas man reported his horse had frozen to death in his stable. Every fire hydrant in the city was frozen solid and water pipes froze a foot underground. One man trying to employ a plumber to mend his broken pipe was told he was 192d on the list. Streetcars did not run for two days. The *Dallas News* of February 12, 1899, described this as "the most biting, penetrating cold ever encountered under a Texas sky in this latitude."

It had been cold in Dallas back in 1856, in 1870, and again on February 1, 1873, when it was 4 degrees below, but those freezes were mild by comparison with 1899. In the 1870 visitation all the ponds and streams were frozen over and four inches of ice on Cedar Springs Lake prompted citizens to cut and store it for use the following summer. Ice skating on the river and ponds was possible on January 28, 1883, and again on December 29, 1894.

Proving every claim of extremes in weather, Dallas official records show that in contrast to these real wintry spells the city has enjoyed some remarkably warm days in winter. One of these was February 25, 1918, when the thermometer climbed from 60 degrees at 7 A.M. to 93 at 2 P.M., dropping back to 56 degrees at midnight. The hottest day recorded by the weather bureau was August 10, 1936, with a maximum of 110 degrees. Unofficial records for earlier years also show some remarkably high temperatures. In this category is the claim that on each of three days, July 7, 8, and 9, 1860, the thermometer reached a reading of 112 degrees. Some commentators of the period claim that the great fire of July 8 in that year was started by heat from the sun and not by rebellious slaves, three of whom were hanged on arson charges. Hottest day of all was Sunday, July 30, 1876, when the unofficial maximum temperature was 114 degrees in the shade.

The coldest summer day in local history was July 5, 1924, when, after falling steadily for 36 hours, the temperature reached a minimum of 56 degrees. Wind attained its highest recorded velocity of 77 miles an hour on July 20, 1936, dropping after a moment to 68 miles, sustained for four minutes. The heaviest rainfall of record was 6.17 inches, September 26–27, 1936. The longest growing season, 280 days, was in 1922, and the shortest, 210 days, in 1936.

An unprecedented storm visited Dallas shortly after 6 P.M. May 8, 1926, hail following a heavy rain. Hailstones ranged in size from smaller than a mothball at the start to larger than a baseball at the crescendo of the icy deluge. Some measured 8 to 12 inches in circumference, composed of five to eight layers of ice, and weighing, after being partially shattered by striking the ground, as much as 22 ounces. Tops of streetcars, automobiles, and roofs of houses were punctured, and hundreds of skylights, windows, and plate glass fronts broken throughout the city, with heavy damage to crops and fruits in the county nearby. Property damage was estimated at more than $900,000. No one was killed, but scores were injured, forty persons receiving treatment at the emergency hospital.

The longest continued fall of hail at one spot was on April 25, 1933, when at one downtown point hail fell for one hour and six minutes. The hail was accompanied by a terrific rainstorm, 2.74 inches falling within an hour and 3.42 inches between 4:15 and 8 p.m. Three persons were drowned as low places in the city were flooded, and much property damage was done, 200 windows being broken in the Cotton Exchange building alone. During the hailstorm an electric temperature recorder in a glass tube lay exposed on the roof of the Cotton Exchange building where the weather bureau is located, and was unbroken.

Dallas fortunately is largely protected from tornadoes, which in this region usually come from the southwest. They follow the line of least resistance and hence, on the few recorded occasions of visitations in the vicinity of the city, have been confined to the valleys of the North Elm Fork and of the main Trinity River. The high chalk ridge bounding the city on the west tends to elevate such storms and diminish their intensity before they reach the main areas of population east of the Trinity.

The only recorded occasion when a cyclone struck this section of Dallas was in 1894, when severe damage was done in the area immediately east of Central Avenue, a boy being killed by falling timbers. Western Oak Cliff has several times suffered from localized cyclones, the last of these being on July 30, 1933, when a number of small houses were wrecked but no lives lost.

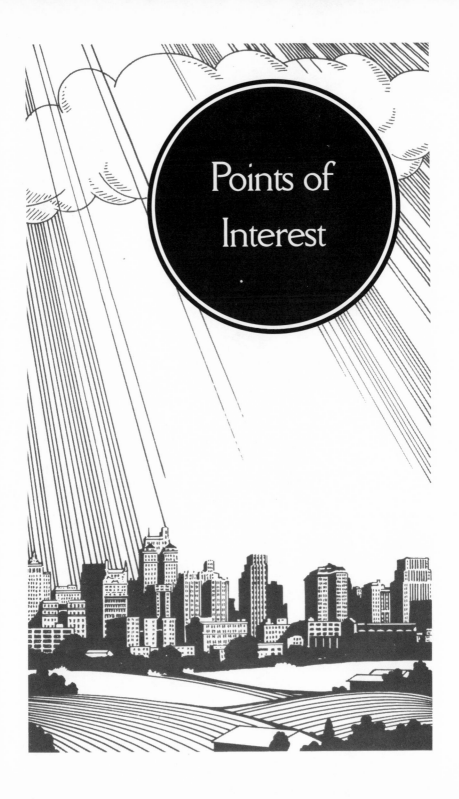

Points of
Interest

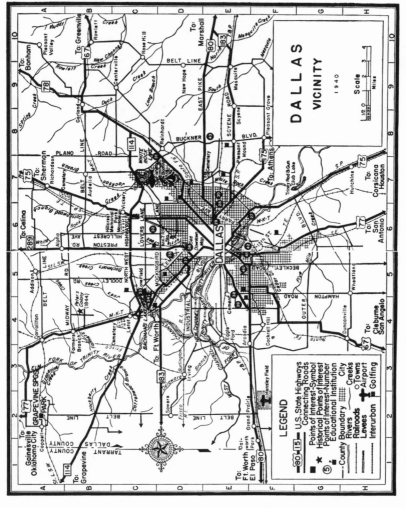

City of Dallas (Numbers correspond to buildings and sites discussed in POINTS OF INTEREST.)

POINTS OF INTEREST

1. The UNION PASSENGER TERMINAL BUILDING *(open day and night)*, west side of Houston Street between Jackson and Young Streets, is a rectangular three-story structure done in the modern classic manner. Two end pavilions project slightly from the main facade and a central pavilion containing three large openings rises somewhat higher than the rest of the structure. Designed by Jarvis Hunt of Chicago, architect, it occupies a frontage of 282 feet and faces a landscaped square, Ferris Plaza.

With this square in front and the wide sweep of the reclaimed Trinity River bottoms behind it, the Dallas Union Terminal is notable among the larger railway stations of the country for its open, pleasing setting, its complete freedom from dirt and grime, and its central location. It stands at the eastern terminus of the Houston Street viaduct, oldest of the five steel and concrete causeways connecting Dallas and Oak Cliff. Streetcar lines on Jefferson Avenue, only a block east, provide direct transportation to Oak Cliff, west of the river, and the main downtown shopping, hotel, and amusement centers, less than a mile away. Several good hotels are just north of the terminal on Houston Street.

Climaxing several years of negotiations between civic leaders of Dallas and the railroads, work was begun on the Union Terminal in January, 1914, and on October 14, 1916, the opening day of the State Fair of Texas, the building was formally dedicated in ceremonies attended by the then Governor James E. Ferguson and other notables. Since that date passenger trains of the eight railroads serving Dallas have used this station. The station cost only $1,500,000, but the total expenditures involved, including purchase of land, laying of new tracks, construction of the express and auxiliary buildings, and installation of the signaling and switching systems, amounted to approximately $6,500,000. It was designed to handle with ease a maximum of 50,000 passengers a day, and is fireproof throughout. The white enameled brick with which it is faced and which gives the building its appearance of dazzling whiteness unusual in railroad architecture, was especially manufactured for use in its construction.

The ticket offices and baggage department are on the first floor. From the main entrance on Houston Street at the south end of the building a spacious staircase divided by brass railings into four lanes sweeps up to the second floor. The main waiting room, lunchroom, and other facilities for the comfort and convenience of travelers are located to the right of this staircase, with the train gates directly in front at the head of the stairs. Entrance to the trains is by means of stairways leading down from a long window-lined corridor extending out over the tracks, at right angles to the body of the building. Underground tunnels are now under consideration, but were impractical at the time the building was constructed, before the Trinity River was leveed, as the tunnels would have been flooded in times of high water. The station is equipped with automatic telephones and an electro-pneumatic signaling system for handling trains from interlocking signal towers. The yards contain 19 miles of tracks with ten parallel tracks in the station.

2. FERRIS PLAZA *(admission free)*, bounded by Houston and Wood Streets,

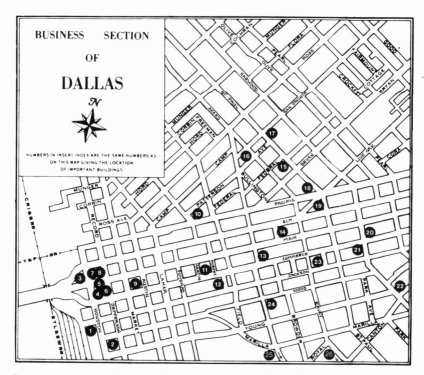

Downtown Points of Interest (Numbers correspond to buildings and sites discussed in POINTS OF INTEREST.)

south Jefferson Avenue and Young Street, is a landscaped square with an electrically illuminated fountain in the center. It is the result of an ambitious proposal advanced by *The Dallas Morning News* at the time the new Union Passenger Terminal Building was constructed; the plan was to surround the terminal for several blocks with an extensive system of concourses, parkways, and trafficways. This it was believed would forestall the possible development of a dingy, squalid slum area around the depot.

The plaza was named for Royal A. Ferris, secretary of the citizens' committee that completed negotiations for the Union Terminal. It is the only part of the extensive early plan ever to materialize. Land for the plaza was bought and cleared by the city in 1918 at a cost of $250,000. The electrically illuminated fountain with its rainbow-tinted and constantly shifting jets of water was donated by Mr. Ferris in 1925, replacing a sunken garden and pergola that formerly occupied the spot. The plaza was remodeled in 1934. A waiting station and information bureau on the Jefferson Avenue side of the park was constructed with funds donated by the Junior Chamber of Commerce. Concessionaires of the park board are on duty from 6 A.M. to 10 P.M. to dispense information. Refreshments and interurban tickets are sold here.

3. **DEALEY PLAZA** *(admission free)*, between the mouth of the Triple Underpass and Houston Street, is a landscaped triangle named for the Dallas publisher G. B. Dealey. The plaza is where the main downtown east and west thoroughfares of the

city—Commerce, Main, and Elm Streets—converge before plunging under the railroad yards of the Union Terminal Passenger Station.

Though only recently a park, the area occupied by this small downtown plaza has seen much local history. Two tall shafts of stone on each side of Main Street, which forms the central avenue of the plaza, proclaim it to be the "Birthplace of Dallas." The first local home, John Neely Bryan's cabin, was erected here. In later years the section of Houston Street that now bounds the plaza on the east was the west part of the old Courthouse Square, the geographical center from which Dallas grew. Here at the corner of Main and Houston Streets stood the Crutchfield House, Dallas' leading hostelry from 1852 to 1888.

4. JOHN NEELY BRYAN'S CABIN *(not open)*, northeast corner Commerce and Houston Streets, on the lawn of the old courthouse, is a reconstruction of the first permanent home of Dallas' pioneer founder. It is interesting both for its association with early events in Dallas County, and as an authentic example of the architecture and living arrangements of the average home of the Southwestern frontier in the early 1840s.

Except for the roof of handmade shingles the cabin has been reconstructed from its old materials used by Bryan. It measures approximately 16 feet square, and is built of 12-inch hewn logs chinked with clay. In the center of the front wall is the only door, made of heavy planks and operated by a latchstring. Against the west wall stands an outside chimney of limestone. There are two windows, one at the east end and one at the rear, both protected by heavy wooden shutters hung on hand-wrought hinges. Partially enclosing the cabin is an old rail fence.

The structure has a single room with a puncheon floor—cedar logs hewn flat— and a limestone fireplace. High over the fireplace rests a heavy log with three auger holes into which pegs were driven. On these pegs game was hung to cure. The wall over the fireplace is decorated with the flags of the Texas Republic, the Confederacy, and the United States, the three banners under which Bryan served his country. In the corner is a crude bed built by inserting cedar poles into holes in the logs of the wall. A lantern fashioned from a hub taken off a wagon driven to Texas by a Mr. Hollifield in 1837 hangs in the center of the room.

The memoirs of the Bryan family and those of other old settlers in Dallas County are often confusing, but the best evidence supports the belief that this was the last of three cabins built by Bryan, and that it served as the earliest store and the first post office in the community. There are records indicating that it was the scene of the first trial held in Dallas County.

John Neely Bryan first visited the present site of Dallas in 1840 in the company of a Cherokee guide called Ned, pitching his camp at the foot of a bluff on the river near the present-day west end of Main Street. He did not settle permanently until later in November, 1841, when he returned with only his Indian pony Neshoba and his bear dog Tubby, and raised a rude hut of cedar poles against the face of the bluff on the site of his former camp.

This was the first of Bryan's three dwellings. While he was absent on a trading expedition to Preston his first habitation was washed away by a rise in the Trinity, and early in the spring of 1842 he built a more substantial one-room cabin farther back from the river channel, close to the spot where the courthouse is now. Here he lived as a bachelor until February 26, 1843, when he married Margaret Beeman, daughter of John Beeman, a pioneer who with his family had settled a short time before at Bird's Fort, now Birdville, Tarrant County. Bryan persuaded Beeman, along with the Gilberts, the Webbs, and other families to join him on the banks of the Trinity in the spring of 1842. Bryan and his bride lived for some time in the earliest cabin, and their first child, Coffee Bryan, who died in infancy, was born here. The child was named for General John Coffee of Tennessee, friend of Bryan and associate and confidant of Andrew Jackson.

Bryan's trading trips appear to have been ill-fated, and while he and his wife were buying supplies in Clarksville on the Red River another Trinity River flood occurred, so badly damaging their cabin that it necessitated the building of new quarters on present-day Commerce Street near Broadway. The cabin now on the courthouse lawn is believed to be a part of that one. It was an airy and commodious structure for those times, being a double house of hewn cedar logs, with an open space or "dog-trot" between the two rooms. The roof was of clapboards and the rooms were large and floored with hand-sawed planks. The west chamber was the family room, the east room (the one now preserved) was the kitchen, dining room, and spare bedroom. In this home were born three of John and Margaret Bryan's children—John Neely Bryan, Jr., on January 9, 1846, Elizabeth F. on December 4, 1847, and Edward T. on June 2, 1849. It also became, as has been indicated, the community center around which revolved the social, economic, and political life of the settlement.

On August 7, 1852, Bryan sold his residence along with other possessions to Alexander Cockrell and moved to Mountain Creek, where in the old Cockrell home was born his fifth child, Alexander L., on October 30, 1854. After the sale of this house the vicissitudes and peregrinations of Bryan's former log cabin residence were almost equal to those of its builder. For a time, while Cockrell was building a new house at the foot of Commerce Street and Bryan was living at Cockrell's former home on Mountain Creek, the cabin was occupied by Cockrell and his family. Later in the 1870s it was moved to what is now the south shore of White Rock Lake and a lean-to added. After the Civil War it was bought by William J. Rupard and moved minus the lean-to to his 40-acre farm east of Dallas.

That farm was purchased on September 25, 1880, by Dr. Robert Cooke Buckner with the understanding that the house should go with the property. With three orphans as residents, the cabin was dedicated as Buckner's Orphans Home on September 27, 1880. When the present chapel of that institution was built in 1908, the cabin was moved, unchanged, to a basement room. In 1928 it was loaned to the State Fair Association for exhibition. During the Fair that year John Neely Bryan, Jr., who had been born in the cabin, lived in it and received there many of the old settlers he had known in pioneer days. After the closing of the Fair the cabin was temporarily stored on the grounds, and half of the old logs lost or stolen. Finally in 1935 directors of the Orphans Home gave the building to the county of Dallas for reconstruction on its present site. Here it was formally dedicated by the county on January 9, 1936, as a feature of the Texas Centennial observance in that year.

5. The **DALLAS COUNTY COURTHOUSE** *(open workdays 9–5)*, Jefferson, Main, Houston, and Commerce Streets, has been the focal point from which the city has spread out fanwise, north, east, and south, and across the river to the west. In all, six structures marking in their appearance and materials the successive stages in Dallas' growth from a straggling frontier trading settlement to a progressive young city have stood on this site, each dedicated to the functions of county government. The first of these, erected while the land was still the private property of John Neely Bryan, was a small one-room log cabin with a board roof and

puncheon floor, where court was held from the organization of the county in 1846 until Christmas Day, 1848, when some of the citizens, inspired by an excess of holiday "spirits," burned their primitive temple of justice to the ground. This was the first of three trials by fire to which the local county buildings have been subjected.

From 1848 to 1850 court was apparently held in John Neely Bryan's double log cabin on the south side of Commerce Street near Broadway. Prior to the election in which Dallas was chosen as the permanent county seat, John Neely Bryan and his wife Margaret Bryan bonded themselves on October 31, 1850, to donate to the county the lots "designated and known on the map or plan of said Town (Dallas) as the public or courthouse square," provided that Dallas won the election. This donation was confirmed by a deed dated January 10, 1851, conveying the lots in question to Amon McCommas in his capacity as president of the County Board of Commissioners.

The local legend, already well established in the 1890s, that the land was deeded to the county specifically as "a perpetual site for a courthouse" finds no support in the text of either the bond or subsequent deed. The same is true of the equally persistent legend that the ground would revert to Bryan's heirs if it ever ceased to be used as a courthouse site. A test has never arisen in fact since this land has been used continuously for courthouse purposes from the original date of the bond down to the present day.

In 1850 the contract was let for a new and enlarged courthouse, 16x32 feet, with nine-foot ceilings, a plank floor, "a good stone chimney in the center of the building and a fireplace in each room." Only five years later this made way for an even more commodious structure, two stories high and 50 feet square, built of the best brick obtainable in the county, with a lead roof and a chimney at each corner, the whole costing $7,400. During the period that followed and well up into Reconstruction days the courthouse apparently stood in the middle of the town common. An outraged journalistic protest in 1870 called attention to the fact that the yard, "one of the most beautiful in the state," had been "converted into a horse-lot, a cow-pen, a hog-pen, a loathsome common for animals to ruin—root up, eat off, and do other things too numerous to mention."

In 1871 the building of 1855 was condemned as unsafe and sold for $465. The new structure that in 1874 arose on the site was of native granite quarried about six miles east of the city. It was two stories high, and crowned by a "splendid" dome. An iron fence around the building supplied an additional touch of elegance. For its time it was imposing. After a fire in 1880, believed to be of incendiary origin, it was completely rebuilt, a third story added, and a tower constructed in the center. Just ten years later, on February 7, 1890, this building also was gutted by fire. Warrants were issued almost immediately, and the present courthouse constructed in the same year.

The building, which cost $350,000, is designed in Romanesque style from rough-cut red Pecos limestone, trimmed with Arkansas gray granite. It has a pointed roof of red slate. Three stories in height, surmounted by eight round towers, fireproof throughout even to the stairways, and with all modern conveniences, the courthouse was a showplace to which the thriving young city once "pointed with pride." Contemporary newspaper accounts record that visitors came from far and near to admire its grandeur and hear its massive two-ton bell boom out the hours from a central tower that rose 205 feet from the pavement. The tower with its clock and bell have long since been removed for structural reasons; and the rapidly expanding needs of a metropolitan county have outgrown and overflowed the facilities once considered so magnificent. Stripped of its former glories, the building stands only as a decayed monument to the grandiose and ornate taste of the nineties. Agitation for its removal as both unsafe and unsightly, and its replacement by a more modern structure, had been unsuccessful in 1940. It still shelters all county courts except the two criminal courts, and a considerable number of administrative offices.

6. The old COUNTY RECORDS OFFICE *(open workdays 9–5)*, northwest corner Jefferson and Commerce Streets, a squat two-story stone edifice once connected with the courthouse by an iron bridge, was built in 1884. After the fire of 1880, in which the county archives were spared from complete destruction, the citizens of Dallas resolved to transfer the records to a fireproof place of safety. For the purpose of providing such a place the present structure was erected. J. E. Flanders was the architect.

The walls are of stone, two feet thick, the floors of cement; there is not so much as a single splinter of wood or other combustible material in the building. It is used as the Dallas County Women's Recreation Building, and contains club and rest rooms.

7. The CRIMINAL COURTS BUILDING *(open workdays 9–5)*, northeast corner Houston and Main Streets, is a nine-story structure of steel and brick trimmed with granite, designed by H. A. Overbeck of Dallas, architect. It houses the two Dallas County criminal district courts, offices of the sheriff, the district attorney, and the county jail. Built in 1913, it cost $585,982.

The jail, designed to make prison breaks practically impossible, is of unusual construction. It is virtually a building within a building; running through the center of nine floors of the main building, its only entrance is on the ground floor by means of elevators, one for freight and one for passengers. There are no stair connections with the jail cells, which are on the sixth floor. Here there are 96 cells three tiers high, with a deck for exercise. On the lower floors are the jail hospital and operating rooms, cells for women, quarters for delinquent girls, jailer's living quarters, jail barber shop, cells for trusties, juvenile and Negro prisoners, and for insane persons who cannot immediately be accommodated in asylums.

The floors above are devoted to the kitchen and dining rooms, quarters of the jail chef, laundry, and storage rooms for belongings of the prisoners, confiscated gambling paraphernalia, and the like. While normally designed to house 200 inmates the jail has at times accommodated as many as 450, including some of the more notorious of the Southwest's latter-day criminals. Clyde Barrow and Floyd Hamilton were confined here for varying periods.

It was from this jail that Harvey Bailey, one of the kidnappers of Charles F. Urschel, escaped on Labor Day, 1933. Testimony in court showed that this escape was effected by inside collusion, for which a jailer went to prison; Bailey, recaptured, was sent to Alcatraz to serve a term of life imprisonment.

8. The COUNTY HALL OF RECORDS *(open workdays 9–5)*, Jefferson Street between Main and Elm Streets, dates from 1928 and contains the county archives. Built at a cost of $700,000, the building was designed in modified Gothic style in one rectangular block of six stories and basement, faced with plain white stone. Lang & Witchell of Dallas were the architects. It contains fireproof vaults for storage of records, and all the fiscal business of the county government is transacted here.

Dallas County Courthouse

Parkland City-County Hospital

Dallas County Criminal Courts Building

Dallas City Hall

Federal Building and Post Office

Medical Arts Building

Dallas Cotton Exchange

In the roistering post-Civil War boom days the north side of the courthouse square where the Hall of Records and adjoining Criminal Courts Building now stand was occupied by a solid row of saloons and gambling dens notorious for brawls and shootings. Following the fire of 1869 that gutted the entire block, other structures were built in this area, and during the latter part of the century as the heart of the city moved eastward, it became part of the wholesale district that gradually grew up north of the courthouse. About 1900 the block on Jefferson Street between Main and Elm Streets was occupied by several two-story brick buildings occupied by implement and machinery companies. On the second floor of one of these there was an engraving company from about 1900 to 1906 where John Knott, the famous *Dallas Morning News* cartoonist, is said to have served his apprenticeship. The land was acquired by the county in 1926–27, and the construction of the Hall of Records commenced in the latter year.

9. The DALLAS MORNING NEWS BUILDING *(open 8–8; six tours daily, conducted by guides; ask at information desk, near main entrance on Commerce Street)* extends for a block on the north side of Commerce Street between Austin and Lamar Streets. This is the home of one of the Southwest's more influential daily newspapers, one closely identified with the growth of Dallas and more than a half century of Texas politics. The A. H. Belo Corporation also publishes in this plant the *Texas Almanac* and the *Semi-Weekly Farm News*.

The Dallas Morning News has had its plant on this location since its first issue appeared on the streets on October 1, 1885. The present building, constructed in three units of no coherent style, represents successive additions in the course of which the newspaper's property has spread across the block. The western unit is four stories in height; the eastern and central units three stories. All three were designed by the late Herbert M. Greene, Dallas architect. The first building, a three-story brick structure costing about $10,000, was erected by Colonel William E. Hughes, prominent local banker of the eighties, and leased to the *Galveston News* when its owner, Colonel Alfred H. Belo, decided to establish a sister journal in Dallas. It had a 50-foot frontage and stood in the middle of the block just west of the city hall and fire station. The site was chosen by G. B. Dealey and other officials of the newspaper because of its location in the center of the then main business section of Dallas, with important banks, business houses, and public buildings within a radius of a few blocks.

The Lamar Street frontage was acquired in 1899 and was at first devoted to a one-story annex built to house the larger presses which the paper installed in that year. The northeast corner of Commerce and Austin Streets was bought by the *News* in 1912, and in the following year, after the death of Mrs. A. H. Belo, Sr., the company ordered constructed its four-story-and-basement fireproof building on this site. The building still houses the mechanical departments of the newspaper; linotyping and stereotyping machinery is on the top floor, presses and power units below.

Its owners have been among the pioneers in trying new printing inventions. The Bullock press, incandescent lamps, and stereotype plates that were part of the plant's earliest equipment fascinated the citizens of Dallas in 1885, and were the subject of some justifiable boasting on the part of the newspaper's editors. In 1891 a Seymour-Brewer inset, web-perfecting press capable of printing 24,000 copies an hour was installed.

When Governor James Stephen Hogg visited Dallas in 1894 he was conducted to

346

the composing room to see "the wonderful Merganthaler typesetting machine," installed a few weeks before. In 1899 the company purchased a new three-deck multiple press, and in the fall of 1911 installed a sextuple press with color attachment that could turn out 72,000 copies of a 12-page paper in an hour. Other similar presses have been added as the growth of circulation required.

The editorials and business offices of the *News* are in the central and eastern units of the building. The circulation, advertising, and other business departments are on the first floor, with direct access from the street by an entrance at the corner of Commerce and Lamar. The editorial offices and libraries, reached by an elevator and stairway in the center of the building, are on the second and third floors. The biographical section of the library or "morgue" is on the third floor adjoining the City Room. The reference library, on the second floor, is valuable as a repository of historical information about Dallas and Texas generally, with records extending back almost a hundred years.

It contains a partial file of the oldest publication of the A. H. Belo Corporation, the *Galveston News*, established in 1842 and not separated from *The Dallas Morning News* until 1923; also complete bound files of *The Dallas Morning News*, the *Texas Almanac* (1857), the *Semi-Weekly Farm News* (1885), and the *Dallas Journal*, an evening paper established on April 1, 1914, and merged on July 1, 1938, with the *Dallas Dispatch* to form the *Dispatch-Journal*. All of the *News* files have been photographed by special arrangement with the Eastman Kodak Company and can be examined through the use of a projecting machine and negative without disturbing the bound volumes. The files have been partly indexed; there is a file containing clippings classified by subject matter. This reference library is maintained primarily for the convenience of members of the *News* staff, and use by the general public is not encouraged. Research students can use its facilities by securing permission of the librarian.

Radio station WFAA, owned and operated by *The Dallas Morning News*, formerly had its studios and broadcasting station in this building, with antennae stretching from a tower on the roof of the *News* building to one on the Mercantile Bank Building. The broadcasting plant has been moved to a site near Grapevine and the studios in 1940 were in the Baker Hotel, but scheduled to open in the Santa Fe Building penthouse late in the year.

10. The TIMES HERALD BUILDING *(open during daylight hours)*, on Herald Square, Pacific and Patterson Avenues and Griffin Street, is the home of Dallas' second oldest newspaper, and is one of the city's best examples of modern functional architecture. The building, three stories and basement, was designed by Lang & Witchell, Dallas architects, and follows the severely simple lines of the modernistic American school, with an absolute minimum of ornamentation. Its exterior is of light pressed brick with stone finish. The main entrance on Pacific Avenue is of carved stone, with matching panel above, bearing a name plate. The first-story steel casement windows extend from floor to ceiling, a height of 22 feet, and permit a full view of the presses in operation.

Business offices are also on the first floor. They occupy a soundproofed lobby finished in green and gold in modernistic style, with counters and wainscoting of verde marble and lighting fixtures in the form of bronze and tapestry glass lanterns, repeating in pattern the fixtures that flank the building's entrances on the outside. The editorial, advertising, circulation, and Associated Press offices, as well as those of the owner and publisher Edwin J. Kiest, are on the second floor.

An information booth to the left of the elevator is on this floor. The newspaper files, dating back to October, 1886, are bound and can be consulted by special arrangement.

The third floor is utilized by the composing room and other mechanical departments. A basement houses the foundation of the presses, storage rooms, machine shop, and boiler rooms, and a covered tunnel at street level extends from Pacific to Patterson Avenues, permitting delivery trucks to load under cover from the pressrooms on the first floor.

The *Times Herald* occupied its present plant in August, 1929. Its first home was in a building that stood approximately where the Adolphus Hotel Annex is today; from here it moved in 1903 to 1305 Elm Street.

11. The CHAMBER OF COMMERCE BUILDING *(open 9–5 workdays)*, northeast corner Commerce and Martin Streets, has unusual present-day functional importance. The building, a very narrow six-story structure, was remodeled in 1915 to serve as the first home of the Federal Reserve Bank of Dallas. Today it is the general headquarters of organized business enterprise in the city.

The Chamber of Commerce and its subsidiary branches—as, for example, the Manufacturers' and Wholesale Merchants' Association, the Retail Merchants' Association, and the Junior Chamber of Commerce—have their offices here. The building also houses various related commercial and civic organizations including the Automotive Trades Association, Bureau of Foreign and Domestic Commerce, United States Chamber of Commerce, Girl Scouts, Hotel Association, Insurance Agents' Association, Open Shop Association, Printers' Board of Trade, Real Estate Board, Stores' Mutual Protective Association, Texas Fire Insurance Department, and the "Welcome Wagon," a hotel greeters' organization.

To an even greater degree than most American communities Dallas is a businessman's and booster's city, and these organizations have had a far-reaching influence in determining its economic and civic fortunes.

The history of commercial associations in Dallas dates back to August, 1874, when during the boom that followed the arrival of the railroads in 1872 and 1873 the Dallas Board of Trade was established. C. M. Wheat was the first president of this pioneer promotional organization. It lasted until 1878 and was succeeded by the Merchants' Exchange, organized on April 15, 1882, with an initial membership of 200. The Merchants' Exchange was almost immediately successful. Two years after its incorporation it had built its own three-story building on the northeast corner of Lamar and Commerce Streets, today called the Gaston Building.

The Manufacturers' Board was established in 1893 with Dr. F. E. Hughes as the first president, and on May 2 of that year the Dallas Commercial Club came into existence with Philip Sanger as its president. In Sanger's words, the latter organization claimed as its province "everything for the growth of Dallas." From this group the present Dallas Chamber of Commerce traces its descent. The Dallas Commercial Club had its offices in the Cotton Belt Building across Commerce Street from *The Dallas Morning News*, and was the first organization in the city to devote itself seriously to the promotion of fair trade practices through arbitration and adjustment of disputes between member firms. It was also the first to organize good will tours over the state to advertise Dallas as a trading center, and in 1895 inaugurated the first campaign urging Texans to patronize Texas merchants and manufacturers.

Despite the Commercial Club's active program and progressive outlook, Dallas

348

eventually outgrew it. About 1908 the need became apparent for a single large, well-integrated organization to present adequately the city's opportunities. In December of that year the Commercial Club, the One Hundred and Fifty Thousand Club, the Trade League, and the Freight Bureau met and formed the Dallas Chamber of Commerce, which included practically every civic organization in the city. L. O. Daniel was elected president. From that time the Chamber of Commerce has functioned as the principal agency through which Dallas has sought to make itself the distributing and financial center of the Southwest.

Three of the important outgrowths of the Chamber of Commerce have been the Dallas Wholesale Merchants' Association, the Junior Chamber of Commerce, and the Open Shop Association. The Wholesale Merchants' Association was set up as a separate organization in 1920 with W. J. Kinsella at its head, but affiliated two years later with the Chamber of Commerce. It sponsors a semiannual Southwestern Style Show that every spring and autumn brings buyers to Dallas from all parts of the Southwest.

The Junior Chamber of Commerce, formed in 1919 with George O. Wilson as its president, has been a very active branch of the Dallas Chamber of Commerce. It is a training school to prepare young professional men and businessmen to assume responsibilities as civic leaders, and every year awards a trophy, the Wilson Cup, to the member who has rendered the most valuable service to the city.

Though the Dallas Open Shop Association has subsequently been divorced from any direct and official connection with the Chamber of Commerce, it was formed at a mass meeting of that organization in 1919, during the wave of industrial unrest that swept the country after the World War.

The many activities of the Dallas Chamber of Commerce include special attention to foreign trade; sponsoring good will tours to Mexico, the Rio Grande Valley, and other places in Dallas' trade area; working for an improved rating of Dallas in public health; furnishing information for tourists and prospective residents about Dallas, Texas, Mexico, and the Southwest generally; and publicizing the city through radio broadcasts, its own publications, and in other regional and trade publications.

The Chamber of Commerce publishes a monthly magazine, *Southwest Business*, and a monthly newspaper, *The Hub*. It also publishes and distributes the Dallas Manufacturers' Directory.

12. The SANTA FE BUILDING *(open daylight hours)*, Commerce Street at head of Murphy Street and extending back to Young Street, bulks large in the foreground of the Dallas skyline and attracts attention because of the distinctive features of modern commercial architecture it embodies.

Designed by L. R. Whitson and F. C. Dale, Dallas architects, and opened in 1927, it is the property of the Terminal Building Corporation, a subsidiary of the Gulf, Colorado & Santa Fe Railway, and stands on the former site of this railway's passenger terminal. It is one of the largest single office and terminal buildings in the Southwest, and consists of four units of graduated height, one behind the other, opening respectively on Commerce, Jackson, Wood, and Young Streets. The first unit, on Commerce Street, is in two levels: the first devoted to offices, 19 stories in height; the second, devoted to loft space, of ten stories. Immediately behind it on Jackson Street—connected with the main building by an overhead bridge—is a second ten-story unit devoted to warehouse space. The third and fourth units facing respectively on Wood and Young Streets are eight-story warehouses. All four of the units are of reinforced concrete throughout except for the exterior walls, which are of terra cotta tile and light buff brick.

There is a system of underground railroad tracks 24 feet beneath the street level, by means of which freight can be unloaded in the basements of the various building units and conveyed directly by 17 freight elevators to the floors above. Tracks that serve the entire group enter from the south on a ramp guarded by retaining walls, and connect directly with the adjacent Santa Fe freight yards. Inside, switches operated from platforms and a system of safety signals prevent any confusion in the handling of trains. A locomotive using steam from thermos tanks hauls the cars.

On top of the second unit is a spacious penthouse surrounded by gardens and protecting walls, with direct elevator service from the building's main entrance on Commerce Street. This was at first used as a clubhouse by the Dallas University Club, and later occupied by Chez Maurice, one of the city's smart night clubs. In 1940 it was being remodeled as studios for radio station WFAA.

13. The 29-story MAGNOLIA BUILDING *(open daylight hours)*, northeast corner Commerce and Akard Streets, is topped by an Observation Tower *(open 2–4 workdays)*, which affords a broad panorama of the city and its environs, particularly of the system of viaducts and railroad bridges that span the Trinity River bottoms between Oak Cliff and downtown Dallas. The building's tall smokestack tower, with its pointed green tile roof, obstructs the view to the east, but it is possible to see for miles in other directions. On a clear day with a pair of binoculars it is possible to see the skyline of Fort Worth. Formerly the platform was open and a connecting runway to the opposite side of the smokestack tower made it possible to get a view to the east, but building authorities experienced considerable trouble with vandalism and schoolboy pranks, making it necessary to completely enclose the platform in a wire cage.

Surmounting the Observation Tower is a thirteen-ton revolving sign 40x32 feet in the form of a red winged horse, the trademark of one of the Magnolia Petroleum Company's subsidiaries. This figure, representing Pegasus, the flying stallion of classical mythology, makes the Magnolia Building a kind of standard-bearer among Dallas skyscrapers. By day this sign, bright red against the blue Texas sky, is by far the most conspicuous feature of the skyline, and by night the one-fifth mile of neon tubing which serves to illuminate it makes it a flaming beacon visible for 75 miles around. The highest point of the sign is 450 feet above the street level. Because of its size it has attracted national and even international attention. The mechanism by which it revolves is automatically cut off when the wind reaches a velocity of from 25 to 30 miles an hour.

The Magnolia Building is the tallest structure in Dallas and completely dominates the skyscrapers massed around it. Begun in 1920 and completed in 1922, it was designed by Alfred C. Bossom of New York, now an English baronet, with Lang & Witchell of Dallas as associate architects. The design is Renaissance, modified by the height of the building; Bedford limestone facing covers a steel frame. The ground floor is occupied by the Mercantile National Bank, and the upper floors are used for offices, including those of the Magnolia Petroleum Company. This structure, with the Tower Petroleum Building and the Continental Building, indicates the position of the city as a center of the oil industry in the Southwest.

14. The PRAETORIAN BUILDING *(open daylight hours)*, northeast corner Main and Stone Streets, is a 14-story-and-basement structure in the Victorian office building style. It dates from 1907. Though of commonplace design and long

since dwarfed by the towering modern structures that surround it, the building has interest as a landmark in the development of the city, being the first steel skyscraper built in Dallas.

It was erected as the home office of the Modern Order of Praetorians, organized in 1899 as a fraternal order to do life insurance business, and at the time of its construction was not only the tallest building in the city, but the tallest in the state. As such it was popular with visitors as an observation point; a bird's-eye view of Dallas could be had from the roof for twenty-five cents.

The Praetorian Building was designed by C. W. Bulger & Sons, Dallas architects. It is faced with white brick, with terra cotta trim, and has a two-story base course motif of pilastered Renaissance detail. Above this is a plain white brick shaft surmounted by a wide overhanging Renaissance style cornice supported on large consoles. Inside, the walls are wainscoted in Vermont marble.

15. The FEDERAL BUILDING AND POST OFFICE *(General Delivery and Federal offices open workdays 8–6)*, on the block bounded by St. Paul, Bryan, Ervay, and Federal Streets, is a five-story-and-basement structure of reinforced concrete and stone designed in a modern Italian style by the Federal Bureau of Architecture in Washington. It was opened for service in 1930.

The building is faced in Indiana limestone, the first story with rusticated finish and the upper stories plain. Ornamental entrance doorways occur on the St. Paul and Ervay Street fronts. A colored stone cornice surrounds the upper part of the building and an ornamental colored band or belt course is at the middle of the main shaft. Terra cotta picture spandrels between the windows of the two upper stories depict in salmon-colored figures on a field of blue the progress of postal transportation from pony express to air mail. Of the many critical comments these have provoked, probably the most amusing was that made soon after the completion of the building; it was quoted by Ralph Bryan in *The Dallas Morning News* thus: "They (the picture spandrels) are as startling as would be the discovery of a colored comic strip in the *Encyclopedia Britannica*." They are part of the designs furnished by the supervising architect to the P. N. Severn Company, who executed them in terra cotta.

The two murals in the interior of the post office, one over the Ervay Street entrance and one over the St. Paul Street entrance, are more conventional. The west mural on the Ervay Street side has for its basic design an ornamental map of Dallas in light brown, with the Trinity River running diagonally across it. The east mural on the St. Paul Street side shows a map of Texas on a light brown field, with directions indicated by a compass. The general designs for these murals were furnished by supervising architects in Washington.

Though Dallas has had only 28 postmasters, the post office is its oldest governmental unit, antedating both the county and city of Dallas. Dallas' first settler, John Neely Bryan, was also its first postmaster; there is evidence that he served in this capacity under the Republic of Texas as early as 1843, though his official appointment dates only from September 26, 1844. Bryan's log cabin was the first post office. The mail, seldom exceeding two letters, was brought on mule back from Bonham to be placed in the alphabetically numbered pockets of a roughly stitched container of cotton sacking that hung on the cabin wall. Postage was uniformly collected under the laws of the Republic from the addressee.

Bryan remained postmaster for the Republic until 1846 when, following the annexation of Texas to the Union, he also received the first United States appointment on May 22. Charles H. Durgin succeeded Bryan on November 12, 1846. Durgin had come to Texas from Massachusetts the year before, and his United States passport is preserved as a relic in the present Federal Building. He had opened the second store in Dallas, on the west side of the courthouse square; he was primarily a store-keeper and only postmaster in his spare moments. Bryan's homemade pigeonholes of cotton sacking were transferred to Durgin's store, and mail continued to be dis-tributed by a grab-bag method. Persons who might be expecting letters fumbled unaided in the alphabetically marked sacks while the postmaster-storekeeper waited on his customers. This cotton bag has also been preserved. Durgin's lax ad-ministration of his duties continued while he remained a bachelor but later, after he had married a "womanly woman" of orderly habits, it is said a reformation was brought about.

Durgin was succeeded in 1850 by Thomas F. Crutchfield, later proprietor of the old Crutchfield Hotel on the northwest corner of the present Main and Houston Streets, in the area now occupied by the Triple Underpass. The post office, after having been housed successively in a home and a store, was moved in 1852 to this hotel and Crutchfield, like his predecessor, delegated most of his active duties as postmaster to his wife. In 1860 there were nine mails a day. In this year the Crutchfield House fell a victim to the disastrous fire of July 8, and though an effort was made to save the mail only the postage stamps were rescued.

Harvey Shepherd served as Confederate postmaster from 1862 to 1865, and for some time after the Civil War Dallas had no post office closer than Waco. The first postmaster to have an assistant was William Jones (1869–75). This first employee of the Dallas post office was Henry H. Smith.

During the late sixties and early seventies the post office had a number of tempo-rary locations. In 1873 it was located on the southeast corner of Pacific Avenue and Austin Street. Later it was moved into a brick building at Camp and Lamar Streets and then into a small frame structure on Main Street near Murphy Street.

Carriers were first employed in 1879, while Arch M. Cochran was postmaster and deliveries began November 1. The city was divided into four districts and Al Mann, T. Hudson Smith, J. M. Cochran, and Charles F. Altermann were engaged as car-riers. In 1940 there were 253 carriers in the Dallas system.

It was not until 1890 when J. S. Witmer was postmaster that employees of the local post office were brought under civil service regulations. In 1885 the post-master was J. H. Cochran, first Democrat to be appointed after the Civil War. The post office was on the southeast corner of Elm and Akard Streets, in the rear of Hunstable's shoe shop; its total gross receipts for that year were $41,736, and the payroll numbered 21 persons, eight clerks and 13 carriers, drawing a total of $3,500 a month. These figures offer an interesting comparison with those of 1935, when the Dallas Post Office showed gross receipts totaling $3,555,390, and had a payroll of 678 persons drawing $120,000 a month. In 1939 receipts were $4,399,914.

By November, 1900, the Dallas post office was depository for 135 counties in Texas, with about 1,600 post offices. Rural free delivery was instituted in October, 1901, with six routes. A postal savings department was opened August 25, 1911. The first parcel post package, a six-pound box of Texas pecans, was mailed to Wash-ington by Postmaster George F. Rockhold on January 1, 1913.

The post office was moved in 1888 to the southeast corner of Akard Street and Pacific Avenue. In 1883 a new and permanent site had been purchased at Main, Ervay, and Commerce Streets (then far uptown), at a cost of $11,000, and work was begun on the initial unit, facing Ervay Street, in 1884. This first unit was completed in 1889, and the Commerce Street section with its clock tower, so long a landmark in downtown Dallas, was erected by 1893. The final unit, facing Main Street farther to the east, and marked by a second tower, was completed in 1904. The entire building was of stone with two towers, in Renaissance design with massive architectural details.

This old structure was sold by the government in July, 1939, for $125, and the purchasers began to clear the site soon afterward. The work of demolition was finished early in 1940. On June 24 the cleared site was sold for $607,000 cash to the Mercantile Bank of Dallas, which announced plans for erection of a 25-story office building. The site of the present Federal Building and Post Office, which first changed hands soon after the Civil War in trade for a saddle, was bought by the government in April, 1914. The old post office was abandoned and the new building occupied on November 16, 1930.

The United States Terminal Annex Post Office *(open 8–6 workdays)*, on Houston Street between the Union Terminal Station and the Triple Underpass, a five-story stone, steel, and concrete building costing one million dollars, was completed in 1937. It replaced the former Young Street Station, on the northeast corner of Young and Austin Streets. In the basement are auxiliary workrooms, storerooms, and service departments. The first floor is devoted to the distribution of first-class mail, registered mail, and incoming parcel post, while the second floor is used exclusively for the handling of outgoing parcel post. Two large murals, one representing a night air mail scene, and the other a pioneer family building a home in the wilderness, were planned for the building when it was first opened, but various delays ensued and they were not begun until early in 1940. They are the work of the nationally-known New Mexico artist Peter Hurd.

For the fiscal year 1938 Dallas ranked 21st among American cities in the volume of its postal receipts.

16. The YOUNG MEN'S CHRISTIAN ASSOCIATION BUILDING *(training department open 9 A.M.-9:30 P.M., club rooms open daily until 10 P.M.)*, west side of North Ervay Street from San Jacinto Street to Patterson Avenue, is 15 stories, of steel frame and concrete construction, with brick facing and stone trim. It was designed by Anton F. Korn, Dallas architect. Problems of arrangement and floor space were decided in advance with the Association's architectural board in order to meet the needs of the numerous departments housed here. The building combines under one roof the facilities of a social club, athletic club, hotel, school, restaurant, and church. It was opened in 1931 and cost $621,212.

The general plan of the building provides separate quarters for men, boys, and members of the Newsboys' Club. Three separate entrances lead to the quarters reserved for these groups. The main entrance on the Ervay Street side of the building opens on the men's lobby, giving access to the public service desk, elevators, checkroom, telephone, fountain, and grill room. Left of the lobby is the beamed and paneled Fellowship Lounge with a reading room at one end and alcoves at the other. The gaily decorated fountain and grill are at the rear, just off the main lobby, with banquet rooms adjoining. Three club rooms are down a short corridor.

The Boys' Division is on the north side of the building. At the front is a large game and recreation room colorfully decorated in tile with Indian designs of bright red, yellow, and green. Back of the game room are club rooms. Directly beneath the Boys' Division is the Newsboys' Club. Here is a game room, adjoining it a club room and secretary's office. Rooms on this floor are used by newsboys and other boys who work in the craft shops, where there are facilities for leather work, basket weaving, and the like.

There are full facilities for indoor sports, including swimming. A health service operated by a trained attendant is housed on the first floor.

A recreation terrace on the seventh floor is one of the most unusual features of the building. This outdoor playground, 132x52 feet, is covered overhead and at the sides with a finely woven wire screen but is open to the sun and air, and provides an ideal spot for sun baths, outdoor gymnastics, and track work. It is equipped with lights, and during the summer is often used at night for entertainments and lectures.

An attempt was made in 1873 to organize a Young Men's Christian Association in Dallas. In 1875 "a number of pious gentlemen" secured a room at 608 Main Street; here prayer meetings were held and a reading room maintained to afford "hundreds of homeless men . . . a place to spend their evenings where with books, papers, and congenial friends and religious exercises, a moral and social restraint might be maintained." The community failed to support this center, and before the end of 1876 it was abandoned. Officers of this pioneer organization were L. C. Reed, president; L. M. Martin, vice president; and J. N. Russell, secretary.

The present Young Men's Christian Association dates from November, 1885, when a permanent organization was formed with R. W. Howell as president and C. W. Harned as secretary. The initial membership was 24. Quarters were rented above H. W. Graber's store at 317 Elm Street. By 1886 the Association had 621 members and a budget of $4,000. Two years later its membership had fallen to 131, and it did not again pass the 600 mark until 1896.

In 1893 the Association moved to the Burford Building, employed a physical director, and initiated its first physical program, consisting of a gymnasium, cycle club, and football team. In 1895 it leased the second floor of the Fakes Building at 1217 Elm Street, then moved to the Jackson Street Natatorium, a three-story brick building. On January 1, 1899, when this latter building was occupied, the membership of the Association was 994. In the following year it passed the 1,000 mark.

In November, 1905, a drive was started to raise money for the erection of a more adequate building. The goal was finally oversubscribed by $10,000, and on May 1, 1909, the Association was able to open its new building at 1910 Commerce Street, now the Savoy Hotel.

In 1915 the Association inaugurated two important local activities, one the YMCA schools offering courses in law, business administration, and other subjects, and the other the purchase of Camp Crockett in Hood County, 75 miles south of Dallas. The former was the culmination of an educational program beginning in 1886 with two classes, one in German and one in stenography, and the latter a significant addition to the Association's work with boys. In 1915 the Association entered the field of work for underprivileged boys with the organization of its free Newsboys' Club. In April, 1919, it entered as an experiment the field of Negro activity, and today maintains one of the best equipped buildings in the South devoted entirely to a YMCA program for Negroes.

As a result of a highly successful financial campaign in 1928, 5,615 Dallas citizens subscribed $1,255,260 to erect three new buildings, the downtown building, the Oak Cliff Branch, 101 East Tenth Street, and the Moorland Branch for Negroes.

The Moorland Branch was completed in 1929, the Oak Cliff Branch in 1931, and the main downtown building in 1930–31. Another branch was opened at the Sullivan Park Field House in January, 1938, but was soon abandoned.

The annual budget for the Dallas YMCA is in excess of $250,000. Its night schools, which are self-sustaining and substantially of college level, have an enrollment of 248 students in 28 classes. It also supervises the Church Recreational League.

17. The COTTON EXCHANGE BUILDING *(market open 8–1)*, southeast corner of St. Paul and San Jacinto Streets, is a 17-story rectangular structure of reinforced concrete with gray brick and front terra cotta trim, located on the northern fringe of the downtown business section. It has 220,000 square feet of floor space and is especially arranged for the convenience of the important Dallas cotton trade whose operations are centered here. The Exchange employs the ground floor for its spot and futures marketing operations and on the floors above are located offices of the brokerage and exporting firms, buyers for domestic and foreign mills, and other agencies associated with the industry.

The Dallas Cotton Exchange, organized in 1907, originally met in the offices of a member, from which it moved to the old Scollard Building at 1315 Main Street. In 1912 a seven-story building was erected at Wood and Akard Streets for the exclusive use of the Exchange, and the present building went up in 1926, with Lang & Witchell of Dallas as the architects. A large part of Texas' cotton crop is handled through the Dallas Cotton Exchange, and from the Cotton Exchange Building far-flung operations are conducted extending to Europe and the Orient.

18. The MEDICAL ARTS BUILDING *(open day and night)*, northwest corner Pacific Avenue and St. Paul Street, with an annex immediately west of Pacific Avenue, is the tallest reinforced concrete structure in Texas, and is believed to be one of the tallest in the world. It has attracted wide attention among architects and builders by reason of its beautiful design.

Nineteen stories in height, it is built in the form of a Greek cross around a central circular shaft, about which are elevators serving four wings of offices. This construction gives every office in the building an outside exposure. Slight offsets at the 15th floor, and a dormer roof of green tile, eliminating the usual penthouse, add to the distinction of its modernistic design and prevailing vertical lines. The building is faced with light buff-colored brick with buff stone trim. The main unit, containing 768 office rooms, was opened in 1923 and was designed by H. C. Barglebaugh, L. R. Whitson, and F. C. Dale, Dallas architects. The annex, containing 400 office rooms, was built in 1928, and was designed by Herbert M. Greene, La Roche and Dahl of Dallas. The two buildings represent an investment of $3,000,000.

Notable as an example of modern functional architecture, the Medical Arts Building is not less notable as a tangible expression of modern organized medicine—depending upon group effort and proper laboratory and clinical facilities. It was built by Dr. E. H. Cary, former president of the American Medical Association, to house the offices of Dallas physicians, surgeons, and dentists, and contains not only offices, but chemical and X-ray laboratories, drug and medical supply shops, a specialized bookstore dealing in medical publications, a hospital (on the top floor of the annex) with 50 beds and thoroughly equipped operating rooms, large medical and dental libraries, and an auditorium above the main floor facing St. Paul

Street, designed to provide a meeting place for the medical and dental societies of the city and county.

The Dallas Medical Arts Building was the first metropolitan medical center in the Southwest to be conceived in these comprehensive terms, and since its construction, has become the prototype of many similar Medical Arts buildings in various cities throughout the country. The name has been registered by Dr. Cary.

19. The DALLAS ATHLETIC CLUB (LIBERTY BANK) BUILDING *(hotel section open day and night)*, St. Paul, Elm, and Live Oak Streets, is one of the institutions that gives Dallas a metropolitan character. The club is entered by a private driveway and porte-cochere on St. Paul Street, and occupies the basement, part of the first floor, and seven more floors of a 13-story combination club, hotel, and office building of irregular shape. It was completed in 1925; Lang & Witchell were the architects. The building is of concrete and brick construction, faced with red brick and limestone trim, and is Georgian colonial in design. Facilities of the club include gymnasiums and swimming pools for men and women, public and private dining rooms, recreation features, and 80 hotel rooms. The club is popular as a social center. Many business and luncheon organizations hold weekly meetings in its dining rooms, and dances given here are popular with the younger set.

Dallas has had other gymnasiums and athletic clubs since the eighties, but the present one dates from a luncheon at the Adolphus Hotel in the spring of 1919, when T. L. Monagan, prominent local sportsman who had previously helped to organize the Texas Baseball League and the Dallas Country Club, met J. L. Osborn, Bob Shelton, and Harry Webster for an informal discussion of plans. Directors were elected in November, 1919. One hundred and thirty-one citizens interested in sports subscribed $100 each toward a promotional fund, and exhaustive data on athletic clubs throughout the country were collected. The new organization was incorporated for $10,000 on January 7, 1920, and employed Mr. Monagan as its executive secretary the following month. A building committee was appointed and the site of the present club building bought on December 1, 1921, for $600,000. Construction was begun in 1923 but was later suspended because of financial difficulties. The project was refinanced in 1924 by Chicago interests, at whose insistence it was made a combination office, hotel, and club building instead of an eight-story structure for club purposes only. The building was later acquired by the Liberty State Bank, which occupies a part of the ground floor.

20. The DALLAS CITY HALL *(open 8–5 workdays)*, fronting on the east side of Harwood Street between Main and Commerce Streets, is a simple rectangular building of Indiana limestone, in the classical style of the French Renaissance. Designed by the Dallas architectural firm of C. D. Hill & Company, it has five stories and a basement. On each end of the main facade is a pavilion, with Corinthian columns between, topped by a mansard roof.

Floors are of terrazzo and marble, the woodwork of mahogany, with windows inset in wide casements. The ground floor is occupied by various city offices. From it, in the center of the building, rises a marble double staircase of monumental design, leading to the second and main floor where are the offices of the mayor, city manager, city secretary, and others, and the council chamber.

A series of murals by Jerry Bywaters and Alexandre Hogue, Dallas artists, encircles the second floor lobby at the head of the staircase. Here scenes depict the Dallas of pioneer days; the city of the eighties and nineties; the unfolding of its

356

Kessler plan of reclamation, zoning, and metropolitan development; and some of the outstanding contributions to modern city life which Dallas claims—automatic traffic signals and radio-equipped police cars. The council chamber contains portraits of each of the past mayors of Dallas, from Dr. Samuel B. Pryor, elected in 1856, to George A. Sprague (1937–39).

The fourth floor houses the City Auditorium *(seating capacity 1,100)* and administrative offices. The fifth floor, commonly called High Five in local crime annals, is occupied by the city jail, which can be reached from the basement, which is used by the police department, with the identification and records bureaus and assembly room occupying most of the floor space. It also contains a police garage extending under the alleyway between the city hall and its annex, and connecting with the street by ramps.

The two units that comprise the City Hall Annex *(open 8–5 workdays)*, Commerce Street to Main Street, were once the E. H. R. Green residence and the site of its adjacent flower garden. The Commerce Street unit, joined to the main building by an open bridge, was at first a schoolhouse but in 1903 Otto H. Lang, Dallas architect, was engaged by the luxury-loving multimillionaire son of Hetty Green to convert it into a gaudy palace with plate glass windows of unusual design, heavy doors, high ceilings, numerous bathrooms, and other elaborate embellishments in the taste of the early 1900s. This unit of the annex today houses the municipal health department, including inspection and vital statistics divisions, city bacteriological laboratories, and the Emergency Hospital *(open day and night)*.

The second unit of the annex, facing on Main Street, stands on ground bought by Colonel Green for a flower garden, which he later disposed of for commercial purposes. A store was built on the site, and when first acquired by the city the building was used as a fire station, which it still resembles in external appearance. It serves as quarters for the corporation court, and as a detention ward for women prisoners, and also houses the Welfare Department.

The seat of Dallas' municipal government has progressed uptown by a series of irregular jumps during the growth eastward of the city. The first mayor, Dr. Samuel B. Pryor, was inducted into office on April 5, 1856, and from this time until 1872 the council met in several rented quarters. In April, 1872, a committee was appointed to arrange for a permanent city hall. Shortly afterward an agreement was reached with a man named Caplin, under which he and his associates contracted to erect a two-story frame structure, 60x30 feet, at the southwest corner of Main and Akard Streets. The second floor of this building was to be used as a city hall in return for a franchise to Caplin permitting him to operate a public market on the first floor. At the end of 12 years the title of the property was to revert to the city of Dallas.

The agreement was carried out, and the second floor quarters were occupied by Mayor Ben Long and his council in 1873. A storm of protest arose over the granting of the market franchise to Caplin to the exclusion of would-be competitors, and public opinion forced the city to buy the property before the end of a year.

This first city hall was used until 1881, when the municipality's offices were moved downtown to the corner of Commerce and Lamar Streets. A bronze tablet on the Lamar Street side of *The Dallas Morning News* building records this fact. The second city hall was a two-story brick building, and contained a fire station on the first floor. On June 29, 1889, the city government's quarters were moved again,

357

this time into a new and much more pretentious turreted building three stories in height on the northwest corner of Commerce and Akard Streets.

This third city hall, which cost $80,000, served until 1910. In that year, pending the completion of the present building, city officials moved into temporary quarters in an old residence on the north side of Commerce Street between St. Paul and Harwood Streets. The present building was completed in 1914 at a cost of $700,000.

The old Green residence was acquired as an annex in 1925 for $85,000. The Main Street unit of the annex had previously become the property of the city.

21. The DALLAS PUBLIC LIBRARY *(open for lending 9–8:30 workdays; for reading and study 9–9 workdays, 2–6 Sunday)*, southwest corner Commerce and Harwood Streets, is a two-story-and-basement structure in the classical style, dating from 1901, and designed by R. Sanguinet and Carl G. Staats, architects. The main body of the building is of Roman brick with stone trim, and a broad flight of stone steps leads to the main Commerce Street entrance, which is in a portico shadowed by Ionic columns.

In this building and in five branch libraries is housed the city's "people's university," having 148,635 volumes, and with more than 97,000 registrants who during 1937–38 borrowed 804,693 books. Courses in various fields are suggested by the Readers' Advisory Service, which the library maintains. In addition to its bound volumes the library carries 500 general and technical periodicals, has 4,200 unbound pamphlets, subscribes to many current newspapers, and maintains a loan collection of 27,000 mounted prints.

Nonresidents of the city are permitted free use of the library's reference facilities, and can borrow books or other material by depositing a returnable sum in cash equal to its value. Books can be borrowed for three-, seven-, or fourteen-day periods, depending on the demand. During 1939–40 the institution's total estimated budget was $75,760. In its special collections the library has concentrated principally on Dallas material; it has the county censuses of 1850, 1860, and 1870 as well as Dallas directories from 1873 to date. There is also, for the use of the blind, the Martha M. Matthews collection in Braille.

The loan desks, offices of the head librarian and her assistants, and the open stackrooms containing both fiction and nonfiction are on the first floor, where also are offices of the Readers' Advisory Service *(open 2–5 daily)*. The reading room is in the basement. In the main corridor, in the center of the building, is a fountain resting on three elaborately scrolled legs. This fountain, in memory of Jules Schneider, was made in Italy of local white marble by an Italian sculptor, and presented to the library by Mrs. Schneider in 1906.

The reference department, containing over 10,500 general and special works, and the children's department with almost an equal number of books occupy the second floor of the library. At the head of a double stairway leading from the first floor there is a large central hall illuminated by a skylight and containing two interesting though very dissimilar pieces of art. The first of these is an exceptionally fine copy of Rembrandt's *The Night Watch*, painted by the Dutch portrait painter J. Van Dix Linde. The other is a rare Navajo ceremonial sand painting designed for curing the sick, and preserved in a glass case in the middle of the hall directly under the skylight. It was presented to the library by Sanger Brothers.

A few of the more literate members of the community struggled courageously to maintain subscription libraries in Dallas during pioneer days. The old *Dallas Her-*

ald appealed for contributions of books or money to the newly established town library in 1857, and in the seventies there began to be organized efforts to establish a city library. In February, 1872, the *Herald* records that the Young Men's Literary Society of Dallas had changed its name to the Dallas Library Association and was planning a musical and dramatic entertainment in order to raise library funds. A year later this rental library, on the second floor of a three-story brick house, had nearly a thousand books, between 200 and 300 geological specimens, and about 75 daily and weekly newspapers. Allowed to lapse for a while, it was reopened in March, 1875, but was always poorly supported.

In the eighties agitation for a public library and sporadic attempts to establish such an institution began. Public funds were not yet available for maintenance. In 1884 the Dallas Public Library Association, headed by Colonel John C. McCoy, rented a room above Charles H. Edwards' music store on the north side of Main Street between Poydras and Murphy Streets and made it into a public reading room.

In June, 1885, the Public Library Association gave an amateur musicale at the opera house to raise money for enlarging its library, and shortly afterward moved its quarters to the south side of Main Street between Murphy and Field Streets. When the new city hall was erected at the northwest corner of Commerce and Akard Streets, space was reserved in the building for a public library and reading room. At this time the library had 1,647 books exclusive of United States Government publications and public records.

The year 1888 produced a Negro library association. Details of its history are not available, but the Dallas *Daily Times Herald* remarked editorially on January 31: "Will some city in the South show up a colored library association? Dallas has one, and it gives teas and luncheons just like the white folks."

The movement that resulted in the present library originated in the spring of 1899, when the City Federation of Women's Clubs, of which Mrs. Henry Exall was president, called a mass meeting on March 1 at the Oriental Hotel. A new library association was formed, of which Mrs. Henry Exall was elected president; Mrs. J. C. Muse, first vice president; Mrs. Jules E. Schneider, second vice president; C. L. Wakefield, third vice president; and Mrs. George K. Meyer, secretary-treasurer. The new association immediately, with the cooperation of local newspapers, launched a subscription drive to which all classes of Dallas citizens responded generously. When $11,000 had been raised the association applied to Andrew Carnegie for help. On September 18, 1899, Mrs. Exall received word that Carnegie would donate $50,000 on condition that the city furnish a site and appropriate at least $4,000 a year for maintenance. Changes in the city charter were necessary before this offer could be accepted, but legislative action at a special session of the state lawmakers in 1899 enabled the citizens of Dallas to accept Carnegie's gift. A site for the building was provided at the southwest corner of Commerce and Harwood Streets, and construction was begun in October, 1900. The library was ready for occupancy on October 30, 1901, and Miss Rosa Leeper was elected librarian.

The Dallas Public Library began operation with only 10,000 books. With meager funds, it had to depend largely for some time on private contributions. But it at once became an important cultural center with varied uses. The present reference room of the library was once an auditorium seating 500 people, and was known as Carnegie Hall. The Dallas Art Association for many years used a part of the second floor for its collection of paintings. Under contract with the city government the library association continues to nominate trustees and to retain its directors, the association and city working closely together to foster the institution's growth.

The Oak Cliff Branch Library was opened in 1914. Four other such libraries date from an expansion program adopted in 1929, and include the Oak Lawn Branch, serving North Dallas; the Alex Sanger Branch in South Dallas; the East Dallas Branch; and the Paul Laurence Dunbar Branch for the Negro population.

22. The SCOTTISH RITE TEMPLE *(open by arrangement)*, South Harwood Street between Young and Canton Streets, is one of the Southwest's most imposing lodge buildings. It was designed by Hubbell & Greene, Dallas architects, and the cost of the building, exclusive of furnishings, was $300,000. The Dallas structure was completed in 1913, almost concurrently with the House of the Temple, the national headquarters of the Scottish Rite Masonic bodies in Washington.

With a frontage of 220 feet the temple occupies an entire block and is set in a wide sweep of landscaped lawn. In the northwest corner of the grounds near the intersection of Harwood and Young Streets is a bronze statue of Samuel Poyntz Cochran of Dallas. He was Lieutenant Grand Commander of the Supreme Council of the Southern Jurisdiction, under whose direction the building was erected. The statue, unveiled in 1920, was a gift of several hundred candidates who had received their degrees at the hands of officers of the Dallas Scottish Rite, and in 1940 was the only one to be raised in the city to a man during his lifetime. Cochran died in 1936.

The building, two stories and a half in height, is of tan brick with stone trim, and is approached by broad flights of stone steps with a symbolic arrangement of landings. At the head of the steps, within a portico supported by six lofty Corinthian columns and ornamented with the doubleheaded eagle of the order in stone, are three arched doorways with massive double doors blazoned with bronze emblems. Above the doorways is an inset balcony with a stone balustrade opening on the second floor. The whole is elaborately lighted by branched lamp posts of bronze on each side of the steps. Bronze bracket lamps flank each of the three double doors and swinging lights are suspended by chains from the roof of the balcony. There are two smaller entrances at each end of the building similar to the central one, the entrance at the south, or Canton Street, side leading to the secretary's office. The interior of the building is notable for the number of period styles represented in furnishings and decoration.

The main entrance opens on the first floor corridor, called Statuary Hall. It contains statues and portraits of prominent Texas Masons, is floored with tile, and has wainscoting, pilasters, and pilaster caps of veined Italian marble. The general design is Doric. The banquet hall, social and billiard room, office of the secretary and library, and drawing room are on the first floor.

A banquet hall, scene of many large social gatherings, extends almost across the entire east side of the building and has space for 1,500 diners. It is finished in white enamel in the style of Louis XIV, with dado work extending three feet above the floor level. Above this the walls are plastered in panels with highlights in colors, and other elaborate decorations.

The library at the southwest corner of the building is finished in Gothic style, with nine-foot paneled wainscoting of stained oak except where it is broken by the library shelves rising to an equal height. The social and billiard room is immediately behind it to the southeast, and is finished in paneled oak, seven feet high, in the Dutch manner. This room can be made part of the banquet hall when desired. The combination parlor and drawing room, at the northwest corner of the first floor, is done in Italian Renaissance design with three-foot paneled wainscoting in white enamel. It has beautiful tapestries.

Degree work is conducted in several rooms on the second floor, each opening off a main corridor similar to that of the first floor except that it is Ionic instead of Doric in design. The big degree room, sometimes used as a public auditorium, has an Egyptian theme and is distinguished by its exceptionally fine pipe organ and ingenious sound effects.

The organ, first heard at the dedication reunion in April, 1913, was at the time of its installation conceded to be the finest instrument in the country, unsurpassed in tonal range and number of stops even by the great organ in the Mormon Tabernacle at Salt Lake City. It was made by the Boston firm of Hook & Hastings. Clarence Eddy of Chicago, leading American organist of the time, wrote concerning it: "With 151 registers it is easily the largest organ in America. Eight thousand speaking pipes means that your organ has about 1,000 more pipes than the famous organ at the Chicago Auditorium, which cost about $50,000." The organ is electric, pneumatic, and automatic, and cost between $25,000 and $30,000. It is divided in half by the proscenium arch, with the pipes arranged over doorways leading to the stage wings. Its equipment includes chimes, echo organ, trumpets, cymbals, kettle drums, and other orchestration, and it can be operated from either of two consoles, one played by hand in the organ room, the other played either by hand or cut music from the right of the stage.

Another unusual feature of the degree room consists in soundproof shutters separating it from the choir loft. These shutters are operated by a director on the first floor in telephone communication with the choir, and make it possible to control the volume of sound so as to give the effect of advancing or receding voices.

The Dallas Scottish Rite bodies, whose total membership is between 5,000 and 6,000, began with the organization of the Dallas Lodge of Perfection in 1898. It and the Lone Star Chamber of the Knights of the Rose Croix, chartered in 1901, met in an old hall on Commerce Street near Lamar Street. These two bodies formed the Dallas Scottish Rite Cathedral Association in 1903 and elected Sam P. Cochran president. A lot was first acquired at the corner of South Harwood and Wood Streets where the First Presbyterian Church now stands. The present site of the building was acquired for $25,000 on June 8, 1905.

Ground was broken for the present building at the fifth annual reunion of the Scottish Rite bodies in Dallas April 19, 1906, and the cornerstone laid with appropriate ceremonies at the seventh reunion on March 21, 1907. The building was not used until the spring of 1909, the Dallas Scottish Rite bodies continuing to hold their semiannual reunions in Turner Hall, across the street from the temple under construction. During this period, the successive stages in the temple's completion were memorialized by special designations bestowed on the classes of candidates to receive degrees during these years. Even though partially occupied in 1909, the temple was not finally completed and dedicated until April 21, 1913.

23. The YOUNG WOMEN'S CHRISTIAN ASSOCIATION BUILDING *(open 8 A.M.-10 P.M.)*, 1709 Jackson Street, between Ervay and Prather Streets, is a five-story brick structure erected in 1921–22 at a cost of $535,000 and designed by C. D. Hill & Co., Dallas architects.

The comprehensive recreational and character-building program of the Young

Women's Christian Association in modern Dallas includes not only provision of supervised and inexpensive living accommodations, but special business and industrial classes; clubs for girls; a riding club; swimming; health education; social activities; classes in speech, marital problems, and the home; handicrafts; dramatics; contract bridge; personality development; social usage; and trend of the times.

The YWCA maintains a year-round camp in Somervell County, and conducts work among Negro girls through its Maria Morgan Branch, 2503 North Washington Avenue. The Association contacts more than 34,000 individuals annually, and has a membership of more than 3,000. Varied activities are reflected in the well-equipped downtown headquarters.

On the first floor of the building are a foyer, the main dining room, reading rooms, a gymnasium, information bureau, and an office for directors of group work activities. An auditorium, corrective gym, rest rooms, and personal service office occupy the second floor. The third floor is devoted to a large reception and recreation room; club rooms and service kitchen designed for luncheons, parties, and dinners; classrooms; and administrative and business offices. The fourth floor is occupied by classrooms, offices, recreation rooms, and library of the downtown branch of Southern Methodist University. The main kitchen, the swimming pool, and health education office with adjoining lockers, showers, and lounge are in the basement. There are no residential quarters in the building; these are in Proctor Hall, 1206 North Haskell Avenue.

The Young Women's Christian Association in Dallas began in 1908, when following a meeting called by Mrs. J. W. Everman, a charter was obtained and quarters secured on the second and third floors of the old *Farm and Ranch*, or Easterwood Building, just west of the Adolphus Hotel Annex on the north side of Commerce Street near Field Street.

A lunchroom for businesswomen was opened, library and restrooms provided, and entertainments, classes, and vesper services held. A short time later organized athletic work was made available. In these early days Mrs. Everman's staff of directors took turns at performing the menial tasks required to maintain these various services on the slender budget allowed them, even to building fires on Sundays when the porter was off duty.

In 1911 a worker was employed to do travelers aid work among young women arriving alone in the city, and in this year a home for employed women, made possible by the gift of a residence belonging to Mr. and Mrs. J. F. Mulkey, was opened at Floyd Street and Haskell Avenue.

In the spring of 1912 Mrs. J. O. McReynolds sponsored a concert given by the Dallas Orchestra Association to start a YWCA building fund. It netted $5,285. In 1913 the Association was able to move to larger quarters at 1219 Main Street. This location permitted the addition of several new activities, including an employment bureau, a loan fund, clubs for working girls, and schoolgirl activities.

With the entrance of the United States into the World War the influx of young women to replace men who had enlisted created a need for a still more comprehensive program. In July, 1918, headquarters were moved to 1307 1/2 Commerce Street, lunchrooms were established at McKinney Avenue and Lamar Street and at the Sears, Roebuck & Co. plant, and clubs for employed women were organized at various centers in the city.

A drive to raise funds for both a downtown YWCA building and a residential hall was begun in November, 1919, and more than $800,000 pledged in ten days. Work

362

was begun on both buildings almost immediately. Proctor Hall was opened in 1921. The downtown building was occupied in August, 1923.

In 1926 the Milam family of Glen Rose, in Somervell County, presented the Association with a ten-acre tract at the junction of Squaw Creek with the Paluxy and Brazos Rivers. Later, through a gift of Mr. and Mrs. W. C. Proctor, 66 acres were added to the tract. This land was made the site of Camp Tres Rios, one of the best equipped outing camps for girls in North Texas.

The Young Women's Christian Association's work among the Negroes of the city began when the Homemaker's Industrial School was turned over to the Association by a committee headed by Mrs. Maria Morgan. A Negro branch was opened in 1927 at 2503 North Washington Avenue. It was named for Mrs. Morgan.

24. The **FEDERAL RESERVE BANK BUILDING** *(open 8:30–5 workdays)*, southeast corner Akard and Wood Streets, marks Dallas as the capital of the Eleventh Federal Reserve Banking District. Designed by Anderson, Probst, and White, Chicago architects, the building has eight stories and a basement, and is a fine example of the adaptation of the classic Doric style to the requirements of a modern business structure. The exterior facing of the building is of Bedford Indiana limestone, with a gray granite base. Four Doric columns on the Akard Street side support an entablature with sculptured figures extending around the structure between the third and fourth floors. The main entrance doorway of bronze, flanked by two bronze light standards, is in a recess in the loggia or porch formed by this entablature and its supporting columns.

Special requirements of the building make necessary a light court with a skylight that extends through all the stories above the ground floor, about the center of which the tellers' cages are grouped. This is only one of the building's many features specially designed to provide a maximum of safety, convenience, and efficiency.

Currency trucks drive into an enclosure at the rear of the building, and are locked in while being loaded or unloaded, a lift conveying their contents directly to the bank's vaults. There is but one opening to the inner enclosure and one entrance leading to the vault.

When the Federal Reserve Bank opened its doors in Dallas on November 16, 1914, it was in temporary quarters at 1305 Main Street. These were soon outgrown and on August 25, 1915, the bank purchased the present Chamber of Commerce Building at Martin and Commerce Streets at an approximate cost of $185,000. At the time it was thought this building would accommodate the bank's needs for many years, but by 1918 it became necessary to lease additional quarters in four other buildings, causing serious inconvenience in the transaction of business. This condition led to the purchase on November 27, 1918, of the site on which the present building stands. It was completed and occupied early in 1921. Two more stories were added in the spring of 1940.

25. The old **CITY, JEWISH, ODD FELLOWS,** and **MASONIC CEMETERIES** *(open sunrise to sunset)*, South Akard and DeSoto Streets and Masonic Avenue, are a group of four burying grounds dating from the days when Dallas was little more than a frontier village. Though lying forlorn and half-forgotten today in an unpaved, out-of-the-way cul-de-sac surrounded by warehouses, shacks, and dilapidated rooming houses a few blocks south of the downtown district, they contain the remains of some of Dallas' best known early citizens.

The **Jewish Cemetery** *(private)*, southwest corner Masonic Avenue and South

Akard Street, is the smallest and newest of the four graveyards but also the best preserved and the most accessible. It was purchased by the Hebrew Benevolent Association in December of 1871. Since 1912 it has been owned by Congregation Emanu-El, which has enclosed it in an old-fashioned ornamental iron picket fence and pays a watchman to mow the little patch of shady lawn and tend the graves. Here are buried several of Dallas' early business and civic leaders, including Aaron Miller, Charles Kahn, Max Mittenthal, and some of the children of the Sanger family. The gate to this little cemetery is locked, but a good view of the gravestones bearing inscriptions in both English and Hebrew can be obtained through the fence.

The **Old City Cemetery** *(open sunrise to sunset)*, north of Masonic Avenue some distance back from South Akard Street, was established in the early fifties in an area then a cedar brake on the southern edge of Dallas. Today the graves have been levelled and there are only a few scattered markers, the earliest dating back to 1854. It is recorded that the English actor-manager William H. Crisp, the father of Charles Frederick Crisp, one-time speaker of the House of Representatives, is buried in this cemetery. On the far side of this area, where two wooden posts mark the dividing line between it and the Odd Fellows and Masonic Cemeteries, stands a small white cottage with a flagpole in front of it, and around it some humble attempts at beautification in the form of flower beds. This is the residence of an elderly watchman in the employ of the city. In return for the use of the cottage he gives the four old graveyards the scant care they receive. He has occupied his present post for 18 years, and furnishes information to visitors.

The **Masonic and Odd Fellows Cemeteries** *(open sunrise to sunset)*, overlooking the Santa Fe freight yards beyond DeSoto Street, contain by far the largest number of markers, including pretentious family shafts and ornate headstones in the taste of the last century. But except for a few plots that are privately maintained, this cemetery presents a dreary appearance of weed-and-bramble-grown desolation amid which many of the smaller stones are hardly visible. Here are buried Dr. J. W. Crowdus, once mayor of Dallas; Thomas F. Crutchfield, postmaster and proprietor of the pioneer Crutchfield House; John J. Good, district court judge and mayor of Dallas; W. C. C. Akard, for whom Akard Street was named; T. L. Marsalis, who developed Oak Cliff; Jefferson Peak, early merchant and farmer; James K. P. Record, prominent landowner; J. W. Latimer, publisher of the old *Herald*, Dallas' first newspaper; and many others who made local history.

These two adjoining burial tracts, at first covering about three acres, were donated in 1857 by Judge J. M. Patterson, his partner J. W. Smith, William L. Murphy, and W. P. Martin to Tannehill Lodge No. 52 of Masons and Dallas Lodge No. 44, Independent Order of Odd Fellows for their joint use, the Masonic lodge receiving the north tract and the Odd Fellows the south tract.

On February 21, 1857, the Dallas Lodge appointed "Brothers Good, Nicholson, and Jones as a committee to secure a deed to the cemetery." On January 1, 1859, Tannehill Lodge adopted a resolution requiring that a charge of five dollars be made for cemetery lots, except to the donors of the land. The burial of W. P. Martin was the first in the cemetery from Tannehill Lodge; it occurred on January 13, 1858. The second one was that of William H. Keen, on November 4, 1858. There was at least one burial earlier than either of these—as indicated by a headstone in the Masonic part of the cemetery to a child named Harriet S. Masten, who died in 1857.

Since the beginning of the twentieth century controversy has developed over titles to the land occupied by the Masonic and Odd Fellows Cemeteries. This has caused much of their present neglect. In 1907 excavations for the railroad along the western boundary of the south side of the burial grounds removed many of the bones. An option was also taken on the site for the construction of a large warehouse in 1922. The proposal aroused so many protests that it was abandoned, and the twin cemeteries were left to slow decay amid the growing city around them.

26. SULLIVAN PARK *(admission free)*, between Gano, South Ervay, and Pocahontas Streets and Park Avenue, covers 19 acres in South Dallas, and was long known as City Park. Though surrounded by a frowzy big-city no man's land where the downtown business section is gradually encroaching on a once fashionable neighborhood of sprawling old residences, the park is distinguished by a quiet charm compounded of the mellowness of age and its character as a poor people's outdoor community meeting place. It is the oldest municipal park in Dallas, acquired in 1876, when J. J. Eakins gave the city ten acres of land. This gift was enlarged by purchases in 1881 and 1885. The name of the area was changed to Sullivan Park in 1936 in honor of Dan L. Sullivan, first local water commissioner.

In the early 1900s, scattered along the banks of the little stream called Mill Creek that flows sedately through the park between sunken walls of masonry, were the cages of the city's first zoo. Still earlier, in the seventies, Browder Springs in the park was Dallas' only public water supply. Today Sullivan Park is used chiefly as a play area and breathing space for the poorer residents of South Dallas. It has four tennis courts which occupy an area where the city's herd of deer once roamed, a swimming and wading pool for children, modern playground equipment, and a rock shelter house near the northeast corner. Scattered through the park are rock tables and benches where workingmen during the noon hour, and the unemployed at all hours of the day, gather to eat meager lunches, play dominoes, and discuss politics, economics, and plain hard luck.

Sullivan Park has a certain local reputation as a sort of Union Square. Some itinerant preacher can generally be heard holding forth on pleasant Sunday afternoons from the bandstand near the center of the park. Since the onset of the depression in the early 1930s and the beginning of local unemployment this has been the scene of sporadic working class demonstrations, including a minor riot in the summer of 1937, when a vigilante mob smashed the projection machine and sound truck of a socialist organizer attempting to show a militant labor film, and dragged the operator away to tar and feather him in the Trinity River bottoms.

The Confederate Monument, northeast corner of the park, was erected in 1896 by the United Daughters of the Confederacy, and was the first monument raised in Dallas. It was designed by Frank Teich of Llano, sculptor, who created it in five units. The central shaft is surmounted by the figure of a Confederate soldier, with a bust of General W. L. ("Old Tige") Cabell, twice mayor of Dallas, organizer of the quartermaster's department of the Southern Army, and honorary commander of the United Confederate Veterans. At the base of the shaft the four surrounding units are figures of Jefferson Davis, General Albert Sidney Johnston, Brigadier General Stonewall Jackson, and General Robert E. Lee.

The City Greenhouses *(open daylight hours)*, near the Ervay Street side of the park, are used by the Park Board for storing delicate plants during the winter months. Presided over by Charles Bilger, veteran Alsatian city gardener, these greenhouses are on the site of the reservoir and pumping plant of Dallas' first waterworks. A well house nearby covers the original Browder Springs.

Tower Petroleum Building

Santa Fe Building (first three units)

Magnolia Petroleum Building

27. The PROCTER & GAMBLE COMPANY PLANT *(open 9–5 workdays, guides available on application)*, 1226 Loomis Street at Parnell Street, between Metropolitan and Romine Streets, is a branch of the parent company in Cincinnati, opened in Dallas in 1920 for the utilization of Texas cottonseed oil in the manufacture of edible fats. Among the nationally advertised and distributed food products manufactured in this plant, claimed to be the largest of its kind in the world, are Crisco, Flakewhite, Fluffo, Puritan Oil, and Marigold Oil; the plant also serves as a warehouse and distributing point for other of the company's products. Plans were announced early in 1940 for the building of a soap factory to cost $1,000,000 to be built on land adjoining the present plant.

Tours through the plant, conducted by guides, are organized each year for college students and public school pupils. For the general public the manufacture of Crisco, explained in nontechnical terms, is usually emphasized. Visitors are first conducted to an assembly room where the various processes involved in the transformation of crude cottonseed oil into cooking and salad oils, shortening, frying fat, and margarine are graphically explained with the aid of a chart. They are then shown the departments where the crude vegetable oil is refined by means of sodium hydroxide, bleached with fuller's earth (another product obtained in Texas), and deodorized by agitating the oil, increasing temperature, and decreasing pressure. These are the only processes involved in the manufacture of the cooking and salad oils, except for "winterizing" or chilling the latter in refrigerator rooms. But the shortenings, frying fats, and margarines are in addition hardened by hydrogenization and put through a special creaming process. Most of the products are automatically packed, sealed, and labeled by special machinery, and there is an elaborate testing process for both the products and their containers.

The Dallas factory maintains a chemical laboratory for analysis of products at each stage of their manufacture and a physical laboratory for testing under all conditions to which they are likely to be subjected, including mixing with various ingredients and actually baking them into bread, cakes, and pastry. Some minor experimentation with new processes is also carried on, but most of this is conducted in Cincinnati, where the company maintains a special research staff.

The Dallas company has its own power and hydrogen plants and extensive oil storage tanks, and owns about 100 acres along the edge of the Trinity River bottoms, although only about 25 acres are now in use. Adjacent to the factory buildings are tennis and croquet courts, horseshoe pitching grounds, and other recreational facilities for employees. A cafeteria, dispensary with trained nurse, and restrooms are also maintained at the factory. The Procter & Gamble Company has pioneered in the field of improved employer-employee relations, and in force at the Dallas plant, as at their other branches, are their distinctive time-bonus, profit sharing, and sickness and death compensation plans. Their special pension plan still applies to old employees, but has been discontinued for others since the passage of the National Social Security Act.

28. FAIR PARK *(admission free, except during State Fair, 50¢)*, Parry, Second, and Pennsylvania Avenues and Texas & Pacific Railroad, surpasses other Dallas parks in the diversity of its appeal. Covering 173 acres of landscaped grounds and with 103 buildings, amusement devices, and other structures within its boundaries, it is not only a large exposition site offering a variety of exotically colorful modern architecture, but is a year-round cultural and recreational center.

Though it has been the scene of local fairs since 1876 and state fairs since 1886, and has been a city park since 1904, Fair Park, as it exists today, is largely a creation of the Texas Centennial Exposition of 1936 *(see STATE FAIR OF TEXAS: EMPIRE ON PARADE)*. This exposition found Fair Park a city of wood and left it a city of stone—a city of massive, glittering white classic and modernistic buildings, sweeping drives, and broad squares commemorating the names of the men who helped build the State Fair; of luxuriant semitropical gardens; splashing multiple fountains; artificial lakes and lagoons, heroic statues, and vividly stylized, ultramodern murals covering whole sides of buildings—all proclaiming the theme of Texas' romantic history and abundant natural resources. The main entrance, on Parry Avenue opposite the end of Exposition Avenue, is through a double gateway flanked by squat, massive concrete pylons bearing the dates 1836–1936, and dominated in the center by a tall white shaft ornamented with a frieze of historical figures and the Lone Star of Texas in gold.

Fair Park, with the exception of the land on which the Hall of State stands, is owned by the city of Dallas. The greater part of the grounds is leased to the Texas State Fair Association, which subleases some of the buildings to concessionaires and other organizations. Among the concessions operated all year are various devices along the Midway; a miniature golf course; a rollerskating rink; the English Village, an indoor and outdoor cafe featuring old-time melodramas; and the Globe Theater, where one of the city's amateur drama groups presented performances about once a month during the 1938–39 season.

In addition to the Municipal Swimming Pool (1925) and the Municipal Broadcasting Station WRR, located in the Municipal Radio Building, the city of Dallas controls and operates the Hall of State, Museum of Fine Arts, Museum of Natural History, Aquarium, Amphitheater and Band Shell, Museum of Natural Resources, and the Horticultural Museum. This group of permanent buildings was constructed for the Texas Centennial Exposition in 1936; each is in a harmonizing neoclassic design. With the exception of the Hall of State, they are in or adjacent to a 26-acre tract called the Civic Center, laid out around a beautiful, winding, landscaped lagoon with terraced banks, artificial islands, and rustic bridges. This area lies between Second Avenue and Knepfly and Olmstead Drives and extends from the Grand Avenue entrance to the Forest Avenue entrance.

With the exception of the municipally owned museums and the permanent concessions, most of the buildings in Fair Park are used only for exhibition purposes during fairs, or for special occasions.

The **Esplanade of State**, between Holland Court and the State Court of Honor, suggests in its proportions and arrangement the approach to some ancient Egyptian or Babylonian temple. Down its center runs a sunken lagoon, with a terraced fountain at the eastern end adorned with gilded allegorical figures. On each side tower white statues of cast stone 31 feet high emblematic of the six sovereign powers—Spain, France, Mexico, the Republic of Texas, the Confederacy, and the United States—that have ruled over what is now Texas. Three of these were executed by Lawrence Tenny Stevens of New York and the remaining three by the naturalized French sculptor Raoul Josset. On one side the Esplanade is flanked by the General Exhibits and Hall of Gold Building, and on the other by the Automobile, Machinery, and Foods Building, both offering a continuous succession of brilliant and arresting murals in the modern manner, broken by inset courts filled with trees, plants, and shrubs native to the four principal geographic regions of Texas.

Fair Park

These buildings are of uniform modernistic architecture with straight, formal lines, sharp angles, and large unbroken planes predominating. The prevailing materials are cream- and rose-colored Texas granite, and the structures are chiefly notable for the murals and cameos that cover a large part of their exterior wall space. These were executed by the Italian mural painter Campo Ciampaglia and the French artist Pierre Bourdelle, whose cameos on the southwest side of the Esplanade represent a new technique which makes their colors practically indestructible.

The **Auditorium** *(open during productions)*, Gaston Court, southwest corner of the fairgrounds at the Parry Street and First Avenue entrance, is in a modified Spanish mission style, built of light, buff-colored tapestry brick. It was constructed in 1925 at a cost of $575,000, including landscaping, and was designed by Lang & Witchell, architects of Dallas. The main facade is dominated by twin towers with corner buttresses topped by a dome. Between the buttresses is a loggia broken by five arched openings, with one-story wings ornamented with small pylons projecting on each side. The auditorium, largest in Dallas and one of the largest in the Southwest, is really a building within a building, and has a seating capacity of 4,309.

The building is constructed so that four hidden columns carry the entire weight of the roof, and the balconies are supported on the cantilever principle. Thus there are no pillars to obstruct the view of the stage, which has an expanse of 70 feet, with dressing rooms in an annex. The auditorium is fan-shaped. Acoustical improvements make it ideal for operas, concerts, musical comedies, and conventions.

The Sydney Smith Memorial Fountain, in the center of Gaston Court, often called the Gulf Cloud, occupies a circular plot of flowers and grass directly in front of the auditorium. It consists of a bronze group 13 1/2 feet high of four female figures representing "the dewy benediction that the Gulf gives to Texas." It was executed by Miss Clyde Chandler, a young Dallas woman who became the pupil of Lorado Taft, and was erected in October, 1916, in honor of Captain Sydney Smith, who served for 26 years as secretary of the State Fair of Texas.

The Globe Theater *(open during productions)*, Sliney and Trezevant Drives, architecturally is one of the most interesting structures in Fair Park. It is a wooden reconstruction according to scale of the Globe Theater of London's Elizabethan era. It was built for the presentation of Shakespearean drama during the Texas Centennial Exposition, and differs from the English building only in that here the pit was roofed over. The newly formed Civic Theater secured the building in 1938, and had the stage modified for the presentation of modern plays. But the theater, which seats 500, retains a quaint charm with its exposed beams, continuous double galleries decorated with Elizabethan scrollwork, rough wooden benches, and lighting fixtures in the form of wrought iron lanterns.

The Hall of State *(open 9–5 workdays, 2–6 Sunday)*, is in the very heart of the exposition grounds, commanding a magnificent view of the Esplanade of State. The building is in the neoclassic style, built of Cordova cream limestone. It cost $1,300,000. Architects collaborating on its design were Walter Sharp, Ralph Bryan, H. B. Thomson, Arthur Thomas, T. J. Galbraith, and Flint & Broad of Dallas, and Adams & Adams of San Antonio. The main facade has a central dominating concave entrance feature with vertical fluted shafts flanked on each side by vertical pylons. Entrance doors are of bronze and plate glass, with the statue of a Tejas brave in gilded bronze above them. Two wings extend on each side from the main entrance, with full-length loggias of plain stone shafts supporting an entablature on which are inscribed the names of early-day Texas heroes.

The main entrance opens upon the Hall of Heroes, where six lifesize bronze portrait statues of Texas revolutionary heroes executed by Pompeo Coppini stand on marble pedestals. The Hall of Heroes opens upon the Great Hall of Texas, 66x90 feet, with a beamed and skylighted ceiling rising 45 feet. The floor is made of blocks of red antique marble interspersed with squares depicting the fauna and flora of Texas. Walls are paneled in black marble to a height of eight feet. Above this paneling they are decorated with immense murals by the New York artist Eugene Savage, assisted by Reveau Bassett, James Buchanan Winn, Jr., William Smith, and Lennie Lyons. These murals are among the largest in existence, and tell of the history and resources of Texas. A bronze star disc 24 feet in diameter is at the far end of the Hall. Regional rooms decorated with murals representative of the sections, and containing cases and cabinets for museum display purposes, make up the two front wings. The basement, reached by a flight of marble stairs leading from the Hall of Heroes, contains a lecture room equipped with 408 seats.

Since 1938 the Hall of State has been used by the Dallas Historical Society, organized in 1922, which maintains in the building a museum of statewide interest with Herbert Gambrell as director (1940). It contains General Sam Houston's report on the Battle of San Jacinto, a large and varied assortment of aboriginal artifacts, mostly from the region around Dallas, and the valuable Howard Collection of Texana and Mexicana, including portraits, autographs, letters, documents, and illuminated manuscripts, presented to the museum by Dr. William E. Howard of Dallas in 1938.

The **Bust of Prospero Bernardi**, southeast corner of the State Court of Honor, was erected in honor of an Italian pioneer who participated in Texas' struggle for independence. Executed by Pompeo Coppini, sculptor, of San Antonio, it is five feet in height and stands on an 18-foot base of Texas granite. It was dedicated on October 12, 1936, during the Texas Centennial Exposition, by the then Governor James V. Allred.

The **Education Building (open during State Fair)**, south of Hall of State, facing Herold Plaza, was built as the Federal Building for the Centennial Exposition, and today is used as headquarters by the State Fair Association. It is a masonry structure in classic style designed by George L. Dahl of Dallas, architect, and costing $325,000. Its 175-foot vertical shaft is crowned by a spread eagle inlaid with gold. The exterior is ornamented with the seal of the United States and a frieze in bas relief depicting the basic institutions of the nation and episodes in the history of Texas. Responsibility for its complete decoration was entrusted to Julian Ellsworth Garnsey, mural painter of New York and California. Two cameos on the walls above the entrance doors represent War and Peace, with the figures of a man and woman mutually supporting each other in each cameo.

The central rotunda has a gigantic seal of the United States in full colors; two quotations, one from the Declaration of Independence and the other from the naugural address of Mirabeau B. Lamar, second president of Texas; and four murals by Garnsey assisted by Jerry Bywaters, Thomas M. Stell of Dallas, and G. Henry Richer of Dallas depicting the chief characteristics of the four quarters of the United States—North, East, South, and West. Three figures representing the three branches of the Federal government—legislative, judicial, and executive—decorate the rear lobby of the building.

The **Cotton Bowl Stadium**, Tennison, Cochran, Coke, and Jackson Circles, erected in 1930 at a cost of $360,000, occupies a large area behind Otto Herold Plaza. It is a concrete bowl with sloping sodded walls on the outside, three entrances, ramps and approaches of concrete, and seats and flooring of Washington fir. The seating capacity is 46,400. Its name was changed from Fair Park Stadium to the Cotton Bowl in 1936 in recognition of the highly advertised intersectional college football game played here each New Year's Day.

The **Texas Woofus**, J. S. Armstrong Parkway, is an imaginative symbol of the Agricultural, Livestock, and Poultry buildings grouped around it in the area north of the Cotton Bowl Stadium. It is a cast stone and chromium figure nine feet high on an 18-foot base, executed by Lawrence Tenny Stevens, representing a composite beast composed of parts of six different domestic animals and fowls.

The **Race Track** *(not in use)*, along Pennsylvania Avenue from Duke Circle to the Texas & Pacific Railroad tracks, occupies the northeastern corner of the park. A grandstand seating 1,200 is at the southern end and a group of barns at the northern end. Since legislative action prohibiting pari-mutuel betting in Texas it has been used chiefly as a parking area.

The **Museum of Natural History** *(open 8–5 workdays; 2–7 p.m. Sunday)*, west end of lagoon, south of Knepfly Drive, is built of Cordova cream limestone and was designed by Mark Lemmon, C. H. Griesenbeck, Frank Kean, and John Dana, Dallas architects. The plan of the building is that of a simple rectangle with a plain facade relieved by fluted pilasters forming panels. The main entrance features three high openings with aluminum-finished windows and doors, with the title of the building excised in stone at the top. The lobby, which is in the central part of the building, has six columns of Italian marble supporting a lofty ceiling. It is appropriately paneled in Texas shellstone containing fossils. A stairway leads to the second floor, which is closed to the public and devoted to the assemblage of specialized paleontological and biological exhibits. The two east halls on the first floor are devoted to Texas mammals, present or extinct, and the two west halls to the bird life of Texas.

Exhibits are arranged in illuminated glass cases to form three-dimensional still life pictures with background scenes painted by Reveau Bassett, J. D. Figgins, and Walter Stevens of Dallas. Incidental exhibits include prehistoric bison skulls, a collection of wildflower paintings done by Mrs. Dloise R. Thompson of Houston, a cast of the 12-foot skeleton of *Mosasaurus tylosaurus*, an aquatic lizard which during the cretaceous period frequented the region now known as Texas, and synthetic gems and specimens of the state's minerals—this latter collection presented to the museum by Arthur A. Everts. W. M. Miller in 1940 was director of the institution.

The **Museum of Fine Arts** *(open 8–5 workdays; 2–7 p.m. Sunday)*, between the lagoon and Second Avenue, is built of Cordova cream limestone, cost $500,000, and was designed by DeWitt & Washburn, Herbert M. Greene, La Roche and Dahl, and Henry Coke Knight of Dallas, architects. It has for its main facade a central pavilion projecting in front of two wings of solid, plain wall surfaces. The main entrance has three openings with bronze doors and windows set just back of a loggia of three similar openings. Bronze lanterns rest on buttresses on each side of the entrance steps. The plan of the building is a simple rectangle, with one wing projecting at the left side. A central court contains a fountain which has a figure created by Harriet Frishmuth. There are nine exhibition galleries; an auditorium where illustrated lectures, concerts, and other programs of cultural value are given; lounges; offices; and a kitchen for the preparation of refreshments served at teas and receptions. The left wing is occupied by the Dallas Art Institute, where art classes are held. The Dallas Art Association is custodian of the building, and in 1940 Foster Howard was the director.

The museum contains, in addition to its general exhibits, a print collection mainly of old masters donated by the Junior League. The Munger Collection belongs to the museum and includes Van Dyck's "Countess of Oxford"; the Karl Hoblitzelle loan collection is of old masters; the Joel T. and Catharine Howard loan collection is of nineteenth-century paintings; and there are several miscellaneous exhibits of art objects and local sculpture. *(For a description of individual paintings in the museum see PAINTING AND SCULPTURE: ESTHETIC ASSETS.)*

The **Aquarium** *(open 8–5 workdays; 2–7 p.m. Sunday)*, Olmstead and Mangold Drives, is a simple rectangular building faced with cream-colored tapestry brick. It was designed by H. B. Thomson and Lester Flint of Dallas, architects. The main facade is dominated by an entrance feature projecting in front of the main wall. In the center of the entrance is a loggia built on a segmental curve and flanked on each side by a square stone pylon. The otherwise plain walls on each side of the entrance are broken by stone panels featuring a sea horse design. The building contains 44 specimen tanks constructed to give an authentic underwater picture of fishes and other water creatures. Among the exhibits are trout, tropical fishes, coral, nacre, sea anemone, abalone shells, turtles, eels, salamanders, an octopus in alcohol, the Arthur A. Everts collection of pearl culture, and numerous fresh and salt water fishes from Texas waters.

The **Museum of Natural Resources** *(open 1–5 workdays; 2–5 P.M. Sunday)*, Yopp Drive and Ranger Circle, is an L-shaped building faced with ashlar cream Cordova stone and designed by Anton Korn and J. A. Pitzinger of Dallas, architects. Its severe neoclassic lines are modified by Georgian and modernized colonial influences expressed in a semicircular porch supported by four columns and two pilasters at the main entrance, and with cut stone architraves around the openings. There is a paved patio at the rear enclosed by low walls, and a graceful projecting chimney rises from one wing. It houses the exhibits (as yet incomplete) of the Texas Institute of Natural Resources, including samples, pictures, charts, studies, and models representative of Texas' major resources and industries.

The **Horticultural Museum** *(not open; used only for storage purposes)*, Mangold Drive between Ranger Circle and Yopp Drive, is surrounded by spacious botanical gardens. It resembles the other buildings of the Civic Center in its design, created by Arthur A. Thomas, architect. It is faced with cream-colored smooth brick and is trimmed with ornamental stone depicting the flowers and plant life of Texas. The facade is broken by a simple bronze door entrance feature, with windows in the center of the pavilions at each end. There is a special heating plant for the protection of fragile and semitropical plants. The cost of the building was $220,000.

The **Amphitheater and Bandshell** *(admission free)*, Olmstead and Mangold Drives and Ranger Circle, is constructed of rough-faced concrete, plastered in the bandshell only. It cost $118,000 and was designed by W. Scott Dunne and Christensen & Christensen of Dallas, architects. The bandshell, 143x53 feet, fully equipped with acoustical devices, has space for 300 musicians; the seats slope to a height of 25 feet, and can accommodate an audience of 5,500. Pylons containing loudspeakers and spotlights encircle the structure at the rear. It is used for summer concerts and local high school graduating exercises, also for daily band concerts during the Fair.

The **Alamo Chapel** *(open only on special occasions)*, extreme southeast corner of fairgrounds, off Ranger Circle, is a full-scale enlargement of a half-scale model of the Alamo, widely known shrine of Texas liberty in San Antonio. The model was presented to the State Fair Association by *The Dallas Morning News*, and was moved to this site and a reproduction built in its present form in 1936. The James B. Bonham Chapter of the Daughters of the Texas Revolution acts as custodian.

The **Texas State Police Building** *(open day and night)*, Ranger Circle, is built of East Texas pine logs, and is interesting as an example of the state's ranch house architecture. A lifesize statue of a Texas Ranger stands in the central corridor or "dogtrot" of the building. It has two rooms, the one on the left being used as the offices of the State Police, and the one on the right by the license division. Both are furnished in rustic style.

The **United States Naval Reserve Building** *(open 9–5)*, off Ranger Circle on Second Avenue, was built to house Civilian Conservation Corps exhibits during the 1936 Centennial. The interior is equipped and arranged to represent the bridge of a naval destroyer.

29. The MURRAY COMPANY PLANT *(open 8–4:30 on application to office)*, Canton, Hickory, and Chestnut Streets and Gulf, Colorado & Santa Fe Railroad, occupies an extensive area and a number of large buildings in the Southeast Dallas industrial district adjacent to the Santa Fe railroad yards.

This company (founded in 1900, when it took over a small gin manufacturing plant in East Dallas), is one of the largest manufacturers of cotton gin machinery in the world. It has a capital stock of $1,814,896 and maintains a plant in Atlanta, Georgia, as well as the one in Dallas, marketing cotton gin machinery in all cotton-producing states in the Union as well as in foreign countries where the crop is grown. The company maintains a staff of consulting and research engineers and utilizes its own patents and developments in the manufacture of its various machines and equipment.

Among the important contributions the Murray Company has made to the improvement of cotton ginning processes have been an all-steel, highspeed, airblast gin; the Murray elevating system, an all-steel, selfcleaning, fireproof condenser; an improved airline cleaner; and the Hancock Cotton Picker. It was also the first company to perfect a machine for cleaning cotton at the gin and the first to build a gin to run at 700 revolutions a minute with a loose roll.

At the Murray Company's plant, which is equipped with the most modern machinery, the visitor may see the casting and stamping out of the individual parts as well as the assembling of the complete gins. The manufacturing process is highly mechanized and includes many labor-saving devices, which make it possible to build all-steel gins that sell at practically the same price as wooden gins. Huge power machines and stamping dies shape a piece of metal with the greatest speed and precision, and modern electric welders weld the parts together with the ease of a simple household task.

30. The FORD MOTOR COMPANY ASSEMBLY PLANT *(open Monday through Thursday, 9 A.M., 10 A.M., 12 N., 2 P.M., and 3 P.M.)*, 5200 East Grand Avenue, assembles automobiles from parts furnished by the company's Detroit factory. The Ford Motor Company first established an assembly plant in Dallas in an old red brick building at the corner of Canton and Henry Streets which soon was outgrown. The present plant with its extensive landscaped grounds and elaborate provisions for showrooms and outdoor displays illuminated with batteries of floodlights was opened in 1925. Plans were announced early in 1940 for a $300,000 addition.

The plant serves Ford dealers over a wide trade area linked by the many arterial highways radiating from Dallas. When running at capacity it employs 2,500 men and turns out 400 automobiles a day. Visitors are shown through the factory in groups at the times designated, and can see the various phases of the Ford assembling system.

31. WHITE ROCK LAKE PARK *(admission free)*, in the extreme northeastern part of the city between the Northwest Highway and US 67 (the Garland Road), with an area of 2,314 acres, 1,350 of which are covered by the waters of White Rock Lake, is one of the largest municipal parks in Texas.

White Rock Lake *(fishing licenses 25¢, obtainable from Dallas Park Board)*, fed by White Rock Creek, serves the city of Dallas as a reserve water storage basin. It has a capacity of 5,700,000,000 gallons and is one of the major pleasure resorts of North and Central Texas. offering picnicking, horseback riding, fishing, boating, bathing and aquatic sports, including annual regattas for sailboats and inboard and outboard motor craft. The lake is stocked annually with bass, crappie, bream, channel cat, and other edible fishes. It is also the natural winter habitat of large numbers of ducks, geese, coots, cranes, and other waterfowl, and was formerly dotted with duck blinds used by hunters during the autumn season. Shooting is prohibited within the boundaries of the park. Five police motorboats patrol the lake for safety and the enforcement of park regulations.

White Rock Park was acquired by the city in 1909 at a cost of $176,420, and was an outgrowth of Dallas' desperate search for an adequate water supply. The idea of an artificial lake in this area was at first ridiculed by many as chimerical, but the project, spurred by the acute water famines of 1910 and 1911, was nevertheless soon realized. Tne contract for a dam to impound the waters of White Rock Creek was let to the Fred A. Jones Company on March 8, 1910. at a price of $253,070, with the stipulation that it be completed in 350 days.

A pumping station and filtration plant was built near the dam, and the lake was filled in a much shorter time than had been anticipated, doing much to ease the water problem in Dallas. The project was at first under the control of the municipal water department. Comparatively little was done to beautify and improve the area for recreational purposes until after it was taken over by the park board in 1930. A beach and bathhouse, boathouse, and fish hatchery were constructed almost immediately. Since 1936, with the cooperation of the Civilian Conservation Corps, the park board has undertaken an extensive program of building, dredging, and roadmaking. This has included the construction of a rock gateway at the main entrance to the park, the erection of two rock concession houses, beautification of the picnic grounds, the building of retaining walls along the shores, and dredging operations designed to drain the marshy area at the northern end of the lake and to construct from the silt removed an archipelago of small artificial islands.

Extending from the gateway that marks the main entrance to the park on US 67 for about two-thirds the distance around the lake and following the contour of the shoreline runs Lawther Drive, named for former Mayor Joe. E. Lawther in 1923. It was paved in 1931. Along its winding course and in the wooded areas bordering the road are picnic grounds equipped with stone ovens, benches and tables, and numerous private fishing and boating camps, on sites leased by the park board. Several private clubs, including the Dallas Anglers Club, Dallas Boat Club, and Dallas Sailing Club, also have their clubhouses and piers along the lake shores. Concessionaires rent boats for a moderate fee and sell fishing tackle and bait.

On the hillside to the right of the road, about a mile down the east shore from the entrance, can be seen the flagpole and yellow frame buildings of the Civilian Conservation Corps Camp *(open 4-6 daily)*. This camp is maintained by the Park Service Division of the Civilian Conservation Corps and was established in 1935 and is one of the largest and best equipped in North Texas. It serves as a concentration point for enrollees bound for various camps throughout the Eighth Corps Area.

Along the water's edge a short distance north of the Civilian Conservation Corps Camp is the Municipal Bathing Beach *(open daily, May to September, 6–10, admission 25¢ for adults, 15¢ for children)*. The beach, which is a semicircular concrete slab 612x162 feet, and the bathhouse (which contains 908 steel lockers, 268 steel dressing rooms, and 29 showers), were built in 1930 at a total cost of $121,603.

Lawther Drive connects with the Northwest Highway at the northern end of the lake and continues south along the western shore, turning west a little north of the Filtration Plant, Municipal Fish Hatchery, Municipal Boathouse, and County Prison Farm *(each open daylight hours)*, grouped along the southwestern shore of the lake at the northern end of the dam and spillway. This filtration plant is reserved for emergency use, and the prison farm has been abandoned since 1935. The

Municipal Boathouse was constructed in 1930, and has 36 stalls which are rented for $60 a year. The fish hatchery was built by the Dallas Park Board in 1930. In 1934 it was turned over to the State Game, Fish, and Oyster Commission in exchange for the Fair Park Fish Hatchery, then in 1936 was restored to the Dallas Park Board.

Below the dam, on the banks of White Rock Creek in a grove between the spillway and the highroad, is a newsboys' camp maintained since 1930 by the Young Men's Christian Association. Equipment includes an all-concrete shelter house, barbecue pit, and playground apparatus, all of which was donated by the Kiwanis Club.

32. SOUTHERN METHODIST UNIVERSITY *(campus open at all times, buildings during daylight hours)*, Hillcrest Avenue, Mockingbird Lane, Airline Road, and Daniels Avenue, is supported by the Methodist Church, and occupies a 133-acre campus on the edge of the fashionable residential suburb of University Park.

The history of this university—which opened with 706 students in the autumn of 1915, during the disturbed period immediately preceding the entrance of the United States into the World War—has been one of rapid expansion, balanced development, liberally administered education, and close integration with the life of Dallas. Today, with a cosmopolitan student body of more than 3,800, it ranks as one of the leading denominationally supported coeducational institutions of higher learning in the Southwest, and has come to occupy an important place in the intellectual, artistic, and sports life of the city and North Texas. Enriched by numerous benefactions, it has a total endowment, including plant equipment, amounting in 1940 to $6,121,672.

The land on which Southern Methodist University stands was donated by Mr. and Mrs. J. S. Armstrong of Dallas. Twenty-five years ago it was a bare, treeless expanse of prairie on which stood a single building. In 1940 the campus with its 13 substantial main buildings of uniform stone and red brick Georgian architecture suggested a group of dignified English country houses set in the midst of formal gardens conceived in the precise, conventional taste of the eighteenth century. Broad, straight, tree-lined esplanades intersect the campus at right angles; and neat flower beds, clusters of clipped shrubbery, and walks and hedges radiating from ornamental fountains combine to form varied geometrical patterns. The total effect, though in no way suggesting the Southwest, is pleasing with a quiet sense of classical fitness, at once academically traditional and topographically functional.

Virginia Hall *(public rooms open day and night)*, southeast corner Hillcrest Avenue and Roberts Parkway, one of two dormitories in which undergraduate women are required to live unless married, living with relatives, or working in a home, was completed in 1926. The building was made possible by the donation of $158,947 by the people of Dallas and other Texas cities. Named for Mrs. Virginia K. Johnson, who was largely responsible for raising the money, it accommodates 136 students and contains the general dining hall for women.

Snider Hall *(public rooms open day and night)*, adjoining Virginia Hall to the east and connected with it by a colonnade was erected in 1926, and serves as a dormitory and social center for 100 women. It was presented to the university on an annuity basis by Mr. and Mrs. C. W. Snider of Wichita Falls, and cost $162,147.

McFarlin Auditorium *(open 7:30–6, later for programs)*, southwest corner of the Quadrangle, is considered to be one of the finest university auditoriums in America. Costing $440,108—the most expensive building on the campus—it was a

VII. SETTINGS FOR SIGHTSEEING

Education Building, Fair Park

Esplanade of State during State Fair

Hall of State, Fair Park

Museum of Fine Arts, Fair Park

Museum of Natural History, Fair Park

Aquarium, Fair Park

Horticultural Museum, Fair Park

Bandshell and Amphitheater, Fair Park

Globe Theater (reproduction), Fair Park

Arlington Recreated, Robert E. Lee Park

White Rock Lake, Man-made Inland Resort

Along Scenic Turtle Creek Drive

gift of Mr. and Mrs. R. M. McFarlin of San Antonio. It was dedicated on March 24, 1936, in memory of Mr. McFarlin's father and mother. The spacious, modern, and classically proportioned auditorium can accommodate nearly 3,000 people. The building houses the School of Music, for which complete facilities have been provided, including a pipe organ. The editorial offices of the *Southwest Review*, a quarterly literary magazine which since 1924 has been closely identified with the rise of the "indigenous culture" movement in the Southwest, are in the basement. In addition to its use by the Arden Club, Choral and Glee Clubs, and other student organizations, the facilities of McFarlin Auditorium also serve the needs of the Dallas Symphony Orchestra, visiting concert artists, local dancing studios, and other groups not directly associated with the university.

The **Perkins Hall of Administration** *(open 8:30–6)*, northwest corner of the Quadrangle, is one of the newest buildings on the campus. It was financed by Mr. and Mrs. J. J. Perkins of Wichita Falls. The first floor, used for offices and the University Cooperative Store, was opened in 1926; the remaining two stories were added in 1938. This building houses many administrative offices of the university, including those of the president, dean of women, dean of students, business manager, registrar, and publicity director.

The **World War Monument**, Hillcrest Avenue and University Boulevard, is a memorial to 11 SMU men who fell in France during the World War. Presented to the university by the class of 1924, it consists of a square granite shaft with a bronze tablet bearing the names of the student-soldiers.

Kirby Hall *(open 7:30–6)*, University Boulevard, houses the School of Theology. It was erected in 1924 through a gift of $100,000 from Mr. and Mrs. R. Harper Kirby of Austin. The bronze plaque in honor of the donors is left of the main entrance; a quotation from John Wesley embedded in the flagging at the foot of the central staircase seems an apt expression of the spirit of Southern Methodist University. It says: "Let us unite the two so long divided, knowledge and vital piety." Kirby Hall is provided with classrooms, library, chapel, and offices. The library contains some 3,000 volumes, including a fine collection of Wesleyana. Kirby Hall contains the **Lane Museum** *(open by application to the curator)*, left of the main entrance on the first floor. The museum, which is popular with school children for its odd and interesting miscellany of Aztec, Inca, Graeco-Roman, Oriental, and African curios, is named for Alvin Valentine Lane, Ph.D., of Dallas, who contributed a valuable collection of clay tablets and cylinders from Babylon and papyri from Egypt. Among the interesting exhibits are 12 Babylonian tablets earlier than 2000 B.C.; an extremely rare cylinder composed by Nebuchadnezzar, describing the Walls of Babylon and the Tower of Babel; and an Egyptian mummy reputed to be that of a princess of Rameses II, brought to this country by Judge A. W. Terrell, one-time minister to Turkey. Authentic translations of the Babylonian tablets and cylinders, and of the Greek and Egyptian papyri, have been secured by the curator. Soon to be added to the museum are casts of the Rosetta Stone, the Moabite Stone, and Hammurabi's Code, and a collection of pottery illustrating the evolution of that art from earliest times.

Dallas Hall *(open 7:30–9)*, north end of the Quadrangle, is a four-story structure surmounted by a dome, with massive porticos of white Corinthian columns on the south and west sides. This was the first building to be erected on the campus and is the focal point of student life. There is a fine view from the south portico, about which academic tradition clusters. Many of the ceremonies connected with graduation exercises in the spring take place here, as well as the annual Shakespearean or Greek play presented by the Arden Club. The lofty rotunda rising from the second or main floor to the top of the dome does much to give character to the building, and has been commemorated in the name *Rotunda* borne by the student yearbook.

In the basement are the university postal substation, the main library, and the periodical library. These libraries contain some 90,000 volumes, 15,000 pamphlets, current numbers of 550 general and technical periodicals, and bound files of periodicals chosen to serve the practical needs of the student body. Special collections include the historically valuable E. L. Shuttles collection, the Edmund Montgomery collection of scientific and philosophical works, and the recently acquired philological library of Dr. Morgan Calloway of The University of Texas. Departmental units are the Law Library, the Science Library, and the Theological Library.

The main reading room and reference library is in the east wing on the second floor of Dallas Hall and has an alabaster model of the Taj Mahal, brought from India by Mr. and Mrs. J. W. Blanton. The model stands at the far end of the room. Also housed in Dallas Hall are the offices and classrooms of the Liberal Arts College and Law School.

In the west wing of Dallas Hall, on the fourth floor, there is a small workshop theater where one-act plays are given. Here and scattered through the classrooms of the speech department are the exhibits of the **McCord Theater Museum** *(open on application to curator)*, an institution organized in 1933 and named for Miss Mary McCord, professor of speech and founder of the university's dramatic society. This museum is the only one of its kind in the South, and is intended to serve the dual purpose of preserving a historical record of the theater in the Southwest and providing a reference library for students and research workers. It has been enriched by donations of valuable material from Stark Young, L. Stoddard Taylor, and Eli Sanger, and includes a wide variety of photographs, prints, drawings, designs, paintings, programs, masks, puppets, costumes, stage models, scenery, and lighting equipment from famous old theaters, prompt books, scrapbooks, manuscripts, letters and autographs, dramatic slides, "stills," and dramatic books and periodicals. These mementos are representative not only of the theater in the Southwest but of the Continental, Shakespearean, Chinese, and Mexican theaters, the circus, vaudeville, ballet, and opera.

The **Blanton Observatory** *(open by special arrangement)*, east side of the parking space in the rear of Dallas Hall, is a small domed edifice, 16 feet in diameter, revolving on ball bearings, and driven by an electric motor. It is equipped with a telescope having a 16-inch Clark refractor with a graduated circle, and was built in 1934 at a cost of $925, obtained mostly from funds provided by Mr. and Mrs. J. W. Blanton of Dallas.

Hyer Hall of Physics *(open 7:30–6)*, northeast corner of the Quadrangle, was built in September, 1925, at a cost of $140,469, and is named for Dr. Robert Stewart Hyer, first president of the university—a scientist of some note who, local legend says, anticipated Marconi by a few days in the discovery of wireless telegraphy. Hyer Hall contains the offices and classrooms of the science departments and is interesting for its astronomical, geological, and anthropological exhibits. The most extensive collection is that of the Teaching Museum of the Geological Department on the second floor, which contains more than 10,000 specimens including a very fine specimen of *Elasmosaurus serpentinus*, a sea-lizard of the Upper Cretaceous epoch, donated by A. J. Anderson of Cedar Hill. It also has some rare minerals and a large collection of the bones of Pleistocene mammals taken from Dallas sand pits. The anthropological exhibits, also on the second floor, include a collection of artifacts from the Neolithic and Early Bronze periods collected in Kent, England, by Gilbert Floyd of London, and the A. W. Webb collection of Australian aboriginal weapons and ceremonial objects. The latter exhibit has two of the much-feared and extremely rare "kau-kau" or "death-pointing" bones made from the arm of a murdered man and used by his relatives to determine his murderer. The astronomical exhibits consist of a small planetarium right of the main entrance on the first floor, and an interesting model, to the left up the north corridor, illustrating the size of our sun compared with that of some of the larger and better known fixed stars.

The new **Fondren Library** *(open 7:30–9)*, southeast corner of the Quadrangle, completed early in 1940, was built with $400,000 donated in 1935 by Mr. and Mrs. W. W. Fondren of Houston. It is a modern university library building, four stories in height, air conditioned, and with space for approximately 300,000 volumes. The ceiling of the main reading room is decorated with seven sculptured panels, representing scenes from English and American literature, which were executed by Harry Lee Gibson, Dallas sculptor who designed the bronze figure of a Tejas Indian over the door of the Hall of State at Fair Park. In addition to stack and reading rooms it contains an auditorium, seminar rooms, and cubicles for the use of graduate students. Some units of the university, now inadequately housed elsewhere, will be transferred to the fourth floor of the library.

Atkins Hall *(public rooms open day and night)*, Roberts Parkway east of the Quadrangle, affectionately known to students as The Barn, was made possible through a subscription of $179,000 by the North Texas Conference of the Methodist Church. It is a fireproof four-story building, and provides living quarters for 139 men. The west wing is used by the School of Engineering, the Chemistry Department, Journalism Department, and the SMU Students' Publishing Company, which publishes the *Semi-Weekly Campus*, *The Rotunda* (a yearbook), and the *Student Directory*.

The **Engineering Building** *(open 7:30–6)*, east on Roberts Parkway near Airline Road, is a two-story brick building erected in 1928 and contains laboratories, classrooms, offices, and drafting rooms. It also houses the university's steam plant. Service tunnels conduct light and electricity, gas, steam, and water to all campus buildings. The university is supplied with water from artesian wells.

Fraternity Row *(private)*, a series of seven lodge houses, extends south from the Engineering Building. Here live a large number of the male students of the university. There are no sorority houses, but Greek letter societies for both men and women are numerous and influential on the campus.

Ownby Stadium *(open for athletic events)*, southeast corner of the campus near Mockingbird Lane, is the home gridiron of the widely known SMU Mustangs, a football team whose string of Southwestern Conference championships and participation in the Rose Bowl and other intersectional games have brought Southern Methodist University national recognition in the sports world. The stadium, the western unit of which was completed in 1926, seats 20,000 and cost $222,688 of which $16,676 was contributed by Jordan C. Ownby. Athletics are officially encouraged at Southern Methodist University. Adjacent to the stadium are a practice field, tennis courts, a basketball pavilion accommodating 3,000, and a gymnasium containing a swimming pool, boxing and wrestling room, lockers for men and women, and the offices of the director of Physical Education. An indoor cinder track runs underneath the stadium.

The **Statue of Peruna I,** north of Mockingbird Lane near entrance to Ownby Stadium, is an interesting memorial to the university's most beloved mascot, a diminutive Shetland pony named for the school song, *Peruna.* The pony gained nationwide publicity when it accompanied the football team to New York for the Fordham game in 1934. A short time later the mascot was killed by an automobile, and funds were raised by student subscription to erect this memorial, designed by Mike Owen, young Dallas sculptor. It is a recumbent figure of a pony in marble cast stone, resting on a base of the same material.

The **Forest of Arden,** southwest corner of the campus, extending from the intersection of Potomac and Hillcrest Avenues to Bishop Boulevard, is a large grove of trees so named by the students because it was here that the Arden Club gave, as its first production in the spring of 1916, an outdoor performance of *As You Like It.*

The **University President's House** *(private),* west side of Hillcrest Avenue between Shenandoah and Binkley Streets, is just off the campus. It was erected in 1920 and cost $38,994. The occupant in 1940 was Dr. Umphrey Lee.

33. **LOVE FIELD AIRPORT** *(open day and night),* Love Field Drive, Lemmon Avenue, Lovers Lane, and Burrus Street, in 1940 was one of the five largest municipal airports in the United States. It is served by three of the country's important air transport companies—American Airlines, Inc., Braniff Airways, Inc., and Delta Air Lines—which provide direct connections north, south, east, and west, with the Middle West and Great Lakes region, the Gulf Coast and Mexico, and the Atlantic and Pacific seaboards. It is on the main trunk line of American Airlines and is the operating and overhaul headquarters for Braniff Airways, Inc.

Extensive air service makes Dallas a favorite stopover for transcontinental flyers and air travelers, and every year swells the number of celebrities who make brief visits in the city. A total of 48 mail and passenger planes in addition to numerous private planes arrived and departed from the field daily in 1940, handling 84,903 incoming and outgoing passengers during 1939.

The Dallas School of Aviation gives instruction to amateur and commercial flyers at the field, and takes sightseers aloft for short flights over the city. The field also serves as a center for various government activities connected with aviation, including a United States aerological weather forecasting bureau maintained by the Department of Agriculture; teletype lines extending to Wichita, Kansas, and Nashville, Tennessee; the office of the supervising inspector of the Seventh District, Bureau of Air Commerce, Department of Commerce; and a training class for Army flyers, established in cooperation with the Dallas Aviation School on July 1, 1939.

Love Field occupies a rectangular 278-acre tract of level land on the northwestern edge of the city, and is controlled by the city manager through a field supervisor. It is an all-direction field, with eight hard-surfaced runways on which planes can alight or take off. The entire area is sodded with bermuda grass and is well drained by means of perforated corrugated iron pipes placed in trenches parallel to the runways. There are 13 wooden, sheet steel, and steel and masonry hangars on the field, of which 11 are in active use. These are owned or leased by private companies. Lighting equipment includes an aerial traffic signal for planes in the air; a ground traffic signal for planes on the ground; floodlights at both ends of the runways; a 24-inch rotating beacon on top of the control tower; a code flasher

389

beacon, green in color, on top of the rotating beacon, which flashes DL, the identifying signal of the field; a neon sign, M-Dallas, mounted on the roof of the hangar behind the control tower; and a neon-lighted wind tee mounted on the roof of the adjacent hangar.

A **Monument**, northwest corner of the field at the intersection of Lemmon Avenue and Love Field Drive, has been erected in memory of the aviators killed at Love Field during their training for the World War. On this monument have been placed 12 bronze plaques, one for each soldier, inscribed with his name, rank, and year of birth and death.

Love Field began as an Army flying field during the World War, at which time it covered a square mile, with hangars on one side and repair depots on the other. After the war about half the field was returned to other uses, and the remainder, 167 acres, retained as an airport. The United States Army maintained a base here, and the remaining hangars were bought by private operators for various services. The city of Dallas acquired the landing field in 1927, buying the land from the privately owned Love Field Company for $325,000. In 1931 the city bought approximately 90 acres more and installed the present runways and lighting system in 1931–32. Since that time it has been further enlarged. *(For outstanding flights and flyers see AVIATION: OVERNIGHT TO EVERYWHERE.)*

34. The **TEXAS TEXTILE MILLS** *(open 2–4 Monday through Friday)*, Maple Avenue and Love Field Drive, is a company representative of the large manufacturing plants that have been established since the World War in a new industrial area around Love Field airport. The mills also symbolize the importance of Dallas as a center for the manufacture of cotton goods.

The plant has 358 looms, 15,504 spindles, is modern in construction throughout and equipped with improved safety devices. It employs approximately 400 people. The principal products are tickings, chambrays, seat covers, and suitings. More than 1,500,000 yards of cotton suitings were manufactured for foreign export trade during 1938–39.

The Texas Textile Mills, as a company, dates from 1900, and draws from the Central and North Texas cotton growing region, also having mills at Waco and McKinney. Visitors are welcome at the plant and may see the various steps in the spinning, weaving, dyeing, and cutting of cotton cloth.

35. **CRADDOCK PARK** *(admission free)*, Hawthorne Street, Lemmon Avenue, and the St. Louis & Southwestern Railway tracks, is one of Dallas' newer parks, in a fashionable residential section on the northern edge of Oak Lawn. It is a small triangular stretch of level meadowland covering nine acres, and was donated to the city by L. Craddock in 1922. Its equipment includes two tennis courts, a baseball diamond, comfort station, and playground apparatus.

The park was the site of Cedar Springs, one of the earliest known settlements in Dallas County. The springs that were here were visited in 1840 by Colonel William G. Cooke and his expedition, during the preliminary exploration undertaken by the Republic of Texas of a highway route from Austin and Bastrop to the Red River. In 1843 the community known as Cedar Springs was established in the vicinity by Dr. John Cole. This settlement was the rival of Dallas in an election to determine the permanent location of the county seat, four years after Dallas County was formed. It was in August, 1850, that first Cedar Springs, and later Hord's Ridge, were eliminated as contenders.

Craddock Park has the **Municipal Rose Garden** *(open daylight hours)*, in its northwestern corner. This garden, designed by Wynne B. Woodruff, landscape art-ist, and laid out by the park board in cooperation with the Public Works Adminis-tration in 1935, is approached by a graveled walk that winds around from the en-trance to the park at Lemmon Avenue and Loma Alto Drive, across a rustic bridge spanning a narrow stream confined within masonry walls. The garden is laid out in three courts defined by arbors, wrought iron gateways, hedges, shrubbery, rock seats, and short flights of stone steps, with a sunken pool in the central court. Just inside the entrance is a sundial, and at the far end a rock pavilion with benches from which the garden can be viewed. The rose bushes, which are from the widely known rose growing region around Tyler, Texas, include 35 varieties and are set out in marked beds. From April 1 to November 1, or later in mild seasons, many different varieties can be seen in bloom, and in the late spring and early autumn there is a profusion of blossoms of all shades and sizes.

36. ROBERT E. LEE PARK *(admission free)*, bounded by Hall and Hood Streets, Lemmon Avenue, and Turtle Creek Boulevard, and until 1936 called Oak Lawn Park, is a comparatively small area acquired by the city from the street rail-way company for $38,000 on April 24, 1909. It covers 17 acres of rolling hillside overlooking the winding, tree-shaded course of Turtle Creek, whose bridges, land-scaped banks, and clear rippling waters form a natural extension of the park area and add to its charm.

The park has four tennis courts, a softball diamond, five roque courts, play-ground apparatus, and a comfort station, and is equipped for picnics with stone benches, tables, and ovens. It has been beautified as part of the park board's 1936–38 improvement program, undertaken in cooperation with the Work Proj-ects Administration. Natural rock bridges and retaining walls have been built, and a new **Field House** *(open on special occasions)*, on a hill facing Turtle Creek Boule-vard, has been constructed at a cost of approximately $30,000. This house, com-pleted late in 1939, is a two-story structure of yellow brick with a portico of mas-sive white columns extending across the main facade. The auditorium is rented for parties and dances; the other wings of the building are reserved for a display of Confederate period furniture. The building is an accurate reproduction of General Robert E. Lee's home at Arlington, Virginia, and was inspired by the equestrian **Statue of General Lee** at the southwestern corner of the park where Hall Street intersects Turtle Creek Boulevard. This monument was erected by the Southern Memorial Association of Dallas in 1936, and is of Lee and an armed orderly. Two bronze figures portray the revered commander of the Confederate armies riding bareheaded with an armed orderly at his side. The group is a spirited and dignified piece of sculpture about 18 feet high, mounted on a granite base approached by a flight of steps. A granite bench encircles its outer edge. An inscription describing Lee's "everlasting fame" is carved in the circular back of the bench. Around the bot-tom of the base and at each side of the steps are set ornamental shrubs, the whole forming a single harmonious composition strikingly placed on the hillside with an unbroken view in every direction. The statue is illuminated by floodlights at night.

The cost of the bronze figures, $40,000, was raised by a campaign conducted by the Southern Memorial Association. An additional $18,000 was appropriated by the park board for the base and incidental landscaping. Part of the latter amount was supplied by a Work Projects Administration grant. A. Phimister Proctor designed the statue, which was cast in bronze by the Roman Bronze Works of Corona, Long Island, New York. The architect was Mark Lemmon.

37. REVERCHON PARK *(admission free)*, Welborn Street, Maple Avenue, the Missouri-Kansas-Texas Railroad and St. Louis & Southwestern Railway tracks, formerly known as Turtle Creek Park, was purchased by the city in 1914 for $31,128. It was named for Julien Reverchon, noted botanist who came to Dallas with the La Reunion colony. Its 39 acres lying along Turtle Creek were formerly a slum area called Woodchuck Hill, occupied by the makeshift shacks and hovels of a squatters' colony. But this has been transformed into one of the beauty spots of Dallas, popular for picnics, sports, and outings. The park contains a comfort station, concession stand, grandstand, three baseball diamonds, two tennis courts, roque and croquet courts, benches and tables for picnics, an iris bowl, sunken garden, and an open-air theater on the creek banks where each year the various playgrounds of the city compete in the finals of a one-act play contest.

For the visitor the park is interesting chiefly for its trees and springs. The former include the tallest oak tree in Dallas, and the latter Raccoon Spring, famous as a stand for deer hunting in pioneer days; both are in the northeast corner of the park. The Gill Well mineral springs are near the south entrance on Maple Avenue. The discovery of the Gill Well, which occurred at about the turn of the century, was an accidental by-product of Dallas' perennial search in early days for an adequate water supply. It cost the city about $25,000, and flows at a rate of 500,000 gallons a day.

About two-thirds of the water is from the mineral flow, which is 900 feet below ground. The water, which resembles in many respects the mineral waters of European resorts and is used in several county and city institutions, is carried to the surface in pipes and can be drawn from taps arranged around a semicircle of masonry near the entrance to the park. Here cars stop at all hours of the day, and people alight to drink the water or to fill bottles and pails. Caution is advised in its use, as it is a powerful purgative. An analysis made by M. J. Dorns of the Science Department of Fort Worth University in 1904 revealed the following contents in terms of grains to the gallon:

Sulphate	4.05
Chloride	14.4
Calcium	48.0
Silicon Dioxide	5.2
Carbonate	17.0
Lithium	.1
Sodium & Potassium	134.0
Magnesium	6.2

When this water was analyzed by the Chemistry Department of the University of Texas in 1924, the following minerals were discovered in one gallon:

Sodium Sulphate	338 grains
Magnesium Chloride	65 grains
Magnesium Sulphate	65 grains
Calcium Carbonate	65 grains
Calcium Sulphate	65 grains
Ferric Hydroxide	60 grains
Sodium Carbonate	60 grains

38. FISHTRAP CEMETERY *(open sunrise to sunset)*, west side of Fishtrap Road, 0.5 miles north of Eagle Ford Road, sometimes called the Old French Cemetery, is neither the oldest burial ground in Dallas nor the most notable for its monuments, but is one of the most interesting. It contains amid its almost impenetrable jungle of vines and weeds the graves of many of the French socialists who in 1855 established the ill-fated utopian colony of La Reunion in this vicinity. The most recent of these graves is that of Emanuel Santerre, last surviving member of that band of colonists, who died on April 20, 1939. He arrived in Dallas in 1855 at the age of five, and resided for 84 years on the site of the long-abandoned communal settlement.

Fishtrap Cemetery lies on the border of a marshy gravel slough in the midst of the West Dallas suburban slum area, which has bred and provided hideouts for some of the Southwest's more notorious criminals of the postwar, machine-gun generation. Buried in a bare sandy plot under a mesquite tree near the southern edge of the cemetery is Bonnie Parker, who gained nationwide notoriety in the early 1930s as the outlawed, golden-haired, cigar-smoking gun moll of the killer-bandit Clyde Barrow. She also acquired a certain romantic glamour as a sort of Maid Marian of modern crime for the manner in which she stuck by her lover throughout his long career as a hunted fugitive.

Both Bonnie Parker and Clyde Barrow came from the so-called poor white class, were born on Texas farms, and grew up in the Dallas slums, Bonnie attending school at Cement City not far from her present resting place. When they met in West Dallas in January, 1930, Bonnie and Clyde were only 20 years old. She had been married and was separated from her husband, and he had served several jail sentences for car thefts and stickups in Oklahoma and Texas. When the pair met, it was apparently love at first sight. Clyde was arrested again soon afterward and imprisoned in Waco, and Bonnie followed him there and slipped him a gun with which he made a daring jailbreak. Clyde was recaptured in Middletown, Ohio, after another robbery, and was brought back to Texas where he was committed to the state penitentiary on April 21, 1930, to serve a fourteen-year sentence. He was pardoned on February 2, 1932, and immediately rejoined Bonnie in Dallas.

From this time on she was his constant companion in crime. She received her first jail sentence for participation in a robbery at Kaufman in March, 1932. In April Clyde was charged with his first murder, the Bucher killing in Waco. For a brief period after Bonnie's release they were separated; then she joined Clyde in Wichita Falls where they lived with the almost equally notorious bandit Raymond Hamilton in a tourist camp. Soon afterward Clyde, Bonnie, and Raymond Hamilton committed another murder at Atoka, Oklahoma, and from this time on Clyde's and Bonnie's lives were those of two hunted beasts of prey—a continuous succession of killings, holdups, mad flights, periods of enforced hiding, ambushes, hairbreadth escapes, and running fights with law enforcement officers—making their names a headline legend and leaving a trail of blood across the length and breadth of the Southwest from Arkansas to New Mexico, and from Louisiana to Kansas and Missouri.

Impelled it seems mainly by a sentimental attachment for their respective families they kept returning to Dallas, and it was in this area that some of their more daring exploits were performed, the last of these being the murder on April 1, 1934, of two highway patrolmen who dismounted from their motorcycles near Grapevine to investigate Barrow's parked car. Less than two months later, on May 23, Clyde and Bonnie ran into an ambuscade near Arcadia, Louisiana, and died together behind the wheel of their car, literally riddled with machine-gun bullets. Their mutilated bodies, the clothing torn from them by morbid souvenir hunters, were brought back to Dallas for burial and were the occasion of a gruesome Roman holiday; 20,000 persons crowded the street in front of the undertaking establishment where Bonnie's body lay in state in a silver casket, clad in a blue silk negligee, with marcelled hair and polished fingernails. Crowds of the curious also fought to get to the gravesides when Bonnie and Clyde were buried, and aviators swooped down in planes dropping flowers on the biers. They were not buried together as they wished. Bonnie was interred in Fishtrap Cemetery, and Clyde in the neighboring Western Heights Cemetery beside his brother Buck, who died of wounds received while fleeing south from Iowa with Bonnie and Clyde in July, 1933.

In contrast with the broken stone slabs, tin signs, old bottles, crockery, fruit jars, and other improvised markers that dot this neglected resting place of the poor, Bonnie's grave is marked with a low, slanting headstone bearing a large bright plate of chromium steel on which is inscribed the epitaph:

BONNIE PARKER
Oct. 1, 1910-May 23, 1934

As the flowers are all made sweeter by the sunshine and the dew, so this old world is made brighter by folks like you.

This marker was a tribute from a local monument maker.

39. The SITE OF LA REUNION, north of the Fort Worth Cut-off Road, at Westmoreland Road, on the northwestern edge of Oak Cliff, is marked by the mouldering ruins of a single house. Along with the untended and largely unmarked graves in Fishtrap Cemetery *(see POINTS OF INTEREST, Fishtrap Cemetery)*, these ruins are all that remain of the ill-considered French utopian colony that in the early days of Dallas did so much to enrich the struggling frontier village with Old World talent, culture, and craftsmanship. Until comparatively recent years, this house, a small but substantial one-story structure of limestone in French cottage style, was in a fair state of preservation with roof, walls, and floor still intact, but vandalism, added to the ravages of time and weather, has reduced it to a heap of crumbling stones, mortar, and rubbish on the border of a shallow ravine some little distance back from the road. Its restoration as an historical landmark has been urged but no practical steps have been undertaken, and only the foundations and a fragment of two adjoining walls are still standing.

The house was built in 1859 for the widow of Alphonse Delord shortly after the colony had ceased to function as a Fourierist *phalange*, or self-contained, cooperative community, as its founders had intended. Madame Delord had invested heavily in the short-lived La Reunion Company, and when it dissolved, received forty acres of land as her share of the communal property. On this tract Pierre, Joseph, and Francois Girard, three brothers who had come to Texas with their father in 1856 and had taken up the occupation of architects and builders, constructed a house for her. She resided here until the outbreak of the Civil War in 1861 when she returned to France with her children.

The commissary and other main buildings of the colony constructed in 1855 and 1856 lay a considerable distance to the north of the Delord house, close to the present Eagle Ford Road. They were abandoned and rapidly fell into ruins after the dispersion of the colonists, and no trace of them remains today, the limestone bluff on which they stood having been blasted away during the development of the cement industry in this vicinity.

40. **FRANK REAUGH'S STUDIO** *(open 2–5 Thursday)*, 120 East Fifth Street, called *El Sibil*, stands on an eminence overlooking Oak Cliff and houses the living quarters, workrooms, storage vaults, and exhibit room of one of the Southwest's best known painters of cowboy scenes. The building was erected in 1928.

The vaults and the exhibit room—the latter has a large skylight and special lighting features for displaying canvases—contain Reaugh's complete collection including his best known cycle of range paintings—"Twenty-four Hours with the Herd." These paintings, preserving for posterity a vision of the vanished longhorn herds that once grazed the Texas plains, have been willed to the University of Texas; but even after their removal there will remain enough of Reaugh's canvases, large and small, to comprise an extensive collection.

In addition to Reaugh's own paintings the exhibit room contains a plaster bust of a young girl, by Lorado Taft, given by the sculptor; Robert Bringhurst's "Awakening of Spring," a piece that won the first prize at the Chicago World's Fair and Tennessee Centennial; Clara Phifer's "The Piper"; an Indian pottery jar by Edward Keney, from which bronzes have been cast; and a small model of Manulita by Herman A. McNeil. Miscellaneous curios and heirlooms that grace the exhibit room include buffalo skulls, antique chairs, old sewing tables, a spinning wheel, and a chair from the old Windsor Hotel in Dallas.

Frank Reaugh came to Texas in 1876 and first settled on a ranch near Terrell. There he became acquainted with the Texas longhorn cattle that are the subject of so many of his pastels. He settled in Dallas in the early 1900s; there was only one other professional artist in the city, R. J. Onderdonk, father of Julian Onderdonk, known for Texas landscapes and bluebonnet paintings. In a small brick building on Elm Street near Akard Street Reaugh established a studio and organized an art class, made up for the most part of youngsters. There was no art association in the city, but Reaugh gradually developed local interest in such a group and donated a picture to the association—its first. He took charge of the loan exhibits brought to early state fairs. The Reaugh Art Club, organized by his pupils, in 1940 had more than 50 members.

41. The **HORD HOUSE** *(open on application to the custodian of the Marsalis Pumping Station across the street)*, southwest corner Opera and Thirteenth Streets, is a story-and-a-half edifice of cedar logs with a broad rustic porch across the front and a white stone chimney at one end. It sits well back from the road at the entrance to Marsalis Park, in enclosed grounds amid dense clumps of crepe myrtle and groves of chinaberry, cedar, oak, and pecan trees. Old-fashioned flower beds line walks leading to the front and side doors, and a carriage entrance gate stands at one side of the well kept lawn.

The old house, a reconstruction of the first one to be built in Oak Cliff and one of the oldest still standing in the city limits, is considered by many the most interesting architectural relic of pioneer days in the metropolitan area of Dallas. Built in 1845 it is almost as venerable as the cabin of John Neely Bryan on the courthouse lawn, and retains much more of its early homelike atmosphere, lacking the somewhat artificial museum character of the reconstructed Bryan cabin.

The builder of the house, Judge William H. Hord, for whom Hord's Ridge (now Oak Cliff) was named, came to Texas from Tennessee in 1845 with his wife, three children, and three Negro slaves. He settled on 640 acres of land and first erected as a temporary shelter some dirt-floored cabins with chimneys of sticks and mud, but in the following year built a better house. Large cedars and oak trees were abundant in the neighborhood, and these Judge Hord and his slaves hewed with a broad-axe into logs 12x18 inches square, from which they built the walls of the house, covering the roof with oak boards split by hand with a frow. The floors were made of cedar planks split by hand with a crosscut saw; the cutting was accomplished by laying the logs across a gully, with one man in the bottom of the channel and the other standing on top to pull the saw. The chimney was built of blocks of white stone about twice the size of bricks.

As Mrs. Hattie Hord Crawford, Judge Hord's daughter, recalled the home of her childhood many years afterward, it at first consisted of a single room 20x20 feet, with a fireplace at one end, built-in bunks around the walls, and a small staircase in one corner leading to the attic in the half-story above. A couple of years later, about 1847, an annex was added making possible a second room. Slave quarters were also added in the rear. At the time when the Hord residence was built it was the only house between Dallas and Lancaster, but it soon became the nucleus of the settlement called Hord's Ridge, which by 1850 had grown to such proportions that it proved to be a formidable rival of Dallas in the election held in that year to determine the permanent location of the county seat. The settlement later became Oak Cliff, which was an independent municipality until 1904 when it was annexed to the city of Dallas.

The reconstruction of the Hord house dates from 1927, when Martin Weiss, prominent in civic and philanthropic work in Oak Cliff and Dallas, acquired possession of the property with the understanding that it be donated for public use. It was under the control of the courts, after prolonged litigation. The appearance of the house, which was in a bad state of repair, had been altered almost beyond recognition by the addition of clapboarding and other changes. Weiss transformed it into an authentic historical monument, making the house and grounds available to worthwhile organizations for parties and picnics. About 300 social and civic groups use the place annually for such purposes. There is a spacious screened and glassed-in porch for dancing, cooking facilities in one of the rooms of the house, and chairs and tables which can be used inside in winter and outside in summer.

42. MARSALIS PARK *(admission free)*, bounded by Opera Street, Clarendon Drive, Ewing and Storey Avenues, with the main entrance at Marsalis and Crawford Streets, three blocks south of East Jefferson Avenue, was once called Forest Park. It covers about 50 acres of hilly, heavily wooded land along Cedar Creek, in the older southeastern residential section of Oak Cliff. An earlier tract of 36 acres was acquired by the city in March, 1909.

Though by no means the largest park in Dallas the deep, winding ravine that the creek has cut through it and the dense groves of pecan, cedar, hackberry, and oak trees that mantle its white limestone cliffs give it a natural scenic beauty unequaled in the city. Landscaping dates from the inauguration of the George E. Kessler City Plan of 1910. An extensive system of concrete, log and natural stone bridges, park and animal houses, winding walks, hillside stairways, and retaining walls along the creek banks, carried out at a cost of $100,000 with Work Projects Administration labor between 1935 and 1938, add to its picturesqueness and charm. Marsalis Park is equipped with stone benches, picnic tables and fireplaces, two tennis courts, a swimming and wading pool for children, concession stands, play apparatus, and a pony track.

The park's chief attraction is its Zoological Garden *(open daylight hours, free)*, which is one of the ten largest in the country, valued at $150,000, and containing over 700 individual mammals, birds, and reptiles. The zoo is housed in pens and cages on both sides of the creek, in the habitats best suited to the various species. The illusion of natural environment is created by the surrounding cliffs, woods, and water. Monkeys, reptiles, and tropical birds are housed in enclosed buildings. Among the featured exhibits in 1940 were a saddle-backed Malayan tapir, two male chimpanzees called Henry and Duffy, and two female elephants named Queenie and Tootsie; the latter are kept in a pit with concrete-lined walls, where spectators can look down from the road over a low coping and watch as they are bathed, fed, and exercised.

Among other zoo specimens are rhesus, Java, and spider monkeys; pig-tailed macaques; Hamadryas and mandrill baboons; a pair of large Nubian lions; a Sumatran tiger; bobcats; jaguars; pumas; black and spotted leopards; Mexican black bears; cinnamon bears; llamas; yaks; water buffaloes; goats; deer; and a number of miscellaneous animals indigenous to Texas, including badgers, foxes, jackrabbits, raccoons, opossums, wolves, coyotes, and peccaries. Until recently the zoo had a longhorned steer, but this typically Texas specimen died of old age in 1937.

Birds include parrots, cockatoos, and other tropical birds; American golden eagles; canaries; doves; quails; pheasants; pigeons; ostriches; emus; rheas; peacocks; Mexican turkeys; game chickens; and a large variety of waterfowl. There is also a collection of reptiles, most of them native to Texas, which includes rattlesnakes, bull snakes, adders, moccasins, garter snakes, chicken snakes, horned toads, a Gila monster, alligators, and loggerhead turtles. In addition to the caged denizens of the zoo, Marsalis Park swarms with birds and squirrels that are attracted to this protected area to raise their young and feed on wild berries and nuts.

All zoo animals are carefully sheltered from the weather, and the more delicate species kept in heated quarters during the colder months. Their diet is carefully prepared. The monkeys and small animals are fed at 8 A.M. and 4 P.M. The carnivorous animals are fed once a day, at 4 P.M.

The idea of a city zoo in Dallas is believed to have been advocated in 1890; on October 29 of that year the city had purchased two young black bears, "very playful," and City Clerk McGrain presented the zoo management with a choice collection of black and white rabbits. It was reported under this date that Street Commissioner Spahr was "rustling" for deer and other animals and that the council would be asked to appropriate money for the purchase of cages and the like.

Charles Bilger, veteran employee of the park board, recalled that when he first assumed his duties about 1900, the city owned a large herd of deer which were kept in an enclosure in the old City Park, now Sullivan Park, and which were thinned out every year at Christmas by shooting a selected number and selling their meat to Dallas hotels. He recalled a pair of bears, one of which drowned the other in a fight.

In 1904 when the park board was created and assumed control of Fair Park, the city acquired from the State Fair of Texas 27 animals, including three monkeys, one bear, two anteaters, five deer, one coon, two foxes, one wolf, one eagle, three squirrels, and eight peafowls. These were housed in cages along the banks of the creek in City Park amid picturesquely landscaped settings. The zoo was apparently allowed to deteriorate. A newspaper article on the parks of Dallas in 1910 indicated that City Park had three javelinas or wild hogs, two cinnamon bears, one crane, 100 rabbits, and a family of squirrels.

The Marsalis Park Zoo dates from a subscription campaign in 1912, conducted with the cooperation of the Dallas newspapers. After this campaign the remaining inmates of the City Park Zoo were transferred to Marsalis Park, and the zoo was greatly enlarged by the purchase of additional animals. Among the principal exhibits in the period immediately preceding the entrance of the United States into the World War were a small herd of bison and a flock of ostriches.

In 1920 Frank "Bring 'Em Back Alive" Buck, who began his career as an animal collector trapping wildlife along Turtle Creek, Mill Creek, Cedar Creek, and other streams in the vicinity of Dallas, contracted with W. Foster Jacoby, superintendent of Dallas parks, to furnish the city with a complete zoo. As a result Dallas received in the fall of 1921 a shipment of many rare specimens of animals, birds, and reptiles from the jungles of the Malay Peninsula, Borneo, Sumatra, India, and Africa. These acquisitions were transported in bamboo cages from the freight depot to Marsalis Park along the downtown business thoroughfares of Dallas, and the parade of snarling and roaring carnivora, chattering and screeching monkeys, bright-colored tropical birds, and deadly reptiles, including two enormous blue-black pythons, is an event still remembered in the city. Hundreds of men, women, and children followed the trucks to the park, where Frank Buck, who accompanied the shipment, made a personal presentation of an auburn-haired baby orangutan which he carried under his overcoat.

Many of the animals supplied by Buck are still living, and their progeny, particularly that of the lions, panthers, and monkeys, have been sold or traded to zoos in other parts of the country. In this way the zoo has been built up and new specimens secured. In 1936, through the cooperation of the park board and the Work Projects Administration, the animals acquired more commodious quarters designed by Walton Carlton, who for many years has been zoo superintendent. In 1940 further improvements were contemplated, including a new bird house and a commissary building; in the latter there will be, according to accepted plans, a large hospital room for sick animals. Rare specimens are preserved after death by taxidermy.

Many of the animals in the Dallas zoo have become great favorites with children and adults, and have furnished material for innumerable feature stories in local newspapers. Among these have been the elephants. The birthdays of Queenie and of Wilbur, a large bull elephant that ran amuck in 1934 and killed himself by charging into the cement wall of the elephant pit, were celebrated for a number of years with birthday parties that were attended by hundreds of children from all over the city. This custom, which was allowed to lapse after the death of Wilbur, was revived in the summer of 1938 on the occasion of Tootsie's sixth birthday. Another favorite was Dr. Wham, a peg-legged Egyptian stork that was accidentally locked out of his sleeping quarters during a blizzard, and froze to death on his feet standing in the snow outside his house like a sentry at his post. Jimmy, the baby orangutan presented to the zoo by Frank Buck, recovered from a severe attack of pneumonia and learned to do many tricks during the four years he lived, including that of riding a bicycle. He died of lead poisoning from eating a paint brush left within his reach. A second orangutan, born in captivity and purchased along with his mother when only six months old at a cost of $3,500, attracted much attention by his surliness, bad manners, and mimicry of visitors. When he died in the spring of 1939 from a malignant tumor, his body lay in state on a slab, and his pelt and skeleton were preserved by mounting.

43. BUCKNER ORPHANS HOME *(open daily except Saturday)*, Samuell Boulevard (East Pike) and Buckner Boulevard, occupies a tract of more than 2,000 acres approximately three miles due east of the city. Here are a neatly landscaped campus, a profitable and scientifically cultivated farm, a modern dairy, and small burying ground. The plant consists of 20 buildings and includes three six-story dormitories, administration building, high school, elementary school, physical education building, hospital, chapel and auditorium, nursery, kitchen and dining room, and a number of smaller structures.

All these buildings are of harmonious architecture in the Georgian style, built of red brick with red tile roofs, white stone trim, and wood colonial entrance features, the principal ones including the Administration Building with its portico of Greek Doric columns facing a circular drive around a central plaza. Seventeen of them, including all of those in which the children live and carry on their daily pursuits, are of brick and concrete construction throughout and as nearly fireproof as practicable. The home possesses a power plant, two artesian wells, two water storage tanks, one mile of fire mains with plugs, three miles of sewer mains, 17 1/2 miles of farm terraces, 12 miles of fences, and a symmetrical plan of walks and driveways.

In the middle of the central plaza is a bronze **Statue of Robert Cooke Buckner**, founder of the institution, affectionately known to the children as Father Buckner. The statue is seven feet, four inches high and rests on a gray granite base. It was created in the studio of Lorado Taft by one of his associates, was erected by former inmates of the home on June 1, 1936, and formally unveiled at annual homecoming ceremonies on October 11, 1936.

Buckner Orphans Home, which is maintained by endowment, private contributions, and the Baptist General Convention of Texas, admits boys and girls of any or no religious faith. During the 60-odd years of its existence it has cared for some 45,000 children, having 647 residents in 1940, of whom the majority were boys. An effort is made to keep families together by permitting children to be adopted into private homes only when there are no brothers or sisters. The orphans are cared for until they have finished high school. The home has fully accredited grammar and high schools with a combined enrollment of 557 at the beginning of 1940, and gives physical, religious, and occupational training to the children entrusted to its care. They are also provided with medical, surgical, and dental attention; eyeglasses are furnished those whose vision is defective.

An effort is made to secure jobs for boys and girls leaving the home, and each is provided with a complete wardrobe. Twenty-five graduates of the home in 1940 were attending colleges and technical schools. Baylor University, maintained by the Baptist church in Waco, admits the home's graduates at half the regular tuition price.

Historically Buckner Orphans Home represents the lengthened shadow of one family. For the forty years of its existence, from 1879 to 1919, it was under the direct charge of its founder, Robert Cooke Buckner, who was succeeded by his two sons, Joe Dudley Buckner and Hal F. Buckner. Joe Buckner died in 1936 and his brother has been general manager from that time. All have been Baptist ministers.

The inception of the home dates from December 7, 1876, when Dr. Buckner of Dallas, editor of the *Texas Baptist*, began to publish a series of open letters to the deacons of Texas, unfolding the idea of founding an orphanage under their control. The home was first opened in a rented cottage in Dallas on December 2, 1879, with only three children. On September 25, 1880, 44 acres of land were purchased for $500 from Elder J. F. Pinson on the present site of the home, which was then seven miles beyond the city limits. Two days later the home was formally dedicated in the 16x18-foot log cabin, one-time home of John Neely Bryan, which then occupied the land *(see POINTS OF INTEREST, John Neely Bryan's Cabin)*.

In the spring of 1881 a frame house with capacity for 25 children was constructed at a cost of $841, and on April 5 a formal opening took place with eight children representing both Protestants and Roman Catholics. There was $59.45 in cash on hand. By July 14, 1881, the home had come into the possession of 300 acres, and its property then was valued at $4,000. The provisions of the home's charter had forbidden the directors to incur indebtedness, and its growth was hampered by lack of funds. Its nondenominational character was stressed in the newspapers, and an appeal made for donations of money, food, clothing, livestock, and farming implements.

By 1886 the home was able to care for the children orphaned by the flood at Sabine Pass. In 1890 it had 720 acres and domiciled 130 children, of whom 86 were enrolled in school. There were then four two-story frame dwelling houses, a combination school and chapel, farms, and barns. The annual budget had grown to $12,468. Excavations had been begun for a new main building of brick, to cost $40,000.

On the night of January 15, 1897, the boys' dormitory, a frame building, caught fire and 20 orphans perished in the flames. This tragic incident spurred the construction of fireproof buildings. A new dormitory of brick was completed soon after the fire. This was followed by the construction of a nursery in 1906, a chapel in 1908, a powerhouse in 1910, and Manna Hall in 1911. By 1917 ten schoolrooms had been completed, two at a time. Dr. Buckner went to Galveston after the storm and tidal wave which swept that island city in September, 1900, and returned to Dallas with 36 children who had been made orphans by the disaster. By 1918, just before Dr. Buckner's death, children in the home numbered 600, of whom 500 were enrolled in the school that had been extended by this time to include eight grades. The annual budget had risen to $165,382.

Another fire occurred on January 2, 1923, consuming one of the dormitories and resulting in the loss of two lives. A building program launched at the Baptist General Convention of Texas in November, 1919, resulted between 1921 and 1938 in the construction of the 19 buildings. Thirteen of these were erected through special gifts and the resulting buildings designated by the names of the donors. The new $40,000 physical education building was formally opened January 3, 1940. The educational program has been pushed, leading to the recognition by the State Department of Education in 1923 of the high school as a first-class institution. In May, 1925, a graduating class received the first diplomas to be awarded from the high school.

DALLAS COUNTY TOUR

Dallas—Lancaster—Cedar Hill—Grand Prairie—Irving—Carrollton—Richardson—Garland—Mesquite—Seagoville—Hutchins—Dallas

Roads paved with asphalt, cement, or brick except for a few sections of connecting roads, which are graveled and rough in places: the latter when in river and creek bottoms are sometimes subject to overflow, but are otherwise passable.

Texas Electric Ry. parallels US 77 and US 75 on the east and west; Houston & Texas Central RR (Southern Pacific System) parallels US 75 on the east.

Accommodations in the county, outside Dallas, limited to tourist lodges along main highways.

This route gives access to all main points of interest in Dallas County within six or eight hours, and offers a variety of suburban and industrial developments, wooded river bottoms, and fertile farm and grazing lands. The metropolitan environs of Dallas, marked by charitable and corrective institutions, flying fields, radio broadcasting stations, and a succession of taverns, tourist lodges, and roadside filling stations, stretch out along the arterial highways in all directions from the city. Outside of this area the county is predominantly open farm land, but with a large number of small rural communities, many of them dating back to the 1840s and 1850s and remaining to this day primarily trading, milling, ginning, and shipping centers.

Along the Trinity River that cuts across the county from northwest to southeast, and its maze of tributary creeks, a large area of level bottom lands is covered with a dense growth of vines, bushes, willows, postoaks, pecans, cedars, bois d'arcs, hackberries, chinaberries, elms, and cottonwoods. The streams may be roaring torrents of muddy water, making a half-inundated marsh of the surrounding countryside, or narrow, half-stagnant trickles meandering across parched mud flats, depending on the season and amount of rainfall. The lakes and watercourses, as well as numerous gravel pits, offer excellent hunting and fishing. These bottom lands once had little use; large sections have been reclaimed by levees, cleared and converted into pasture lands or cotton and corn fields.

Most of Dallas County consists of rolling upland prairies dotted with sparse clumps of mesquite and other trees and covered in the spring with tall grass and a profusion of wild flowers. This upland prairie is gashed by frequent shallow ravines, and where the road dips down into these the gleaming white limestone that forms the geologic base of the rich, waxy, black soil is exposed.

Dallas County lies in the center of an extremely fertile farming region, and most of its 52,594 inhabitants who live outside of Dallas and the suburban cities of Highland Park and University Park depend directly or indirectly on agriculture, poultry farming, and dairying for a livelihood. The lands are ideally adapted to the growing of cotton, which constitutes the chief pay crop. Large quantities of wheat, corn, oats, milo maize, kaffir corn, hay, and other grains are grown. Onion production is important in the northeastern part of the county. In several regions, particularly in the southeast where black land gives way to sandy loam, there is considerable truck farming and fruit growing. Dallas is east of the cattle country, and stock raising

401

except for dairying and poultry farming is a sideline. The dairy industry flourishes, especially in the northwestern part of the county, which is adapted to the raising of hay and other feed crops. Some horses and other blooded stock are raised on the large country estates of the northeastern sections.

Aside from agriculture the chief occupations are cotton ginning, gravel mining, and the manufacture of cement. Both of the last are important in the northwestern quarter of the county, and most of the gravel used in construction work in Dallas comes from local pits. There are some small miscellaneous factories in the larger towns. The commuting population that finds regular daily employment in the city is comparatively small.

Historic pioneer sites are numerous but not particularly conspicuous or well marked.

S. on Houston St., crossing Houston St. viaduct to Oak Cliff; S. at W. end of viaduct on Lancaster Ave., route of US 77; follow highway signs to city limits, S. on US 77.

The **UNITED STATES VETERANS HOSPITAL, *7.0 m. (L)*,** in 1939 was scheduled for completion in 1940. Extensive facilities will be open to veterans of all wars under certain prescribed conditions of eligibility. The site occupies a tract of approximately 244 acres. When the plant is completed it is planned that it will include a large main building of five stories and basement with 250 beds for general medical and surgical cases, a dining hall, kitchen building, attendants' quarters, nurses' quarters, storehouse, garage, boiler house, and residential buildings for the staff and personnel. Provision has also been made on the plat plan for two additional patients' buildings and a recreational building. All the buildings have been designed in a uniform Georgian style with red brick walls, trimmings of stone, and slate roofs. They will be fireproof throughout. Clinical facilities will consist of a complete pharmacy; eye, ear, nose, and throat unit; laboratory service; dental operating and X-ray facilities; minor operating rooms; and a complete X-ray suite comprising radiography, cystoscopy, and fluoroscopy. A modern operating suite will consist of two major operating rooms and separate units for eye, ear, nose, and throat, and orthopedic work.

US 77 follows a long winding grade protected with railings, and cutting through chalk cliffs mantled with cedars and scrub oaks to Five Mile Creek, then winds across high rolling farmlands.

LANCASTER, *13.7 m. (512 alt., 1,133 pop.),* is an old and sedately prosperous farming community and trading center. It was laid out in 1847 by A. Bledsoe, who named the town in honor of his birthplace, Lancaster, Pa. It was the site of a small arms and ammunition factory for the Confederacy during the Civil War. US 77, down the center of which runs the tracks of the Texas Electric Railway, constitutes its principal thoroughfare, with the town square and Central Avenue, the other main street, on which red and yellow brick school buildings are located, lying to the east. The business section, composed of one- and two-story brick buildings, is clustered about the square which has a small circular park in the center.

There are forty-three commercial establishments, a national bank, and five churches. Residential sections are made up of dignified old one- and two-story frame houses, most of them in an excellent state of repair, interspersed with neat, modern brick bungalows. Spreading hackberry, chinaberry, bois d'arc, and elm trees shade the streets, and the houses set far back in the midst of well kept lawns, flower beds, and clusters of crepe myrtle, redbud, and other flowering shrubs. Essentially a trading center located in a region growing cotton, wheat, oats, corn, pecans, and diversified farm products, Lancaster has no industries except two cotton gins.

The route is west on the Belt Line Road, through wooded creek bottoms abounding with small game, to DE SOTO, *21.4 m. (528 alt., 97 pop.),* a straggling cluster of frame houses and stores around a water tank. It dates from 1877 and was named for its first postmaster, Dr. Thomas Hernando DeSoto Stuart. The surrounding farming land is generally rocky and poor but grows some cotton, corn, wheat, oats, and small grains.

CEDAR HILL, *27.0 m. (750 alt., 500 pop.),* is the highest point between Galveston and the Red River, and takes its name from the extensive cedar brakes along Mountain Creek to the west of the town. It shares with one other community the claim that it is the second oldest settlement in the county, having been established in 1842. Its weatherbeaten frame houses testify to the many long years they have withstood the storms of this windy hilltop, of which the most violent occurred in 1856, destroying much property and several lives. The ruined walls of a granary built more than 50 years ago of stones hauled from the valley by ox teams before the coming of the railroad are standing today at the intersection of the Belt Line Road with the Gulf, Colorado & Santa Fe Railway, a picturesque reminder of the village's age. The town has a cotton gin and a creamery.

West of Cedar Hill the road loops over high rolling uplands blanketed with dense, dark green masses of scrub cedars. At *28.7 m.* it swings northward and plunges abruptly down between steep walls of white rock into the woods and meadows of the Mountain Creek bottoms. At this point, as the road begins to descend, is one of the finest views in Dallas County. The silvery surface of Mountain Creek Lake, rimmed by low hills, shines in the distance. This lake has been formed by damming the creek of the same name to form a body of water covering 3,500 acres as an adjunct to a generating plant of the Dallas Power & Light Company. It produces 31,250 kilowatts of power, which supplements that of the central plant in Dallas. The Mountain Creek plant was completed early in 1938 and supplies power for electrified farms over a large part of the county.

FLORENCE HILL, *32.2 m. (620 alt., 20 pop.),* is a scattered settlement, named about 1895 for two men named Florence and Hill, and is strung out for five miles or more along the Belt Line Road. An athletic field, general store, school, and church are encountered in succession northward, with a few frame houses between. Alfalfa, corn, oats, wheat, milo maize, and other small grains are the chief crops of the vicinity.

GRAND PRAIRIE, *40.2 m. (528 alt., 1,529 pop.),* is a busy industrial center, with several factories manufacturing truck bodies, trailers, rock wool, brooms, breakfast food, and stoves. The town was established in 1867 and takes its name from the Grand Prairie region of North Texas, on the eastern edge of which it is situated. Hay, grain, and cotton are grown in the vicinity, and there is considerable dairy and poultry farming. US 80 constitutes the main street, and along it flows a continuous stream of traffic between Dallas and Fort Worth. The business section has an appearance of spruce modernity and urban bustle in contrast to the somewhat dingy and rundown appearance of the residential sections, lying back from the highway, where houses are mostly frame and in a poor state of repair.

Eastward, the route is on US 80; then, at *45.3 m.,* is Ledbetter Drive; at *47.4 m.,* at the juncture of Ledbetter Drive with the Eagle Ford Road, it turns northwest on the Eagle Ford Road. The small town of **EAGLE FORD** *(75 pop.),* dominated by its red brick cotton gin, is visible a little to the east.

The Eagle Ford Road at *47.8 m.,* crosses the leveed channel of the Trinity over an old plank-floored iron bridge. The route is north on the Eagle Ford Road to its juncture with Irving Boulevard; at *49.9 m.,* turn west on Irving Boulevard.

IRVING, *50.7 m. (500 alt., 731 pop.),* is a pleasant, homelike little town shaded with numerous oak and pecan trees. It is in a rich dairy, poultry, and truck farming district, and has a weekly newspaper, the *Herald.* Thirty-five business establishments are housed in one- and two-story frame and brick buildings built in the form of a cross, extending for a block in each direction from the intersection of Britain Road with Irving Boulevard. Many of the residents have businesses or employment in Dallas.

The route is in a northwesterly direction over the Irving-Sowers Road to **SOWERS,** *53.8 m. (512 alt., 121 pop.),* a crossroads settlement dating from 1868, consisting of a school, a church, and two or three stores arranged around a triangle. It is in open rolling country dotted with mesquite thickets, suitable for dairying and the growing of grains and feed crops; the town serves as a trade center.

In **SOWERS** the route is north on the Belt Line Road; at *62.3 m.,* it jogs west and then north again, following the Belt Line Road to a gateway of natural stone that marks the entrance to **GRAPEVINE SPRINGS PARK,** *62.8 m.,* a public park *(R)* donated to the county in May, 1936, by Mr. and Mrs. J. D. Thweatt of Wichita Falls and Mr. and Mrs. A. B. Miller of Dallas County. Here for thirty days in August and September, 1843, Sam Houston, then president of the Republic of Texas, made his temporary headquarters while he awaited the outcome of negotiations between his Indian commissioner, Joseph C. Eldridge, and the chiefs of the North Texas Indian tribes. This effort culminated in the Bird's Fort treaty and circumvented the Mexican General Santa Anna's scheme to enlist these tribes in a second invasion of Texas. At the same time Houston watched from a strategic distance critical developments—at his capital at Washington-on-the-Brazos—that were to result in the annexation of Texas by the United States. Houston hurried back to Washington-on-the-Brazos before the Bird's Fort treaty was signed to attend to affairs of state and see his firstborn son, and the annexation of Texas by the United States was not consummated until six months later; but both the conclusion of the treaty and annexation, together marking the climax of Houston's career as a statesman, passed through their critical stages while "The Raven" was inactive in his camp at Grapevine Springs.

The park, covering twelve acres, is a natural beauty spot. The clear spring from which it takes its name is located in a miniature ravine formed by a small creek that flows in a winding course across the park from north to south. The spring itself is sheltered under an old-fashioned, rustic-type well house. The spreading old pecan tree under which Sam Houston made his encampment stands about ten yards north of the spring. It constitutes a part of a large grove of pecan, elm, and oak trees with gnarled and serpentine old grapevines twisting about their trunks; they make the grounds a shady retreat for motorists and picnic parties. With the cooperation of the Works Progress Administration, Dallas County expended $25,000 in the autumn of 1936 on the beautification of the park, constructing retaining walls of natural rock, gravel walks, a dam, and bridges. The park was landscaped, and benches and picnic tables installed.

404

The route continues on the Belt Line Road to **COPPELL**, *63.6 m. (561 alt., 200 pop.)*, a small and undistinguished place with one cotton gin, three places of business, one school, and two churches. The surrounding country is black land and grows cotton, wheat, oats, sweet potatoes, peanuts, and melons.

At *73.2 m.[sic]* the way is east on the Thweatt Road, which at *65.3 m.* intersects US 70 at a point known as Midway; eastward on US 77, the route passes numerous taverns, inns, and roadhouses, marking the northern fringe of Dallas' metropolitan area.

At *68.2 m.* US 77 crosses the Elm Fork of the Trinity River at Carrollton Crossing. A concrete dam south of the highway is a favorite fishing spot. Surrounding country is low and densely wooded, and subject to overflows that often make the highway impassable at this point. At *69.9 m.* US 77 makes a right-angled turn and the way is south.

CARROLLTON, *71.0 m. (448 alt., 689 pop.)*, is at the junction of three railroads, which explains the present location of the town. The first settlement in the vicinity was known as Trinity Mills, several miles to the north, but the population shifted to Carrollton in 1872 when the Missouri-Kansas-Texas Railroad was built to this point. The town was named for George Carroll, pioneer citizen of the community, who was from Carrollton, Maryland. The deserted appearance that the wide, bare, dusty town square frequently presents on weekdays is deceptive. Carrollton's bank, cold storage plant, and 40 business houses attract a thriving Saturday trade, drawn from the surrounding farming country which produces large quantities of cotton, corn, wheat, oats, sweet potatoes, cane, sheep, and dairy products. Gravel mining in the pits west of the town also is important.

FARMERS BRANCH, *73.2 m. (465 alt., 300 pop.)*, a row of sleepy weatherbeaten stores and houses strung out along the highway and Missouri-Kansas-Texas tracks, shares with Cedar Hill the distinction of being the second oldest settlement in Dallas County. The town was first known as Mustang Branch; its name was later changed to Farmers Branch because of the prolific crops grown by early settlers. It was here that the first Peters' Colony immigrants took up homesteads in 1842.

The Texan Land and Emigration Company, commonly known as Peters' Colony Company, was organized in Louisville, Kentucky, by W. S. Peters, and in 1841 contracted with the Republic of Texas for the settlement of a large number of colonists in the Dallas area, its grant covering a region of about seven present day North Texas counties. About 10,000 persons settled on this grant between 1844 and 1854. The first men to obtain rights from the company at Louisville for homesteads in the vicinity of Dallas were Isaac Webb and William M. Cochran. The two families remained on land near Farmers Branch and Isaac Webb, a Methodist, established at this site Webb's Chapel, the first formal house of worship in Dallas County *(see RELIGION: BRUSH ARBOR TO TEMPLE)*. The first resident agency of the company established in 1845 was about a mile north of this point. All remains of the chapel and other buildings have long since disappeared, and the only trace of these pioneer settlers' presence here is the old burial ground in which many of them rest.

The route from Farmers Branch is east on the Valley View Road. At *74.6 m.* it turns north on Webb's Chapel Road, traversing open, rolling, grazing country. At *76.6 m.* the way is east again on the Belt Line Road and enters the prosperous farming section of the county extending to Richardson and Garland. The growing of cotton, wheat, corn, oats, and onions and the raising of fine stock and poultry are the chief occupations, and there are a number of large, well kept farms of the country estate type—with modern homes, barns and silos, miles of white board ranch fences, and artistic rock entrances with neat name plates. Occasionally airplanes can be seen resting on private flying fields beside the houses. Some of these deluxe farms, presenting a striking contrast to those in other parts of the county, are owned by old families who have been on the land since pioneer days, others by retired businessmen who live in Richardson, Garland, and Dallas.

The route leaves the Belt Line Road at *80.5 m.* and veers north on US 14; at *80.9 m.* it turns east again on the Belt Line Road to its intersection with the Coit Road *83.0 m.* and then at *83.1 m.* goes east again on the Belt Line Road. At *85.7 m.* the way is southwest on US 75.

RICHARDSON, *86.6 m. (620 alt., 629 pop.),* is a clean, prosperous community of one- and two-story brick and frame stores, modern school buildings, numerous churches, and neat bungalows with well kept lawns and landscaped grounds—a community of well-to-do home owners. Located in the rich blackland area, growing wheat, oats, corn, cotton, hay, and onions, it has two cotton gins, and is an important onion shipping point.

The entrance to The Garden of Memories Cemetery is at *87.9 m. (R),* and at *88.3 m.* is the entrance to Restland Memorial Park *(R).* Both of these new cemeteries are of the modern type, without raised graves or visible markers of any kind, resembling artistically landscaped parks rather than burial places.

At *89.3 m.* the route is east again on the Belt Line Road.

AUDELIA, *90.8 m. (600 alt., 35 pop.),* is a tiny crossroads village with one store and a church.

GARLAND, *95.2 m. (551 alt., 1,584 pop.),* grew out of the consolidation of the villages of Embree and Duck Creek in 1891, and developed into a flourishing trading center and suburban homesite. Ravaged by a cyclone in 1929, the town has been completely rebuilt and the visitor is struck by its newness and up-to-date urban appearance, city lighting, automatic traffic signals, and other evidences of progress. The business section, composed of substantial one- and two-story brick buildings, draws trade from Dallas as well as the surrounding farming country and is arranged around a square which has an ornamental fountain in its center. The residential sections have unusual suburban charm, containing a large number of fine homes, most of them fireproof and of all types of modern architecture set among well kept lawns, trees, flowers, and shrubbery. There are also a number of large country estates on the edge of the town. A park with a swimming pool provides recreational facilities. Situated in the very heart of the onion growing region and on two railroads, Garland is one of the most important onion shipping points in North Texas. Freight platforms east of the square are piled high with sacks of white and yellow onions during picking and shipping season in the late spring and early summer. Cheaper operating conditions than those found in Dallas have attracted the large Byer-Rolnick Hat Factory, whose modern plant with its ornate buff brick entrance and all glass and steel-sash workshop, is visible in the center of a large bare field south of the town. This plant was the scene of a brief but sharply contested strike in the summer of 1939, when the workers demanded the right to organize and a city wage scale.

In Garland US 67 continues east to **ROWLETT,** *100.1 m. (500 alt., 108 pop.),* which has an old and dilapidated appearance, with only a sprinkling of new homes. It is a trading center of some importance, however, deriving much of its revenue from the heavily traveled highway on which it is situated. It has 13 places of business, one school, four churches, and three cotton gins.

Southward, the route is Rose Hill Road to its intersection with the Belt Line Road, *104.3 m.*, hence south on the Belt Line Road to **NEW HOPE**, *107.2 m. (474 alt., 100 pop.)*, once a place of some importance justifying the name bestowed on it in 1887 by its first merchant, W. Tinsley, when the post office was established. The railroads and main highways passed it by in favor of the nearby town of Mesquite, and it is today only an active country trading center built up around the large, old-fashioned general store of Frank Ellis & Son, "Dealers in Everything."

MESQUITE, *110.6 m. (491 alt., 729 pop.)*, was settled in 1872 and was named for the many mesquite trees in the vicinity. It was the scene of a train holdup by Sam Bass' outlaw gang in the seventies *(see HISTORY: CITY IN THE MAKING)*, and was the second town in Dallas County to be incorporated, in 1887. State 183, known as the Scyene Road, forms the northern boundary of the town square, surrounded by one-story brick and frame buildings. It is a flourishing trading center situated on the main line of the Texas & Pacific Railroad, with 40 business houses, two cotton mills, and one grist mill. It also has good school and church facilities, a weekly newspaper, a bank, and post office.

At *113.3 m.* the Belt Line Road crosses Mesquite Creek. South of Mesquite Creek the country becomes lower and is covered with a ragged growth of mesquite trees and scrub oaks, the black lands farther north being replaced by a sandy loam. Orchards of fruit trees appear, and the principal crops are fruits, berries, vegetables, melons, pecans, cotton, corn, and hay. Large numbers of hogs, sheep, and poultry are also raised.

The route leaves the Belt Line Road at *114.0 m.* and veers south on the Balch Springs Road; then at *115.6 m.* turns southeast on old US 175.

SEAGOVILLE, *121.5 m. (451 alt., 604 pop.)*, is an active trade center established in the 1870s and named for a pioneer merchant and land owner, T. K. Seago. The "ville" was added when the post office was opened in 1878. Drawing its trade from the fertile truck growing area in which it is located, it has two gins, 41 places of business, and five churches. Most of the buildings are old one-story brick and frame structures clustered along the highway.

At Seagoville the route is retraced to Simonds Road; at *123.7 m.* the way is west on the Simonds Road.

The **FEDERAL REFORMATORY FOR WOMEN**, *124.3 m.*, has its entrance *(L)* on the Simonds Road. It was opened October 10, 1940. This institution, intended to house all women prisoners having sentences of more than a year from states west of the Mississippi, as well as offenders with sentences of less than a year from neighboring judicial districts, occupies an irregularly shaped tract of land containing approximately 780 acres.

Completed it will accommodate 550 prisoners and will consist of 18 separate buildings, including administration buildings, a staff house, auditorium and school, individual room buildings for housing, a receiving and hospital building, power-house, warehouse, garage, shops, and an industrial building. All the buildings are to be of brick and stone of modernized Virginia plantation design. The housing units have been designed to avoid the appearance of a prison. Inmates will be quartered in individual rooms; the cells are to be guarded with ornamental grilles over the windows, and there will be electrically controlled doors rather than steel bars.

The Belt Line Road intersects the route at Parsons' Slough, *128.0 m.*, in the midst of the low, marshy, heavily wooded Trinity bottoms, thence it continues southwest across the Trinity River through the bottoms. Considerable wood is cut in this area, which otherwise supports only subsistence farmers. Sorghum cane and molasses making is sometimes visible in farm yards along the highway.

WILMER, *132.2 m. (472 alt., 250 pop.),* is a straggling town irregularly strung out along US 75, most of its houses of frame and badly in need of repair. Most of the older part of the town is situated west of the highway and has been largely abandoned since a destructive fire occurred a number of years ago. The town has two cotton gins and 19 places of business. Cotton, corn, oats, livestock, and diversified farm products are raised in the rich bottom land area surrounding the town.

In Wilmer the route is north on US 75. The new brick WILMER-HUTCHINS SCHOOL, *135.3 m.,* is left of the highway. This school plant serves both communities.

HUTCHINS, *137.3 m. (476 alt., 500 pop.)* resembles Wilmer in nearly all essential respects and is equally dingy in appearance. Its one-story frame and brick stores are old, and trailer camps fringe the road. The east side of the highway is lined with loading platforms along the railroad, where piles of miscellaneous farm produce await shipment.

At *138.2 m.* the red brick buildings of the DALLAS COUNTY CONVALESCENT HOSPITAL are visible *(L)* and the white buildings of the CITY-COUNTY BOYS INDUSTRIAL SCHOOL can be seen about a mile to the east *(R)* across the railroad tracks. These institutions are part of the city-county social welfare system *(see SOCIAL SERVICE: SOUL OF A CITY).*

Northward there are numerous gravel pits and truck farms, and near the city limits are railroad repair shops, oil refineries, a basket factory, and a large dairy plant, also a number of taverns, roadhouses, and eating places.

US 75 at *143.3 m.* crosses the Trinity River over a long concrete causeway. The city limits are at *144.7 m.;* the route continues on US 75 to the corner of Main and Lamar Streets, then turns west on Main Street to the courthouse and the starting point of the tour.

CHRONOLOGY

1542   *June-July*—Luis Moscoso and survivors of DeSoto's Spanish exploring expedition cross northeastern part of present Dallas County, seeking route to Mexico City.

1712   Antoine Crozat and Bernard de La Harpe, French traders from Louisiana, visit Anadarko Indians on Trinity River.

1760   Friar Calahorra y Saenz, Roman Catholic missionary from Nacogdoches, visits area of modern Dallas, making treaties with Indians, giving name of Trinity to river previously called Arkikosa, because of its three forks.

1771   Athanase de Mezieres, Frenchman acting for Spaniards, concludes treaty with Indians in territory now including Dallas, Waco, and Wichita Falls.

1818   Caddo Indians in battle with Cherokee near three forks of Trinity drive latter to the eastward.

1837   *November*—Ten Texas Rangers are killed in battle with Indians fifty miles north of the present city. Survivors retreat to site of Dallas, camping first at Turtle Creek, then at present Murphy and Commerce Streets.

1840   Colonel William G. Cooke and John Neely Bryan make separate scouting and surveying trips within present city limits of Dallas.

1841   *November*—John Neely Bryan, founder of Dallas, pitches camp on the east bank of the Trinity River, establishing first permanent settlement.

1842   *April 8*—John Beeman and family arrive from Bird's Fort to join Bryan, followed closely by other Bird's Fort colonists.
       Isaac Webb and other immigrants of Peters' Colony Company settle on Mustang (later Farmers) Branch.

1844   John Neely Bryan is appointed postmaster by Republic of Texas, his log cabin serving as first post office.

1845   Trading post is established at Cedar Springs, three miles from Dallas.
       First school in county is opened at Farmers Branch.
       William H. Hord residence, oldest house still standing in the city, is erected in present Oak Cliff area.
       Dallas votes, 29 to 3, for Texas' annexation to the United States.

1846   J. P. Dumas is employed by John Neely Bryan to survey and plat town site.
       March 30—County is organized.
       April 18—Town of Dallas is made temporary seat of government and a log courthouse erected.
       May—First church congregation is organized in Dallas by Orin Hatch, Methodist minister.
       First church structure in county, Webb's Chapel, is built at Farmers Branch.
       First horsepower grist mill is erected on west side of river.

1847   Henry Harter built the Dallas Tavern, first hotel.

1849   J. Wellington (Weck) Latimer, journalist, arrives in Dallas, bringing first piano and first printing equipment, and establishing first newspaper, the *Cedar Snag,* shortly renamed the *Herald.*

First cotton gin in the county is erected at Farmers Branch.

1850 Dallas is made permanent county seat, second courthouse erected.
First census shows population of 2,743 for county, 430 for the town.

1852 Crutchfield House, leading hotel for many years, is opened.
Cotton is first moved from Dallas into commercial channels by J. W. Smith, pioneer merchant.
Maxime Guillot, carriagemaker, builds first factory.

1853 *May*—First legal hanging occurs, that of Jane Elkins, a slave.

1855 First bridge is constructed across the Trinity River.
John M. Crockett builds first two-story residence.
June—Main body of La Reunion colonists under Victor Considerant arrive in Dallas.

1856 First town charter is granted; Dr. Samuel B. Pryor elected first mayor.
First stage coaches enter Dallas.

1857 First brewery is established by M. Monduel of La Reunion French Colony.
First subscription library established.

1858 Drought and floods beset Dallas, Trinity bridge collapses.

1859 Dallas County Agricultural and Mechanical Association holds first fair in county.

1860 *July 8*—Dallas is practically wiped out by fire, believed at time work of slaves.

1861 Four Dallas companies are formed to fight for the Confederate cause, and march to Austin.

1864 *December*—Ladies' Welfare Association establishes soldiers' home.

1865 Civil War ends, 1,250 Dallas residents take oath of amnesty. John M. Crockett appointed mayor by Reconstruction government.

1866 *May*—Trinity River flood reaches unprecedented height.

1868 First bank in Dallas is organized by Gaston & Camp.
May—Steamboat arrives in Dallas and ties up at foot of Commerce Street.
In first election under Reconstruction, Negro voters outnumber the whites.
The Ku Klux Klan appears.

1869 *October*—The first Dallas Jockey Club is organized.
First tent road show gives a performance.
Systematic mass extermination of the great buffalo herds cause Dallas to boom as hide market.

1870 Population 3,000.

1871 *April*—A city charter is substituted for town charter.
November—First Dallas County Medical Society is organized.
December—Dallas County Bank receives first state bank charter.

1872 *July*—First train (Houston & Texas Central) steams into Dallas.
Dr. Matthew Cornelius made first "City health doctor."
First iron bridge is built across Trinity.

1873 *February*—Second railroad (Texas & Pacific) is extended to Dallas.
Mule-drawn street cars begin operation.
First telegraph service to eastern points is established.
Field Opera House is opened, starring the Crisp Sisters.

1874 *June*—City is illuminated with artificial gas for the first time.
July—First National Bank is chartered.
Board of Trade, first commercial organization, is established.

1875 *May*—Jefferson Davis on tour of Texas speaks to an enthusiastic crowd at McCoy Grove.

1876 Dallas County Medical and Surgical Association is formed to succeed Dallas County Medical Society.
Dallas Musical Society is organized.

1879 *December*—Buckner's Orphans Home is founded.
First telephone is installed, connecting waterworks and fire department.

1880 John Jay Gould, railroad magnate, visits city.
Population 10,358.

1881 The first telephone exchange is opened.
August—The Texas Trunk Railway is opened from Dallas to Kaufman.

1882 *January*—City acquires water works from Dallas Hydrant Company.
September—Town of East Dallas is incorporated.
The Knights of Labor is organized.
First electric light plant is installed.
Texas Marriage Aid Association is formed in Dallas.

1883 The town's first strike occurs, a railway walkout.
Dallas Opera House is opened.
Dallas Amateur Baseball Association is formed.
New and permanent site is purchased for post office.
First cotton gin is manufactured.

1884 Gaston Building is erected to house cotton traders.
First highway is macadamized in Dallas County—Cedar Springs Road.
The Idlewild Club, exclusive social club, is organized.
July—First street paving is laid with bois d'arc blocks.

1885 *October 1—Dallas Morning News* begins publication.
October 6—Typographical Union No. 173, oldest local in Dallas, is chartered.

1886 The first State Fair of Texas is held.
December—T. L. Marsalis purchases land west of Trinity and begins development of Hord's Ridge (Oak Cliff) the following year.

1887 John Henry Brown writes first history of Dallas County.
Dallas joins newly organized Texas Baseball League.

1888 Six-story North Texas Building, regarded as first "skyscraper" in North Texas, is erected.
First cotton mill is established.
January—Thomas W. Keene, famous actor, visits city and organizes first lodge of Elks.
The *Times Herald* is established by consolidation of *Evening Times* and *Dallas (Evening) Herald*.

1889 *April*—East Dallas is annexed to Dallas.
First electric street cars make their appearance.

1890 Present county courthouse is erected.
Population 38,067.

1891 *June*—Oak Cliff is incorporated as a town with H. F. Ewing as first mayor.
October—First major football game is played by teams representing Fort Worth and Dallas.

1893 North Texas National Bank, Central National Bank, and Bankers & Merchants Bank fail in nationwide panic.

411

May—Dallas Commercial Club, forerunner of present Chamber of Commerce, is organized.

May—Trinity River navigation believed assured with docking of steamer, *H. A. Harvey*, at foot of Main Street.

October—Oriental Hotel, famed throughout Southwest, opens doors.

1894   State National and Ninth National Banks fail in panic.

Democratic State Convention, meeting in Dallas, backs "Cleveland and sound money."

Survey of Trinity River begun from Dallas by army engineers.

1895   World's heavyweight fight in Dallas is banned by action of state legislature.

1896   City goes Republican by majority of 244 votes in presidential race between William McKinley and William Jennings Bryan.

First golf game is played in Dallas.

June—Cornerstone of Confederate Monument is laid in City Park during Confederate State Reunion.

1897   *February*—First motion picture is shown in Dallas.

Buckner's Orphans Home burns, 20 children perish.

City acquires first modern hospital when St. Paul's Sanitarium is erected.

1898   Linz Bros. erect first fireproof building at Main and Martin Streets.

Company of Union and Confederate Civil War veterans is formed for service in Spanish-American War; youngest 48, oldest 60.

May—Dallas troops, 175 strong, leave for service in Cuba following outbreak of Spanish-American War.

The Terpsichorean Club, sponsor of annual society balls, is organized.

1899   *February*—Coldest weather in recorded history of Dallas, 10 degrees below zero, occurs.

November—Charter is granted by the American Federation of Labor to Trades Assembly of Dallas.

William Jennings Bryan visits State Fair.

Cleaner Dallas League is organized.

1900   The College of Medicine, University of Dallas, is established.

Dallas Golf Club, forerunner of Dallas Country Club, is organized.

Funds for Dallas Public Library are contributed by Andrew Carnegie.

Population 42,638.

1901   First cement plant is built.

Dallas Public Library opens.

First art exhibit is held in Dallas Public Library.

1902   *April*—Confederate Reunion brings 3,000 veterans and 100,000 visitors to city, trebling population.

Dallas assumes world leadership in output of saddles.

The first art school in Dallas, still in existence, is established by Vivian Aunspaugh.

Interurban electric lines begin operation.

1904   Oak Cliff is annexed to Dallas.

Wireless messages are transmitted between Fort Worth and Dallas for the first time.

1905   Majestic Theater is erected.

April—President Theodore Roosevelt visits Dallas; first president to visit city while in office.

Metropolitan Grand Opera Company comes to Dallas for the first time and gives *Parsifal*.

Dallas Red Cross Chapter is organized.

1907   Restricted suburb of Highland Park is opened.

April—Dallas Cotton Exchange is granted charter.

Commission form of government goes into effect with Stephen J. Hay as mayor.

May—The first auto license is issued to J. M. Oram.

Fourteen-story Praetorian Building, first actual skyscraper, is built in Dallas.

1908   *Aerial Queen*, first airship seen in Dallas, is brought here by a carnival company.

May—Trinity River flood is worst in recorded history of Dallas County.

1909   *Dallas News* initiates the movement for a city plan.

President William Howard Taft visits State Fair.

1910   *February*—First flight of heavier-than-air machine in Dallas is made by Otto Brodie in Curtiss biplane.

Acute water famine leads to impounding waters of White Rock Creek to provide city with reserve water supply.

Dallas City Plan and Improvement League is organized and George E. Kessler employed to prepare a city plan.

Population 92,104.

1911   Woodrow Wilson, governor of New Jersey, speaks at State Fair.

Elm Street becomes "great white way" by installation of 110 street lamps.

1912   Adolphus Hotel is erected.

February—Houston Street viaduct is opened and acclaimed as the longest concrete bridge in the world.

City suffers severe outbreak of meningitis.

1913   County Criminal Courts Building erected.

1914   *April*—Dallas is awarded Federal Reserve Bank for the Eleventh District, under Federal Reserve Act of 1913.

1915   City Welfare Department is established.

Southern Methodist University is opened.

1916   *January*—Labor Temple is dedicated by Governor James E. Ferguson.

Union passenger station is erected.

1917   *January*—First airplane flight is made from Love Field airport.

April 11—City holds great patriotic parade following America's entry into World War; 15,037 register later for army service.

September—Dallas votes for prohibition, 10,625 to 8,551; saloons close October 20.

November—Love Field is established as an army air training base.

Dallas has 5,000 men under arms by the end of the year.

1918   Camp Dick is established at Fair Park.

Hospitals taxed to the limit in great influenza epidemic.

November 14—Dallas celebrates Armistice ending World War.

1919   *March*—First troops, belonging to the 133rd Field Artillery, return from overseas and parade through downtown streets.

Greatest strike in history of Dallas when building trades throughout North

Texas go out in sympathy with striking linemen of Dallas Power & Light Company.

Dallas voters ratify 18th and 19th Federal constitutional amendments by large majorities.

1920　George E. Kessler revises his first city plan to meet needs of rapidly growing Dallas.

Dallas Little Theater is organized.

Population 158,976.

1921　*April*—New Ku Klux Klan appears.

May—"Bank run" on Security National Bank, only run in history of Dallas, causes much excitement.

Station WRR, first municipal radio broadcasting station in America, is established.

1922　*June*—Radio Station WFAA is established.

Ku Klux Klan candidates carry election in Dallas County.

Magnolia Building is completed—29 stories, the city's tallest building.

1923　Railroad tracks are removed from Pacific Avenue.

November—The Texas Scottish Rite Hospital for crippled children is opened.

1924　Dallas Little Theater wins Belasco Cup with *Judge Lynch*, the first of three successive awards.

1925　Half-Century Club formed by fifty-year residents.

1926　*May*—Most severe hail storm in its history visits Dallas.

First mail plane of National Air Transport is flown to Chicago by Herbert L. Kindred.

October—Work is begun on Garza Dam in Denton County for creation of Lake Dallas, finally solving Dallas' water problem.

1927　*August*—Captain William Erwin of Dallas is lost at sea while attempting to pilot airplane "Spirit of Dallas" from San Francisco to Honolulu.

$23,900,000 Ulrickson city bond issue is voted.

Love Field is purchased by city as municipal airport.

Santa Fe Building is erected, said to be largest single office and terminal building in Southwest.

1928　*June*—Ground is broken for Trinity River levee and reclamation project.

July—First passenger service between Dallas and San Antonio and Houston is instituted by Texas Air Transport.

Hensley Field is purchased by Dallas and leased to U. S. government for airport at $1 a year.

November—Dallas gives majority to Herbert Hoover, Republican nominee, in national election.

1929　Dallas Community Trust is formed.

1930　*September*—Captains Dieudonne Coste and Maurice Bellonte fly from Paris to Dallas for $25,000 prize offered by Colonel William E. Easterwood.

Cotton Bowl Stadium is erected, seating 46,400.

Present Federal Building and Post Office is opened.

October—City manager form of government is approved at polls.

Population 260,397.

1931　Unemployment reaches serious proportions. Emergency committee asks $100,000 for relief.

1932   City and county apply jointly to Reconstruction Finance Corporation for $450,000 loan to provide relief work programs.

1933   Only State Trust and Savings Bank fails to reopen after bank holiday.

         August—City votes for repeal of prohibition by heavy majority.

1934   Dallas wins central Exposition for Texas Centennial in open bidding.

1935   *March*—Eighteen striking women garment workers sent to jail after outbreak of violence.

1936   Triple underpass completed, linking Main, Commerce, and Elm Streets with Oak Cliff.

         Museum of Fine Arts at Civic Center in Fair Park is opened.

         Radio Station KRLD is established.

         Texas Centennial Central Exposition is held at Fair Park.

         June—President Franklin D. Roosevelt and Vice President John N. Garner speak at Texas Centennial Exposition.

1937   Pan-American Exposition is held.

         Strike of millinery workers and attempt of CIO to organize Ford assembly plant causes numerous outbreaks of violence. Governor Allred dispatches a detail of Texas Rangers to Dallas to restore order.

1938   Dallas is cited as an economic bright spot in midst of nationwide recession. Dallas ranks twenty-first among American cities in the volume of its postal receipts.

         October—State Fair of Texas is resumed and observes Golden Jubilee, after having been suspended for three years to make way for expositions.

1939   *September*—Dallas school girls welcomed home after rescue from SS *Athenia*, torpedoed in the North Atlantic following outbreak of Second World War.

1940   *January*—Population (estimated) 380,927.

BIBLIOGRAPHY

The following bibliography is selected from the many hundreds of books, articles, and documents consulted in the preparation of the *Dallas Guide and History*. Files of Dallas and Texas newspapers, among them the *Dallas Herald* from 1858 to 1885, the *Dallas Mercury*, the *Dallas Times Herald*, the *Dallas Journal*, *The Dallas Morning News*, the old *Texas Register and Telegraph* of Houston, the *Galveston News*, and a great number of miscellaneous publications also have been utilized for historical research. The history of newspapers in Dallas will be found in the essay on newspapers. For fiction and poetry the essay on literature should be consulted, while other titles will be found in the essay on the theater.

Acheson, Sam. *35,000 Days in Texas*. Macmillan, New York, 1938. 360 pp. History of *The Dallas Morning News*.

Agatha, Sister *M. Texas Prose Writings*. Banks Upshaw & Company, Dallas, 1936. 168 pp.

Asbury, Herbert. *The French Quarter*. Alfred A. Knopf, New York, 1936. 455 pp.

Baer, Carl J., and Brigadier General Charles W. Kuts. "Trinity Waterway in Dallas." Transcript of Testimony before Army Engineers, mimeographed, Fort Worth, 1935.

Bancroft, Hubert Howe. *History of the North Mexican States and Texas*. The History Co., San Francisco, 1889. Vol. 11, 1801–1889. 814 pp.

Barns, Florence Elberta. *Texas Writers of Today*. Tardy Publishing Company, Dallas, 1935. 513 pp.

Barton, Henry. "A History of the Dallas Opera House." Southern Methodist University, Dallas, 1935. Thesis. 135 pp.

Bolton, Herbert E. *Athanase de Mezieres*. Arthur H. Clark Company, Cleveland, Ohio, 1914. 2 vols.

Bolton, Herbert E. *The Spanish Borderlands*. Yale University Press, New Haven, 1926. 320 pp.

Bolton, Herbert E. *Spanish Explorations in the Southwest*. Charles Scribner's Sons, New York, 1916. 487 pp.

Bolton, Herbert E. *Texas in the Middle of the 18th Century*. University of California Press, Berkeley, n.d. 501 pp.

Brown, John Henry. *History of Dallas County, 1837–1887*. Milligan, Cornett & Farnham, Dallas, 1887. 116 pp.

Bryan, Ralph. "Twelve Texas Buildings." *Southwest Review*, January, 1931. Vol. 16.

Bryant's Railroad Guide and Tourist's and Emigrant's Handbook of Travel from Canada to Mexico. Privately printed, Austin, 1875. 130 pp.

Burks, J. *Texas Almanac and Immigrants Handbook*. Houston, 1883. 224 pp.

Carpenter, Miles. *Sociology of City Life*. Longmans-Green, New York, 1931. 502 pp.

Castaneda, Carlos Eduardo. *Myths and Customs of the Tejas Indians*. Von Boeckmann-Jones Company, Austin, n.d. 349 pp.

Castaneda, Carlos Eduardo. *Our Catholic Heritage.* Von Boeckmann-Jones Company, Austin, 1936. 2 vols.

Cline, J. L. *Annual Meteorological Summary, with Comparative Data.* U. S. Department of Agriculture, Weather Bureau, Dallas, 1938.

Cochran, John H. *Dallas County, A Record of Its Pioneers and Progress.* Mathis-Van Nort Publishing Company, Dallas, 1928. 296 pp.

Considerant, Victor. *Au Texas.* Librairie Phalansteriere, Paris, France, 1854. 334 pp.

Cordova, Jacob de. *The Texas Immigrant and Travellers Guide Book.* Austin, Texas, 1856.

Dallas Cotton Exchange. *Dallas Cotton Market.* Southwest Printing Company, Dallas, 1935. 34 pp.

Dallas, James. *History of the Family of Dallas.* T. & A. Constable, Ltd., Edinburgh, Scotland, 1921.

Directory of Organizations. The Civic Federation of Dallas, Dallas, 1938.

Dallas City Directories. 1875–1939.

Dixon, Samuel Houston, and Louis Wiltz Kemp. *The Heroes of San Jacinto.* Anson Jones Press, Houston, 1932. 462 pp.

Dixon, Samuel Houston. *The Men Who Made Texas Free.* Texas Historical Publishing Co., Houston, 1855. 345 pp.

Dixon, Samuel Houston. *Poets and Poetry of Texas.* Sam H. Dixon & Co., Austin, 1885. 360 pp.

Dodson, Dan, Arthur Blair Crutchfield, and Stella Nance. "A Sociologic Survey of the Religious Life of Eight Ethnic Groups in the City of Dallas, Texas." Southern Methodist University, 1936. Thesis. 185 pp.

Eagleton, Davis Foute. *Writers and Writings of Texas.* Broadway Publishing Company, New York, 1913. 390 pp.

Fisk, Frances Battaile. *A History of Texas Artists and Sculptors.* Abilene, Texas, 1928.

Fulmore, Zachary Taylor. *Origin of Texas Counties, 1846–1923.* Steck Co., Austin, 1935. 312 pp.

Gard, Wayne. *Sam Bass.* Houghton Mifflin, New York, 1936. 262 pp.

Greer, Hilton R. *Best Short Stories from the Southwest.* The Southwest Press, Dallas, 1931. 380 pp.

Gregg, Josiah. *Commerce of the Prairies, or the Journal of a Santa Fe Trader.* Southwest Press, Dallas, 1932. 438 pp.

Hammond, W. J. "La Reunion, A French Colony in Texas." *The Southwestern Social Service Quarterly.* Norman, Oklahoma, September, 1936.

Handbook of Texas Libraries. Texas Library Association, Houston, 1935. 151 pp.

Hanscom, Otho Anne. *Parade of the Pioneers.* Tardy Publishing Company, Inc., Dallas, 1935. 266 pp.

Harman, S. W. *Hell on the Border.* Phoenix Publishing Company, Fort Smith, Arkansas, 1898. 320 pp.

Hazard, Lucy Lockwood. *The Frontier in American Literature.* Thomas Y. Crowell, New York, 1927. 308 pp.

Head, Louis P. *The Kessler City Plan for Dallas, Genesis and Development of the Plan of 1910; the Supplement Plan of 1920; Progress in Fifteen Years.* A. H. Belo Corp., Dallas, 1925. 76 pp.

Head, Louis P. *Measuring the Efficiency of a City's Government.* W. B. Munro-Harvard University, Cambridge, 1927. 80 pp.

Hill, Robert T. "The Geologic Formations That Made Dallas Rich." *Dallas Morning News,* October 1, 1935.

Hodge, F. W. *Hand Book of American Indians.* J. Grant, Edinburgh, 1933–34. 2 vols.

Holden, William Curry. *Alkali Trails, 1846–1900.* The Southwest Press, Dallas, 1930. 253 pp.

Holley, Mrs. Mary (Austin). *Letters of an Early American Traveler, 1784–1846.* Southwest Press, Dallas, 1933. 216 pp.

Jackson, George. *Sixty Years in Texas.* Wilkinson Printing Company, Dallas, 1908. 384 pp.

James, Marquis. *The Raven.* Bobbs-Merrill Co., Indianapolis, 1929. 389 pp.

Jeffries, Charles. *Early Texas Architecture.* Bunker's Monthly, 1928. Vol. 1. 947 pp.

Johnson, Allen. *Dictionary of American Biography.* Charles Scribner's Sons, New York, 1929. Vol. II. 613 pp.

Kendall, John Smith. *History of New Orleans.* The Lewis Publishing Company, Chicago and New York, 1922. Vol. II.

Kimball, Justin F. *Our City—Dallas.* Kessler Plan Association, Dallas, 1927. 384 pp.

King, Edward. *The Great South, a Record of Journeys in Louisiana, Texas.* American Publishing Co., Hartford, 1875. 802 pp.

Life and Adventures of Sam Bass, the Notorious Union Pacific and Texas Train Robber. Commercial Steam Press, Dallas, 1878. 89 pp.

Lindsley, Philip. *A History of Greater Dallas and Vicinity.* Lewis Publishing Company, Chicago, 1909. 2 vols.

Lomax, John Avery, and Alan Lomax. *American Ballads and Folk Songs.* Macmillan Company, New York, Dallas, 1934. 625 pp.

Lomax, John Avery. *Negro Folk Songs as Sung by Leadbelly.* Macmillan Company, New York, 1936. 242 pp.

Lutz, Eusibia. "Almost Utopia." *Southwest Review,* April, 1929. Vol. XIV.

Major, Mabel, Rebecca W. Smith, and T. M. Pearce. *Southwest Heritage.* The University of New Mexico Press, Albuquerque, 1938.

Martin, Charles Lee. *A Sketch of Sam Bass, the Bandit.* Privately printed, Dallas, 1880.

McConnell, H. H. *Five Years a Cavalryman or Sketches of Regular Army Life of the Texas Frontier.* J. N. Rogers & Co., Jacksboro, Texas, 1889. 319 pp.

McConnell, Joseph Carroll. *The West Texas Frontier.* Gazette Print, Jacksboro, Texas, 1892. 334 pp.

Memorial and Biographical History of Dallas County: The Lone Star State. Lewis Publishing Company, Chicago, 1892. 1,011 pp.

Morphis, J. M. *History of Texas From Its Discovery and Settlement.* United States Publishing Company, New York, 1874. 592 pp.

National Cyclopedia of American Biography. James T. White & Co., New York, 1931. Vol. 21.

Newton, Lewis William, and Herbert P. Gambrell. *A Social and Political History of Texas.* Southwest Press, Dallas, 1932. 422 pp.

Nickens, Bess. "History of Cumberland Hill School." Dallas Morning News, Dallas, 1928. 12 pp.

O'Brien, Esse Forrester. *Art and Artists of Texas.* Tardy Publishing Company, Dallas, 1935. 408 pp.

Paddock, Captain B. B. *A Twentieth Century History and Biographical Record of North and West Texas.* Lewis Publishing Company, Chicago and New York, 1906. 2 vols.

Parker, Emma, and Nell Barrow Cowan. *Bonnie and Clyde: Fugitives.* Edited and compiled by Jan Isbelle Fortune. The Ranger Press, Inc., Dallas, 1934. 255 pp.

Payne, Leonidas Warren, Jr. *Literature of the Southwest.* Rand McNally, New York and Chicago, 1873. 76 pp.

Personal Narrative of Exploration and Incidents of Texas, New Mexico, California, Sonora and Chihuahua. D. Appleton & Co., New York, 1854.

Pickrell, Annie Doom. *True Stories in Texas.* The Naylor Company, San Antonio, 1936. 365 pp.

Rankin, Melinda. *Texas in 1850–1875.* Chase and Hall, Cincinnati, n.d. 214 pp.

Reagan, John H. *Memoirs: with Special Reference to Secession and the Civil War.* Neale, New York, 1936.

Roberts, Oran M. *A Description of Texas.* Gilbert Book Co., St. Louis, 1881. 133 pp.

Rock, James L., and W. I. Smith. *Southern & Western Texas Guide for 1878.* A. H. Granger, St. Louis, 1878. 278 pp.

Ruggles, William B. *The History of the Texas League.* The Texas Baseball League, Dallas, 1932. 240 pp.

Savardan, Dr. E. *Un Naufrage au Texas.* Translated by Eloise Santerre in "La Reunion," Thesis, Southern Methodist University, Dallas, August, 1936. Gannier Freres, Paris, 1857. 496 pp.

Schmitz, Joseph William. *Thus They Lived.* The Naylor Company, San Antonio, 1935. 141 pp.

Shuler, Ellis W. *The Geology of Dallas County.* University of Texas Bulletin, No. 1818, University Press, Austin, 1918. 54 pp.

Smith, Edward. *Account of a Journey Through North-Western Texas, Undertaken in 1849, for the Purpose of Emigration.* Privately printed, London, 1849. 188 pp.

Smith, Goldie Capers. *The Creative Arts in Texas.* Cokesbury Press, Dallas, 1926. 178 pp.

Speer, William. *Encyclopedia of the New West.* The U. S. Biographical Publishing Co., Marshall, 1881. 1,014 pp.

Texian Who's Who. Texian Company, Dallas, 1937.

Trent, Lucy C. *John Neely Bryan.* Tardy Publishing Company, Dallas, 1936. 80 pp.

"University of Texas Bulletin on County Government, No. 1732," *Texas Law Review.* Austin, February, 1936. Vol. XIV.

Wilbarger, J. W. *Indian Depredations in Texas.* Hutchings Printing House, Austin, 1889. 672 pp.

Williams, David R. "Toward a Southwestern Architecture." *Southwest Review,* January, 1931. Vol. XVI.

Winter, Nevin O. *Texas the Marvellous: the State of the Six Flags.* L. C. Page & Co., Boston, 1916.

Who's Who in Texas. Who's Who Publishing Co., Dallas, 1931.

Who's Who in the Theater. Sir Isaac Pitman & Sons, Boston, 1914.

Young, Stark. *Southern Treasury of Life and Literature.* Charles Scribner's Sons, New York, 1937. 747 pp.

INDEX